103418 X

a30103001034185b

OCT 1 1 1955 REC'D

THE LIBRARY, UNIVERSITY OF SUSSEX

Please return this book as soon as you have
finished with it, and in any case not later than
the last date stamped below.

11. NOV 1966

18. NOV 1969

-17. JUN. 1974

15. JAN. 1975

11. JAN 1988

25. JUN 1997

D1422504

McGraw-Hill Series in Political Science

JOSEPH P. HARRIS, *Consulting Editor*

GOVERNING URBAN AMERICA
Structure, Politics, and Administration

103418

SUSSEX
UNIVERSITY
LIBRARY

McGraw-Hill Series in Political Science

JOSEPH P. HARRIS, *Consulting Editor*

ADRIAN · Governing Urban America: Structure, Politics, and Administration

BONE · American Politics and the Party System

CHASE · The United Nations in Action

FERGUSON AND MCHENRY · The American Federal Government

FERGUSON AND MCHENRY · The American System of Government

FERGUSON AND MCHENRY · Elements of American Government

FIELD · Governments in Modern Society

FRANK · Cases on the Constitution

GOSNELL, LANCASTER, AND RANKIN · Fundamentals of American National Government

GROSS · The Legislative Struggle

HARTMANN · Basic Documents of International Relations

HARTMANN · Readings in International Relations

HOLLOWAY · State and Local Government in the United States

LEONARD · Elements of American Foreign Policy

LEONARD · International Organization

MANGONE · A Short History of International Organization

MILLETT · Management in the Public Service

NEUMANN · European and Comparative Government

REED · Municipal Management

RIEMER · Problems of American Government

ROCHE AND STEDMAN · The Dynamics of Democratic Government

STRAUSZ-HUPÉ AND POSSONY · International Relations

SVARLIEN · An Introduction to the Law of Nations

TURNER · Politics in the United States: Readings in Political Parties and Pressure Groups

VANDENBOSCH AND HOGAN · The United Nations—Background, Organization, Functions, Activities

WALDO · Ideas and Issues in Public Administration: A Book of Readings

WILSON · The American Political Mind

WILSON · Police Administration

GOVERNING URBAN AMERICA

Structure, Politics, and Administration

CHARLES R. ADRIAN

Assistant Professor of Political Science
Michigan State University

McGRAW-HILL BOOK COMPANY, INC.

New York   Toronto   London

1955

GOVERNING URBAN AMERICA
STRUCTURE, POLITICS, AND ADMINISTRATION

Copyright © 1955 by the McGraw-Hill Book Company, Inc. Printed in the United States of America. All rights reserved. This book, or parts thereof, may not be reproduced in any form without permission of the publishers.

Library of Congress Catalog Card Number 55-7264

THE MAPLE PRESS COMPANY, YORK, PA.

PREFACE

The government of cities is a part of the political process. Since this is the case, I believe that a course in American city government should be taught as a part of the offerings of political science in the liberal arts tradition. I have tried to write this textbook with that purpose in mind. It will, therefore, not serve as a handbook for the local government official, and it will not teach applied administration to a student who is a would-be city manager. Perhaps it may inspire a few students to take further courses toward a career in municipal administration, but that is not its major purpose. Principally, this textbook will, I hope, teach the college student, whether a political science major or otherwise, some of the things he, as a citizen, needs to know about his city and its governmental operations.

I have made three basic assumptions in writing this book. One is that a general text on city government should deal not only with structure and policy making, but also with functions and administrative operations. This volume is designed to be used as the text for either a one- or a two-semester course, but the current trend toward a single-semester course has been considered in the allocation of space. A second assumption is that city government is meaningful only if studied as part of the whole urban culture. I have therefore made considerable use of the materials of urban sociology, social psychology, and other related disciplines. A third assumption is that the process of urban government is primarily a *political* process. I have emphasized this point throughout the text. Functions are discussed from the point of view of what the lay citizen needs to know, and emphasis has been placed upon current issues of policy. The administrative organization of functions is not ignored, but detailed treatment of technical engineering and administrative problems has been omitted in the belief that these are properly material for professional courses in public administration as distinguished from academic courses in political science. I believe that the apathy so often found in connection with municipal government can be overcome only by convincing more people that good municipal government is a matter not alone of administration of a professional quality, but also of protecting one's stake in a local political process—a process that does not differ fundamentally from that on the state or national level.

The writing of a textbook involves essentially the assembling and organizing of the works of others so as to make them more effective for teaching purposes. To those who have created the literature in the field, I am therefore indebted. I must also acknowledge the helpful advice and criticism of several of my colleagues, Harvey Brazer, Merrill Case, H. Warren Dunham, Theodore B. Fleming, and William Monat. Special thanks go to Louis L. Friedland and Stephen B. Sarasohn for their comments on large portions of the manuscript, and to Mary Kukkonen, who did a fine job in typing the manuscript. My wife, Audrey, scarcely complained when my study remained in disarray for months on end, and she offered encouragement at those many times when the task seemed too difficult.

It is conventional, and quite proper, to add that all errors of fact and all disputable conclusions are those of the author, and are his responsibility alone.

CHARLES R. ADRIAN

CONTENTS

Preface v

1. The Trend toward an Urban Nation 1
2. The Urban Fringe 30
3. Theories of Local Self-Government in America 48
4. Municipal Elections 67
5. The Political Process and the City: I 99
6. The Political Process and the City: II 118
7. The Law of Municipalities 137
8. Forms of Government 172
9. Mayors and Managers 208
10. The City Council 226
11. Government in the Metropolitan Area 242
12. Intergovernmental Relations 257
13. Municipal Administration 268
14. The Municipal Civil Service 285
15. Financing Modern City Government 305
16. The City and Organized Crime 339
17. Public Safety 352
18. Public Utilities and Transportation 372
19. Urban Housing 396
20. Planning and Zoning 407
21. Public Health and Welfare 417
22. The Future of American City Government 432

Index 443

CHAPTER 1

THE TREND TOWARD AN URBAN NATION

The college student of today is, according to the best available estimates, by all odds a favorite to spend his lifetime in an urban community.
This textbook is designed to help him, as a lay citizen, gain a better
understanding of the operation of city government. Particular stress is
laid throughout the text upon those issues in city politics that are political in nature, that is, that are controversial and possess alternative patterns of solution. As such, these issues may require the ordinary citizen
to make a choice and take a stand, either at the polls or as a member of
an interest group. It is not the function of this text to urge any specific
viewpoint upon the student; the purpose is rather to aid the citizen in
making an *informed* choice, or at least to help explain some of the basic
factors that will influence his views on urban issues. This is not to suggest that the author is without opinions on these issues or that he will be
utterly "objective" in his presentation. It has been his observation that
one of the surest recipes for a dull, uninspiring book is for the author
meticulously to avoid stating his conclusions or discussing controversial
subjects.

THE CITY AND THE URBANITE

The City Today. American city government has matured rapidly in
the last fifty years. Within that time, many of our cities have changed
from the worst-governed to almost the best-governed of American political units. Unlike most state and county governments, cities have undergone extensive modernization of their structure, so that they are prepared
to furnish the services demanded by modern society. Most city political
machines and bosses have been destroyed. The remaining ones are adopting a more modern viewpoint toward government. Blatant corruption and
spoilsmanship have given way before the need for governmental services
performed by technical specialists.

The realities of government in the contemporary American city are not
well understood by the typical citizen. The folkways and folk tales of
Americana saddle city government and city politicians with a stereotype

1

that has little basis in fact. The stereotype does, however, have a *historical* basis.

The Public Attitude toward City Governments. Nearly everyone has at one time heard of the famous comment by the great British political scientist Lord Bryce, who called "the government of cities the one conspicuous failure of the United States." That statement was made more than sixty years ago. Yet many Americans think of it as being appropriate today. Partly for this reason, citizens, including college students, have developed an unfortunate, almost a dangerous, cynicism regarding municipal government. This viewpoint is highly undesirable in any democracy. It is worthwhile, therefore, to inquire into the following causes which formerly resulted in corrupt and incompetent city government.

1. *Rapid Growth of Cities.* In the first place, difficulties in achieving good government in cities are partly a product of the rapidity with which the American city grew after the Civil War. This nation was predominantly an agricultural one until (roughly) the last half of the nineteenth century, and its democratic traditions were oriented toward the frontier and the farm, not toward the city. The same traditions do not necessarily fit each of them equally well. Furthermore, effective *democratic* government is built largely upon a sound foundation of customs, attitudes, and traditions that require time to build and to work into the normal behavior patterns of a society. A nation of farmers cannot overnight discover methods of honest and efficient government of industrial cities. Furthermore, when blossoming cities of the nineteenth century had added to their populations shiploads of immigrants, ignorant of the customs, laws, beliefs, and even language of an adopted country, the possibility of good government became a thousandfold more remote.

2. *City as Creature of State.* A second factor is to be found in the position of the city as a creature of the state. With minor exceptions (to be discussed in Chapter 7), the relationship of a city to the state in which it is located is the relationship between a child and its parent. A city can perform only those functions authorized for it by state law. These functions are generally of two kinds: (1) those in which the city acts simply as the agent of the state, and (2) matters of local concern. An example of the former is the protection of the public health; of the latter, the provision for transit service. American courts historically have given a very narrow intepretation to the powers of cities. This has been based on the theory that, if in doubt, power belongs to the sovereign state and not to one of its corporate subdivisions. The result has been that the state legislature—usually dominated by farmers and small-town lawyers who are inexperienced in city government—has often not given the city the power needed to deal with local problems. This situation may lead to dissatisfaction, cynicism, and a tendency on the part of the

public to look elsewhere for the solution of the problems of the city. The typical citizen, casually interested in politics and law, is not concerned with *why* the city cannot perform a function felt to be needed—he wants it done, and if the city cannot do it, he will look for another unit of government that can and will.

Especially restrictive of the power of the city to perform services wanted by its citizens has been the state-imposed limitation upon the power of the city to tax. American cities have been, and still are, overwhelmingly dependent upon a levy that was designed to fit the needs of a frontier society—the general property tax. Because legislatures have not been anxious to allow cities to use other types of taxes, municipalities often have found that their limit of services renderable comes at whatever point the property tax seems to reach a saturation point. Again the impatient and annoyed citizen is likely to turn to the state or national government for a service for which the city has no money.[1]

Picayunish control over local matters has been carried to such an extent by many state legislatures that cities have sometimes been given almost no chance to decide any really important matter for themselves. This type of action by the lawmakers turns the legislature into nothing less than an *administrative* overseer of city government. While the practice appears to be on the decline today, it continues in many states to give the citizen the impression that the really important decisions are made, not in the city hall, but in the state capitol and that, therefore, city government is not of sufficient consequence to rate his attention. Such supervision by the state government has also had its adverse affect upon the municipal officeholder, whose creativity becomes dulled and discouraged by being constantly told that he is exceeding or is in danger of exceeding his authority. When his powers are interpreted narrowly by the courts and he must go to the legislature whenever he wishes to make a departure from customary policy, the city official soon begins to orient his job toward the annotated statutes and the opinions of the attorney general, instead of toward the economic and sociological needs of the city. The ordinary citizen, impatient with legalism, is likely to view the plight of the harassed official without sympathy. The explanations he hears will sound to him like excuses for inaction.

3. *Experience in Depression.* A third item discouraging citizen faith in city government stems from the experience of the Great Depression that began in the fall of 1929. Municipalities, supported by a tax base often deceivingly inflated by the artificial real estate boom of the twenties, found themselves financially unable to meet the suddenly enormous costs of the public relief load, the costs of the municipal payroll, or the costs of the interest upon bonded indebtedness. In many parts of the United

[1] City financing will be examined in some detail in chap. 15.

States, states had to shore up the finances of their cities, and then the national government had to do the same for the states. The reformer, the New Dealer, and the ordinary citizen, seeking to overcome the paralyzing depression, turned from the city to the state, and especially to the national government, for aid and support. The phenomenon of a municipality nearly or actually bankrupt in a time of great public need is well remembered by millions of persons alive today. The memory does not enhance the prestige of our cities.

4. *Corruption.* A fourth consideration has been the persistency with which American cities have been plagued with varying degrees of corruption. It has become a veritable tradition in our larger municipalities and has affected a great many of our cities of any size, at one time or another in history. Corruption may enter city government, in the first place, as a result of the commonplace lack of public interest in the operations of the city which permits lax administration. Dishonesty and irregularities breed a greater lack of interest and a cynicism which merely allows for more of the same. Another cause stems from circumstances which demand that city officials enforce formally enacted laws that do not accord with the prevailing public mores. Examples of this may be found in the case of liquor prohibition during the twenties, and of gambling today.[2] Such anomolies place city officials in positions of great temptation, yet the same citizens who drink illegal liquor or insist upon gambling will be among those who will censure public officials who do not enforce the law. Individual Americans are quite capable of expecting tougher moral fiber in their public officials then they themselves possess.

Corruption is far less widespread and certainly less overt today than it was formerly. Yet in 1948 Philadelphia was rocked by a series of scandals during which embezzlers were uncovered in the city's purchasing department, amusement-tax division, and other agencies. Several extortionists were convicted, and at least four city employees committed suicide. Shortly thereafter, the Kefauver committee uncovered widespread instances of alliances between racketeers and municipal officials in various parts of the United States.

5. *Apathy.* Finally, however, we must face the fact that our cities have not been better governed primarily because most of the general public has not been interested enough to insist upon good government. The ordinary citizen is a busy person with many demands upon his time. As a consequence, he must budget his interests—and municipal government has rated a low priority. This has been true in part because the city dweller has viewed his local government as one that performs primarily

---

[2] The effect of organized crime upon our cities will be examined in chap. 16; the influence of the old-time boss as a "broker of privilege" will be considered in chap. 6.

routine service functions. Who, he wants to know, can become interested in such prosaic problems as the supplying of water, the maintenance of streets, the disposal of sewage? Are these not routine matters to be handled by civil servants? Why should he concern himself? Unfortunately for the welfare of good city government, many advocates of the reform movement of a few decades ago advanced the misconception that municipal government is nothing more than the application of the principles of "good business management" from which the politician ought properly to be excluded.[3] Undoubtedly, city governments exist primarily to render services to patron-citizens. These services, however, are often far from routine, and the existence of alternative approaches to public policy offers the basis for lively citizen participation in genuine political issues. Much of this book will be taken up with the consideration of nonroutine political issues in urban functions.

Until recent decades, citizen interest was often at low ebb because "respectable people" thought they could not be connected (at least not openly) with city administrations that all too often were under the control of a boss or a machine or were cooperating with professional criminals. It was uncommon for a representative of the "best people" of the community to become involved in municipal politics prior to the advent of the reform movement in the 1880s, which helped to make that sort of thing respectable. Even today, many persons still believe that city politics is corrupt, and hence to be shunned by good citizens. Such viewpoints severely retard efforts to achieve adequate, able, and modern city government.

The high mobility so characteristic of contemporary American cities, combined with the extreme heterogeneity of their populations, has militated against most people having a sense of "belongingness" in the community. This in turn has resulted in a low degree of civic pride and morale, which produces lack of interest in the local political process. Irvin S. Cobb once said, "There is this to be said for New York City: it is the one densely inhabited locality—with the possible exception of Hell—that has absolutely not a trace of local pride." Mr. Cobb to the contrary notwithstanding, the same problem exists in most large cities.

Another aspect of low citizen interest as a cause of poor government may be found in factors related to the phenomenon that the psychologists call identification. The individual, in his fantasies—in his daydreaming—tends to associate himself with the heroic, the "important" things in life. The dramatic, glamorous activities of the national government attract the layman, appeal to his imagination, and help him to form opinions about controversial matters on that level of government, but the commonplace problems of health and of police and fire protection will have much less

[3] This movement, its philosophy, and its results will be studied in chap. 3.

appeal. When the President of the United States discusses national problems over radio and television and asks for the assistance and support of the citizen, the individual is flattered. If, however, the mayor of the city appears on the television screen to talk to the citizenry about the daily problems of the municipality, the response of the citizen is not likely to be the same. Unless the mayor is an unusual individual, the citizen is likely to switch to another channel. His busy mind, with a thousand attractions calling for attention, can be directed only toward those things that are "important" or "interesting."

It can be seen, therefore, that many factors have combined to keep our cities from being as well governed as they might be. Of all of them, however, the most important is the failure of the lay citizen to take a full measure of interest in the government that is the most intimate, the most observable, and the closest to him of all the coercive agents of society. The first thing that the ordinary citizen must learn is that whenever governments fail him in performing a demanded service, whenever there is a lack of imagination, of ability, or of zeal on the part of city officials, and whenever there is a lack of honesty in city government, it is because the citizenry has not insisted that it be otherwise.

METROPOLITAN PANORAMA

Cities come in all sizes and shapes. Some are large, some are small. No two are exactly alike. We can speak of statistical averages and "typical" cities, but we can only approximate what we would find if we were to give an intensive examination to any one city. An impressionistic glance may, however, furnish a few generalizations which can be examined in greater detail farther on in this text.

What, then, are the characteristics of the metropolis? It is a smoky, grimy sea of television aerials, noisome slums, bright neon signs, impatient traffic, mammoth factories with fantastic productive capacity, manicured suburbs desperately seeking to imitate a fond memory of a county-seat town in grandfather's day, with its frenetic citizens earnestly striving to be as exactly like the next-door neighbor as possible, dreading a slip that might engender the anathematic charge of being "different." It is a Champaigne fair of conflicting cultures where thousands of human beings live in close proximity to other thousands whom they dislike in one degree or another because—though they would not so state it—their values and cultural habits do not coincide. For the human being dislikes what he fears, he fears much that he does not understand, and there is much in the modern city that he does not understand. It is a land of coolness in a nation of supposedly friendly people, where émigrés from rural places find an absence of the primary social relationships to which they are accustomed, and where people, in the midst of the greatest possible variety of activities, often lead basically dull lives, although they seek to hide that fact from their own consciousness.

The City Hall. The people of the city have little interest in their local government and treat it with a lack of respect which, in their opinion, is its due. Somewhere downtown in an area sadly lacking in parking space —as is the entire city, for that matter—stands a hideous monstrosity

Fig. 1. City Hall, Birmingham, Ala. Victorian and "General Grant gothic" city halls are giving way in many cities to modern buildings in contemporary design. The change is symbolic of the change that has taken place in city government. SOURCE: Courtesy of C. E. Armstrong, Birmingham, Ala.

decorated with Victorian gingerbread and contemporary pigeon droppings. This is the city hall. The interior of it is a prime example of poor utilization of space, and the taxpayers meet an abnormally large light bill, since the windows would not furnish adequate natural light if the building were located in the center of the Sahara (but see Figure 1).

The city officialdom is headed by the mayor, who is quite likely to be a man of broad smiles, firm handshakes, and modest talents. There are probably several other elective administrative officials—most of them glorified bookkeepers or file clerks, but the public insists upon electing them.

The members of the city council are perhaps somewhat more difficult to classify. Depending upon the city, a few or even perhaps most of them may be men chosen from the business and industrial world, who often are more concerned with the interests of the groups that selected them to run for office than with trying to determine a concept of the public interest. The council is apt to include in its membership one or more representatives of organized labor, who similarly are primarily concerned with labor interests. Usually it includes several lawyers, often those who are politically ambitious and who would use membership in the council as a steppingstone to higher political careers. It is not uncommon for lawyers to run for the council in the hope that the prestige and public notice gained in councilmanic membership will advance them in their profession. There may be a number of political hacks on the council: men who know nothing but the art of politics and to whom defeat would spell threatened starvation.

Although the citizen may pay little attention to local politics, he is quite likely to consider himself a very competent "Monday morning quarterback." While he is quick to offer criticisms of state and national officials, he is even more convinced of his competence in evaluating problems of municipal government. Furthermore, since municipal officials are close at hand, it is much easier for the citizen to make his complaints known.

Services of the City. Transportation is a real problem in the city. Not only is there a serious shortage of parking facilities, but there is probably no form of public transportation that can serve even generally as a substitute for the auto. The bus and streetcar system is operating at a deficit, be it privately or publicly owned, chiefly as the result of one simple fact: in 1918 there was one automobile for every eighteen people, today there is one for every four. Of course, the inadequacy is blamed on just about anything but this. If a private company owns the system, the pundits are screaming for purchase by the city. If the city is already in possession, the fault is found to lie with this misguided application of un-American socialism and the whole system should be returned posthaste to private hands. (Not that any entrepreneur in his right mind would undertake to buy it.) If no other scapegoat can be found, the fault must lie with "politics."

Some expressways, belt lines, and cutoffs are beginning to appear several decades after their need first became apparent. The sunken highways do, in some cases, hurry you downtown, but they do not help you park the auto once you arrive there.

The Urban Personality. The streets of the city are not likely to have the fascinating names of those in a European metropolis. Our cities must have efficiency, not uniqueness. Many an American town is laid out with consecutively numbered streets running in one direction. The streets running at right angles to these may well be numbered "avenues." In 1952, the city of Toledo changed Wausonoquette Boulevard to 290th Street, and in one American city unimaginative residents petitioned the council to give a new name to a street called Spike's Alley. The main artery of Philadelphia is called simply Broad Street; Columbus has High Street; Davenport, Second Street. Although Boston has the Hoosac Docks, most of its place names sound as dull as the love life of a Puritan. Even mighty New York shows its tourists such names as Madison Avenue, Wall Street, Fifth Avenue and, at best, Broadway. At least in Manhattan. Of course Brooklyn does somewhat better with the Gowanus Canal and Flatbush Avenue.

All is not lost, however: there is Cane Run Road in Louisville; Sepulveda Boulevard and Topanga Canyon Avenue in Los Angeles; Cottage Grove Avenue in Chicago; and John R. Street in Detroit. St. Louis has Gravois; Minneapolis, Nicollet; Atlanta, Ponce de Leon; and Omaha, Saddle Creek Road. Even the nation's capital has Fighting Alley and Donnybrook Lane. Probably no city in America can come close to legendary New Orleans with its properly romantic street names: Canal, Carondolet, Bourbon, Beauregard, and the immortal Rampart Street. Nor are all American cities named for the local frontier banker, or called -burgs, -cities, -villes, or -ports. To name only a few, there is Fuquay Springs, Conshohocken, What Cheer, Aliquippa, San Luis Obispo, Wauwatosa, Irondequoit, Nacogdoches, Walla Walla, and Waxahachie. The chances are, however, that the First National Bank stands at the corner of Third Street and Sixth Avenue in Williamsburg.

Unlike the cities of Europe, each of which possesses a distinctive individuality, American cities for the most part have a dull monotony about them. To be sure, there are exceptions. There is only one Boston, New Orleans, New York, Atlantic City, San Francisco, or Washington. But the typical city has little to distinguish it as a personality. It has failed to develop its own individuality, to exploit latent traditions, to use its every opportunity to make the community a place where life is richer because of its own particular attributes. In the past, most pillars of the community and local politicians have been too busy in a frenetic world to concern themselves with such an expendable as local color.

Chaotic Development. Inadequate zoning—too little and too late—is a part of the picture, for somehow the concept of individual initiative and individual use of one's own property has been misinterpreted to mean a right to damage property values of others indiscriminately and to destroy the physical beauty and utility of an area. On the fringe of the city in particular will you find chaotic land use at its worst. Even in zoned areas, residential subdivisions are often laid out on the traditional gridiron pattern, highly desirable in downtown and factory areas but indefensibly severe for contemporary residential building. Happily, however, since the end of World War II there has been a trend toward well-planned residential subdivisions.

The City Is a Playground. From the hinterland for miles around, people flock to the city when they seek recreation and relief from the chores of everyday. The informal amusement patterns of rural America have given way to commercialization. The metropolis offers the theater, the symphony or an occasional opera, professional sports, the public dance hall, skating, billiards, and bowling. The saloon and its more elaborate relative, the night club, interest many. Some wish to visit museums, art galleries, zoos, parks, beaches, or playgrounds.

Any kind of recreation demanded by its hordes of people will be furnished by someone within the city. In a day when people feel more than ever the need for escape from the humdrum, gambling serves as a way out for increasing numbers. Except for operations at the gaudy track laid out in the suburbs, this business is illegal, to be sure, but it is controlled by a syndicate of gangsters who welcome its illegality. This same syndicate is likely to be involved in furnishing other illegal services: prostitution and narcotics. Illegal occupations produce enormous problems for the police—and city officials receive no sympathy from a public that simultaneously demands law enforcement and illegal services.

The City Is a Magnet. In comparison with the rural life that once dominated America, contemporary city life produces more crime, especially of the organized and professional type, more neurotics, more insanity, more lung cancer (possibly because of the greater amount of hydrocarbon irritants in its polluted air), greater extremes of wealth and poverty, more social and economic interdependence and hence more insecurity, more juvenile delinquency, more wrecked marriages, more suicides, and more deaths per thousand people.

Why, then, do increasing numbers of people come every year to the metropolis? And why do those who are already there only *talk* about giving up the struggle and taking "a little place in the country"? Because there is in the city a greater freedom for individually chosen behavior patterns; greater tolerance of diversity (but only in the more crowded parts of the city); more and better schools at all educational levels; a greater variety of entertainment mediums; far more institutions of fine art —libraries, museums, theaters, art cinemas, symphony orchestras, and the ballet; and a much greater opportunity for advancement in accord with the American pattern of values.

The city contains greater extremes of wealth and poverty than does the country, but for most people it means a higher standard of living. It suggests more material things and more of an opportunity for "the good life." The older pattern has been reversed: ours is now a society based largely upon urban values, with the rural dweller more and more imitating the ways of the urbanite. The contemporary American dream is housed among the millions in our cities.[4]

PORTRAIT OF A SMALL CITY

The metropolis, as it has just been described, is only part of the picture. In addition to those large cities of over, say, 100,000 people, there are a number of middle-sized cities in the United States ranging within the general limits of 40,000 to 100,000 people. Smaller than these and less complicated politically, but still a most important part of America, are hundreds of small cities.

The County Seat Today. Storville (we shall call it) is a Middle Western city of about 5,000 inhabitants. While it is hardly possible to pick out *the* typical small city in America, or even one for a particular section of the country, Storville certainly reflects many of the characteristics of a city of its size, and its governmental pattern is not atypical.

Storville is a county seat and trading town in a dairy region. It contains a goodly number of elderly retired farmers, but many of its young people have left to live in larger cities. There are several small manufacturing plants in town, all of them unionized, but the unions are not active in local politics, as they would be in a large city. Most of the people of the community have conservative political, social, and economic views, and they are Republicans in state and national elections. Churches are important local institutions—there are eight of them to serve the city and its rural trading area.

The local school board is building new schools, partly because Storville is growing in size, but largely because of the consolidation of school districts and the closing of surrounding "country schools." People in the city feel they are paying too great a share of the cost of educating the rural students.

The Manager, the Council, and Local Politics. Storville has operated as a council-manager city since the middle 1920s. The present manager, the city's sixth, is a civil engineer. He is about fifty years old, has spent most of his life in private employment, and is now serving in his second city as manager.

The council, which is elected at large, consists of five men, all of whom are under forty-five, except for the mayor. One is a grocer, another operates a men's store, a third is a hatchery owner, and the fourth is a plant

---

[4] For unfavorable criticisms of the contemporary city and of urban life, see E. T. Peterson, *Cities Are Abnormal* (1946), and Lewis Mumford, *The Culture of Cities* (1938).

superintendent in a middle-sized city forty-five minutes away by automobile. The mayor, who presides over the council and has no veto power, is a motel operator, is fifty-eight years old, and has had eighteen years of experience in city government—much more than any of the councilmen. He shares policy leadership with the manager.

Elections are on a nonpartisan ballot and campaigns on an informal, personal basis. There is some pressure-group activity before the council and at elections, but most relationships between candidates or officeholders and the public are direct. State and county politicians do not take part in city campaigns. There is no single outstanding political leader in the city, although on some matters of local public policy people defer to the judgment of the president of the local bank. The principal interest groups in Storville politics are the chamber of commerce, acting for the downtown merchants, the League of Women Voters, and the American Legion. The last time an incumbent councilman decided to retire, the Legion solicited support in the community for one of its leaders and he was elected to fill the vacated seat.

Councilmen try to determine the public's viewpoints on important issues through personal contacts. They have no direct way of measuring their success in discovering cross-section opinions, but they believe that they "do all right"—at least an incumbent is seldom defeated for reelection.

Issues and Problems. The people of Storville are quite satisfied with their police department. It consists of a chief, seven policemen, two patrol cars, and a two-way radio system, and it enjoys a close relationship with the county sheriff's office. The fire department suits them, too. It has a paid chief with one full-time fireman. Other members are volunteers, each of whom has a radio in his home for receiving fire calls.

Water supply—from deep wells—is adequate, although another well will be needed in a few years. The manager will recommend that it be built at the east end of town—in the direction of population movement. The cost of water in Storville is nearly twice that of the largest cities in the state, since there is no large volume of sale which would reduce unit costs.

The city is faced with greater problems, however. County taxes are poorly equalized, and the city dweller pays a disproportionate share of them. City property taxes are high and produce many complaints. Storville, from the time sewers were first installed, has dumped its raw sewage into the local river. This practice is creating a hazard to fish and to human health, so the city must now raise $350,000 for a sewage-treatment plant.

The capital-improvements program of the city has not kept pace with the increase in the number of people—or automobiles. The greatest number of complaints heard by councilmen and the manager deal with the condition of the streets. They are in poor repair—poorer than the streets in a typical large city—and maintenance has not equaled the rate of wear in recent years. There is no demand, however, as there is in some nearby cities, for belt lines to take state highways around the city. Traffic is not heavy enough in Storville, and the main street is not on a highway, as it often is in small cities. The manager has recently convinced the council that it should pass an ordinance authorizing the council to install street paving, curbs, and gutters without first securing permission from a majority of the abutting property owners. This will give the manager much more flexibility in planning street improvements.

There is a serious shortage of parking spaces in downtown Storville, and the city government is trying to acquire a number of off-street parking lots. The weekly *Storville Star* has criticized this action by the city as adding a further burden to the overworked property tax. (The *Star*, unlike newspapers in many small cities, has been very critical of the mayor and the manager, irresponsibly so at times. The parking lots, for example, are to be paid for exclusively from parking-meter receipts, not from general taxes.) Parking meters were installed in 1948, and they blanket all of the commercial areas of the city. They have been profitable from the start. People no longer complain about them.

The parking situation, plus a need for more space and a desire for lower taxes and cheaper land, has led some merchants and small manufacturers to move outside the city limits. A recent headline in the *Star* warned, "Tax Loss to City Seen in Decentralization Trend." A fringe-area problem has resulted. Two adjacent townships have found it desirable to adopt zoning ordinances to control developments. Storville has been asked to supply water outside its limits. A slum area of dilapidated shacks has grown up on the fringe to the west, but a subdivision of expensive homes lies outside the taxing limits to the north. The fringe is growing along the main traffic arteries.

A new planning and zoning ordinance was adopted a year ago to replace an outmoded one. It was prepared by a professional planner. But it was greatly altered by the council after hearings revealed the views of interested individuals.

Closing Statement. The small city and the metropolis differ from one another in many ways. But they are both cities, and they share many characteristics, problems, and issues. This text will be concerned with their similarities and their differences.

THE COMING OF THE CITY

Meanings and Usages. Nothing much can be learned concerning the nature of an area simply because it is called a city. The term itself descends from the Latin *civis* (citizen) and was restricted in England to application to cathedral towns. (Other urban areas in England were known as boroughs—a term used today in the city of New York and to some extent in Connecticut, New Jersey, Minnesota, and Pennsylvania.)[5] A city in the United States is a *legal*, not a *sociological*, concept. City limits may be greater or smaller than the *de facto* urban area. In most states a city may or may not be larger than the largest villages in the state. Villages may be tiny rural trading centers, or they may be sizable urban areas, as in the case of several of Chicago's large suburbs. There may or may not be meaningful legal differences between cities and villages. In this text, what is said to apply to cities will also generally apply to villages as well. As a matter of fact, the smaller urbanized areas of a state may be legally called villages (as in Minnesota), or they may be called towns (as in Iowa). The smallest *rural* unit of government is usually the township—except in New England, where they are unique institutions and are called towns. To add to the confusion, however, townships do not exist at all in some states, especially in the South; in Minnesota they are legally (although not popularly) known as towns; and around some of our cities they have become urbanized and constitute virtually another form of city government (for example, in Michigan and New Jersey).

The largest urban communities are often popularly (although not legally) known as metropolitan areas (from the Greek *mētēr*, mother, and *polis*, city-state). These "mother-cities" are ordinarily made up of an agglomeration of cities, villages, townships, special districts, and other units that may total several hundred in number. In the United States, these sociologically cohesive units are virtually never treated as legal units; the metropolitan area is almost never a single city.[6]

The student should be warned, therefore, against any hasty conclusions concerning the meaning of the terms usually used in connection with urban areas. Without a standard terminology he must be prepared to adapt his understanding of terms to conditions prevailing locally. For purposes of this text, an urban area is conceived of as a sociological com-

[5] The word *town* is from the Anglo-Saxon *tun*, a homestead surrounded by a hedge or other fence (from Old High German, *zûn*, a hedge). *Borough* is from the Anglo-Saxon *burh*, a fortified town. Today, in the four states named above, it represents an incorporated area occupying a position between that of a city and a village. The five administrative subdivisions of New York are also called boroughs. *Village* is from the Italian and Latin *villa*, meaning originally a farm or country house. The term *municipality* is from the Latin *municipium*, which referred to certain Italian towns that enjoyed special privileges under Rome. In the United States today, the term is popularly (and in this book) used interchangeably with *city* or *village*.

[6] Problems arising where sociological and legal boundaries do not coincide are examined in chap. 2.

munity wherein the individuals are engaged primarily in diversified non-agricultural pursuits and where distinctive, nonrural patterns of behavior prevail. A city, village, borough, or (sometimes) town is a legally described region which seldom coincides with the actual urban area.[7]

Urbanization of the Western World. The city in western civilization is primarily a product of the industrial revolution. To be sure, there were cities in Europe before 1770 (roughly the time of the beginning of the "revolution," which lasted for over a century thereafter), but they were chiefly capitals or trading centers.[8] In 1550, Paris, both a trading center and a great seat of government, was, according to W. B. Munro, the largest city in Europe, and its population did not exceed 300,000. Mighty London was a village during the Middle Ages, having only about 40,000 people as that period came to an end. It grew very rapidly in the sixteenth and seventeenth centuries as Britain became the trading center of the rising new economic world. By the time of the American revolution, it had become the largest city in Europe, with a population of around three-quarters of a million people.

With the rise of a machine technology, steam power, and the factory system, cities grew at phenomenal rates. Europe and America, predominately rural from prehistoric times, rapidly became urbanized nations. In the United States, there were only small towns at the time of the Revolution. They were growing, however, and they continued to grow. From the turn of the nineteenth century, cities expanded at an ever increasing pace. Between 1820 and 1840 the number of people engaged in manufacturing increased by 127 per cent. Between 1840 and 1850 alone America's urban population increased by nearly 50 per cent.[9]

After the War between the States (1861 to 1865), urban growth, which earlier had occurred on the east coast and especially in New England, spread into the Middle West. The rise of the great corporations and the never-ending developments in technological knowledge continued to raise the American *standard* of living even as it changed the American *mode* of living. Immigrants who before had hurried to the rich clay loams of the Middle Western farm belt now remained in New York, or Cincinnati,

[7] It is neither realistic nor necessary to try to make a sharp break between rural and urban living, especially in present-day United States. For the difficulties involved in trying to define a city, see Noel P. Gist and L. A. Halbert, *Urban Society* (3d ed., 1949), pp. 3–8; or Stuart A. Queen and David B. Carpenter, *The American City* (1953), pp. 16–22.

[8] For a most interesting account of ancient and medieval cities, see W. B. Munro, *Municipal Government and Administration* (1923, with subsequent revisions), vol. 1, chaps. 1–4; or his article "City," in *Encyclopedia of the Social Sciences,* vol. 2, pp. 474–482. See also Lewis Mumford, *The Culture of Cities* (1938).

[9] An account of the coming of industrial society to America is especially well done in Arthur M. Schlesinger, Jr., *The Age of Jackson* (1945).

or Chicago to become a commodity called "labor" in the factory, the steel mill, or the stockyard.[10] The children of country bumpkins yearned to become city slickers and hurried off at the earliest opportunity to what was often their disillusionment. And they continue to do so today (see Figure 2).

The City Today. The population of cities doubled between the beginning of the War between the States and 1900. By 1920, over one-half

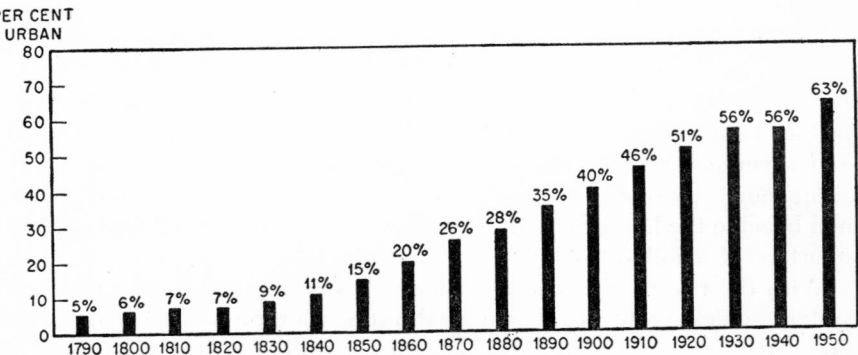

Fig. 2. Percentage of population in urban areas. Figures have been rounded off. At the time of the first United States census in 1790, less than 5 per cent of the population lived in urban areas. Today, virtually two-thirds of all Americans are urbanites. SOURCE: U.S. Bureau of the Census.

(51.2 per cent) of the American people were living in cities.[11] The percentage is now past 62 and continues to climb. We live in an urban nation. The world today depends upon no man more than it depends

[10] See Arthur M. Schlesinger, *The Rise of the City* (1933); and his "The City in American History," *Mississippi Valley Historical Review,* vol. 27 (June, 1940), pp. 43–66.

[11] For statistical purposes, the U.S. Bureau of the Census classifies cities as incorporated places with 2,500 or more inhabitants. Legal definitions differ from this in the various states.

In the census of 1950, the Bureau defined urban, as distinguished from rural, areas as (1) places of 2,500 inhabitants or more incorporated as cities, boroughs, or villages; (2) the densely settled urban fringe, whether incorporated or unincorporated, around cities of 50,000 or more (the limits of this area determined more or less arbitrarily, based upon physical features); (3) unincorporated areas of 2,500 inhabitants or more outside of the urban fringes; and (4) towns of 2,500 or more except in New England, New York, and Wisconsin.

The Bureau has also undertaken to define large urban places. "Standard metropolitan areas" contain at least one city of 50,000 or more population. The nucleus of the area is the county or counties containing the core city or cities. Contiguous counties are included in the area if they are densely settled by nonagricultural workers and are socially and economically integrated with the core city. For technical criteria, see *1950 Census of Population,* vol. I, pp. xv and xxxiii. The Bureau has also defined "urbanized areas," not to be confused with "urban areas"; see *ibid.,* p. xxvii.

upon the American farmer. But he is no longer a member of the dominant group in our society. And his cultural patterns and sets of values are rapidly being replaced by new ones more in keeping with our own, rather than our parents' or grandparents', world.

Today more than one-half of the American population lives not merely in an urban, but in a *metropolitan* community. Approximately one-fourth of it lives in the twelve largest metropolitan areas. About 220 counties hold one-half of the nation's population. The other half is scattered over 2,800 rural counties.

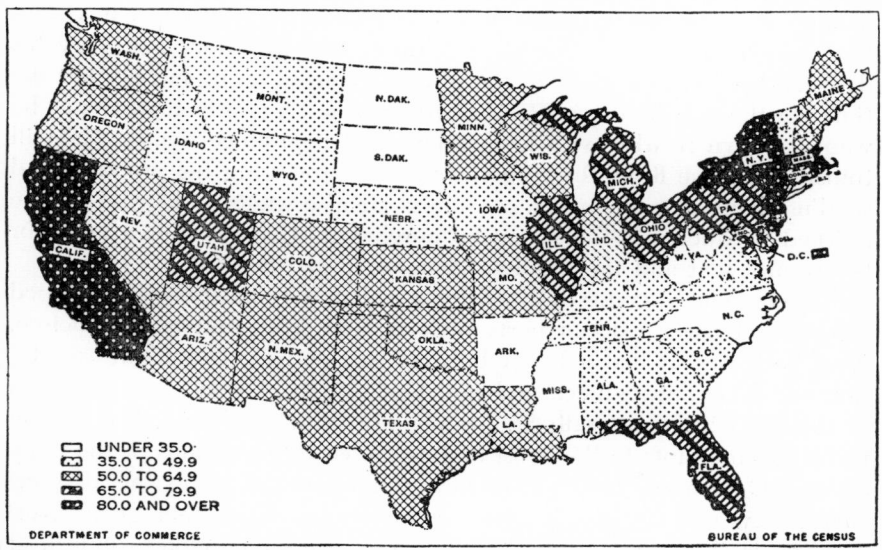

Fig. 3. 1950 urban population as per cent of total population. SOURCE: U.S. Bureau of the Census, reproduced in *Municipal Year Book* (1953), p. 20. Used by permission.

The movement toward the cities is indicated by the fact that one-half of the counties in the nation showed a population decrease between 1940 and 1950. These were, of course, the rural counties.

The 170 metropolitan areas, as defined by the Bureau of the Census, account for two-thirds of the total retail volume and about 90 per cent of the total wholesale volume of the nation. It was in these areas that about 80 per cent of the nation's population increase took place in the decade preceding 1950. The greatest increase took place in cities along the coast of the Pacific Ocean and the Gulf of Mexico, and also on the Great Lakes (see Figure 3).

Most of the net population increase took place in the suburbs. While the core cities of metropolitan areas increased by 13 per cent during the decade prior to 1950, the suburbs increased by 34.7 per cent. Nearly one-half of the total population increase in the United States took place in the suburbs of the 170 metropolitan areas.[12]

LOCATION OF CITIES AND FACTORS IN GROWTH

The Break-in-transportation Theory. One theory concerning the location and growth of cities is the break-in-transportation thesis, which holds that wherever the flow of goods is interrupted, either on the way to the manufacturer or from him, a city will grow up.[13] A snowball effect follows, with one institution creating the need for another, one business making it profitable for another to locate there, until a diversified city has been built up. The Wisconsin farmer ordinarily does not carry his dairy and poultry products to the ultimate consumer; he has neither the time nor the need to do so. He is a producer, not a middleman. Hence he wants a town nearby with a creamery and a produce dealer. He will transfer to these firms the responsibilty for processing his products and sending them on to the urban consumer. He also wants a place where the finished products of others may be purchased. There is thus a need for the county seat and the smaller towns of rural America.

More obviously, goods destined for an inland city must be transshipped at excellent natural ocean ports such as New York and San Francisco. New York was at first a break between sea and river-canal transportation and later between sea and rail. Dodge City, Kansas, was the head of the old Chisholm Trail; St. Joseph, Missouri, served as an outfitting point for emigrants to the West and as the eastern terminus of the pony express; Omaha and Council Bluffs were ferry points across the Missouri River; New Orleans was located on the estuary of another great river; Chicago is at one of the western heads of the Great Lakes, Duluth at another.

Chicago is close to some of the world's richest farm land, to iron ore, and to coal. Cheap water transportation was essential in the utilization of these resources. With these advantages, with a relatively central location between East and West, and with Lake Michigan jutting deep into the Middle West, Chicago acted as a magnet in drawing railroads to it as a terminus, becoming perhaps the greatest rail center in the world. Duluth transships wheat sent by rail from the Red River Valley and iron ore from the nearby Mesabi iron range.

---

[12] Population shifts and patterns are analyzed in Victor Jones, "Local Government in Metropolitan Areas," in Coleman Woodbury (ed.), *The Future of Cities and Urban Redevelopment* (1953), pt. IV, chaps. 1–2; and in *Population and Its Distribution* (7th ed., 1951).

[13] See Charles H. Cooley, "The Theory of Transportation," in *Sociological Theory and Social Research* (1930); and A. F. Weber, *The Growth of Cities in the Nineteenth Century* (1899).

Of course, changes in transportation techniques may vitally affect cities. With the rise of the railroad some formerly important river towns and, especially, canal towns became stagnant. The rise of motor transportation in the twentieth century in the form of the auto and the semitrailer truck provided a previously unknown flexibility of movement. It was now possible for smaller cities to become more important industrially, and larger cities no longer had to have single "factory sections" on the waterfront or the rail spur. Inhabitants no longer had to crowd together, but could decentralize, as happened in the great suburban movement, depending upon the auto to get them downtown or to other business centers. The airplane has aided in freeing transportation from the rigidity of the stream and the rail, but has not had the great impact of the auto.

Proximity to Natural Resources and Other Factors. Wherever iron, coal, oil, and other raw materials are to be found, cities will arise to house and feed the workers. Manufacturers making use of these raw materials will also try to locate reasonably close by. Adequate transportation must be available or a possibility, however, and another prerequisite is a plentiful water supply. It costs much more to move water over great distances than it does to move electricity—and our estimated water needs within the next quarter century are double the present.

The accident of a rail-junction location may help produce a city, as in the case of Moberly, Missouri, or Wichita, Kansas. A capital city may be created primarily out of political considerations—even if it means building in an unhealthful humid swamp—as in the case of Washington and St. Petersburg (now Leningrad). Ancient cities were often located with a serious eye on the military defensibility of the site. Climate is worthy of consideration, but many American and foreign cities are located in areas affording physical discomfort. Pity the resident of New Orleans with its high summer humidity; the nigh-frozen dweller in Fargo, North Dakota, in February; the rain-drenched Seattle citizen in November or December.

War, with its modern emphasis upon assembly-line production of complex weapons and equipment, aids in bringing more people off the farms (where the continued increase in mechanization and other modern techniques and discoveries has been freeing manpower for the last two and one-half centuries) into the cities. World Wars I and II have aided in the rapid building up of such areas as Los Angeles, Detroit, Wichita, and Houston, to name a few. The future may see a dispersion of war industries as a protective measure, and hence the rise of new cities in inland areas away from the coast.

Proximity to Power. The city is chiefly a product of an industrial age, and industry requires power sources. At first, in America, this meant water power. It was available in New England, along the fall line, where this nation's manufacturing first developed. The same phenomenon was important elsewhere. For example, the Falls of St. Anthony located in the Mississippi River not far from rich grain fields helped account for Minneapolis, a milling center.

Later steam power became dominant, and this established a familiar pattern: steam required coal; coal could be moved most cheaply by water. Furthermore, disposal of industrial wastes from large plants required availability of water. Rail transportation also became vital once it was available, but only as a supplement and especially to haul away finished products. These conditions were usually fulfilled in an industrial town, and they dictated, for the most part, large industrial units. Today a new source of power—electricity—has allowed the old pattern to be modified somewhat. The trend today is toward the building of smaller plants in the suburbs rather than large plants on the waterfront, near the downtown section. Electrical power combined with modern motor transportation is also tending to make middle-sized cities more important in relation to the largest cities. While this trend is evident, there is no danger that Chicago and Philadelphia are about to become ghost towns. The differential advantages between Chicago and Kokomo to be found in lower wages, taxes, land values, and other costs in the smaller city only slightly offset the greater advantages in Chicago of a larger market immediately surrounding the factory and a ready supply of skilled and unskilled labor. Furthermore, electrical power is still far more expensive than steam for most uses. Our cities will decentralize somewhat, but it will be chiefly in the well-established pattern of movement to the suburbs, where many of the advantages of the smaller city can be combined with those of the large city.[14]

A great new power source, atomic energy, if adapted to industrial use, may greatly alter the pattern of cities in the future. It may considerably accelerate decentralization.

Eclectic Factors as Causes of Growth. Cities are seldom created as the result of a single causal factor; and if they grow and become powerful, it is not necessarily for the same reasons as those of their founding. Break-in-transportation may provide the initial impetus, but subsequent growth may be a result of manufacturing and other diversified factors. Detroit was a quiet shipbuilding town in the nineteenth century, but it boomed with the rise of the auto industry. Hibbing, Minnesota, was a small trading center until the Mesabi range was discovered literally underneath it. Wichita, Kansas, was a rail junction that grew as an aircraft and diversified manufacturing center. Rochester, New York, was a tiny frontier trading post until the Erie Canal reached it.

[14] W. C. Hallenbeck, *American Urban Communities* (1951), a textbook, furnishes a collection of geographic, historical, governmental, economic, and social data on American cities.

A single city is not necessarily tied by destiny to a certain industry or function. Detroit had all of the prerequisites to make it an auto-manufacturing center—iron ore and limestone for steel to the northwest, the steel industry and coal fields around Pittsburgh and Youngstown to the southeast, the rubber industry at Akron, and the Great Lakes as a connecting link to bring in raw materials and to haul away finished products. Yet but for the accident of Henry Ford being born and reared in what is now suburban Detroit, and other early auto pioneers locating there, the industry might well have centered (perhaps even more logically) in Cleveland, Toledo, Sandusky, or even Chicago or Milwaukee.

Many factors beyond mass-production techniques and rapid forms of transportation and communication have contributed to the growth of cities: The almost miraculous development of modern medical techniques, especially in the field of communicable-disease control, has permitted hordes of people to live healthfully in close proximity; the urban way of life itself has become a part of our cultural values, making the city symbolic of "excitement," a way out of the "dull" country life where "nothing ever happens," and hence a desirable place to live; the development of engineering techniques has made possible the skyscrapers so necessary to a concentration of business in a small, closely knit area and has overcome the technical difficulties of furnishing germ-free water and disposing safely of thousands of tons of sewage.[15]

Cities are founded and grow—or languish—as the result, then, of an admixture of many factors—economic, political, technological, and cultural. In the next few decades we may expect a continuing trend toward urbanism in America, although the pattern will change somewhat: middle-sized cities will flourish, while large cities will "flatten out" to some extent, with a rush of dwelling areas, factories, and business and shopping areas toward the periphery.[16]

URBAN ECOLOGY

Theories of Urban Development. The term *ecology* refers to the study of the distribution of people and institutions in space. It is evident, of course, that cities have "sections" and "districts." The causes, effects, and interrelationships of these areas must be left to a course in urban sociology, but the fact of their existence is a matter of immediate concern in the politics and administration of cities. Urban areas are divided into several zones. There is a downtown or *central business district*. Next is a surrounding *zone of transition* where retreating higher-class residents

[15] Luther Gulick, *Our Cities Today and Tomorrow* (1947), discusses factors making urban growth possible.

[16] The present tendency toward the development of several nuclei in metropolitan areas rather than a single downtown sector is referred to by some sociologists by the term *polynucleation*.

have left an area now made up of rooming houses, cheap hotels, and business places that need not put up a good front for the public. Here live the casual laborers, the recent migrants from the rural South and other parts of America (for our cities depend upon rural America for much of their population as they once depended upon immigrants), the second-story men and other professional criminals, usually of the petty type, the prostitutes, gamblers, bootleggers, and, as a result of the social system rather than by fault of their own, many of the foreign-born and

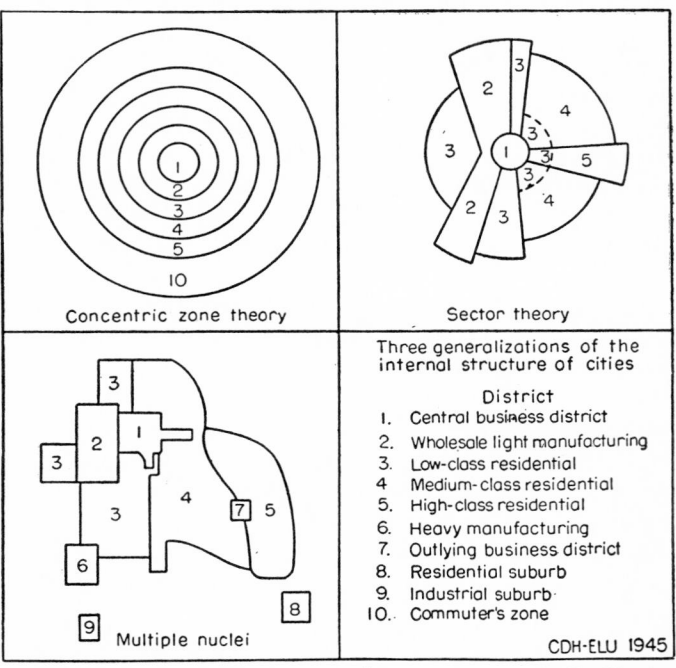

Fig. 4. Generalization of internal structure of cities. SOURCE: C. D. Harris and E. L. Ullman, "The Nature of Cities," *The Annals of the American Academy of Political and Social Science*, vol. 242 (November, 1945).

the Negroes. This is the area of low home-ownership rates and high crime, death, insanity, suicide, juvenile delinquency, and public welfare dependency rates. This is the area in which the city must spend the greatest percentage of its budget and from which it receives its smallest contributions to the cost of government.

Next there may be a *zone of workingmen's homes* gradually improving into the lower-middle-class and finally the well-to-do living areas. The theory that these areas are to be found in *concentric circles* about the main business area has been put forward by E. W. Burgess,[17] but it re-

[17] E. W. Burgess, "The Growth of the City," in R. E. Park, E. W. Burgess, and R. D. McKenzie, *The City* (1925).

quires considerable modification to fit the facts in most cities (see Figure 4).

To overcome some of the objections to the Burgess theory, Homer Hoyt has advanced the *sector theory,* which holds that the city is sliced up to look somewhat like a pie, the wealthy sections to be found at the outer edge of one or more sectors and poor areas in another sector, with areas moving out along the radial spokes—the main arteries of transportation.[18] Other sociologists have held that no general theory of urban growth patterns can be hazarded. For the purposes of the political scientist, it is enough to know that cities do have various sectors serving various clienteles.[19] The chapters on politics and public policy will make clear their political import.

SOME CHARACTERISTICS OF URBAN LIFE

The urban dweller, and especially the middle-class suburbanite, of today is motivated in the direction of pleasing others—particularly strangers and near strangers. He is afraid of the cold, impersonal world in which he finds himself. He desires power, prestige, and security. But these are hard to find in the metropolis. Yet they seem to be fundamental human needs. What is modern man to do?

The Lonely Escape. Erich Fromm, a social psychologist, has suggested that the contemporary urbanite seeks to avoid the isolation of modern life in "automaton conformity."[20] Man fears freedom and individuality. In an interdependent world, he is afraid to "go it alone." He does not desire to emphasize creativity or opportunity for individual action. The person who deviates from the norm, even very slightly, is subject to immediate criticism from a mediocre, unimaginative, fearful society. It is *safer*—it is more conducive to security—if he conforms. No one will attack him, no one will persecute him, no one will single him out for criticism, no one will have a reason to exclude him from the children's play group, the country club, the Kiwanians, or a deaconship in the church if he loses his individuality in entire, uncritical conformity. He becomes *accepted*—and it is a deep-seated need for social acceptance that he feels.

More recently David Riesman, building on the concepts presented by Fromm, has shown that until late decades Americans sought security in

---

[18] Homer Hoyt, *The Structure and Growth of Residential Neighborhoods in American Cities* (1939), chap. 6.

[19] If the student has not had a course in the sociology of urban areas, it would be profitable at this point for him to read Gist and Halbert, *op. cit.,* chaps. 6–10, or Queen and Carpenter, *op. cit.,* pt. 3.

[20] Erich Fromm, *Escape from Freedom* (1941); see also Margaret Mary Wood, *Paths of Loneliness: The Individual Isolated in Modern Society* (1953).

conformity to parental, and particularly paternal, authority.[21] The middle-class urban American of today, however, seeks social approval, not from his family and close personal friends, but from his associates and for the most part from associates in secondary relationships. And this process begins before he, as a child, enters school and does not end until sometime after the funeral.

The individual seems doomed to frustration in Riesman's analysis, however, for he desires to come closer to other people by conforming to whatever they tell him to do, yet because almost all of his contacts with others are superficial rather than warm and personal, "he remains a lonely member of the crowd."

In the postwar years, orthodoxy and conformity have become particularly enforced upon "the lonely crowd" as a result of accommodation to the justified, but immaturely expressed, fear of the threat of communism. Lack of conformity has recently become non-American and, by implication, un-American.

Between the security of the womb and that of the grave, the contemporary middle-class urbanite apparently wishes for little more than a few obscure years bending and swaying with the crowd.

Urban Classes. Although it has always been popular among tellers of the great American myth to say that this nation is lacking in classes, that all are equal, that anyone can do anything that his ability and determination dictate, less romantic sociologists point out that while we have a good deal of mobility between classes, the classes do, indeed, exist. Some sociologists would go further and say that, because of the inferior social position of the Negro, America has both a class and a caste system.[22] A social class is a division of society in which individuals are recognized as belonging to a certain social-status group. These people have a sense of *belongingness* to one another and of separateness from others. A social caste exists when the status position of the individual in society is determined by birth and cannot be changed by any personal efforts made by the individual.

Class systems are based upon relative wealth, occupations, education, manners, mode of life, and such things as membership in an "old family" or a recent immigrant family. Americans regard millionaires with awe, but frequently despise the poor as lazy and shiftless; physicians rate so highly that they almost cease to be human beings and become "doctors"; teachers receive much of their pay in inedible prestige rather than in readily convertible dollars; but professional gamblers, who also perform a service that much of society demands, are low on the social scale. There

---

[21] David Riesman, *The Lonely Crowd* (1950). The conclusions expressed in this work are somewhat modified in *Faces in the Crowd* (1952).

[22] Gist and Halbert, *op. cit.,* chap. 14.

is in general a positive correlation between one's educational level and his social status; but members of the Adams, Lodge, Roosevelt, or Taft families enjoy a high social position by that very fact alone, while persons whose names are Rakosi, Rabinowitz, Rannuci, or Rzadkowolski must start off lower down on the scale.

America's caste system is separate from, and parallel to, its class system. A criterion of caste is the ban against intermarriage, a prohibition which exists by formal law as well as by social dictate in many states. This unhappy system, which is in contravention of basic American ideals and hence leads to guilt complexes, is an important cause of political problems in our cities.[23]

Politics and Classes. Politically, a class or caste system is an important determinant of strategy and tactics of campaigning. Politicians appeal to Negroes, foreign-born, Jews, Puerto Ricans, Americanized Mexicans, homeowners, renters, and other socially or economically identifiable groups. These appeals may be basically harmless or they may arouse virulent intergroup prejudices.[24] Because of the prestige factor, which in turn has economic repercussions that affect, for example, property values, many political battles—in the city council chamber, in the mayor's office, on the campaign platform—are fought over the issue of what the sociologist so innocently calls *invasion.* "The process of invasion is a convenient name for what happens when a new type of people, institution, or activity enters an area previously occupied by a different type."[25] Much social, and hence political, tension is caused when a rapid increase of Negro population, as in Chicago and Detroit, forces rapid invasion. The question of intended policy, expressed or implied, toward invasion has been important in postwar mayoralty campaigns in Detroit, especially in 1945 at the height of the housing shortage, but also in the 1949 contest. The question sometimes takes the form of policy toward proposed public housing units. Should they be built only after tearing down existing slums, or should vacant areas be used where there may be alterations of the character (and hence the property values) of existing communities?

Tensions may also result from counterinvasions, as in the case of the re-expansion of Boston's Beacon Hill into the surrounding slums, or the white "colonial restoration" of the largely Negro Georgetown section of Washington, D.C., in the thirties. Residential areas may be invaded by

---

[23] For detailed illustrations of class and caste in operation, see the following. A New England city: W. Lloyd Warner and Paul S. Lunt, *The Social Life of a Modern Community* (1942). A Middle Western city: Robert S. Lynd and Helen M. Lynd, *Middletown in Transition* (1937). For classes within the Negro community of Chicago: St. Clair Drake and Horace R. Cayton, *Black Metropolis* (1945).

[24] For an example of the latter, see Carl O. Smith and Stephen B. Sarasohn, "Hate Propaganda in Detroit," *Public Opinion Quarterly*, vol. 10 (Spring, 1946), pp. 24–52.

[25] Queen and Carpenter, *op. cit.*, p. 109.

commerce and industry, which also causes resentment and political strife, because it, too, threatens property values. So-called "improvement associations" have been created in many neighborhoods of our cities, chiefly "to protect property values." Many times these organizations exist primarily to keep "inferior" groups out of the area. In the past, they and subdivision developers have had legal assistance in the form of "restrictive covenants" in deeds to property. Such covenants prohibited conveyance of the land to specified groups of persons (e.g., Negroes, Jews, persons of the yellow race) for a certain number of years, or permanently. In 1948, however, the United States Supreme Court, taking note of the fact that the United States Constitution prohibits a state from denying "to any person within its jurisdiction the equal protection of the laws," declared all such provisions unenforceable.[26]

Many improvement associations have a broader interest. Nearly all of them concern themselves with all threats of commercial and industrial invasion and many of them spend much of their time on the little things (good street lighting, prompt repair of chuckholes, countless stop signs, etc.) that interest the people of the neighborhood. Chicago's Commission on Human Relations, the Commission on Community Relations in Detroit, and perhaps other such groups in other cities have encouraged a new type of improvement association designed to further tolerance and understanding and to help all groups in a neighborhood to seek to improve the area further.

Hearings before city councils or appeal boards on the rezoning of an area often conceal interclass or interracial conflicts behind ostensible arguments concerning property values. A public or cooperative multifamily housing project which is to be nonsegregated is likely to become a political issue. Opponents may not state their real objection but may advance other arguments, such as a complaint that the proposed project will destroy the single-family-homes character of the neighborhood. If the apartments were designed to rent to restricted clientele at $150 per month, the community attitude might be much different.

Invasion by a different class or caste may even cause the established residents of an area to encourage their own law-enforcement officers to violate the law. In the notorious Cicero riot of 1952, where a well-educated, middle-class Negro family attempted to move into a lower-middle-class all-white suburb of Chicago, not only did many members of the community encourage unlawfulness on the part of spectators, especially of impressionable teen-agers, but they actually encouraged the chief of police to refuse to extend the protection that the law grants to all peaceful persons. Refusal of the police to perform their duty when it involves the rights of members of minority groups is an old, though fortunately a

[26] *Shelly v. Kraemer*, 334 U.S. 1 (1948).

gradually more uncommon, story. It is also the story of the political effects of caste and class consciousness.

Impersonalization of Life. Cities are based upon a money economy. Many business relationships are impersonal and devoid of sentiment, in contrast with these same activities in rural and small-town situations. In the city one is lost in anonymity, having casual contacts with many persons rather than intimate contacts with a relatively few. One is judged by what he can do, not by what he is—by his *reputation* rather than by his *character*. So relationships among people are brief and stylized. People are cool toward one another, quick to take advantage, and, in the view of many ruralites, hardhearted. If one journeys to a large department store in a city in order to make a purchase, he will probably find the clerk uninterested, possibly even impertinent. After all, the transaction may take only five minutes, after which neither person will see the other again. What is at stake? The store management is interested only in the question: Does the clerk keep the inventory moving at the expected rate? The clerk is interested only in the question: How much do I have to do in order to keep my job or to get that possible raise? The customer may suspect that the clerk has a heart, and possibly even a soul, but he will not find out whether his suspicions are correct (the clerk will resist any attempt). After the transaction is completed, the customer leaves the store and boards a bus where he finds a driver who gives him change grudgingly and what may appear to him to be thirty-five other soulless automatons who block the aisles, step on his toes, and look bored. And so life in the city goes on and on, with each person seeing a façade of the other—never the whole person.

In the small town and on the farm, society is subjected to social controls characterized by *primary,* that is to say close and personal, relationships. Some of these exist in cities, too, but to a much smaller degree. *Secondary* relationships and controls predominate there, and these are impersonal, fragmentary, and ephemeral. Social distance—the degree of relative lack of intimacy that one person has with another—is much greater. Urban society, therefore, becomes organized more formally, through more *laws,* than is the case in rural areas. The political process becomes more important in the city.

This textbook cannot take the space to examine the *why* of the characteristics of urban behavior, but it is important to note that this new way of life has immediate effects upon the political institutions of the community. The rural society is policed largely by its system of primary social controls. Gossip and community opinion strongly discourage deviations from accepted values. The back-fence tattler may be a nuisance, but she is also a protectress. Crime rates are low, and there may not be a professional law-enforcement officer within thirty miles or more. In the city, things are not the same. The absence of most primary controls means that the crime rate in cities is higher. It means that mores must be enforced by policemen and by more laws instead of by gossips and community opinion. It means that the courts are kept busier settling civil disputes. It means bigger government, reaching more people in a more formalized, institutionalized manner.

Mobility of Population.[27] Physical mobility of population has been a characteristic of American life from earliest colonial times. When Horace Greeley suggested that young men "go West," he was merely reflecting traditional American practice. Since the War between the States and especially since the beginning of World War I (1917), Americans have been following a somewhat different migration—from farm to city. If, after a young person or family arrived in the city, he were to settle down in a stable neighborhood and take up a life not too different from his previous mode of living, no great change in the American pattern would be noted. But such is not the case. Persons migrating to the city often do so in times of very high employment, only to return to the old home town at the first slackening off. They may shuttle back and forth several times during a lifetime—although others, of course, do make the move and remain permanently fixed, even eventually becoming suburban home-owners. Depending upon economic conditions, from 1 to 4 million Americans make the farm-to-city or city-to-farm migration annually. During the war years, from December, 1941, to March, 1945, over 15 million civilians migrated, not to mention the millions of servicemen who moved about the country.

Physical mobility has been of advantage in opening up new opportunities for people who feel that they have reached a dead end in their present location. It makes manpower available wherever it may be needed; it gives variety to otherwise jaded life interests. Without the willingness of so many people to move to places where they were needed, our war effort in both world wars would have been seriously curtailed.

High physical mobility has, however, some serious liabilities connected with it. The breakdown of primary controls in the rooming-house and deteriorated apartment-house areas where migrants as a rule first locate leads to higher crime rates, increased insecurity feelings, and all the other characteristics of the zone of transition. Since migrants are usually "marginal" workers—last to be hired and first to be fired—their presence in large numbers in a city makes the public welfare problem more complicated. From the viewpoint of the study of municipal government, the

---

[27] A. W. Boutemps and J. Conroy, *They Seek a City* (1945); F. G. Boudreau and Clyde V. Kiser, *Postwar Problems of Migration* (1947); Robert McMillan, "Boom Migration: Incidence and Aftermath," *Rural Sociology,* vol. 7 (June, 1942), pp. 145–155.

most important effect of the high-mobility factor in growing cities is to be found in the failure of large numbers of these migrants to *identify* themselves with their adopted communities.[28] Their civic pride is likely to be almost nonexistent. To them the city is likely to be a place to live—it just happens that the factory is surrounded by a cluster of streets and houses. There is no loyalty to the city as an institution, or as "home." If the migrant happens to live in a suburb, he may not even know whether it is actually an independent unit of government. Politically, this means that appeals to community responsibility will fall on deaf ears. It means that municipal elections will be ignored. The city government will be left in the hands of others—and the others may be grossly unrepresentative of the interests of the newer arrivals. Detroit, for example, has a very large number of recent immigrants, Negro and white, from the near and deep South. Most of them are labor-union members and have labor-union interests politically. Yet the CIO has been dramatically unsuccessful in its efforts to elect persons politically sympathetic to its views in city elections, even while it has delivered the votes for national elections and for the state governorship and legislature. The failure of thousands of its members to sink their roots into the soil of the community and to identify their interests with its interests is a major (though not the exclusive) reason for this failure. One could go further and say that the broad lack of community spirit or civic pride both in Detroit and in most of its suburbs may be laid to the fact that to thousands of people dwelling there, the city is a place to earn money "while the earning's good." But it is not "home," or the place where one would *want* to live, or a place where one should retire. In Detroit and in every other city where expansion is taking place at a rapid rate, one can expect this condition to prevail. It will disappear of itself as the expansion rate decreases and the community becomes more stabilized.[29]

The shallow roots in the community that are a result of a high mobility rate have a direct effect upon the pattern of municipal politics and upon the problems of municipal administration. After the rate of rural-to-urban migration of the last two decades declines, it is likely that the stabilization of city populations will permit or encourage the feeling of belongingness, of civic pride, of civic interest, that is now so badly lacking in nearly all of our cities of any considerable size.

[28] See Robert C. Angell, "The Moral Integration of American Cities," *American Journal of Sociology*, vol. 57 (July, 1951), pt. 2.

[29] Arthur Kornhauser, *Attitudes of Detroit People toward Detroit* (1952), indicates that some supposed attitudes such as those above have been exaggerated. He concludes, however, that "the problem is to develop in the ordinary citizen the conviction that this is *his* city and that its improvement is *his* responsibility."

CHAPTER 2

THE URBAN FRINGE

The American city today is much more than a legal entity existing within carefully described boundaries and headed by a single government. It is actually a sociological complex consisting of a downtown sector, a blighted and decaying older portion, newer sections of a principally residential character, and, beyond the legal limits but an intrinsic part of the community, the suburbs. A suburb may be defined as a community beyond the legal boundaries of the core city, but lying within its economic and sociological limits and with a population at least partially dependent for a livelihood upon the core city.

There are sections within some large cities (e.g., Los Angeles and, until recently, Minneapolis and Detroit) that are relatively undeveloped and assume some, but not all, of the characteristics of the suburb. The movement toward the urban fringe is overrunning both types of areas.

THE MOVEMENT TOWARD THE SUBURBS

Why Move to the Suburbs? What is behind the centrifugal force that is pushing our urban population toward the periphery of the community? No doubt the increasing size of the urban population is itself a factor, for additional population is likely to require increasing area. But this alone is not a sufficient reason to explain the great suburban movement of the last thirty-odd years and especially that since the end of World War II.

Rather we should ask, what do most American people want out of life? Where and under what conditions can their desires best be fulfilled?

A recent summary of the findings of social-psychological research into these questions has been reported as follows:[1]

The goal which, if reached or reasonably approximated, will fulfil the basic needs of the urbanite is a community that will combine some qualities of both small town and large city. Neither, in its present form and at the current stage of cultural development, satisfies all of the fundamental human requirements. The small town provides ample opportunity for companionship

[1] William L. Slayton and Richard Dewey, "Urban Redevelopment and the Urbanite," in Coleman Woodbury (ed.), *The Future of Cities and Urban Redevelopment* (1953), p. 367. By permission of the University of Chicago Press.

and friendship, for easy access to local services, and for certain forms of security. On the other hand, it may fall short of fulfilling man's need for recognition and variety of experience. The large city does provide insurance against boredom, affords wider opportunity for choice of occupation, freedom from unwanted interference with one's personal life, and permits one to identify himself with the city's greatness or, at least, bigness. Nevertheless, it may fail to meet other basic social needs of man. The city can be a very lonesome place. It can thwart natural human friendliness. It can breed suspicion and misunderstanding. It often has dissolved long-established values as to behavior while putting nothing comparable in their place.

The suburb, more and more urbanites believe, is the best available compromise, especially if the medium-sized city is not a possible choice. In addition to allowing the urbanite to keep *some* of the best of both the large city and the small town, there are other subjectively determined values held by Americans today that add to the attractiveness of the suburb. Studies show that people want to own their homes, that they want single-family dwellings, and that they want more space than is available within built-up cities at a cost they can afford. They want to avoid, or at least reduce, dirt, noise, congestion, traffic, and taxes. They want vegetable gardens and rosebushes. They want a private play yard for the children.

People want better government than they think they are getting in the core city. They want "services without politics." The suburbanite, as a good conformist, talks of the desirability of a council-manager government, which the large city, as a rule, does not have. A "better, more honest" government is something that many think is available in the suburb, although this is a much less important factor than are many others. Neighborliness, the re-establishment of some of the primary controls of the rural and small-town society, is something that many yearn for. A suburban address is also a symbol of higher prestige than the typical core-city address, and this fact does not escape many urbanites, for social climbing of this sort is very important as a source of recognition in an impersonal society.

The suburb keeps within hailing distance of the variety of scene and activity, of job opportunities, and of accessibility to multiple and specialized services that people want from the large city. Most people would like to have nearby, at walking distance—even in the suburbs—a corner grocery for last-minute shopping (the supermarket for the large weekly shopping list may be driving distance away), a drugstore, a playground, and a grade school. Other services, entertainment media, and places of work may be considerable distances away, for the automobile, people believe, will take them there within the limits of a tolerable amount of sacrifice. The commuting time and effort, within present value systems, is not too great a price to pay for the advantages of not living near the manufacturing or business districts.[2]

What Makes Suburban Living Possible? A brief answer might be simply this: modern techniques of transportation and communication. To the extent that a decentralization of industry is also a factor, the availability of highly mobile sources of *power* in the form of electricity has also been important. Together with prosperity after World War II, the Federal government's policy of aiding purchasers of new homes through a loan guarantee to the mortgage holder has been another important factor. The Veterans' Administration and the Federal Housing Authority have thus been substantial contributors to the suburban movement by making low-interest mortgages a possibility for large numbers of families who could not otherwise have afforded homes of their own.

World War I brought an acceleration in the rate of urbanization in the United States. People began to look for additional space to occupy. They found it outside of the city proper. They also found that a prewar novelty, the automobile, had now become commonplace. In fact, it had become a necessity for members of the middle class, and Henry Ford was building a "poor man's" car in the famous Model T. There were suburbanites and commuters before the 1920s, to be sure, for those were the days of the electrified interurban lines and there were commuter trains operated by the railroads out of the largest cities, but it was the coming of the automobile that made suburban living as it is known today a possibility.[3]

Modern methods of communication are also contributors to the suburban movement. Without the effective, inexpensive telephone service of today, few would isolate themselves from the core city. The telephone is used to obtain services rapidly, for the employer in town to contact his employee in his suburban home, for the husband at work downtown to "check on things back at the house," and for all to keep in contact with relatives and friends in other parts of the city even when many miles of crowded highways separate them.

Without the automobile and the telephone, it is possible that the present-day value patterns previously discussed would never have evolved. Even if they had, it is certain that few would have been able to take advantage of them.

Rate of Suburban Growth. How rapid has the increase in population of the outlying areas been? Between 1940 and 1950, 80 per cent of the

[2] This section draws heavily upon Slayton and Dewey, *op. cit.*, pt. III. The empirical research justifying the above statements is there summarized and cited. See also an article on the suburban movement in *U.S. News and World Report,* June 30, 1950; reprinted in Charles M. Kneier and Guy Fox, *Readings in Municipal Government and Administration* (1953), pp. 13–18.

[3] The early movement toward the fringe is discussed in H. P. Douglass, *The Suburban Trend* (1925).

population increase took place within the *standard metropolitan areas*[4] and most of the remainder could be found in smaller urban places. Nearly one-half of the increase took place in American suburbia alone. This general trend has continued after 1950, perhaps at an accelerated pace.

Chicago, which is almost completely built up within the legal city limits, gained 7 per cent in population between 1940 and 1950, while its

Table 1. Metropolitan-area Population Trends

City	Coun-ties in area*	Metro-politan population	Per cent in-crease 1940-50	Core-city population	Per cent in core cities	Per cent in-crease in core cities 1940-50	Per cent in-crease outside core cities 1940-50
1. New York.............	16	12,911,994	10.7	7,891,957	66.8†	5.4†	23.2
2. Chicago...............	6	5,495,364	13.9	3,620,962	65.9	6.6	31.2
3. Los Angeles...........	2	4,367,911	49.8	1,970,358	45.1	31.0	69.8
4. Philadelphia...........	8	3,671,048	14.7	2,071,605	56.4	7.3	26.1
5. Detroit...............	3	3,016,197	26.9	1,849,568	61.3	13.9	54.8
6. Boston................	4	2,875,876	8.3	801,444	33.8	4.0	11.5
7. San Francisco–Oakland..	6	2,240,767	53.3	1,159,932	51.8	23.8	105.8
8. Pittsburgh.............	4	2,213,236	6.3	676,806	30.6	0.8	8.9
9. St. Louis.............	5	1,681,281	17.4	856,796	51.0	5.0	33.8
10. Cleveland.............	2	1,465,511	15.6	914,808	62.4	4.2	41.6
11. Washington...........	7	1,464,089	51.3	802,178	54.8	21.0	117.1
12. Baltimore.............	3	1,337,373	23.5	949,708	71.0	10.5	72.9
13. Minneapolis–St. Paul....	4	1,116,509	18.7	833.067	74.6	6.8	76.2
14. Buffalo...............	2	1,089,230	13.6	580,132	53.3	0.7	33.1
15. Cincinnati.............	3	904,402	14.9	503,998	55.7	10.6	20.8

* City-counties and the District of Columbia are included as counties.

† In calculating this percentage, Newark and Jersey City are counted as core cities, too.

SOURCE: *1950 Census of Population*, vol. I, tables 27 and 28.

suburbs increased by 32 per cent. Los Angeles, which has vast areas within its huge city limits that are not yet built up and that, it is esti-mated, will not be fully utilized until after 1980,[5] increased by only 31 per cent. The rest of the area increased by 70 per cent, and some of its suburbs more than doubled in population. There was little population increase within mature Manhattan, Brooklyn, and the Bronx, but Nassau County, on Long Island, increased by 65 per cent, and many other parts of New York, New Jersey, and Connecticut made very great gains. About 750,000 people moved out of the city of New York and into its suburbs between 1940 and 1950. The population of St. Louis grew by 5 per cent between 1940 and 1950, but the increase in adjacent St. Louis County amounted to 48 per cent. New Orleans increased by one-fourth, but its

[4] Standard metropolitan areas are defined on p. 16, n.

[5] The estimate is made by C. C. Jamison of the Security–First National Bank of Los Angeles in *Newsweek*, Aug. 3, 1953.

suburban fringe doubled in population. San Francisco–Oakland increased by over 50 per cent, but suburban Contra Costa County almost tripled in population, as did Washington's suburb of Falls Church, Virginia. This story could be repeated over most of the nation.

TYPES OF SUBURBS

Suburbs may be of many types. They are likely to be somewhat difficult to classify, and it is probable that most of them will include characteristics of more than one of the following types: first of all, the "dormitory" suburbs, especially built up on undeveloped land for the purpose of absorbing the overflow from the city; second, the industrial suburbs; third, suburbs, or *enclaves,* that have become completely surrounded by the core city; fourth, recreational suburbs; fifth, communities that were once independent, autonomous municipalities, probably serving as marketing towns, and that have been overrun by a metropolitan community; last, the heterogeneous suburbs that serve many purposes and for that reason cannot be classified readily.[6]

The Dormitory Suburbs. The residential suburbs are characterized by the fact that they are living places, primarily, for persons who earn their living within the core city or the industrial suburbs. The suburb may have a well-developed business district, but many of the newer ones have only a series of shopping areas along the main highways. There may be very little community spirit and almost nothing to give the area the appearance of a natural community. In fact, its boundaries may well be determined by following main traffic arteries.

Dormitory suburbs may be made up of very expensive subdivisions, or working-class areas with modest frame homes, or anything in between. Some of them allow only individual homes under the strictest zoning and subdivision regulations, while others will allow the more moderately priced mass-production projects of the Levittown type. Some will even permit apartment houses. Some seek to exclude industry altogether, while others are of a mixed type, admitting industry in order to give some backbone to the tax base.

Industrial Suburbs. Industrial suburbs or satellite cities have been described by two sociologists as follows:[7]

These are usually built around one or a group of large manufacturing establishments. Frequently marked physiographic features cut them off from

[6] A more elaborate classification is described and developed in Stuart A. Queen and David B. Carpenter, *The American City* (1953), pp. 119–130. Another is to be found in Grace K. Ohlson, "Economic Classification of Cities," *Municipal Year Book, 1946,* pp. 32–70.

[7] Queen and Carpenter, *op. cit.,* p. 120.

the rest of the metropolitan area. Sometimes they are larger, and usually they are more congested, than other suburbs. Satellite cities live more to themselves because their people dwell, shop, worship, play, educate their children, earn their living, and spend most of their time within their own communities. Their people read the metropolitan newspapers less than do the residents of other suburbs. However, the industries of the satellite city are dependent on the central city for financing, managing, sale of products, and extra labor supply, and the inhabitants go to the central city for some forms of recreation and for specialized shopping.

In addition to such long-established suburbs of heavy industry as Gary and Dearborn, there has been a strong postwar trend toward the building up of light and medium industrial plants in the suburbs. It would probably not be justified to make the flat statement that industries are decentralizing,[8] but it is certainly true that *some* industry is decentralizing. It appears that various groupings of industry are following different trends. Factories that do not need railroads, bodies or streams of water, or heavy power sources nearby, and particularly the supplier sections of large industries, seem to be looking to the suburbs.

From the turn of the century until World War II there was a slow, rather persistent diffusion of industry within the major areas of industrial concentration. It appears to be continuing, especially in the Middle Atlantic, East North Central, and Pacific industrial regions.[9]

Industries seem to be leaving the core cities not primarily because of being squeezed or pushed out, but rather in response to positive factors. Suburbs offer some hope of lower taxes; they offer cheaper land, a vital consideration since a properly laid out, healthful, physically attractive factory needs a good deal of room; they offer better parking facilities for workers; they bring the factory nearer the workers' homes; they eliminate the need to bring large semitrailer trucks into the heart of the city, for the factory can be located near important highway intersections; and they aid in reducing congestion on the commuter highways and in the central portion of the core city.

In addition to a pattern of diffusion for some industries in our larger manufacturing cities, there has also been a certain amount of dispersion of industry.[10] Smaller cities are acquiring more industries and becoming more important economic units. This pattern is especially to be noted in

[8] See Coleman Woodbury and Frank Cliffe, "Industrial Location and Urban Redevelopment," in Coleman Woodbury (ed.), *The Future of Cities and Urban Redevelopment* (1953), chaps. 5 and 6.

[9] *Diffusion* is defined by Woodbury and Cliffe, *op. cit.*, p. 209, as "the redistribution of industrial plants and facilities from a major area of concentration, such as a central city or metropolitan area, to a nearby or adjacent area."

[10] *Dispersion* means a wider redistribution of industry than in the case of diffusion, "as from a major industrial concentration in a large city or metropolitan area to a number of smaller localities." Woodbury and Cliffe, *op. cit.*, p. 209.

the South Atlantic states and in the South in general. These cities are expanding partly at the expense of the metropolitan areas and partly as the result of industrial emigration from New England's cities. The Department of Defense has encouraged dispersion as part of a pattern of protection against attack by thermonuclear weapons, but its efforts appear to have had little net effect.

Gary and Hammond were deliberately set up as industrial suburbs of Chicago. Their favorable location on Lake Michigan was well suited to the needs of the steel industry. Kansas City's suburb Argentine is a semi-autonomous industrial suburb, and St. Louis has three heavy-industry suburbs: Granite City, Madison, and Venice, all in Illinois.[11]

Enclaves. Some American cities have grown so rapidly that they have quite literally swallowed up their suburbs. A city that suddenly becomes economically more important and therefore creates a population vacuum as job opportunities increase may stretch its boundaries outward quite rapidly. Independent suburbs on the urban fringe may choose to remain approximately static in areas while this is happening. The core city may then surround them on all sides, making something of a mockery out of their independent legal status and their suburban appellation. Los Angeles has about fourteen such enclaves, Cincinnati three, and Detroit two.

Recreational Suburbs. This type of suburb probably seldom exists by itself, and the term should be taken to mean places where people go to play, to escape. Sometimes there is a lake or the sea near the core city. Beaches, dance halls, and picnic places are built up, with perhaps a carnival or amusement-park area included. Excelsior in the greater Minneapolis area and Walled Lake, near Detroit, are examples of this type.

Some suburbs become havens of gambling establishments and houses of prostitution. This is sometimes the result of advance knowledge that these localities will not enforce the law strictly. They may be across a county or state line and in the case of some, such as Tijuana and Windsor, across an international boundary. Race tracks, because they require a great deal of room for the physical plant and for parking space, and because they cause dust and a good deal of noise both day and night, are nearly always located in a suburban area which is (at least at first) not too heavily populated.

Formerly Autonomous Communities. Not only does the core city sometimes swallow up its suburbs, but it may sometimes draw into its economic and sociological (but rarely into its *political*) orbit communities that were once independent of it, that were created for and developed as the result of factors other than those that created the core

[11] Queen and Carpenter, *op. cit.*, p. 126.

city. Chicago has drawn many cities into its orbit, including Joliet and much of northern Indiana. The Minneapolis–St. Paul metropolitan area has come to include the county-seat town of Anoka, the prison and river town of Stillwater, and the resort towns around Lake Minnetonka. Detroit has expanded its magnetic field to include the county-seat and manufacturing city of Pontiac and the county-seat and resort town of Mt. Clemens, and is even beginning to encroach upon the county-seat and university town of Ann Arbor. The city of New York has socially annexed the old towns of southwestern Connecticut and dozens of others in New Jersey.

Heterogeneous Suburbs. It should not be assumed that suburbs are planned to perform a single function or that many will be found that would fit exclusively into any of the above categories. To illustrate from the Detroit metropolitan area: Livonia contains a race track, a large amount of medium industry, and some fairly heavy industry (including a tank arsenal), but it also has a great deal of living area and many of the residents of the community work in the core city. Furthermore, the homes are not of a homogeneous value pattern, for they vary from working-class sections to extremely expensive subdivisions. Dearborn, containing the mammoth River Rouge plant of the Ford Motor Company, is also to a large degree a dormitory suburb and contains some very wealthy areas. Hazel Park is basically a working-class dormitory town, but it also has a race-track industry.

PROBLEMS OF THE CORE CITY

The centrifugal movement of population and industry to the periphery of the urban area is causing a multitude of problems for both the core city and the suburbs. Some of these problems are severe and are likely to prove to be chronic.

Loss of the Tax Base. While the cost of operating municipal governments has increased along with almost everything else in the postwar years, the movement toward the suburbs has seen the core cities lose more and more of their tax base. Industries have been moving out. Retail stores are following the shoppers. The large department stores of many core cities are expanding their facilities to meet the increases in population in the community—but they tend to build in the suburbs, where land is cheaper and more plentiful and where the customers are nearby. In two years in the early 1950s, San Francisco lost 289 retail stores to the suburbs. From 1939 to 1952, 10 per cent of the retail trade in the St. Louis area transferred from the core city to the suburbs.[12] In 1939, suburban

---

[12] See *Newsweek*, July 29, 1952, and *U.S. News and World Report*, June 30, 1950, for statistics. Also J. D. Carroll, Jr., "The Future of the Central Business District," *Public Management*, vol. 35 (July, 1953), pp. 150–153.

stores of that city accounted for 31 per cent of the retail trade of the metropolitan area. By 1948, the percentage had increased to 37. It was surely over 40 per cent in 1954.

A 1953 study of thirty-two metropolitan areas indicated that in the core cities of twenty-seven of these areas, the number of retail stores had decreased by as much as 20 per cent in recent years. In contrast, the suburban tax base had been strengthened by increases in the number of retail stores by as much as 67.6 per cent in some areas.[13]

Between 1930 and 1951, the central business district of Flint, Michigan (1950 population: 163,143), declined in value by 37.2 per cent in relation to the total city assessed valuation.[14] It decreased in assessed worth from 15.6 per cent of total valuation of the city to 9.9 per cent during that period. The real drop may have been even more than this, for it is probable that in most cities the sale value and probably also the assessed value placed on downtown property is today unrealistically high in proportion to values in the remainder of the city. Choking traffic, lack of parking space, and the general centrifugal movement of population are lowering the worth of the downtown sector, which has always been the hard core of the tax base.

The people who are moving to homes in the suburbs are the people best able to pay taxes, for the movement is dominated by members of the middle and upper middle classes. They build their immodest expressions of consumption and leisure outside the taxing limits of the city. On the other hand, the great majority of the very poor continue to live within the core city. To heap trouble upon trouble, as the prosperous citizens move out, part of the population loss is made up by the rural-to-urban migration that supplies the extra manpower to cities—but the newcomers to the core city are likely to be a financial liability rather than an asset. The majority of migrants will settle first in the city, probably in the decaying zone of transition.[15] Because they are culturally marginal people—that is to say, they live in the culture of a large city, but still have many of the values they earlier received from a quite different rural culture—they are likely to create a police and juvenile problem. They are insecure and confused people. They are very unlikely to be homeowners, and those who own their blighted dwellings do not pay as much in taxes as the city must spend in the area.

[13] From a speech by C. C. Choyce of Sears Roebuck and Company, quoted in *Time*, Feb. 1, 1954.

[14] Carroll, *op. cit.*, table 3.

[15] Studies made on this point and the need for more research on it are discussed in Victor Jones, *Administrative Consequences of Demographic Change*, a paper delivered before a panel of the American Political Science Association meeting, September, 1953. The pressing need for much further research on the whole matter of the metropolitan area is stressed in G. S. Birkhead, "Metropolitan Areas Demand Attention," *National Municipal Review*, vol. 42 (June and July, 1953), pp. 305–310, 364–368. Birkhead presents a fine bibliography of recent research.

Furthermore, as the density of population in the core city decreases, the value of homes also decreases, since demand for them becomes less. The eroding of the tax base is therefore a cumulative phenomenon.

Subsidization of the Suburbs. In addition to its decreasing tax base, the core city has been forced, in most states, to subsidize the suburbs. As the tax base declines, the amount and number of subsidies increase. There are at least two ways in which the core city is forced to help the suburbanite pay for his governmental services: by furnishing services of the city free or below cost; and by paying a disproportionately large share of state and county taxes in return for a disproportionately small share of their services.

The core city furnishes services free to suburbanites in many ways. Whether it likes it or not, it builds strong, wide commuter highways to carry the load into the city each morning and back to the dormitory towns each evening. After the morning rush hour is over, it must be prepared to handle another miniature rush hour as the shoppers come into the city. The city pays for the repairs on the highways that deteriorate rapidly under the pounding of an ever increasing traffic load. The city hires extra policemen to handle the nonresident traffic.

Table 2. Cities Furnishing Water and Sewer Service to
Properties outside City Limits

Population group	No. of cities in group	Water service		Sewer service	
		No. of cities	No. with higher rates	No. of cities	No. with higher rates
Over 500,000........	18	9	6	9	7
250,000–500,000.....	23	15	13	12	9
100,000–250,000.....	65	39	25	22	16
50,000–100,000......	129	61	38	33	18
25,000–50,000.......	276	111	76	67	37
10,000–25,000.......	836	278	198	151	95
Total............	1,347	513	356	294	182

SOURCE: *Municipal Year Book, 1953*, p. 287.

Some cities subsidize their public transportation system from taxes but allow it to operate in the suburbs and to carry suburbanites without their sharing in the subsidy. Parks and recreational facilities of the core city are available to suburbanites, although quite a few suburbs restrict their own parks to residents. The city must expand its public health department in order to inspect the restaurants where the noontime hordes of suburbanites eat—blissfully unaware that it costs other people money to see to it that they are not poisoned. Many core cities make their tax-supported libraries available to nontaxpaying suburbanites, especially to those who are employed in the city.

Some core cities are required by state law—the rural legislature is likely to listen more sympathetically to suburban pressure groups than to those of the metropolis—to furnish fire protection, water, sewage disposal, or other facilities to the suburbs at less than cost. Because of the lesser density in population and in order to build up a protective reserve, most cities charge somewhat more to the suburbs to which they furnish water than they do to their own residents. (If rates to core-city residents prove to be too low, or depreciation reserves inadequate, the deficit can be made up from taxes. This is not true of suburban customers; hence the protective reserve.) Chicago, however, is prohibited by law from charging a higher rate to the suburbs. As a result, in 1951 Chicago sold water to forty-eight of its suburbs at twelve cents per thousand gallons. The suburbs in turn sold it to their residents at an average markup of 200 per cent. In the extreme case of Forest Park, the water purchased at twelve cents was being sold to residents at seventy-three cents.[16] To add insult to inequity, many suburbanites undoubtedly blamed Chicago for their high water bills. Chicago has tried unsuccessfully since 1904 to get permission from the legislature to charge a differential rate to suburbs.

The core city also subsidizes the urban fringe through the payment of a disproportionate share of the county taxes. The county is traditionally a rural unit of government. In many urban communities it performs almost no functions within the core city. There are some exceptions to this in those areas where the county has been modernized, but for the most part the county collects most of its taxes within the city and spends them outside, particularly in unincorporated areas. The inequity is increased by the fact that core-city properties are assessed at a higher rate than are those in most suburbs. Property in the core city, for example, may be assessed in practice at 60 per cent of market value, while that in some suburbs may be assessed at 40 per cent. In theory, such inequities are illegal and should be corrected by the board of equalization. In practice, they exist almost everywhere.

In Minneapolis in 1949, about 87 per cent of the Hennepin County taxes were paid by city taxpayers who received no benefits, or only very small benefits, from nine of the county functions, including some of the most expensive ones. Residents of Dallas pay twice as much per capita toward the city-county hospital as do suburban taxpayers. Detroiters pay not less than 75 per cent of Wayne County taxes, yet during some heavy snowstorms the residential streets in unincorporated suburbs are plowed by the county, while those in the city remain snowbound. Suburban

[16] For the political factors involved in this situation, see Illinois Legislative Council, *Chicago Sanitary District* (1953), pp. 27–31.

roads are often maintained by the county, but few core cities receive any such aid.

The large cities also pay most of the state taxes, since they are centers of concentration of wealth.[17] Yet the state tends to spend most of its money in the rural and suburban areas. The core city thus helps to subsidize the suburbs in many of their functions. The state police, for example, will often lend assistance to the amateurish efforts of suburban policemen, but seldom operate within the core city. The state detective bureau, health department, highway department, and many others are likely to furnish more services to the suburbs than they do to the core city which is paying most of the bill.

The cities, it has been said, must learn to accept their fate in a decentralizing urban community. But it would not seem that they should be victimized, and state law should not require them to be. There is a need for the development of a tax system whereby the core city can force wage earners within the city to pay for their share of the services rendered regardless of the place of residence.[18] There is also an urgent need to revitalize the county, or at least not force the core city to pay its expenses without deriving service benefits from it.[19]

PROBLEMS OF THE SUBURBS

The politically atomized pattern of contemporary American suburbia results from the fact that this was a rural nation in the days when laws of annexation and attitudes toward large cities were developing. Rural-dominated legislatures have for the most part kept the traditional legal situation unchanged. As a consequence, the boundaries of a city are almost always artificial and arbitrary and have nothing to do with economic and social realities.

The entire community is an organic whole, despite its artificial compartmentation, and most suburbs, if they were moved fifty miles away, would wither and die. Because of this, suburbanites should properly support and help finance the government of the core city. Instead, the prevailing pattern produces independent suburbs that, because of their extravagant use of the resources of government, are expensive. Furthermore, most suburbanites wish to retain the present arrangement. Some of their reasons are valid; others are not.

The Demand for Independence. Not only has the population of the fringe area grown rapidly, but the number of suburbs has been increas-

[17] For one example, see Mayor's Committee on Management Survey, *Modern Management for the City of New York* (1953), vol. I, chap. 7.
[18] See chap. 15.
[19] See chap. 11.

ing at a great pace. In 1911 there were eight incorporated municipalities in St. Louis County. In 1940 the number had increased to thirty-nine, and the postwar expansion raised the total to ninety-four by 1952.[20] A similar pattern is to be found around most metropolitan areas. These figures would indicate not only that the population is expanding in many directions from the core cities, but that there is a tendency toward a *governmental fragmentation* of the fringe area. As each group of subdivisions becomes partially populated, it tends to seek incorporation for itself rather than annexation to another suburb or to the core city.

Why do people want "their own" little suburb? Partly for the same reasons that people want to live on the fringe of the urban area. Government is likely to be more personal. One may easily come to know the suburban officials personnally or by reputation. The city hall is more personalized and humanized.[21] The suburb may even have its own personality. There may be a certain amount of civic pride in one's suburb. This is not true in a great many of them, but it is more likely to be the case than it would be in the core city, where such pride is usually notably absent. (While core-city dwellers often have little pride in their city as a whole, *community* interest does not require independent governmental status. Many local areas within core cities have community improvement associations, local civic and social institutions, and a high level of community identification.) Many people are also influenced by a belief that suburban government is more honest and efficient than government in the core city.

The most important reason for incorporation in most areas, however, stems from a need for services. In many states it is difficult or impossible to provide these services without either incorporation or annexation to a nearby core city or suburb. It is commonly believed by the layman that services can be secured more cheaply by incorporating the area than by becoming annexed. And, once a municipality is established, there is resistance, usually led by local officeholders, to merging with a larger city.

Wasteful Duplication. The social waste of a legally atomized urban area is great. With the community broken up into a series of small units, it becomes very difficult to make use of the advantages of specialization of personnel and mechanization of equipment. Any urban area with a

[20] St. Louis County Planning Commission, *Let's Get Together: A Report on the Advantages of an Integrated Community* (1952).

[21] Suburban living often requires many hours spent weekly in travel. This means that the commuter has little time to enjoy the fruits of autonomous, personalized government. Local businessmen, elderly retired people, and housewives are likely to dominate community affairs and organizations in the suburbs. For a case study in Claremont, California, see A. H. Scaff, "The Effect of Commuting on Participation in Community Organizations," *American Sociological Review*, vol. 17 (April, 1952), pp. 215–220.

host of suburbs will have a great deal of wasteful duplication of services and of equipment needed to perform services. Police and fire departments are found in great numbers, as are water-supply systems, sewage-treatment plants, and health, welfare, and recreation agencies. Furthermore, each of them is likely to be going in its own direction, with little or no coordination or long-range planning.

There are 46 law enforcement agencies within Los Angeles County. The Chicago metropolitan area has some 350. This implies a lack of coordination and sometimes of cooperation. It is not only difficult to obtain justice by treating all alike before the law, but it gives many advantages to lawbreakers and to professional gamblers, prostitutes, and racketeers. There is not likely to be a systematic approach to traffic control, either.

The social loss is also great because large and expensive installations or pieces of machinery are not utilized to the maximum in some parts of the area, while other areas are utterly lacking in modern equipment. There are six fire and law-enforcement radio stations in the St. Paul–Minneapolis area. Sewage-disposal and water-filtration plants require such a large capital investment and have such high fixed costs that they are not economical unless they are in constant use. This implies that there should, for reasons of economy, be only one for each urban area. Suburbs that do not join the core city in sewage disposal often do an inadequate job of treatment, or dump raw sewage into public streams, polluting them. If they finally decide, or the state forces them to decide, to build a treatment plant of their own, the cost is almost prohibitively high.

Amateurism. In the midst of specialists of every type, many of the suburbs try to get along with untrained amateurs. While the suburban policeman is not quite the bumbling constable presented in the motion pictures, many suburban officers have only the most general idea of what to do if called to the scene of a murder or other major crime. Actually, such an officer will probably conclude that it would be best to call the state police or the sheriff's office—in which case the core-city taxpayers will pay most of the cost. Many suburbs have volunteer, or partially volunteer, fire departments—sometimes even in localities with very expensive homes. Still, just a few blocks away a professional and completely equipped fire system is available. Fires are actually a responsibility and problem for the entire community and are not respecters of legal boundaries, although the present system seems to assume that they are.

The use of amateurs where professional personnel are available is a strangely expensive method for approaching government. It is interesting to note that many urban businessmen, who would hire nothing but qualified specialists in their businesses, will permit amateurs to furnish services to their suburban homes.

Lack of Services. Not only are some services performed by amateurs, who are likely to do it inadequately and expensively, but services that most people expect in an urban community are not available at all in many outlying areas. There may be regions without collection or disposal of trash and garbage, very commonly no sewers are available, and sometimes there is not even a water-distribution system. Streets are not likely to be paved, and there are often no storm sewers. Street signs may be absent, even though they are vitally needed in any urban area. There may be no street lighting. "Taxes are lower in Perambulator Park," the real estate advertisements proclaim—they are less likely to mention that they are lower because almost no services are provided.

Lack of Cooperation. Suburbs tend to become intensely jealous of their independence, and they attribute ulterior motives to all suggestions of cooperation with the core city, or even with another suburb. This attitude is likely to increase the lack of coordination and of efficient use of equipment. Suburbs sometimes refuse to work together with other units in police, fire, health, and other services. This may be good political strategy for local politicians, who can claim that they are protecting the residents from the "evil" core city, but it actually deprives the local residents of needed protection. There is even a case on record of one Chicago suburb refusing to pool its fire equipment for use in the emergency of an air raid.[22]

Schools. While the educational plants of the nation are almost everywhere under the control of separate units of government called school districts, it is worthwhile to note that their cost of operation becomes part of the tax bill of the homeowner and he is likely to view it as part of the cost of city government. Most of the recently developed suburbs have inadequate educational systems. The schools are too far apart for small children. New buildings are becoming inadequate in size even before they are finished. Teachers are often less well qualified and less experienced than those of the core city. Huge bond issues for schools have steadily been raising suburban taxes since the end of World War II.

Unequal Tax Bases. The accident of boundary lines contributes to the creation of suburbs with highly unequal financial facilities for supporting local government. There may be very wealthy suburbs alongside of a core city that is desperately in need of more taxable wealth to support its services. Other suburbs may be very poor even though they are located in the heart of a prosperous urban area. Often the suburbs most needing services are the least able to afford them. Since an urban area is

[22] *Newsweek*, July 28, 1952.

an interdependent social and economic community, vast and arbitrary differences in taxable wealth would seem to be unjustifiable.

Inadequate Planning and Zoning. The metropolitan community usually develops in an uneven, unsystematic manner because of a lack of planning and zoning in suburban areas. Even when there is planning and zoning, it is usually established after a great deal of blighting has taken place, or after physical resources and property values have been badly damaged by the intermixing of residential, commercial, and manufacturing units.

While metropolitan planning commissions have been set up in most areas of the nation,[23] they seldom have any but advisory powers; and the fact of the matter is that there is almost no real planning on an area-wide basis in the United States. Each suburb gallops off in its own direction, damaging property values in the next municipality, making for a chaotic highway system, allowing unsightly blighted areas (especially in unincorporated suburbs) far from the center of the core city where such blight might be expected, and in other ways making poor use of physical facilities and preventing the maximum development of property values.

The Illusion of Suburban Economy. In the rapid expansion of America's cities in recent years, the problem of the urbanite has been to establish a household for himself and his family that is at the highest possible social level in an economy in which the cost of living has been constantly rising. Efforts to cut costs have been earnestly sought. In particular, the homeowner has struggled desperately to get out from under the property-tax load. It has been a fond illusion of many that moving into the suburbs will accomplish this goal. Actually, such a result is unlikely under most conditions.

It is true that there are a few ways in which savings in taxes can be made by establishing a suburban home. In the first place, if the core city is seriously corrupt and the suburb is not, a saving of the amount of waste through corruption can be made in the suburb.

In the second place, very large cities suffer from increasing costs per capita. Beyond some certain point, cities lose any advantage of large-scale operations and begin to encounter cost increases. For example, the costs of procuring water may increase greatly if a city becomes very large. This has happened especially to New York and Los Angeles, which must bring some of their water great distances. The per capita cost of police in cities of over 500,000 is more than twice that of cities in the 10,000 to 25,000 class.[24] The difference is almost as great in the case of fire pro-

[23] See chap. 20.
[24] See *Municipal Year Book*, 1953, p. 417.

tection.[25] The per capita cost of operating a city of over 1 million people is roughly twice that of a city of 25,000 to 50,000.

In the third place, crime rates, health and slum problems, and welfare expenses are all likely to be greater in the core city and hence more expensive. Lastly, by moving into the suburbs, it may be possible to have the state and county, most of whose costs are paid by core-city taxpayers, perform services that are performed by the municipality itself within the core city.[26]

The picture of large savings is likely to be illusory, however, and for many reasons:

First, a move to the suburbs almost certainly means an increase in fire-insurance rates. In one fringe area in Champaign County, Illinois, using a valuation of $9,000, the higher cost of insurance would take all but $9.00 of the annual property-tax savings.[27]

Secondly, any real tax advantages caused by location in the suburbs (advantages in site value of land) tend to become capitalized in the sale price and hence to accrue to the seller and not to the buyer. It might be added that the suburban buyer is frequently victimized through jerry-building or skimping of materials made possible by inadequate building codes.

Thirdly, "low taxes" is likely to be only a polite way of saying "no services." It has been noted above that many suburbs do not have all of the services that urbanites expect. If one moves some distance out from the core city, it will be necessary to dig a well and install a septic tank. This is followed by worries about contamination and a falling water-table level. Eventually, as the density of population increases, it will be necessary to install sewers and a water-distribution system, both of which cost a great deal of money. Furthermore, this will cause an almost total loss in the investment in the well and the septic tank.

Fourthly, as has been pointed out above, services that *are* available are likely to be performed by amateurs. This means that they are not likely to be either satisfactory or inexpensive.

Fifthly, taxes may start at what appears to be a much lower level than those of the core city, but the suburban buyer can be assured that they will increase at a rapid pace. The major portion of one's property-tax bill goes toward the support of schools, and in contemporary suburbia one school-bond issue has followed another with regularity since the end of the war. Each issue raises taxes. Furthermore, if one family is attracted to a particular suburb, many others will be, too. As population density

---

[25] See *ibid.*, p. 371.

[26] See above, pp. 39–41.

[27] Don Dickey, "Fringe Areas and Rural Communities," *Local Government Notes* (University of Illinois), Feb. 3, 1953, p. 6.

increases, the need for urban services increases. Each new service must be paid for by additional taxes.

Water and sewerage systems must be installed. Soon the neighbors want to have the street paved and a storm sewer laid. Street lights, which were not installed originally, become desirable. Fire and police service must be expanded. The sewage-disposal problem, not merely the financing of sewerage lines, must be solved.

Urbanites demand many services. And they can be secured only by paying for them. The discovery of this fact sometimes results in bitter disillusionment to the suburbanite who had believed that "suburban living" included the having of the cake as well as the eating of it.

Closing Statement. This chapter has discussed some of the characteristics of current urban decentralization and the difficulties that it involves for both the core city and the suburb. Some attempts to meet the inadequacies and inequities presented here are discussed in Chapter 11.[28]

---

[28] Bibliography for this chapter is given in the last footnote of chap. 11. A rather complete bibliography may be found in Barbara J. Hudson, *The Urban Fringe Problem* (1952). As a case study, the New York area is discussed in a series in *The New York Times,* Aug. 7–11, 1950.

CHAPTER 3

THEORIES OF LOCAL SELF-GOVERNMENT IN AMERICA

THE FRONTIER PRECEPTS OF JACKSONIAN DEMOCRACY

The British-colonial Background. It was an agricultural nation that declared its independence from the mother country in 1776. Only about 3 per cent of the people lived in nonrural communities, and there were not more than twenty-four incorporated municipalities in all thirteen of the new states.[1] The city having the largest number of people living within its legally defined area was New York, which fourteen years later, in the first census of the United States, claimed a population of 33,131. The urban area, including suburbs, with the largest number of inhabitants was Philadelphia with 42,444. Today the United States possesses hundreds of cities of that size or larger, and an urban area in the 30,000 to 40,000 population class is often summarily dismissed as a "small city." In fact, a New Yorker of today would probably refer to it as "a wide place in the road."

These few statistics are cited to indicate that there was little *need* for Americans of the late eighteenth century to devote their time to the development of a theory of urban government. As a matter of fact, the cities and villages of the time used a governmental structure modeled upon a system that had been familiar to the colonists in their native England. There was no separation of powers between the legislative and executive branches. The council possessed virtually all power. It was headed by the *mayor,* who had no veto power and practically no executive power. His task was to preside over meetings of the council as one of its members and to perform the ceremonial functions of the city. He was appointed, usually for one year, by the colonial governor, by the council as a whole, or by the aldermen. It a very few instances he was elected under the restricted suffrage rules then prevailing. Another appointed officer was

---

[1] In New England, urban and rural areas alike (including Boston) were ruled by the same unit of government, the *town.* In its pristine form, the town was a form of direct democracy, with the town meeting serving as the policy-making body. At this time, New England had no legally described villages or cities.

the *recorder,* who held his post for an indefinite period. He was a member of the council and a member of the local court,[2] and served as the corporation counsel (city attorney). In addition to these two, the council was made up of *aldermen* (distinguished citizens of the community who were usually selected by the common councilmen from their own membership) and *councilmen.* The latter were the only members of the city government to be elected directly by the "people"—i.e., by the comparatively few eligible electors.[3] Furthermore, nearly one-third of the boroughs (the English term for an incorporated municipality and the one generally used in the United States in the early years) were "close corporations" in which no popular elections at all were held. In these cities, the original charter named the members of the council, and vacancies were filled from time to time by surviving members of the body.

The city actually had a plural executive. Administrative supervision was exercised and minor appointments were made by the council as a whole, by committees of the council, or by the municipal court.

This plan, largely removed from the supervision or participation of the common citizen, remained in effect without basic change for the first few decades after independence. (In England, this same fundamental structure is in use today. It has been made operable under modern conditions by the installation of permanent, professionally trained department heads, a competent civil service, and an extension of voting privileges on the principle of universal suffrage.) That alterations might be expected was, however, presaged in one change that took place at the time of the Revolution. Under colonial rule, no charter could be made or amended without the consent of the city or village. With the cessation of British rule, control over charters passed from the Crown to the state legislatures rather than to the logical successor, the governor, for executives fell into disrepute during the Revolution. Since the legislatures appear to have assumed that their powers were plenary and unrestricted (excepting in a few cases of state constitutional limitations), the trail was opened for domination of the city government from the state capital—a phenomenon that characterized nineteenth-century American city government.

This potential for domination probably would never have been developed—the British tradition of local self-government being to the contrary—were it not for the evolution in the early decades of the nineteenth

[2] The court was usually made up of the mayor, the recorder, and the aldermen (but not the common councilmen). Jurisdictions varied but usually covered misdemeanors in violation of state law and of municipal ordinances. Powers of a justice of the peace were also included. From this court came the term *recorder's court,* which we still find in North Carolina for minor courts, in the city of Detroit for the major criminal trial courts of the city, and in others places in the United States.

[3] To find out exactly who was eligible in a rather complicated system, see A. E. McKinley, *The Suffrage Franchise in the Thirteen English Colonies in America* (1905).

century of a genuinely American philosophy of government. This philosophy came out of the everyday experiences of the American frontiersman, and as such it was pragmatic rather than introspective, functional rather than universal; and it was applied to state, county, township, village, and city governments alike. We usually refer to its rather unsystematic precepts by the use of the term "Jacksonian democracy."

Jacksonian Theories and City Government. The rustic idyl that was the America of the dreams of Thomas Jefferson began to disappear as an actual possibility well before that philosopher and statesman had completed his days on earth. Jefferson firmly believed that democracy, if it were to be successful, must find its strength in the individual farmer working in soil that he could call his own. Directly, he did not know very much about large cities (except for what he had seen in Paris), but he was an insatiable reader, and what he read about them did not please him. His opinion was stated trenchantly in *Notes on Virginia* (1782): "The mobs of great cities add just so much to the support of pure government, as sores do to the strength of the human body." So long as he lived, he urged that the United States remain an agricultural nation.

But the cities came anyway, and with them the urban proletariat that Jefferson thought spelled doom for democracy. With the rise of the city came also a philosophy for its proper government. That philosophy came via Jefferson and the frontier to the rising urban centers, where it was embraced by the workingman. It was an attitude toward government taken by those who labored on the farm and in the city alike; it was a philosophy of a rapidly growing nation, constantly pushing westward, founding new towns, building up old ones through the rise of a new industrialism; it was a viewpoint of a people constantly in debt, yet perennially optimistic as they realized, or at least hoped for, the unearned increment of increasing site value of land; and it was the thoughts of the common man about a nation that was now his own and that no longer belonged to an oligarchy of propertied aristocrats. Together it made up the political myth of Jacksonian democracy and it provided a rationalization for city government that survived nearly intact the remainder of the nineteenth century and is still important in our thinking today.[4] Its general principles are not difficult to summarize.

Jacksonian Principles. Probably antecedent to all others in importance was the concept of *government by the common man.* Government existed, not for a privileged class, but for the general citizen. Any one man was equal to any other man. Jefferson had said so in 1776, when the country was controlled by an aristocracy; now the words were to be taken quite

---

[4] For a background picture of the era in which the American industrial city was born and in which the ideas for governing it matured, see Arthur M. Schlesinger, Jr., *The Age of Jackson* (1945), especially chaps. 2–4, 24, 26, 37.

literally.[5] If this were the case, then it followed that any man was as good as any other man *in a public office*—no special qualifications were needed, no special training, nothing other than status as a human being willing to serve the community.

Out of this concept came the principle of *universal manhood suffrage*. It followed logically from egalitarianism, it was necessary to the development of Jacksonian thought, and, furthermore, it was the natural result of the effect of inertia upon the already existing tendency to broaden the electorate—a tendency that had begun even before the Revolution. When the Constitution was written (1787), only about one man in seven or eight could vote, and even when Andrew Jackson was first elected president (1828) only about one adult male in five could vote in the cities, although the electorate had broadened somewhat in rural areas.[6] The next decade saw a tremendous change, and by 1850 virtually all property restrictions had disappeared from voting requirements and universal manhood suffrage had been achieved. (The extension of the vote to women in later decades proved to be of very little immediate political importance.) From thenceforth, the general public possessed the potential for the control of government in its own interests.

Universal manhood suffrage made it possible for any man to run for office, to get support from all kinds of people, and to be elected. Jacksonians were not greatly concerned with the education, background of experience, or private calling of a candidate. It might be noted in passing that this viewpoint made a career as a professional politician or even as a political hack legitimate.[7]

Following from the above, Jacksonians believed that public officeholders, as servants of the people, should hold their mandates directly from the people. It was therefore held desirable to elect public officials rather than to appoint them. Gradually this came to mean the election of virtually all top-level officers, thus imposing upon Americans the unique institution of the long, or "bedsheet," ballot. To further ensure proximity to the people, a short term of one or two years in office and rapid turnover of personnel was advocated. In the small village or city, government could be *personal*, and the long ballot was therefore less of a handicap to the casual voter, for he probably knew all or most of the candidates either personally or by reputation. Similarly, while rapid turnover of personnel

[5] But only the visionary extended the concept beyond the *white* man in the 1820s.

[6] The estimate is made in W. B. Munro, *Municipal Government and Administration* (1923), vol. I, p. 95, n.

[7] The frequently used term *political hack* may be said to refer to the individual who has never "made good" at anything else, who is a perennial office seeker, and who depends for a livelihood upon scraps from the political table. His competence and public faith in him are questionable. The term *professional politician* is here used to refer to a person who secures his livelihood from political jobs, but whose competence is assumed or has been demonstrated.

meant inexperienced officeholders, this was no great problem where government was on a neighborly basis and administration was simple and nontechnical.

The movement toward the direct public oversight of officeholders through the use of the ballot was begun when the office of mayor was made elective. This was initiated in Boston and St. Louis in 1822 and spread rapidly throughout the nation. It was but a start, however. The Detroit charter of two years later not only made the office of mayor elective, but in true frontier spirit added the other city administrative offices to the list. This idea spread less rapidly than did that of the elective mayoralty, but gradually along the frontier the council was deprived of its power to appoint administrative officials. Some or all of the following became elective in various cities: the offices of tax collector or city treasurer, clerk, assessor, and city attorney, and, somewhat later, the myriad posts on the various boards and commissions that became a part of city government.

The rise of the independent board or commission for administrative purposes came about gradually as a protest against inadequacies in the performances of council committees as administrative overseers. It also reflected the growing distrust of city government and the desire to take certain functions "out of politics" by setting up independent commissions —sometimes appointed by state officials—to administer them. The New York charter of 1830 replaced the committees with single officers or boards (still, however, appointed by the council). In 1849 New York made their offices elective, and a similar plan was applied in Cleveland in 1852. After the War between the States, the use of the independent board and commission gained headway rapidly, and throughout the remainder of the nineteenth century this was the general practice. It might be noted that while the use of multimember boards did not originate in the springtime of Jacksonianism, it was a direct and logical outgrowth of its tenets.

Deterioration of Responsible Self-government in the City. By the time of the War between the States, a system of city government based on Jacksonian principles had matured. Now it is usually referred to as the "weak-mayor" plan. It dominated the last half of the nineteenth century, and even now it is found in more cities and villages in America than is any other structural form.[8] Its characteristics included a mayor who usually had a veto power but who was very weak administratively; a large council that dominated the scene, performing both legislative and administrative functions; a long ballot with many elective administrative officials, each independent of the others; numerous elective or appointive (but almost unremovable) boards and commissions; many ex officio

[8] A detailed examination of structures of city government will be made in chap. 8.

positions; and an extreme deconcentration of both legislative and executive responsibilities.

Legislative Interference. During this period there was a strong tendency for the state legislature to interfere in the control of the profitable or politically important aspects of city government. This it did in a variety of ways: by reserving for itself the power to grant public utility franchises for gas, water, electricity, and street railways; by granting special act charters to specifically named cities, amendable only at the legislature's discretion; by removing many local powers from a city if it fell to the control of a party not in a majority in the state legislature; by direct state administration of particularly patronage-laden local functions through special commissions (so-called "ripper" legislation); and by many other techniques. After about 1850, special legislation (i.e., legislation affecting exclusively a specifically named city) became so common that in many states its consideration took up more of the legislature's time than did legislation directed at the state as a whole. In many instances it had the effect of making the legislative delegation from each city a veritable supercouncil, far more powerful than the members of the real council.

Political differences between the state legislative majority and the largest cities of the state led to reduction in the degree of local self-government in many cities. As early as 1861 Chicago was Democratic while the legislature was Republican; this resulted in a struggle for control of the city that has lasted intermittently for nearly a century. Similar differences caused trouble between the city of New York and the state, between Boston and Massachusetts, and between St. Louis and Missouri. A feud within the party resulted in the temporary abolition of self-government for Pittsburgh and other Pennsylvania cities in 1901. In 1879, the Alabama legislature actually abolished Mobile, and Memphis suffered the same fate in Tennessee. In the latter case, the city had become bankrupt and the creditors applied pressure on the legislature to help them save their investments.

Special commissions controlled by the governor or legislature to take control of police, health, and other functions of cities became common after 1850. At various times, the police departments of New York, Chicago, Boston, Detroit, Baltimore, and St. Louis, among others, were removed from local control. It should not be assumed that the legislature was never motivated by any other desire than to secure control of luscious patronage pastures: often municipally controlled departments were so corrupt that responsible and honest citizens rushed to the legislature asking that certain functions be transferred to state control with the hope, at least, that an improvement might be effected.

Legislatures often were not beyond paying out the city taxpayer's money for the benefit of favored businessmen. Note, for example, the elaborate set of city buildings erected for Philadelphia in 1870 by the state legislature without consulting the citizens of the city—but with the uninvited bill being turned over to them. Individual legislators in those days were far more often guilty of questionable ethics and even of sheer venality than is the case today. Members were frequently in the pay of railroads, land speculators, liquor interests, and the like. Gas, electric, street railway, and other franchises were sometimes virtually auctioned off by legislators to the highest bidder. Public faith in the state legislature as the guiding authority for cities could not be great under such circumstances. The rise of the city boss and machine as a phenomenon of the new industrial city did not furnish a very satisfactory alternative to any citizen interested in honest and competent government.[9]

Reaction to State Control. Protests and reactions to this situation could be expected, and they were not long in coming. However, reforms proved to be much easier to suggest than to make effective. As early as the 1820s specific provisions were written into constitutions granting voters in cities certain privileges, such as the power to choose their own principal officers. Special legislation—the most direct technique of state control—was prohibited by the Ohio constitution of 1851. Similar provisions are found today in most of the state constitutions. A further development in the effort to free the city from excessive control by the state legislature came with the provision for constitutional home rule in the Missouri constitution of 1875. Home rule refers to the right of the voters of a city (or their representatives on a charter commission or city council) to frame, adopt, and amend their own city charters, as distinguished from the practice of having this done for them by the state legislature.[10]

These attempts often met with frustration. The courts commonly permitted legislatures to continue to enact special legislation so long as it was thinly disguised as general legislation. Constitutional home rule, likewise, did not of itself establish autonomous and capable self-government in cities.

While these experiments were failing to solve the problem of securing urban self-government, the unwieldy, uncoordinated, complicated, irresponsible weak-mayor system was becoming increasingly inadequate as a form of government for America's rapidly growing cities. Something more was needed.

[9] For the city boss and machine, see chap. **6.**
[10] See chap. **7.**

THE INHERENT RIGHT OF LOCAL SELF-GOVERNMENT

A Romantic Legalism. Under the theory of "home rule," advanced in protest against excessive legislative meddling in local affairs, the community has an inherent right to rule itself on local matters without interference by the state. The doctrine enjoyed but a brief life as a *legal* theory; yet overtones of the concept were felt in American thinking long before Judge Thomas M. Cooley of Michigan first expressed his often-cited dictum, and they are still felt today whenever the "rights" of city government as against state control are argued by citizens at civic-association, council, charter-commission, and similar meetings.

The lay citizen, arguing for a "right" of the city to control local affairs, is not likely to give a closely reasoned argument for his view, but the crux of it is likely to hold that there are three levels of government in the United States and that each has certain areas of exclusive control. The legal argument is somewhat more sophisticated, but it comes to the same thing. In 1871, Judge Cooley, asserting that local self-government was a matter of "absolute right," gave a historical argument augmented by some concepts from the eighteenth-century natural-rights philosophers. The historical argument holds that local self-government was well established as an Anglo-American tradition long before an American state was created and that this practice was transferred to American municipalities through the common law. Unless the state constitution specifically turned over control of local government to the states, the argument ran, it remained as it had long been established. Writers sought to show that the principle of local self-government predated the establishment of the Kingdom of England, that it had, in fact, been the greatest contribution to government of the Angles and Saxons before William the Conqueror, and that its origins were to be found in the democracy of the ancient German tribes in the days before that part of Europe fell under the influence of Rome.

The argument as presented by Judge Cooley was actually an obiter dictum—that is to say, his remarks were not absolutely necessary, since he had already settled the case before him upon other, more conventional, grounds. His remarks suited the spirit of the times, however, and were used by judges at one time or another in California, Indiana, Iowa, Kentucky, Michigan, Nebraska, and Texas. The doctrine, however, never became established, for the courts generally followed the opposite principle, that the state is supreme and the city is its creature. This is hardly surprising, since the doctrine of the inherent right of cities to home rule was a wistful, fanciful notion based upon very weak legal reasoning and largely manufactured by judges who were sympathetic to local self-government.

Actually, local government in England is not, and probably never has been, independent of the central government. Since the days of William I there certainly has been no question but that any "rights" that cities may have are actually privileges extended by the Crown. Sovereignty over the former colonies passed from the British Crown to the American states, which have since retained such powers as were not relinquished to the national government. And as for any "rights" of cities existing under the common law, all judges, and most certainly the scholarly Thomas M. Cooley, knew that the unwritten common law is automatically super-seded by any contrary provisions in statute or constitutional law. More important, there is no natural cleavage to separate local from state powers. Probably all "local" concerns have within them some element of state-wide interest, and state powers must often be administered, when it comes to detailed application, in specific local areas. The definition of "local" concerns is therefore not natural at all, but a fairly arbitrary legalism that has historically been determined in the United States by the state legislatures and the state courts.[11]

Short-lived as was the legal protest, a legacy remains in the widespread belief among Americans that the municipality has, or should have, a "right" to rule itself in local matters without detailed supervision by the state.

PREMISES OF THE MIDDLE-CLASS BUSINESSMAN: THE EFFICIENCY AND ECONOMY MOVEMENT

The Organization of Protest. Well-meaning but poorly organized amateurs began their efforts to reclaim city government from the boss and the political machine as early as the 1870s. They lacked experience and organizational skills and were often politically naïve. The movement, like its Jacksonian predecessor, was pragmatic, unsystematic, and loosely coordinated. It had no single intellectual leader and was not part of a general philosophy, although it did have definite Hamiltonian overtones. Its strength was centered in the middle-class businessman with additional aid coming from a handful of academicians. The businessmen had a particular motivation for action. They paid a large portion of the taxes to city governments that were not noted for cautious expenditure of public

[11] The principal legal case is *People of Michigan ex rel. LeRoy v. Hurlbut*, 24 Mich. 44 (1871). A supporting argument is given in A. M. Eaton, "The Right of Local Self-government," *Harvard Law Review*, vol. 13, pp. 441 ff., 570 ff., 638 ff. The reasoning in the Cooley doctrine is effectively rebutted in H. L. McBain, "The Doctrine of an Inherent Right of Local Self-government," *Columbia Law Review*, vol. 16 (March and April, 1916), pp. 190 ff., 299 ff.

funds, and they lived under their own code of civic obligations (see Figures 5 and 6).

The difficulties which confronted reformers were at first almost overpowering. Political machines, often headed by a well-known boss, resisted by using any technique that would destroy or discourage the neophytes. The machine was usually well organized, with an army of precinct workers and large numbers of voters who were obligated to it, and hence was generally able to defeat any attempts at reform. The minority of businessmen who turned reformers were in a particularly vulnerable position. A strong political machine in control of the city government had many weapons at hand to injure those who dared to oppose it, as, for example, increasing the assessment of their properties, refusing them permits and licenses, or harassing them through overadministration of fire, health, or other city codes.

Many industrialists and businessmen refused to cooperate with reformers because they followed a belief popular among their kind that it was cheaper to buy off the machine than to fight it. The reformers were also confronted by a public that was almost completely cynical regarding the possibilities for honesty in municipal government, and they had to fight that greatest of all opponents of change, public apathy.

Attitudes and Antidotes. Nevertheless, reforms took place. Some were the result of political accidents and compromises, such as the adoption of constitutional home rule in the Missouri constitutional convention of 1875. Others were the result of organized pressures upon the state legislatures, as in the case of the New York and Massachusetts acts of 1883 establishing civil service for all cities in those states. A nationwide organization, the National Civil Service Reform League, had been organized in 1877. In that same year, the report of a governor's commission in New York condemned the use of national political parties in municipal elections, giving an opening wedge to the concept of election without party designation, an idea that became a favorite of reformers.

In answer to demands for a more modern type of city government, a version of the *strong-mayor plan* was put into effect in Brooklyn in 1880 and Boston in 1885. This plan is one in which the council is restricted to a sharing of the legislative power with the mayor, while the entire administrative structure is integrated[12] under the control of the mayor, who is also a powerful policy maker. After about 1820 many cities imitated the American national government by adopting a bicameral (two-house) council and mayoralty appointments subject to council ap-

[12] By an *integrated* administrative structure, political scientists mean one in which all administrative authority and responsibility is in the hands of a single individual or body. The administrative structure is arranged so that each employee or officer is responsible to some one superior who in turn must answer to his superior, until ultimately department heads are each responsible to a single chief executive.

THE TAMMANY TIGER LOOSE—"What are you going to do about it?"

Fig. 5. "What are you going to do about it?" In the early 1870s, Thomas Nast was offered $500,000 to stop drawing cartoons such as this one denouncing the Tweed ring of Tammany Hall.

proval. This trend was later abandoned. The strong-mayor plan, however, was found by reformers to be a much more workable, systematic approach to the problems of city government than was the weak-mayor plan, for the latter had not been conceived of for use in the larger cities

ELECTION TIME GIMMICKS

Fig. 6. The Tammany tiger has been a target of cartoonists for over eighty years. During that time, however, the animal has been partly domesticated. SOURCE: Copyright, 1953, New York Post Corporation. Cartoon by John Pierotti from the *New York Post*. Used by permission.

of an industrial age. Although varying considerably in detail from one city to another, the strong-mayor plan met with the approval of an increasing number of state legislatures during the 1890s and today is the plan generally used in America's largest cities.

The reform movement developed through organizations on the local level. The Municipal Voters' League was formed in Chicago in 1896, and before long such groups, supported by and made up chiefly of local businessmen, began to appear in nearly all large and medium-sized cities, although they were, of course, not all of equal effectiveness. They were characteristically known as "voters' leagues," "citizens' leagues," "taxpayers' associations," "nonpartisan reform committees," "committees of 100," or by similar titles.

An important effort to coordinate these local groups was made through the National Municipal League, which was formed in 1894. This organization became the center, and a veritable symbol, of the movement. In its "model" charters and laws, its booklets and pamphlets, it made available to local groups ammunition that included all of the most recently developed reform favorites. It became an effective and respected leader of the struggle.[13]

Another key step toward effective organization was taken with the creation of a Bureau of Municipal Research in New York in 1906. Dozens of imitations appeared in other cities in the next decade and after.

The municipal research bureaus were often formed with the thought that attempts to elect reform administrations were doomed to failure and that the best way to secure improvement in the administration of cities would be to work with city officials, furnishing them with research data. The bureaus were privately financed. They concentrated upon problems of finance and administration.[14]

More organizations followed: the Proportional Representation League (to further the plan designed to give every significant interest group or political party representation in proportion to its voting strength at the polls); the National Popular Government League (to secure the public ownership of local utilities[15] and to urge the adoption of the *initiative, referendum,* and *recall*[16]); the National Short Ballot Organization (to fight the "bedsheet" ballot); taxpayers' leagues (sometimes chiefly to protect the interest of the largest taxpayers); local government committees of chambers of commerce; many different women's clubs; and the League of Women Voters (which does not confine its activities to reform or to local affairs). By the early years of the twentieth century, reform

---

[13] The story of the League is told, largely from its own viewpoint, in Frank M. Stewart, *A Half Century of Municipal Reform* (1950); see also Richard S. Childs, *Civic Victories* (1952).

[14] See N. N. Gill, *Municipal Research Bureaus—A Study of the Nation's Leading Citizen-supported Agencies* (1944). On the relationship of research groups and direct-action groups, see a note in the *National Municipal Review*, vol. 41 (March, 1952), pp. 165–167.

[15] Public ownership of public utilities was neither socialistic nor radical in concept. It was merely an attempt to get rid of racketeering or gouging private organizations in this area by adopting the standard European practice of public ownership.

[16] These terms are defined on p. 61.

was still largely in the hands of amateurs, but it was now effectively organized and the amateurs were experienced in politics.

Institutions of Reform. Practical results of "reform" began to be made evident. The commission plan of city organization appeared in Galveston in 1901, shortly received the endorsement of many reformers, and in the next few years it spread rapidly throughout the nation wherever the movement was effective. This plan, which provides for elected "commissioners" (usually five) who serve collectively as the legislative body and individually as heads of administrative departments, was an improvement over the weak-mayor system, especially in providing for a shorter ballot and for some semblance of an integrated administrative structure, but it contained fatal defects which caused it to pass into eclipse after about 1917.[17] It was succeeded by the council-manager (or city manager) plan, which got its start about 1908. It is characterized by a governmental structure that places legislative power in a small, preferably lay, council and administrative authority under a professional "manager" who is appointed by and responsible to the council.

The reform movement also generally included the initiative, referendum, and recall, although some conservatives at first feared that they would serve the causes of radicals. The *initiative* (which allows the voters themselves to enact legislation or amend city charters without resort to the legislative body) was first authorized by city charter in San Francisco in 1898. This charter also provided for the *referendum* (which requires popular approval, under certain conditions, of acts of the legislative body before they become effective). The *recall* (removal of an elective public official from office by a vote of the people prior to the expiration of his term) seems to have been authorized first by the Los Angeles charter of 1903.[18] In an attempt to write a "model" reform charter and apparently under the assumption that if a little medicine is good, a lot of medicine is better, reformers in Des Moines combined the commission plan with the initiative, referendum, and recall (1907). For some years the "Des Moines plan" symbolized reform. (As a word of caution to the zealot who may be in the habit of devising an "ideal" solution and then dogmatically defending it as a permanent panacea, it might be noted that in 1949 Des Moines abandoned the "Des Moines plan" and adopted a council-manager form of government.)

During their heyday—the first and second decades of the present century—reformers sponsored other organizational and procedural changes: preferential voting, such as the Bucklin and Ware systems, which did not catch on; reapportionment of urban representation in state legislatures; "model" plans of budgeting, accounting, contract procedures, elec-

[17] See chap. 8.
[18] See chap. 4 for more details.

tion procedures, and bond issuing; the direct primary election system of nomination for city offices and a shorter ballot. Underlying nearly all reform efforts were two basic assumptions: (1) that the political party and politicians in general were not to be trusted and (2) that the principle of "efficient business management" could and should be applied to city government. The muckraker at the turn of the century had shown the low moral tone to which the professional politician of the day had descended, and the reforming businessman wanted no part of it in his city.[19] In contrast, he viewed the structure of the private corporation and the "business methods" of the nineteenth century with pride and respect. He made famous the assertion that "there is no Democratic way to lay a sewer and no Republican way to pave a street" and that running a city is simply a matter of applying the "principles of good business management."

An Appraisal. The reform movement made a real contribution to local self-government by recovering a certain amount of responsibility, by replacing the checks and balances of Jacksonian democracy with a more modern system of centralized leadership, and by reestablishing at least a modicum of public respect and confidence in local government. However, it did some damage, too. It placed a misleading overemphasis upon *forms* and *structures* of government. It led people astray in its constant preaching to the effect that there are few, if any, partisan issues in city government—that it is a mere matter of "efficient business management." Not only was this concept false, it also did a great deal to discourage interest in local politics, which in turn has continued to leave endangered the institution of local self-government.

The reform movement failed, for the most part, to make local government in large cities more representative of a cross section of the community.[20] The old-style politician was rather thoroughly repudiated, true enough, but the balance of power in government was not fundamentally altered. The business community continued to dominate city government. Formerly it had had to do this indirectly, through the machine. Now a new type of control grew up. Businessmen began to participate directly in government. Control of the voter was now achieved, not through the traditional devices, but through control of the media of mass communication. Nonpartisan elections, in particular, made it easy for the conservative business interests to run the city government.

The movement—and especially what is left of it today—has in most

---

[19] The most famous muckraker was Lincoln Steffens. See his *The Shame of the Cities* (1904), which originally appeared as a series of magazine articles; and his *Autobiography of Lincoln Steffens* (1931).

[20] The failure of the movement to include a "solid basis in mass support" was pointed out many years ago by John A. Vieg, "Advice for Municipal Reformers," *Public Opinion Quarterly*, vol. 1 (October, 1937), pp. 87–92.

places become closely associated in the minds of workingmen and labor leaders with the business community and its interests. Workingmen and labor leaders know that the reformers have produced a more efficient type of government, but they feel that it is often more concerned with saving taxpayers' money than with solving the problems of the whole community. This situation is partly responsible for the manner in which organized labor has turned to the national-government level for legislation.

Many of the "citizens' action" groups and bureaus of municipal research (there are exceptions) have changed a good deal from their original character and purpose. A quarter of a century ago these groups had life, ideas, and a set of goals planted in the future. Today too many of them have become tools of large taxpayers who want attacks on municipal taxes and essentially on municipal government itself. In seeking to minimize city-government services and expenditures, they have in effect become organizations *opposing* municipal government.

Helpful and necessary as the reform movement was, its philosophy is no longer adequate for present-day needs, at least not those of the large city.

CURRENT THEORIES OF CITY GOVERNMENT

The City and the New Deal. The worst depression in the history of the United States began in the autumn of 1929 and did not actually end until the country began preparing for war about a decade later. The election of 1932 produced a huge protest vote that resulted in (1) the election of Franklin D. Roosevelt and (2), as it proved, the New Deal. The New Deal attempted to do at least two things simultaneously: to combat the depression and to effect social reforms. It developed programs for almost every area where extensive demands for improvement were heard: social security for the aged and dependent; farm-price supports; slum clearance; soil conservation; protection for organized labor; emergency "make-work"; and a host of others.

The farmer, worker, banker, small businessman—almost everyone, in fact—began turning to the national government for whatever aid they felt was needed. The states and cities were bypassed, either because their financial resources or their legal authority was hopelessly inadequate, because they were unwilling to tackle the problems, or because the scope of the problems was so broad that they could be handled adequately only by the national government.

However, some effort was made by the New Deal to utilize local agencies. PWA projects (such as new city halls, water standpipes, sewerage systems, bridges, even public housing units) were determined upon the approval of recommended plans submitted by local governments. Perhaps the most outstanding case of New Deal reliance upon municipalities came as a result of the United States Housing Act of 1937.[21]

Most people probably think of Franklin D. Roosevelt as the very symbol of centralized authority in Washington, yet one of his long-time advisers tells us that although he favored business regulation and credit control through the national government:[22]

Aside from this, he would be against the development of strong central government, would indeed be in favour of minimum Federal powers . . . and [would want] most governmental functions to be decentralized—carried on by the states and municipalities.

This was in fact the kind of programme President Roosevelt would have liked to carry out. It was the furniture of his mind down into 1932; and his mind was never entirely purged of these preferences. . . .

To some [projects], such as the building up of a Federal (central) relief organization, he gave only the most grudging consent and got rid of it at the earliest possible instant. . . .

And when a permanent social security system came to be worked out, he settled an internal argument in his official family by coming down on the side of state rather than Federal administration. This was a momentous and revealing choice; it showed what side he would like to be on if he could.

Perhaps this is overstating the case somewhat, or possibly circumstances soon forced these preferences to the back of Roosevelt's mind. In any case, the same writer ten pages later speaks of "the President's incorrigible tendency to think in terms of national rather than local administrative units. . . ."[23]

The Need for a Contemporary Theory. It should be clear by now that municipal self-government faces a real problem in the future—the problem of finding a satisfactory mid-twentieth-century niche for itself. The preceding brief review of American theory indicates that the concepts of the Jacksonian frontiersman and the resulting institutions (such as the weak-mayor system and the city boss) are not adequate to meet the needs of an industrialized, urbanized, specialized, technological society. The theory of an "inherent right" of local self-government is quite dead, in addition to being legally and sociologically impossible. The efficiency and economy movement did much to modernize local government. But its modernity was that of fifty years ago, before the advent of either powerful organized labor or the social-service state. The movement never had a strong base in mass support, and its institutions have not often included in their membership a cross section of the general public. If these people do not find a more acceptable theory, they will continue—as they do today in a host of American cities—almost to ignore city government and

---

[21] See chap. 19 for a closer look at housing.

[22] R. G. Tugwell, "The Experimental Roosevelt," *Political Quarterly*, vol. 21 (1950), pp. 239–270. The quotation is from p. 241. By permission.

[23] *Ibid.*, p. 251.

its politics and to concentrate their attentions and hopes upon the national-government scene.

We stand today in very real need of a theory of municipal government which will evoke interest from both the conservative and the liberal; one which will cause people to take an active interest in municipal affairs and to participate in them, to vote in as large numbers in a mayoralty election as they now do for the presidency; one that will not allow a handful of professional politicians (as was the case in the nadir of Jacksonian disintegration), or a handful of businessmen (as has happened in some cities as a result of the triumph of the efficiency and economy movement), or a handful of labor leaders (as could happen if the future produces an inadequate theory) to control without responsibility; one that will possess sufficient legal authority to perform demanded functions.

We need a theory, not in the narrow sense of a panacea, but one that will produce government representative of a cross section of the urban population. We must decide which functions ought properly to be performed on each of the levels of government. Once this is decided, we must free the city from its legal bondage so that it may proceed to furnish the services of these functions. We must find adequate structures of government, but we must not become overly absorbed with them. We must strive for flexibility and avoid dogma—in contrast to what happened to some reformers of the past.

A truly useful theory becomes absorbed into the political-myth system of the day. We must find one that will become accepted by the businessman, the labor leader, the politician, the rich man and the poor man— and, perhaps most difficult of all, by a substantial bloc of state legislators. The problem, then, is to find the ingredients for an acceptable contemporary theory.

The Pattern of Contemporary Reform. The initial impulse toward municipal reform came, as has been explained, from businessmen, academicians, and their citizens' organizations and governmental research agencies. Today, efforts to solve most of the remaining problems in achieving good municipal government are being made by professional organizations. They have interested themselves in the development of standards and techniques of administration and have become increasingly important in recent years. These groups include organizations of managers, mayors, city attorneys, engineers, police chiefs, fire chiefs, recreationists, social workers, librarians, and officers in the fields of correction, housing, public health, public works, planning, municipal finance, and personnel. The state leagues of municipalities are also important agents for governmental improvements today.

These voluntary associations of public officials provide many of the services which in other countries are furnished by the central government.

They sponsor national and regional conferences, publish newsletters and periodicals, answer technical inquiries, publish technical manuals of standards and procedures, conduct training courses, and otherwise seek to improve their professions.[24]

Betterment of standards and techniques of administration is a desirable thing, and organizations such as the above are undoubtedly continuing the trend toward better government. However, most of these groups have had little influence in making municipal government a better *political* instrument by improving its responsiveness to, and representativeness of, a cross section of the public. It is in this area that many problems of good municipal government remain unsolved.

[24] *Municipal Year Book,* 1953, pp. 143–144.

CHAPTER 4

MUNICIPAL ELECTIONS

Probably the simplest, most common, and ultimately most important *direct* contact the typical citizen has with his city or village takes place when he steps into the booth and exercises his privilege of voting. Unlike voting in national-government elections, the local suffrage imposes a duty to vote for many offices (in most cities), in addition to numerous proposed chapter amendments, bond issues, and referred and initiated municipal ordinances. While the simple *act* of voting is easy enough, its conscientious exercise requires serious efforts.

THE ELECTORATE

Who Is Eligible? Time was when more persons were eligible to vote in state than in municipal contests. As a matter of fact, some American cities in the colonial period were "close corporations" where no one at all, not even the wealthiest men, enjoyed the suffrage. Until after World War II (1945), Great Britain had one set of suffrage laws for parliamentary elections and another, less universal, set for municipal voting. In the case of the latter, occupancy as owner or tenant had traditionally been a prerequisite for voting in local contests. In Canada, voting restrictions for municipal elections are still generally greater than for other elections.

Today, with but a few exceptions, the right to vote in American municipal elections is determined by eligibility to participate in state elections. The usual prerequisites include American citizenship, a minimum age of twenty-one (eighteen in Georgia), a minimum period of residence in the state, county, and polling district, and registration. Other requirements are sometimes added.[1]

---

[1] The basic historical reference is Kirk H. Porter, *A History of Suffrage in the United States* (1918). Dudley O. McGovney, *The American Suffrage Medley* (1949), discusses voting restrictions in the various states. He is critical of unnecessary disenfranchisements and urges a uniform national suffrage law as a remedy. One may learn more about voter qualifications by consulting the current issue of the annual *Book of the States,* published by the Council of State Governments, or by consulting the local official in charge of elections, usually the city or county clerk.

Special Local Requirements. During the Great Depression, Arizona, Michigan, Montana, Nevada, Texas, and Utah provided that only property-tax payers could vote on questions of direct appropriation of public money or the issuance of bonds.[2] One study has indicated that the Michigan law prevented more than half of the Detroit electorate from voting on such issues during the depression.[3] Since World War II, the Michigan Supreme Court has shown a tendency toward a narrow interpretation of the application of the state constitution on this point. While these provisions apply to all such questions coming up in the state, they most often affect municipal issues.

A very few states make, or are constitutionally permitted to make, an actual distinction between eligibility for municipal, as against general, elections. The Mississippi legislature (in a state with one of the most restricted suffrages in any democracy) is authorized to prescribe municipal qualifications over and above the general requirements. The Virginia legislature is permitted to establish a property qualification of up to $250 in any city (and in certain other political subdivisions). Until 1928, the state of Rhode Island required that anyone who wished to vote in a municipal election own taxable property with a minimum value of $134, although there was no property requirement for general elections. The Nevada Supreme Court has held that the legislature of that state may restrict voting to direct property-tax payers on the question of issuing municipal bonds for certain purposes. Most Canadian provinces allow only property owners or property-tax payers to vote on local bond issues. But all of these provisions are unusual, are seldom resorted to, and are far off the course being steered by contemporary democratic theory. The almost universal rule is that persons who are eligible to vote in national and state elections may also vote in municipal elections.

VOTING AND NONVOTING

The Apathetic Ones. In March, 1951, the mayor of Roselle, New Jersey, declared that a tax should be levied upon all nonvoters. Compulsory voting supported by a tax, fine, or other punishment is used, or has been used, in nearly thirty nations, including Australia, Austria, Belgium, Czechoslovakia, the Netherlands, and Switzerland. President Truman blamed nonvoting on "laziness" and urged the American Political Science Association to study ways of getting out the vote. The American

[2] By property-tax payers is meant property owners, of course. Contrary to popular misunderstanding, a renter pays just as much in property taxes as an owner, although it is hidden in the rent. While there may well be a *psychological* difference between owner and renter when it comes to taxation; there is no *economic* difference.

[3] Donald S. Hecock and Harry A. Trevelyan, *Detroit Voters and Recent Elections* (1938).

Heritage Foundation conducts a "Get Out the Vote" contest, as do various local civic groups. Labor's League for Political Action of the AFL, the Political Action Committee of the CIO, and the National Association for the Advancement of Colored People operate registration and voting drives at every major election. (Members of organized labor and Negroes, even in areas where the latter are not discriminated against at the polls, fall below the national average in election participation.)

In comparison with the people of such advanced democracies as Great Britain and the three Scandinavian countries, Americans take their voting responsibilities lightly. Studies indicate that only about one-third of the eligible voters are in the habit of going to the polls regularly. Even in presidential elections, which regularly attract the greatest number of people, the record is not impressive. In 1948, barely one-half of the eligibles managed to get to the polls, although the 1952 turnout was better (62.0 per cent). In nonpresidential elections for Congress or state offices, few people ordinarily vote. And for municipal elections—elections dealing with matters in very close physical proximity to the voter— participation is typically at its lowest. It is not uncommon for the vote in municipal elections to drop to less than one-fourth of the qualified voters.

The extent of voting varies in different sections of the country, and even between different cities in the same section. Each city has its own tradition of participation or nonparticipation in municipal elections. Sometimes a matter of particular interest will bring out a larger vote for a municipal election than was the case in the corresponding presidential vote. The degree to which the electorate is organized or to which organized groups are active in municipal elections influences the size of the turnout. In almost all jurisdictions and at all levels of government, the primary election is of considerably less interest than the general election. (Exceptions are to be found in one-party areas, such as the deep South and parts of New England.)[4]

Nonvoting: Three Studies. A study made in St. Louis a few years ago indicated the usual differential between presidential and municipal elections in the degree of participation. It also showed the over-all apathy of the American voter. In 1944, despite a presidential election in the offing, only 59 per cent of the *eligible* voters of the city bothered to register. In the Roosevelt-Dewey presidential contest, 83.8 per cent of those registered voted, but this amounted to only 49.4 per cent of those who were eligible.[5]

If less than one-half of those upon whom voting rights have been

---

[4] On voter participation, see the *Municipal Year Book, 1937;* James K. Pollock, *Voting Behavior: A Case Study* (1939); and the St. Louis and Los Angeles studies cited above.

[5] E. B. Olds and D. W. Salmon, *St. Louis Voting Behavior* (1948), sec. C.

bestowed bother to vote in a contest for the highest office in the land, how many would consider it worthwhile to help choose a mayor for St. Louis? In the election of 1945, 42.7 per cent of the registered population went to the polls, but this was only 25.2 per cent of those eligible. It must be remembered that these elections were affected by the absence of thousands of citizen-soldiers who could vote only if they bothered with the extra work of an absentee ballot, but even so the result is a poor showing. A mayor was elected by less than one-half of those who had registered and by only one-fourth of the potential electorate.

An ambitious voter-participation study has been conducted by the Bureau of Governmental Research at the University of California, Los Angeles, under the direction of Lawrence W. O'Rourke.[6] It found that in the average city of Los Angeles County between 1935 and 1952, voter turnout at the average state and national election amounted to 77.2 per cent of the registered voters. For the average municipal election, however, the figure was only 41.1 per cent of those registered. These statistics compare closely with those in the less comprehensive St. Louis study.

The Los Angeles–area study indicated that participation did *not* vary inversely with the size of the municipality. The city of Los Angeles ranked twenty-sixth out of the forty-five cities in local elections, but ranked lower in state and national contests. Tiny Avalon had a very good record, but San Marino, only slightly larger, had the poorest of all records in local elections. Some cities had very good records in state and national elections, but very poor ones in local elections, and vice versa.

The study found that there was no correlation between distance from the core city and amount of voter participation. It was found, however, that predominantly Republican cities had better voting records than did those that were predominantly Democratic.[7] But wealthy communities did not necessarily have good records in *local* elections. Beverly Hills, for example, had next to the poorest record.

Among the important conclusions of the study were these:[8]

1. . . . People tend to vote *against* candidates and propositions rather than for them. . . . People attend city council meetings more often to protest than to affirm some proposed action.

2. . . . Voter turnout is dependent upon the degree of *opposition* that can be generated in the minds of voters.

3. . . . There is a sizable number of citizens who consistently participate in state and national elections, but *never vote* in municipal elections.

[6] Lawrence W. O'Rourke, *Voting Behavior in the Forty-five Cities of Los Angeles County* (1953).

[7] The municipal elections themselves are nonpartisan in California.

[8] O'Rourke, *op. cit.*, chap. 2. Italics added.

4. . . . Percentages of the registered electorate remain fairly *constant* in each city for almost all municipal elections. This may be contrasted with the somewhat more erratic percentages found in voting for state and national offices. . . . *There is a small core of citizens in each city who sustain municipal government.*

Why such a poor turnout? Part of the answer seems to be furnished by a study made in Detroit.[9] A representative sample of persons was asked the question: "Do you feel that there is anything you can do to improve the way the city is run? What do you feel you can do?" *More than one-half the people declared that they can do nothing.* One-third could suggest only voting. Only one person in twelve believed that he could exert influence by means of personal criticisms, or by joining in group action.

The study added that "the indifferent or helpless types of reply are much more common at low educational and low economic levels than at higher levels. They likewise occur more among women than men, and more among older than younger people. Those who belong to no organizations answer no differently than members of organized groups. Labor union members say there is nothing they can do as often as do non-union people."

The feeling of futility appears to be widespread. Before the 1945 election in the city of New York, one-third of those eligible to vote told pollster Elmo Roper that "no matter which of the candidates is elected, the city will be run about the same."[10]

Consequences of Nonvoting. At virtually every election the local newspaper, bent upon demonstrating that it is "civic-minded," will conduct a vigorous campaign to get individuals to register and then to vote. All of the clichés concerning the responsibility and privilege of living in a democracy will be trotted out. The newspaper will assure the reader that it does not care how he votes (which is not quite the case, as a rule), but that it certainly wants to see him in that line-up on election day. The fact that the poor fellow who is stampeded into line does not know who is running, cares less, and can be counted upon all too often to cast a totally ignorant vote seems not to bother the writer of the front-page editorials. If people really *want* to vote they will without doubt do so. And a bonfire need not be built under them to get them to the polling place. If they do not want to vote, what is democratic about forcing them to cast an uninformed vote, or to choose between equally undesirable candidates, or to do something that is in some other way distasteful?

Just how serious is our high percentage of nonvoting anyway? The

[9] Arthur Kornhauser, *Attitudes of Detroit People toward Detroit* (1952), p. 28.
[10] Elmo Roper, "New York Elects O'Dwyer," *Public Opinion Quarterly*, vol. 10 (Spring, 1946), pp. 53–56.

chances are that its dangers have been greatly exaggerated. Most people who stay away from the polls do so deliberately and by their own choice. They are not interested, and they feel that voting in the particular instance will avail them nothing. The important question is not whether people *do* vote, but rather whether they *may* vote if they so choose. Studies made of why people do not vote show that, outside of illness or a broken fan belt on the way to the voting booth, most people stay home because of *lack of interest*.[11] To most people, choice of candidates is of *marginal* interest. They believe that "changing horses" will not effect a change in the economic-social situation. When something they consider to be truly important comes up, they will appear at the polls. Americans are more interested in voting *against* candidates than for them.[12] They become excited about elections in which they can register a *protest*.

There is only one aspect of nonvoting that seems to have truly unfavorable implications for the mental health of our democracy. That is to be found among those who do not vote, not because of apathy, but because of *cynicism*. To some extent since Jackson's time, Americans have accepted the attitude that "all politics is crooked." It is a popular, if highly erroneous, belief that all politicians make money "under the table" and that one set of politicians is just as bad as another. If this is carried very far by very many people, it can become serious, for it carries with it an implicit distrust of the democratic process.

The major danger in a light vote lies in the fact that highly organized groups, whether of the nature of old-fashioned city machines or of special-interest groups of any type, will thereby be able to control the government, for the lighter the vote the easier it is for such groups to win. They have a solid nucleus of dependable voters. A small turnout *does not* result in the same percentage distribution of the vote among the various segments of the population as would be found in a large turnout. Hence it is fallacious to rationalize failure to vote with the argument that "my one vote wouldn't make any difference anyway."

Who Goes to the Polls? Certain generalizations can be hazarded concerning the qualitative make-up of our voting population. We know that in terms of *percentages*, more men vote than do women, more whites vote than do Negroes, more people who are property-tax payers vote than do those who are not, more conservatives vote than do liberals. Except for persons who must stay at home because of the infirmities of old age, people vote in larger proportions as they grow older. Almost twice as

[11] For studies, see C. E. Merriam and H. F. Gosnell, *Non-voting* (1924); P. F. Lazarsfeld, *The People's Choice* (1944); Michigan Survey Research Center, *A Study of the Presidential Vote, November, 1948* (1952); J. K. Pollock, *Voting Behavior* (1939). These citations are also the basis for the following section on "Who Goes to the Polls?"

[12] The Roper and O'Rourke studies, cited above, lend support to this statement.

many vote at the age of fifty-one as vote at twenty-one. This seems to support the general theory that people do not vote because they theoretically *ought* to, or because they feel it is a duty or a great privilege, but rather they vote when they feel that they have a direct *stake* in the outcome. It should be further noted that there is a direct relationship between size of income and participation in elections; and between amount of education and participation.

The white-collared middle class votes in greater proportion than does the working class. This is of particular significance in municipal elections, although it is important at all times in politics. Democracy had its beginnings in Western civilization as a middle-class movement, and persons who identify themselves with this group absorb the tradition that calls for alert interest in public affairs and a civic-minded attitude. Members of the middle class also have a vested property interest to protect, or identify themselves with those who do, and tend to pay a large share of the taxes levied by government. Hence there is considerable social and economic pressure for these people to go to the polls.

Organized labor, which is usually associated with liberalism, has a more difficult problem at election time. Marginal voters—those who go to the polls only when they are convinced that something special is involved—come very largely from the working class. Their value patterns place less emphasis upon voting than do those of the middle class, and in the past they have had much less of an economic stake in the outcome of elections. Labor leaders, in conducting get-out-the-vote campaigns, are not merely engaged in teaching "good citizenship"; they know that their task in getting workingmen to the polls in a municipal election is a difficult one.

Improving Our Record. It has been suggested by some that voting should be made compulsory, but this is not likely to be the answer to voter apathy. Great Britain, the Scandinavian nations, and some of the British Commonwealth nations have a very high voter participation record without resort to any kind of coercion. These countries have developed their high sense of public interest, level of political intelligence, and public responsibility without attempting to require voter participation. Forcing people to be democratic comes close to being a philosophical contradiction. The constitutions of Massachusetts (since 1918) and North Dakota (since 1899) authorize the legislatures to compel voting, but no action has ever been taken in those states. The people of Oregon in 1920 voted down a similar constitutional amendment. Kansas City once had a charter provision in effect levying a fine for not voting, but the Missouri Supreme Court, using an argument based upon the philosophy of John Locke, held it unconstitutional. The court said that voting is a right of the sovereign people, that the sovereign is above the law, and that therefore voting could not be made compulsory.[13] There is little interest in, and certainly no enthusiasm for, compulsory voting in America today.[14]

This is not to suggest that people should not be encouraged to become interested in, and informed about, politics. An increasingly alert general public is probably a prerequisite to progress in the art of democratic government. It is highly desirable that we remove as many obstacles as possible from the path to the polling booth.

BALLOTS, NOMINATIONS, AND ELECTIONS

American cities use both partisan and nonpartisan ballots in their municipal elections. In a few cases, a system called proportional representation is used. The ballot itself may take several forms.[15]

General Parties on the Local Scene. From necessity, the basic strength and organization of a political party is in the local community. Until nonpartisan elections came into use around 1910, municipal election campaigns were invariably conducted by the local party organizations. In that earlier day, many large cities were dominated by well-organized political machines, particularly of the majority party of the community. The minority party was usually less well organized and often had very little chance for success at the polls. In most cities the ward was, and is today, the basic unit of party organization. It was often subdivided into precincts.

Today few political machines remain, and partisan elections are used in only about 40 per cent of American cities. Despite the trend away from partisan municipal elections, quite a number of informed persons believe that such elections are desirable, at least for large cities, because the strength of our vitally necessary state and national parties depends upon effective local organization and because public policy today is executed simultaneously on all levels of government. The functions performed by cities are interdependent parts of the whole process of government. Politics and politicians on the local level do not differ fundamentally from their counterparts on the higher levels. Charles A. Beard once asserted that many local problems can be solved only by cooperation with either the state or the national government or both. Today this is surely true of such functions as public health, welfare, safety, housing, and unem-

[13] The case is *Kansas City v. Whipple*, 136 Mo. 475 (1896).

[14] Compulsory voting is discussed pro and con in H. J. Abraham, "What Cure for Voter Apathy?" *National Municipal Review*, vol. 41 (July, 1952), pp. 346–350.

[15] Details concerning political parties and elections that cannot be further treated here may be found in a course in political parties or in any one of several good textbooks. See, for example, Hugh A. Bone, *American Politics and the Party System* (1949); V. O. Key, Jr., *Politics, Parties and Pressure Groups* (3d ed., 1952); H. R. Penniman, *Saits' American Parties and Elections* (5th ed., 1952).

ployment. Since political parties serve as a liaison between politicians and since a party approach toward a public problem may include plans that require action at all levels of government, partisanship on the local scene may be definitely desirable.[16]

Opponents of partisanship, on the other hand, argue that running a city is not a matter of skillful politics, but rather one of efficient business management. The editors of the *National Municipal Review,* for example, argue in the following vein:[17]

> There is, after all, no valid reason for national and state parties to be involved and every reason why they should not.
>
> It has been amply demonstrated that, to be effective and self-reliant cities must be emancipated from the tyranny of the national and state political parties. Good citizens who agree on vital local issues should not be divided by blind loyalties that serve only to confuse these issues.
>
> The way to decency and honesty in national as well as local politics is to eliminate parties from the local scene and thus make all voters "independent."

The arguments on both sides are doubtless exaggerated. Many municipal officers elected on a nonpartisan ballot do cooperate successfully with partisan state and national officers. Our general parties have not proved to be very effective in a liaison role, neither do they stand on definite principles or policies.

Local organizations of the national and state parties, on the other hand, are often quite independent of the higher party structure, especially on local questions. The "blind loyalties" of party exist without doubt, especially in cities where the remnants of political machines are to be found, but this phenomenon may be exaggerated, too. Devoted members of a political party in national and state elections may well vote quite independently in municipal elections. This is especially true if city and general elections are held at different times.

Certainly party leaders often try to inject state or national issues into local campaigns. Sometimes they are successful, sometimes not. Surely, however, it is a fallacy in logic to say that local campaigns in which candidates run as Republicans or Democrats cannot be conducted on local issues.

Whatever the merits of the conflicting arguments presented, there remains one very serious obstacle to the effective use of national parties for city elections: most of our cities, instead of having two well-balanced parties where one stands ready at all times to take control away from

[16] See Charles A. Beard, "Politics and City Government," *National Municipal Review,* vol. 6 (March, 1917), pp. 201–205.

[17] Editorial, "Revolt of the 'Independents,'" *National Municipal Review,* vol. 40 (December, 1951), pp. 564–565.

the other, actually have only one strong party. This is highly undesirable, for our political system is conceived of as an in-party-out-party relationship. Where one party dominates almost to the total exclusion of the other, there is no effective criticism, there is no control of the party in power, and there is no real responsibility to the electorate. The city with a working two-party system is rare. Unhappily the pattern in New York, where the Democratic party is rarely defeated except by its own dissidents, or in Philadelphia, where the Republicans controlled the city government for over eighty consecutive years, is a common one. It is this situation, and not some of the more often cited objections, that forms the greatest weakness of partisanship in municipal affairs.

An Illustration. The type of interrelating of national and local politics which has often been criticized can be illustrated in the April, 1953, mayoralty election in St. Louis. The Democratic candidate was Raymond R. Tucker, Washington University Professor of Engineering. His Republican opponent was a little-known real estate dealer. On local issues, the Democrats sought to defend the record of their incumbent administration, while the Republicans argued that it had been a "defeatist" administration, lacking in any willingness to solve the city's acute financial problem. The national party organizations hailed the city election as a test of strength and presumably of the popularity of the newly inducted Eisenhower administration. The chairman of the Democratic National Committee came to town to speak, while Harold E. Stassen, then Mutual Security Administrator, spoke for the Republicans.

Tucker was elected by the greatest plurality in the history of the city. The Democrats also elected the controller and eleven of the thirteen ward aldermen, a gain of three seats. No one, however, appeared to be able to give a very confident estimate of the relative importance of the personalities of the candidates and of local and national factors in the outcome of the election.

Nonpartisan Elections: The Hope of the Reform Movement. Early in the twentieth century, many members of the reform movement began to advocate the use of nonpartisan elections. They argued that city government was a matter of efficient business administration and that state and national politics had nothing in common with local politics.

Today, almost 60 per cent of American cities of over 5,000 population use a nonpartisan ballot. In some, perhaps most, of these cities the machinery and personnel of national parties and local politics are effectively separated. This is generally true in Minneapolis, Detroit, Dallas, and San Francisco, for example. On the other hand, in many cities there remains some degree of regular party activity despite the nonpartisan ballot. In Boston and Jersey City, until recently, Democratic machines were able to retain their control despite nonpartisan municipal elections. Most of the states west of the Mississippi have provided for nonpartisan elections for all cities, and in California and Minnesota they have been extended to counties as well. Over 85 per cent of council-manager cities use nonpartisan elections.

The Effects of Nonpartisanship. In small cities and villages, where government is largely on an informal, personal basis, nonpartisanship has worked satisfactorily. Some observers feel that it has been a major factor in recent decades in the improvement of the quality of government in such cities.

In quite a few cities, nonpartisanship has improved the quality of candidates for office. Business and professional men have been willing to become candidates on a nonpartisan ballot who would not wish to risk the condescension which often greets the politician representing one of the regular parties.

Many scholars are convinced, however, that in the largest cities nonpartisanship has not succeeded in producing a satisfactory degree of representative and responsive government. Without a guiding label on the ballot, the large-city voter has difficulty in identifying candidates, especially for council. The most important thing for the candidate is therefore not to have a platform, but rather to have a name that rings a bell in the voter's mind. Publicity becomes all-important, and the election is normally won by those who can control the media of mass communication, the newspapers in particular. This has been largely the pattern, for example, in Dallas, Fort Worth, Los Angeles, San Francisco, San Diego, and Detroit.

In large cities, nonpartisanship makes it difficult for voters to cast a protest vote. Discontented voters will normally vote against the "in party" and for the "out party." They cannot do this under nonpartisanship. The incumbent is thus given an advantage in a campaign, for his name is often the best known to the voter. Nonpartisanship in large cities also has a definite tendency to benefit the cause of conservatism.[18]

Some observers would agree with Charles A. Beard, who long ago said that "nonpartisanship has not worked, does not work, and will not work in any major city in the United States."[19] Others believe that it can be successful, even in large cities, providing that it is not accompanied by

---

[18] See Charles R. Adrian, "Some General Characteristics of Nonpartisan Elections," *American Political Science Review,* vol. 46 (September, 1952), pp. 766–776; Richard S. Childs, "500 Non-political Elections," reprinted as an appendix to his *Civic Victories;* A. W. Bromage, "Partisan Elections in Cities," *National Municipal Review,* vol. 40 (May, 1951), pp. 250–253, which argues for nonpartisanship. For the effect of nonpartisanship in Minneapolis upon both city and state politics, see Robert L. Morlan, "City Politics: Free Style," *ibid.,* vol. 38 (November, 1949), pp. 485–490.

[19] Beard, *op. cit.,* p. 205.

the long ballot. And in smaller cities, where the voter knows the candidates personally or by reputation, this type of election seems to work very well; in these cities a trend toward nonpartisanship has accompanied the trend toward the council-manager plan.

Local Parties: The Hope of the Future? Some political scientists have urged the necessity for local political parties as a compromise between nonpartisanship and the use of the regular state and national parties, neither of which is particularly satisfactory in large cities. Such parties would appear to have real merits: they could stand on platforms dealing with local matters without becoming involved in national issues and without having the election turn upon such national questions; at the same time the best aspects of partisanship, including channels for protest voting, responsiveness to changes in public opinion, and collective responsibility for councilmanic actions, could be retained.

There have been numerous examples of local parties in municipal politics, although they have in no way become an integral part of the American political system. Americans in overwhelming numbers have taken the attitude that efforts toward third parties are a waste of time, and this viewpoint probably spills over into local politics. Local parties for the most part fall into three classes: (1) the Socialist party; (2) small-town parties; and (3) reform parties.

Sewer Socialism. The Socialist party is, technically at least, not a local party at all, since it was conceived of as a national organization. Its success has been restricted almost entirely to the local level, however, and in several cities (especially in Milwaukee and in Bridgeport, Connecticut) the party has acted and has been pictured by the public as being largely a local party.

The rise of the Socialists came simultaneously with the rise of the middle-class reform movement. Their program of action, with perhaps a few exceptions, does not sound very radical or even surprising today. It stood for most of the principles of the reform movement plus much of what we would call today New Deal policies. The Socialists differed from the Republicans and Democrats in that they held to a series of platform planks that dealt with genuinely local matters. While the great parties straddled the fence on local issues or ignored them entirely, the Socialists of the second decade of this century came out strongly for such things as proportional representation, the initiative, referendum, and recall, relief of unemployment through public works, and the municipal ownership of all public utilities. In part their successes, such as they were, could be attributed to the fact that cities were, of course, centers of the working classes, to which socialism made its primary appeal.[20] The great majority of people who voted for Socialist candidates were, however, not

[20] See Ira Kipnis, *The American Socialist Movement* (1952).

Socialists or sympathetic to socialism. Voters no doubt often felt that Socialists could provide more competent, honest reforms in local government than could or would their opponents.

During the years before the conservative reaction of the twenties, several cities elected Socialist mayors or councilmen, including Reading, Schenectady, Minneapolis, Seattle, Milwaukee, Butte, and Bridgeport. A Socialist came within 1,600 votes of becoming mayor of Los Angeles in 1907. Daniel W. Hoan of Milwaukee, one of America's most famous mayors, was a Socialist.[21] Socialist mayors and councilmen have, for the most part, acted independently of party discipline, and many of the more idealistic members of the party have referred disdainfully to municipal reform activities as "sewer socialism."

Socialism was revived in a handful of cities during the Great Depression, and a very few cities continue to elect Socialists today. The relative success of the municipal reform movement and later of the New Deal largely eliminated the *raison d'être* of the local Socialist party. In 1954 there were Socialist mayors in Milwaukee and in Bridgeport and Norwalk, Connecticut.

Local Parties for Small Towns. Local parties are to be found, secondly, in many villages and in small and even middle-sized cities where politics is on a personal basis, national parties are not desired, and yet for one reason or another (perhaps local custom, or state laws which do not permit nonpartisanship) a party label must be used. A small Iowa city, for example, may have a municipal contest between members of the People's party and the Citizen's party, or the Liberal party and the Temperance party, or the Progressive party and the Conservative party. These labels are most often nothing more than collective terms for slates of candidates which have no organization, platform, or treasury. Politics is on a personal basis, and the label is meaningless.

Reform Parties. Reform parties have been organized from time to time in various cities chiefly for purposes of driving out existing machines or corrupt politicians, or for establishing some of the principles of "efficiency and economy." Most of these parties have been short-lived, and their general failure has caused most reform groups to organize themselves as *pressure groups* rather than political parties, endorsing candidates and policies, but not putting men of their own into the field. This is true today of the New York Citizens' Union, the Chicago Municipal Voters' League, and the Detroit Citizens' League, for example.

Some of these groups, such as the one in New York, began as local parties but found this impractical for one reason or another (the Citizens' Union was nearly taken over by a Tammany Hall fifth column). They

[21] He tells his story in D. W. Hoan, *City Government: the Record of the Milwaukee Experiment* (1936).

then proceeded to work toward their goals on a bipartisan or nonpartisan basis.

New York City had a genuine local party created during the Great Depression in the form of the Fusion party with Fiorello H. LaGuardia as its principal driving force. The organization was made up of Citizens' Unionists, many Republicans (including LaGuardia), sundry persons not usually politically active, and antimachine Democrats. Although the party still exists, it was greatly weakened with the death of its able, imaginative, and colorful leader. It was quite unsuccessful when it ran Newbold Morris for mayor against Tammany Hall in 1945, the year that William O'Dwyer was elected. The party was, however, one of several groups backing the successful candidacy of Rudolph Halley, of Kefauver investigation fame, for council president in 1951.

There are two other local parties in the city of New York. Both of them are state-wide parties in form but draw nearly all of their support from within the city. The American Labor party was organized in 1936 chiefly by several labor leaders and some Socialists who had broken with their national party. It campaigned against Tammany Hall and proclaimed itself the "true" New Deal party of New York. It reached its greatest power in the city election of 1937, following a practice of endorsing other candidates or running its own, whichever might prove most advantageous in each individual case. The party became infiltrated with Communists, and a long fight ensued for control of the organization, culminating in 1944 with the withdrawal of the bulk of the non-Communists, who then formed the Liberal party.[22] Since that time, the Liberals (dominated by the Hatters and International Ladies Garment Workers unions) have usually preferred to endorse other candidates (generally Democrats on the state level and Republicans in city contests) rather than run their own, although they do run their own whenever they think it desirable. The American Labor party now serves as a Communist front in local politics. Since other candidates will no longer accept its endorsements, it runs its own candidates or none at all, but with very little success.

The Charter Party. Perhaps the best-known and most successful local party in the United States is the City Charter Committee of Cincinnati, often referred to as the "Charter party." Although the organization does not formally call itself a party and although its name does not appear on the Cincinnati nonpartisan ballot following the names of its candidates, it is thoroughly organized in the general pattern of urban parties, and it functions very definitely as a local party.[23]

[22] The Amalgamated Clothing Workers of America (CIO) did not withdraw until 1948.

[23] For detailed information see the pamphlet by the National Municipal League, *Citizen Organization for Political Activity; the Cincinnati Plan* (3d ed., 1949).

Cincinnati had long been controlled by a powerful Republican machine when, in 1924, a reform effort secured the adoption of the council-manager plan and proportional representation. It was in order to safe-guard these achievements that the Charter party was formed immediately after the election. The organization is today as well organized as the best of political machines of the old type: it not only has complete men's and women's ward and precinct organizations, but is actually built upon a broad base of the block worker. It has publicity, literature and speaker's committees, poll watchers, telephone brigades, and all the other para-phernalia necessary to get out the vote. Perhaps most important of all, it has a permanent and effective organization for financing its efforts. The party differs from traditional machines in that it is interested in good government per se and makes no political promises in return for volunteered efforts. That is, it is not based on patronage, as are other political machines, but relies entirely on unpaid citizens.

From its inception, the Charter party has been opposed in elections by the regular Republican organization. About one-half of the time the Charterites have organized the city council. At other times, either the Republicans have taken control or there has been a 4-4-1 split, with an independent holding the balance of power. This spirited and closely balanced two-party system has forced the regular Republican organiza-tion to reform itself (a large number of Charterites are Republicans in state and national elections), and regardless of which party is in power, the city has enjoyed high-quality government.

Groups in several smaller cities, especially with council-manager forms of government, have sought to imitate the Cincinnati type of local party with varying degrees of success. Generally they fail to solve the problem of how to establish themselves as a party if no labels are on the ballot, or of maintaining a permanent organization, or both. In many cities, how-ever, reform or business groups put candidates into the field and help finance their campaigns. These groups often have the backing of the local press. They should perhaps be classified as pressure groups rather than local parties, although the line between the two is not easy to draw in this case.

Local Parties: an Appraisal. Although local parties seem to have some advantages, especially in large cities, they suffer from serious handicaps that make the Charter party or even the Fusion party rare successes in America. It is often argued that such parties would quickly become mere adjuncts of national parties—the same old parties under different names. While this does not necessarily follow and it would be quite possible to maintain these parties as separate entities, some very real problems do confront local parties.

In the first place, local parties require constant attention and interest from a large part of the public. This is difficult to secure, and the normal result is that after "the rascals" are thrown out, or a few elections later, the party begins to disintegrate. This has happened many times in the United States. A permanent organization with permanent electioneering on the Cincinnati model is imperative for longevity of local parties. Secondly, local parties are difficult to organize in any case. Political-party structures are complex and require much coordinated effort. It is virtually impossible to organize a successful local party except under unusual circumstances (a deep economic depression, a particularly corrupt administration), and even then it is not easy. Thirdly, attempts to organize local parties, as such, are likely to be resisted by the informal ruling group of businessmen who put up candidates, finance them, and —in lieu of having an organized party structure—control the media of communication. Lastly, local parties have a great deal of difficulty in securing enough funds for survival. People will not make contributions unless they believe in the cause to begin with and further believe that a particular organization is capable of advancing that cause. The Cincinnati Charter party has been successful because it has been able both to develop an effective money-raising organization and to get the confidence and support of businessmen who have funds that can be tapped. The American Labor and later the Liberal party could survive in New York because they had a firm financial base in labor-union support. A poorly financed party has no chance of survival.

Methods of Nomination. Before there can be an election, the individuals who are going to make the race must first be nominated. There are numerous ways of placing candidates in nomination. Although the method has proved to be far from satisfactory, the overwhelming majority of nominations on the local (or any other) level made in the United States today are by way of either the partisan or the nonpartisan direct *primary* election. There are, or have been, however, numerous other techniques, including caucus or convention nomination, sponsorship, and petition.

Early Nomination Devices. The *caucus,* the oldest form of nomination in the United States, consisted originally of an informal meeting to choose candidates deserving of support for the various public offices becoming vacant. In America's early days the caucus members could print a ballot and distribute it themselves.

With the development of cities, the caucus system degenerated. A more formal method and one that would make known the desires of the common voter, rather than those of the organized few, was needed. The *convention* method called for nominations at a formal gathering whose membership was chosen by caucus at the precinct level. With the organization of nineteenth-century political machines, both the caucus and the convention tended to be dominated by a few people, with the general public having little real choice in the nomination—and in most cities nomination by the dominant party was tantamount to election.

Reforms in Nomination. Beginning at the turn of the century, the reform movement produced a change in nomination procedure. The *direct primary election* was substituted for the caucus and convention. It is now almost universal in the United States, although a few states do not use it for important state offices and there are cities in such populous states as California, Texas, New Jersey, and Massachusetts that do not use it.[24]

Strictly speaking, a primary election is nothing more than a *nonassembled* caucus. That is to say, in an earlier day every eligible voter was entitled to take part in the selection of candidates. Next, part of this job had to be turned over to what were theoretically his representatives acting at a *convention.* When the convention proved to be unrepresentative and boss-ridden, the primary election was devised to return nominations "to the people." The plan in large measure transfers control of the nomination machinery from the party to the state, all parties choosing their candidates on the same day under the supervision of public election officials, with ballots standardized and printed at public expense (except in a few Southern states) and with a secret ballot (in contrast with most caucus and convention systems).

The primary election has never been understood by the vast majority of American voters. They are annoyed by the fantastically long "bedsheet" ballot with which they are confronted; they bitterly resent the fact that they must usually reveal their party preference in order to vote, and even when the open primary is used, they become incensed when they discover that splitting the ticket is not permitted.

Types of Primaries. Primary elections are of two types, nonpartisan and partisan. The latter is subdivided into two classes, open and closed. In the *nonpartisan* primary, we have what is actually an elimination contest. Names appear on the ballot without party designation. The first election, popularly and sometimes legally called a primary, serves to eliminate all candidates except twice the number to be elected. Hence if seven file for the office of mayor, only two will survive the primary—the two with the highest number of votes. If seven councilmen are to be elected, the fourteen highest at the primary are nominated. In some cases, such as in many California cities and in elections for the Chicago council, if any candidate receives a majority of the vote cast in the primary he is declared elected, and the taxpayer is saved the cost of placing him on the final ballot.

[24] See Spencer D. Albright, *The American Ballot* (1942); Charles E. Merriam and Louise Overacker, *Primary Elections* (1928); or the textbooks on elections. Strong criticism of the primary method may be found in Penniman, *op. cit.*

In nonpartisan as well as partisan primaries, one gets on the ballot in the first place by one of three ways: by a simple formal declaration, by signature petition (in either of these two a small filing fee to defray part of the expense of putting the name on the ballot may be charged), or by filing a forfeitable deposit.

The *partisan* primary may be open or closed. An open primary is open to any eligible voter regardless of which party may be his own, or whether he is a party member or a confirmed independent. He need not demonstrate or declare anything other than that he is a qualified voter in order to receive a ballot. A closed primary, on the other hand, is closed to everyone except members of the political party concerned.

Other Nomination Devices. Some California and Wisconsin cities make use of nomination by *petition* directly onto the final ballot. This method saves the expense of a primary election, and usually has satisfactory results in small cities. But when the plan was used in Boston, the mayor was often a plurality rather than a majority choice, for there were nearly always more than two major candidates.[25] Boss James Michael Curley, as the best-known mayoralty candidate, sometimes found this plan of considerable help to him.

The *Model City Charter* of the National Municipal League recommends a plan, especially in connection with proportional representation, called the *sponsor system.* It has been used in some California cities for several years. It is similar to the British system of nomination, for it requires a petition signed by ten persons who are listed as "sponsors" of the candidate and the filing of a sum of money, to be returned under certain conditions.[26]

EXPERIMENTS IN DIRECT DEMOCRACY

The Initiative and Referendum.[27] With the deterioration in the quality of city councilmen during the last half of the nineteenth century came also a public lack of faith in representative democracy. In order to compensate for this situation, what was then considered a radical solution was proposed. These reformers renovated and reorganized some old American institutions, introduced some new ones, and hopefully pre-

[25] A *plurality* is more votes than any other candidate. A *majority* is at least one vote more than one-half of the number cast.

[26] *Model City Charter,* 5th ed., art. 9.

[27] Some useful references are: W. B. Munro (ed.), *The Initiative, Referendum and Recall* (1913); J. V. Zeitlin, *Initiative and Referendum: A Bibliography* (1940). Studies of the initiative and referendum in individual states have been made by W. W. Crouch in California (1943 and 1950); the Colorado Legislative Reference Office in that state (1940); L. L. Pelletier in Maine (1952); J. K. Pollock in Michigan (1940); and J. G. LaPalombara in Oregon (1950).

sented us with techniques for direct democracy as a check upon excesses and incompetence. The *initiative* permits a legally defined number of voters to propose changes in the city charter or ordinances which are then accepted or rejected by the voters at the polls. This device permits legislation to be effected with no recourse at all to the legislative body. The *referendum* permits the voters to accept or reject at the polls council-proposed changes in the city charter or ordinances. The referendum differs from the initiative in that it *follows* favorable action by the legislative body, whereas the initiative takes place independently of the legislative body.

The Procedure. An initiated proposal is normally drafted by the attorneys for the particular interest group seeking the legislation. Petitions to put the proposal on the ballot are then circulated, either by volunteers or by persons hired for the purpose, often at the price of a certain amount per signature. The total signatures required may be a specific number or a certain percentage of voters (registered, or voting for a certain office at the last general election, or some other formula). Where such a percentage is used, it is generally from 5 to 10 per cent but may be higher. In most instances the proposal is adopted if a majority of those voting on the proposal vote in its favor, although in some cases a majority of those voting *in the election* is required (this means that if a voter ignores the proposal he is in effect voting "no"), or some special formula may be used. It is often provided that an initiated ordinance may not be amended or repealed by the city council, at least within a certain prescribed time limit.

The initiative and referendum (I. and R.), particularly the latter, date from early times in America and elsewhere. Antecedents are to be found in the direct democracy of ancient Greece, the ancient tribal governments of Germany, the right to petition the king in medieval England, the town meeting of colonial New England, and the direct democracy of Switzerland.[28] As early as 1825, the Maryland legislature provided for a referendum on the question of establishing a public-school system. It later became very common to hold referendums on liquor questions, charter amendments, public utility franchises, bond issues, and other matters. California, Iowa, and Nebraska in the late nineteenth century authorized municipal use of the initiative and referendum. The San Francisco home rule charter of 1898 was the first such document to provide for them. From then the movement spread rapidly, and it is today widely authorized for municipal governments.

Around the turn of the century, when many cities adopted the initiative and referendum, proponents made greatly exaggerated claims of

[28] See Munro, *op. cit.*, chap. 1.

their merits. Opponents were equally vociferous, viewing with alarm the potentiality for hamstringing of the governmental process by their use. The results have not borne out the claims of either side.

Arguments Concerning I. and R. Proponents of direct democracy argued that corrupt and low-quality city councils made it necessary for people to have a check upon the government. Reformers also took note of the trend toward a concentration of authority in government and a breakdown of the traditional check-and-balance system. The initiative and referendum could serve to replace some of these disappearing checks. It was argued that the use of these devices strengthened popular control over city government by giving the people "a gun behind the door" which could serve as a means of requiring greater alertness, honesty, and responsiveness on the part of council members.

It was believed that I. and R. would protect the people from political tricks and steals from the public treasury. Some argued that it would encourage voters to become better informed on issues, since they would have to vote on so many of them directly and since they could now feel that they had a real chance to get things done in local affairs.

Opponents of the system argued that it confused legislative responsibility, lengthened an already overly long ballot, created a bad psychological effect upon the city council, expected more than was reasonable from an uninformed and uninterested electorate, would promote radicalism and a disrespect for property rights, was opposed to the best principles of Americanism (since the Constitution is based upon *representative,* and not direct, democracy), and would allow well-organized pressure groups representing a minority of the population to exercise an inordinate advantage.[29]

I. and R.: an Appraisal. The debate over the use of I. and R. has subsided in recent years, but there is little doubt that the two devices are still often misused. Perhaps it is necessary here to make only two points without discussing the merits of the arguments briefly outlined above.

First, the I. and R. seem to carry the implicit assumption that the individual voter is always informed and rational in his choices. Actually, of course, this assumption is false. Furthermore, democracy as we know it does not require such an assumption. In an ordinary election, the voter is merely asked whether or not he is relatively satisfied with things as they are. According to the state of his satisfactions, he votes for those in power or he casts a protest vote. His reasons for his vote are his own, and they need not be rational, logical, or informed. He is not asked to rule, but merely to choose those who are to rule. But the I. and R. ask more than this of the voter. They ask him to help rule himself **and to**

[29] Extensive arguments on the pros and cons are presented in Munro, *op. cit.,* chaps. 1–11.

make policy decisions on questions that are often complex, technical, and minutely detailed.

It is not uncommon, for example, for the voter to be asked a question such as the following:[30]

GENERAL RETIREMENT SYSTEM AMENDMENT

Do you favor an amendment to Title IX, Chapter VI, General Retirement System, of the Charter of the City of Detroit, changing membership service pension from $\frac{1}{120}$ of average final compensation to $\frac{1}{100}$ average final compensation times years of membership service; to increase maximum city pension from $1,800 per annum to $2,400 per annum; to provide for optional benefit to widow or dependent husband for member who continues in service after becoming eligible to retire and to provide for increase of employees' annuity contributions from 5% on $3,600 to 5% on $7,200 or under per annum?

YES ☐

NO ☐

Where the law permits or requires questions that are properly those of the council to be submitted to the general public for direct action, the results are sometimes humorous—or would be if government were not such a serious business. In the November, 1952, election, the voters of Waldwick, New Jersey (1950 population: 3,963), on the edge of the New York metropolitan area, voted to establish a full-time police force, but on another question refused to appropriate the additional $10,000 a year to finance the project, and on a third question voted to retain the existing part-time system. And this all at the same election!

Second, opponents of the I. and R. are wont to overlook the fact that the American political structure is pluralistic and not neatly integrated, and that the American political process is typically based upon the interaction of pressure groups. American cities, for the most part, do not have responsible political-party structures, and few cities have a two-party system of any kind regularly competing for voter support. Furthermore, it is unlikely that this pattern will be changed much in the foreseeable future. Since this system may result in city councils that are neither responsible nor representative of a cross section of the population, the I. and R. may well be used as a check, a "gun behind the door."[31]

On the basis of these two points, then, perhaps the following conclusions could be drawn:

[30] Proposed Amendment E to the Detroit City Charter, election of November 6, 1951. Incidentally, the proposal passed, 119,717 to 110,234, after city employees urged a favorable vote. Probably most voters did not know that they were raising city expenses by one-half million dollars a year.

[31] In this connection, see J. G. LaPalombara and C. B. Hagan, "Direct Legislation: An Appraisal and a Suggestion," *American Political Science Review*, vol. 45 (June, 1951), pp. 400–421.

1. The I. and R. should be used sparingly, and then only as a check against irresponsible government.

2. The I. and R. should deal with questions of a fundamental nature and not with trivia or technical matters. The referendum should be used, of course, for home-rule amendments and possibly for certain types of bond issues. It is of doubtful use, however, in connection with tax levies or other questions where the voter will be sorely tempted to vote his short-run, rather than long-run, interests.[32]

The Recall. The third member of the triumvirate that was to produce "popular control" of city government was the *recall*. This is a device whereby any elective officer may be removed from office by a popular vote prior to the expiration of his term. Although it is often popularly mentioned in connection with the initiative and referendum, the recall may exist independently of them. It was brought into extensive use by the same people and for largely the same reasons. It was argued that a faithless or incompetent public servant should not be inflicted upon the people for the duration of his term—that he should be removed as soon as his shortcomings are discovered. Again, Jacksonians who were none too happy over the increasing popularity of the four-year term as against the traditional two years found it easier to accept the longer term if "continuous responsibility" were maintained through the availability of the recall. The mechanism was probably first provided for in the Los Angeles home rule charter of 1903; unlike its two sisters, it has no direct precedents in American political practices.

The Procedure. In order to recall an official, a petition must be circulated. Since a large number of signatures are usually required—such as 15 to 25 or even as high as 51 per cent of the vote cast for the office of mayor in the last election—an organized group with a good deal of motivation and a sizable treasury is usually required. After sufficient signatures are procured and certified by the city clerk or other appropriate election official, an election becomes obligatory.[33]

Arguments pro and con. The principal arguments for the recall are that it provides for continuous responsibility (especially important with the four-year term) so that the public need not wait in exasperation and frustration until the term comes to an end. It is similarly argued that with a sword constantly hanging over the head of the public official he will feel a need to remain alert at all times.

[32] For additional material, see E. F. Dow, "Portland Limits Initiative," *National Municipal Review,* vol. 40 (July, 1951), pp. 347–350; A. A. Schwartz, "Initiative Held in Reserve," *ibid.,* vol. 41 (March, 1952), pp. 142–145. The National Municipal League recommends limited use of the I. and R. See editorial, *ibid.,* vol. 40 (July, 1951), pp. 345–346.

[33] There are several variants of the recall ballot. An adequate discussion of details not covered in this text may be found in almost any textbook on state and local government.

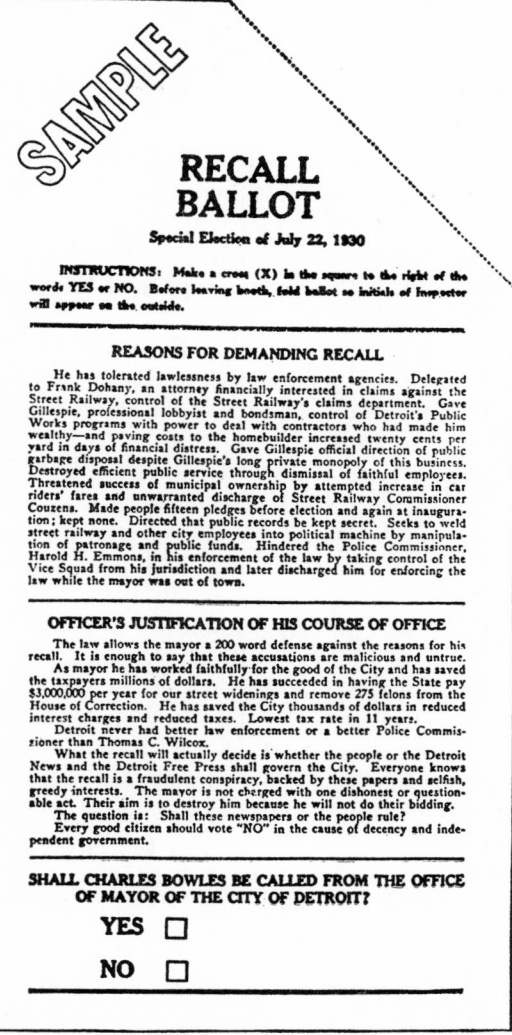

RECALL BALLOT

Special Election of July 22, 1930

INSTRUCTIONS: Make a cross (X) in the square to the right of the words YES or NO. Before leaving booth, fold ballot so initials of Inspector will appear on the outside.

REASONS FOR DEMANDING RECALL

He has tolerated lawlessness by law enforcement agencies. Delegated to Frank Dohany, an attorney financially interested in claims against the Street Railway, control of the Street Railway's claims department. Gave Gillespie, professional lobbyist and bondsman, control of Detroit's Public Works programs with power to deal with contractors who had made him wealthy—and paving costs to the homebuilder increased twenty cents per yard in days of financial distress. Gave Gillespie official direction of public garbage disposal despite Gillespie's long private monopoly of this business. Destroyed efficient public service through dismissal of faithful employees. Threatened success of municipal ownership by attempted increase in car riders' fares and unwarranted discharge of Street Railway Commissioner Couzens. Made people fifteen pledges before election and again at inauguration; kept none. Directed that public records be kept secret. Seeks to weld street railway and other city employees into political machine by manipulation of patronage and public funds. Hindered the Police Commissioner, Harold H. Emmons, in his enforcement of the law by taking control of the Vice Squad from his jurisdiction and later discharged him for enforcing the law while the mayor was out of town.

OFFICER'S JUSTIFICATION OF HIS COURSE OF OFFICE

The law allows the mayor a 200 word defense against the reasons for his recall. It is enough to say that these accusations are malicious and untrue.

As mayor he has worked faithfully for the good of the City and has saved the taxpayers millions of dollars. He has succeeded in having the State pay $3,000,000 per year for our street widenings and remove 275 felons from the House of Correction. He has saved the City thousands of dollars in reduced interest charges and reduced taxes. Lowest tax rate in 11 years.

Detroit never had better law enforcement or a better Police Commissioner than Thomas C. Wilcox.

What the recall will actually decide is whether the people or the Detroit News and the Detroit Free Press shall govern the City. Everyone knows that the recall is a fraudulent conspiracy, backed by these papers and selfish, greedy interests. The mayor is not charged with one dishonest or questionable act. Their aim is to destroy him because he will not do their bidding.

The question is: Shall these newspapers or the people rule?

Every good citizen should vote "NO" in the cause of decency and independent government.

SHALL CHARLES BOWLES BE CALLED FROM THE OFFICE OF MAYOR OF THE CITY OF DETROIT?

YES ☐

NO ☐

If you want Bowles PUT OUT of office, make a cross (X) in the square after the YES.
If you want Bowles to REMAIN IN office, make a cross (X) in the square after the NO.

Fig. 7. SOURCE: Reproduced in Carl O. Smith, *A Book of Ballots* (1938).

Opponents of the recall point to its costliness: a *special* election is imperative for its use, since it would be grossly unfair to conduct such an election in connection with other questions (although this is sometimes done). A second objection to the recall is that it is not an attempt to *prove charges* against an officeholder, but is merely an attempt to persuade the electorate, by whatever means, to remove the incumbent. A third objection is that the recall is unnecessary. In all states, improper conduct by public officials is grounds for removal by other judicial, councilmanic, or sometimes gubernatorial action.[34]

A final objection to the recall centers in the assertion that it serves as a tool for well-organized pressure groups and for political recrimination. Similarly, it is said that the threat of the recall is a constant and perfectly legal means for intimidation of public officials who must therefore slavishly follow public whims and sentimentality. In many instances, a strong leader with a positive program will find that some interest group will stand in his path threatening him with a recall action if he seeks to carry out his plans—even if those plans represent the planks of the platform upon which he was elected.

It may be quite safely concluded that the recall is unnecessary baggage that need not be carried in any modern city charter. The trend today is away from it, and the National Municipal League and most political scientists no longer advocate it.

The Faceless Man: a Case Study in Irresponsibility.[35] Roger Dearborn Lapham was a businessman. He had been born in New York and educated at Harvard, and had then proceeded through a career in the shipping industry, ultimately becoming chairman of the board of the American-Hawaiian Steamship Company. In 1943, as he was approaching retirement age, he was prevailed upon to run for the office of mayor of San Francisco to succeed Angelo Rossi, the florist who had held that position for twelve years. Lapham had not run for political office before, but he was a bluff extrovert and enjoyed campaigning. As a long-time business administrator, he was in the habit of giving orders and expecting them to be carried out, and this lifetime habit he carried not only into the campaign but also into the mayor's office after his promises to take a "nonpolitical approach" and to run the city on a "businesslike" basis proved successful.

Lapham managed to get into difficulties almost immediately. He appointed two department heads from minority groups that had never before been represented in these positions. He dropped one of Rossi's park commissioners, who had served ten years in the office. He supported higher taxes for badly needed postwar developments of the sewerage system, city purchase of the public transit system, a fare increase to repair its dilapidated and overworked equipment, and in general launched into an ambitious plan for making up the time lost from public improvements because of World War II.

It took the opponents of an assertive municipal policy and of higher

---

[34] See chap. 9.
[35] The material for this section is drawn from John M. Selig, "San Francisco Upholds Mayor," *National Municipal Review,* vol. 35 (October, 1946), pp. 465–470; and *Time,* July 15, 1946.

taxes, together with disgruntled politicians, three years to make use of a weapon that seemed to be begging for them to come after it. The recall petition was the work of a group led by the dismissed park commissioner, who was also the publisher of a daily throwaway and a municipal employees' magazine.

The recall petition and pamphlet (which in San Francisco is published at public expense, each side being allowed 300 words) asserted, among other things, that Lapham had:

1. Failed to reappoint a "good public servant"—the park commissioner
2. Raised trolley fares three cents in an "arrogant" manner (public hearings had been held)
3. Raised taxes
4. Refused to declare an emergency so that trolley operators could get wages boosted by edict
5. Refused to endorse a "Dimes for Manila" campaign—or for that matter any "days," "weeks," or "months" on the ground that they were inane
6. Failed to obtain the permanent United Nations headquarters for San Francisco
7. Acted like a dictator

Clearly none of the charges suggested that Lapham had acted in an illegal or immoral manner (unless the last name caller is taken seriously). Clearly, too, some people did not like his appointments and his policies—something that is true of any mayor, but especially true of one who tries to get things done.

It would not be part of Lapham's character not to fight back. Besides, under the San Francisco charter, an official against whom an unsuccessful recall attempt is made is entitled to reimbursement for campaign expenses within prescribed limits. He argued that no one had charged him with anything more serious than a difference in opinion; that a successful recall would disgrace the city and discourage office seeking; and—not giving the opposition a monopoly on the use of the cliché—that the recall was contrary to the principles of American democracy. He signed his own recall petition and urged that the election be gotten over with.

Lapham supporters bought space on signboards and showed pictures of a ghostlike creature and the admonition: "Don't surrender your city to the faceless man. Vote NO on recall." This was a reference to the fact that the board of supervisors[36] would choose his successor. Board members had made no statements, and so no one could know for certain who the next mayor would be.

The well-known "women's" novelist, Kathleen Norris, sent a postcard

---

[36] The city and county of San Francisco are consolidated, and the board of supervisors also acts as the city council.

to every registered voter in the city urging a "no" vote, and somehow *Time* magazine was prevailed upon to devote its cover story of the issue before the election to a defense of Lapham.

On July 16, 1946, the voters of San Francisco—actually only a modest turnout of them—decided that they had been right the first time. Roger D. Lapham was retained by a vote of 109,526 to 73,946.

The election had cost the taxpayers a great deal of money, and Lapham had been forced to save from ruin a reputation that he had spent a lifetime in establishing. And all this over an issue that would not have lasted five minutes before a court or an impeachment proceeding.

PROPORTIONAL AND PREFERENTIAL VOTING SYSTEMS

The Hare System of Proportional Representation.[37] One of the more promising but least prospering of the schemes advocated by members of the reform movement was the Hare system of proportional representation by single transferable vote.[38] P.R. reflected the untiring efforts of reformers to reduce the power of political machines and constituted a definite improvement over other attempts to remove objections to both the old ward system and the newer at-large system of councilmanic elections.[39] The ward system unduly encouraged parochialism in politics, while election at large could give 100 per cent control of the council to whatever group might receive a plurality in the voting.

[37] The outstanding proponent of what appears to be a losing cause is George H. Hallet, Jr. See his work, *Proportional Representation: The Key to Democracy* (2d ed., 1940). An outstanding councilman discusses the most successful application of the Hare system in Charles P. Taft, *City Management, The Cincinnati Experiment* (1933). The quarterly *P.R. Review* covered developments from 1914 until 1932. Since that time, they have been reported in a special section of each issue of the *National Municipal Review*. This is edited by Mr. Hallet and William R. Woodward.

Articles supporting P.R. in New York include: Belle Zeller and Hugh A. Bone, "The Repeal of P.R. in New York City—Ten Years in Retrospect," *American Political Science Review*, vol. 42 (December, 1948), pp. 1127–1148; G. M. McCaffrey, "Proportional Representation in New York City," *ibid.*, vol. 33 (September, 1939), pp. 841–852; Hugh A. Bone, "Political Parties in New York City," *ibid.*, vol. 40 (June, 1946), pp. 272–282.

Detailed criticism of P.R. will be found in three works by F. A. Hermans, *Democracy or Anarchy? A Study of Proportional Representation* (1941); *Democracy and Good Government* (1943); and *Europe between Democracy and Anarchy* (1951).

[38] In addition to the Hare system, the *list system* of P.R. is extensively used in European nations, where political parties play a more important role than they do in the United States. It is used in Belgium, the Netherlands, Scandinavia, and Switzerland in one version or another. For a balanced view of the use of P.R. on the national level and for further bibliography, see G. Lowell Field, *Governments in Modern Society* (1951), pp. 132–138.

There are also other versions of the single transferable vote system than the Hare plan, which itself has dozens of variations.

[39] On the at-large versus ward system of election controversy, see chap. 10.

Table 3. Uses of Proportional Representation in the United States

Cities adopting P.R.	Adopted	Repealed	Reasons for repeal
Ashtabula, Ohio.........	1915	1929	Voted out on referendum to rid city of uncooperative minority on council
Boulder, Colo..........	1917	1947	On fourth referendum, repealed—lack of interest
Cleveland, Ohio........	1921	1931	Not provided for in new charter adopted in 1931
Coos Bay, Ore.........	1945	1948	Eliminated collaterally in fight to oust city manager
Gloucester, Mass.......	1948	1951	Declared unconstitutional
Kalamazoo, Mich......	1918	1920	Declared unconstitutional
Long Beach, N.Y.......	1943	1947	Dissatisfaction with P.R. council; newspaper hostility
Medford, Mass.........	1947	1952	Lack of interest
New York, N.Y........	1936	1947	Presence of Communists on council; regular-party opposition
Norris, Tenn...........	1936	1947	Ceased corporate existence
Quincy, Mass..........	1947	1952	Opposed by mayor, chamber of commerce; lost 3 to 1
Revere, Mass..........	1947	1952	Apathy, no organized defense; lost 2 to 1
Sacramento, Calif......	1920	1922	Declared unconstitutional
Saugus, Mass..........	1947	1951	Lack of interest; 23.4% of registered voters turned out on repeal
Somerville, Mass.......	1949	1951	Declared unconstitutional
Toledo, Ohio...........	1934	1949	On fifth referendum, repealed; regular-party opposition; apathy
West Hartford, Conn...	1921	1923	Prohibited by state legislature; Republican party opposition
Wheeling, W.Va........	1935	1950	Lack of interest; poorly qualified councilmen blamed on P.R.
Cambridge, Mass......	1940		
Cincinnati, Ohio.......	1924		
Hamilton, Ohio........	1926		
Hopkins, Minn........	1948		
Lowell, Mass..........	1941		
Oak Ridge, Tenn......	1948		
Worcester, Mass.......	1947		

SOURCE: Chiefly *National Municipal Review*, various issues.

Some cities experimented with the St. Louis practice of nominating by wards and electing at large; many others elected part of the council at large and part of it by wards. Some (including New York, Boston, and the present Philadelphia charter) tried *limited* voting, by which each elector was required to vote for less than the total number of councilmen to be elected. This gave the minority representation, as a rule, but not necessarily in any systematic proportion.

How It Works. The Hare system, named for an Englishman, Thomas Hare, is designed to give representation upon a multimembered body in direct proportion to the numerical strength of the various interest groups in the community.[40] In contrast to current political theory, which holds that some group or party should have a majority in each legislative body and be responsible for the program it enacts, P.R. seeks to give every significant group in the voting population voice on the body in proportion to its numerical strength and works on the principle that a multiplicity of views is preferable to a single view and that a spokesman for each voter is more important than collective responsibility by a majority party or group. The system is used extensively in Eire, to a lesser extent in Australia, and to a small extent in Canada, New Zealand, and the United States.

Only a brief explanation of the Hare system need be given here. Its whole object is to give each voter but one vote for the council (or such multimembered bodies as school, park, and library boards, if elective), but to make every effort to see that the vote is eventually used to help someone get into office—a someone who then acts as a representative of that particular voter.

The voter chooses from among the candidates in the order in which he prefers them for office. The traditional "X" is not used; rather, the individual places a "1" beside his first choice, a "2" beside his second, and so on for as many choices as he may have (or, in some jurisdictions, up to the maximum of the number of seats to be filled). After the voting has been completed, the ballots are taken to some central counting house where the total vote for the election is determined and a quota established. The quota is simply the total needed for election, one which is mathematically established so as to ensure that no more persons can meet the quota than there are seats to be filled (see Figure 8).

Choices are initially distributed according to first choice votes, and all who meet the quota are, of course, elected. As the counting proceeds, some votes will be transferred to second, third, or even more remote choices, either because the choices of higher preference are already elected or because they appear to have no chance of securing election. The counting proceeds by eliminating the man with the fewest votes at the end of each tally and continues until enough candidates have reached

---

[40] Thomas Hare began to write on P.R. in 1857. John Stuart Mill gave the plan prestige by endorsing it in *Considerations on Representative Government* (1861). Its support in England came primarily from conservatives seeking to reduce the electoral strength of the working classes following their enfranchisement by the Reform Acts of 1832, 1867, and 1884.

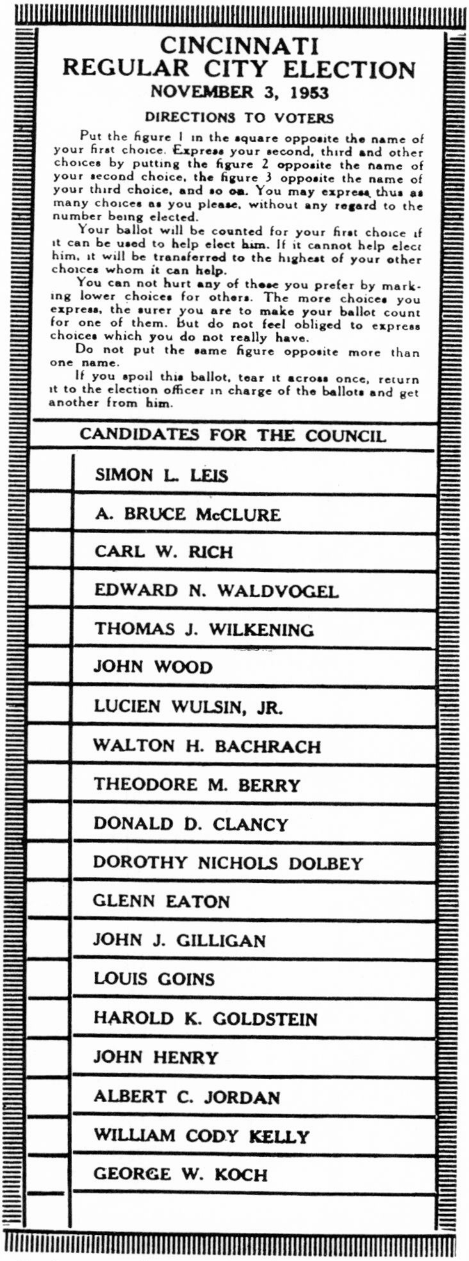

CINCINNATI
REGULAR CITY ELECTION
NOVEMBER 3, 1953

DIRECTIONS TO VOTERS

Put the figure 1 in the square opposite the name of your first choice. Express your second, third and other choices by putting the figure 2 opposite the name of your second choice, the figure 3 opposite the name of your third choice, and so on. You may express thus as many choices as you please, without any regard to the number being elected.

Your ballot will be counted for your first choice if it can be used to help elect him. If it cannot help elect him, it will be transferred to the highest of your other choices whom it can help.

You can not hurt any of these you prefer by marking lower choices for others. The more choices you express, the surer you are to make your ballot count for one of them. But do not feel obliged to express choices which you do not really have.

Do not put the same figure opposite more than one name.

If you spoil this ballot, tear it across once, return it to the election officer in charge of the ballots and get another from him.

CANDIDATES FOR THE COUNCIL

SIMON L. LEIS	
A. BRUCE McCLURE	
CARL W. RICH	
EDWARD N. WALDVOGEL	
THOMAS J. WILKENING	
JOHN WOOD	
LUCIEN WULSIN, JR.	
WALTON H. BACHRACH	
THEODORE M. BERRY	
DONALD D. CLANCY	
DOROTHY NICHOLS DOLBEY	
GLENN EATON	
JOHN J. GILLIGAN	
LOUIS GOINS	
HAROLD K. GOLDSTEIN	
JOHN HENRY	
ALBERT C. JORDAN	
WILLIAM CODY KELLY	
GEORGE W. KOCH	

Fig. 8. An actual proportional-representation ballot.

the quota or until the candidates remaining equal the number of seats to be filled.

Use of P.R. In the United States P.R. has had little use, and, while its prospects looked fairly bright in the thirties, there appears to be very little likelihood of a movement in its direction in the foreseeable future. Ashtabula, Ohio, in 1915, was the first United States city to make use of the British import, followed two years later by Boulder, Colorado. Both cities have since abandoned the plan. While P.R. has been used in such large cities as New York, Cleveland, Toledo, Sacramento, and Cincinnati, only the last of these still uses it today (see Table 3 for a complete list). In some cities P.R. was cut down by adverse court or legislative rulings, in others by public apathy, and in New York and two suburbs by "fear of communism." Without doubt the adoption of P.R. in the city of New York in 1936 gave proponents great hope. Two of its suburbs followed, and after World War II several cities adopted it, especially in Massachusetts under optional charter Plan "E" (council-manager plus P.R. charters). But in 1947 Tammany Hall, which did not like its reduced representation on a P.R. council, and various other groups, which did not like the presence of Communists and their supporters on the council, teamed up to jettison the plan. The fact that P.R. allows representation for radical minorities makes it especially unpopular today. Since 1947, P.R. has been losing ground almost everywhere. In Massachusetts, which once had nine communities under the system, a hostile legislature has been pruning away at Plan "E" and has refused to allow any further adoptions in that state. By 1954, only seven communities used the Hare system in electing the council.

There is little likelihood that P.R. could or will play an important part in any long-range solution to the severe problems confronting local self-government. P.R. struggled along for decades against great odds, but with some cause for hope. The postwar abandonments in Boulder (after thirty years), New York, Toledo, and Yonkers, among others, appear to have delivered an already frail institution the *coup de grâce.*

Because of the small use made of P.R. in the United States today and because there appears to be no future for it in this country, a discussion of its pros and cons seems unnecessary.[41] P.R. results in nearly perfect representation of the various segments of society, but it also produces a legislative body which is likely to be leaderless and ineffectual and in which no single group is likely to be able to dominate in putting forth a systematic program. Most political scientists, and probably most of the general public, feel that it is more important to elect a body that can govern than it is to elect one that is precisely representative.

Taking the long view, there appears to be a better solution to the

[41] They are discussed in the major works on P.R. already cited.

Table 4. P.R. Elections for New York City Council†

Party or group	1937			1945		
	No. seats	% seats	% votes	No. seats	% seats	% votes
Democratic.....................	13	50.0	47.0	14	60.0	59.0
Republican.....................	3	11.5	8.5	3	13.0	15.0
Insurgent Democratic.............	2	8.0	7.0			
American Labor.................	5	19.0	21.0	2	9.0	10.0
Fusion........................	3	11.5	10.5			
Liberal........................	..	.....	.....	2	9.0	7.0
Communist.....................	..	.....	2.5	2	9.0	9.0
Other.........................	..	.....	3.5			
Total......................	26	100.0	100.0	23	100.0	100.0

† Note that P.R. affords representation that is almost perfectly in proportion to the distribution of the vote.

SOURCE: Adapted from Belle Zeller and Hugh A. Bone, "The Repeal of P.R. in New York City—Ten Years in Retrospect," *American Political Science Review*, vol. 42 (December, 1948), p. 1132. By permission.

political needs of our cities: a responsible party system (national or local organizations or a combination) with a program of action, with one group or another assuming leadership, and with a collective responsibility for results. Unfortunately for the future health of local self-government, this situation appears to be almost as remote as is the general use of P.R.

Preferential Voting Systems.[42] While reformers were concerned, on the one hand, with ensuring extensive representation for minority groups through P.R., they also desired, on the other hand, to devise a system to prevent minorities from manipulating elections by promoting additional candidates designed to split the vote of the person who would otherwise be expected to win. Several mechanisms have been devised that seek to prevent a minority from gaining control by splitting the majority. In effect, these devices reassemble the atomized majority vote. All of them attempt to do so by allowing the voter to make more than one choice for each individual office. If his first choice will not help elect

[42] No contemporary studies have been made of preferential voting in the United States. For material from the hopeful days of the system, see R. G. Mott, "Preferential Voting and How It Works," *National Municipal Review*, vol. 1 (July, 1912), pp. 386–400; L. J. Johnson, "Preferential Voting," *ibid.*, vol. 3 (January, 1914), pp. 83–92; *Preferential Voting*, Bulletins for the Massachusetts Constitutional Convention, no. 27 (1917).

The curious student can find more information than is given in this text in E. B. Schulz, *American City Government*, pp. 215–221, which discusses each of the four systems; also O. Douglas Weeks, "History and Present Status of Preferential Voting," *Southwestern Social Science Quarterly*, vol. 18 (June, 1937), pp. 64–67.

a candidate, the mechanism is designed to allow his second or later choice to aid in selecting the winner.

The earliest plan, the Bucklin system, was first used in Grand Junction, Colorado, in 1909 and eventually gained some fifty-five adoptions. All of these cities have since abandoned the plan. Three other preferential voting systems have had a total of only two adoptions among them. These systems have never been popular in the United States, little use has been made of them, and they are almost forgotten today, except for state elections in Maryland.

CHAPTER 5

THE POLITICAL PROCESS AND THE CITY: I

Politics is not an evil thing. It is the catalysis that changes citizens into public officials and individual wishes into public policy. It is essential to democracy. On the local scene it operates largely in the same manner as it does for state and national governments. Only the emphasis and the relative balances of forces are changed.

THE NATURE OF THE POLITICAL PROCESS

Politics as Demand and Supply. In order to have an understanding of the nature of the political process, it is necessary to be able to picture it, not as the principal purpose of a certain type of human activity, but rather as a *by-product*. Human life in Western culture is a struggle for power, prestige, and security. Some people, in their search, turn to politics to secure this. They become the relatively small group of politically active people. The general public, politically passive though it may be, becomes a collection of clientele groups, seeking services from government in order to help themselves, in turn, achieve these same ends. Or, alternatively, they seek to *prevent* government from launching certain types of services if they feel that their goals can be reached by some alternative type of activity.

The politician, then, is a person who seeks to determine what a considerable portion of the public is asking of government and to make this available to them if possible. Since the individual normally has a certain amount of actual choice in selecting public offices and is free to join various groups that exert pressure upon government, government is responsible to the people—the essential characteristic of a democracy.

In order to achieve his desired objectives in public policy, the individual may choose to work through a political party. If the party stands for a definite set of principles, this approach is worthwhile and is the common method used in European democracies. In the United States, however, political parties are loose coalitions, each covering a great variety of political viewpoints. This is true very often even at the local level. The individual belongs to a political party for a variety of reasons

99

connected largely with economic status, geographic location, and family tradition. He can, however, seldom go to the polls and vote for a set of policies.

He may choose to become active in a political party, of course, and seek to influence its policies. But by the simple act of voting for the slate of a particular party, he will not be able to assure himself that he has selected a group of public officials who are philosophically in accord with himself. If he wishes to influence public policy, therefore, he will usually find it more expedient and fruitful to join forces with like-minded persons in a pressure group. In fact, the individual normally belongs to a number of such groups, not all of which have like views toward the same questions of policy. It is this overlapping of membership in groups which helps to mitigate their conflicts and to enable a workable system to develop.

What Is a Pressure Group? A pressure group differs from a political party chiefly in that it does not seek to capture offices for its members, but rather attempts to influence public policy. It also differs from most political parties in the United States in that it is made up of persons with basically the same interests and viewpoints—it is normally much more philosophically cohesive than is a political party in this country. Much has been said of the evil influences and dangers of pressure groups in politics. It has even been suggested by some critics that they be legally abolished or stringently controlled. Most such suggestions are, unfortunately, naïve. If we had a system of two or more political parties, each standing upon a definite platform of proposed action to which the parties could be held, pressure groups, or at least their lobbying[1] activities, could be greatly reduced. Such is not the case in the United States, however. Neither is it practical to say that a public official can determine the viewpoints of a cross section of the citizenry simply by noting the comments of those who contact him personally—not in any but the smallest villages, at any rate. And only the naïve or foolhardy would suggest that the officeholder should be elected with no promises to the public and then be entrusted to use his own free will and best judgment in doing as he sees best "for all the people" while in office. He must constantly be reminded of the nature of the shifting viewpoints of his constituents.

A pressure group is not only not an evil, it is an absolute necessity in a democracy lacking in disciplined political parties. It serves the purpose of marshaling individual opinions, organizing them, and presenting them in a skillful way to the proper governmental officials. While individual

---

[1] *Lobbying,* often performed by professionals, consists of seeking to influence legislative and administrative officials in a variety of ways so that their actions will be favorable to the group doing the lobbying. Lobbyists are also frequently in charge of the dissemination of propaganda to the general public. In this book *propaganda* is used to mean any communication designed to create a desired effect, impression, or opinion.

pressure groups no doubt do sometimes go beyond the bounds of the mores of society, do fail to give an accurate picture of the interests, desires, and aspirations of their individual members, and do act otherwise irresponsibly, most of them are kept in check quite automatically by the fact that for nearly every pressure group that comes before government, there is a counter pressure group. In this fashion, most of the potential dangers of the organized power of such a group are neutralized by the watchful eye of an opposing group. And each watcher is also watched. In fact, *public policy* might be defined as the end result of the interaction of the various interested pressure groups upon one another. It is the sum of the vector forces, where each vector represents the total force and direction of each group as determined by its age, respectability, size of membership, wealth, ability of leadership, skill at lobbying, inside connections, intensity of interests, and other pertinent factors.[2]

Characteristics of Groups. Several things should be kept in mind in classifying these interest or pressure groups. Remember that some of them are especially created for the single purpose of lobbying, while to others lobbying is only a side line. Some are temporary organizations created for a special problem, while others are permanent groups. Some, in large cities and in state and nation at any rate, are always present and lobbying at the seat of government, while others do not lobby except when a matter of particular importance to the group is under consideration.

Remember, too, that pressure groups are forever realigning their forces as expediency demands. It should not be naïvely assumed that politics is simply business versus labor, or that businessmen always work together, or that various groups operate in fairly permanent alignments. The *fluidity* of the pressure-group system is one of its greatest advantages. To take an example, we might find a hearing before a committee of the city council in which a Fair Employment Practices Commission (FEPC) ordinance is being considered. The local chamber of commerce and the teamsters' union local might well be lined up against the proposal, with a CIO local fighting for it. Here we have a labor union joining forces with the very symbol of the business community. Furthermore, we have one labor union fighting another, conceivably very bitterly. Yet when the committee hearing adjourns, it would not be unrealistic to picture the two labor lobbyists strolling down the hall side by side and turning into another committee room where the two erstwhile opponents might well join together, this time perhaps in a fight to retain rent control in the city.

[2] For further analysis of pressure groups, see any good introductory textbook on American government. Probably the best reference on the nature of the political process is David B. Truman, *The Governmental Process* (1951); see his bibliography. Also E. P. Herring, *The Politics of Democracy* (1940); E. E. Schattschneider, *The Struggle for Party Government* (1948); A. N. Holcombe, *The Middle Classes in American Politics* (1940).

Businessmen, likewise, are constantly finding themselves in such shifting positions of supporting and opposing one another. Ours is a dynamic system.

URBAN PRESSURE GROUPS

Pressure groups operate in basically the same pattern whether on the national, state, or local level. To be sure, there may be differences in the relative balance of power of the various groups. On the national and state level, for example, agricultural groups tend to be the most powerful of the lot, while in cities they ride in the back seat. Liquor lobbyists tend to be more powerful before state and local bodies than before the national government. Real estate groups and downtown merchants tend to be extraordinarily powerful in city politics.

Good-government Groups. The so-called good-government groups are among the few who restrict most of their organized efforts to the local scene. These groups have been mentioned above in connection with the reform movement.[3] Examples of them include the Citizens League of Pawtucket, the Richmond Civic Association, the Municipal League of Spokane, the Cleveland Citizens League, the Citizens Union of New York City, Citizens Action of Grand Rapids, the New Boston Committee, the Worcester Citizens Plan "E" Association, and the Hartford Citizens Charter Committee.[4] While many of these groups date back to the reform era, new ones continue to be formed, just as old ones become inactive. The Miami Citizens Action Committee was formed as a reaction against the conditions described in the report of the Kefauver committee; the Citizens Civic Association of Terre Haute was formed in 1951 "after an indignation meeting of citizens disgusted with gambling and vice";[5] the Citizens League of Greater Minneapolis was formed in early 1952; and the Colorado Springs Charter Association was organized in September of that year.

In general these groups lobby for the lowest possible taxes and the greatest possible value from each tax dollar. They often seek to promulgate the basic aims of the reform movement, such as the council-manager plan, a professional civil service, modern personnel and fiscal practices, municipal home rule, nonpartisan elections, and sometimes proportional representation. They are interested in "good government" as such, usually with no immediate personal benefits expected except in the belief that

[3] See above, pp. 59–61.
[4] The activities of good-government groups are reported in the "Citizen Action" section of each issue of the *National Municipal Review*. The *Review* does an excellent job of collecting and reporting municipal-government activities that are otherwise not readily available outside of each immediate locality.
[5] *National Municipal Review*, vol. 41 (September, 1952), p. 417.

more modern forms of government will save taxpayer dollars. Some members belong to these groups as something of a hobby, while others consider it to be a civic obligation. The groups often work in close cooperation with municipal research bureaus (such as the Citizens' Research Bureau of Milwaukee, the St. Louis Governmental Research Institute, and the Cleveland Bureau of Governmental Research).

Because these groups are interested in keeping taxes low through keeping city expenses down, they often find themselves arraigned against labor unions in struggles for higher pay for city employees, the extension of old services, the assumption of responsibility for new services by the city, or a change or increase in the city tax structure. While these groups were considered "progressive" and forward-looking forty years ago during the reform movement, quite a few of them are today aligned with the largest taxpayers on the side of conservatism. Others, however, continue to be primarily interested in studying municipal issues and advancing rational attitudes toward them.

These "leagues" and "unions" often follow the practice of making recommendations concerning initiative and referendum propositions at each election and of endorsing a slate of candidates on a nonpartisan or bipartisan basis. These recommendations receive much newspaper publicity in many cities, including New York, Chicago, and Detroit, for the groups often enjoy the open support of at least some of the newspapers. The effect of these endorsements varies greatly, however, depending upon the degree of political organization, local traditions, and many other factors. The Detroit Citizens League is far more effective, for example, than the Municipal Voters League of Chicago. Some groups, such as the Seattle Municipal League, do not make recommendations for voting, but do give their opinions as to whether or not each candidate is qualified for the office he seeks.

Related to the above type of group are various other middle-class clubs and endeavors. Women's clubs, particularly the League of Women Voters, often work for good government per se. The League gets out a voter-information sheet in many cities. Being strictly nonpartisan, the League usually has a prepared set of questions on current issues which it submits to candidates. The questions are generally not "loaded" (the League *does* sometimes endorse certain policies—for example, perhaps, the council-manager plan, or a four-year term for elective officials), and the answers are printed verbatim (unless, of course, the candidate gets carried away too far). The Parent-Teachers Association (PTA) is also a powerful pressure group, much more interested in the affairs of the school board, of course, but where its interests overlap with those of the city, the PTA may be found lobbying before the council, or before the voters if a referendum is involved.

Improvement Associations. In many cities virtually every neighborhood shopping area has an association for the safeguarding and furthering of the interests of the businessmen operating in that community. Likewise, in many sections of the city, similar groups will be found for the various residential subdivisions. These groups serve many purposes. If the city is growing or shrinking in size, they fight to keep property values high. If the city or neighborhood is losing population, the slackening of demand for homes demands diligence in order to save as much as possible of the homeowners' investment. If the city is increasing in size, older neighborhoods are constantly undergoing transition in character. In this case the association fights—usually without ultimate success if there is real demand for space—to keep Jews or Negroes or Mexicans or some other socially unwanted group out of the area.

These groups often appear before the council or administrative officers of the city, for they have almost countless bases for making such contacts. They are interested in every proposed rezoning of the area, since this has a direct effect upon property values. They do not want commercial or industrial areas nearby, they want the factory eight blocks upwind to stop making all that smoke and noise, they want more stop signs in the neighborhood ("trucks are using our street for a through street"), they want the chuckholes repaired immediately (though this must not result in a tax increase), they want the squad car to drive past the house more often at night (but "Look at all the money the police want to run that lousy department for next year!") and they want only single-family dwellings in the neighborhood if such has been the previous character of the area.

The improvement associations also serve other functions. Americans seek to lessen insecurity by joining together with others who feel as they do, and the neighborhood civic association gives the individual another club to add to his list. There are also offices to be filled, and Americans like to be presidents or vice-presidents of almost anything. They will appoint a committee at the first excuse, and neighborhood associations present a multitude of reasons for appointing committees: to "investigate the situation of 81st Street," or to "see the police chief." The associations also help to satisfy the urban dweller's longing to restore the primary relationships characteristic of the small town and rural community, for most of these groups are limited to a fairly small, truly neighborly area. If the group is made up primarily of homeowners, as a suburban group is, or if it is a businessmen's association, the organization also affords an opportunity to identify oneself more closely with these socially honorific classes. Members of neighborhood associations are fond of talking about the rights and responsibilities of homeowners and taxpayers, while members of a businessmen's group remind one another that they are indeed businessmen and hence the mainstays of the American economy. In fulfilling these psychological needs for prestige, the improvement associations, like many other pressure groups, serve a useful social function beyond that of exerting political pressure alone.

Taxpayers Groups. As something of a cross between the good-government groups and the business groups in the community, there are often organized "taxpayers leagues" of one title or another. In general they stand for lower taxes and fewer government activities and services and have their support in the more conservative business community—the large taxpayers. They often publish propaganda based upon either real or pseudo research on taxation, budgeting, and borrowing policies. Their membership is normally not large, and their influence on government varies greatly from place to place. Some of these groups have broader interests, more in the nature of the good-government groups.

Business Groups. There are so many business groups exerting pressure upon government that they would probably overshadow and overpower all of the others if it were not that they spend so much of their time opposing one another. There is an organization equipped to lobby for every business interest in the city. To name only some of them: there is often an association of downtown merchants, representing the owners, or in a large city probably the managers, of the large, usually retail, stores downtown. That these people would have numerous interests is obvious. They pay much of the general property tax of the city and so have an interest in tax rates; they want ample parking spaces, paid for, if possible, from taxes and not from their own pockets; they want superhighways that will bring people downtown to shop and will discourage the development of competing neighborhood shopping areas.

The downtown merchants and property owners are of tremendous influence both in determining the outcome of elections and in setting policy afterward. In middle-sized cities without political machines they are often the dominant group, and even in large cities, they wield great power. In Detroit and Los Angeles, for example, their influence is all-pervasive, although it is kept unpublicized and *sub rosa* by choice.

If a political machine exists, these groups must use a somewhat different approach. The traditional arrangement, as it exists in Chicago, is described by John Gunther:[6]

> Recently I asked an eminent Chicagoan what ran the city, and he answered "State Street and the Irish." The great merchants in the Loop have great influence, together with their allies such as the packers. . . . What the State Street oligarchy tries to stand for is civic and social leadership. The tycoons live in subdued beautiful estates along the Lake Shore or on the "Gold Coast" in town; it is they who sponsor such manifestations of civic energy as the Chi-

[6] John Gunther, *Inside U.S.A.* (1947), p. 372. By permission of Harper & Brothers.

cago Planning Commission and the like; their impregnable inner citadel is the Commercial Club. The Irish meantime, the most articulate of the great immigrant bodies that grew up under the layer of oligarchs, allied with other racial [and ethnic] groups, run the city politically. There is a kind of unspoken, unwritten deal. "We let the Irish have the government, if they let us do what we please," is one way I heard it put.

General Business Groups. The chamber of commerce is interested at the local level, as at the state and national, in tax rates, labor legislation, and other matters that affect business activity and costs. In quite a few cities, the chamber serves as the principal spokesman for business before the council and city officials. Often it acts in lieu of a downtown property association and exerts the same type of pressure.

The so-called service clubs, the Rotarians, Lions, and Kiwanians, are basically for businessmen, but their interests are not primarily political and they are not likely to act in this capacity, except perhaps in connection with a summer playground program or some such community service project.

Banks. Banks and related financial institutions are important pressure groups for several reasons. In the first place, they are businesses and have the interests of the businessmen. In the second place, bankers being among the most respected of all businessmen, their views are likely to be taken into the bosom of other businessmen, who then present them as their own. Furthermore, because the banker decides who is to be able to borrow money and under what conditions, he may in dozens of subtle or open ways influence the thinking, or at least the behavior, of other businessmen. Thirdly, bankers have a direct stake in local legislation affecting public utilities, in which banks have a pecuniary interest, and in bond issues and sinking funds, since banks act as brokers in servicing these. Banks are also interested in public policies that may affect businesses to which they have loaned money; hence they are interested in such matters as business regulation, taxation, zoning, and housing.

Utilities. Public utility companies in a great majority of cities are today dependent upon a state body for determining rates and service, but they also have many local interests. They must guard against movements to place their utility under public ownership, they are often dependent upon the good will of the city administration in order to extend or restrict the area covered by their services, and since the city is responsible for the public safety, the city's interpretation of what is safe or adequate equipment is of vital interest.

Contractors. The city has the power of inspection over all sorts of construction within the city. The building, plumbing, lighting, and other codes are hence of great interest to contractors, as is the manner in which these are enforced.

Businessmen who are particularly desirous of procuring public contracts are, of course, unusually interested in the political scene. Some businesses, such as road-grading and -surfacing companies, depend for most of their work upon public contracts, and they can be expected to seek to do their utmost to influence both elections and policy decisions.

Taxicabs. Taxicab owners (and their drivers' unions) also play an important role in municipal politics. The city council normally determines the number of taxi licenses to be issued and decides the question of who is to get them. The council can thus make or break any given company. Furthermore, both the owners and the drivers are interested in *restricting* the number of licenses below that of actual need—so that they may charge monopoly rates. The driver and his union are just as interested in keeping down competition as is the company itself.

In almost every American city, taxicab rates are outrageously high (especially if one includes the tip, which is really a hidden portion of the charge) and the number of cabs available is greatly insufficient. This is a direct result of pressure-group activity upon the council and is a good illustration of the council acting in the interest of the organized few rather than the unorganized many. (An outstanding exception to this situation is Washington, D.C., where sanity prevails in setting rates, but this is because the taxis are much used by Congressmen and by their constituents, who must not be unduly irritated while visiting the seat of government—the citizen might vote against the Congressman who allows his constituent to be fleeced while visiting the capital.)

Taxicab companies, and often their drivers, find it necessary to pick candidates and support them in municipal campaigns. Those who bet on the winning candidates will have the lion's share of the licenses for the next term of office, while those who are wrong will get the crumbs. Taxicab companies also seek ordinances against "jitneys" and strict enforcement of these ordinances.

The Professions. Professional organizations have a stake in government. Some of them, such as medical and dental groups, are more important as lobbyists before state and national governments, but others, and particularly the city or county bar association, are also active locally. The bar association is interested in city government for a variety of reasons. Lawyers make up a large portion of the candidates for public office and are likely to view this field as a private hunting ground. Lawyers and their organizations look upon themselves as singularly responsible for guarding the law and its traditions. They are particularly concerned over the modern tendency to use administrative tribunals rather than law courts in the settlement of many public matters, since the former need not always be made up of lawyers and do not necessarily use the traditional processes of the courts of law. Lawyers, furthermore, often consider themselves to be trained in the problems of public policy formulation and peculiarly qualified to comment upon them, even though the law is not a social science and most lawyers have had very little training in sociology, economics, psychology, or even political science.

Real Estate Groups. The local real estate board and other similar groups have a special interest in local government. The city zoning ordinance and building code are of the greatest interest to them; the city tax rate is important, since the general property tax is the major source of city revenue; the cost of paving streets is a factor in the selling of homes; public housing is anathema to them. Builders and real estate speculators are often among the most influential groups before a city government, and this is particularly true in suburban areas in a period of expansive home building. A builder may often contribute to the campaign funds of *all* candidates for office in a modest-sized suburb, especially if he is of the large, assembly-line type of "project" builder. There are often conflicts before the city council between "project" builders and improvement associations representing subdivisions of individually built homes and also between homeowners and large real estate companies interested in the development of commercial and industrial properties.

Liquor Interests. Time was, around the turn of the century, when the two most powerful pressure groups in most cities were the public utilities and the liquor interests. Since the turn of the century there has been a considerable decline in the power of the liquor and beer industry. Prior to prohibition, licensing of beer and liquor stores was largely a local function, making the interests of these occupations in city government obvious. Of course, there was also the question of the attitude the local police would take toward laws dealing with closing hours, selling to minors, selling on Sunday, engaging in such socially disapproved but financially profitable side lines as the narcotics trade and prostitution, and the like. During prohibition, the liquor industry continued (with public approval) quite unabated. In order to do so, it was necessary to buy off local governments whose officials were in a position to work an easy shakedown racket. Bootleggers in many instances virtually captured whole city governments, even in very large cities, as when the infamous Capone gang dominated Chicago in the twenties. Today liquor interests are less powerful in most cities, but they still exercise considerable influence, especially where the law and local mores are not in accord. The policing of the liquor industry, now largely in the hands of state government, has relieved city officials of some of the problems and temptations that existed before prohibition.

Illegal Occupations. The gambling, prostitution, and narcotics businesses are almost everywhere illegal, but they operate to some degree in most of our larger cities, as well as in many smaller places. They may be beset by peace officers from all three levels of government, but they persist because they are profitable; and they are profitable because of the highly inelastic character of the demand for their services. Because they are illegal, they must be particularly concerned with politics. Where they cannot purchase protection, they must seek to establish a pale wherein their operations are allowed by either tacit or explicit arrangement. Failing this, or as a preferable substitute, they may seek to operate in a suburb if the core-city administration is especially hostile. The narcotics trade is probably the least thriving of these businesses, for, despite the cruel cravings suffered by the drug addict that will make him go to any extreme in order to obtain supplies, Federal government officers have ruthlessly sought to exterminate the trade, usually, although not always, with the cooperation of state and local peace officers. On the other hand, gambling and prostitution are likely to be with us for some time to come.

Newspapers. Newspapers, as has often been pointed out, tend to be conservative influences in the community because big business is conservative and newspaper publishing, at least of the city dailies, is big business. It is also true that newspapers which are middle-of-the-road or responsibly conservative on national and international questions may well become much more conservative or even reactionary on matters of local politics. A daily which recognizes that labor unions are here to stay when discussing national labor law may speak of unions in the same terms it might have used in the nineteenth century when speaking of them in connection with local politics. Physical proximity and the immediacy of the economic interest involved may be a factor in producing this phenomenon. There is the further consideration that businessmen are dependent on the city government for all types of permits, licenses, favors, and sympathies in order to operate freely and successfully. A government controlled by labor or by unsympathetic liberals is a frightening specter to most businessmen and hence to newspaper editors.

Newspapers often work together with good-government groups and give them much free publicity. They may even print their press releases on the front page as news stories and not mention that it is partisan propaganda of an interest group. In many cities, newspapers have been important forces in achieving honest, efficient, and modern government.

Reasons for the Importance of Newspapers. The over-all effect of the opinion of a newspaper editorial board would probably not be great if the publication's effect were limited to its editorial opinions. Probably only a tiny percentage of newspaper readers pay any attention to the editorials, and those who do for the most part agree with them already. Yet a newspaper can be very influential in a dozen different ways. It can influence individual opinion by playing up or burying an item; by distorting the relative importance of the various facts involved in a story; by choice of location of the story; by choice of adjectives and adverbs; by phrasing of headlines; by its use of cartoons (picture editorials that reach far more people than do the ordinary ones). A newspaper that would not permit the "loading" of a story on a national matter may make its stories during a local election into veritable editorials. It may play up the speeches and pictures of Candidate Twitingham and bury those of Candidate Torkelson on page 37. Individual newspapers vary greatly in their use of these available weapons. Some seek to give balanced attention to all events. Others, for example the Hearst newspapers, normally pay relatively little attention to local issues, being more concerned with the national and international scene. A locally owned newspaper is more likely to play up local issues (and to take sides) than is one that is chain-owned or one whose editorial policy is determined by a person who lives elsewhere.[7]

Newspapers and Local Politics. Some newspapers have energetically, if not too successfully, fought political machines and especially corruption in local government. In the summer of 1871 the *New York Times* was offered no less than 5 million dollars to suppress evidence against the Tweed Ring. The *Times,* then as now, was incorruptible, but lesser newspapers were taken into the machine's orbit. Thomas Nast, the famous cartoonist of *Harper's Weekly,* was offered a half-million dollars if he would stop attacking the Tweed organization. This, too, failed.

The *Times* today, like another of the nation's great newspapers, the *New York Herald-Tribune,* supports reform, antimachine (in New York, usually Republican) candidates. The influence of the two would appear to be generally very limited in city politics, however. As another example, the *Philadelphia Inquirer* also supports reform groups (in that city, usually Democratic). Many other urban dailies have taken a firm stand, often a much firmer stand than have other businessmen, against machines.

The *Chicago Tribune* follows the line of least resistance in local politics and has gotten on well in the past with the Democratic Kelly-Nash machine, although the newspaper is avidly Republican (of its own sort). Like the State Street merchants, the *Tribune* has not crusaded against the machine despite the newspaper's great power. It does, on occasion, support opposition candidates where they have a chance to win. This policy has often been followed in the past in newspaper-machine relationships of other cities, perhaps because the business community in general has taken the same attitude.

The *Detroit News* has great influence in city elections through edi-

---

[7] Here would be a good place to study, either in a term paper or in class discussion, the power of the press, its attitudes toward local politics, and its methods of furthering its attitudes in the home community of the student. It might be interesting to contrast small towns with large cities in this respect.

torials, choice and location of copy, and dissemination, free of charge, of the propaganda (especially the candidate recommendations) of the Detroit Citizens League. The *Los Angeles Times* performs a similar role in that city. Both newspapers have the advantage of publishing in cities with nonpartisan elections and no semblance of a political machine. (The *Times* is sometimes opposed by the middle-of-the-road *Los Angeles News.* The Detroit newspapers rarely disagree on local politics.)

In many cities, especially large ones, limited-circulation weekly newspapers may be of more influence in elections than are the large downtown dailies. These newspapers are usually aimed at a definite clientele: residents of a suburb or of a neighborhood area in the core city, foreign-language-reading members of an ethnic group, members of a labor union, Negroes, Catholics, or Jews. Since they emphasize the interests of particular groups, they are able to call specific candidates or issues to the attention of the voter and to discuss them in terms of his interests.

The suburban and neighborhood newspapers are especially influential since they are not viewed as "commercial" or "partisan." Because they reflect the interests and values of the neighborhood, they are thought of rather as agents of "community welfare and progress."[8]

Radio and TV. Radio and television are important media in large cities for reaching voters and people to be propagandized over local issues. In the days before television, radio was not too successful for conveying ideas concerning local matters. People would listen to the President, but not to the mayor, and almost certainly not to a local labor leader or the president of the local chamber of commerce, unless the issue were of the most unusual importance. There is reason to believe, however, that television, with a hypnotic quality lacking in radio, will be able to catch the eye and thought of citizens where radio failed.

Organized Labor. Probably no event in the last thirty or more years is likely to have so great an effect upon the future pattern of urban government as the coming to power of organized labor. Especially important as a long-range factor is the rise since 1937 of the Congress of Industrial Organizations (CIO) with its organization of the unskilled and semi-skilled workers and its fresh supply of imaginative, able, and ambitious leaders. The full effect of organized labor as a political-action group has not yet been felt, partly because the leaders have so far not succeeded in persuading the members to support the union position in local politics. While the leaders deliver the votes quite well on national and even state matters where they can convince members that they have a real and immediate stake, there has been less success in convincing them that

[8] Morris Janowitz, "The Imagery of the Urban Community Press," *Public Opinion Quarterly*, vol. 15 (Fall, 1951), pp. 519–531. This is a report on a study made in Chicago.

local politics is of equal importance to the labor movement. Progress is undoubtedly being made in this direction, however, and this is why the political activities of organized labor seem to be destined to change the picture of municipal politics in the future.

At the present time, however, "Unions have a long way to go before they achieve a community position equal to that of older and better established groups."[9] Neither the labor leaders nor the membership have yet fully recognized the opportunities and advantages for collective action in the political realm. In time they likely will.

Labor groups have always had some effect upon urban politics in the largest cities, but the coming of the CIO with its definite social philosophy has made a great difference. The older craft unions of the AFL were interested primarily in what is called "business unionism"—the highest possible wages, best possible working conditions, shortest possible hours. Few of them, however, had developed a social philosophy. The AFL sought essentially to achieve a monopoly of skilled labor and to make its members better and more prosperous members of the middle class. The CIO, on the other hand, has sought to inculcate into its members the idea that the working class has a set of interests to pursue that are different from those of the business-oriented middle class. It is therefore to be expected that they would seek to challenge the business community for control of city government.

The Goals of Labor. Organized labor has a whole list of wants it desires from government, and a large number of them result in a conflict with other interest groups. Labor expects that the many services it demands be paid for on an ability-to-pay theory of taxation, rather than on a benefit theory. This brings labor into conflict with those who are expected to foot the bill. Labor is more interested in services than in the tax rate. Many workingmen feel that the burden of the general property tax is of no concern to them because they do not own homes. This assumption is, of course, fallacious, since the renter pays the property tax as part of his rent. It does, however, change his attitude.

The considerable increase in the rate of ownership of homes by members of the working classes since the end of World War II as a result of liberal financing provisions of the Veterans Administration and the Federal Housing Authority is likely to change this attitude in time. Many workingmen, especially in the skilled trades, have today become members of a new middle class of suburbanites quite different from the traditional pattern. They are sometimes called the "blue collar" class. While

---

[9] For a case study of one union local (of the United Steel Workers) in one city (probably Gary), see Joel Seidman, Jack London, and Bernard Karsh, "Political Consciousness in a Local Union," *Public Opinion Quarterly*, vol. 15 (Winter, 1952), pp. 692–702. The quotation is from this study.

these people tend to be Democratic in state and national politics, they are likely to assume the conservative characteristics of homeowners on the local level.

Labor is also interested in such things as a subsidized public transportation system in contrast to the businessman's views on a pay-as-you-ride system, preferably privately owned. It wants public housing with low rentals, perhaps an FEPC ordinance, and high wages for city employees, all of which is likely to run it into various conflicts with business, good-government, and other middle-class groups. Labor also wants to control the city administration, if possible, partly in order to ensure a sympathetic police force in the event of strikes or other labor disturbances. It well remembers the time, not long ago, when the local police department was often considered available to any manufacturer for strike-breaking purposes.

The CIO does not have a nationally adopted municipal program—each local CIO council works out its own program and policies to fit local expediencies. The AFL appears to follow the same pattern. Both carry on their conventional practice of seeking to support friends and defeat enemies in local elections. The national CIO-PAC (Political Action Committee) compiles an annual list of all city and county elections taking place during the year and follows this up with a reminder to the local PAC sixty days before the election that the time has come to get to work.[10]

While no statistics are available to indicate the number of labor-endorsed mayors and councilmen in the United States, some idea of the aggressiveness of this new force in municipal politics can be derived from the 1949 figures on the number of CIO *members* holding local office. In that year, there were 26 mayors, 244 council members, and 390 other officials who were dues-paying members. The number of endorsees must have been many times this figure.

Racial and Ethnic Groups. Although there is no logic from a theoretical standpoint in having democratic representation on the basis of racial or ethnic groups and no particular reason why such groups should be separated off from one another in such a manner as to require them to act as pressure groups, such is nonetheless the case. Minority groups find that they are beleaguered and feel the need to protect themselves from further encroachment by an unsympathetic dominant group in society. Negroes, Jews, Mexican-Americans, and sometimes Poles, Italians, or Irish groups find that by banding together they can seek protection in the law.

Minority groups are interested in such things as FEPC, the protection of their equal right to civil-service jobs, equal police protection and

---

[10] Information on CIO activities is from a letter from Henry Zon of the CIO-PAC to the writer, May 5, 1953.

treatment, and a fair share of housing. Minorities often vote in blocs in political campaigns, resulting in such situations as that in New York where the mayor, the controller, and the president of the council must always be of different ethnic or racial groups. For a well-balanced city-wide ticket, there must be an Italian, an Irishman, and a Jew, while a fourth important position could well be found for a Negro. A similar recognition of political realities may be found in many cities where identifiable groups are important.

For pressure purposes, there are many organizations for these people. Negroes, for example, will be represented at council hearings by the National Association for the Advancement of Colored People as well as by the local Urban League. The NAACP has been more active politically than has the League, which has been interested mainly in making more jobs, more economic opportunities, available to Negroes. Both are potent organizations, especially in large cities, even though they cannot by any means claim to speak for all Negroes.

Religious Groups. Virtually all religious and church-related organizations represent political forces. Perhaps the only exception would be those sects that are opposed to political action. Since a religion—any religion—is based upon some kind of faith or set of beliefs, it is to be expected that political and social questions will be interpreted in the light of these moral-value scales and viewpoints taken in accord with them.

In almost any important councilmanic hearing, ministers, priests, rabbis, or leaders of religious lay groups will be found testifying for their members. Because Catholics tend to be concentrated in cities and because the Church is disciplined and dogmatic, its views are often particularly powerful and effective. The Church has dozens of lay organizations that act as pressure groups. Protestants are less well organized, but may be equally active. Methodist groups may work for a policy of restricting the number of retail liquor permits; Quakers may be interested in the humane treatment of prisoners in the local workhouse; a group of ministers may lobby for an FEPC ordinance.

Municipal Employees. Employees themselves are organized into pressure groups and can exert influence on the administration and council for matters that interest them, particularly wages, hours, and conditions of labor. Because many employees belong to labor unions that have close association with the other AFL and CIO unions of the city, they are in a position to bring up reinforcements at important times.

There are professional organizations such as the International City Managers' Association, the Civil Service Assembly of the United States and Canada, and the American Society of Municipal Engineers. Others are regular labor unions, the most powerful of which are the American

Federation of State, County, and Municipal Employees (AFL) and the Government and Civic Employees Organizing Committee (CIO). There are also the International Association of Fire Fighters (AFL), Fraternal Order of Police, and the United Public Workers of America. Purely local unions commonly exist, either because they are old, respected, and powerful, or because other types of unions are discouraged by local public policy. Examples that might be cited include the Milwaukee Government Service League and the Detroit Police Officers Association.

Veterans. After each war, veterans—at least many of them—organize themselves into interest groups. They are particularly powerful because, unlike ordinary groups, they have no organized opposition, no counter pressure group. It is not easy for a politician or another pressure group to oppose the interests and demands of a well-known veterans' group. In local politics, returned servicemen are interested in such things as tax exemptions, civil-service preferences on job certification, "patriotism," taxicab licensing, and all other types of licensing with an eye toward privileges for veterans.

The largest and most powerful veterans' groups on the local as well as the national scene are the American Legion and the Veterans of Foreign Wars, both of which have members who served in the two world wars and in the Korean conflict. Products of World War II, such as the Amvets and the AVC, are smaller and less powerful. There are also groups that represent two special interests simultaneously, such as the Catholic War Veterans and the Jewish War Veterans.

Who Are the Decision Makers? Every human organization (at least in Western civilization) is made up of a leadership group and a general following. Pressure groups, too, have leaders. Sometimes they are closely subjected to the will of the rank and file, sometimes they are quite independent, making political decisions for the group and later seeking to convince the group that this action was justified. Many factors influence the standing of the leader within his group.[11]

Who are the decision makers in city government, the men who pull the strings that make or unmake politicians, administrations, regimes, and councilmanic majorities? The answer, of course, varies with the particular time and city. One reliable observer, looking at Los Angeles in 1945, prepared a list of eighteen men.[12] The group included the executive vice-president of the *Los Angeles Times;* two prominent attorneys whose clients include persons and firms that stand to be particularly affected by municipal activities; a retired millionaire who seems to make politics a hobby and who is an important source of campaign contribu-

[11] On this matter, see Truman, *op. cit.*
[12] Aldrich Blake, *You Wear the Big Shoe* (1945).

tions; the head of the Southern California Edison Company; the general counsel for the Downtown Business Men's Association; a multimillionaire oil man; the president of a large manufacturing firm who is also an expert fund raiser; four leaders in the local American Federation of Labor organization, middle-of-the-roaders generally, with one a definite conservative; four members of the Congress of Industrial Organizations, starting at the middle of the road and moving toward the left; and lastly the president of a restaurant chain who makes a hobby of politics and prefers a direct appeal to the people rather than working behind the scenes as most king makers prefer to do.

Some of these leaders are well known to the voting public; others have names that would not be recognized even by a fairly well-informed citizen. This is the way of politics in every American city.

Another study,[13] of a Southern city of about a half-million people (perhaps Atlanta), has indicated that local officials are the pawns of the principal policy makers in the community. A very few men make the important decisions on behalf of the whole community and a few hundred carry them out. The top men confer by telephone or by meeting in the home of one of the members of the group. After they reach a decision, the word is passed down to the next lower level of the pyramid for action —or inaction. In the study, no Negroes and no labor leaders are included in the inner circle, although they are growing in importance. *All* of the top decision makers are also the top leaders in the business community. Their power is greatest in relation to city government and grows progressively less at the higher levels of government.[14]

Public Awareness of the Political Power Structure. Just how aware is the typical citizen of the identity of the decision makers in his community? What does he know of the relative influences exercised by various forces in the political process? In order to find out something about this, a recent study asked the following question: "Who runs Detroit?"

Before the answers are given, it should be pointed out that Detroit government has been dominated almost without interruption from the time of World War I by the businessmen of the community: members of the board of commerce, the downtown merchants, and the real estate groups in particular. This is accomplished through a community of interests with the daily newspapers, whose control of the principal means of local communication is all-important in a system of nonpartisan elections. Detroit political parties are weak, and there are no political bosses in the traditional sense. The labor unions, despite the huge membership of the UAW-CIO, have been very weak in local politics. Jews and Negroes have

---

[13] Floyd Hunter, *Community Power Structure: A Study of Decision Makers* (1953).
[14] The student might try to determine the decision makers in his own community.

had little representation in either the legislative or the administrative branch of city government. Organized racketeering has not been influential in Detroit government for many years.

The answers to the question were classified as follows:[15]

Answer	Per cent
No special group: "the public," don't know, etc	42
Special groups named:	
Total	58
Businessmen, industrialists, the rich	18
Labor unions, organized labor	11
Politicians, political bosses	11
Jews	6
Negroes	5
Racketeers, gamblers, underworld	2
Others	5

The survey showed interesting variations of response among different population groups. The better-educated were most convinced that special groups "really run the city." Only 30 per cent of those who went beyond high school named no groups that had most influence, while 50 per cent of people with eighth-grade education or less named no particular groups. High-school and college graduates and the upper socioeconomic groups almost never named Jews or Negroes. It is significant that the more education a person had, the more likely he was to believe that businessmen and "people with money" had most influence in the city.

[15] Arthur Kornhauser, *Attitudes of Detroit People toward Detroit* (1952), pp. 13–15. This is a summary of a longer, more technical study, *Detroit as the People See It* (1952). By permission of Wayne University Press.

CHAPTER 6

THE POLITICAL PROCESS AND THE CITY: II

Basic election machinery was described in Chapter 4, pressure groups and the principal media of communication in Chapter 5. The task of putting the pieces together remains for this chapter.

At one time in American history, the political process in the city would have had to be explained in terms of the boss and the machine. Today that is no longer the case. This chapter will therefore briefly describe the cause of decline of bossism and then examine the political process that has replaced it.

THE CITY BOSS AND MACHINE: A PASSING PHENOMENON

The Function of the Boss and Machine. In American folklore, in newspaper editorials, in magazine articles, in political campaigns, and in suburban gossip, it has been all too common to picture the nineteenth-century city boss and machine as if they were a contemporary phenomenon. It is not uncommon even today to hear the phrase "boss-ridden cities." Actually, the boss and machine performed a necessary social function in their day, but they have outlived their usefulness and have been disappearing from the American scene. William Marcy Tweed of New York, "Ed" Flynn of the Bronx, "Big Bill" Thompson of Chicago, "Doc" Ames of Minneapolis, "Abe" Ruef of San Francisco, and a host of others have left the front pages of the newspapers and are taking their place in the history books, where they will become a romantic, if not exactly an honored, memory.[1]

There is probably no need to describe in detail the *modus operandi* of the old-time machine. A few points should be made concerning it, however.

In the first place, the machine did not exist *in spite of* society. It existed because it filled a real need. It served as a highly effective, if inefficient, system of social welfare. To the poor in the slums of cities, the machine provided needed services: it found jobs, or tided the family over

[1] See Suggested Readings at the end of this book for a bibliography on bosses and machines in various cities.

during periods of unemployment; it buried the dead; it cared for widows and orphans; it organized youth activities; it provided a multitude of neighborhood social functions; it contributed to the churches of poor neighborhoods; it provided bail bonds and legal advice; it furnished assistance in finding housing and helped tenants talk their landlords out of rent increases. It provided literally hundreds of services, the need for which was not recognized by a callous society.

Secondly, the machine was a product of universal suffrage, perhaps its first important manifestation. The services provided were offered in the expectation that the recipients would cast their ballots in support of the machine. If the ordinary worker in the slum had not been enfranchised, as he was in the 1830s and 1840s, the pattern of urban politics during the remainder of the nineteenth century would have been quite different.

Thirdly, the machine raised the great amounts of money that were needed for the services it provided (and often for the personal profit of its leaders) by acting as a broker for the city's services. It raised most of its money from businessmen and industrialists; and owing to the then current belief that it was cheaper to buy off the machine than to fight it, the business community often worked hand in glove with the machine.

The organization raised its money in a great variety of ways. It made available, for a price, building permits, all types of licenses, utilities franchises, and ordinances that might be helpful to a business. Sometimes it resorted to simple blackmail, or the shakedown racket. Much money was made through contract rebates. Contracts were granted to a firm that was working closely with the machine with the understanding that part of the profit would be returned to the machine. Municipal employees were very commonly assessed part of their pay, and other funds could be raised by the purchase of land by inside members of the organization for resale to the city. It was this type of profiteering that was made famous as "honest graft" by George Washington Plunkitt of Tammany Hall. It was Plunkitt who stated the code of the more sincere organization worker when he said, "If my worst enemy was given the job of writin' my epitaph when I'm gone, he couldn't do more than write 'George W. Plunkitt. He Seen His Opportunities, and He Took 'Em' "[2] (see Figure 9).

The Decline of Bossism. Opportunities, as seen by Plunkitt, began to fade away as the effects of the reform movement came to be felt. The decline of the boss and machine began to accelerate after World War II in particular, and by 1950 the boss and machine in almost every American city had been either destroyed, badly mangled, or profoundly modified in its pattern of behavior.

There were many reasons for this. Since World War I, there has been a

[2] See the fascinating profile by W. L. Riordon, *Plunkitt of Tammany Hall* (1905).

steady decline in the percentage of foreign-born in American cities, and it had been to the needs of this group that machines had particularly appealed. Negroes and other rural-to-urban migrants likewise became less subject to machine control after they became more sophisticated in urban ways. Another factor was the high employment after 1940, which allowed large numbers of people to escape the extreme poverty that had forced them to be partly dependent upon the machine.

IT'S A BUSINESS LIKE ANYTHING ELSE
—*Boss Pendergast.*

Fig. 9. SOURCE: By permission of Daniel R. Fitzpatrick and the *St. Louis Post-Dispatch.*

The general adoption of the officially printed, secret ballot made it more difficult for the machine to stuff ballot boxes, falsify election returns, or conduct other election frauds. Lincoln Steffens tells us that the voting lists of Philadelphia at the turn of the century were padded "with the names of dead dogs, children and non-existent persons." Success in such practices has become increasingly difficult in recent years. Yet as recently as 1936 the *St. Louis Post-Dispatch* won a Pulitzer Prize for uncovering 45,000 false registrations in that city.

The whole reform movement damaged machine government by helping to arouse citizens from their apathy and by rallying businessmen to fight the machine instead of buying it off. The stabilizing of the population of some of the older cities in the nation has helped produce a sense of identification with the city in its inhabitants. A stable population, one with a low physical-mobility rate, helps to develop a civic pride and political awareness that does great damage to machine control. The rise to power of organized labor has upset the traditional balance of control in many cities and has caused a shift in loyalty of the worker from the machine and its leadership to the trade union and its leadership.

Lastly, and perhaps of greatest importance, a modern and professionalized approach to the problems of social welfare has taken away from the political machine its principal means for achieving loyalty and support. The development of government control of such functions as workmen's compensation, unemployment compensation, old-age pension, and old-age insurance, and their administration by professionally trained civil servants rather than by political hacks, proved a mortal wound to the old-time machine.

Machines in Decay. Beginning with the reform movement around the turn of the century, an entire procession of machine defeats has paraded across the front pages of the newspapers of the nation. The one-time organizations in St. Louis, Minneapolis, and San Francisco are long dead. The once-powerful Republican machine in Cincinnati was defeated and permanently disabled by reform efforts in the elections of 1924 and those that followed. The castle of Thomas J. Pendergast and his Democratic machine in Kansas City came crashing down in 1939 and today lies in ruins, nearly if not quite entirely destroyed.[3] Tammany Hall in New York has been losing ground since the 1932 Seabury investigation of the "Jimmie" Walker administration. It was greatly weakened during the long period when its enemy, Fiorello H. LaGuardia, served as mayor.[4] Tammany has undergone considerable modification and today, despite the fact that reformers still denounce it in each campaign, operates with a far more modern concept of politics than it did in former years.

By the time of the coming World War II, bosses and machines were thoroughly outmoded. Nearly all of those that remained were liquidated during the period of postwar readjustment. The Republican machine of Philadelphia, which had enjoyed uninterrupted control of that city since shortly after the War between the States, lost important ground in the election of 1949 and was thoroughly routed in 1951, when it lost control of the mayor's office and of a majority of the council to a reform

[3] Miniature portraits of some of the more recent city machines are painted in John Gunther, *Inside U.S.A.* (1947).
[4] See the views of LaGuardia in his article, "Bosses are Bunk," *The Atlantic Monthly*, vol. 180 (July, 1947), pp. 21–24.

Democratic group. The old Democratic Kelly-Nash machine, now under "Jake" Arvey, still held control of the city of Chicago in 1954, but the quality of city government there had improved in postwar years.

James Michael Curley of Boston long ruled that city by building up a Robin Hood legend about himself. He was known as a builder of schools, a provider of jobs, and a man who got things done. He was strongly supported by the great bulk of the minority ethnic groups in the city. He was so effective in personal contacts that as recently as 1945, 10 per cent of the Boston voters claimed to know him *personally*.[5] Yet in 1949 a reform group, called the New Boston Committee, defeated him, elected a mayor, and took control of the council. In the next election, Curley again lost.

In 1940, Dayton D. McKean wrote that the Hague machine in Jersey City "is so nearly perfect that other machines may be measured against it."[6] Yet Hague's candidate was defeated in 1950 and in succeeding elections, although the destruction of his machine did not signal the rise of a reform administration, as happened in many other cities. In Memphis, Edward H. Crump managed to keep an effective machine together until his death in 1954. But like so many who exercise power for a long time, he had made no adequate provision for a successor, and a shadow was therefore cast over the future of his machine.

There can be no doubt that the nineteenth-century machine system has outlived its usefulness. Some of its techniques are being adopted by a few men and organizations of a new type of middle-class, twentieth-century development such as is discussed below in connection with the political structure of Dearborn, Michigan. Most American cities today, however, are based upon quite a different pattern of politics, characterized by an informal, loose political structure and with primary importance being placed, in large cities, upon control of the media of communication. This pattern is explained below.

TWO CASE STUDIES

The Depression Years: Kelly-Nash in Chicago.[7] Chicago proper has a population of 3,620,962 (by the 1950 census), yet it received its first

[5] J. S. Bruner and S. J. Korchin, "The Boss and the Vote," *Public Opinion Quarterly,* vol. 10 (Spring, 1946), pp. 1–23.

[6] D. D. McKean, *The Boss: The Hague Machine in Action* (1940).

[7] The best sources on Chicago are C. E. Merriam, *Chicago: A More Intimate View of Urban Politics* (1929); H. F. Gosnell, *Machine Politics: Chicago Model* (1937); J. Bright, *Hizzoner Big Bill Thompson* (1930); H. Andrews, *The Battle for Chicago* (1946); and an entertaining, although essentially hostile, panorama painted by one of America's greatest reporters, A. J. Liebling, *Chicago: The Second City* (1952). A worthwhile bit is to be found in Gunther, *op. cit.*, chap. 23.

charter, as a village, only in 1833. In a century and a quarter it has grown from sand dunes and prairie to the second largest city in the nation and one of the largest in the world. Its rapid growth has made it a natural target for machine rule and corruption. Even so, it has not, as popular belief would have it, always been one of the worst-ruled cities in the United States. As a matter of fact, during the periods of worst corruption in American cities, Chicago was relatively restrained and its government was far more effective and honest than that of most large cities. Under the two Carter H. Harrisons, Chicago had capable administration.[8] It has been since 1915 that it has most often blackened its own eyes.

"Big Bill" Thompson: Republican. While most Americans probably think of Chicago as a stronghold of Democratic strength, the colorful William Hale ("Big Bill") Thompson, who was mayor from 1915 to 1923 and again from 1927 until the depression-year election of 1931, was a Republican. As a matter of fact, throughout the twentieth century, both major parties in Chicago have been divided into factions, and the political picture has been made up most of the time of constantly changing alliances, with little regard to party membership.

It was under Thompson that Chicago descended into a "saturnalia of corruption, more disgraceful, if possible, than any that had preceded it. In this new outburst of municipal greed almost nothing escaped, beginning with the plunder of the schools [which most bosses were wise enough to avoid] and extending to almost all branches of the municipal service."[9]

Thompson had an organization "resting upon patronage and spoils, and flanked by the support of predatory business interests, with open defiance of the press and the independents. . . . The utility interests centering around Samuel Insull became the chief [financial] bulwark of the later flowering of the Thompson group."[10]

Thompson was born into wealth and social position. Unlike many politicians who had not chosen their parents with equal care, he had little interest in graft for personal gain. As Gosnell puts it, "He liked the

[8] See C. O. Johnson, *Carter H. Harrison I, Political Leader* (1928); and for the son, Carter H. Harrison, *Stormy Years: The Autobiography of Carter H. Harrison, Five Times Mayor of Chicago* (1935). The elder Harrison was mayor from 1879 to 1887 and for a few months in 1893; The younger, from 1897 to 1903 and from 1911 to 1915.

[9] Merriam, *op. cit.*, p. 22. Merriam, late University of Chicago professor of political science, was once a city alderman and, in 1911, was nearly elected mayor. This and the following quotation by permission of the Charles E. Merriam estate.

[10] *Ibid.*, pp. 185–186. Thompson was mayor during the heyday of the notorious "Scarface Al" Capone, and some of Thompson's lieutenants were friends of Capone and his gang.

game and the crowds."[11] He clowned before the public while his hench-men pillaged the city. He was a genius at showmanship. He campaigned to make Chicago the "wettest city in the country"; he believed in "America first" and campaigned against King George, Marshal Joffre, and the League of Nations. He would use such stunts as that of bringing two rats on the stage and carrying on a "conversation" with them, calling them by the names of his political opponents, or bringing his "opponent" on the stage in the form of a bridled donkey. The voters of the roaring twenties loved him. He had color and, behind him, Insull's money. Never before had people been more cheerfully plundered.

But Insull's pyramided empire of utility holding companies collapsed, an honest state's attorney began to bring indictments against some Thompson men, and the Great Depression brought on everywhere a demand for a change.

The Depression and Cermak. It was through these circumstances that the Democrats were able to build a political machine, after the greatest day of that social phenomenon had passed elsewhere, more powerful than any the city had previously known.[12] They were not too well organized when the great day came. Roger Sullivan, the old-time boss, had passed the mantle on to George Brennan, but his death in 1928 had left the party temporarily leaderless and with a threatened struggle for control. Leadership, and the successful 1931 mayoralty choice, passed, however, to the Czech-born president of the County Board of Supervisors, Anton J. Cermak.

Cermak had the social philosophy of a businessman and of an organization politician. In the 1931 campaign he did not talk about ameliorating the distress of the unemployed, but concentrated on promises for reducing the city budget and saving taxpayer money. Thompson replied with the accusation that "Saving Tony . . . saved six million out of a $10,000 salary" while on the County Board.[13]

Not only was Cermak lacking in a social philosophy with which to meet the city's depression problems, but he quickly got into bad odor with Franklin D. Roosevelt and with James A. Farley, who became chairman of the Democratic National Committee, when he backed Alfred E. Smith for the 1932 Democratic presidential nomination. It was in February, 1933, that he went to Miami in order to talk over with Roosevelt the unhappy prospect of federal patronage control in Illinois being turned over to another Democrat. While he was conversing with the President-elect an assassin aimed his pistol at Roosevelt. The aim was bad and Cermak fell with a fatal wound.

[11] Gosnell, *op. cit.*, p. 11.
[12] *Ibid.*, p. 12.
[13] *Ibid.*, pp. 13–14.

Kelly and Nash: Democrats. Control of the organization now passed to the chairman of the Cook County Democratic Committee, aging Patrick A. Nash, who preferred to run things from the background. He had the Illinois General Assembly pass legislation permitting the city council to name the new mayor. The council, at Nash's "suggestion," named Edward J. Kelly, president of the South Park Board and chief engineer of the Chicago Sanitary District. Kelly was a personal friend of Colonel Robert R. McCormick, publisher of the *Chicago Tribune* (who had disliked Republican "Big Bill" Thompson), he was a trusted friend of Nash, and he was favorably known to many of Chicago's businessmen. He had the good wishes of the press and the general public.[14]

How did the Kelly-Nash machine operate in the depths of a pervasive depression? Gosnell tells us:[15]

Seven years of depression in the city of Chicago [he wrote in 1936] have made practically no changes in the fundamental character of party organization, methods and leadership. It is true that the fortunes of individual politicians and parties have been greatly altered, but the party system has remained about the same. The party which controlled only a minority of the local offices when the financial crash came was greatly benefited by its connection with the new national administration, but it did not change its outlook. *Jobs and spoils were the currency of Chicago politics in 1936 as well as in 1928, and not issues which concerned the functions of municipal government in times of great economic stresses and strains.*

The political bosses who found themselves in power in the great metropolis of the Middle West in the 'thirties were, for the most part, self-made men. Chicago, in contrast to New York, has been a center abounding in self-made men—industrialists, grain merchants, large department-store owners, and real estate speculators. . . . The self-made politicians understood the self-made business men, as they talked the same language. While the sources of revenue available for local governmental purposes were greatly reduced, the politicians were able to use what there was to consolidate their positions. They said, in effect, to the business men: "You leave us alone and we will leave you alone." *The economic crisis in Chicago was met not by the local governments but by the national government. . . .*

Economic hardships undoubtedly created feelings of discontent which might have been used to bring about political changes, but the city lacked the kind of leadership which was necessary to guide the inarticulate demands of the masses. The new Tammany which was created on the ruins of its opponents' machines was led by men who were thoroughly in sympathy with the philosophy of big business. The conservative political outlook of the political, industrial, and financial leaders and a lack of local constitutional powers prevented the city government from becoming a major instrumentality of the citizens in meeting their problems during the crisis.

[14] *Ibid.,* pp. 15–16.
[15] *Ibid.,* pp. 24–26. Italics added. By permission of the University of Chicago Press.

The political machine had failed to meet the needs of modern society.

Mid-century Style: Hubbard in Dearborn.[16] Politics, to Orville L. Hubbard, is public relations. It is one long publicity stunt. It is neither graft nor corruption, nor is it service to the underpriviledged or personal profit. For Hubbard represents a new, mid-twentieth-century style of political leader. He symbolizes the modern successor to the old boss and machine: the political leader of the middle-class suburbanite. Just as the old boss is moribund, so the new system of Hubbard or of J. Russel Sprague in Nassau County, Long Island, is in the ascendant.[17]

The Suburb. Dearborn, Michigan (1950 population: 94,994), is a south-western suburb of Detroit. With the exception of one slum area immediately adjacent to the mammoth River Rouge plant of the Ford Motor Company, it is made up of lower- and upper-middle-class residents, with several very expensive neighborhoods. It consists of single-family dwellings for the most part, although there are some expensive apartment buildings of the type known in the Detroit area as "terraces." Over 80 per cent of the families living in Dearborn are homeowners. The population of the city has grown rapidly during and since World War II.

In 1941, three important things happened in Dearborn, things which were subsequently intertwined and confused in the minds of many of the voters. In the first place, the Ford Motor Company was unionized that year by the UAW-CIO after a long and at times bloody fight. In the second place, a grand-jury investigation uncovered officially the already well-known fact that Dearborn was a wide-open town for gambling and prostitution with little or no interference from the police, and the city was cleaned up. In the third place, Orville L. Hubbard, who had been a perennial candidate since 1933, was elected mayor. By 1954, he had been elected to his seventh consecutive term and had survived, in addition, a 1950 recall attempt. Almost from the beginning he has been called a "boss" or "dictator" by his many opponents. He is hated by many, yet he wins elections easily. How does he do it?

The Middle-class Appeal. Hubbard does not have a machine in the traditional sense. He has almost no patronage appointments. There are no ward or precinct organizations. Nor does he have the support of the regular party organizations, for Dearborn has a nonpartisan city ballot. Instead he depends upon personal contacts, professional public relations activities, municipal services of good quality, and trouble-shooting department heads. Each department head is assigned a district

---

[16] This section is based in large part upon personal interviews and observations by the present writer. Two newspaper feature serials are helpful: *The Detroit Free Press*, Nov. 16–17, 1949; *The Detroit News*, Apr. 17–19, 1950. There is also an article in *Time*, Aug. 21, 1950.

[17] A paragraph on Sprague may be found in James M. Burns and Jack W. Peltason, *Government by the People* (2d ed., 1954), p. 369.

within the city. He is expected to cover that area constantly, looking for things to be done, anticipating complaints of residents, keeping the service departments on the alert.

Hubbard is aware of the continuing value of some of the techniques of the old-time machines. The personal touch is a good vote getter, he knows, and sometimes he will appear in person at the home of a complainer to say that the problem has been taken care of—and to the satisfaction of the resident, he hopes. He knows that the propaganda technique of *transfer* is especially useful in connection with religious activities. Hubbard attends many different churches within the city. Can he help it if the members of each congregation receive the impression that he is a member? Under his administration the city has erected two signs for each church in the city in locations selected by the pastor and pointing toward the church. Municipal parking lots are located with a mind to their use for free Sunday church parking.

Dearborn has some of the best municipal services in the Detroit metropolitan area. It is a policy of Hubbard to start at least one new service before each election. In 1953 sidewalk snow removal and sweeping was introduced—a service that is otherwise available only in the expensive Grosse Pointe suburbs. Camp Dearborn, a "private country club" for Dearborn residents and their guests only, was established in 1949.[18] Under Hubbard a "tot lot" has been established in every subdivision. He has provided for dozens of baseball diamonds, ice-skating rinks, hockey rinks, fireworks displays on the Fourth of July and Labor Day, thousands of trees and shrubs, and hundreds of new street lights and street signs.

All of this costs a great deal of money, for these services are normally available only in "millionaires'" suburbs. How does he do this without being driven from office as a spendthrift? Hubbard is fortunate, for he is mayor of an unusual city. It is tremendously wealthy, with most of its wealth held not by the homeowners who get the superior services, but rather by industry. Something like two-thirds of the assessed valuation of the area is in industrial property, about one-half of it in the hands of the Ford interests alone. Only this makes the unusual services budgetarily possible, but Hubbard gives the credit to Hubbard.

Techniques of Appeal. Hubbard is a great campaigner, and he loves campaigning. His electoral support at the polls varies inversely with the income of the voter. In the slums of south Dearborn he gets nearly all of the votes; in the Springwells Park section, made up largely of Ford executives and engineers, he can expect to be defeated by as much as ten to one. His greatest support, numerically, comes from the lower

[18] It has lakes, over 500 acres of timber, picnic areas, camping areas, a trout brook, a large beach, 100 aluminum rowboats usable without charge, but no canoes—a drowning would cause bad publicity and a loss of votes. Buses haul children the 35 miles to the camp, where they can stay at a charge far less than cost.

middle class, and his campaign platform contains three *implicit* planks: better services for a cleaner Dearborn; a firm stand against the Ford interests; and a preservation of property values especially by keeping Negroes out of the city. The platform is aimed directly at the hopes and fears, the aspirations and the insecurities, of the lower-middle-class property owner. It has proved greatly effective.

The better services have already been explained. He has delivered on his promises. When he talks of keeping Dearborn "clean," he means not only that he will keep the garbage and rubbish cleaned up and the alleys free of dead dogs, but that the area will be "spiritually clean," for like Crump in Memphis, he will not tolerate organized gambling or prostitution. If a policeman seeks to line his pockets from this source, he ceases to be a policeman. Hubbard understands how to appeal to middle-class values.

The feud with the Ford company and family is largely window dressing, but with a symbolic purpose. Dearborn contains many skilled and some unskilled workers from the• great River Rouge plant which dominates the life of the whole community. In the old days, before the plant was unionized, it was a common thing for the Dearborn police to be used for strikebreaking purposes and for the prevention of labor disturbances. Hubbard asserts that he is an "unbossed mayor," which in Dearborn means that he is independent of the Ford company, something unusual in the history of that city. Many who remember the earlier days count on him to keep the city government from becoming "annexed" once again. (The Ford Motor Company operates under an entirely different philosophy today from that of 1939 so far as labor relations are concerned, but fear is a convenient tool for the politician.) He finds many ways to badger the company and the family, sometimes with resulting gifts to the city. Yet he named his youngest son Henry Ford Hubbard, and once when accused of driving Ford gifts out of the city and into Detroit, he ordered "Home Town of Henry Ford" printed on all city stationery.

There are no Negroes in Dearborn, and no Japanese-Americans have moved in while Hubbard has been mayor. In an industrial area with an ever increasing Negro population, the lower middle class tends to become obsessed with a fear of Negro invasion and of "lowering property values." Because this is so, some politicians in Detroit and many of its suburbs find it politically profitable to exploit this fear. Hubbard has found ways of using this gimmick effectively in irrelevant situations. In 1948, the John Hancock Mutual Life Insurance Company sought to build a multimillion-dollar private housing development in the city. There seemed to be no objection to the proposal until Hubbard decided to oppose it, probably on the theory that his stand would be popular with owners of single-family homes. Once he had spoken it became necessary for him to win, since a defeat on a major issue can be disastrous for any politician. He called upon the voters to defend themselves against "an invasion of renters." He called the expensive units a "bunch of row houses" and a *"public* housing project" (which it was not). He attacked the Ford interests for selling the land for the project to the insurance company. But his trump card was played on the day of the referendum. He sent his department heads around to the polling places, distributing cards bearing the injunction: "Keep the Negroes out of Dearborn. Vote against the John Hancock Housing Project."[19] That did it. There had never been any intention of renting the homes and apartments in the project to Negroes, but that did not matter—Hubbard had won. In his 1951 campaign for re-election, he emphasized that he had stopped a proposed Wayne County park from extending into Dearborn since it would have "attracted all types of undesirables." One of the greatest attractions of Camp Dearborn to prejudiced whites is that it, unlike other public parks, is not open to Negroes. If you ask a Hubbard man about the administration's Negro policy, he will explain that the city does nothing to keep anyone out. It just so happens that there are no homes for sale if a Negro wishes to buy.

Politics as Showmanship. Like many of the bosses of old, Hubbard is an expert in public relations and is an excellent judge of public opinion. For sheer color and campaigning skill, he is on a par with "Big Bill" Thompson of Chicago of the twenties. He keeps a dossier of his contacts with every constituent. He thus not only knows who is indebted to him, but can also give his correspondence a personal touch. He sends a letter or makes a personal call whenever there is a birth, death, wedding, house fire, or the arrival of a new resident in Dearborn. He signs his name in green ink with a special pen and in letters up to an inch high. His name and picture appear almost everywhere in the city. He was at the station to say good-by to every Dearborn inductee during the war and was there to greet him on his return as a civilian. He created the Dearborn Navy during World War II to protect the city from the German submarine menace. (When city employees began to use the boats for pleasure cruises, the navy was scuttled.) He takes the city directory with him on vacations and sends home hundreds of postcards to citizens— who are flattered by the mayor's thoughtfulness. He sees to it that some department head is a member of every club or organization of any size in the city. He himself belongs to as many as possible. (In the 1951 campaign he listed membership in twenty-five, including everything from the National Sojourners to the Michigan Academy of Science, Arts and Letters.) Like so many of his constituents, he started from the

[19] *Detroit News,* Apr. 19, 1950.

bottom of the social ladder, and, again like so many of them, he was born and raised on a farm before coming to the big city. (On this score, among many others, he differs from the traditional boss.) Like "Big Bill" Thompson, he is an expert at substituting irrelevancies for issues and in covering up embarrassing situations with confusion.

The final stage of an election campaign is completely professionalized. A meeting is likely to be held at Fordson High School, with a professional master of ceremonies, a professional show, and professional chorus girls. All of the good sign spots, parking places near voting booths, and auditoriums are taken up well in advance of the campaign—and usually well in advance of the less alert opposition.

In 1945 a jealous council (often he elects enough members of his slate to control the council, but before the next election he is usually feuding with many of them) passed an ordinance prohibiting the mayor from talking business with his constituents either personally or by telephone. Through the newspapers he received national attention. After having milked the publicity possibilities dry, he had himself arrested for deliberately violating the ordinance (more publicity) and then had the whole thing declared unconstitutional. An embarrassed council repealed the ordinance.

In facing his enemies—and they are many—Hubbard can be as merciless as any old-time boss. His path is strewn with the political bodies of those who have opposed him. He will do whatever is necessary, his opponents say, to destroy a man whom he has turned against. He has triumphed over all opponents and has dismissed some of his department heads (including his own law partner) even though they had been instrumental in his own advancement. After the *Dearborn Press* turned against him, the publisher's personal property assessment was increased 50 per cent.[20] Hubbard's opponents do not think it a mere coincidence. They claim that other property assessments have taken sudden, unexplained dips and increases while Hubbard has been mayor. But there has been no graft or corruption. The worst charge that a one-man grand jury investigation into the Hubbard administration could levy was that after the 1950 tax assessments of a large Dearborn retail store were reduced by $120,000, Hubbard was offered and accepted a television set as a gift from the company.[21] But Hubbard, like many old-time bosses, has no interest in money. He wants power and publicity.

Interpretation. Hubbard seems to represent a new trend in urban political organization. He is a characteristic leader, appealing to the middle class of a metropolitan suburb with things they want to hear, in contrast to the older pattern of appeal to the working class in the slums of the core city; a leader with little interest in patronage or

[20] *Time,* Aug. 21, 1950.
[21] Wayne County, Michigan, Circuit Court, Misc. 78616 (1953).

personal financial gain, but with a desire to give effective, professionalized services that the voters demand.

Allowing for local environmental and personality differences, this pattern is likely to become more and more in evidence. The Sprague Republican organization in Nassau County on Long Island is an efficient political machine. It receives its support from upper-middle-class New York commuters—businessmen, bankers, and lawyers. The county is organized with a county manager. J. Russel Sprague is both the manager and county Republican chairman. His department heads are also leaders in the machine. Sprague is a power in state politics and an ally of former Governor Thomas E. Dewey. His organization is efficient, disciplined, and honest.[22]

The Hubbard and Sprague organizations illustrate the adaptability of political institutions to changing environments. They and their kind will bear watching.[23]

THE MORE TYPICAL CITY

Cities without Machines. While a few cities have well-organized political machines which control the local government, others, especially large cities, tend to be controlled by pressure groups. Though organized labor is the largest of these, it is usually not this group, but the business community, which assumes control. If the downtown businessmen, the chamber of commerce, the real estate groups, and the newspapers can unite, they can normally control the city.

We have already seen that the big businessmen and manufacturers in the past often supported machines. Where there is no machine, they are likely to go along with the merchants or perhaps to ignore local politics in favor of the state and national scene. The motion-picture and aircraft industries do not dominate Los Angeles politics, for example. In fact, they have far less influence than do the large merchants. Contrary to what an outside observer might expect, the automobile industry does not control Detroit city government. In fact, it has almost nothing to do with it. (But in sharp contrast, the UAW-CIO is perhaps the dominant group in control of the Michigan Democratic party, while the automobile manufacturers, and especially the General Motors Corporation, tend to dominate the Michigan Republican party. Both groups look beyond city government for the protection of their positions in society.[24])

[22] Burns and Peltason, *op. cit.*, p. 369.

[23] Additional case studies may be found in R. S. Allen (ed.), *Our Fair City* (1947), which discusses eleven cities.

[24] Stephen B. Sarasohn, "The Regulation of Parties and Nominations in Michigan: The Politics of Election Reform," unpublished doctoral thesis, Columbia University (1953).

The Business Point of View. Wherever possible, and for the reasons discussed above,[25] businessmen seek to control nominations for the principal city offices. If the city has partisan elections but the party or parties are not organized effectively enough to be called a machine, business groups seek to back an acceptable candidate in the primary election in the party that is likely to win. Whether that party is Republican, Democratic, or a local party depends upon local circumstances. Sometimes they can get men with acceptable viewpoints nominated by all important parties.

If the city has nonpartisan elections, business groups (they do not always agree among themselves, however) seek out a likely person, or they choose one who has already entered the lists and back him. The principal opponent in either partisan or nonpartisan elections may be the candidate of another business group or, in an increasing number of cities, he may be the labor-backed candidate.

The Rise of Labor. When the AFL was the only major organization of unions, it was either not active in local politics, or it tended to back business candidates and to participate in the political process in much the same way as another business pressure group, for the interests of its members did not differ much from those of the merchants and other businessmen. The rise of the CIO has made a great difference, however. That union is more and more supporting policies sharply in contrast with those of the business community. Sometimes the CIO has the genuine support of the AFL under such circumstances; often it does not.

The influence of the CIO and other unions that will join with it has not yet been fully felt. For several reasons, the union has not yet been greatly successful in selling its endorsees to the rank and file. To begin with, the CIO is a relatively recent arrival on the scene. Further, the union and many of its members tend to look toward the larger units of government as the first areas to be conquered. Finally, many of its followers have lived in the city where they are now located a comparatively short length of time and have not yet identified themselves closely with the community. There can be little question, however, but that the CIO is rising in the municipal area of political activity and that its increasing influence is changing and will continue to change the basic pattern of politics in large American cities.

Illustrations of Business-supported Mayors. The professional politician is sometimes supported by businessmen for city offices, but businessmen often prefer, where practicable, to take one of their own kind. (Labor unions, in cities where they are strong enough, generally prefer a member of the union bureaucracy or a union attorney to a professional politician.)

[25] See pp. 105–109.

Harley Knox of San Diego was the operator of a dairy business in the city until other businessmen drafted him for the city council in 1939.[26] In 1943 they were successful in putting him into the mayor's office, a position actually of president of council in a manager-type city. Roger D. Lapham of San Francisco was another business choice.[27] He was board chairman of the American-Hawaiian Steamship Company and had not run for public office until he was asked to run for mayor. Both of these cities have nonpartisan ballots. Since most large American cities are normally predominantly Democratic, while most businessmen identify themselves with the Republican party, nonpartisanship is of considerable aid to large-city business groups in political action.

Business support helped make Eugene Van Antwerp mayor of Detroit in 1947, but by 1949 these groups withdrew their endorsement for a variety of reasons and transferred it to Albert E. Cobo, a former Burroughs Adding Machine Company accountant who had for some time been city treasurer. Cobo easily won the election over the CIO-endorsed candidate in a nonpartisan election. Van Antwerp, running for re-election despite a lack of group support, ran third in the primary.

In Los Angeles, Fletcher Bowron became the choice of business and other reform forces to succeed Frank Shaw, who was recalled in 1938. (Shaw had been charged with running a wide-open town.) Bowron had been a Hearst reporter, secretary to the governor, and a superior court judge. He was sold to the public as "a decisive, aggressive, dynamic, politically courageous personality,"[28] although much of his supposed character appears to have been manufactured by a public relations staff.

Bowron began to lose much of his business support after he backed a multimillion-dollar Federally aided public housing project and other business-disapproved policies. In May, 1953, Bowron tried for re-election depending upon his well-known name and the support of one newspaper and much of organized labor (because of his housing policy). His opponent, Congressman Norris Poulson, however, now commanded the support that mattered—the downtown merchants, the realty groups, the chamber of commerce, middle-class neighborhood improvement associations, and three of the newspapers. Poulson was able to defeat the man the business community had jettisoned.

These few sketches indicate the type of person who is likely to be elected mayor in a machineless city of medium or large size today. It should be noted that not one of the persons mentioned above has what politicians call "color." In fact, they are quite definitely colorless, in contrast to most machine mayors. Businessmen are not interested in

[26] See John Gunther, *Inside U.S.A.* (1947), pp. 55–56.
[27] On Lapham, see pp. 90–92.
[28] Aldrich Blake, *You Wear the Big Shoe* (1945), p. 39. For additional information on Los Angeles, see G. W. Finney, *Angel City in Turmoil* (1945).

color. They prefer a man with a fairly dependable business orientation, if possible with some business experience of his own, for that adds to his stability. These men are sturdy and honest, but they are not popular heroes.

THE POLITICS OF SUBURBIA

The Preservation of Property Values. The suburban movement of the years since World War I has produced a value pattern in which at least two things have been deified: conformity and property values. The suburbanite is nearly always a homeowner in a community where some of the primary relationships of the small town have been restored. Gossip is a factor in social control; contacts with people are more likely to tend in the direction of meeting the whole person on a warm, personal basis; and politics is likely to revolve around property values, for the individual who holds title to property will, in local politics at least, tend to be conservative in his desire to protect his investment.

In a few suburbs organized labor is important, but not in most of them. Even the skilled machinist, die maker, or truck driver who graduates to the ranks of the "blue collar class" is likely to be very conservative on local matters once he buys a suburban home, even though he may continue, for a time at least, to take labor's liberal view on state and national matters.

The Pattern of Suburban Politics. If the suburban community elects its officers on a partisan ballot, the Republican party will quite certainly dominate, for it is the party of middle-class respectability. We would find an exception, of course, in most Southern suburban communities. Even though many suburban newcomers are, or recently were, Democrats, they will find themselves in the minority, and there will be great social pressure applied for them either to switch parties or at least to remain discreetly quiet. Women appear to succumb to this pressure even more readily than do their husbands. Suburban America is today the greatest stronghold of the Republican party.[29]

On the local scene, the national party may be well organized, with a disciplined group of active workers, as it is in Nassau County, New York. But it is much more likely, especially for local purposes, to be made up of a series of small cliques, like the pattern in suburbs having nonpartisan elections. These cliques may have a rapport established with the district and state organizations of a major party, or they may exist only to take part in local elections. They are made up, for the most part, of political amateurs who are in politics for a hobby or for prestige or,

[29] See the comments of Stephen Mitchell as Chairman of the Democratic National Committee in *Time*, Oct. 26, 1953.

less frequently, for the sake of power and the ability to manipulate the process from behind the scenes. As in the core city, however, the vast majority of citizens are politically passive.

The women of suburbia, bored with dishes and diapers, are more likely to be active in the League of Women Voters and other women's clubs of varying degrees of political activity.[30] Neighborhood civic associations are particularly alive and of very considerable influence in community policy making. They frequently have a lobbyist whose duty it is to represent the association at city or village council meetings and to report back to the group. Sometimes the associations endorse candidates in election campaigns. Local businessmen's groups are also important in the local political process.

Suburbia is especially the home of small political-action groups with such names as "The Taxpayers' Protective Association of Sequoia Grove," "The Azalea Park Citizens' League," and "The Nonpartisan Voters of Vertigo Heights." These are generally nothing more than small cliques which have assumed general (and often important- and neutral-sounding) names in an attempt to give their propaganda greater prestige and influence. They usually accept viewpoints on public policy that are already predominant in the community.

Issues in Suburban Politics. During an election campaign, the suburbanite will be assured by each politician in turn that the candidate is a "homeowner and taxpayer," or that he is a "local businessman." The voter will be urged to "elect candidates who will work for you and protect your property values."

There may be red-hot issues on preventing invasion by socially "inferior" groups. There may be bitter debate over the question of whether to allow the development of industries within the community, and if so, their proper location (which, so far as the individual voter is concerned, is usually on the opposite side of town from his home). There may be taking of sides on whether the community should become incorporated (a very common problem as the population increases in density), or whether a village should become a city, or whether the council-manager plan should be adopted in preference to the mayor-council. There is the question of how to solve the sewage-disposal problem, or the water-supply problem, or the problem of water in the basement every spring.

While violently fought campaigns may appear from time to time on such issues as the above, it is more likely that the platform of a slate of candidates for the city council in suburbia will look something like this:

---

[30] The higher one's position on the class continuum, the greater one's participation in political and civic organizations. This is especially true of women. Mirra Komarovsky, "The Voluntary Associations of Urban Dwellers," *American Sociological Review,* vol. 11 (December, 1946), pp. 686–697.

THE ABOVE CANDIDATES ARE PLEDGED

1. Not to raise taxes. We believe that we can give you more services with no increase in taxes by achieving greater efficiency and economy.

2. To legislate only for the benefit of the entire community.

3. To protect your tax dollar through sound budgeting, controlled expenditures, and other scientific budgetary practices.

4. To protect homeowners' rights. We will insist upon strict and adequate zoning laws. There will be no duplexes, motels, or apartments illegally pushed on certain subdivisions. There will be no shanty towns and no faulty home construction below subdivision and zoning standards. We will oppose the rezoning of any residential area for light or heavy industrial use.

5. To provide adequate police protection for your home and your business and to ensure safety of school children.

6. To continue and enlarge your parks and recreation program.

7. To improve the condition of our neglected streets and to secure better and safer traffic control.

This, then, is the pattern of suburban politics. It may be a jumble of amateur politicians fighting for control and attention, or it may be an organization led by a strong leader such as J. Russel Sprague or Orville L. Hubbard, for the conditions exist for this type of system, too. Most of all, the suburbanite wants an "efficient," economical, honest, conservative government that gives him the services he wants, when he wants them, at less cost than he would have to pay in the core city.

CHAPTER 7

THE LAW OF MUNICIPALITIES

Americans have a penchant for discussing problems of public policy in terms of constitutional law rather than in terms of public policy. This is particularly true in municipal affairs, for the legal position of the city is one of lowest priority: "The city is a political subdivision of the state, created as a convenient agency for the exercise of such of the governmental powers of the state as may be intrusted to it."[1]

May a city perform whatever functions a substantial proportion of its residents want to have performed? Not at all. It may perform only those functions that the state legislature or the state courts allow it.

THE CITY AS A CORPORATION

The Problem of Sufficient Authority: A Case Study. Let us suppose that the city council wishes to eliminate a group of ugly billboards that surround a city park. The council recognizes that the billboards are destroying the natural beauty of the park and that people use the park in order to get away from the prosaic, hurried, commercialized world of everyday. The council has had numerous complaints about the billboards, and a majority of the members promised in their campaigns for election to vote them out of existence. Is this sufficient justification for council action? Certainly not.

Before any action can be taken effectively, these questions, and perhaps many more, might have to be answered: Does the city charter authorize regulation of billboards? And because the legal mind is razor-sharp and hence capable of splitting hairs, the further question, perhaps: Does the city charter authorize regulation of billboards *on the periphery of public parks?* If the city charter does authorize regulation, is there a contravening general act of the legislature? Is such regulation, in any case, *reasonable?* Would it somehow violate the state or Federal constitution? Would this particular regulation constitute, according to the common law, an *abuse of discretion* by the council? And is the proposed ordinance for a *public purpose?* Before World War I, roughly speaking,

[1] *Trenton v. New Jersey*, 262 U.S. 182 (1923). This is the standard rule, and its substance may be found repeated in dozens of cases.

regulation of billboards was considered by the courts an invasion of the rights of private property.[2] Then the courts began to allow regulation on the basis of the police power.[3]

In order for a city ordinance regulating billboards to be valid, it must be shown that such regulation is necessary to the safety and welfare of the people. The city must show that a rickety billboard might topple over on an unsuspecting pedestrian, or that a billboard might well be used as a place of ambush by a rapist, or that a billboard might serve to collect flammable newspapers and leaves.

It was not until 1935 that a high court was willing to allow regulation of billboards on a simple basis of aesthetics in the public interest. "Grandeur and beauty of scenery," the Supreme Judicial Court of Massachusetts said, "contribute highly important factors to the public welfare." This concept, while gaining in recognition, has not become the generally accepted rule.[4] Note the skepticism of an Illinois judge: "Authorities in general agree to the essentials of a public health program, while the public view as to what is necessary for aesthetic progress greatly varies. Certain legislatures might consider that it was more important to cultivate a taste for jazz than for Beethoven, for posters than for Rembrandt, and for limericks than for Keats. Successive city councils might never agree as to what the public needs from an aesthetic standpoint, and this fact makes the aesthetic standard impractical as a standard for use restriction upon property."[5] The judge said, in effect, that he can determine better than can the council the point at which the public interest becomes more important than the private interest.

If all of the many questions that may be raised can be answered in a satisfactory manner, the city may, perhaps after paying expensive court costs, proceed with its drive to eliminate the offensive billboards. Such are the limitations under which city government must operate.

The Nature of a Corporation.[6] The city, in lawyer's language, is a

---

[2] *Massachusetts v. Boston Advertising Company*, 188 Mass. 348 (1905); *New York ex rel. Wineburgh v. Murphy*, 195 N.Y. 126 (1909); and other cases. See also Illinois Legislative Council, *Regulation of Billboards* (1953), pp. 17–20.

[3] The *police power* is usually defined as the power of the state to "protect the health, safety, and morals" of society. See *St. Louis Gunning Advertising Company v. St. Louis*, 235 Mo. 99 (1911) and nearly all subsequent cases where billboard regulation was upheld.

[4] *General Outdoor Advertising Company v. Massachusetts Department of Public Works*, 193 N.E. 799 (1935).

[5] *Forbes v. Hubbard*, 180 N.E. 767 (1932). In accord with this more common opinion, see *Youngstown v. Kahn Brothers Building Company*, 148 N. E. 842 (1925); and *Wondrak v. Kelley*, 195 N.E. 65 (1935).

[6] The most current of the outstanding commentaries on municipal corporation law is Eugene McQuillin, *The Law of Municipal Corporations* (3d ed., 1949). Held in even higher esteem by legal authorities, but now partially outdated, is John F. Dillon, *Commentaries on the Law of Municipal Corporations* (5th ed., 1911). Much illus-

municipal corporation. A corporation, in turn, is an artificial *person* created by the state. In this sense, the city is something of a cross between the national or state governments on the one hand and the private corporation on the other. It differs from both, however. In theory, both the United States and the states are *sovereign*, or at least share sovereignty. A sovereign body is one possessing supreme temporal power, a state that owes allegiance to no one. Actually, of course, neither the United States nor any of the states possesses full and true sovereignty. The plenary powers of government are divided in a federal system in such a manner that the ancient concept becomes somewhat obscured. It is perfectly clear, however, that cities, villages, and other municipal corporations possess no sovereignty at all. They are children of the state, created usually by the action of the state legislature; and even in those states most dedicated to the principle of home rule, the *state* courts remain the final arbiters of what are local concerns.[7]

The municipality, like any other corporation, derives its powers from the state, and those powers granted to it are expressed in a *charter*. A charter is the fundamental law of a corporation which establishes (1) the structure or form of government, (2) the powers that may be exercised by it, and (3) the general manner in which the powers granted may be exercised. The charter is almost never a single document, but includes all state laws and judicial opinions that affect the structure, powers, or manner of exercising the powers of the corporation.

The city, in some respects, has a legal position not unlike that of a private corporation. In fact, it has been only in the last two centuries or so that a definite distinction has developed. The two are still similar in that each has an existence independent of the members of the corporation, may own property, may make contracts, may exist, normally, in perpetuity, and may sue and be sued. They possess very important differences, too. A private corporation is created entirely by the *voluntary* request of a group of people who wish to form a corporation. They know the corporation law in advance and hence know the conditions under which they will operate. Furthermore, once the corporation charter is granted it becomes a *contract* which cannot be altered or taken away (except under the rarest circumstances involving an overriding public interest).[8] A public corporation, on the other hand, may be created with or without the consent of its membership (the persons living in the area), the terms of its charter may be quite different from what the people of

---

trated material may be found in such casebooks as Murray Seasongood, *Cases on Municipal Corporations* (1941), and J. B. Fordham, *Local Government Law—Text, Cases and Other Materials* (1949).

[7] See section on home rule, pp. 152–161.

[8] The contract could be altered or taken away, of course, if provision for this existed in the contract itself.

the community desire, and, even more important, the charter is *not* a contract and is hence subject to constant, involuntary, and sometimes arbitrary changes. It can even be taken away without advance notice, unless the state constitution specifically prohibits this.

There are two other important differences between public and private corporations. A public corporation can act only in the *public* interest and for a public purpose. A private corporation must always have the public interest in mind (one could not long exist, for example, if it were organized for the purpose of robbing banks), but it may also have private interests (such as profit making for the individual owners). The two also differ in the amount of control the state exercises over them. A private corporation can carry on any activities it wishes, so long as it does not violate some law; a public corporation can do only those things that it is authorized to do. A corporation producing cigarettes, for example, could take on a side line of producing, say, plowshares without seeking an amendment to its charter or any other kind of permission from the state. (It could not, however, put in a side line of marijuana cigarettes, since this would not be in the public interest and could be curbed by the state under its police powers.) A municipal, or public, corporation, on the other hand, could not decide to enter into such side lines as, say, municipal parking lots or a municipal theater or to adopt a new form of taxation without having first the specific authority to do so.

The Elements of a Corporation. What are the elements necessary in order to have a municipal corporation? Stated by McQuillin in the language of the law, they are:[9]

1. Incorporation as such pursuant to the constitution of the state or to a statute.
2. A charter.
3. A population and prescribed area within which the local civil government and corporate functions are exercised. However, the inhabitants of the municipality are not a separate legal entity and do not themselves constitute the municipality, and the common council or other governing body of the municipal officers does not constitute the corporation.
4. Consent of the inhabitants of the territory to the creation of the corporation, with certain exceptions [actually, the legislature in most states may act without consulting the local residents].
5. A corporate name.
6. The right of local self-government, although in most states this is held to be not an inherent right.[10] Unless otherwise provided by statute, a test as to whether an organization is a municipal corporation, using the term in its strict sense, is whether it has the power of local government as distinguished from

[9] McQuillin, *op. cit.*, vol. I, sec. 2.07. By permission of Callaghan and Company.
[10] This is an example of the cautious legal mind. It is safe to say that in *no* state is the concept of local self-government as an inherent right legally acceptable. See above, chap. 3.

merely possessing powers which are merely executive and administrative in their character. The characteristic feature of a municipal corporation beyond all others is the power and right of local self-government.

The Corporation and the Quasi Corporation. In the above passage, McQuillin suggests that there may be local units of government that are not in the strict sense municipal corporations. He is referring to a legal distinction that is made between corporations and quasi corporations. The former includes cities, villages, and the relatively few *incorporated* (under a separate written charter) counties and school districts. The latter includes most of the counties, townships, unincorporated New England towns, and the so-called special districts such as sewage-disposal, airport, drainage, mosquito-abatement, fire, and irrigation districts.[11]

So far as the lay citizen is concerned, the principal distinction between genuine corporations and quasi corporations is to be found in the fact that quasi corporations serve only as an administrative agent of the state—while the true municipal corporation serves a dual purpose. It not only acts as a local agent for the state, but also performs certain local functions exclusively in the interests of the people living within the corporate boundaries of the city.

In theory, the city acts as an agent of the state whenever it performs a function in which the state as a whole has a certain interest; for example, when it enforces the law, or maintains public health standards, or collects taxes. On the other hand, the city may perform some tasks purely for the comfort and convenience of the local inhabitants, in theory at least. In this classification we find such things as the operation of a water-supply system or a street railway. Counties and school districts, in contrast, perform only such functions of state-wide interest as the maintenance of records, the prosecution of crimes, the maintenance of roads, and the education of children.

Since the city acts in a dual capacity, it is said that the city performs two types of functions, *governmental* (as an agent of the state) and *proprietary* (as an agent of the local inhabitants and for their comfort and convenience). This distinction is less important for laymen than it is for lawyers. As will be seen later, the line of demarcation is in any event difficult to draw, is an artificial legalism, and has probably created more problems than it has solved. Property owned for carrying on governmental functions is in theory held for the state, which may dispose of it without consulting the city and without payment to it. On the other hand, property owned by the city for carrying on its proprietary functions cannot ordinarily be taken by the state without compensation, on the theory that constitutional guarantees of property rights extend to property

[11] The special districts are discussed in chap. 11.

held by the city in its proprietary capacity.[12] The same distinction is followed in the law of municipal-tort liability.[13]

Powers of the Corporation. The subordinate legal status of cities makes it necessary that the question of whether or not a particular city has the power to perform a particular function in a particular way must be decided by the courts. Because the city is merely a creature of the state while the state itself is a sovereign body, the courts have established a rule of a narrow construction of municipal powers and a broad construction of state powers. To put it another way, the courts say that, if in doubt, the city does *not* have the power to do something it wishes to do. The authority that is almost invariably cited by courts in support of this interpretation is the famous *Dillon's rule*. John F. Dillon, a renowned Iowa judge and author, summarized the legal position of cities in the following words:[14]

It is a general and undisputed proposition of law that a *municipal corporation possesses and can exercise the following powers, and no others:* First, those granted in *express words;* second, those *necessarily or fairly implied* in or *incident* to the powers expressly granted; third, those essential to the accomplishment of the declared objects and purposes of the corporation—not simply convenient, but indispensable. Any fair, reasonable, substantial doubt concerning the existence of power is resolved by the courts against the corporation, and the power is denied.

It is this rule that explains why a city might have to spend weeks of time and thousands of dollars in actions before the state courts seeking to justify its decision to finance a municipal parking lot from the parking-meter fund rather than from the general-revenue fund. Or seeking to find some theoretical justification for an FEPC or a smoke-abatement ordinance. That the community should demand them and that they should be adopted according to democratic procedures is not enough (see Figure 10).

It should be evident that Dillon's rule allows the courts a good deal of leeway in determining what a city may or may not do. What are necessarily or fairly implied powers? What powers are essential to "the accomplishment of the declared objects and purposes" of the city? Only the judges know. They base their decisions as much as possible on the principle of *stare decisis*,[15] of course, but much is left to their discretion. It may

---

[12] See McQuillin, *op. cit.,* vol. II, sec. 4.132. The United States Supreme Court makes no such distinction so far as the Federal Constitution is concerned. *Trenton v. New Jersey,* 262 U.S. 182 (1923).

[13] See below, pp. 166–168.

[14] Dillon, *op. cit.,* vol. I, sec. 237. By permission of Little, Brown & Company.

[15] *Stare decisis:* "let the decision stand." The basic principle of the common law under which a rule of law in one case becomes the basis for deciding subsequent cases that are the same in essence.

Ridiculous, Isn't It?

Fig. 10. Most of America's wealth is to be found in its cities. Yet because they are creatures of the state, city governments can normally raise taxes only as the state permits. SOURCE: By permission of Frank Williams and the *Detroit Free Press*.

be implied, for example, that a city may offer a reward for the arrest and conviction of an *ordinance*[16] violator, but not for the violator of a state law, even for the murderer of the city's chief of police.[17] An implied power

[16] Legally an ordinance has a lower priority rating than a law. Laws are enacted by sovereign institutions. Ordinances, in theory, simply clarify or apply laws. City councils cannot enact laws, except where they have special constitutional authority to do so.

[17] Compare *Choice v. Dallas,* 210 S.W. 753 (1919), and *Madry v. Scotland Neck,* 199 S.E. 618 (1938).

may vary greatly from one state to another. For example, it *cannot* be implied from anything in the Cleveland charter that the city has the right to spend its money in order to send councilmen to the state capital as lobbyists,[18] but it *can* be implied from the Minneapolis charter that aldermen may be sent to attend meetings of the Rivers and Harbors Congress in Washington.[19]

Creation and Dissolution of the Corporation. Cities and villages are normally created upon the receipt of a *charter*. The charter may be granted in any one of several different ways.[20] It is also possible, however, for a municipality to be created in other ways. The people of a city might *think* that the community is incorporated and act accordingly over a long period of time, only to discover later—perhaps years later—that there was somehow a mistake made when it was "incorporated" and that the precise requirements of the law were not met. In such a case, it would be unreasonable to try to undo all of the presumed legal acts that the city had committed up to that time. The courts, therefore, provided that the legislature has in the meantime treated the supposed city as if it were indeed a city, will say that the area is a municipal corporation *de facto* (in fact), even though not *de jure* (in law).[21]

Some years ago, the Minnesota Supreme Court discovered that when the state constitution granted a city the power to "frame a charter for its own government," it meant that it could do so only once and that subsequent changes would have to be in the form of amendments and not in a completely new charter.[22] This bit of divination had the immediate effect of changing every home rule city not using an amended form of its original from a *de jure* to a *de facto* corporation. The people living in the affected cities were not seriously shaken by the development; in fact, they were hardly aware of any difference.[23]

Some cities and villages flourish, and others become "ghost towns." There are deserted shacks that once represented cities and villages in the mining areas of the mountain and Pacific states, in the timbering regions of Minnesota, Wisconsin, and New England, and in the hill country of North Carolina and Tennessee. There are decaying crossroads trading centers throughout the nation—victims of the automobile, the telephone, and the migratory movement toward the large cities. It sometimes hap-

---

[18] *Cleveland v. Artl*, 23 N.E. 2d 525 (1939).

[19] *Tousley v. Leach*, 230 N.W. 788 (1930).

[20] See below, p. 145 ff.

[21] *Tulare Irrigation District v. Shepard*, 185 U.S. 1 (1901).

[22] *Leighton v. Abell*, 31 N.W. 2d 646 (1948). This highly technical decision destroyed the results of months of effort by the Minneapolis Charter Commission.

[23] Municipalities may also be created by implication or prescription. See Charles M. Kneier and Guy Fox, *Readings in Municipal Government and Administration* (1953), pp. 32–34, and McQuillin, *op. cit.*, vol. II, sec. 7.09.

pens, therefore, that an incorporated municipality loses its original need for a charter. The question arises as to when a municipality ceases to be a corporation.

In actual practice, when a community becomes so depopulated as no longer to need a municipal government, it usually simply stops electing officers, collecting taxes, and functioning as a municipality. In legal theory, however, the corporation does not cease to exist merely because it is not functioning. It has simply gone into hibernation, from which it can reawaken at any time by resuming its activities. Permanent destruction of the creature that was created by the state can be accomplished only under the laws established by the state. Formal dissolution normally takes place after a petition by a sufficient number of residents, either to the municipal council or to a designated court. Depending upon the state, the council or court then either orders dissolution or provides for a popular referendum on the issue. It is also possible for a corporation to be dissolved by being wholly absorbed by another corporation or by a specific act of the state legislature. Whenever a corporation ceases to exist, its debts must be settled, its property disposed of, and other administrative details cleaned up. These minutiae are accomplished according to state law.

Charters: General and Special Act. While the concept of the city as a corporation dates back to Roman times, and noblemen granted charters of special privileges to unincorporated cities of Europe as early as the eleventh century, the modern practice of incorporating urban communities and prescribing their powers did not appear in England until the fourteenth century.[24] Often these charters merely legalized the informal situations that already existed. In any case, the Crown (or an important lord or colonial governor) began to grant special charters *wherein the specific city to be incorporated was named and its powers enumerated.* This plan became the standard practice in England, on the continent of Europe, and in the British colonies of North America.

It was not until the French Revolution that the *general charter* came into use. As one of the reforms of 1789, the French established *a general municipal code to apply to all communes, giving them equal status and powers.* From that time on, the use of the general charter became standard in European democracies, although the pattern was somewhat modified in the United Kingdom, where the general laws were often supplemented by special laws and administrative ("provisional") orders granting special powers to particular municipalities.

[24] A good general survey of the history of city charters may be found in W. B. Munro, *Municipal Government and Administration* (1923), chap. 9. Further useful reading includes S. Griffith, *The History of American City Government: The Colonial Period* (1938); E. Martz, *How Colonial Cities Grew* (1939); (for Europe) H. Pirenne, *Medieval Cities* (1925), and C. Stephenson, *Borough and Town* (1933).

The Special Act Charter. The special charter plan, inherited from the mother country, was standard practice in the American colonies and remained so until well past the middle of the nineteenth century. In 1851, Ohio, and a few months later, Indiana, outlawed special legislation, including special act charters of incorporation.[25] The following century produced a series of attempts to eliminate or modify the use of the special act charter. The major objection to its use was to be found in the tendency of the legislature to substitute its own desires for those of a locally elected city council on important matters of public policy. In theory, there was nothing wrong with the special act: it provided a tailor-made charter to fit the special circumstances of the particular city. In actual practice, however, the legislature often refused to allow local governments to run their own affairs. Local urban dwellers, therefore, sought to find ways of retaining or recapturing local control.

Where special legislation was not completely outlawed, an attempt was made after about 1870 to allow it only after due notice had been given that the legislature was considering changes in the fundamental law of a city and after an open hearing at which interested persons and groups could testify. This plan was modeled on the British technique. It is in use in several states, but has met with considerable success only in Massachusetts. Legislators will usually not cooperate with devices that have the effect of restricting their powers, as this plan does.

In a few states, special legislation was permitted only if the proposed legislation received local approval. The New York constitution of 1894, for example, allowed special legislation if the proposal, after passage in the general assembly, was approved by the mayor in a first-class city (New York, Rochester, and Buffalo) or by the mayor and council in other cities. The bill would then go to the governor for his consideration in the usual manner. If disapproved either locally or by the governor, it could be repassed by the legislature and become law nonetheless. The New York plan appears to have given considerable protection to localities, although quite a few bills continued to be passed despite local disapproval.[26] The adoption of home rule in 1923 made the plan obsolete.

An amendment to the Illinois constitution in 1904 sought to give Chicago some protection for its local self-rule. It provided for a referendum on all special legislation applying to Chicago. The plan had the effect of protecting Chicago from what it did not want, but it provided for no method by which the city could obtain what it did want.[27] As a result, the provision has had little use, and the Chicago charter is seldom amended.

[25] The abuses of excessive state legislative control over cities, and attempts to curb these abuses, are discussed in chap. 3 above.

[26] H. L. McBain, *The Law and the Practice of Municipal Home Rule* (1916), gives a detailed account.

[27] As has been pointed out in Munro, *op. cit.*, pp. 180–181.

Some states outlawed special acts only if it was possible for a general act to "be made to apply" to the situation. This rule contained a loophole that could be discovered by even the dullest legislator. Since the courts are normally inclined to resolve doubts in favor of the action of law-makers, a pretense could almost always be found to argue that a given situation could not possibly be met by general legislation.

It should not be assumed that special legislation is in itself an evil. In Iowa, when special act charters were used, "the people of the local community not only had in many instances a considerable share in formulating their charters in accordance with local needs, but they also had in effect authority to amend their charters. Special charter cities had little difficulty in securing amendments from the legislature. . . . While such charters and their amendments were subject to legislative control, the records do not show the existence of a meddlesome attitude on the part of the General Assembly."[28] But the picture was, and is, different in other states, and it aroused considerable urban resentment.

Despite its unpopularity in urban communities, special legislation continues in use. It is to be found especially in New England and the South, particularly in Alabama, Florida, Maryland, North Carolina, Tennessee, and, at least prior to the adoption of its postwar constitution, Georgia. In Maryland, for example, 70 per cent of the bills passed by the 1951 legislature were local in character. About one-half of the states are constitutionally authorized to grant special charters or special acts, and a number of the states still employ this system either exclusively or predominantly. In more than one-half of the states, there will be found old special act charters still in existence, but no new ones are being created, either as a matter of policy or as a result of subsequent constitutional prohibition. About twelve states provide, at least in some instances, for a local referendum on new special act charters.

The General Act Charter. The general act charter, designed to provide for uniform powers, privileges, and structures for every city in the state, has not met with much real success, except where it has been modified by home rule or local option. Since American towns vary from hamlets to empires of millions of people, it is unrealistic to expect that every city government should be exactly like every other in powers and structure. There must be some variation. The failure of general acts is, however, more importantly attributable to the fact that legislators have been largely unwilling to vacate traditional areas of authority over local government. They have sought for loopholes of evasion and have met with a success that forces one to pause and admire their resourcefulness.

Constitutionally required use of general legislation has been circum-

[28] George F. Robeson, *The Government of Special Charter Cities in Iowa* (1923), p. 178.

vented by three techniques, principally by the passage of laws that purport to be general but are not in fact; by the erection of special districts other than cities; and by prostituting the classification device. If special legislation is prohibited, the question arises: What *is* special legislation? The answer, of course, must come from the courts. Following the general rule of a broad construction of legislative powers of the sovereign state, the courts have hesitated to rule against the legislature. Most of the state high courts have therefore been willing to allow as "general" any legislation that *on the surface* appears to be general, or any legislation that may *potentially* apply to another city, even though at the moment it affects only one. In one case, pointed out by Munro,[29] the Ohio legislature, despite a constitutional prohibition against special legislation, passed an act applying to "any city having within its limits an avenue more than 100 feet wide known as Lincoln Avenue." Is this special legislation? Not at all. Practically any city could qualify if it chose to build such a street. If, however, the legislators had added "on January 1, 1900," or some such prohibitive qualification, the supreme court would almost be forced to void it. In point of fact, however, it has been easy to achieve special legislation without judicial proscription.

Another method of avoiding the ban on special legislation has been by establishing special districts: for parks and recreation, sewage disposal, police, and the like. This has been possible because the prohibition on special legislation applied only against "municipal corporations" or "cities."

Some state constitutions, while outlawing special legislation, did recognize that, say, the city of New York and the village of Au Sable Forks in the northern lakes country of the state could not be treated adequately with the same legislation, and therefore permitted the *classification* of cities. In some states the constitution set up the classifications, in others it authorized the legislature to do so, and in a third group of states, where the constitution was silent, the courts permitted the legislature to classify, holding this to be general legislation. Whatever the source of authority for classification, it was permitted because it was generally recognized that the equal treatment of all cities, large and small, was impractical. General acts did not allow for unique problems.

In some states, for example in Wisconsin in the last quarter of a century, classification legislation has been used sparingly and for valid purposes. In other states, however, the legislators have deliberately sought to use the classification device as a disguise for special legislation. Sometimes the courts have insisted that classifications be reasonable, but in most cases they have been tolerant when the legislators resorted to subterfuges. True, the courts did on occasion prohibit some types of

[29] Munro, *op. cit.*, p. 178.

classifications, especially those using a *geographical,* rather than a population, basis,[30] but the lawmakers usually had their way. Classification made it particularly easy to pass special legislation for the largest cities.

In Pennsylvania the three largest cities were each placed in a separate class, while in Ohio the *eleven* largest cities at one time stood each in its own class.[31] Although some classification is necessary because the problems and needs of large cities are not the same as those of small cities, state legislatures under the guise of classification have deprived the larger cities in many states of much of their powers of local self-government.

Classification in Indiana: an Illustration. The Hoosier state was second in outlawing special legislation in 1851—following Ohio by only a few months. Together with Arkansas and Louisiana, it was one of three states which in 1954 still did not permit the council-manager plan. It has neither home rule for municipalities nor optional charters. Instead, Indiana operates under a system of general act charters imposed upon the hundred-odd cities of the state in accordance with a classification system based upon population. The inhabitants of each city have no choice at all in the type of government they are to have, either as to structure, powers, or functions. For example, cities of the second class have prescribed for them a common council of nine members, three elected at large and six by districts. The structure is that of the strong-mayor system, but the clerk and treasurer must be elective officials.

There are five classes of cities in Indiana, divided as follows after the 1950 census:

	Population	Number
Cities		
First class.............	250,000 and over	Indianapolis only
Second class...........	35,000–250,000	13
Third class............	20,000–35,000	6
Fourth class...........	10,000–20,000	19
Fifth class.............	2,000–10,000	91
Towns*................	Under 2,000	About 433

* Small nonrural communities in Indiana may simply be part of the local township, but if they incorporate they become "towns" until they have a population of 2,000.

[30] The *form of government* (commission, council-manager, home rule charter, etc.) is sometimes used as a basis, as are other criteria.

[31] After classification had been reduced to an absurdity in Ohio, the Supreme Court belatedly outlawed *all* classification in *State of Ohio ex rel. Knisely v. Jones,* 64 N.E. 424 (1902). The legislature then unsuccessfully attempted to treat all cases alike. The dilemma was resolved in 1912 with the introduction into the state of municipal home rule.

General Act Charters: Cafeteria Style. In those states without home rule or special act charters, it has been necessary to devise some way of meeting the particular needs of particular cities. Variations in needs occur in connection with both powers and forms of government. A large city might want the strong-mayor form, a middle-sized city the council-manager, and a village the traditional weak-mayor. In order to meet these variants, some states have adopted *optional charter laws.* More than one-half of them make use of this device, with about one-third of them using it as the principal source of city charters.

Under this plan, upon petition of a prescribed number of voters, or by resolution of the council, the council or the voters of a city may decide which *form* of government they wish to adopt. They are limited in choice, of course, to the type of options the legislature provides. There may be two or three basic charters, or five, as in Massachusetts, or as many as fourteen, as in New Jersey. The people of the city may go through the cafeteria line, picking from among the offerings set out by the state. They may take only those things offered, however, and without variations or alterations. There can be no substitutions on the menu. This plan is convenient for the state, and it offers some real choices as to type of government, although the *powers* that the city is authorized are normally much less variable. The plan is gaining in popularity in the United States. Of course, the legislature still determines the structure of government for each city, and *all* amendments to charters must still be obtained from the state,[32] but the local population at least can determine whether it prefers a more modern structure of government than the weak-mayor form, for example, or perhaps whether it wants the council-manager form with or without an added provision for proportional representation.[33] A liberal optional charter plan, such as that of New Jersey, may be a very satisfactory method of bestowing charters.

[32] In several home rule states, charters originally granted by general (or special) acts of the legislature may subsequently be amended by the home rule process.

[33] Because variations are so great from one state to another, each student will have to do some independent research in order to get a picture of the situation in his own state. At this point, it might be well for the student to attempt to answer the following questions: Does *your* state have a constitutional provision seeking to control special legislation? If so, what limits does it attempt to set? What has been its *practical* effect upon legislative action measured in terms of judicial decisions? Are there any cities in your state operating under special act charters? Does the legislature create or amend special act charters by special acts (either openly or by subterfuge)? Does your state have a system for *classification* of cities? If so, is it established by constitutional provision or legislative policy? Is the *number* of permitted classes determined in the constitution? Are the specific classifications themselves set out in the constitution (as they are, for example, in Kentucky)? How many classes are there? If there are more than four, can the large number of them be reasonably justified? Does your state have both a classification system and municipal home rule? If so, what is the purpose of this arrangement? Does the state have an optional charter law? If so, what are the options? Are some options preferred more often than others? Why? Is there a *pattern* of adoptions (by size of cities, location, or other criteria)?

Appraisal. Efforts to prevent or reduce legislative interference with local self-government have been made through such devices as the constitutional prohibition of special legislation, constitutional control of classification of cities, and the use of the optional charter plan. These efforts have met with only limited success. The legislature remains paramount, and its members have found it relatively easy to legislate for specific cities whenever they have desired to do so.

But in seeking to grant independence to cities, advocates of general legislation tended to minimize the fact that cities do have unique requirements that must be met by specific legislation. As a matter of fact, no state today has a single general act to cover the powers, functions, and structure of all of its cities.

While legal safeguards against legislative meddling were circumvented by imaginative legislators, often with the cooperation of the courts, and while legislative meddling in local affairs is still excessive in several states, notably in the South, the legislatures of an increasing number of states have, as a matter of public policy, given the people of cities a good deal of autonomy in local affairs. In some states, home rule has helped provide considerable local autonomy. This is especially true in California, Michigan, and Wisconsin, as well as perhaps Minnesota and Texas. Optional laws work reasonably well in many states, enabling cities to modify their forms of government as to details, and sometimes such laws establish permissive, as distinguished from mandatory, legislation which each locality may avail itself of as it sees fit. This is especially true in Wisconsin, Washington, and Nevada.

It should also be noted that some types of state control and supervision have been helpful to cities and not harmful. Furthermore, in many cases city officials, instead of chafing under the existing degree of state controls, approve of this control or are unconcerned with it.

If local self-government is to prosper, legislative action should be limited to the protection of the genuine and legitimate interests of the state at large. While progress has been very uneven if one compares the experiences of the various states, the direction of trend in the twentieth century has been toward this goal.[34]

It is important to remember, however, that cities will inevitably be

---

[34] See Hallie Farmer, "Special Legislation and Home Rule," *The University of Tennessee Record,* vol. 51 (January, 1948), pp. 7–10; reprinted in Kneier and Fox, *op. cit.,* pp. 85–88.

On the general topic of legislative control over cities, the standard reference is still H. L. McBain, *The Law and the Practice of Municipal Home Rule* (1916). The best recent discussion is the Council of State Governments, *State-Local Relations* (1946). Useful cases and articles are reprinted in Kneier and Fox, *op. cit.,* pp. 75–88.

An old article, still useful, is Harry Hubbard, "Special Legislation for Cities," *Harvard Law Review,* vol. 18 (June, 1905), pp. 588–604. For Nebraska as a case study: A. C. Breckenridge, "The Mockery of Classification," *National Municipal Review,* vol. 36 (November, 1947), pp. 571–573.

subject to a great deal of legislative control. Nearly every function performed by them affects the people of the state as a whole. In a day of large economic units and rapid means of transportation and communication, it is impossible and undesirable, in any case, for the cities to isolate themselves. Furthermore, there is no natural cleavage between state and local interests and functions. Because one tends to grow out of the other gradually, the state and its cities must of necessity learn to work together and avoid feuding with each other.

Charters: Municipal Home Rule.[35] As towns were founded in colonial Rhode Island, "the local communities . . . organized and managed their own local affairs and services. Each town retained its own individuality and functioned to a great degree without reference to any higher authority, except for those few laws which were commonly accepted by all communities."[36] It was not until after the Revolutionary War that the general assembly of Rhode Island, together with the legislatures of other states, began to enforce claims of sovereign and plenary powers over matters of local concern. In the new United States, the earlier idea that local communities should be left alone as much as possible all but disappeared. Municipal home rule charters represent a somewhat romantic attempt to return to an earlier situation that is often pictured as ideal. The home rule movement was another device that won the support of early-twentieth-century reformers in their drive to free the local community from the all-powerful grasp of the state legislature.

Municipal home rule, which is a genuinely indigenous Americanism, may be defined as the power granted to municipal corporations to frame, adopt, and amend a charter for their government and to exercise all powers of local self-government, subject to the constitution and general laws of the state.[37] Home rule may be provided for in the state constitution or simply by enabling acts of the state legislature. It may be available to all cities and villages (e.g., Oregon and Wisconsin), or only those

[35] The two basic reference books on municipal home rule are: H. L. McBain, *The Law and the Practice of Municipal Home Rule* (1916); and J. D. McGoldrick, *Law and Practice of Municipal Home Rule, 1916–1930* (1933). The story of the origin of home rule in Missouri is told in T. S. Barclay, *The Movement for Municipal Home Rule in St. Louis* (1943). A series on "What Municipal Home Rule Means Today" gives a picture of the situation in ten states some two decades ago, in vol. 21 (January–December, 1932) of the *National Municipal Review*.

A more recent argument for home rule is found in Rodney L. Mott, *Home Rule for America's Cities* (1949), which summarizes developments to that time. Students should also read the skeptical appraisal by Harvey Walker, "Let Cities Manage Themselves," *National Municipal Review*, vol. 36 (December, 1946), pp. 625–630. The title of this article is misleading. Other material is given in Kneier and Fox, *op. cit.*, chap. 4.

[36] Robert J. M. O'Hare, "Cities Rush Home Rule Gate," *National Municipal Review*, vol. 42 (February, 1953), pp. 73–77.

[37] This definition is based upon the home-rule provisions of the constitution of Ohio, art. 18. The term "general laws" does not apply in a few home rule states.

of over a certain population (e.g., California and Colorado), or to a very limited number of cities (e.g., three in Louisiana, eleven in Washington by the 1950 census, and Baltimore alone in Maryland). It may be a self-executing provision of the state constitution (e.g., Arizona and Nebraska), or it may require legislation before a city can avail itself of the authorization (e.g., Texas and Wisconsin).[38] It may be used by many municipalities in the state (e.g., in Oregon and Michigan), or by relatively few of them (e.g., in Ohio, Missouri, and West Virginia).

The coming of home rule produced a very important difference in the procedure for securing charters and subsequent amendments to them. Under the older system of special and general act charters, a charter is secured through the process of lobbying before the legislature, and *every amendment* to the charter must be secured through the method of sending city officials and other interested persons to the state capital to harangue, threaten, and bargain with legislators. Under home rule, this is not necessary: the amendment is proposed (usually) by the council and is voted upon by the eligible voters. Under general act charters of either the classification or optional charter type, a city that lobbies for an amendment may find itself in the peculiar position of being opposed by another city in the same class or using the same option. This never happens under home rule.

Framing a Charter. The procedural rules for drawing up a new charter or making major revisions in an old one vary, of course, from state to state. In states having self-executing constitutional home rule, the procedures are outlined in the constitution itself. About one-half of them do not go into these extensive details, however, but simply authorize the legislature to make the rules. The constitution of Wisconsin, for example, provides simply that "The method . . . shall be prescribed by the legislature."[39] All states operating under legislative home rule, of course, use procedures established by the legislature.

The common procedure is for the people of the city to elect a charter commission. In Minnesota, the commission is rather illogically appointed by the local district judge, while in Oregon the city council acts as the charter commission, or a charter may be presented through the procedure of the initiative. The commission is usually given a certain length of time in which to draft a charter for submission to the voters, who must then approve (usually by a simple majority vote). It may sometimes be necessary to elect a second or third commission if the first cannot agree upon a charter or if its proposed charter is defeated at the polls. Sometimes (see

[38] For the preference of the American Municipal Association, see their Committee on Home Rule, *Model Constitutional Provisions for Municipal Home Rule* (1953); and the National Municipal League, *Model State Constitution* (1941). The former is not self-executing; the latter is.

[39] Constitution of Wisconsin, art. 11.

Tables 3 and 4), state approval is required in addition to that of the voters.

Once a home rule charter is adopted, it may be amended from time to time. In some states the charter commission is a permanent body that can propose amendments at any time (e.g., Minnesota and West Virginia), but the most common system is to have the proposals for amendment come from the city council, or through the use of the initiative. Ratification is normally by popular vote.[40]

Because of the practical effects of Dillon's rule, city charters must be lengthy, complex, and technical in some sections. (The index to the Los Angeles charter alone contains more words than does the United States Constitution.) The result is that in many home rule cities the voters are

Table 5. States with Constitutional Home Rule

State	Year adopted	Cities eligible	Cities with home rule*	Self-executing	State approval
Arizona.........	1910	Over 3500	3	Yes	Governor
California......	1896	Over 3500	57	Yes	Legislature
Colorado......	1912	Over 2000	12	Yes	None
Louisiana......	1947	Three largest	3	Partly	Governor
Maryland......	1915	Baltimore	1	Yes	None
Michigan......	1912	Each city & village	180	No	Governor
Minnesota.....	1898	Any city or village	81	No	None
Missouri.......	1875	Over 10,000	3	Yes	None
Nebraska......	1912	Over 5000	3	Yes	None
New York.....	1923	Every city	7†	No	None
Ohio..........	1912	Any municipality	33	Yes	None
Oklahoma.....	1907	Over 2000	55	Yes	Governor
Oregon........	1906	Every city or town	107†	Yes	None
Pennsylvania..	1922	Over 10,000	1	No	None
Rhode Island..	1951	All cities & towns	4	Yes	None
Tennessee.....	1953	Any municipality	0	Yes	None
Texas.........	1909	Over 5000	99	No	None
Utah..........	1932	Any city or town	0	Partly	None
Washington....	1899	Over 20,000	8	No	None
West Virginia..	1936	Over 2000	8	No	Attorney general
Wisconsin.....	1924	Cities and villages	†	No	None

* Data on number of cities with home rule are approximate.

† Numerous amendments to existing charters by home rule.

SOURCE: Adapted from Rodney L. Mott, *Home Rule for America's Cities* (1949), pp. 60–62, by permission of the American Municipal Association, and various issues of the *National Municipal Review*.

[40] Much technical detail on home-rule procedures in the various states may be found in E. B. Schulz, *American City Government* (1949), chap. 7.

constantly being called upon to consider amendments to the charter, often many of them at a single election. Furthermore, many of the proposed amendments are of minor importance, while others are highly technical. The public is often either apathetic or confused, or both. In order to overcome this handicap to the effective operation of home rule, the New York constitution has made an interesting and very desirable provision. It allows the local council to draft and *adopt* all charter amendments of a minor character without submitting them to a popular vote. If, however, there is organized opposition to the action of the council, a referendum can still force a public vote, and for certain types of amendments involving important questions of public policy the conventional type of referendum is always required. A similar rule applies in Wisconsin, while Oregon and West Virginia (for third-class cities) allow charter amendment without popular vote under certain conditions. There is much merit in these methods, for they reduce the length of the already overcrowded ballot and remove some, at least, of the technical amendments from decision by the voters.

Table 6. States with Legislative Home Rule

State*	Year adopted	Cities eligible	State approval
Connecticut.............	1951	Any city, town, borough	None
Florida.................	1915	Every city and town	None
Iowa...................	1858	Special charter cities	None
Mississippi.............	1900	Special charter cities	Governor
Nevada.................	1924	Any city or town	None
North Carolina..........	1917	Any municipality	None
South Carolina..........	1899	Any city or town	None
Virginia................	1920	Any city over 50,000 population	Legislature

* Some of these states allow only the amendment of existing charters. Others allow only a suggestion of home rule—for example, by allowing a local charter commission to draw up the charter, which is then submitted to the legislature in the form of a recommendation and may be adopted by it with or without amendments, or may be rejected.

SOURCE: Rodney L. Mott, *Home Rule for America's Cities* (1949), pp. 60–62; N. N. Gill and M. S. Benson, "Classes and Forms of Municipal Government," *Municipal Year Book, 1945*, pp. 90–123; and various issues of the *National Municipal Review*.

The Origin and Spread of Home Rule. Like so many American political institutions, including the United States Constitution itself, municipal home rule had its origins in the expedient actions of practical politicians. The first state to establish a version of it was Iowa, which did so under an 1851 act of the legislature. After operating since territorial days under the special act charter system, the legislature in that year established a single method of charter adoption for newly incorporated communities or for towns desiring to become cities. If the inhabitants decided to incorporate, the law provided that an election would be held to choose persons to prepare a charter. The legislature provided the general limits of authority that could be granted by the charter, but these were broad. The charter, once written, was submitted to the voters for approval or disapproval.[41]

Unfortunately, this unique and liberal law was not given a full opportunity to show its merit and hence was not actually the beginning of the home rule movement. Few uses seem to have been made of it. Most of Iowa's municipalities had already been established by earlier special charters. In 1858 the law was repealed, for the new Iowa constitution adopted the preceding year followed the contemporary fashion and required the use of a general incorporation act. However, the new law allowed the already existing city charters to be amended locally, and the four remaining cities to which this applies still exercise this privilege.[42]

The Missouri constitutional convention of 1875 furnished the stage for the first provision for *constitutional* home rule. The people and politicians of St. Louis had long been dissatisfied with legislative oversight of the city government and the need to secure the approval of the legislature to any changes in the fundamental law of the city. The St. Louis delegation, therefore, came to the convention with a set of proposals for the government of the city, including one for what is now known as home rule. This plan was included in the constitution and was adopted by the voters of the state, although home rule was restricted to St. Louis at that time. The reform period that followed helped to spread the idea of home rule throughout much of the nation.

Home Rule Today. In 1954, home rule was provided for in the constitutions of twenty-one states, was actually in use in some cities of all but two of these, and in eight other states was provided by legislative act, without constitutional authorization or safeguards.[43] Of the cities of the United States with populations of over 200,000, some two-thirds have home rule. It is in these larger cities, of course, that home rule charters to meet unique situations are most important. Of the ten largest cities in the nation, only Chicago, Boston, and Pittsburgh do not have home rule. The movement, which appeared to have spent itself with the decline of the

[41] State of Iowa, *Code of 1851*, chap. 42. For even earlier antecedents for home rule, especially in New York, see H. L. McBain, *American City Progress and the Law* (1918), pp. 22–29.

[42] George F. Robeson, *The Government of Special Charter Cities in Iowa* (1923), pp. 178–180.

[43] Based upon Mott, *op. cit.*, and, since 1949, reports in the *National Municipal Review*. See Tables 5 and 6.

reform spirit after World War I, enjoyed a revival after World War II with the granting of home rule for the first time to Baton Rouge, Philadelphia, and potentially to all cities and towns in Tennessee, Connecticut, and Rhode Island.[44] In Rhode Island the home rule amendment was adopted in June, 1951. By November, 1952, seven home rule charters had been written, four of which were adopted by the voters.[45] The Connecticut law appears to be unworkable in practice, however, unless it is further amended.

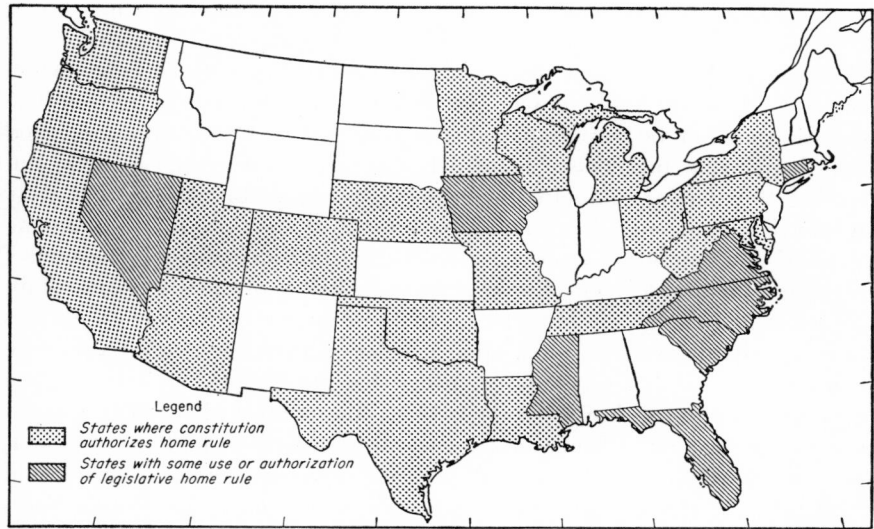

Fig. 11. The use of home rule. SOURCE: Chiefly, R. L. Mott, *Home Rule for America's Cities* (1949), pp. 60–62. Used by permission of the American Municipal Association.

A 1953 amendment to the Tennessee constitution provides for self-executing home rule for all municipalities that choose to adopt it[46] (see Figure 11).

The Maryland Commission on Administrative Organization of the State, in its second report in June, 1952, noted that only the city and county of Baltimore was granted home rule under existing law in that

[44] In 1951, Rhode Island adopted self-executing constitutional home rule and Connecticut cities, towns, and boroughs were granted legislative home rule. See the *National Municipal Review*, vol. 40 (July, 1951), pp. 360–362.

[45] Robert J. M. O'Hare, "Cities Rush Home Rule Gate," *National Municipal Review*, vol. 42 (February, 1953), pp. 73–77. In 1951 the Georgia legislature passed a municipal home rule act using a clause of the state constitution authorizing uniform optional charter plans as authority. This was held unconstitutional by the Georgia Supreme Court. However, the movement for Georgia home rule has been continued.

[46] A letter to the author from Lee S. Greene, Mar. 1, 1954.

state and recommended that "a constitutional provision should authorize municipalities to amend their own charters or adopt new ones."[47] In March, 1953, a bipartisan joint resolution was approved by the Indiana legislature calling for a constitutional amendment to permit home rule, but the proposal must go through the slow Indiana amending process. Local politicians, good-government groups, chambers of commerce, and other interests over the nation continue to press for home rule.

The Practical Meaning of Home Rule. Some reformers have assumed that municipal home rule results in the granting of greater powers to cities, with more independence from the state legislature. Students should not make the same mistake. That the granting of home rule makes for changes in several aspects of the political scene is not to be questioned, but does it grant more power or greater independence to cities? The question cannot be answered categorically, but a 1938 study suggested that home rule had been "helpful but not of great importance in enlarging the zone of municipal activity."[48] A commentary upon that study found that home rule gives cities their greatest freedom in choosing the *form* of government they are to employ and in exercising routine housekeeping functions (civil-service rules, the fixing of salaries, the establishment of pension systems, etc.). In these areas, non–home rule cities must nearly always secure enabling legislation from the state. Home rule cities may *possibly* be freer on matters that are fairly definitely *local* in interest (the establishment of parks, zoos, the control of building regulations), but "their freedom is not measurably greater in matters of education, general police control and utility rates and services (except in Colorado)."[49] On financial matters, in which the state can always claim an interest, home rule cities have virtually no advantage at all over special and general act charter cities, except in California.

In many states, home rule has helped to give municipalities greater power of discretion in solving their day-to-day problems. Cities without home rule must often go to the legislature in order to get an authorization to perform some minor function or to exercise some power that most laymen would consider to be obviously a local responsibility. For example, in recent years a North Carolina town had to have the legislature pass an act in order that the council might declare it a misdemeanor to use roller skates on the public sidewalks. A Maryland city had to get special permission to increase the salary of a stenographer by $300 a year. A Nevada city had to get legislative permission in order to purchase a rotary pump

[47] See *National Municipal Review*, vol. 41 (July, 1952), p. 351.
[48] George C. S. Benson, "Sources of Municipal Powers," *Municipal Year Book, 1938*, pp. 149–165.
[49] Council of State Governments, *State-Local Relations* (1946), pp. 164–166; reprinted in Kneier and Fox, *op. cit.*, pp. 101–103.

for the fire department. An Iowa town discovered that it lacked power to purchase uniforms for the members of its police force.[50] Home rule is not a guarantee against such municipal impotence, but it has been helpful in overcoming it.

While home rule cities often, in fact, enjoy greater powers than do non–home rule cities, most of them are *potentially* just as subject to state control over their affairs. In most home rule states, the legislature enjoys concurrent or superior power to the city government in matters of local concern. And the legislature is, of course, supreme in those areas that the courts deem to be of state, rather than of local, concern. In most states, general acts of the legislature, or what purport to be general acts, take precedence over ordinances or charter provisions. Under these circumstances, the question of whether municipal home rule will work, and the extent to which it will work, is a question not of law, but of *public policy* determined by the legislature, at whose sufferance home rule actually exists.[51] To be sure, the enactment of a constitutional amendment providing for home rule places an implied moral obligation upon the legislature to carry out the spirit of its provisions, and this moral pressure appears to have had an effect upon the legislatures of several states.

A somewhat different, more autonomous kind of home rule is to be found in California, Colorado, Ohio, Oklahoma, and perhaps Arizona and Nebraska. In these states, a distinction is made either by the courts, or by the constitution plus the courts, between matters of local and of state concern. The legislature has definitely less power over localities, and general laws do not supersede local ordinances or charter provisions.

In some of these states, the constitution attempts to define some, at least, of the powers that are properly those of the municipality, but it cannot define them all, nor can it attempt detailed definitions of powers so as to explain where they end and state-wide interests begin. Because this is so, this type tends to *transfer* control from the state legislature to the state courts (Ohio offers the clearest example). Whether this is an improvement is questionable. The courts, in most cases, strongly tend to resolve doubts in favor of the state. Furthermore, the judges under this system become even more important supercouncilmen than they are under ordinary methods of local government—and judges are not chosen for purposes of making public policy on the local level. A leading authority has pointed out that "after all, it seems clear that the determination of the actual extent of power to be exercised is wholly a question of

[50] Examples from among those cited in Nevada Legislative Counsel Bureau, *Home Rule in Nevada* (1952).

[51] An interesting attempt to classify home rule cities according to the extent to which they remain subject to legislative control is made in E. B. Schulz, *American City Government* (1949), pp. 130–131.

policy and not at all a question of law."[52] The task belongs properly to the legislature.

An attempt to circumvent the problem of distinguishing between state affairs and municipal affairs has been made by J. B. Fordham.[53] He has suggested that the state constitution authorize a city to "exercise any power or perform any function which the legislature has power to devolve upon a non–home rule charter municipal corporation."

While this plan is ingenious in theory, there is room for much doubt as to whether it would expand municipal powers in actuality. Certainly the courts could give "power to devolve" a narrow interpretation and just as certainly actual municipal powers would still be left to the mercy and discretion of the courts. However, a very broad interpretation of the clause, similar to that given in recent years by the United States Supreme Court to the delegable powers of Congress, would give cities a free hand in performing those functions demanded of it by the public.[54]

Legislative Home Rule. A word should be said about *legislative* home rule. Under this plan, there is no constitutional authorization for home rule; the legislature simply provides for it as a matter of public policy. In the past, it has been common to disparage this device as an inferior grade of the product. It is true that what the legislature gives it may take away, but the plan requires nothing more than a responsible attitude on the part of legislators. Furthermore, once home rule is granted, it tends to remain alive not because of legal restraints upon the legislature, but because a vested interest has been established which is then protected through the normal process of lobbying and applying other political pressures upon the legislature.

Iowa has used legislative home rule to amend special act charters since 1858. It now applies, however, to only four municipalities. In Nevada, "a framework of home rule is provided for both incorporated and unincorporated cities and towns, but it appears that the provisions are not sufficiently broad and flexible to meet the needs of many Nevada cities and towns."[55] Connecticut adopted a potentially liberal legislative home rule law in 1951, and there are other instances of its use[56] (see Table 6).

---

[52] H. L. McBain, *American City Progress and the Law* (1918), p. 7. The opposite view, arguing for constitutionally enumerated powers for the states, with *all other powers* reserved to the cities, is argued in R. L. Mott, "Strengthening Home Rule," *National Municipal Review*, vol. 39 (April, 1950), pp. 174–176.

[53] J. B. Fordham, for the Committee on Home Rule, American Municipal Association, *Model Constitutional Provisions for Municipal Home Rule* (1953).

[54] The Fordham theory has been given limited application by judicial construction in Texas. See John P. Keith, *City and County Home Rule in Texas* (1951).

[55] Nevada Legislative Counsel Bureau, *Home Rule in Nevada* (1952), p. 8.

[56] For a view that legislative home rule is not satisfactory, see Rodney L. Mott, *Home Rule for America's Cities* (1949), pp. 14–15. A weakness of legislative home rule is that it may be declared an unconstitutional delegation of legislative power, as were early laws in Wisconsin (1912) and Michigan (1899). In an almost forgotten

Home Rule: an Appraisal. On the whole, home rule has been beneficial to cities. It allows charters to be tailor-made to suit the needs of the particular community and permits them to be more flexible than the types provided by the legislature in allowing for changing exigencies and in taking advantage of new developments in administrative techniques. Home rule probably makes it easier to experiment with charter provisions, since the amendments are locally proposed and adopted.

Perhaps the greatest advantage of home rule lies in its psychological value. To those interested in local government, it gives the impression of granting more independence to the city than is often the actual case. This produces a healthy frame of mind, if nothing else. It gives encouragement and incentive to those who would improve local government and thus fends off defeatism and gives the reformer the feeling that if he fails, he has only himself to blame. The psychological effect upon legislators is also a desirable one. Most legislators have been willing to accept the mandate of the voters when a home rule provision is written into a constitution and to permit home rule to operate properly even where legal authority to commit sabotage lies with the legislature. This is not always the case (as for example, in Utah), but it usually is. In home rule states, bills which would deal with local matters are sometimes opposed by legislators who wonder if they would not "interfere with the rights of local self-government" or "violate the principle of home rule." Home rule is hence more often an *attitude* toward local government than it is a legal injunction against legislative action.

Multiple Charter Systems in Nebraska: an Illustration.[57] City charters, as has been indicated, may be provided for in general acts, special acts, classification systems, optional charter acts, or home rule. Rather than use one of these devices to the exclusion of all others, it is common for the state to allow charters under several of them. Nebraska offers a good illustration of this.

The basic law of the state provides for a *general act charter* of the mayor-council type. It applies to all cities of from 1,000 to 40,000 population and applies automatically to all cities that do not specifically adopt some other kind of charter. Since there are provisions for minor structural differences between first- and second-class cities, the plan might be called a classification-type charter rather than a simple general act charter.

The state also has a provision for two *optional* forms of local government. One establishes a commission structure for which all cities of over

---

discussion, the greatest authority on the subject makes a strong argument in favor of *legislative* home rule: H. L. McBain, *American City Progress and the Law* (1918), pp. 1–29. See also Harvey Walker, *op. cit.*

[57] This section is based on a note by A. C. Breckenridge in the *National Municipal Review*, vol. 42 (February, 1953), pp. 84–85.

2,000 population are eligible. The other permits municipalities of 1,000 people or more to adopt a specified council-manager plan. A third system is provided for in the Nebraska constitution, which permits *home rule charters* to be adopted by all cities of over 5,000 population.

In 1953, only one city was operating under the commission option. Nine were using the council-manager option. Several cities had home rule charters, under which it is of course possible to adopt any governmental structure. The two largest cities, characteristically, had taken advantage of the home rule provision. Omaha uses the commission plan. Lincoln, the second city, has a mayor-council charter. This demonstrates the flexible use to which home rule can be put. The majority of Nebraska cities, it should be added, operate under the general act charter.

THE CITY AND THE STATE

It should be clear by now that the city is a child of the state. It has been noted that the state has been most unwilling to allow its child to grow up. A theory of perpetual infancy was adopted by nineteenth-century legislatures in their attitudes toward their offspring. Efforts at achieving independence for municipalities through the legal device of constitutional limitations were largely unsuccessful. Cities in most states did achieve more independence and less legislative supervision of their affairs after the first decade or so of the twentieth century, but the change seems to have been produced principally by a changing climate of opinion toward cities that accompanied the urbanization of the nation, together with a slight increase of public trust in the politician, both state and local.

Legislative oversight of local government declined in the twentieth century for another reason: government got to be too complicated to be sufficiently understood by amateur legislators meeting for a few weeks annually or biannually as an interlude away from other occupations that took the whole of their time. City government became professionalized and technical; its complex details came to be understandable only to the professional, full-time technician. Flexibility, which legislatures did not possess, was needed. So was continuous, rather than sporadic, oversight. It could therefore be said that the twentieth century represented a period during which state legislators were somewhat reluctantly, but inexorably, forced to transfer increasing amounts of supervision over local government to the professional bureaucracies of the administrative branch of the state government.

It is perhaps desirable to postpone an examination of the details of state-local administrative relationships until a more appropriate place is reached.[58] In addition to legislative and administrative oversight of cities,

[58] Set chap. 12 on intergovernmental administrative relationships.

the judicial branch also acts in a supervisory capacity, and some facets of this control require development.

State Judicial Oversight of Cities.[59] Standing behind every city official, looking over his shoulder as the baseball umpire looks over the shoulder of the catcher, is a judge. He is the individual who settles all disputes between the city and the state, a taxpayer and the city, one local government and another. He is the umpire. While he makes a determination only when asked to do so and then upon the basis of laws and ordinances made by other people, he is himself in a real sense a lawmaker, for the judge decides ultimately what the law *means* and hence what the city can and cannot do.

Because the city is not a sovereign body, its standing at law is approximately the same as the standing of a private corporation, except when it is acting in the name of the sovereign (the state). Because of this legal position and because it enjoys only those powers granted to it under the principle of Dillon's rule, the city is constantly faced with the task of proving in court that it has the power to do what it seeks to do.

The Taxpayer's Action. The court actions in which the municipality constantly finds itself embroiled may in some cases be brought by a state official, but most of them are brought by a taxpayer resident in the city, or by a corporation that is a taxpayer, since a corporation is an artificial person at law.

It is a well-known principle of ancient Anglo-Saxon common law that "the King is the fountainhead of all power" and that therefore "the King can do no wrong" and likewise that "the King cannot be sued without his own consent." This principle was transferred to the American republic, where the word "people" was substituted for "King" in the first quotation, but "state" was used in the last two. The United States Supreme Court has consistently held that status as a taxpayer does not give one sufficient interest in the matter to test the legality of an act of Congress in a judicial action,[60] and this rule also applies in most of the states. The same protection does not extend to municipalities, however, for they are normally subject under the common law to taxpayers' suits even where there has been no statutory grant of the right.

Taxpayers' suits may be brought for three purposes: (1) to enjoin acts of the municipality that are unauthorized, unlawful, or *ultra vires;*[61] (2) to compel unfaithful officers, or even third persons, to repay into the

---

[59] In addition to the great commentaries on municipal law by Dillon and McQuillin, contemporary developments are reported in the annual volume by the National Institute of Municipal Law Officers, *Municipalities and the Law in Action.* Beginning with the 1953 edition, the name was changed to the *NIMLO Muncipal Law Review.*

[60] *Massachusetts v. Mellon,* 262 U.S. 447 (1923).

[61] *Ultra vires* actions are actions legally beyond the power of the municipal corporation or its officers.

treasury sums illegally paid out; and (3) to protect the interests of the municipality where its officers wrongfully refuse or neglect to perform their duties. This third type may involve legal actions by the taxpayer in the name of the city to protect municipal powers and rights that the officers of the city fail to protect.

In theory, taxpayer actions are analogous to the actions that a stockholder may bring against the officials of a private corporation (who are merely acting as his agents). The purpose of the action is to stop acts that are allegedly illegal, or to stop or remedy situations that give evidence of fraud, corruption, or other wrongdoing. It is important to protect the public from potential wrongdoers, and the taxpayer suit has often been used to prevent the granting of fraudulent contracts, the issuing of improvident bonds, or the granting of illegal franchises. The student who will later be a local taxpayer might well keep in mind his right to this legal protection.

Unhappily, the taxpayer action is often abused. Theoretically, such an action cannot be brought simply because the taxpayer disagrees with the judgment or doubts the wisdom of the city officials or because their policies might damage the profits of one's business. In practice, however, these are often the real reasons behind suits. Almost any public policy that deviates even slightly from traditional municipal behavior will result in an action in which the policy is claimed to be *ultra vires*. The individual or corporation in such a case may be seeking to protect his own economic interests or personal philosophy as against the general interest and the will of a larger number of people. The courts are often the last resort of the obstructionist. Unfortunately for the health and vigor of local self-government, state court judges have usually lent a sympathetic ear, and the road toward modernized city government has again and again been obstructed by expensive, time-consuming legal actions. The exasperated interest group looking for an expanded governmental service is thus encouraged to turn to the national government, which is almost free of this problem.

Should a parking-lot owner have a right to bring action to prevent the city from going into the parking-lot business on the somewhat comic ground that it is *ultra vires* to use money from the parking-meter fund (rather than the general-revenue fund) for this purpose? Should a home builder be permitted legal action to stop a public housing project on the ground that such a project is not for a public purpose? Should a television-station owner be permitted legal action to prevent the city from operating a municipal television station on the ground that the city charter permits only a radio station? Assuming good faith on the part of the council in each action, this writer is inclined to answer "no" to each question.

It is not suggested that there should be no remedy at law, or that municipal officials should enjoy *carte blanche* in determining the functions they wish to perform. Certainly in all cases where fraud, corruption, negligence, or bad faith on the part of public officials is suspected, the taxpayer should have the right to bring action. It is the view of this writer, however, that a major deterrent to effective, modern city government is the freedom which the individual citizen has to bring nuisance or delaying suits against the city each time it launches a new project or new policy. The frustrating of proposed municipal actions on the basis of highly technical legal decisions has undermined both the self-confidence of the municipal official and public confidence in municipal government as an alternative to centralization in Washington.

THE CITY AND THE CITIZEN

Because cities are corporations and not sovereignties, they are responsible for contract violations and torts.[62] They become answerable before the courts in much the same way as do private corporations. The basic rules of municipal liability are established in the common law, but they are subject, as is any part of the common law, to statutory variations in the individual states.

Municipal Contract Liability. Cities, as would appear obvious, enter into countless contracts with individuals and corporations. In general, cities must be answerable for these contracts in the same manner as private corporations. Even where there is no question of good faith involved in the carrying out of a contract, many other problems may arise —problems of interpretation of the contract, of determining when its conditions have been completed, of making settlement when performance of the conditions of the contract become impossible. Cities may therefore find themselves in court in the normal course of carrying out their activities.

The principal problem that faces the courts in the interpretation of contracts to which the city is a party is that of determining the conditions under which a contract is either valid or invalid. In general, a valid contract is one that the city is authorized to make, that is made by the proper officer according to law, and that has been adopted according to proper procedures (for example, the law may require that certain contracts be let only after advertising for bids, and then only to the lowest responsible

---

[62] Almost every culture, even the most primitive, distinguishes between a *tort,* or wrong against an individual, and a *crime,* or wrong against society. A tort is a violation of a personal right established and protected by law. A violation of a contract is the violation of a personal right established by mutual agreement and protected by law. For purposes of this text, a tort is an injury to a person that is neither a crime nor a violation of a contract.

bidder). An *ultra vires* contract is normally invalid, but the courts of the various states sometimes order monetary settlements where the city has benefited from the contract. Similarly, a contract made by the wrong officer or without following proper procedures may sometimes be validated, but at other times it may not be, and the other party to the contract may have to assume any loss. Court practices vary from one state to another.[63]

Municipal-tort Liability. In a large American city a few years ago, an elderly lady tripped over a loose floor board at the head of the stairs in a city-owned building, fell down the stairs, and was seriously injured. Was the city liable for damages for maintaining a defective stairway, as a private business firm would be? It may well come as a surprise to the layman to discover that the law would make the answer depend, in most states, upon the *use* to which the building was put by the city. If it was used as the offices of the city-owned water supply system, the injured person could recover damages, but if it was used as a police station, no claim would be allowed against the city.

If a university student walking down Main Street is struck by a runaway bus belonging to the city-owned transit system, he will be in an entirely different legal position than if the vehicle had been a fire truck. A broken leg or a caved-in chest hurts as badly in either case and is just as costly to repair, yet in most states the student could collect if he were hit by the bus, but could not if it were the fire truck.

Why should this be? The answer is to be found largely in historical accident and in a failure to modernize the municipal-tort liability law. There is a legal argument to justify the arrangement, but it is not likely to impress the layman.

It will be recalled that the city was earlier described as performing two different types of functions: those which it does involuntarily as an agent of the state, and those done at local option as a service to the immediate community. In performing the former type of activity, the city becomes a veritable department of the state government and as such becomes cloaked in the state's mantle of sovereignty. It is said to be performing a *governmental* (or public) function. In performing services of comfort and convenience to the immediate community, however, the city acts very much as if it were simply a private corporation doing the same job. It is said to be performing a *proprietary* (or corporate, or sometimes private) function.

Clearly a theoretical line could well be drawn between those functions where the city directly represents the sovereign, and hence cannot be sued without its own consent, as is the rule with the sovereign power,

---

[63] Details of municipal-contract liability are developed in McQuillin, *op. cit.*, vol. 10, secs. 29.01–29.04.

and where the city acts as an ordinary corporation and hence could reasonably be expected to assume the same responsibilities as other corporations. The difficulty with such a legal fiction arises when an attempt is made to classify the multitudinous activities of a modern city. The theory requires a perfect bifurcation, with every function being either governmental or proprietary, and with no messy edges or leftover pieces. The functions themselves, however, are not very cooperative when a classification is attempted.

Is the parks and recreation function, for example, carried on only for the comfort and convenience of the community, or is it part of the sovereign's responsibility to protect the health, safety, and welfare of the inhabitants of the state? How about airports, hospitals, or garbage disposal? The answers to these questions are not easy to find. Furthermore, the law of municipal-tort liability is not the same in any two states of the union.

The classification of functions is done in the various states either by legislative statute or, in its absence, by the judges. The legislature is free to overrule the judges and can, if it chooses, make functions that are the most clearly governmental in character subject to tort action. The whole law of tort liability is based upon the judge-made common law, however, and most of the legislatures have been content to allow the judges to work their way through the problem on their own.

What criteria do the judges use in trying to determine whether a function is governmental or proprietary? Even on this question, there is no agreement. There are three principal criteria, but they are not given the same weighting or precedence in the various states. First, the judges sometimes use a historical test. Since the whole question has been one that has gradually developed over time, it is felt that the historical usage or treatment of the function should be given weighty consideration. The difficulty with this approach is to be found in the tendency for the judges to call "old" functions—those long performed by municipalities—governmental and newer ones proprietary. But there is no logic in denying suability because the function has been performed by governments for too many decades or centuries.

A second criterion sometimes used is based upon the question of whether the function is performed involuntarily by the city at the insistence of the state or is voluntarily assumed at the option of the local community. But the degree of compulsion imposed upon the city varies greatly from state to state, and it is not often easy to determine the meaning of the term *voluntary.*

A final criterion is one based upon the question of whether or not the function is revenue-producing. A function that does, or may, return a profit resembles the functions of private corporations, it is argued, and is therefore more likely to be proprietary in nature. But how about a profit from, say, garbage collection that is incidental to the operation of the function? Or profit from the operation of a miniature railroad at a park that represents only one small segment of the whole function of parks and recreation? None of the criteria are consistently or systematically applied. They vary from state to state, and none of them can mark a satisfactory trail through the wilderness of tort liability.

The courts almost invariably place certain functions in the governmental category, for which the city may not be sued. These include police, fire, education, libraries, traffic signals (they act in lieu of policemen), and public health. Functions that are nearly always held to be proprietary include city-owned public utilities, such as water, public transportation, gas, and electricity. There are many functions that vary considerably from state to state in their classification: parks and recreation (which tend to be governmental), hospitals (likewise), airports (which tend to be proprietary), street lighting, street cleaning, garbage collection and disposal, and the construction and maintenance of sewers.[64]

There are certain functions which are generally recognized as being essentially governmental, but for which the municipalities must nonetheless maintain responsibility for torts. These are functions dealing with the *public ways.* Historically, the state has expected the municipal corporation to be responsible for torts committed in the maintenance (but usually not in the construction) of streets, sidewalks, bridges, culverts, and the like. The citizen has a right to expect that a bridge will not collapse under him or that he will not walk into an open manhole in the sidewalk. Even in these cases, however, doubts are resolved against the individual. It is always held, for example, that the city must be given a reasonable time in which to correct a fault or post a warning.

The Rule on Discretion. Regardless of whether a function is claimed to be governmental or proprietary, most courts will ask another question before deciding whether tort liability exists. That question deals with whether the action in litigation involved a *discretionary* or a *ministerial* act. That is to say, is damage claimed because the city decided to do or not to do something, or is it claimed because of the manner in which city officials or employees carried out established policy? Discretionary acts involve the making of public policy decisions, and they are *not* subject to tort action. Ministerial acts involve the carrying out of established policy, and they are normally the only type of acts that will allow for a legal action. For example, if the city council decides not to extend a water main or not to build a bridge across a stream, or if a police officer (acting in good faith and upon probable cause) decides to arrest a person who

---

[64] In the absence of statutes to the contrary, quasi corporations such as school districts, counties, and townships are not responsible for *any* torts. The theoretical reasoning holds that all of the functions of a quasi corporation are involuntarily performed as an agent of the state.

subsequently proves to be innocent of any crime, there could be no maintainable action, since these all involve decision making. On the other hand, once a bridge is built, the public has a right to expect the ministerial function of maintaining it to be carried out, and once the city decides to operate a bus line the public has a right to expect that individuals will not be injured while riding on the buses.

The Rule of Respondeat Superior. According to the common law, the master is responsible for the actions of his servant, providing that those actions may reasonably be said to follow from the orders given to the servant. This is the rule of *respondeat superior*. In municipal-tort liability, it means that the city must answer for the action of its officers and employees, providing that the city is suable for the particular function involved and that the officer or employee was acting in general compliance with the requirements of his job.

If a city official or employee does something not called for in the performance of his duty, his actions are *ultra vires* and the city bears no responsibility for them. Since an individual is responsible for his own actions where there is no master-servant relationship to protect him, this means that the citizen who is wronged may sometimes be able to sue the *individual* city official or employee when he cannot sue the city itself. This may sometimes protect the injured person when he is wronged in the course of the city's performing a governmental function. But the individual, it must be remembered, is not responsible when the city cannot be sued unless his actions are *ultra vires*. If a city policeman arrests an innocent man against whom he holds a grudge, or if a fire-truck driver operates his vehicle in a grossly negligent manner, or if a public health officer quarantines a hotel while drunk, the individual who is harmed may be able to collect from the officer or employee as an individual. The chances are excellent, however, that even if he gets a court judgment, the city employee will not earn enough from his job to pay for such damages.

Recapitulation. A tort is an injury to a person that is neither a crime nor a violation of a contract. Cities and villages are responsible for torts committed by their officers and employees (generally speaking) when the tort was committed in the performance of a ministerial act, by an employee who was not acting in an *ultra vires* fashion, in connection with a municipal function of a proprietary character, or in connection with the public ways, and not one of a governmental character. In most states, if any one of these conditions is not met, the city is not responsible in tort action.[65]

---

[65] The basic material on municipal-tort liability is to be found, of course, in the treatises by McQuillin and Dillon. A lengthy bibliography is cited in Murray Seasongood, *Cases on Municipal Corporations* (1941), p. 784, and many cases are given in his chap. 13. Another important work is Leon T. David, *Tort Liability of Public Officers* (1940). Convenient illustrative material may be found in Kneier and Fox, *op. cit.,* pp. 48–64.

An Appraisal. Nearly all political scientists, and most lawyers and public officials in the field, agree that the present law of municipal-tort liability is unsatisfactory. The layman, looking at what appear to him as arbitrary distinctions, is hopelessly confused. Even the judges sometimes admit that they are, too. Yet they continue to try to make the theoretical principles of the law into practical applications of justice. Only the judges of South Carolina and Florida have given up and have decided to face reality. They have taken opposite routes toward a solution, however. In South Carolina, the courts will entertain a suit only where the clearest authorization for it exists in state law. The few existing statutes are given a very narrow interpretation against liability.[66] In Florida, on the other hand, the distinction between governmental and proprietary functions has been abandoned—all of them are treated as proprietary, even police and fire protection—and the cities take the same chances as private corporations.

In a few states, the judges have expanded the concept of proprietary functions by tending to include newer functions in that category. In other states, the legislature has increased liability by statute, as has been done in California and Illinois, for example, in connection with the operation of fire trucks.[67] The trend in this direction has been slow, however, and at its present rate will scarcely bring about the reform that is so often demanded.

There is some dissent from the view that reform is needed, chiefly upon the basis of the arguments that cities would have to pay too much tax money that should go for public purposes to individual litigants; that juries would be too liberal in allowing claims if they knew the city, rather than an individual, would have to pay the bill; and that many spurious suits would be started by persons looking for easy money. The general view, however, is that equity to those injured requires that municipalities be made fully liable for their torts. This seems only fair to the individual who is run down by a squad car while minding his own business. It would have the effect of forcing the city to be as responsible in performing its functions as a corporation or an individual must be. Cities could be protected from overzealous juries by statutes giving the judge an extra amount of discretion in such cases.

George A. Warp, in a widely cited article,[68] has presented the view that a full assumption of tort responsibility is likely to be financially dangerous only to very small towns. He suggests that the answer might

---

[66] G. R. Sherrill and R. H. Stoudemire, *Municipal Government in South Carolina* (1950), pp. 26–28.

[67] See *Raynor v. Arcola*, 77 P.2d 1054 (1938); and *Bryan v. Chicago*, 20 N.E.2d 37 (1939).

[68] George A. Warp, "Can the 'King' Do No Wrong?" *National Municipal Review*, vol. 21 (June, 1942), pp. 311–315; reprinted in Kneier and Fox, *op. cit.*, pp. 48–55.

lie with some form of state or cooperative insurance which the small towns would be required to carry so as to be able to pay their claims without facing bankruptcy. Except for the special provision needed for small towns (many of which, together with cities up to the size of San Diego, already have liability insurance), a study conducted under Warp's direction concluded that there is "no justification for fears of excessive litigation, fraud, and unreasonable cost if tort liability were to be further extended." Most students of municipal government would like to see at least some of the state legislatures put this conclusion to the test.

CHAPTER 8

FORMS OF GOVERNMENT

A Minneapolis alderman once told the writer that forms of government have nothing at all to do with the effectiveness or honesty of government. He felt that Minneapolis, which has a nineteenth-century form, operates under a government as good as could be had under any of the newer forms which are so often advocated by political scientists. The viewpoint was scarcely new with him, however: similar expressions have come from Alexander Pope, Edmund Burke, and Lincoln Steffens.

It is true that Americans have been rather obsessed, in recent decades, with the idea of a relationship between structure and effectiveness of government. Many advocates of reform have been guilty of overstatement in this direction. Much literature may be found urging the commission or council-manager plan, for example, on the ground that these plans follow the organization form of the business world, the corporation. The implication is that the success of the one should ensure the success of the other.[1]

The truth of the matter, it would seem, is that structural arrangements do have an effect upon the quality of government, but they neither guarantee good government nor prevent it. Why is the structure of consequence? Perhaps an answer to this question can be approximated through asking other questions. Are all forms of city government equally good in providing needed *political leadership?* Do they provide equally for responsible, effective *administrative leadership* that will meet the social and economic needs of the day? Do they provide equally for representative government of the type expected by contemporary democracy? Do they provide equally well for the use of modern methods of budgeting, personnel recruitment, and other housekeeping functions?

The answer to each of the above questions is assuredly "no." There are limitations to each form of government which the informed citizen should understand so that he may better know his own city and so that he may determine which form best suits the needs of his or any other particular community.

[1] The overemphasis upon forms of government is discussed in J. C. Phillips, "Good Government Under the Old Forms," *The Annals of the American Academy of Political and Social Science,* vol. 199 (September, 1938), pp. 91–98.

The Basic Forms. There are three basic forms of city government in the United States, the mayor-council, commission, and council-manager plans. To this must be added the New England town meeting and its accommodation to modern urban conditions, the representative town meeting. It must also be noted that there are many variations of the mayor-council plan, and that there are important differences between so-called strong-mayor and weak-mayor plans of this type.

A word of caution should be given at the outset in examining forms of government: there are probably no two cities in the United States that have *exactly* the same structure of government. There are very few that fit the theoretical ideal of the general plan they follow. Nearly every charter commission or state legislature, in considering structure, finds it politically expedient to add its own improvisations on the given theme. For example, the strong-mayor–council system calls for the appointment of department heads by the mayor, yet many such cities have elective clerks and treasurers.

Boston and Cleveland are the only large mayor-council cities that do not elect any administrative officers other than the mayor. New York, Baltimore, Buffalo, and Houston elect the controller. Philadelphia elects the controller and treasurer. San Francisco elects not only the city attorney and treasurer, but the assessor as well.

The mayor of Chicago has great administrative powers, which are characteristic of strong-mayor cities, but a council committee, rather than the mayor's office, prepares the annual budget. Detroit clearly has a strong-mayor government, yet the organization chart is cluttered with a series of *advisory* boards and commissions that are vestiges of the old weak-mayor *administrative* boards and commissions.

The manager plan calls for the manager to appoint all department heads, yet in most cities with this form, some administrative officers are either elective or selected by the council. The variations are quite endless, and the structural descriptions that follow must be thought of as models which city charters tend to imitate. The difference between the weak- and strong-mayor systems, in particular, is a relative one. The models of each are at opposite ends of a continuum, and the various mayor-council cities must be thought of as being located somewhere along that continuum, rarely if ever at one of the extremities.

CITIES WITH A SEPARATION OF POWERS

The general historical context in which the structures of American city government developed has already been discussed.[2] During nearly all of the nineteenth century, American cities were operated under the weak-

[2] See above, chap. 3.

mayor–council (or weak-mayor) system. Near the end of that century, what is now called the strong-mayor system gradually evolved. In recent years a third principal derivative of the plan, a result of efforts to correct a major weakness of the strong-mayor system in large cities, has evolved. For purposes of this text, it will be called the strong-mayor–council plan with chief administrative officer (or strong mayor with CAO). This plan will be described later.

The various types of mayor-council cities taken collectively make up more than one-half of all cities of the nation under any form of government.[3] Fifty-four per cent of American cities of over 5,000 population are of the mayor-council types. So are most smaller cities, except in New England, where the town-meeting form is common. All but two of America's seventeen largest cities use the mayor-council plan, usually of a strong-mayor type. Nearly two-thirds (64.7 per cent) of the small cities of 5,000 to 10,000 people have the mayor-council form, usually of a weak-mayor type.

The Weak-mayor–Council Plan. In the early decades of the nineteenth century, America's budding cities borrowed from rural government certain essential concepts. Today we call it the weak-mayor–council plan (see Figures 12 and 13).

Characteristics. The weak-mayor plan is a product of Jacksonian Democracy. It reflects the spirit of the frontier, with a skepticism both of politicians and of government itself. It grew out of a time when the functions of city government were few, when the need for a single executive was not recognized, and when people were afraid to give powers to a single executive. Implicit in the weak-mayor plan is the belief that if a politician has few powers and many checks upon him, he can do relatively little damage and that if one politician becomes corrupt, he will not necessarily corrupt the whole city government.

The council is both a legislative and an executive organization under the weak-mayor plan. In small cities today, the council is small—five or seven members—but in larger cities it is usually a fairly large body of perhaps eleven to fifty members. At one time councils might be as large as two hundred. Members are (except in small cities) ordinarily elected by wards on a partisan ballot.

In addition to making policy, the council appoints several administrative officers, such as the city engineer and the city attorney. Councilmen (often called aldermen if they represent wards) often serve on several ex officio boards and commissions.[4] A committee of the council

---

[3] *Municipal Year Book, 1953,* p. 59.

[4] Ex officio boards and commissions have a membership of persons who hold office by right of holding another office. For example, the airports commission might be made up of the mayor, the clerk, the treasurer, and two aldermen.

usually prepares the budget and may even appoint the controller, who administers the expenditures of the budget.[5]

The mayor is not "weak" because he lacks policy-making power—he normally has a veto, can recommend legislation, and may even preside over the council. He is "weak" because he lacks administrative power.

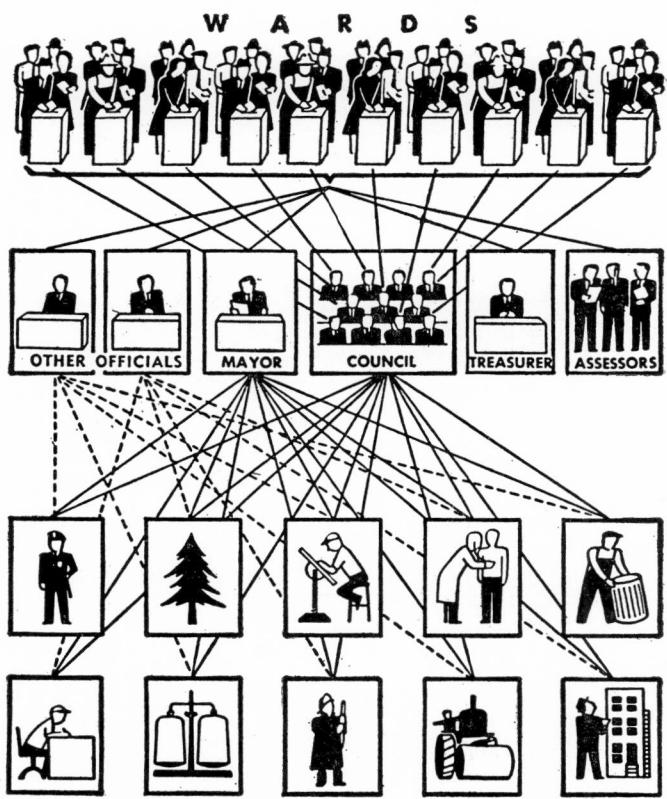

Fig. 12. Weak-mayor–council form. SOURCE: Used by permission of the National Municipal League.

There is, in fact, no single individual charged with the responsibility of seeing to it that the laws and ordinances are properly carried out, or that the city administration proceeds in accord with an over-all plan. The mayor has very restricted appointive powers; even when he is allowed to make appointments, he may not be able to remove those he places in office, so that he is deprived of any real control over them or responsibility for them.

Ordinarily several of the principal city offices are filled by direct election—the long ballot is a characteristic of the weak-mayor plan. (See

[5] See chap. 15 on fiscal administration.

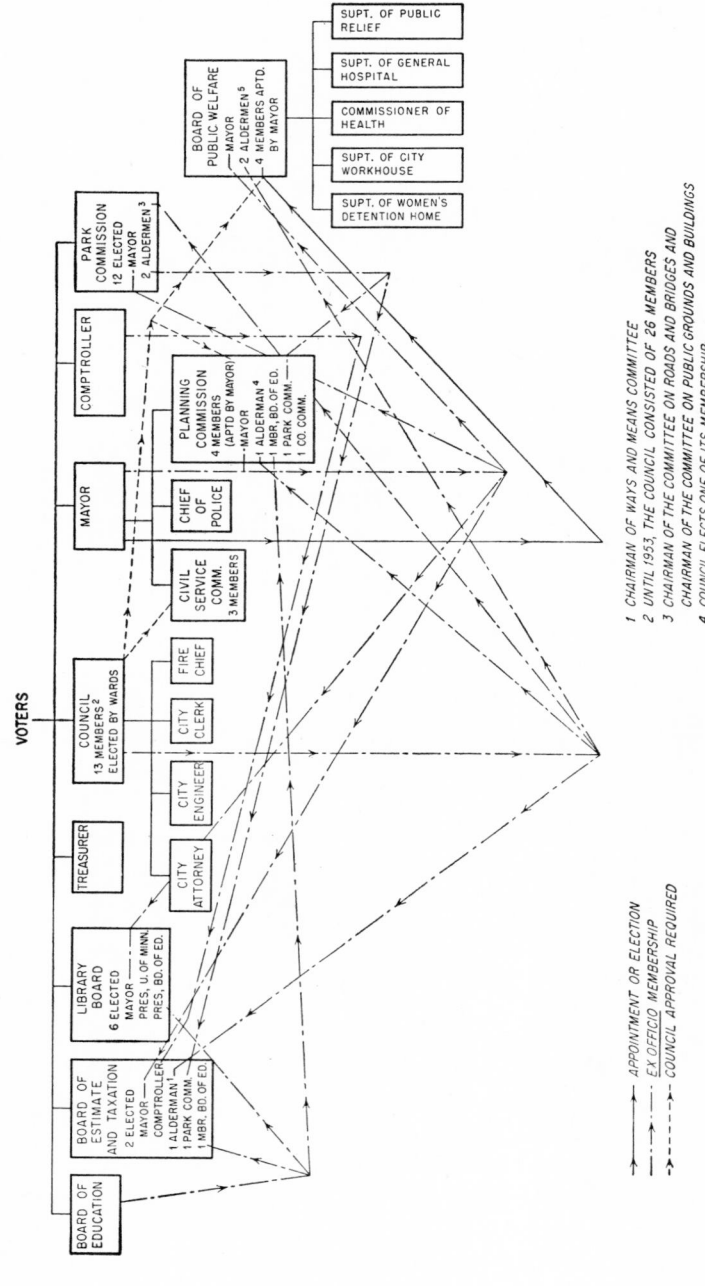

Fig. 13. An actual weak-mayor–council city: Minneapolis, Minn. Note: There are many other appointive and ex officio boards and commissions which are not shown. Departmental subdivisions are also not shown.

Table 7). Other offices, in addition to those filled by election and the council, may be of the ex officio type. Even the governor or some other state official may make some appointments, such as that of the police chief. Without a chief executive, the weak-mayor system is likely to be one in which the various departments are independent of one another and without coordinated effort.

The weak-mayor system requires the voters of the municipality to choose members of sundry boards plus such administrators as, perhaps, the clerk, treasurer, assessor, controller, and attorney. Two candidates for the park board might well offer differing platforms of policy (one might want a new park on the west side, while the other might prefer a new swimming pool on the east side), but will the voter have the time and energy to look past the mayoralty contest as far as the council-manic contests, much less to that for the park board?

In electing a clerk, treasurer, or assessor, the voter is even more sorely beset. Most of the voters will not know which candidate is best qualified to be the assessor, and they will not even know what functions are exercised by the clerk, treasurer, or, especially, the controller. In most cities, the clerk is a glorified file clerk, keeping the records of the city, while the treasurer is a bookkeeper, maintaining the financial records of the city. Both officers are important, but they are ministerial rather than policy-making. They are normally routine jobs of an office-manager type

Table 7. Municipal Elective Offices in Cities over 5,000, Exclusive of the Mayor and Council

Title of office	Per cent of cities electing*	Number of cities electing
Treasurer..........................	36.2	883
Clerk..............................	26.9	657
Assessor...........................	15.8	386
Auditor............................	12.3	299
Attorney..........................	9.8	238
Police chief	4.9	119
Controller.........................	4.6	112
Public works director..............	2.1	51
Welfare director...................	0.7	17
Finance director...................	0.6	14
Engineer...........................	0.3	8
None of the above elective.........	45.7	1,115

* There were 89 cities not reporting that are not included in the above statistics. The above list includes *all* forms of government. Percentages for mayor-council cities alone would be higher.

SOURCE: *Municipal Year Book, 1953*, p. 66.

that could well be performed by either appointive or civil-service personnel. The voter, unacquainted with criteria usable in selecting persons to serve in offices such as these, is likely, in a large city, to vote for the person whose name is best known to him—usually the incumbent—regardless of the candidate's qualifications. In small cities, the voter is likely to support a candidate on the basis of sympathy. A qualified person may be passed over in favor of his opponent who is a veteran, or a handicapped person, or one with a large family who needs the pay, but who is not qualified.

Appraisal. The arguments for the weak-mayor plan are based upon the precepts of Jacksonianism. Many of these ideas are still popular with a large number of American people. For example, Americans may not know which officers are elected and which are appointed, but they are likely to insist that those who are elected should continue to be elected. They may not know what tasks are performed by a particular officer or what the criteria are for choosing an officer for the post, but they want him elected.[6] The weak-mayor system encourages this frontier concept.

The weak-mayor plan was a product of a different world from that which Americans occupy today. It was never intended to serve large, impersonal urban communities, and it cannot serve them well. The plan does not encourage modern methods of housekeeping—budgeting, personnel, purchasing, and the like. In fact, it fosters the use of the spoils plan, with its resort to performance by amateurs acting without coordinated leadership. For example, the city engineer (in charge of maintenance of public ways) may well be appointed by the council in a weak-mayor city. If this is the case, the ward aldermen on the council may personally direct the activities of the engineer's office within each of their wards and will probably have considerable control over selection of the employees of the office. Street maintenance becomes not a matter of professional judgment and performance, but one of doing repairs where they will be of the most help in the next election. The mending of political fences rather than of public ways becomes the first order of business.

Most of the great nineteenth-century machines operated under this plan, for it encourages the boss by its very clumsiness and lack of coordination. The plain fact is that the voter can scarcely determine, after the most conscientious effort, who is responsible for what, or even what functions are being performed by whom. With no clear-cut locus of answerability to the voter, the boss can move in stealthily and can be

[6] Donald S. Hecock, "Too Many Elective Officials?" *National Municipal Review,* vol. 41 (October, 1952), pp. 449–454, offers a case study of this phenomenon on the state level.

most difficult to dislodge. To be sure, bosses have existed under every form of city government: under the strong-mayor plan (Boston under Curley), the commission plan (Jersey City under Hague), and even the much-lauded council-manager plan (Kansas City under Pendergast). Even so, the weak-mayor plan is the most easily corrupted and bossed because of the lack of clear responsibility to the voter.

Probably the greatest defect in the weak-mayor plan, and the one that makes it completely unacceptable for use in a modern community beyond the size of a hamlet, is to be found in its lack of provision for administrative leadership. The mayor, with very limited appointing powers and even more limited removal powers, is not a true chief executive. There is no officer to coordinate the various activities of the city. The mayor may not even make up the budget, which would serve at least to give an over-all picture of the needs of the city and of the relative importance of the proposed expenditures of one department as against another. Suppose, for example, that the city is short of funds (and all cities are short of funds). In a form of city government where one person is responsible for all of the administrative branch, it would be possible to determine that the parks and recreation department should spend less for the coming year so that more streets could be repaired. Under the weak-mayor plan, however, the park board is a law unto itself, answerable to neither the mayor nor the council, especially if it has its own mill levy and hence funds independent of the council, as might well be the case. Each department is likely to gallop off in its own direction with no one empowered to instill teamwork and hence to make the city into a single functioning unit. The effect of all of these independent agencies is to make city government into a series of many little governments rather than one for the whole municipality. There is one city government for parks, another for libraries, another for airports, another for sewage disposal, and so on.

Despite the great amount of criticism that has been levied against the weak-mayor plan, modifications of it remain the most common form of municipal government in the United States today. This is so in large part because the traditional form of village government throughout the United States is that of the weak mayor. Furthermore, the form of government is less important in the smaller municipality because government is more personal, performs fewer functions, and has less elaborate machinery. It has therefore been less important for smaller cities to experiment with newer forms of government, and there has been less agitation for them to do so.

While the weak-mayor system is characteristically found in small cities and villages, there are still quite a few cities of considerable size with relatively weak mayors, especially in the South. Minneapolis (1950 population: 517,277) is the largest city in the United States with what is clearly a weak-mayor system. Until recently, the ballot in each ward there contained candidates for fourteen offices (including local judicial offices) and the city had a twenty-six-member council, with the aldermen elected by wards. Effective in 1953, the council was reduced in size to thirteen, but the city government remains in every way a weak-mayor city. Other cities include Providence (1950 population: 247,700) and Atlanta (1950 population: 327,090). Chicago, with its huge council of fifty members elected by wards, retains many of the characteristics of the weak-mayor system, as does Los Angeles, where administrative boards and commissions are extensively used.

Rather extreme examples of the weak-mayor system may still be found in many places. Stevens Point, Wisconsin (1950 population: 16,550), is an excellent example. The voters select directly a mayor, a controller, a clerk, a treasurer, an assessor, a city engineer, a health officer, a street superintendent, a park superintendent, a city attorney, and ward aldermen, in addition to school officials. The pattern is even more complicated, for control of the police and fire departments is vested in a commission separate from the council.

The structure of the weak-mayor–council plan is not satisfactory for modern government. It is a clumsy, uncoordinated, amateurish, irresponsible, expensive system that provides adequate services, if it does at all, only by accident.

The Strong-mayor–Council Plan. The development of a strong-mayor system of government in the last two decades of the nineteenth century was a gradual one. The new plan differed only in degree from that of the weak mayor. It was not conceived of as a distinctly new form of government, nor was it one. Actually, the weak-mayor form resembled the structure of most state governments of that day and this. The strong-mayor system, on the other hand, was modeled on the national government, with its integrated[7] administrative structure under the control of the President.

It must be kept in mind that there are few, if any, cities that meet exactly all of the conditions of the theoretical model of the strong-mayor system as it is described below and in Figure 14. Most mayor-council cities represent a compromise between the very weak and the very strong mayor plan. The typical one is actually very difficult to classify.

Characteristics. In the strong-mayor–council city, administrative responsibility is concentrated in the hands of the mayor, while policy making is a joint function of the mayor and the council.[8] The plan calls

---

[7] For a definition of *integration,* see p. 57.

[8] The strong-mayor plan is sometimes called the "federal" plan, because it follows roughly the plan of the Federal government, but this term is confusing and will not be used in this text.

for a short ballot with the mayor as the only elected administrative officer. He in turn appoints and dismisses department heads, preferably without councilmanic approval. The mayor thus becomes the officer responsible for the carrying out of established policy and for coordinating the efforts of the various departments. The mayor is also responsible for the preparation of the annual budget and for the administration of the budget once it is adopted by the council. This allows the whole financial picture and the needs of the various departments to be com-

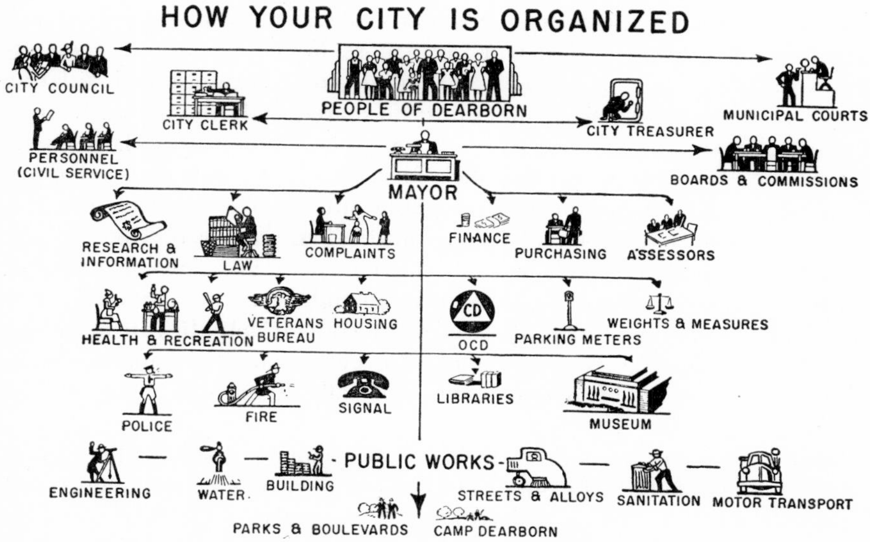

HOW YOUR CITY IS ORGANIZED

Fig. 14. An actual strong-mayor–council city: Dearborn, Mich. Note: There are twenty boards and commissions. A few of them perform staff functions (e.g., Board of Assessors, Civil Service Board); others are for appeal purposes (e.g., Plumbing Board of Appeals, Zoning Board of Appeals); the remainder are advisory (e.g., Plan Commission, Recreation Commission). SOURCE: City of Dearborn, *A Diary of Service, 1950–51.*

pared in financial policy making. This is in contrast to the piecemeal methods by which these things are approached under the weak-mayor plan.

The mayor's legal position allows him to exert very strong *political* leadership in addition to his powerful administrative leadership. Not only does he have the veto power and the right to recommend legislative policy to the council, as is the case under the weak-mayor system, but his complete control over administration gives him constant oversight of the needs of the city as a whole and furnishes a vantage point from which to recommend policy. Furthermore, his strong administrative position rightfully allows the newspapers to give him credit or blame for events that take place within city government. The resultant publicity makes the public keenly aware of his activities and of his recommendations to the council. As in the case of the President of the United States, when a strong mayor speaks, he receives far more attention than does even the most experienced or most respected member of the legislative branch. The fact that the mayor presents a comprehensive budget to the council for consideration also adds to his dominant political position, for by this very act public attention is focused on the mayor and the burden of proof for any changes in the budget is placed upon the council.

The council plays a very subordinate role in a strong-mayor city. It does not, as in the weak-mayor city, share in the performance of administrative duties. Its functions are limited to the exercise of legislative policy making, and even this role must be shared with the mayor. If there is an aggressive member of the council, that body may seek to make policy for itself. But it is more likely that the mayor's recommendations, backed as they are by the greater public attention focused on him, by his constant oversight of the city administration, and by his veto power, will be dutifully enacted by the council, perhaps after insignificant changes or after a symbolic show of independence. The average citizen is not likely to have much knowledge of council activities in a strong-mayor city. In a large city he is unlikely even to know the names of more than one or two of the councilmen, especially if the council is elected at large, as is often the case.

Because the council is exclusively a policy-making body for the city as a whole, it is likely to be small (typically seven or nine members) and elected at large on either a partisan or a nonpartisan ballot. Unless the city is very large, members are likely to serve on a part-time basis, since they have no administrative duties to perform and are not expected, as they are in the weak-mayor system, to serve as errand boys for residents of their wards. When council members serve only part time, the effect is to give the mayor even greater powers, since he has the advantage of spending the whole of his day studying the needs of the city. This may tend to place the council in an even more subordinate position. It will certainly place its members at a disadvantage in obtaining and evaluating information from the various departments and will place an even greater burden of proof upon the council when it disagrees with the proposed policies of the mayor. Terms of office for both mayor and council are likely to be four years in length. This is the result of the reform-movement attitude that public officials should be given time enough in office to prove themselves.

In addition to performing part of the legislative function, the council is also entrusted with the important task of serving as critic. This is a function of all legislative bodies, of course, but it becomes unusually important where complete administrative power is vested in one official. The council is usually given full power to conduct investigations into any department or any phase of administration. In addition, an officer, usually called the auditor and responsible to the council, checks upon the way in which the administrative branch of the city has spent the moneys appropriated by the council.[9]

Appraisal. Because of its provision for vigorous political leadership, the strong-mayor plan is especially desirable for use in large cities, where the complexities of government require someone to give firm leadership and direction. No other form of government in use in American cities makes an equal provision for leadership. It is significant to note that nearly all of the nation's largest cities have some version of the strong-mayor plan. In smaller cities, where the functions performed are fewer and simpler and where government is more personal, the need for this type of leadership is somewhat less.

The strong-mayor plan has several distinct merits in comparison with the weak-mayor–council plan: it allows for the placement of responsibility by the voters; it allows for modern methods of budgeting and of personnel; it permits the coordination of administration; and it allows for over-all policy planning.

It has some disadvantages, too. Perhaps the major one is that it expects too much of the mayor. In addition to serving as ceremonial head of the city, he is supposed to be both an adroit politician and an expert administrator. This combination is not easy to find. The able politician is likely to be either inexperienced with administration or bored by it, or both. The person whose training and interest are in administration or some specialized phase of it is very possibly a colorless campaigner or one who finds politics personally distasteful. While the popular view that all politicians are extroverts and all public bureaucrats are introverts is not correct, it is true that political and administrative leadership is not often combined in the same person. The strong-mayor system expects that it will be.

Another problem in the strong-mayor system is that of getting persons of the proper qualifications to run for office. A person who can do all of the things expected of a strong mayor is usually highly successful in business and industry and is ordinarily unwilling to give up a position which pays a high salary and in which he has reasonable security to conduct a political campaign for a position which carries far less salary and no security.

In selecting a mayor, many voters would no doubt like to consider the qualifications of each candidate as a capable administrator, but they are necessarily unable to do so. Judging whether or not a person is a

[9] See chap. 15 on fiscal administration.

good administrator is very difficult—more difficult than judging whether a person is technically qualified as an engineer or a physician. The candidates themselves are not of much help to the voter; the one who makes the greatest claims of administrative ability may be the one least qualified. The voter must always decide whether the candidates have suitable qualifications of two different sorts, political and administrative, and it is usually the political appeals that determine the outcome of the contest.

It has sometimes been said that the strong-mayor plan is undesirable because it "mixes politics with administration," but this is not a very valid argument. As a matter of fact, this could be offered as an argument *for* the plan. The mayor is able to place administrative problems in their political context—where they must eventually be placed in a democracy. He can compromise between these two inseparable aspects of government.

A final weakness of the plan must be mentioned. Because it is based upon that American favorite, the separation of powers, in combination with its obverse, the checks-and-balances system, the possibility of a deadlock between the mayor and the council on the formulation of policy is always present. On the national level, where the same system exists, most students are aware of serious deadlocks that have taken place—during the last two years of Wilson's administration, the last two of Hoover's, and almost the whole of Truman's after 1946. Where the mayor urges one set of policies and the council another, they can scarcely both be said to be representing the desires of the people, yet this situation does occur. It is perhaps less common on the local level than on the national, however, because the strong mayor so often tends to dominate the political scene and is in a position to keep the council in line. The weakness is, however, inherent in the system.

The Strong-mayor–Council Plan with Chief Administrative Officer. The chief executive in a strong-mayor city may well recognize his shortcomings as an administrator and attempt to do something about it. The most common method of buttressing his position is to appoint an able, professionally experienced administrator to the position of chief fiscal officer, usually called the controller. He may act as something of a deputy mayor and attend to many details of administration.

Unfortunately, the typical politician-mayor is not always willing to choose professional deputies. To remedy this weakness of the strong-mayor plan, a recent trend has been toward establishing by charter or ordinance an official known by various titles but perhaps best called a chief administrative officer (CAO) (see Figure 15). His powers vary considerably from one city to another, and sometimes he can scarcely be differentiated from the chief budget or fiscal officer, but according to

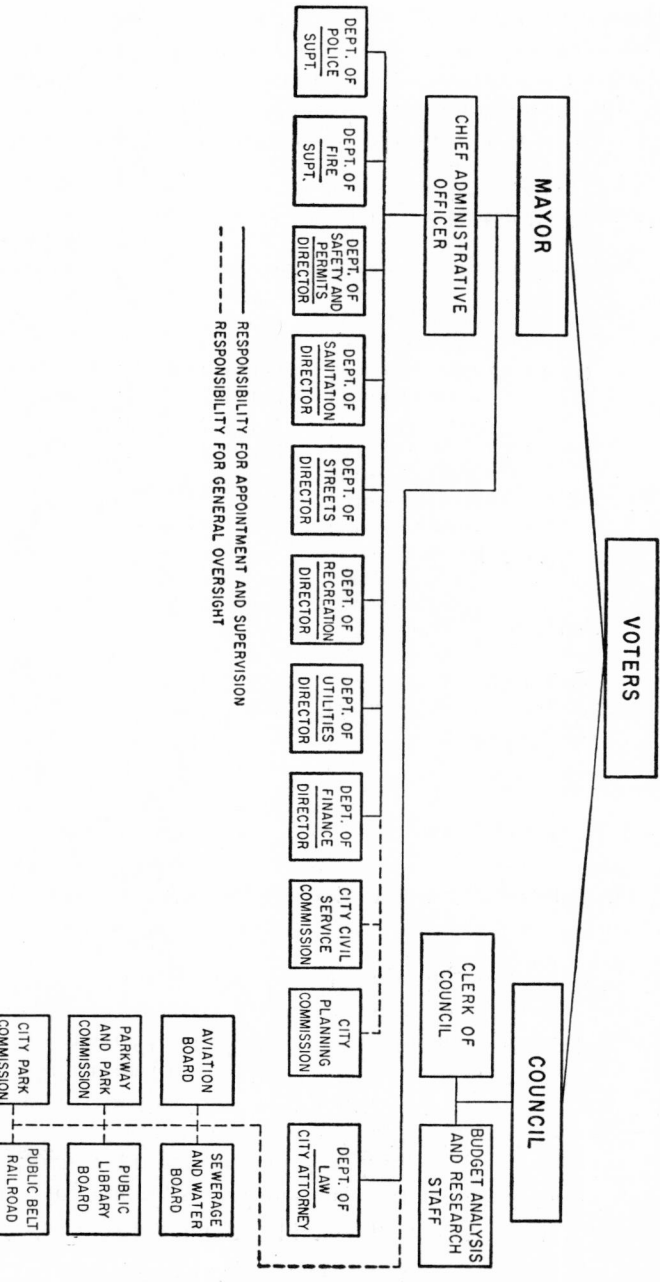

Fig. 15. An actual strong-mayor-council city with chief administrative officer: New Orleans, La. Note: Not all agencies are shown.
SOURCE: Adapted from City of New Orleans, *Annual Report of the Mayor* (1952–1953), pp. 2–3.

Governing Urban America

the theory of the position he should be appointed by the mayor and should perform, in general, such functions as the supervision of heads of various departments, preparation of the budget (or supervision over the budget director), and personnel direction. It is his task to correlate the various departments in the important routine of day-to-day administration, to give technical and professional advice to the political mayor, and hence to free the mayor for his other two major jobs of serving as ceremonial head of the city (greeting the governor, laying cornerstones, and crowning the latest beauty queen) and of proposing and launching broad over-all policy.

Table 8. Structures of Government in America's Largest Cities

City	Population, 1950, within city limits	Structure of government*
New York...............	7,891,957	Strong mayor
Chicago................	3,620,962	Moderately strong mayor
Philadelphia............	2,071,605	Strong mayor with CAO
Los Angeles............	1,970,358	Moderately weak mayor
Detroit................	1,849,568	Strong mayor
Baltimore..............	949,708	Moderately strong mayor
Cleveland..............	914,808	Strong mayor
St. Louis..............	856,796	Strong mayor
Washington............	802,178	Special commission†
Boston.................	801,444	Strong mayor
San Francisco..........	775,357	Moderately strong mayor with CAO
Pittsburgh.............	676,806	Strong mayor
Milwaukee.............	637,392	Moderately weak mayor
Houston...............	596,163	Strong mayor
Buffalo................	580,132	Strong mayor
New Orleans...........	570,455	Strong mayor with CAO
Minneapolis...........	521,718	Weak mayor
Cincinnati.............	503,998	Council-Manager

* It must be remembered that all these cities have unique forms of government that fit only roughly into categories.

† Washington is governed by a commission appointed by the President with the approval of the Senate. There is no local self-government in the city.

The origins of the CAO are somewhat obscure, since it grew out of the garden-variety mayor-council plans, but the city and county of San Francisco appointed one in 1931 who must have been one of the earliest.[10] Many CAOs have been appointed in California in the postwar years, but these all appear to be *managers* with reduced administrative authority.

[10] John C. Bollens, *Appointed Executive Local Government: the California Experience* (1952), pp. 12–14. See Lent D. Upson, *A Proposal for an Administrative Assistant to the Mayor* (1931); reported in *The American City*, vol. 44 (June, 1931), p. 93.

These so-called CAOs are appointed by the council, as is a manager, rather than by the mayor. In California, only San Francisco has a CAO in the sense defined in this book, and even in that city he heads up a group of city offices dealing with public works. He does not make up the budget or coordinate city departments.[11]

Some authorities believe that the CAO plan should be classified as a variation of the manager plan, rather than of the mayor-council plan. It combines some of the characteristics of each, and its classification is probably not too important. It is listed here in this text because it is a plan that continues the use of the separation-of-powers theory and places ultimate responsibility for administration in the hands of the mayor, rather than the council as is the case with the manager plan. In states where there are broad home rule powers, many of the advantages of the council-manager plan can be incorporated under the strong-mayor form. As a result, there is no rigid dividing line between the two forms. The reader is reminded that forms of government in the United States do not fit readily or neatly into categories.

The Current Trend. Large-city interest in the strong-mayor plan with CAO has been very definitely on the increase since the end of World War II. The Philadelphia charter of 1951 provides for a CAO, as does the 1952 model of the New Orleans charter. Both are home rule cities. The New Orleans charter, for example, calls for a council of seven, five elected by districts and two elected at large, for four-year terms. The mayor has the usual powers in policy making and in addition appoints a CAO, who serves at his pleasure. The CAO, with the approval of the mayor, appoints the heads of departments, except for those whose positions are filled according to state law. The CAO, of course, has supervisory and coordinative powers over the departments whose heads he appoints.[12]

A CAO established by ordinance has served in Louisville under two mayors. St. Cloud, Minnesota, adopted the CAO plan in its 1952 charter. A director of administrative services, with some of the powers of a CAO, has been established in Boston.

A 1951 charter amendment provides for an administrative officer for Los Angeles. He is appointed by the mayor with majority confirmation by the council and is removable by the same process or by a two-thirds vote in the council. This officer cannot properly be called a CAO, since Los Angeles is basically a weak-mayor city and the administrative officer at present is principally the mayor's budget officer. In that city the council has numerous administrative duties, and there are a score of departments controlled by five-man commissions appointed by the mayor

---

[11] See Bollens, *op. cit.*, pp. 9–11, 119–123.
[12] See *National Municipal Review*, vol. 41 (May, 1952), p. 250; vol. 41 (December, 1952), p. 570.

with the check of councilmanic approval and with a limited removal power. The city attorney and controller are elected officials.

A 1953 report of the Los Angeles Commission for Reorganization of City Government recommended, among other things, that the office of the administrative officer be strengthened so that he could become a true CAO.[13] He would retain his present budget powers and in addition would be given supervisory control over twelve operating and service departments. The present method of divided responsibility between mayor and council would continue on his appointment and removal. These and other recommendations of this commission would change Los Angeles into a moderately strong mayor city with CAO.

The 1950 Faulkner Act in New Jersey provides for optional charters that are adopted in the various cities after a local charter commission decides to present one of the options to the voters for approval. It makes the strong-mayor plan with CAO one of the options. A 1952 charter commission in Hoboken, New Jersey (1950 population: 50,676), recommended, and the voters adopted, this plan as a replacement for the commission plan which the city had been using for thirty-seven years. Newark, New Jersey, adopted the same option the following year.

Adoption in New York. In 1953, two study groups recommended the CAO plan for use in the city of New York. After a three-year study (it cost $2,200,000) the Mayor's Commission on Management Survey in its final report recommended against a general overhaul of the city's organizational structure and suggested the creation of a new office, that of a CAO to be called a director of administration. It was also suggested that a "management cabinet," to consist of seven ex officio members, be appointed to aid the mayor.[14] The director of administration would perform supervisory and coordinative functions over most of the city's departments and agencies. The deputy mayor would be assigned nearly all of the ceremonial duties of the city.

The governmental problems of the city of New York are constantly being studied. Governor Thomas E. Dewey proposed in 1953 that the general assembly set up a *state* commission to study the city's organizational structure—and the general assembly was happy to do so. A third study, this one by the City Manager Study Committee which was appointed by the Citizens' Union of New York, also recommended the creation of the office of a CAO.[15] This report said that the commission was not

---

[13] *National Municipal Review*, vol. 42 (July, 1953), pp. 338–339.

[14] See *National Municipal Review*, vol. 42 (May, 1953), pp. 232–233.

[15] The study committee was made up of seventeen members. Since the Citizens' Union carries the banner of reform and good government in New York, the make-up of the committee is especially interesting. It included twelve representatives of business, four academicians, and one representative of labor. A great weakness of the reform movement has been in its failure to include a cross section of the population.

prepared to recommend the council-manager plan for the city at that time.

Immediately after his election as mayor of the city in November, 1953, Robert F. Wagner, Jr., announced that he would appoint a CAO to the new post of City Administrator. For this task he selected a widely known student and practitioner of public administration, Luther H. Gulick.

Appraisal. The strong-mayor plan with chief administrative officer seeks to correct a major defect in the ordinary strong-mayor plan. It would appear to be a desirable development, since it would free the mayor for policy making, which is his more proper field, and would give the city a professionally competent man to head administration. This new variation on the old theme would appear to be especially acceptable in large cities, and these are the ones that, in fact, seem most interested in the development. The use of the strong-mayor plan with this modification would, however, leave that system still with at least one major potential defect: the continuing threat of a legislative-executive deadlock. It would appear, too, that there would be a great potential for jealous rivalry between the mayor and the CAO or for an uncooperative mayor to appropriate for himself the powers and functions of the appointive CAO.

CITIES WITHOUT A SEPARATION OF POWERS

The Commission Plan. A hurricane in September, 1900, almost completely destroyed the city of Galveston, Texas, and in doing so created the conditions under which the commission plan was produced. Actually, as Richard S. Childs has pointed out, the commission structure was not planned; it was the result of an accident.[16] During the period of rebuilding Galveston, the legislature suspended local self-government in the city and substituted a temporary government of five local businessmen—the Galveston *commission,* hence the name for the system. The commission, working with great zeal under extraordinary conditions, accomplished much more at less cost than had its almost bankrupt predecessor. A new charter in 1903 tried to retain the system that had been working well and provided for a continuation of the commission, with three of its members appointed by the governor and two to be elected within the city. The courts held this unconstitutional, since an emergency no longer existed. The legislature then made all five commissioners elective.[17]

[16] Richard S. Childs, *Civic Victories* (1952), pp. 134–136. Earlier precedents for the commission idea are cited in E. B. Schulz, *American City Government* (1949), pp. 319–321.

[17] Many state constitutions guarantee municipalities the right to elect their own officers.

The success of the commission plan in Galveston soon attracted wide attention. Other Texas cities adopted the plan, and it quickly became popular in many parts of the nation. A Des Moines attorney, visiting Galveston, was impressed with the new "businessman's government" and proceeded to persuade the Iowa legislature to permit his city to adopt the plan. The legislature added other reform devices to the new charter—nonpartisan elections, and the initiative, referendum, and recall. It then became the "Des Moines plan."

The commission plan was adopted in Houston in 1905 and in Des Moines in 1907, and by 1910 it had spread to some 108 cities. By 1917 at least 500 cities were using the plan. Then a reversal took place. The number of commission-governed cities stopped increasing and then began to diminish. Municipal reformers lost interest in the commission plan and began to advocate the council-manager plan as the true embodiment of a business form of organization. There have been almost no new adoptions since the 1930s, and the total number of commission cities has declined steadily since World War I.

Characteristics. The commission plan's outstanding feature is the dual role of the commissioners. Each of them serves individually as the head of one of the city's administrative departments, while collectively they serve as the policy-making council for the city. In this plan, unlike the various mayor-council structures, there is no separation of powers. The commission performs both legislative and executive functions (see Figures 16 and 17).

The commission is always small, usually consisting of five members, as did the original Galveston model. Some cities, especially small ones, have only three members, and quite a number have seven. There is a mayor, but in the theoretical model he has no powers beyond those of the other commissioners, except that he performs the ceremonial duties for the city and presides over the council. He has no veto power. In most cities the office of mayor is specifically named on the ballot and is hence filled by popular vote. In some cities, however, the council chooses one of their own members to serve as mayor, and in a few places the person who happens to receive the highest number of votes among all candidates becomes mayor.

Because the plan is a product of the reform movement, the commissioners are usually elected on a nonpartisan ticket. This is the case in about three-quarters of the municipalities. The commissioners are usually expected to serve as full-time public servants, even in fairly small cities; and in the original plan it was hoped that they would possess business or engineering experience and not be "mere politicians." They are nearly always elected at large, and four-year terms are most common.

There is a short ballot. According to the original plan, only the commissioners are elected. Often staggered terms are used so that only two or three members of a five-member commission are elected at one time.

Appraisal. The commission plan was a real improvement over the prevailing weak-mayor systems of the turn of the century. It concentrated responsibility in the hands of a few men so that the general public could assess credit or blame for municipal activities. It greatly shortened the

COMMISSION FORM

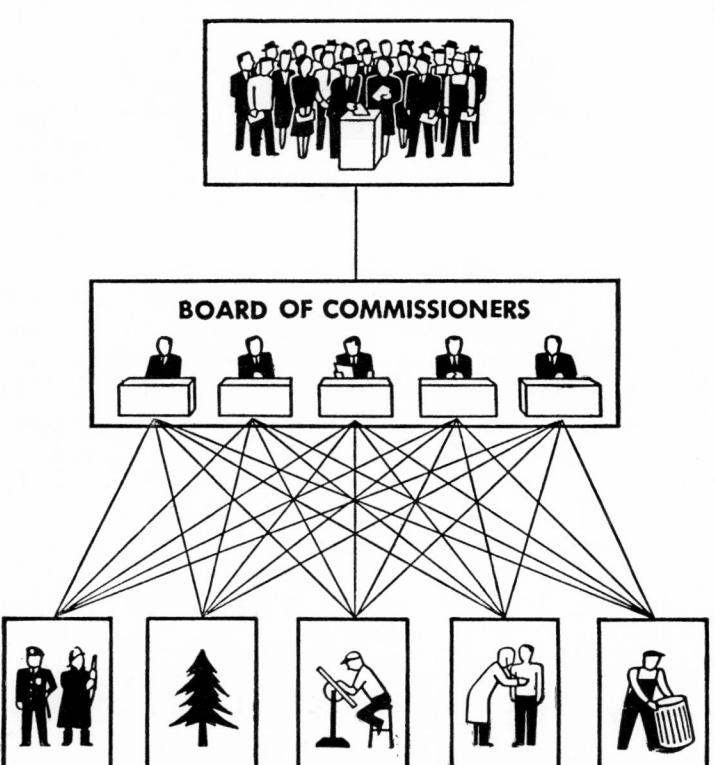

Fig. 16. SOURCE: Used by permission of the National Municipal League.

ballot from that which existed under the weak-mayor, or even most strong-mayor, systems. This gave the average voter a chance to know something about the character and qualifications of the candidates. Furthermore, only policy-making officers were chosen. Voters were not asked to select persons to fill routine offices (such as clerk or treasurer) or technical offices (such as controller or assessor). Since the separation-of-powers theory was not followed, there was no problem of the deadlock between the legislative and executive branches that is always a threat in any mayor-council city.

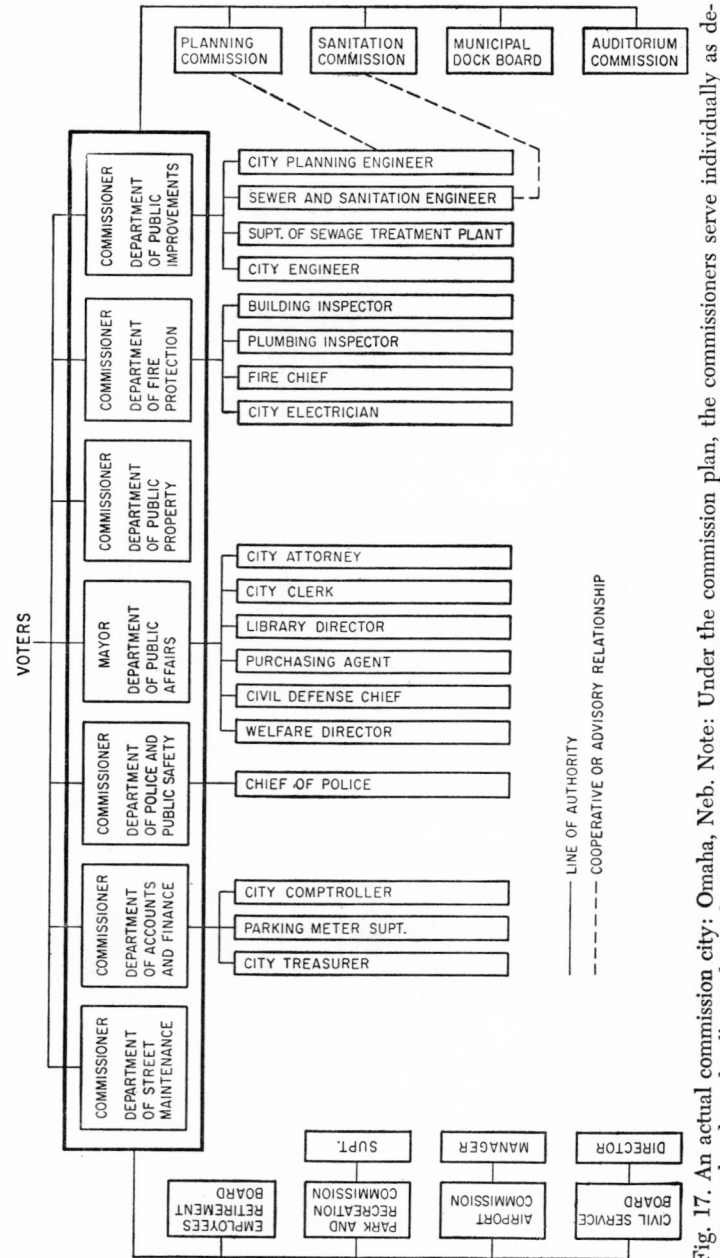

Fig. 17. An actual commission city: Omaha, Neb. Note: Under the commission plan, the commissioners serve individually as department heads and collectively as the governing body. Public health, not listed above, is a city-county function in Omaha and Douglas County. SOURCE: Adapted from City of Omaha, *A Financial Report for the Year 1952.*

The commission plan had, however, too many disadvantages to make it workable. It was supposed to provide for a city policy-making body on which businessmen on leave from their ordinary pursuits would be willing to serve. Sometimes this was the case—for a few years. Actually, as a regular practice, it was not possible to select commissioners from among successful businessmen, or successful persons from any walk of life, for they were unwilling to give up their own businesses and run for an office that paid a low salary.

Responsibility to the public was not definitely fixed; it was divided among the several commissioners. The plan did not eliminate amateur administrators as department heads. In this respect the situation was not changed much from the Jacksonian weak-mayor plan. A local citizen might well be able to help make basic policy for the police department or for public ways, but he would be able to serve capably as *administrative* head of either department only as the result of political accident.

The commission was often too small to provide for the function of *criticism.* It is of the essence in a democracy that the actions of public officials are constantly subjected to critical evaluation. While the mayor-council system might lead to deadlocks, it at least provided a mechanism of criticism. This was not true of the commission plan. There was no separation of powers, so that only the commission members were left to criticize one another. In theory they could do so, but three to seven people seeing one another day after day put their relationships on a personal basis. As politicians they are certain to desire to avoid criticism. The commission very often, therefore, became a fraternity of tolerance.

Instead of watching one another, the commissioners would agree that "if you stay out of my department, I will stay out of yours." Criticism came to an end. There was no minority party to watch the majority. There were no "backbenchers" eagerly awaiting the chance to replace a member of the cabinet, as there is in the parliamentary system of government. There was no mayor with policy message and veto ready. The mutual hands-off policy went even further. In many cities it meant that there were really several different city governments, each operating independently of the others, but with an occasional five-power conference being held to satisfy the demands of the charter.

There were two further serious weaknesses of the commission device, both of them dealing with a lack of leadership. The plan, it developed, did not provide for either a chief *administrator* or a chief *policy* leader. The strong-mayor and manager forms provide for administrative integration with a top official ultimately answerable to the council for all administrative operations. No such person existed in the formal structure of the commission plan. And jealousy of the rights of independence of one's department was likely to keep it from existing in actual practice.

The top of the administrative pyramid was sawed off. Each department ran off in its own administrative direction with no coordination at the top. This might be true to a degree even exceeding that found in the weak-mayor system.

There was no provision for top policy leadership either, except fortuitously. The commissioners were equals and were likely to guard their equality with great zeal. There was no top policy maker, as under the strong-mayor system. It is true that an individual commissioner might by personality, experience, or skill at political organization come to dominate the council, but this was not the rule.

The plan was an improvement over the weak-mayor system of its day, but it was in turn quickly outmoded by the new manager plan and the development of a modern strong mayor. The inherent weaknesses of the commission plan then rapidly became manifest.

Present Status. A large number of commission-governed cities remain in the United States today (383 in 1952), although all of the many Canadian cities that once used it have by now abandoned it. The total number of cities under the plan has been on the decline since about 1917, and the drop has been especially sharp since 1946. Even so, about 15 per cent of the cities with a population of more than 5,000 still use it. Its principal use is in three states. New Jersey had sixty-one cities under the plan in 1952,[18] but a new state optional charter plan offered the possibility that this figure would drop off sharply in the next few years. All third-class cities in Pennsylvania, about forty-seven of them, are required by law to use the commission plan. In 1952, there were about seventy Illinois cities under this form of government, but the number has subsequently decreased rapidly, since the larger cities of that state have been permitted to adopt council-manager charters for the first time under a 1951 law. The largest city still using the commission plan in 1954 was Memphis (see Table 9).

Abandonments, especially in larger cities, have come at a rapid rate in the postwar world. The "Des Moines plan" was abandoned in Des Moines in 1949 in favor of the council-manager form. San Antonio, after thirty-seven years as a commission city, switched to the manager plan in 1951. The Hoboken, New Jersey, charter commission denounced the commission plan in that city as having been "a complete failure," and the city changed in 1952 to the strong-mayor plan with CAO. So did New Orleans.

Inadequacy of political and administrative leadership is felt most in the largest cities. Medium-sized and small cities, however, are also abandoning the commission plan. The trend in these cities might be symbolized

[18] According to a note in the *National Municipal Review,* vol. 41 (September, 1952), p. 407. Childs, *op. cit.,* p. 139, gives the figure as fifty-nine.

Table 9. Largest Commission Cities in the United States

City	1950 population	Size of council	No. at large	Type of election*	Term years	Salary 1952	Other elective officers
Memphis......	396,000	5	5	NP	4	$ 6,000	Assessor
Portland, Oreg.	373,628	5	5	NP-s	4	10,080	Auditor
Birmingham...	326,037	3	3	NP	4	7,000	
St. Paul.......	311,349	7	7	NP	2	6,500	Controller
Jersey City....	299,017	5	5	NP	4	7,500	
Omaha........	251,117	7	7	NP	3	4,500	

* Under "Type of Election," "NP" refers to nonpartisan elections, while "-s" following means that commission terms are staggered so that all do not expire at once. "Salary" refers to that of commission members.

SOURCE: *Municipal Year Book, 1953*, pp. 70–71.

by the action of Beatrice, Nebraska (1950 population: 11,813), which abandoned the commission plan in 1952 after using it for forty years. The city now operates under the mayor-council plan.

Outmoded structures of government live beyond the time when they deserve to die, as do all human institutions which suffer the rigidity of being organized on a formal basis. The voters of Duluth, for example, in 1952 refused to adopt charter amendments that would fundamentally alter the commission structure and in effect abandon the plan. But such actions move against the stream. There is no future for the commission structure of government.[19] Those commission cities that remain do so as a result of apathy or because officeholders have a vested interest in the *status quo.*

The Council-manager Plan. The origin of the idea for the council-manager plan is not known with certainty. It seems that one of the first instances in which it was urged was in an editorial in the August, 1899, issue of *California Municipalities.* Haven A. Mason, editor of the magazine, urged that there should be "a distinct profession of municipal managers." He listed desirable qualifications, saying that a manager should know something about engineering, street construction, sewers, building construction, water and lighting systems, personnel, accounting, municipal law, fire protection, and library management. "Every city that receives or expends $50,000 annually," he said, "ought to have a salaried

[19] The view of reformers toward the plan during its most popular years is expressed in E. S. Bradford, *Commission Government in American Cities* (1911); and Henry Bruère, *The New City Government* (1912). The failure of the plan as a solution is expressed in C. M. Fassett, "The Weakness of Commission Government," *National Municipal Review,* vol. 9 (October, 1920), pp. 642–647. Criticisms of the plan are offered in Charles M. Kneier and Guy Fox, *Readings in Municipal Government and Administration* (1953), pp. 288–291.

business manager." He even went so far as to say that "when we require adepts to run our cities, our universities will establish a department to specially fit our young men to enter the new profession of conducting municipal business."[20]

The claim for having the first council-manager city is sometimes disputed between Staunton, Virginia, and Sumter, South Carolina. In 1908, Staunton, with a weak mayor and a bicameral council, felt the need for a more modern form of city government. Getting a new charter from the legislature would not have been easy. It was decided, therefore, to hire a "general manager" for the city on the basis of an ordinance. He was to be a full-time employee in charge of administration, was to be hired by the council, and could be dismissed by it at any time.

While the Staunton experiment did not produce a neat organization chart and was not based upon a carefully calculated theory, it may correctly be said to have become a manager-plan city in that year. Richard S. Childs, a businessman who was at that time secretary of the National Short Ballot Organization and who later was to become president of the National Municipal League, took a leading part in the development and popularizing of the plan. In 1911 he drew up a proposed city charter which was endorsed by the Board of Trade (chamber of commerce) of Lockport, New York. As it happened, the state general assembly refused to allow the city to use this model manager charter, but the charter attracted a good bit of attention and was adopted by Sumter, South Carolina, in the following year.

The manager-plan idea spread with great speed. During 1913, several small cities and towns adopted the Childs charter. At the same time, the Chamber of Commerce of Dayton appointed a committee to study the need for a new charter in that city, for the state of Ohio had just granted to its municipalities the power of home rule. The committee, which was headed by John M. Patterson, president of the National Cash Register Company, came to favor the manager plan. While the group was pursuing its efforts, the Miami River, which passes through the city, overflowed its banks in spring flood. The ineptitude of the existing city government in meeting the problems that followed gave unexpectedly dramatic support to the efforts of the charter-study committee. The people adopted the proposed new charter in August. It went into effect on January 1, 1914, and the new council promptly hired the city engineer of Cincinnati as manager, thus setting a precedent for the type of person that is still very commonly preferred for the position.

The Dayton episode, partly because it occurred in a large city, partly because of the personal publicity efforts of Patterson, and partly because of the extraordinary drama connected with it, gave a tremendous boost

[20] The editorial is reprinted in Bollens, *op. cit.*, appendix III.

to the council-manager plan. By 1915, there were 49 manager cities. Five years later there were 158. The number has increased uninterruptedly ever since. On January 1, 1954, there were 1,229 manager cities and other local governments in the United States and Canada.[21] Over 35 per cent of the cities of over 25,000 population had managers, as did almost one-third of those between 10,000 and 25,000 (see Figure 18).

Only Arkansas, Indiana, and Louisiana had no manager cities of any kind in 1953. There were none in Rhode Island until a constitutional amendment was passed in 1952. No charters providing for the manager plan were authorized in Illinois for cities over 5,000 until 1951, when a general enabling act made it available to all cities, except Chicago, on

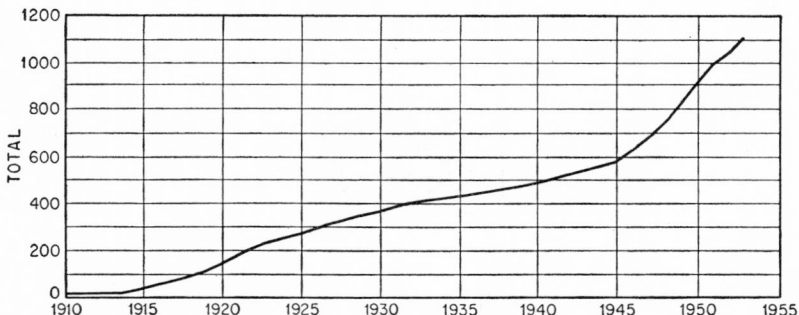

Fig. 18. The growth of the council-manager plan. The table is based only upon adoptions still in effect Mar. 1, 1953, and includes only municipal corporations, towns, and townships in the continental United States. Note the post–World War II spurt and contrast it with the depression years (1929–1939). SOURCE: "The City Manager Directory," *Municipal Year Book* (1953), pp. 521–540.

an optional plan. At the time of the passage of the act, Illinois had fifteen small cities operating under a manager, mostly on the basis of *ordinances.* The manager plan has enjoyed a rapid expansion in the period following World War II.

Characteristics.[22] The outstanding identifying marks of the council-manager plan include a council of laymen responsible for policy making and a professional administration under a chief administrator responsible to the council. The theoretical structure rivals that of the British parliamentary system in its simplicity (see Figures 19 and 20).

The council is small, five to nine members, and is commonly elected at large, on a nonpartisan ballot, often for four-year staggered terms. It is responsible to the public for all policy making and ultimately for the over-all

[21] *National Municipal Review,* vol. 43 (February, 1954), p. 81.
[22] The National Municipal League has issued several pamphlets in popular form. See especially *Forms of Municipal Government* (revised, 1951); and *The Story of the Council-Manager Plan* (revised, 1952).

character of administration. Under the model charter,[23] members of the council are the only officers who are popularly elected. The intended purpose of the short ballot is to concentrate responsibility upon these people and to ask the voters to fill only important policy-making positions in which they can reasonably be expected to take an interest.

COUNCIL-MANAGER FORM

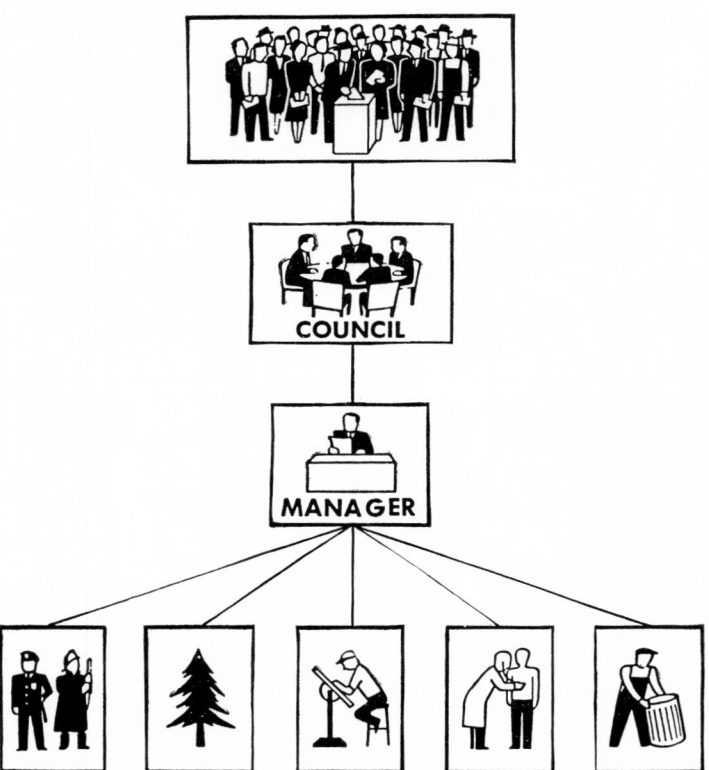

Fig. 19. By permission of the National Municipal League.

There is no separation of powers or checks and balances. There is a mayor or president of the city or village, but he normally performs only ceremonial functions and presides over the council. He has no administrative powers, except in the case of an emergency, and has no veto. In more than one-half of the cities over 5,000 population (57.2 per cent in 1952), the council chooses the mayor from among its own membership.

[23] See the *Model City Charter* (revised, 1941) of the National Municipal League. The manager plan has been endorsed by the League since 1916.

In most other cities he is directly elected, although a few give the post to the person with the most votes in the councilmanic race.

The administration of the city is integrated under the control of a professional manager, who is hired by the council. He serves, in the model plan, for no definite term of office, but rather at the pleasure of a majority of the council. He is not subject to recall by the voters, for they did not

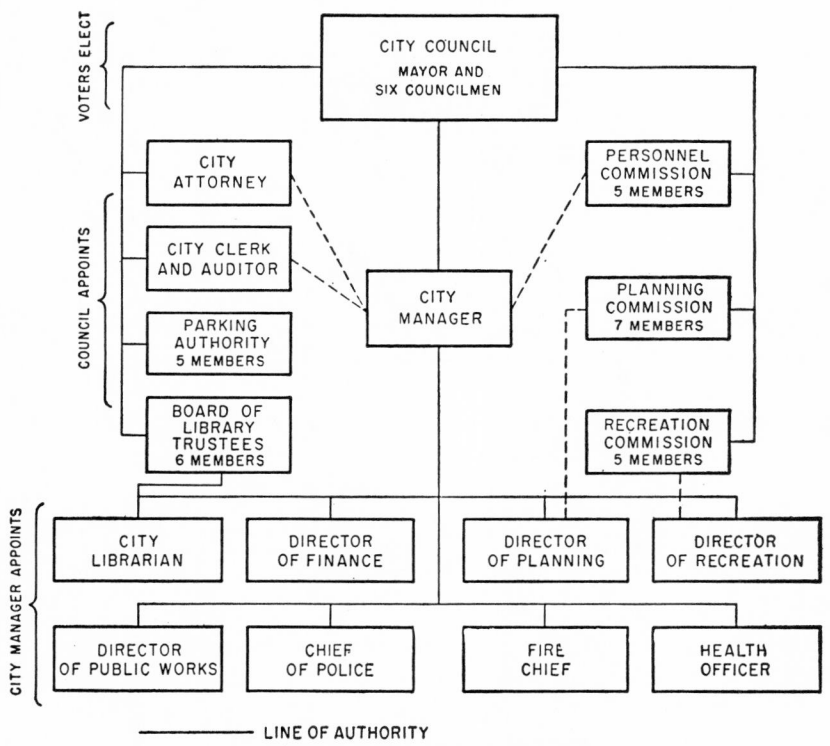

Fig. 20. An actual council-manager city: Modesto, Calif. SOURCE: Adapted from City of Modesto, *A Report of Progress* (1951–1952).

hire him, and furthermore, ultimate responsibility for the quality of the administration belongs to the council. No manager may serve effectively if he does not enjoy the confidence of a majority of the council, and therefore the credit or blame for what he does rests with the council.

Not only is the manager a professional person, but he is expected to hire professionally competent technicians to run the various departments of the city. The lower administrative positions, roughly those below the department heads, are also filled with persons who are technically competent. They are usually chosen by civil-service merit examination.

Appraisal. Municipal reformers have tended to accord to this plan inordinate praise, often attributing to it miraculous powers to bring about efficient and economical city administration regardless of the traditions of city government, the kind of personnel which it employs, and whether the public understands and supports the basic principles of the plan. These exaggerated claims for the plan, as well as some of the specious arguments used against it, should be discounted by the sophisticated student of municipal affairs.

The council-manager plan is indeed a good one, although it possesses certain faults that are inherent. The plan calls for lay citizens, commonly political amateurs, to serve on the council and make public policy as representatives of the community. This is a personification of democracy at work. There are no professional politicians seeking to make a living from the position, for the councilmanic jobs normally pay only a very nominal salary or only a per meeting allowance.

The plan has an advantage over other plans, however, in turning over the execution of policy as determined by the council to a professional staff of administrators headed by the manager. All administrators and technicians are especially qualified for their jobs—an important fact in a day when government performs many complicated and technical functions. The chief administrator can be selected by the council, not from among only local politicians of one party, as would be the case if it were a patronage appointment, but rather from among trained persons from anywhere in the nation. The choice is limited only by what the council believes it can afford to pay.

But while the manager plan emphasizes professional administration, it does not turn the city over to the whims of an independent bureaucracy. The manager and his subordinates are constantly responsible for their actions to the political branch of the government. They normally attend council sessions, where they are expected to answer questions, report on progress of various projects, and explain any of their actions that involve matters in which the council is interested. And there are none of the legislative-executive conflicts that arise from time to time in the mayor-council city, since, as in the parliamentary system, those who carry out policy serve at the pleasure of the legislative branch.

In contrast to the commission plan, however, there is a provision for criticism. There is no dividing up of the administrative spoils among the council members, and hence there is less of a need for a collusion against criticism. The legislative branch remains free to oversee the operation of administration, and it is especially important to note that the people who appropriate the funds are not the people who spend them. The council votes the funds and then checks upon the manager and his staff both through their own supervision and through the receipt of auditors' reports.

Although the manager plan is a simple mechanism, it is not always understood by the general public. An important factor contributing to this is the carry-over to the present day of many elements of Jacksonian philosophy. For example, the plan is sometimes challenged as "dictatorial" or "un-American" because the chief administrator is not elected. To be sure, this fact violates an almost sacred precept of Jacksonianism. But the argument is invalid, since there is full responsibility for administration. The absence of a check-and-balance system also troubles those dedicated to Jacksonian tradition.

Some people argue that the manager plan costs too much for small cities, because the position of manager must command enough pay to attract competent personnel. It is also argued that the manager would not have enough work to keep him busy in a small city. These arguments would seem invalid for most small places, however, for the plan is in operation in a large number of municipalities of under 5,000 population.[24]

There are more serious objections to the plan, however. The number of cities needing managers and professional department heads has increased so rapidly in the postwar era that there is a shortage of able managers. The ample number of positions in private business for administrators and engineers has also helped to reduce the number of persons available to cities. Some cities have tried the plan, only to complain bitterly that the manager was incompetent. In many cases the complaint is undoubtedly justified.

Managers are sometimes criticized on another legitimate ground. Many of them are engineers who have had no training in the social sciences. As such, some of them may tend to view issues of public policy as a series of engineering or budgeting problems rather than as matters of economics and sociology.

Some advocates of the manager plan have made the· erroneous and unrealistic assumption that a sharp· distinction can be made between politics and administration. No such line· exists. One shades off into the other. Their theory holds that the manager is a nonelective employee who should not make policy but should concern himself only with the details of administration. Actually, it is almost a necessity for the lay, part-time council to look to the professional, full-time manager for recommendations concerning policy. If harmonious relations exist and the manager and the council are competent, the council will ordinarily not

---

[24] The pattern of managership in these cities· is described in W. C. Busby, "The Small Council–Manager City," *Public Management,* vol. 35 (July, 1953), pp. 154–156.

act on any policy matter without first getting the recommendations and a statement of the pertinent facts from the manager.[25] On some types of highly controversial issues a manager, if he is wise, will avoid taking a stand, but apart from these, it is his job to make recommendations and, in fact, to initiate policy recommendations. He is nearly always in a better position to recognize the needs of the city than is the council. If the council accepts the recommendations of the manager with regularity, it does not necessarily mean that it is a rubber stamp; it may mean merely that the council has hired a competent manager.

Among managers themselves there are two philosophies (perhaps it is more a matter of two personality types) which deal with the proper relationship of the manager to the council. Some managers center their attention on administrative operations and routine matters, carefully avoiding taking a stand on any city issue; others center their attention on policy matters and the development of the city. Both types have their merits. A city in one period of its history may need one type, at a different period the other type.

In some instances—Berkeley and East Cleveland at one time were examples—a well-entrenched manager, long in office, may completely dominate a council. He may not only make it into a rubber stamp, but may even have considerable influence in determining who should be elected to the council.

While the manager may tend to dominate the council in some cases, it is also true that the policy-making arm may tend to invade the area reserved for professional administrators. If the manager is weak, or if several members of the council do not accept the spirit of the manager plan, there may be a good deal of "political" interference in administration. Councilmen may bypass the manager and deal directly with members of departments, or seek to influence administrative decisions on the basis of political expediency rather than professional judgment.[26] Hostile councilmen may even appoint a local politician to the post of manager. In cases such as these, the manager plan cannot operate properly. It is the responsibility of the people to elect councilmen who will abide by the rules of the game. If they are not willing or able to do so, the possibilities for sabotage are very great.

It is not uncommon to find, especially where a modified manager plan leaves some administrative powers with the mayor, a disrupting and

[25] See A. W. Bromage, "Reducing the City Council's Work Load," *Public Management,* vol. 34 (April, 1952), pp. 74–76.

[26] For a case study of a city where several of the phenomena discussed in this section were found, see Dorothy I. Cline, *Albuquerque and the City Manager Plan, 1917–1948* (1951). Only about 4 per cent of the cities adopting the manager plan have later abandoned it. See A. W. Bromage, *Manager Plan Abandonments* (rev. ed., 1949); and E. O. Stene and G. K. Floro, *Abandonments of the Manager Plan; A Study of Four Small Cities* (1953).

undesirable power struggle between the mayor and the manager. This is also true in cities where the mayor does not understand or accept his role under the manager plan. If the public does not understand the principles of the plan, it is likely to support the mayor in such a fight, for the title of his office implies to many people that he ought to be the chief administrator. In some cities, certain officials, such as the city attorney, the city engineer, or the police chief, may be appointed by the mayor rather than by the manager. In such a case, there are really two managers, one amateur and the other professional. It often follows that the council members are eventually forced to "choose up sides" if either the mayor or the manager launches into a policy of aggrandizement. The results are usually a dead, or at least badly wounded, manager plan.

Perhaps the greatest potential weakness in the plan is to be found in connection with the problem of policy leadership. No adequate provision for it is made in the plan. The council is a body of equals. One of them may emerge as a leader in policy making, but if this is so it is the result of an accident. It is more likely that the council will flounder about or turn to the manager. This problem is seldom important in middle-sized cities, for these places perform fewer functions and the solving of issues of policy is normally not as complicated as it is in larger cities.

It is because of the leadership problem, however, that some political scientists have held that the manager plan is not well suited for the largest cities. Certainly not many of these cities have turned in its direction. It is pointed out that San Antonio is the only really large city to adopt and retain the plan since the depression years. Ten cities of over 250,000 were employing managers in 1954, however, and with apparent success, except perhaps in San Antonio, where the plan was under attack. Cincinnati and Kansas City have used the plan successfully for many years (see Table 10).

Governor Thomas E. Dewey, discussing the need for governmental reform in the city of New York, said in a 1953 message to the General Assembly: "I believe that a city manager form of government offers the brightest prospects to the people of our greatest city."[27] Many political scientists would be skeptical, however, although some would agree. There is little actual evidence, and there are certainly no systematic studies, to demonstrate either the desirability or the impossibility of manager government in very large cities.

The lack of a chief policy maker causes another problem from a different angle. In large cities, especially, it is difficult for the general public to know much about the various candidates for the council or about the voting records of incumbents. The problem is especially great when the

[27] Quoted in the *National Municipal Review,* vol. 42 (April, 1953), pp. 179–180. See also note on p. 191, same issue.

council is elected at large on a nonpartisan ballot, as is often the case. It is therefore not necessarily true that concentration of responsibility in the council will result in intelligent voting. In cities small enough for candidates to be known by reputation, this is not likely to be as serious a problem, if indeed it is a problem at all.

Table 10. Largest Council-manager Cities in the United States

City	1950 population	Date in effect	Size of council	No. at large	Type of election*	Term, years	Other elective officers
Cincinnati.....	503,998	1926	9	9	NP	2	
Kansas City...	456,622	1926	9	5	NP	4	
Dallas.........	434,462	1931	8	2	NP	2	
San Antonio...	408,442	1952	9	9	NP	2	
Oakland.......	384,575	1931	9	9	NP-s	4	Auditor
San Diego.....	334,387	1932	7	1	NP-s	4	Attorney
Rochester......	332,488	1928	9	5	P-s	4	
Toledo........	303,616	1936	9	9	NP	2	
Ft. Worth.....	278,778	1925	9	9	NP	2	
Long Beach....	250,767	1921	9	9	NP	3	Auditor Attorney

* Under "Type of Election," "NP" refers to nonpartisan and "P" to partisan elections, while "-s" following means that council terms are staggered so that all do not expire at once.

SOURCE: *Municipal Year Book, 1953*, pp. 70–71.

Actual Results.[28] A half century of experience with the council-manager plan indicates that it has accomplished much, even though it is no panacea. Where the plan has been adopted, it has not always done away with partisan patronage; professionally qualified managers are not always appointed; the manager is not always kept from becoming a symbol of controversy; and better city government has not always resulted. But despite important exceptions, the over-all result of the adoption of the council-manager plan has been better city government, politics, and administration and the development of a better community in which to live.

In considering typical results, we find that the adoption of the council-manager plan has resulted in increased prestige for the council and in greater control by it over municipal affairs. Managers have generally been appointed by the council without regard to political affiliation, and tenure for the manager has, in most cases, not been interrupted by political considerations. Most managers have given impartial administra-

[28] This section is based upon the findings reported in H. A. Stone, D. K. Price, and K. H. Stone, *City Manager Government in the United States* (1940), which is a report on a three-year survey of fifty cities.

tion and have brought far more coordination to the activities of their governments than had existed before. They have furthered long-range policy planning and have encouraged the employment of experts for advice on technical problems. They have brought about a definite improvement in personnel administration, have raised the standards of public employment, and have increased the interest of employees in their jobs. Managers have improved budgeting methods and have provided more financial information and better financial management than was afforded under the older forms of government.

The adoption of the council-manager form has not reduced the size of the total budget in most cities, but it has instead increased the public's confidence in municipal government so that cities have been asked to perform an increased number of community services. While the plan has not reduced the *total* cost of city government, it has reduced *unit* costs by eliminating graft and waste and by utilizing personnel and methods of greater efficiency. This has meant that any competent manager, regardless of the size of the city, will save his own salary many times over each year and that the plan has therefore been a practical one, even for very small cities.

The council-manager plan, then, suffers from some weaknesses, as do all human institutions. All in all, however, it is a very good form of government.

Proponents and Opponents: the Politics of Reform.[29] The council-manager plan is often launched and supported by good-government and business groups, chambers of commerce, property owners' associations, taxpayers' associations, civic associations, citizens' action groups, women's clubs, and, very often, newspapers. Opposition to proposals for adoption frequently comes from organized labor, politicians in office (especially mayors who stand to lose considerable power in their offices by the employment of a manager), and political parties. Political leaders often dislike the manager plan both because it offers little in the way of patronage and because it is so often coupled with nonpartisan elections.

In many cities, the two leading contenders in campaigns over manager charters have been the local chamber of commerce and local organized labor. This tendency appears to be decreasing, but the impression that the plan is antithetical to the best interests of organized labor has damaged its standing in many cities in various parts of the country.

Though labor has tended to be skeptical, the plan has been accepted with enthusiasm by business groups. There are many reasons for this. It

[29] For case studies on the adoption of council-manager government in various cities, see H. A. Stone, D. K. Price, and K. H. Stone, *City Manager Government in Nine Cities* (1940); F. C. Mosher and others, *City Manager Government in Seven Cities* (1940); Harold Stein (ed.), *Public Administration and Policy Development* (1952).

was the Board of Trade of Lockport that first endorsed the Childs plan, and it was the Chamber of Commerce in Dayton that was responsible for the first large-city adoption. The plan is often lauded as a "businesslike government" in imitation of the corporate form of private business.

The upper-middle-class suburbs which are the homes of metropolitan businessmen are characteristically administered by a manager. Very many managers are engineers, and some are trained in schools of business administration. This means that they received much of their education in the most conservative colleges of our universities. They are likely to be personally conservative in political views. They are business-oriented in their social values. Many of them have had experience in private business before becoming managers; others may hope to move into good positions in private business after serving for a number of years in city government. Whether their conclusions are justified or not, labor leaders have often decided that the circumstantial evidence against the managers is sufficient to warrant grave suspicion.

In contrast to the general pattern, some unions have taken the lead in urging the manager plan. Furthermore, it would appear that labor usually supports the plan once it is well established in a city.

The manager plan enjoys labor support in Cincinnati, Kansas City, and Toledo. Neither the AFL nor the CIO takes a national stand on forms of local government; both allow local organizations to decide positions in local campaigns for themselves. In 1950, union leaders in eighty cities where the plan had been in effect for twenty years or longer overwhelmingly approved of the plan. In only three of the cities was definite opposition expressed.[30] Labor is being reassured concerning the motives of those who favor the manager plan. It is likely, however, that the device will remain especially the favorite of chambers of commerce and good-government groups.[31]

OTHER FORMS OF GOVERNMENT

The New England Town. The direct democracy of the town meeting characterized local government in New England until the urbanization of that area began to force the acceptance of modifications. In some urban

[30] See the pamphlet *Labor Unions and the Council-manager Plan* (1950), issued by the National Municipal League and designed to be read by workingmen.

[31] In addition to material already cited on the manager plan, see C. E. Ridley and O. F. Nolting, *The City-manager Profession* (1934); and R. S. Childs, *Civic Victories* (1952). Contemporary developments in the field are reported annually in the *Municipal Year Book* from 1934 on, and before then in the *City Manager Year Book*. The year books are publications of the International City Managers' Association. There are pamphlets describing the manager plan in each of at least eight states. See, for example, C. L. Ringgenberg, *Council-manager Government in Iowa* (1953).

areas, the town-government feature has been abandoned, while in others it has been made into a representative form.

The town makes no distinction between rural and urban places. As an area becomes more and more urbanized, it continues under the town system, sharing the same government with the neighboring rural area. The town is governed by a meeting of all the qualified voters, who choose officers and make basic policy. There is an annual meeting, traditionally in March, with as many other meetings as may be necessary. After making basic policy, the people choose a board of selectmen, usually three but in some places as many as nine, and a fairly large number of other officers. The selectmen and elective officers are then entrusted with carrying out the basic policies established by community action.

The urbanization of many towns has been accompanied by a sharp decrease in attendance at town meetings and a consequent decline in the democratic effectiveness of this form of government. In many areas of New England, therefore, a *representative* town meeting plan has been developed. Under this plan, the voters choose a large number of citizens, perhaps a hundred or more, to attend the meeting, represent them, and vote. Any citizen can attend and take part in debates, but he no longer has a direct vote. This plan is used in such large urban places as Brookline, Massachusetts (1950 population: 52,300).

Town government, outside of the meeting feature, resembles the weak-mayor or, more particularly, the American village form, except that there is no mayor at all, only a president of the council, and no one has a veto power. It is becoming more and more common for the selectmen to choose a manager and turn actual administration over to him. This is particularly the case in Maine and Vermont and is to be found in all New England states except Rhode Island.[32]

Concluding Statement. Structures of government are tools. They are important, but like other machinery they may be modern or antiquated and are hence not all equally suited for present-day government. A tool will not operate itself, however, nor will the same one be equally effective in various kinds of soils. Local cultural circumstances will determine the type of structure that is needed and the quality of government that will be produced from any chosen form.

[32] On town government, see William V. Holloway, *State and Local Government* (1951), pp. 400–403, or one of the other texts in state and local government. Canadian cities offer further variations on British municipal government. On Canada, see Horace L. Brittain, *Local Government in Canada* (1951).

CHAPTER 9

MAYORS AND MANAGERS

The mayor of today's American small town is commonly a moderately successful small businessman, long active in local politics and civic affairs and well liked by his neighbors. In the large city of an earlier day, the mayor was often corrupt and incompetent—although there were outstanding exceptions. Today our large cities seem to be producing an increasingly large number of capable chief executives. Still, many contemporary mayors are amiable mediocrities, lacking in ability and imagination and under obligation to a few pressure groups that put them in office.

An impressive list of public servants can be made up from among the names of men who have served as mayors of American cities, especially since the early 1900s. Samuel M. ("Golden Rule") Jones, Mayor of Toledo at the turn of the present century, was a great humanitarian and fighter against domination of cities by public utility interests. He was succeeded by one of the most famous of all mayors, Brand Whitlock, an exponent of the principles of municipal reform. There were several other reform mayors at the turn of the century and during the second decade, among them Joseph W. Folk of St. Louis, Patrick Collins of Boston, and Mark Fagan of Jersey City.

The Socialists offered America several mayors who had both imagination in meeting problems and administrative ability in carrying them out. Emil Seidel, the first Socialist to be elected mayor of Milwaukee (1910), and later Daniel W. Hoan were at the top of this list. New York has had many mayors of doubtful ethical standards and many who were mere voices for the hidden machine, but it also had flamboyant, honest, energetic, and imaginative Fiorello H. LaGuardia. Earlier in the century, the nation's largest city also had mayors of considerable administrative ability in Seth Low and John P. Mitchel.

Murray Seasongood, a prominent attorney and law professor, demonstrated in Cincinnati that a mayor-councilman under the manager plan can offer political leadership without interfering improperly with the functions of administration. Frank Murphy, Detroit's depression mayor,

208

was able enough and had sufficient political acumen to move on to higher political office. He later served in several high positions and finally was appointed to the United States Supreme Court. Many members of Congress were at one time mayors of their home towns.

Cleveland, with a strong mayor elected on a partisan basis,[1] has been an exceptional city so far as chief executives are concerned. It has not only had able reformers, but has sent several men on to more important positions in state and national government. Thomas L. Johnson (1901), a prominent businessman, became famous for fighting the "special interests." His campaigns were carried on by his successor, Newton D. Baker (1909), who was chosen a few years later to be President Wilson's Secretary of War. In 1935, Harold H. Burton was elected mayor of Cleveland. After being re-elected for two more terms, he was promoted to the United States Senate and finally became a member of the United States Supreme Court. While he was not outstanding in these positions, his record is an indication that the mayor's office can be used as a step toward more important jobs. Burton was succeeded as mayor in 1941 by Frank J. Lausche, a man of little administrative ability but with a great deal of political skill and ambition as well as a special reputation for honesty.[2] He was re-elected in 1943 in an election in which he received almost three-quarters of the votes cast, before moving on to become Governor of Ohio. In 1953, Lausche appointed his successor, Thomas A. Burke, to fill a vacancy in the United States Senate. But the Cleveland system of consistent promotion to higher office is not really typical.[3]

The problem of securing able men as mayors of large cities is particularly complicated, however, by the fact that such men are likely to be under obligation to interest groups with political axes to grind. This is so because someone must furnish the money for the expensive large-city campaign. While a mayor so obligated could in theory be representative of a substantial portion of the population, could be imaginative and aggressive in meeting problems, and could be responsive to changing demands of the people of the city, in practice it appears that often he is not.

[1] Cleveland uses a nonpartisan ballot, but since all councilmen are elected by wards and the mayor and president of the council are the only other persons elected, the resulting short ballot has produced elections which are, in effect, partisan in character.

[2] Lausche attributes his decision to run for mayor to dramatic and mystical circumstances; see John Gunther, *Inside U.S.A.* (1947), p. 425.

[3] There are some interesting autobiographical works that may be examined profitably. See especially Thomas L. Johnson, *My Story* (1911); Brand Whitlock, *Forty Years of It* (1925); and Daniel W. Hoan, *City Government, the Record of the Milwaukee Experiment* (1936). A series on eighteen mayors of all types is to be found in the *National Municipal Review*, vols. 15–18, various issues from 1926 through 1929.

POWERS OF THE MAYOR

The powers exercised by the mayor vary widely throughout the United States. The person called the mayor in a commission or council-manager city normally has few powers other than those of presiding over the council and performing the ceremonial role for the city. The mayor in a mayor-council city may have a great many powers, or he may be merely one of many virtually coordinate members of the city administration, as is the case in a very weak mayor city.

Legislative Powers. It will be recalled from the preceding chapter that there is no necessary difference between weak and strong mayors so far as their legislative powers are concerned. In virtually all instances, the mayor has the right to submit messages to the council and hence to recommend policy. These messages carry with them the prestige and the publicity potential of the mayor's office and must be considered by the council in light of this. Some mayors have the right to attend council sessions and to introduce measures. In those municipalities that have remained closest to English precedents, the mayor is actually a member of the council and presides over it. This is true in a very common form of village government and is also the case in nearly all commission and council-manager cities.

Most mayors in mayor-council cities have a veto power (see Table 11).

Table 11. Veto Power of Mayors in Cities over 5,000

Form of government	Per cent of mayors who may			
	Veto all measures	Veto budget only	Veto selected items	Not veto anything
Mayor-council............	42.7	1.0	19.3	37.0
Commission...............	7.7	0.0	1.1	91.2
Council-manager...........	8.3	0.0	5.9	85.8
Town meeting.............	0.0	0.0	0.0	100.0
Rep. town meeting.........	0.0	0.0	0.0	100.0
All cities over 5,000.........	27.0	0.6	12.4	60.0

SOURCE: *Municipal Year Book, 1953*, p. 60.

This is, of course, a substantial supporting weapon when the mayor recommends policy. The greatest power of the veto, in the hands of a mayor as of a president, is measured by its threatened use rather than by the number of times it is actually invoked. A veto may be overridden either by a simple majority or by some extraordinary vote such as two-thirds or three-fourths. In a few cities, notably Boston, a veto is absolute. This does not, however, appear to be truly compatible with the checks-and-balances theory and would seem almost to turn the policy-making function over to the mayor.

In strong-mayor cities, it is not uncommon to find that the mayor is so powerful that the council does not attempt to make policy independently of him. Under such circumstances, he need rarely use the veto. The use to which the veto is put will depend, of course, on local custom, prevailing circumstances, and the personal philosophy and political strategy of the incumbent mayor.

In some cities the mayor has the power of casting a vote in case of a tie, even though he may not be a member of the council. If he presides over the council, he is quite certain to have this power (see Table 12). Where the mayor is an actual member of the council he, of course, has a vote.

Table 12. Voting Power of Mayors in Cities over 5,000 Population, by Form of Government†

Form of government	Per cent of mayors who may vote	
	On all issues	In case of tie only
Mayor-council................	10.6	65.8
Commission.................	94.0	3.5
Council-manager.............	42.4	53.0
Town meeting...............	80.0	13.3
Rep. town meeting..........	100.0	
All cities over 5,000.........	28.7	53.8

† Statistics include only mayors directly elected by the people (see Table 13).
SOURCE: *Municipal Year Book, 1953*, p. 60.

Powers over Administration. The characteristic differences between the weak and strong mayors of America are to be found in connection with their powers over administration. The strong mayor, unlike the weak mayor, is given powers to make him the chief administrative officer. He has supervisory and coordinative powers over the activities of the various departments and is in charge of the preparation and administration of the budget. In a few cities he has so much power in budget preparation that the council is empowered to do no more than decrease or strike out items in the budget. The controller, who supervises expenditures by the operational departments, is normally an appointee of the chief executive in a strong-mayor city. At the opposite extreme, the budget is sometimes prepared by a committee of the council well out of the hands of the mayor, and the controller may be an elective official or a council appointee. However, if the mayor is to be chief administrator, he must have executive budgeting powers.

Law Enforcement. Most city charters impose upon the mayor the executive function of seeing to it that the laws and ordinances are enforced and that peace and order are maintained. Actual power to do this is not always granted. It is significant, however, that because this is a traditional power, it is common to give the mayor control over the police department. If he has no other exclusive power of appointment, he is usually given the right to hire and dismiss the police chief or commissioner. Sometimes, however, the mayor is given the responsibility of enforcement of laws and ordinances, but is at the same time deprived of any control over the law-enforcement agency. St. Louis and Kansas City have police heads appointed by the state. The original purpose of this was to give these cities honest police forces, yet ironically today both cities have good governments and far fewer scandals than the state government. A few cities elect the police chief, in some he is responsible to the council, and in others he is chosen by a semi-independent police board.

Appointments. In order to have full power over administration and to coordinate its activities, the mayor must have the power both of unrestricted appointment and of removal. Weak-mayor cities are likely to have several administrative officers elected by the people and others selected by the council. In a strong-mayor city, these officers are appointed by the mayor. In some cities, such as New York and Detroit, his powers extend to virtually all of the department heads in the administrative branch and he need not consult the council or anyone else in making appointments. He is in full charge of administration. He may appoint the heads of the major subdivisions within the departments, or this power may go to the department heads. In actual practice, it does not make much difference which method is used, since a serious conflict between mayor and department head over any matter would mean the resignation or dismissal of the recalcitrant department head.

In many cities the mayor must have the approval of the council in making appointments. This is the more common pattern and is in keeping with the system of checks and balances upon which the mayor-council plan is based. It is in accord with American traditions, but it is probably quite undesirable, for at least two reasons. In the first place, it confuses responsibility for administration; the public cannot directly fix the blame, since several persons have a hand in each appointment. In the second place, it provides a gratuitous system of patronage to council members. The mayor must, in practice, consult the council to a degree in making appointments, and as in the case of the President in relation to the United

States Senate, in practice many or perhaps most of the appointments become patronage items for the council members. It must be remembered that councilmen are not elected in order to make appointments, and placating their patronage demands is not likely to provide a good system for procuring able administrators in the city government. The mayor, clearly answerable for administration to the public, will more probably pick persons of ability. He is likely to combine patronage and competence considerations in making choices, while councilmen will consider only patronage. There is no pressure upon them to do otherwise.

Removals. At least as important as the power to appoint is the power to remove. In the strong-mayor city, the chief executive can remove any member of his administration in whom he has lost confidence. Only by the possession of this power can he be responsible to the people for the acts of his subordinates. In New York and Detroit, the mayor can remove almost all of his appointees at pleasure, even those who are nominally appointed for a specific term of years.

Because of the frontiersman's distrust of government, however, it is more common to find restraints on the removal power. Unlike the President of the United States, who commonly must have the approval of the Senate in order to make appointments but may remove all except members of the independent regulatory establishments at pleasure, the mayor often must have councilmanic approval for both appointments and removals. This pattern is found, for example, in Los Angeles. It is subject to the same criticism as is approval for appointment. The mayor cannot control the acts of those nominally subordinate to him where this system exists.

It is also common to restrict the mayor's removal power by providing that he may make removals only "for cause." This means, usually, removal only after notice and hearing, and the action of the mayor is in such cases normally subject to review by the courts. It should be clear that the operation of the city cannot be smooth if the mayor's appointees may defy him or if he loses prestige in the eyes of officials and employees by being forced into a court fight over a dismissal. If a mayor loses such a fight, the morale problem is especially likely to become acute. Logically, the mayor should be authorized to dismiss persons in whom he has lost confidence. It is perhaps fortunate that in practice the notice-and-hearing requirement frequently does not seriously impair the removal power of the mayor. It does discourage him from making hasty decisions in a fit of temper. In general, however, simple power of appointment and removal places responsibility clearly upon the mayor and gives him adequate power so that he will have no excuse for shirking that responsibility.

It should be noted that in most cities, department heads are usually civil-service employees. Despite this, however, the mayor should have the right to choose his department heads and to remove them if he thinks they are not doing a good job. In the event of the removal of a department head who has civil-service tenure, he is reduced in status and given other assignments, but is not dismissed from the service.[4] It is unlikely, however, that a chief executive would be *required* to choose his chief assistants from the civil service.

Ceremonial Functions. In every city there are beauty queens to be crowned, conventions to be greeted, presidents to be introduced, parks to be dedicated, cornerstones to be laid, baseball seasons to be opened, parades to be led, and charity drives to be launched. The mayor is expected to do all of these things. In fact, it is partly because he must do them that the office of mayor is retained under the commission and council-manager forms. He is the symbol for the whole city.

Probably the typical mayor enjoys the attention that is his at these occasions. He is surely aware of the free publicity attendant upon them. In smaller cities, this duty of the mayor is not burdensome or time-consuming, as it is in larger cities. In the very largest cities, the ceremonial function becomes a real burden, taking up valuable time that could be better spent upon the pressing problems of administration or policy making. It is partly for this reason that a deputy mayor is appointed in New York.

Whatever the size of the municipality, Americans are always likely to "try to get the mayor to be there" whenever a committee plans some function, modest or mammoth. If the mayor is interested in his political future, he will usually be on hand.

Duties as a Lobbyist. Since cities are largely at the mercy of the state legislature, their officials necessarily follow closely the course of proposed legislation which affects them. The cities are collectively protected in most states by the lobbying activities of the state league of municipalities, just as their interests on the national level are looked after by the American Municipal Association and the United States Conference of Mayors. The largest cities have paid lobbyists who are at the state capital throughout the legislative session.

At times, when legislation of particular importance to a certain city or group of cities is being considered, the mayors of the affected cities may be called to the state capital by the secretary of the league of municipalities so that they may use the prestige of their offices in an attempt to protect the interests of their cities. Political skill is most important at such times.

Judicial Powers. It might be mentioned that in early America the mayor exercised minor *judicial* powers as well as having a seat in the *legislative* body and serving as chief *executive*. For example, a provision

[4] Concerning the removal of civil servants of lesser rank, see chap. 14.

of the 1851 special act charter of Davenport, Iowa, provided that the mayor "shall by virtue of his office be a justice of the peace, and as such shall be a conservator of the peace."

Some cities still have a "mayor's court," and legally the mayor of New York is such a judge, but in practice the use of this power is disappearing. Also, since the mayor is in a position analogous to that of the governor and the President, he usually possesses power to grant pardons for violations of city ordinances (but not of state law). The exercise of this power is today comparatively rare.

THE OFFICE OF MAYOR

Selection of the Mayor. The way in which the mayor is chosen varies a good deal according to the form of government. In all but a few mayor-council cities, he is elected directly by the voters. He is chosen in this fashion in about 73 per cent of the commission-plan cities, but in somewhat less than one-half of the council-manager cities.[5] (See Table 13.)

Table 13. Method of Selection of Mayors in Cities over 5,000 Population, by Form of Government

Form of government	Total number of cities	Per cent directly elected	Per cent selected by council	Highest no. votes in council election
Mayor-council...................	1,370	95.0	4.3	0.7
Commission.....................	383	73.2	25.5	1.3
Council-manager.................	681	41.7	57.2	1.1
Town meeting....................	67	68.2	29.5	2.3
Republican town meeting..........	27	60.9	39.1	0.0
All cities over 5,000..............	2,528	77.0	22.1	0.9

SOURCE: *Municipal Year Book, 1953,* p. 60.

In such large municipalities as Kansas City, Dallas, and San Diego, however, he is elected directly.

The public is accustomed to electing the mayor and probably feels more comfortable with a charter that gives it that privilege. The popular election of the mayor tends to elevate him in public prestige and to provide him with the status which he needs if he is to be a legislative leader. There is, therefore, perhaps some advantage in the direct election of the mayor in council-manager cites as a means of providing necessary

[5] Statistics on the method of selection of the mayor are available in the current issue of the *Municipal Year Book.*

political leadership. Yet there is also the danger that if the mayor is made too important in a manager city, he may challenge the manager for *administrative* leadership.

The mayor may also be selected by the council. This is the method used in over one-half of the council-manager cities. Many commission cities use it. But it is used in less than 5 per cent of the mayor-council cities of over 5,000 population. These appear to be chiefly in places in which the government has evolved from the village or township structure.

In a few cities, the man who receives the highest number of votes for council becomes mayor. This is very uncommon, but can be found, for example, in Hartford and Kalamazoo, both manager cities, and in a very few commission cities, including Everett, Washington, and Provo, Utah. Strangely enough, a few mayor-council cities also make the person with the highest number of votes for council the mayor. This is true, however, only where the structure has grown from the old village type of government, based upon English traditions and without a clear separation of powers. Crawfordsville, Indiana (1950 population: 12,851), chooses its mayor in this fashion.

Salary. The pay of the mayor varies according to both the size of the city and the structure of its government. In general, the salary varies, directly with the size of city, as might be expected. Small cities are likely to pay only a token salary, something less than $1,000 a year. New York, at the opposite extreme, pays a not unreasonable $45,000.

In a commission-plan city, the mayor usually receives the same pay as the other commissioners or a few hundred dollars additional. There are some exceptions where he may receive quite an appreciable amount more. In manager cities, the same general rule applies.

It is not uncommon for the mayor to be paid less than some of his subordinates.[6] The city engineer, the health officer, the attorney, and especially the superintendent of schools, are likely to be paid more than he is, except in the very largest cities.

Since the average length of service of a mayor is approximately four years and in running for and accepting the office he takes a grave risk of damaging his personal reputation, it is not hard to see one reason why mayors are not made of better material. Clearly, persons with administrative and leadership ability can make more money, with a longer professional life, in private endeavor. Yet few arguments presented to the voters are greeted more coldly than those suggesting a higher salary for the mayor.

Term of Office. The Jacksonians insisted upon terms of not over two years, for they believed in keeping government "close to the people." The

---

[6] Extensive data on salaries of various municipal officials are reported in the current issue of the *Municipal Year Book*.

traditional term of office in New England was one year—from one town meeting until the next.

The term of office of the American mayor today depends to some extent upon the type of city-government structure in the particular city. The two-year term was still dominant in mayor-council cities in 1952, especially in those of the weak-mayor type. Most council-manager cities had two-year terms, too. Commission-governed cities, on the other hand, are likely to have four-year terms. (See Table 14.)

Table 14. Term of Office of Mayor in Cities over 5,000 Population

Form of government	Per cent of reporting cities					
	One year	Two years	Three years	Four years	Five years	Six years
Mayor-council................	2.9	58.6	0.7	37.7	0.0	0.1
Commission................	2.1	27.5	13.7	53.9	1.8	1.0
Council-manager*..........	21.0	53.4	2.0	23.3	0.3	0.0
Town meeting..............	41.0	29.5	29.5	0.0	0.0	0.0
Rep. town meeting.........	39.1	17.4	43.5	0.0	0.0	0.0

* The large number of one- and two-year terms for mayor in council-manager cities is partly a result of town-meeting communities adopting this form while retaining the New England traditional short term of office for elective officials.

SOURCE: *Municipal Year Book, 1953,* p. 61.

It is generally agreed by political scientists that terms of less than four years are too short. The mayor must have time to establish a record, and he must have time to devote to his job. With a two-year term he begins his campaign for re-election almost as soon as the results of his first campaign are in. It is also undesirable, in this age, to cling to the cynical rule found in some city charters prohibiting the mayor from succeeding himself. During the palmy days of the Republican machine in Philadelphia (until 1951), the charter of that city had such a rule. It did not appear to weaken the machine in the least, however.

Removals. The mayor who is incompetent, unrepresentative, or callous of the wants of the public is no doubt best removed by allowing his term to expire or by securing his defeat at the next election. There are times, however, when it would appear to be necessary in the public interest to terminate the authority of a chief executive before his regular term expires. This is particularly true when he is thought to be guilty of what the lawyers call non-, mis-, or malfeasance in office. That is to say, if he fails to perform his duties, or does them in an unlawful manner, or does illegal things under the mantle of office. There are several remedies at law in such cases.

First of all, there is the *recall*. As has already been noted, there are numerous objections to this device, and particularly the objection that the case will not be decided on its merits.[7] The recall is especially undesirable in light of the fact that several better (and incidentally older) remedies are available.

In most cities, the mayor may be removed by action of the council—an ancient common-law power. Most charters require a vote of something more than a simple majority to effect a removal, however. It is also possible for the mayor to be removed by a court order for certain causes as prescribed by law. In Michigan, New York, North Dakota, and Ohio the mayor may be removed by the governor. All three of these removal techniques are "for cause" only. The courts have regularly held this to mean that there must be a presentation of specific charges, due notice to the official whose removal is sought, and a hearing, usually public. It also means that the official may appeal to the courts if he feels that the procedural safeguards to which he is entitled have not been followed. These safeguards protect both the official and the public and have been proved through their use in many instances over the years.

Vacancies. If a mayor dies, resigns, or is removed from office, the law or charter provides for the immediate replacement. It is quite important that there always be someone to serve as mayor. Since the mayor leaves the city from time to time for a vacation, a conference, or a convention, it is also necessary for someone to act in his temporary absence.

The succession may pass to the presiding officer of the council or to some administrative officer, most commonly the controller. In some cities if the office is vacated, the council is allowed to choose the new mayor, not necessarily from its own membership. If the next election is some time off, say more than six months or a year, the law may provide for an acting mayor and a special election to choose a person to serve out the term.

Legal Qualifications. In virtually every city, there are charter provisions requiring the mayor to be a United States citizen, to be of a certain minimum age, and to have lived in the city for a certain minimum number of years. It might be required, for example, that the mayor must be at least thirty years old and have been a city resident for three years. These rules are probably largely in imitation of the requirements in the United States Constitution for the presidency. Clearly they are of little practical meaning and could well be left out of the charter, even the citizenship requirement—for no alien could be elected to a mayoralty position in any American city today.

[7] See above, p. 88 ff.

THE CITY MANAGER

Qualifications of the Manager. It is a basic part of the theory of council-manager government that the entire administration of the city should be professionalized. Managers are supposed to be trained to use the tools of administration and, especially in smaller cities, to possess a technical skill, such as engineering, as well. The manager should also be a diplomat, for his job is dependent upon his ability to get along with the council. He is supposed to be a politician of a special sort, too, for his job calls upon him to give advice on matters of public policy without becoming ensnared in the political process when these problems become campaign issues. Are managers actually able to do all of these things? What sort of people are they? A recent study concludes: "The average city manager in office is a college graduate, entered the profession between the age of 30 and 44, is still serving in his first city, has received salary increases averaging $366 per year, spends 52 hours per week on his job, gets two weeks vacation a year, and is covered in a retirement system."[8]

In the early days of the plan, managers were most often engineers, and in smaller cities this profession is still preferred, the manager also serving as the city engineer. The trend in medium- and larger-sized cities is away from hiring as managers, engineers and persons trained in business administration. More and more universities are offering special training in public administration designed to prepare students for the city-manager profession. After graduation, these trainees advance through the administrative hierarchy of city governments until they become managers, many of them then moving on to a larger city with higher pay and greater prestige. This training provides the future manager with more of a background in the social and economic character of the city than was formerly the case.

Only 14 per cent of the managers appointed in 1952 came from nongovernmental jobs; one-half had been employed in other manager cities either as the manager, as his administrative assistant, or as an intern.[9] Managers are thus receiving better on-the-job training today. In 1939, only 23 per cent of those hired came from administrative positions in other cities.

The profession of manager appears to carry enough salary and prestige to make it a worthwhile occupation in which to spend a lifetime. In 1952, 11.1 per cent of the managers left the field, a not unreasonable number, since this included those who died and retired. Only eight of

[8] "An Analysis of City Managers," *Public Management,* vol. 36 (January, 1954), p. 5.

[9] See the *Municipal Year Book, 1953,* pp. 517–520.

fifty-five who left the profession did so in order to accept positions in private business.

Selection and Tenure of the Manager. One of the most important tasks faced by the council is the selection of the manager. How does the council go about doing this? Councilmen, encountering the problem relatively seldom, may not know how to approach it. They may know that there are able persons about the country who might be interested in the position, but they may not know their names or how to go about discovering them. Fortunately, the International City Managers' Association has published a helpful pamphlet for cities on *The Selection of a City Manager* (1937). The headquarters of the Association often assists cities on request in securing qualified applicants and publishes notices of available openings. Similar assistance may also be secured from the state league of cities, Public Administration Clearing House, and departments of political science in nearby universities.

The council will often do well to consider one of the city's department heads for promotion to manager. Leading managers whose names and reputations are known to the councilmen will probably be willing to offer names of possible candidates. From such a list the council can then proceed to invite interested persons to apply and submit vita sheets and other appropriate information. (Some unsolicited applications will be received.) The council may next reduce further the size of the list and then invite those still being considered to appear, if possible, for personal interviews before finally choosing the person to whom the job is to be offered.

The manager is normally selected by the council by majority vote and is dismissable by the council at any time by the same method. For the plan to work successfully, it is essential that the council be allowed to remove the manager at any time, and for any reason that the council majority thinks sufficient. Otherwise the administration of the city becomes autonomous and irresponsible, uncontrolled by the democratic principle of majority rule. Since ultimate responsibility for all that takes place in city government rests with the council, that body must be able to control the policies of the manager.

In some cities, a practice has developed whereby each new council majority chooses "its own" manager, but this is not the general rule. Experts on the manager plan consider it unwise to replace the manager simply because there has been a change in council membership. The manager is supposed to afford professional advice and impartial administration. If he does this, there is no reason why he should not be continued on in his job despite transient council majorities. It is significant to note that the average tenure of a manager in a city today is about seven years and that it would be longer except for the shortage of managers, which has encouraged, in the postwar era, their promotion to larger cities.

A few charters permit the removal of the manager through the use of the recall. This would appear to be highly undesirable, not only because the recall under any circumstances is of questionable value, but also because it allows the council to shirk its responsibility for the manager and because it almost of necessity embroils the manager in politics—he becomes something of an appointive mayor instead of a manager and must play the political waves to prevent his own removal. Political rather than administrative motivations become, of necessity, paramount to him.

The Jacksonian influence dies slowly in American politics, and it is still to be found affecting the hand that writes the council-manager charter. The extraordinary majority, such as two-thirds or three-fourths of the council, sometimes appears in the rules governing the removal of the manager. Charters also may permit dismissal only "for cause." Such a rule has the effect of putting final discretion in the hands of the courts rather than the council. Some charters require advance notice of one or more months to the manager if he is to be removed. This creates lame-duck managers and a stalemated government.

Both theory and practice call for the council to have full power over hiring and dismissing the manager. No argument for limiting the powers of the council can circumvent the fact that the manager plan can work smoothly and effectively only if a majority of the councilmen have confidence in the manager.

Place of Residence. Most council-manager charters logically provide that the manager need not be a resident of the city at the time of his appointment. The council should be free, in this respect, to choose anyone it wishes, for it is not looking for a deserving local politician, it is looking for a professionally competent administrator.

In earlier years it was quite common to hire a person from outside the city. Until 1929, about one-half of the managers hired were nonresidents. With the coming of the depression there was a reversal of trend, and in 1933 only 17 per cent of those appointed came from outside the city. This was probably the result of two considerations: (1) a desire of local politicians to keep scarce depression jobs "at home"; and (2) the possibility of hiring local persons at a lower salary.

During World War II and since, there has been high employment combined with a rapid expansion in the number of manager cities, resulting in a definite shortage of qualified managers. Cities have turned to other cities in order to get chief administrators. The number of appointments from outside the city has accordingly risen to all-time highs. In 1951, 74 per cent and in 1952, 71 per cent of new managers hired were from outside the city. These figures probably also reflect a growing emphasis

upon securing trained and experienced persons, persons who may not be
available locally. Furthermore, the percentage of nonresidents hired as
the first manager of a city adopting this form has always been high, and
the rate of new adoptions has been unusually high in recent years.

Salaries. Obviously, if managership is to become a real profession with
persons willing to make a lifetime career of it, the pay opportunities must
be sufficient to attract able persons. The statistics shown in Table 15 in-

Table 15. Salaries of City Managers, 1953

Cities of a population range	Mean	Lowest	Median	High
250,000–500,000	$18,718	$15,000	$17,886	$27,500
100,000–250,000	17,034	12,000	16,000	25,000
50,000–100,000	12,930	6,600	13,000	22,000
25,000– 50,000	10,499	6,160	10,258	16,092
10,000– 25,000	8,272	3,600	8,000	18,265

SOURCE: *Municipal Year Book, 1953*, pp. 135–137.

dicate that managership affords fairly good salaries. It ranks well above
teaching, for example, in salary opportunities.

There has been some opposition to the manager plan because salaries
are thought to be *too* high. It has already been pointed out, however, that
this is a mistaken viewpoint. Public opinion in this country is often not
sophisticated on this matter and may sometimes oppose the payment of
reasonable salaries. This tendency is one of the common causes of disillusionment in the manager plan. This writer has been told that "we tried
the plan, but we're giving it up—the manager was a nice fellow, but he
was incompetent." In the postwar period of high employment and inflation plus a shortage of trained managers, many of those hired were indeed incompetent—and a city must expect that its manager will not be
capable of doing a satisfactory job unless a sufficient salary is offered.
Trying to trim the budget by giving the manager a low salary is false
economy.

The Duties of the Manager. While charters vary widely and none
conform in all details to the provisions of the *Model City Charter* of the
National Municipal League, a manager has all or most of the following
responsibilities:

1. Overseeing enforcement of all laws and ordinances
2. Controlling all departments, with power to appoint, supervise, and
remove department heads and bureau chiefs
3. Making recommendations to the council on such matters as he
thinks desirable

4. Keeping the council advised of the financial condition of the city and concerning future needs and trends

5. Preparing and submitting to the council the annual budget

6. Preparing and submitting to the council reports and memoranda such as are requested

7. Keeping the council, and indirectly the public, informed concerning the operations of all aspects of the city government

8. Performing such other duties as the council may legally assign to him

In a sentence, the manager has full responsibility to the council for the conduct of the administration of the city.

The Manager and the Council. When a city adopts the manager plan, the function of the council undergoes a considerable change, even if the city has previously operated under the strong-mayor form. The study by Stone, Price, and Stone[10] found that the council was relieved of most of its task of hiring department heads and subordinate employees. In all but a few cities the mayor and council were relieved of the duties of supervising the employees. Because of provisions of charters and state laws, however, councils were not relieved of the great mass of minor details that have historically been handled by that body. Even though the volume of work performed by the council could not be reduced, "the point of view and the approach of the council to municipal policy was different."[11] The difference resulted from reliance upon the manager for many things that could not be furnished in the same fashion by the mayor or a council committee.

In most cities, the manager presents significant matters to the council for consideration. Since they are not initiated by councilmen, these men are normally free to consider such items on the merits of the question, having no vested interest in them. New business coming before the council is normally first referred to the manager for a report at a future meeting. The manager, in making his report, is in a position to consider the effect of possible forms of action upon all departments of the city. No councilman making the report could do this, at least not as well. Furthermore, by leaving the report to the manager, the councilmen remain free to criticize it and to judge it without prejudice.

Most managers prefer to make their reports in writing. Of course, they are also quizzed orally by councilmen concerning various aspects and implications of the report at council meetings. Most managers also make recommendations for action in connection with a report. Some managers present only one recommended line of action, the one they consider the

[10] H. A. Stone, D. K. Price, and K. H. Stone, *City Manager Government in the United States* (1940), chap. 8.

[11] *Ibid.*, p. 174.

professionally sound solution. Other managers present two or more possible approaches, thus affording the council opportunity to choose. The council may not always choose the "ideal" path, but the experienced manager knows that the council may be the best judge of what is most acceptable in prevailing local conditions.

The Manager and Elections. The manager often performs many functions of community leadership similar to those performed by councilmen or the mayor. He is often active in service clubs, charitable organizations, churches, and the like.[12] He may make public speeches in which he seeks to explain a new policy which has been approved by the council (and which he may have originated). He may speak on the positive side of a proposed referendum on a bond issue (as frequently does the school superintendent who holds a parallel position with the school board), but he is wise not to do so if the question involves partisan or factional issues.

In neither theory nor practice, however, should a manager engage in direct political activities. He should never appeal to the voters over the heads of the councilmen, or campaign against councilmen who have frequently opposed his policy recommendations, or support candidates or policies for personal or factional reasons. He can fulfill his almost inevitable role as a policy leader without himself becoming a political issue, by making sure that his recommendations are always "controlled by his expert knowledge and professional interest, never by selfish considerations or political friendships."[13]

The manager who does not observe this rule will eventually lose his job, and his reputation—and hence his employability elsewhere—will likely suffer. Sometimes a manager does offer assistance to one faction in a campaign, as the Cincinnati manager did in 1953, but under those circumstances he ceases to be a professional manager, becomes a politician, and will keep his post only so long as his faction has a majority on the council.

The Manager and Public Relations. Unlike the government of any other type of city, the city with a manager has a nonpolitical person serving in the position upon which chief public interest and attention is focused. Whether he likes it or not, to the manager falls the greatest responsibility for "selling" the manager plan, for making citizens satisfied with their government, and, often, for popularizing policies which the council has decided to undertake. The manager and his assistants meet the public daily, and the nature of these contacts has a great deal to do with the popularity of the manager, of the councilmen by whose leave he holds his job, and of city government itself.

All managers are necessarily aware of the importance of public relations, but they are not all equally adept in handling them. The Stone,

---

[12] *Ibid.*, pp. 243–244.
[13] *Ibid.*, p. 244.

Price, and Stone study found that some managers "had the knack of speaking and acting in a way that won confidence and brought about harmonious relations; others, no matter how hard they tried, never seemed to say in the right way what they wanted to say or to do in the right way what they wanted to do. How the manager spoke, acted, and conducted himself was often more important than what he said or accomplished."[14]

Some managers, like other chief executives, have made the mistake of thinking that the services of the city speak for themselves and have paid little attention to municipal reports to the public, have disliked making speeches, and have sought to avoid newspaper publicity. Most of them have come to realize, however, the importance of informing the public about the functions performed by city government and the manner in which they are performed.[15]

The Manager as a Professional. The International City Managers' Association is the professional organization to which most managers belong. The Association seeks to encourage high standards. It has a code of ethics and a committee on professional conduct. There would probably be legal complications if a city attempted to require formally that the manager be a member of the ICMA, but such a rule seems unnecessary, since the council is always answerable to the voters for the manager and since it might be considered improper for a private organization to determine qualifications for a public position. State licenses are less necessary than in, say, law or medicine, since managers do not practice directly before a relatively helpless and uninformed public, but rather before a responsible council with complete power over the professional life of the manager.

The Stone, Price, and Stone study found that:[16]

Perhaps the strongest support for the position the city managers took in regarding themselves as professional men lay in their attitude and in their conduct. Many city managers thought of themselves as professional executives devoting themselves to a job which required technical skill and a high sense of moral obligation. Many felt that they were selected as managers because they possessed special qualifications for the position and that political and private connections played no part in their appointment. With a large majority of managers, the job was the thing. Because city managers generally lived up to the ideals which they had set for themselves through the International City Managers' Association, they were quite widely recognized as professional men.

[14] Stone, Price, and Stone, *op. cit.*, p. 159.
[15] For more discussion of public relations as a means of increasing citizen interest in city government, see chap. 13.
[16] Stone, Price, and Stone, *op. cit.*, pp. 67–68. By permission of the Public Administration Service.

CHAPTER 10

THE CITY COUNCIL

The pattern of councilmanic functions varies with the forms of city government. The duties of councilmen vary from the situation in weak-mayor cities, where each alderman, in addition to sharing in policy-making duties, serves very often as a ward foreman supervising administrative functions, to the council-manager city, where he has only policy-making duties. The type of person who serves on the council also varies considerably from place to place, but the differences are based upon the size of the city as well as the forms of government.

THE PEOPLE WHO SIT ON COUNCILS

Occupations. In the vast majority of American cities, the typical council member is a local businessman, well respected in the community, active in civic organizations, and often a college graduate. He runs for the council because of the prestige and power the position affords. He may consider the fact that the prominence of the position will help his business, but often he is merely acting out of a sense of community responsibility. He is usually not among the top of the businessmen in his earnings and standing, but generally he is prosperous. He is usually above average in intelligence, but it is not necessary for the council to consist of a group of intellectual giants or the leading men of the community; if it has a few able leaders, that is enough, for there is need also for the plodding type who will accept and follow that leadership.

Outside of the very largest cities, the pay for councilmanic positions is very nominal and the job is thought of as being a community service. An exception to this is to be found in commission-governed cities, where the council (commission) is supposed to be made up, not simply of representative citizens of the community, but specifically of persons with executive or engineering experience. Inadequate salaries, however, have tended to attract ordinary office seekers instead. Topeka, for example, once had a commission made up of a barber, a house mover, and a cub reporter—hardly logical occupations for training in public administration.

In general, the smaller the city, the more likely it will be that council members are the really leading citizens of the community. As cities increase in size, the professional prominence of councilmen, in general, tends to decrease. In the largest cities, the councilmen may well devote full time to work at the city hall and may have run for the office partly because of the salary involved. Although venal and corrupt councilmen were once commonly found in these large cities, they are now a rarity. The greatest sins of the councilmen of the metropolis today are likely to be in their allegiance to particular pressure groups—a real estate board, a labor union, a group of builders, the liquor dealers, the downtown merchants. They are likely to view their function as that of protecting these particular pressure groups, although they invariably pretend to act "for all the people."[1]

The difference between the council in a middle-sized and a large city can be demonstrated by contrasting Davenport with Detroit:

Davenport, Iowa (1950 population: 74,549), might be called a not untypical middle-sized Middle Western city. It has a mayor-council form of government tending toward the weak category. Councilmen receive a $900 annual salary. In 1953, there were fifteen candidates for the eight positions on the council. Among these, there were four insurance salesmen and three real estate dealers or agents. There was one retired minister and one career woman. The remaining candidates were small businessmen or white-collar workers. There were a barber, a bookkeeper, a filling station operator, a baker, a retired grocer, and a tax consultant. It is likely that in a middle-sized city with the council-manager plan and at-large elections, the quality of candidates would have been somewhat higher.

Detroit (1950 population: 1,849,568) has a strong-mayor-council form of government. The council is elected at large and members receive a salary of $12,000 a year. In 1954 the council consisted of four persons who could best be called professional politicians, three lawyers, an automobile saleswoman, and a retired baseball player. Because a council position is ostensibly a full-time job and because long tenure is typical, it is not easy to distinguish clearly between professional and amateur politicians among its membership.

Minority Groups. In small cities, minority-group representation is not likely to be a major problem. In larger cities, the number of minority-group representatives on the city council tends to vary according to

[1] The old-time ward alderman was a little mayor in his own bailiwick and was sometimes, for example, in Chicago, quite independent of the party organization. For brief sketches of colorful Chicago aldermen such as "Bathhouse" John Coughlin, "Hinky Dink Mike" Kenna and "Foxy Ed" Cullerton, see Charles E. Merriam, *Chicago* (1929), pp. 223–225. Lloyd Wendt and Herman Kogan, *Lords of the Levee* (1943), is the biography of Coughlin and Kenna, who ran the "levee"—Chicago's First Ward. A more recent ward alderman, Mathias J. ("Paddy") Bauler, is portrayed in A. J. Liebling, *Chicago: The Second City* (1952), pp. 116–125.

whether or not the council is elected at large. Where the council is fairly large and elected by wards, the ethnic groups that include political-activity patterns as part of their subculture tend to dominate, while in the case of a small council elected at large, the groups that are usually deemed "minorities" tend to be excluded.

There are other factors involved, too. Where political parties play a prominent part in local elections, minority-group representation is likely to be greater, since parties have historically sought the support of these groups in large cities. In cities with nonpartisan elections and a political process dominated by the business community, minority groups are usually quite badly underrepresented on city councils. The only exception to this seems to be in the case of the Irish, an ethnic group that has made political participation a part of its way of life. Other racial groups appear to be too poorly organized or too little interested in local politics to be effective, or at least proportionately effective, in the larger cities.[2]

No Negro or Jew was elected to the Los Angeles council between the time of the adoption of the present charter (1925) and 1953. Only one person of Italian descent had served, and Protestants had dominated the council in a city in which a majority of the inhabitants were and still are Catholic. Precisely the same comments could be made concerning the Detroit council between 1919 and 1953. In the latter city, the large Polish ethnic group has also been greatly underrepresented.

Negroes, lacking in a cultural tradition of political participation and hence often poorly organized politically, have not yet learned to use their ever increasing political strength effectively in most cities. Oscar Stanton DePriest (1871–1951) was the first Negro to serve on the Chicago city council, beginning in 1915. Because that city elects its councilmen by wards, the "black belt" is assured of some representation. There is always Negro representation on the New York council today. As the Negro migration from the southern sharecropper farm to the northern city continues, more and more Negro representation will no doubt appear on councils.

In the South, the increasing enfranchisement of the Negro since about 1944 has taken place largely in the cities, with the result that the political influence of Negroes is beginning to be felt there, too. Negroes have long been influential in San Antonio politics in the Southwest. In 1947, a Negro was elected an alderman in one ward of Winston-Salem, defeating a white opponent. The nine-member at-large council that was first elected in Richmond in 1948 after that city adopted the manager plan included a

---

[2] There is a real shortage of research material on both the mayor and the council. The statements in this section are hence more impressions than the result of statistical studies. On the Los Angeles council, see Aldrich Blake, *You Wear the Big Shoe* (1945); on Detroit, Maurice M. Ramsey, "Some Aspects of Non-partisan Government in Detroit," unpublished Ph.D. thesis, University of Michigan (1944).

Negro as one of its members.[3] Cleveland's council sometimes has as many as three Negro members, and there is almost always one in Cincinnati. Indianapolis, St. Louis, Philadelphia, Louisville, and New Haven have elected Negro councilmen in recent years. Malden, Massachusetts, and Urbana, Ohio, are among other places that have done so.

Women on the Council. It is quite common, and understandably so, to find women serving on school boards throughout the nation. They also often serve on park boards, library boards, and other special-purpose bodies. Their numbers on councils have been smaller, however, although some cities have a tradition of always having at least one woman on the city council. Peoria and Los Angeles did not elect a woman to the council until 1953. In Detroit, the first woman was elected in 1949. Portland, Oregon, elected a woman mayor-commissioner in 1948, but this is rare in so large a city. The occasional "skirt slates" that appear in small-city clean-up campaigns are reported in the newspapers throughout the land for the very reason that they are so unusual. Although the pattern is changing, American men and women both still tend to think of politics as being male territory.

Qualifications. As in the case of the mayor, the city charter commonly provides for certain minimum qualifications in age, residence, and citizenship. Other requirements that may be found include such things as required residence in the ward from which elected or disqualification of persons holding contracts with the city.

Most political scientists believe that the quality of councilmen has improved considerably in the last fifty years. There are no measurements for this, of course, and the degree to which it may be attributed to an improvement in the forms of government, to a decrease in the size of the council, to a change from ward to at-large elections and from partisan to nonpartisan elections, or to other causes is not known.

THE STRUCTURE OF THE COUNCIL

Salary. In the British tradition, councilmanic salaries are deliberately fixed at a low rate in most small and medium-sized cities to discourage candidates who are interested in the salary and to make the job one in which the prestige and honor of it are the decisive elements. For this reason, membership on school and park boards and some others, including city councils, carries no salary at all in many communities.

In larger cities—say of over 50,000—the task of being a councilman requires a good deal of time, even under the manager plan, and those who serve are required to make a considerable sacrifice. High salaries for councilmen in these cities would attract candidates who would make a

[3] Maurice R. Davie, *Negroes in American Society* (1949), pp. 274–282.

profession of officeholding, and this might not raise the quality of personnel on the council at all.

Salaries tend to be highest in commission-plan cities (see Table 16),

Table 16. Salaries of Councilmen in All Municipalities of Over 5,000

Type of city government	Median	High
Mayor-council..............	$ 247	$12,000
Commission................	1,200	10,000
Manager...................	233	5,000
Town meeting..............	300	1,400
Rep. town meeting..........	520	2,500

SOURCE: *Municipal Year Book, 1953*, p. 65.

for here the councilmen are also being paid as administrative heads of departments. Council-manager cities tend to have the lowest salaries, since under this form the council is a part-time body even in large cities and is restricted to legislative functions alone. In 1953, for example, the councilmen in Austin and Hartford received no pay at all, in Des Moines they were paid $300 a year, and in Berkeley $240. There are some exceptions in manager cities; Niagara Falls, New York, for example, paid $3,000 a year, and Medford, Massachusetts, $4,000, which is more than was paid in St. Louis, a mayor-council city.[4]

The most common pay pattern would be something like that in Abilene, Kansas (1950 population: 5,775), a manager city in which the three councilmen received $100 "salaries" in 1953; or Forrest City, Arkansas (1950 population: 7,607), a mayor-council city where they were paid $300; or Creston, Iowa (1950 population: 8,317), a mayor-council city that paid $60; or Brookings, South Dakota (1950 population: 7,764), which paid only $750 although it was governed under the commission plan.

Term of Office. Councilmanic terms range from one year to six years. One-year terms are found in cities with the town-meeting form. The six-year term is found mostly in a few commission cities, but a very few manager cities also use it.

In recent years, the four-year term has become the most common in American cities (see Table 18). In general, the larger the city, the more likely it is to have a four-year term. In about 40 per cent of the cities, the terms of all councilmen expire at the same time. The larger the city, the more likely this is to be true. Overlapping, or staggered, terms are most likely to be found in manager and commission cities, where the emphasis has traditionally been upon imitating the business corporation and in play-

[4] Councilmanic salaries are reported in the current issue of the *Municipal Year Book*.

Table 17. Structure of the Council in Selected Large Cities

City	No. of members	No. elected at large	Type of election*	Salary of councilmen, 1953
New York..................	25	0	P	$ 7,000
Chicago..................	50	0	NP	5,000
Philadelphia..............	17	0	P	9,000
Los Angeles..............	15	0	NP	7,200
Detroit..................	9	9	NP	12,000
Baltimore................	21	1	P	4,000
Cleveland................	33	0	P	4,000
St. Louis.................	30	1	P-s	1,800
Boston...................	9	9	NP	5,000
San Francisco.............	11	11	NP-s	2,400
Pittsburgh...............	9	9	P-s	8,000
Milwaukee...............	27	0	NP	5,687
Houston.................	8	3	NP	3,600
Cincinnati...............	9	9	NP	5,000
Newark..................	5	5	NP	10,000
Portland.................	5	5	NP	10,080

* Under "Type of Election," "NP" signifies nonpartisan and "P" partisan elections, while "-s" following indicates staggered terms for councilmen. In Chicago, only the aldermen and not the other officers are elected on a nonpartisan ballot.

SOURCE: *Municipal Year Book, 1953,* pp. 70–71.

Table 18. Terms of Office, Members of Council, in All Municipalities of over 5,000

Type of city government	Two years	Four years	Other
Mayor-council.............	49.4%	43.3%	7.3%
Commission...............	24.4	54.9	20.7
Council-manager	41.0	47.1	11.9
Town meeting.............	27.3	45.4	27.3
Rep. town meeting.........	18.2	63.6	18.2

SOURCE: *Municipal Year Book, 1953,* p. 64.

ing down the political aspects of city government. There is an argument that staggered terms provide desirable continuity in a council, but this is achieved in any case by the almost universal habit Americans have of giving long tenure in office to councilmen. It would appear to be desirable not to stagger the terms, for to do so interferes with the opportunity that should be afforded the voters to cast a protest vote. The council must, above all, be sensitive to changes in public opinion.

Size of Council. Councils range in size from two members in several cities to Chicago's fifty. In the case of the former, the mayor practically becomes a councilman, for he must break the frequent tie. In an earlier day, councils sometimes ranged in size to above two hundred members. Something of a dilemma is encountered in trying to determine the proper size for a council. A large council is cumbersome and tends to obscure responsibility by working through committees. A small council is sometimes said to lack representativeness and raises some questions concerning the function of criticism. A small council becomes involved in personal relationships that make it difficult for members to criticize other members freely. It is generally held, however, that the small council has not been proved bad, while the large one has. In any case, the trend in recent years has been toward smaller councils.

Very roughly speaking, the size of the council increases as the size of the city increases. A more important factor, however, is to be found in the type of structural form used by the city. In commission cities, the size of the commission tends to remain the same regardless of the size of the city. The commission is made up of five members in a preponderant number of cases. (See Table 19.) Council-manager cities tend to increase from

Table 19. Size of Council

Population of city	Mayor-council		Commission		Council-manager	
	Range*	Median	Range*	Median	Range*	Median
Over 500,000	8–50	16				
250,000–500,000	7–27	9	3–7	5	7–9	9
100,000–250,000	4–33	11	3–5	5	4–13	7
All over 5,000	2–50	7	2–7	5	2–20	5

* "Range" refers to the largest and smallest number of council members within each class.

SOURCE: *Municipal Year Book, 1953*, p. 62.

five to nine members as the size of the city increases, but there are many exceptions to this. In the case of mayor-council cities, it is not possible to find very much of a correlation between size of city and size of council.

Unicameralism. At the turn of the century, about one-third of the cities of over 25,000 population had bicameral (two-house) councils. The figure had once been higher, but never included one-half of the cities. From the days of the reform movement of that period until the present, the number of these clumsy imitations of Congress and the state legislatures has diminished. There is no logical basis for a two-house municipal council. To the extent that bicameralism on the state level makes sense, it is based on the need to compromise the rural-urban split. In the city, it has no justification.

In November, 1952, three Rhode Island cities—Pawtucket, Woonsocket, and Central Falls—voted to abandon bicameralism.[5] Atlanta, Georgia, abandoned its two-house council system in 1953. This left only eight cities in the United States continuing this archaism. New York is included in this figure, but its arrangement is not of the traditional type. Other cities still with a bicameral council in 1953 were Augusta and Waterville, Maine; Everett, Malden, Northampton, and Springfield, Massachusetts; and Danbury, Connecticut. Northampton, as an example, has seven aldermen and eighteen councilmen.

The city of New York has a council elected by wards and a Board of Estimate and Apportionment with an ex officio membership. The board is made up of the mayor, the controller, the president of the council, and the president of each of the five boroughs. However, a system of weighting the votes of each of these elective officers gives control to the first three. The board had the power to make up the New York budget before 1933. Since that time, the board has the budgets of the city submitted to it first. It holds hearings and may alter the budgets in any way it sees fit. After it has passed the budgets, they are sent to the council, which has powers only to reduce or delete. Although the board is basically an administrative body, it is in this sense the upper house of a bicameral council.

Election by Wards. There is a strong tendency today to elect members of the council at large, except in cities of over 500,000. Well over half of the cities of more than 5,000 population now elect at large, and a much greater percentage of the smaller cities do so. Again, the pattern that prevails depends to a large extent upon the structural form that is used (see Table 20). Nearly all commission cities, for example, elect their members at large, since each member of the commission is a department head and almost necessarily is chosen by all the voters. The towns of New England almost always elect at large, since most of these places are quite small and all of them grew out of a rural tradition. The manager plan strongly leans toward election at large. Weak-mayor cities tend to use a ward system, which they have inherited from the nineteenth century. A few cities nominate by wards and elect at large in an attempt to secure better geographical distribution.

The great size of cities such as New York and Chicago seems to suggest the use of ward representation, and this has been traditional in America. It is argued that election by wards provides a short ballot and gives representation on the council to the various ethnic, racial, and economic areas of the city. There are grave disadvantages, however. Aldermen selected from small wards tend to become local errand boys. They are unable safely to consider the needs of the whole city lest they be

[5] *National Municipal Review*, vol. 41 (December, 1952), pp. 539, 570.

Table 20. Method of Electing Members of Council in All Municipalities of over 5,000

Type of city government	Elected at large, per cent	Elected by wards, per cent	Elected by combination,* per cent	Staggered terms, per cent
Mayor-council.............	38.6	37.5	23.9	56.4
Commission...............	98.7	0.8	0.5	43.1
Council-manager...........	73.7	15.8	10.5	71.9
Town meeting.............	95.6	2.2	2.2	30.6
Rep. town meeting.........	100.0	0.0	0.0	51.9
All over 500,000.............	29.4	35.3	35.3	29.4
All over 5,000..............	58.7	25.1	16.2	57.7

* "Elected by Combination" refers to the election of some councilmen by wards and others at large within the same city.

SOURCE: *Municipal Year Book, 1953,* p. 63.

quickly told by their constituents that they were sent to the city hall to protect the interests of their own ward. Attempts at "statesmanship" only produce candidates who say, "If Torkelson can't look after this ward and its interests, I can." Furthermore, city populations are constantly shifting—in general toward the periphery. This means that a ward system, especially one written into the charter, eventually bcomes gerrymandered. The slums and the periphery become underrepresented to the profit of the intermediate areas.

Minority groups sometimes make strong arguments for ward election on the ground that this is the only way for them to get a voice on the council. Negro groups are likely to feel especially strongly about this. Yet it is not difficult for white politicians to gerrymander ward boundaries to keep Negroes off the council. Los Angeles and Detroit each have great Negro populations made up largely of recent arrivals (since 1940). Los Angeles elects all councilmen by wards. Detroit elects all at large. Neither city has ever elected a Negro to the council. Proportional representation would offer Negroes greater opportunities, although this method has many weaknesses.

Election at large, although more popular than election by wards, has disadvantages, too. It lengthens the ballot, forces the establishment of a council so small that it may not be representative in a large city, and gives the election to the candidates who can find financial backers able to pay the expense of a city-wide campaign.

Because large and medium-sized cities encounter a dilemma in seeking to choose between ward and at-large elections, compromises are common. Houston elects three members at large and five by wards. Buffalo chooses nine councilmen by wards for two-year terms and six at large for four-year staggered terms. Nearly one-fourth of the mayor-council cities use some sort of combination of the two devices.

Type of Ballot. Far more than half of the city councils in the United States in places of over 5,000 population are elected on a ballot without party designation. (See Table 21.) The nonpartisan ballot is found most

Table 21. Type of Ballot, Members of Council, in All Municipalities of over 5,000

Type of city government	Partisan, per cent	Nonpartisan, per cent
Mayor-council..................	55.1	44.9
Commission....................	33.3	66.7
Council-manager..............	14.9	85.1
Town meeting.................	50.0	50.0
Rep. town meeting............	20.0	80.0
All over 5,000.................	40.6	59.4

SOURCE: *Municipal Year Book, 1953,* p. 63.

commonly in manager cities, since both nonpartisanship and the manager plan grew out of the reform movement. Because the representative town meeting is a recent development in New England, it, too, is usually nonpartisan. The commission plan, also a product of the early reform-movement years, is predominantly nonpartisan, but to a less extent. Its popularity declined before it received the full impact of the nonpartisan movement.

This leaves only the mayor-council city and the traditional New England town as the centers of partisan municipal activity. City and town governments that have not been reconstructed tend to retain the partisan ballot, and some cities are required by state law to use it.

Large cities might be said to tend to use the partisan ballot for the council, but such a statement would have to be made with caution (see Table 17). Two cities of over 1 million people, Los Angeles and Detroit, use nonpartisan ballots. Chicago is listed in Table 17 as having nonpartisan elections, but this is true only in a formal sense. All offices other than those of the aldermen are on a partisan ballot. All of the aldermen are elected in single-member wards. This makes it so easy for the parties to give direct support to an aldermanic candidate and to have this support made known to the voters that Chicago does not fit into the pattern of most cities with a nonpartisan ballot.[6]

---

[6] The effect of nonpartisanship upon the political process is discussed in chap. 4.

ORGANIZATION AND PROCEDURE

The Presiding Officer. The mayor may preside over the council, or a member of the council may serve as its presiding officer. In the latter case, he may be selected either by direct popular vote, by the council members from among their own membership, or by making the person who receives the highest number of votes for council the president. When the president is elected separately for that specific office, as is the case in several cities, including the city of New York, he is sometimes not considered a true member of the council and often cannot vote except in case of a tie. The function of the presiding officer is in keeping with the usual powers and duties assigned to this officer in American legislative bodies. The council may also select other officers, including a secretary or clerk, although the city clerk usually serves in this capacity.

Committees. Because city governments tend to imitate those of the state and nation, the use of committees for the preliminary work on ordinances was customary in the nineteenth century. Even today almost all city councils make some use of committees. Reformers have generally frowned on this device, since it obscures the nature of the work of the council, confuses responsibility to the public, and allows a majority of a committee (a minority of the council) frequently to determine policy by minority rule. Standing committees also tend to take over administrative functions and for this reason are opposed by advocates of the reform-movement principles.

Standing committees are generally used in mayor-council governments, particularly of the weak-mayor type, but their use is less common in council-manager governments. In manager cities, the council as a whole looks to the manager to do the preliminary work on ordinances, making committees less necessary. Because such committees tend to interfere in administration, they are especially disapproved of by experts on the manager form, although special committees are frequently utilized.

In those cities making extensive use of committees, the system works largely in the same manner as does the committee system of Congress or the state legislatures: the council as a whole becomes chiefly a ratifying body for the actions of the committees. Even if the council can override a committee recommendation or relieve the committee of further consideration of a bill, these things are not likely to happen, since each councilman—like each Congressman—will tacitly agree to allow other councilmen to be supreme in their committee areas if they will extend the same privilege to him. The committee is the tail that wags the dog.[7]

Some cities with small councils make frequent use of the committee of

[7] A description of a large, machine-controlled council working through committees is given in C. E. Merriam, *Chicago: A More Intimate View of Urban Politics* (1929).

the whole, which is not a committee at all, but simply a convenient method for considering legislation in an informal atmosphere. Other cities hold an informal executive "conference session" before each meeting. If the city has a manager, he will probably attend. These sessions may be used to decide in advance the manner in which each item on the agenda will be disposed of. The formal session then becomes a hollow

... AND PEOPLE WANT BETTER SEATS AT THE CITY HALL

Fig. 21. The use of some sort of presession secret caucus, with the result that the regular public meeting of the council is a mere formality, has produced criticisms in several American cities in post-war years. SOURCE: From the *Milwaukee Journal*, with its permission and that of Ross Lewis.

ritual, having given way to an informal, extralegal committee. This device is criticized as creating a "hidden government." Secret council sessions were an issue in Milwaukee in 1953, and Akron banned secret meetings of all city boards and commissions in 1954, indicating that the problem is not confined to the council alone (see Figure 21).

Meetings. The frequency of council meetings depends upon the size of the city, local custom, and the complexity of current issues in the community. In cities with part-time, lay councils, meetings are likely to be at night. In small towns the meetings may be only once a month. In the largest cities the councilmen will probably meet almost daily in committee or committee-of-the-whole sessions, with one formal meeting each week, perhaps at night in order to allow interested citizens to attend.

POWERS OF THE COUNCIL

The functions, and hence powers, of the council are basically the same in mayor-council and council-manager cities. In places operating under the commission plan, the council is also the multiple-executive administrative body. For purposes of this section, this special function of the commission will be ignored.

Determination of Public Policy. The most important task of the council, of course, is to pass ordinances and resolutions establishing public policy for the community. The council passes on public improvements and exercises such portions of the state police power to regulate and control the health, safety, and morals of the community as it is authorized to do. City plans are passed upon by the council, as well as modifications of the zoning ordinance. The council makes policy for the municipally owned utilities and exercises control over those that are privately owned to the extent allowed by state law.

Taxation and Appropriation. While the current trend is toward executive preparation of the budget, the council must still vote the funds. Changes in the city tax structure are also made by the council, subject to the rules of the charter. The council also buys and sells city property. In most cities, the council has the power to pass upon all contracts, or at least upon the large ones. This is really an administrative function, and the right of the council to reject a contract negotiated by the administration may serve to interfere with the smooth functioning of the administration. However, the power traditionally belongs to the council.

Supervision of Administration. In a manager city, the administration is directly answerable and completely subordinate to the council through the manager. In other forms of government, the council has an obligation to check upon the activities of the administration. It does this by receiving auditor's reports, by appointing investigating committees, by requiring testimony or reports from department heads and others, and by reviewing the activities of the various departments at budget hearings. Depending on the provisions of the charter, the council may be able to shuffle functions and bureaus to suit itself and to establish many rules of procedure of the departments.

In weak-mayor cities of the past and present, and especially where aldermen represent wards, the council has carried its oversight of administration to great extremes. Each committee of the council may engage in constant interference with the prerogatives and responsibilities of the department heads, creating problems of morale and confusion as to who is boss. Each alderman tends to supervise functions operating within his own ward, concerning himself with details that should properly be handled by an administrative head. He spends so much time and energy on errand-boy activities that he has no time for comprehensive thinking about municipal issues in policy making or in the development of long-range planning.

Other Powers. The council in many cities serves as the city board of equalization or review, hearing appeals from taxpayers on their property assessments. The council often has the power to pass on the appointments of the mayor, and in many cities it makes a goodly number of appointments of its own. In addition, it has the power to remove the mayor and other officials under certain conditions. Many other minor functions are assigned to the council. Their nature varies considerably from one city to another.[8]

PRACTICAL PROBLEMS FACING THE COUNCILMAN

Certain problems confront the councilman in any city of any size: metropolis, suburb, county seat, or small town. M. Nelson McGeary, a political scientist, while serving as president of the State College, Pennsylvania, borough council made the observations summarized in the following section.

Difficulties in Determining Public Opinion. The councilman always has difficulty in determining the prevailing views of the public. This is the case in cities of all sizes, not just in the large ones. McGeary, for example, found that it was very true in his modest-sized borough of about 9,500. A few people are always vociferous. The great majority are silent most of the time. Because this is so, a councilman quickly learns (or should quickly learn) that he cannot determine public opinion simply by counting the pros and cons expressed by office visitors or in letters to him or to the editor. (The councilman might well remember that letters to the editor in the local newspaper may have been written by the editor himself.) The councilman also soon learns that he will hear from his con-

---

[8] A comprehensive study of the American city council in action is badly needed. Some of the studies of individual city governments and of the manager and commission plans discuss the function of the council. Much organizational detail may be obtained from the annual issues of the *Municipal Year Book.*

Several issues of the *National Municipal Review* for 1924 to 1926 have articles discussing the councils of those days in some of the larger cities. There is also a series of articles in *Public Management* for 1935 dealing with the organization, procedure, and powers of the council. Arthur W. Bromage has written articles for several professional publications dealing with his experiences on the Ann Arbor city council. Some of these are reprinted in two booklets, *On the City Council* (1950), and *A Councilman Speaks* (1951).

stituents more quickly if they disapprove of one of his acts than if they approve.

McGeary found that even when a person expresses himself, he may not state his true opinion. He writes of one case in which a man wrote a lengthy letter to the local newspaper on some current issue. When the councilman said he was glad to know where the citizen stood, the letter writer astounded everyone by explaining that his comments in the newspaper did not express his "real feelings."[9]

Difficulties in Adjusting to Criticism. A citizen is accustomed to the elaborate ritual of criticism by circumlocution found in everyday life. If he is elected to the local council, he finds that his actions now become subjected to a different, more open, more straightforward, and more vigorous criticism. Some of it is deserved, informed, and responsible. Some of it is uninformed and irresponsible. The councilman must learn to hide his feelings and to accept these comments without undue sensitivity. But he must not become so immune as to ignore the warning flags of changing public opinion.

Difficulties in Learning to Trust Expert Advisers. The councilman is usually a lay citizen serving only part time at his job. Even in fairly small cities, and especially in large ones, he must learn to trust the advice given by experts, and to rely upon this in making public policy decisions. If the shade-tree expert says that extensive trimming will help preserve the trees, the councilman must overcome his preference for trimming the budget and instead vote the money for trimming the trees—if any is available. Of course, the councilman cannot simply accept the advice of experts, enact it into an ordinance, and go home. It is not that simple. McGeary points to difficulties that the councilman must face when (1) the experts present, as they often do, original estimates of the costs of large projects that are unrealistically low; and (2) the experts disagree among themselves as to the best solution to a problem. Many a councilman has voted for a sewage-disposal plant only to discover later that it cost 50 per cent more than the original estimates. And disagreeing experts can keep a councilman awake nights. After all, the councilman must choose among their conflicting suggestions—and they may all be wrong!

Difficulties of Informing the Public. The councilman must let the people know what he is doing and why he is doing it. Communication with a preoccupied and often apathetic public is difficult. Some possible approaches to this problem are discussed in Chapter 13.

Difficulties in Making the Right Decision at the Right Time. An inexperienced or impetuous councilmen is sometimes guilty of making a decision too rapidly. All of the arguments pro and con may not appear in

---

[9] M. Nelson McGeary, "The Councilman Learns His Job," *National Municipal Review,* vol. 43 (June, 1954), pp. 284–287.

the first few discussions of an issue. Facts that arise later may make the councilman who has already committed himself look ridiculous. Of course, the man who will not make up his mind, or who always follows the lead of someone else, is of limited value, but "a councilman seems to command respect, and may save himself considerable embarrassment if he takes a definite position only after all the facts are in."[10]

Concluding Statement. McGeary has summarized his experiences by saying that "serving on the council is a headache. But democracy is based on the supposition that some citizens will be willing to endure headaches. Actually the travail is not unbearable. And sometimes, for brief periods, it is forgotten—believe it or not—in the knowledge that some little service is being offered."[11]

[10] *Ibid.*, p. 287.
[11] *Ibid.*

CHAPTER 11

GOVERNMENT IN THE METROPOLITAN AREA

Nowhere in the United States today does the sociological and economic metropolitan area coincide with a single governmental unit that includes the entire area. Many of the problems that result from this have been mentioned in Chapter 2 (see Figure 22). Most political scientists, sociologists, and urban planners hold that the existing situation is unsatisfactory. There is, however, a great deal of inertia, not to mention much overt opposition, to the reorganization of urban government. Why is a change advocated by students of the problem? Victor Jones, a leading authority, has put it this way:[1]

A metropolitan government is desirable (1) when coordination of a function over the whole area is essential to effective service or control in any part of the area; (2) when it is desired to apply the ability to pay theory of taxation to the area as a whole, instead of allowing each part to support its own activities at whatever level its own economic base will allow; (3) when services can be supplied more efficiently through large-scale operations and (4) when it is necessary in order to assure citizens a voice in decisions that affect them at their places of work and recreation as well as at their places of residence.

The strange picture that is presented by the metropolitan-area situation has been demonstrated by one writer:[2]

Within ten miles of the Los Angeles city hall are ten other cities, each with more than 25,000 inhabitants. Within the county are 33 "county islands," territory entirely surrounded by some one of the 45 cities within the county. In addition, there are seven "city islands," surrounded, or nearly surrounded, by other cities; 14 "shoestrings," comprising annexed land a few hundred feet or rods wide and a few blocks or miles long; 13 small cities whose boundaries adjoin, and scores of other boundary irregularities—"peninsulas" and "isthmuses"—which multiply administrative costs, perplex officialdom, baffle students of government, and give people locomotor ataxia.

[1] Victor Jones, "Local Government Organization in Metropolitan Areas," in Coleman Woodbury (ed.), *The Future of Cities and Urban Redevelopment* (1953), pt. IV, p. 508. This is probably the best current work on the subject. See also Jones's earlier study, *Metropolitan Government* (1942). Quotation by permission of the University of Chicago Press.

[2] Aldrich Blake, *You Wear the Big Shoe* (1945), pp. 15–16. By permission of the author.

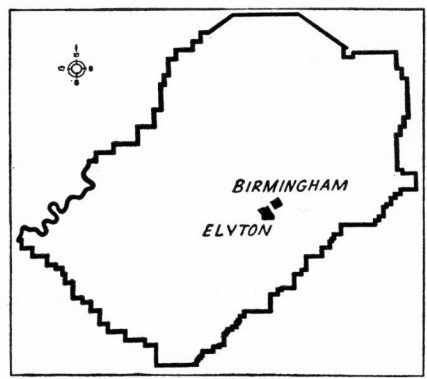

1871. Local government begins: Two villages, little more than frontier settlements, vie with each other for leadership in Jones Valley.

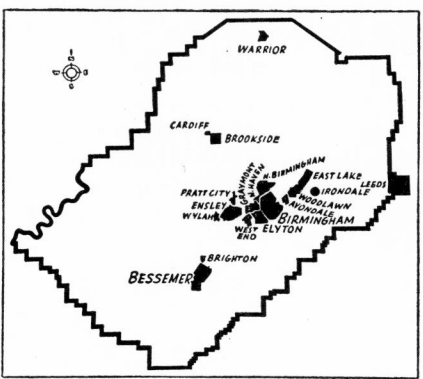

1909. The metropolitan problem asserts itself: Twelve separate and autonomous towns surround Birmingham, by now the undisputed "Magic City."

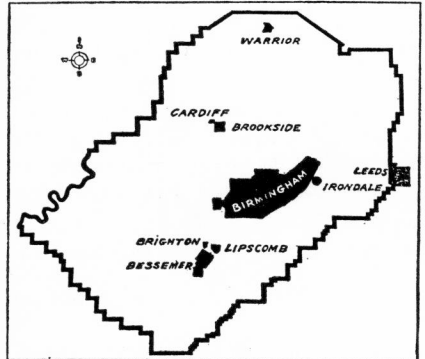

1910. A measure of order is restored: Eleven suburban municipalities give way before a movement which ultimately results in a "Greater Birmingham."

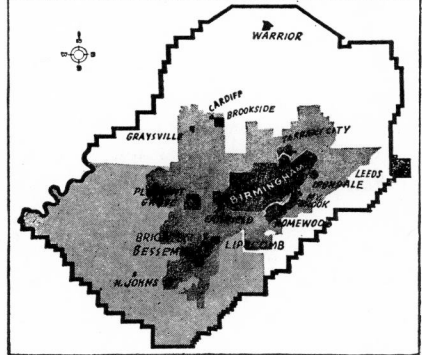

1947. History repeats itself: To the familiar "satellite cities" are added the concept of the metropolitan district, represented by the central shaded area, and the Bessemer "cutoff," indicated by the left and lower shaded area.

Fig. 22. The growth of metropolitan Birmingham, Ala., produced the typical atomization of local government. SOURCE: *Birmingham News*, Mar. 2, 1947; reproduced in Weldon Cooper, *Metropolitan County* (University of Alabama, Bureau of Public Administration, University, Ala., 1949), p. 5.

The outer boundaries of Los Angeles city proper look like a half completed jig-saw puzzle. Competent draftsmen, able to draw the borders of the inner 15 councilmanic districts, find it impossible to describe most of them. Assembly, congressional, supervisorial and councilmanic lines cross each other everywhere in wild profusion and confusion.

And, superimposed upon the whole, are some 450 other districts, mostly with irregular lines, such as school districts, lighting districts, fire protection districts, flood control districts, sanitation districts and what not. . . .

There are even mosquito abatement districts. For in Los Angeles city and county, the citizen who is rendered sleepless by the buzz and sting of this pestiferous creature, has no means to combat his enemy without first creating a district, electing trustees, and voting the money necessary to spray the ditch or pond on his neighbor's privately owned acres. It's all because neither the city nor county health departments may legally appropriate funds for that purpose unless the victim, or his survivors, are able to prove that the bite caused malaria or yellow fever. The catch here is that the mosquito may escape to new breeding grounds, making the organization of still another district, with still more boundary lines, necessary.

Numerous proposals have been made over the years in seeking a solution for metropolitan government. Up to the present time, however, each of these has nearly always proved to be either unsuccessful as a permanent solution, or politically inexpedient.[3] At present there is no trend toward the adoption of a particular solution to the problem, nor has anyone been able to devise a plan that would be both practical and successful. Some isolated exceptions are to be found, however, some makeshift and temporary devices have been put to use in various places, and the past efforts are worth studying, in any case, so that the reasons for their lack of success may be seen. It may also be hoped that a refinement of one or more of these schemes may in time develop into a workable plan for many metropolitan areas.

PROPOSED SOLUTIONS TO METROPOLITAN-AREA GOVERNMENT

Annexation. Superficially, the most obvious method of keeping the sociological and legal cities identical would seem to be for the core city to annex fringe areas as they become urbanized. Formerly this method was widely used to expand the city's legal boundaries to keep pace with the actual urban growth, but it has become increasingly unsatisfactory. Although a considerable number of annexations take place each year in both large and small cities, they seldom succeed in equating the political with the sociological city. Milwaukee, as a not untypical example, has annexed a good deal of territory over the years, but it has not at all solved the problem of metropolitan-wide government. The reason for this situation is quite simple: the laws in nearly all states provide that outlying areas may be annexed only after a referendum has been held and the annexation is approved by the voters of the outlying area as well as those of the core city. Only in a few states, notably in Virginia, is the core city

---

[3] A brief history of these efforts is given in E. A. Cottrell and Helen L. Jones, *Metropolitan Los Angeles: A Study in Integration*, vol. I, "Characteristics of the Metropolis" (1952), chap. 1.

relatively free to expand its boundaries as the surrounding area becomes urbanized.

Annexation is nearly always unpopular in the fringe areas. This is a reflection both of local pride and of the persistent belief that taxes will be higher within the core city, as well as of various other values of suburbanites discussed in Chapter 2. After 1890, there were few large annexations in the United States until after World War II, when several took place. Even so, most recent annexations have been of only a few acres, and the larger cities in particular have not annexed much territory.

Large cities usually cannot annex because they are surrounded, or nearly surrounded, by incorporated territory. When this is· the case, the political community can be integrated only through *consolidation* of municipalities, and this normally involves even more difficult legal procedures than those of annexation of unincorporated territory. In 1951, Atlanta annexed 82 square miles of territory, some of it incorporated, but it did so by fiat of the Georgia legislature and without a vote in the areas affected.

No less than 402 municipalities annexed some land in 1952, and the total amount annexed was more than seven times the 1935 to 1939 average.[4] Perhaps more annexations would have taken place if it were not that cities seldom seek to propagandize outlying areas as to the facts concerning annexation. In 1952, only one city in five where annexation was an issue tried to explain the core city's side of the case to the fringe-area dwellers. By far the largest 1952 annexation was that of San Antonio, which took in 80 square miles. Dallas added nearly 28 square miles. Easily the most important factors encouraging fringe areas to want to become annexed were the sewerage and water-supply services.[5] All other services furnished by cities were of far less interest. Sewerage—and especially sewage-disposal—facilities are very expensive and inefficient if used by small units of government. An adequate *source* of water supply is often a serious problem, too.

A 1952 study indicated that officials in cities annexing territory felt, in more than four-fifths of the cases, that the new areas in the years immediately ahead would not pay as much in taxes as the city would spend on them. But about the same proportion felt that in the long run the areas would pay for themselves.[6]

Most state laws on annexation are unsuited for a solution to the metropolitan-area problem. The requirement of permission of all areas concerned, combined with the fact that suburban dwellers are likely to take a short view, heavily overlaid with misunderstandings, superstitions, and

[4] John C. Bollens, "Metropolitan and Fringe Area Developments in 1952," *Municipal Year Book*, 1953, pp. 33–48, with table of annexations.
[5] *Ibid.*, p. 43.
[6] *Ibid.*

hostility carefully cutivated by fringe-area officeholders protecting their own jobs, all help make this approach unsatisfactory. It is significant that the four largest annexations in 1952 took place where state laws did not require the direct approval of fringe dwellers.

Texas, California, and Virginia lead in annexations in the postwar period. Texas and Missouri allow annexation of unincorporated territory by amendment of home rule charters without a popular vote. Texas also permits annexation simply by an ordinance of the core city, if the home rule charter so provides.[7] This was the technique used in San Antonio.

Virginia has an unusual annexation procedure whose origins are hidden in colonial obscurity. In that state, whenever a fringe area begins to become urbanized, the core city seeks control over the outlying land through a judicial proceeding before a three-judge court. The city is permitted to present the rational case for annexation, and the court is obligated to decide the question on the basis of the public interest of the entire community—not on the basis of the pecuniary interests of the suburban dwellers versus those of the city taxpayers. Under these circumstances, the city usually wins its case. Limited possibilities for judicial annexation also exist in five other states.[8]

Jones, while viewing the Virginia method as more effective than that in nearly all other states, has suggested that annexation questions might best be handled by a state administrative body on the order of the postwar Local Government Boundary Commission in England.[9] It is not easy for a court to settle annexation questions on facts alone or to separate facts from values and interests. This distinction need not be made by an administrative body, which could also be more reflective of changes in public policy, could initiate action rather than wait for cases to come before it, and could settle problems on bases other than those proposed by the parties at issue.

It seems unlikely, however, that annexation to the core city will be the approach used in many metropolitan areas in the foreseeable future. There is no trend toward modernizing existing laws.

Special Districts. If annexation becomes impossible, the next solution that might suggest itself would be to take those functions for which a particularly evident need for metropolitan-wide administration is seen and create one or more special districts to administer them. Hence, covering all or part of a metropolitan area, there might be park, sewerage, water, parking, airport, planning, or other districts.

[7] See A. O. Spain, "Politics of Recent Municipal Annexation in Texas," *Southwestern Social Science Quarterly*, vol. 30 (June, 1949), pp. 18–28.

[8] Victor Jones gives details in "Local Government in Metropolitan Areas," in Coleman Woodbury (ed.), *The Future of Cities and Urban Redevelopment* (1953), pt. IV, pp. 564–566.

[9] *Ibid.*, pp. 568–572.

These *ad hoc* districts may be governed by a body appointed by the state, one appointed by officials from the municipalities making up the district, serving in ex officio capacities, or, sometimes, one elected by the voters of the area. Since the last possibility is not the usual one, special-purpose districts generally do not come within the direct oversight of the general public.

The need for a metropolitan approach to problems has increased as urban populations have increased. Other solutions failing or being politically impossible, an increasing use has been made of the special district. Illinois and California lead in their use. In the latter state unincorporated fringe areas often create special districts in lieu of becoming

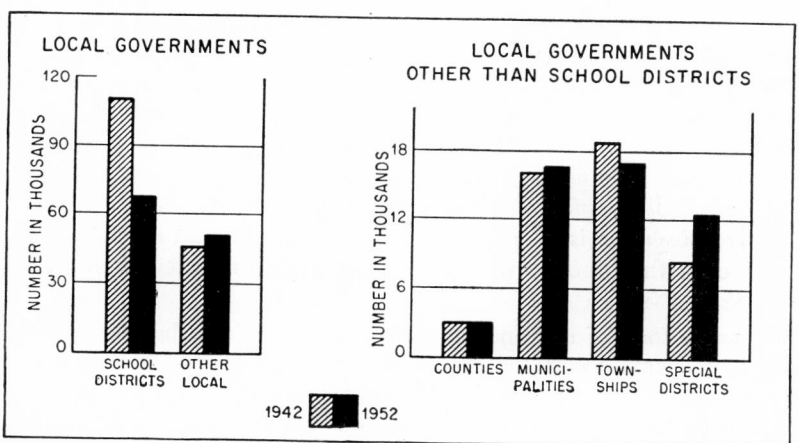

Fig. 23. Number of local governments in the United States, 1942 and 1952. Note the sharp increase in the number of special districts. SOURCE: U.S. Bureau of the Census.

incorporated or annexed.[10] The number of special districts in the nation increased by 48 per cent in the decade preceding 1952 (see Figure 23).

There are several reasons for this trend: Fringe dwellers, needing the services furnished by the districts, do not resist this approach as they do other attempts at metropolitan coordination. Each interest group that may want a service performed by government (amateur pilots wanting an airport, physicians wanting a hospital), together with the professional administrators of particular functions, characteristically wants its special problem handled in a special way by a special organization.[11] School administrators have long ago convinced the American public that they should be independent of the rest of local government, and the school

[10] *Ibid.*, chap. 6. Most special districts are in rural areas (especially fire, drainage, and soil conservation), but large numbers are in urban areas.
[11] As Jones has pointed out, *ibid.*, pp. 527–528.

district is at once the most common and the best-known special district. Others have followed the lead of the educators and the pressure groups supporting them. The special district has also had great appeal to the wistful who would take their pet governmental function "out of politics."

Special districts have often done very good jobs in construction and engineering and sometimes in management. They do not necessarily eliminate political patronage, however, do not guarantee professional administration of functions, and certainly do not remove from the arena of politics governmental functions that involve issues of policy. Special districts often result in increased costs of local government because of the duplication of personnel, the inefficient utilization of equipment, and inability to save through centralized purchasing and other centralized housekeeping activities. They do not balance the various needs for services of a community, do not recognize the interdependence of various functions, and do not usually provide a method of coordinating their activities and budgets with those of the rest of the metropolitan area. If the governing board is elective, this adds to the length of the ballot and asks the voter to choose, in effect, a specialized city council for which the voter has little patience or competence. If the governing board is indirectly chosen, as is usually the case, there is no real responsibility to the public for the function performed. Victor Jones has concluded:[12]

A corporate form of metropolitan government in which the selection of the authority or district commission members is once or more removed from the electoral controls may give us efficient and effective government but it cannot give us good government. It is not necessary, nor is it desirable, for all policy-making officials to be directly elected by popular vote. They should, however, be subject to the budgetary control of popularly elected legislators and their policies should be subject to debate and discussion.

Of course, any legislative body, whether it have jurisdiction over the matter or not, may debate anything it wishes. The object, however, is not futile and irresponsible talk. Our uneasiness should not be allayed by saying that the ordinary municipal governments are frequently corrupt, irresponsible, ineffective, and inefficient. Our job is to make them responsible and efficient. This cannot be done by slicing off the most important functions of local government and handing them over to one or several autonomous bodies.

Multipurpose Special Districts. Most *ad hoc* districts serve a single purpose, such as the Sanitary District of Chicago, which handles sewerage for over seventy municipalities,[13] the Metropolitan Airports Commission

---

[12] *Ibid.,* pp. 585–586. By permission of the University of Chicago Press.

[13] Unifunctional districts normally carry on incidental functions. The Chicago district produces electric power and fertilizer, and its channels are used for navigation. Illinois Legislative Council, *Chicago Sanitary District* (1953), pp. 22–27.

of Minneapolis–St. Paul, and the Metropolitan Water District of Southern California, which brings water some 300 miles from the Colorado River to serve many communities in the Los Angeles area. Where such agencies have met with reasonable success, people have sometimes been encouraged to think that they might be developed into general-purpose super-governments to handle functions that are metropolitan in scope.

There are some multipurpose districts in use and some states, such as Michigan, authorize them where they do not exist. Perhaps the most famous is the Port of New York Authority, which handles many aspects of water, highway, and air transportation. It is, however, a joint agent of the states of New York and New Jersey rather than a unit of local government.

Some observers of local government have supported the use of single-purpose special districts partly on the assumption that they will lead to general-purpose districts for metropolitan government. Such expansion has usually not occurred, however. It has not happened in the Boston, Chicago, Los Angeles, Minneapolis, and Seattle areas. Jones illustrates this failure by pointing to the history of the Massachusetts Metropolitan District Commission. This district is controlled by a commission appointed by the Governor of Massachusetts and is not in any way directly responsible to the local community. It was created in 1919 by the consolidation of three districts which furnished sewerage, water, and park services. In 1923, regional planning was added to its functions (but this has since been transferred to the state), and in 1952 refuse disposal was added. In 1929, however, a separate Boston Metropolitan District was created for rapid transit, and in 1947 a Metropolitan Transit Authority was established to take over the previously privately operated elevated railway system.[14] There appears to be no trend toward making super-governments out of the special districts.

City-county Consolidation. Until recent years, reformers have felt that consolidating the city with the metropolitan county was a desirability second only to annexation and a truer and more permanent solution than the use of the special district. This plan (there are dozens of possible variations of it) calls for an integration of the functions of the core city with the county. The county retains a partial identity, and incorporated municipalities remain independent for local purposes. City and county police, attorneys, clerks, treasurers, and health, welfare, and other departments can be combined to save the core-city taxpayer from paying for county services that he does not use and that in any event duplicate those he is already paying the city to do.

At least fifteen attempts at city-county consolidation have been made

[14] Victor Jones, "Local Government in Metropolitan Areas," in Coleman Woodbury (ed.), *The Future of Cities and Urban Redevelopment* (1953), part IV, pp. 582–583.

in the twentieth century, and only the combination of Baton Rouge with East Baton Rouge parish in 1947 has succeeded. Attempts of this type usually require state-wide approval on a constitutional-amendment referendum, or legislative approval, or a majority vote on referendum both in the core city and in the portions of the county outside. Such approval is not easy to secure.

In Baton Rouge, one of the chronic obstacles to approval was overcome by setting up three taxing districts so that taxes were paid at one rate in urban areas, at another in rural portions of the parish where fewer services were provided or needed, and a third, lowest, one in some industrial areas where no services were provided. Representation, another difficult knot to untie before consolidation can be consummated, was solved by adding two persons elected from the portions of the parish outside of Baton Rouge to the city council whenever that body sits as the parish council.[15]

Not only is city-county consolidation almost impossible politically, but it does not guarantee that the city-county will have sufficient powers to meet all metropolitan problems, and it causes even greater political difficulties if the metropolitan area expands beyond the county limits. Despite the successful development in the Baton Rouge area, this approach to metropolitan government is not likely to bear fruit in many areas of the nation.

City-county Separation. Core-city dwellers, watching the county snowplows at work in the unincorporated reaches of suburbia and remembering that the core city bears most of the cost of county government while securing few services from it, are likely to be intrigued with the idea of separating the city from the rest of the county. This plan is not far different from the preceding one, except that instead of integrating the offices and leaving the county boundaries as they are, separation would create a city-county of the core city and create a new county of the outlying areas.

San Francisco, Baltimore, St. Louis, Denver, and all cities of over 10,000 in Virginia are separate city-counties and have been for a long time. Except in Virginia, there have been no separations in nearly half a century. The plan encounters much the same problems as does city-county consolidation and is no more practical politically. Outlying sections of the county desire to control the county government, as they would under separation, but they also wish to retain the benefits of county services paid for mostly by core-city taxpayers. Furthermore, this is not really an approach to metropolitan government at all, since it traps the city within its own walls (except in Virginia) and instead of treating

---

[15] See T. H. Reed, "Progress in Metropolitan Integration," *Public Administration Review*, vol. 9 (Winter, 1949), pp. 1–10. *Parish* is the Louisiana term for *county*.

metropolitan problems on an area-wide basis, it serves as something of a parochialism, with the core city retreating in a huff to its own enclosure.[16]

Metropolitan Federation. Many functions of government need to be integrated throughout the metropolitan area because of factors already discussed. At the same time there is merit in keeping government as close to the people as possible and a psychological value in retaining the community spirit of the smaller suburb as against the impersonality of the core city. Because of this dilemma, some students of the problem have suggested that a federal plan of government be applied to the metropolitan area with two levels of government, one area-wide to perform functions fitting into that classification and another local community to handle functions of a more parochial interest.

The best example of this device is to be found in the area of metropolitan London, which has twenty-eight metropolitan boroughs plus the ancient City of London proper. Over these, for broader functions, is the London County Council (LCC). The plan is not completely satisfactory, since not all of the metropolitan area comes under the LCC and some functions (such as police and transit) are separately administered. Nevertheless, the federal plan retains the identity of the suburbs and leaves them some powers, but allows a metropolitan approach to the area-wide functions.

Attempts to apply the federal plan have been made in the areas of Oakland, Pittsburgh, St. Louis, San Francisco, Boston, and Cleveland. All have been defeated, although the attempt in the Pittsburgh area in 1929 came very close to success. It should be noted that the metropolitan integrations that took place in New York in 1897 and in Berlin in 1920 did not establish the federal plan, since they called for the creation rather of one large metropolitan city with provisions for *decentralized administration* only and for centralized policy making. In New York, the borough as a unit for administration has become less important over time and today is of little significance.[17]

The Municipality of Metropolitan Toronto.[18] The only example of the federal plan of urban government on the North American continent was established by unilateral action of the Ontario legislature in 1953. With-

---

[16] An important work on city-county separation is J. A. Rush, *The City-County Consolidated* (1941). In 1951, the functions and offices of the coterminous city and county of Philadelphia were joined. A partial integration had taken place as early as 1854. It is difficult to classify this as separation or consolidation, since no boundary changes took place, as happens in separation, and there was no hinterland to provide for, as is the case in consolidation.

[17] Borough representation on the New York Board of Estimate is explained on p. 233.

[18] See Eric Hardy, "Metropolitan Area Merges," *National Municipal Review,* vol. 42 (July, 1953), pp. 326–330; W. W. Crouch, "Metropolitan Government in Toronto," *Public Administration Review,* vol. 14 (Spring, 1954), pp. 85–95.

out a referendum vote in the areas affected, but after extensive public hearings, the legislature created a federal plan with a metropolitan government over the thirteen municipalities of the Toronto area. In addition, the area was disconnected from the county which had had control over it and county functions were assigned to the metropolitan government.

The action established a supergovernment six times the area of Toronto proper. Because of political expediency and lack of study time, the plan is not an ideal one. The metropolitan council of twenty-five consists of the twelve suburban mayors of the cities or reeves (supervisors) of the townships plus twelve representatives from Toronto proper. The chairman is appointed by the provincial government. The Toronto members are the mayor, two of the four elective members of the board of control, and one of the two aldermen from each of the nine city wards.

Not only is this representation ex officio and indirect, but it is not particularly equitable. The city has twelve councilmen for 687,000 people, the suburbs twelve for 467,000. The city population is static, however, and the suburban rapidly expanding; so this gap may be rather quickly closed. Each suburb, regardless of size, has one vote. Two of them have nearly 100,000 population, while three have well under 10,000.

The assignment of powers to the metropolitan and to the local units may not seem entirely satisfactory either. The metropolis controls assessment, water supply and distribution, sewerage and sewage treatment, main highways, public transportation, administration of justice, some welfare functions, land-use planning, and supervision of local zoning. It also has concurrent powers with the local municipalities on public housing and redevelopment, and parks and recreation. Other powers are left to the units, including some that are often thought of as being properly metropolitan-wide in scope: police, fire, libraries, public health, building codes, and direct public relief. No provision is made in the enabling act for a later redistribution of functions.

The Municipality of Metropolitan Toronto represents a major step toward an integrated approach to metropolitan problems and will be the envy of many planners and students of local government. There are some weaknesses in the model established at Toronto, however progressive a step it may be. The dual responsibility of the metropolitan council to the voters is bound to be confusing. All but two of the council members must be elected annually when the "chief goal of the federation is to undertake and implement long-range planning."[19] The two may prove conflicting. Furthermore, the representation is inequitable when measured by a population standard.

The Municipality, as it has been established, does not include quite all

[19] Hardy, *op. cit.*, p. 329.

of the metropolitan area. The plan does nothing about improving the quality of performance of the smaller, often less efficient, units of government. There is some duplication of personnel and equipment because the metropolitan government and the municipalities have concurrent jurisdiction over most functions of government.

Whether American metropolitan areas will follow the lines established by the Ontario legislature will probably depend upon the willingness of American state legislatures to take matters into their own hands and use direct and drastic action. They are not likely to do this so long as they are rural-dominated. Most legislatures today are hostile to large cities and tend to be sympathetic to the views of the satellites. It would seem that the fringe dwellers, in their fear of the core city, are unlikely to assist in the modernization of legislative districting and apportionment. In Northern states, where the core city is usually dominated by the Democratic party and the state legislature by the Republican, conservative suburbanites are torn between favoring a legislature dominated by rural Republicans and supporting one dominated by urban Democrats. Being largely urban Republicans, they are confronted by a dilemma. Because suburbanites are likely to hold, in the future, the balance of power in the politics of many states, the horn of the dilemma which they ultimately choose may indirectly determine whether or not sweeping experiments in metropolitan government will be attempted.[20]

The County as a Metropolitan Unit. It is sometimes suggested that the already existing county governments might be used as a basis for forming a supergovernment over a metropolitan area. There are, however, several handicaps to such a plan. In the first place, the county may be a poor profile of the metropolitan area. The core city may be tucked off in the corner of a county that is in large part basically rural, as is the case of Minneapolis in Hennepin County. Or the metropolis may spread over several counties, as do Chicago, Detroit, Philadelphia, and many others. Secondly, there are many legal objections to the county acting as a municipality rather than as an agent of the state alone. Thirdly, the traditional structure of county government, under either the supervisor or the commissioner system, is wholly inadequate to serve as the base for modern urban government, and this structure is often written into the state constitution. Both county government systems give the county board far too many administrative duties, and there is no administrative system integrated under a county executive.

A very few urban counties have adopted reasonably modern administrative structures that would enable them to become supergovernments.[21]

[20] This paragraph is suggested by remarks in G. S. Birkhead, "Metropolitan Areas Demand Attention," *National Municipal Review*, vol. 42 (July, 1953), p. 366.

[21] Jones has a list in "Local Government in Metropolitan Areas," in Woodbury (ed.), *op. cit.*, pp. 597–601.

Los Angeles County has a chief administrative officer and is quite well integrated, although the Board of Supervisors still performs some administrative functions. Westchester County in New York has, in effect, the strong-mayor plan of government with an elective chief executive. About eleven urban counties use the council-manager form, most of them having adopted it since World War II.

Because of the various factors militating against the use of the county as a senior unit of government, the trend has been rather toward functional consolidation. Either a single function at a time, such as smoke abatement in the Los Angeles area, is turned over to the county, or the function is operated jointly by the county and the core city.

An increasing number of city-county hospitals are being established, especially in Texas. City-county health units, such as that of Pueblo and Pueblo County, Colorado, are becoming more common. Savannah and Chatham County, Georgia, have a joint traffic commission. Many core cities combine with the county to build a city-county building. Newton and Catawba County, North Carolina, have a joint fingerprinting and photography laboratory. Buffalo and Erie County, New York, plan to consolidate their library facilities. Charlotte and Mecklenburg County, North Carolina, have a city-county animal shelter, while Dallas and Dallas County, Texas, have a joint intoximeter and have conducted a joint tuberculosis survey. Planning, zoning, parks, welfare, and correction are among the other functions being turned over to counties or being jointly administered with counties.

As in the other potential plans for solving metropolitan-area government, only one county—Los Angeles in this case—has made long strides toward the use of the county as a unit of government for the metropolis. Elsewhere there has been a slow, piecemeal movement toward a greater use of the county. This approach is not likely to provide an over-all permanent solution to metropolitan needs, but in many cases it is helpful.[22]

Extraterritorial Jurisdiction. Under certain conditions, a city may own and control land outside of its own boundaries. It may do this either under its governmental powers if state law permits, or it may own land in the same manner as a private corporation, in which case its powers are limited to those of the ordinary property owner.

Twenty-eight states authorize some municipal control over the sub-

[22] For Los Angeles, see Helen L. Jones and Robert F. Wilcox, *Metropolitan Los Angeles: Its Governments* (1949); Mel Scott, *Metropolitan Los Angeles: One Community* (1949); various monographs published by the Bureau of Governmental Research, University of California (Los Angeles); G. W. Bemis and Nancy Baschè, *Los Angeles County as an Agency of Municipal Government* (1946); there are sixteen volumes published under the general title *Metropolitan Los Angeles: A Study in Integration* (1952 and later), on a grant from the Haynes Foundation.

division of land outside of the city limits.[23] The areas of jurisdiction vary from 1 to 5 miles. This type of control sometimes enables the core city to require the building up of land within the city before further plats are offered for sale on the periphery. Usually, however, it helps to prevent the uncontrolled growth of suburban slums by requiring suitable standards for new subdivisions. Many heavily urban states, including Massachusetts, Michigan, Missouri, New Jersey, and New York, have no such control.

Extraterritorial powers are sometimes given a city for such functions as controlling roadhouses, securing a water supply, abatement of nuisances, providing for parks (this need is often forgotten until the city is built up and no land within the city limits is left), stone quarries, airports, hospitals for contagious cases, and many others. Many California cities have summer camps and recreational centers in the Sierra Nevada and elsewhere.

The suburbs often resent extraterritorial powers of the core city. Airports may be unpopular in one's neighborhood; yet they are necessary, and there is rarely space within the core city to build one. A careless suburb cannot expect to be left alone if it allows a health menace to exist along the boundary between itself and the core city. If the core city constructs a park in the suburbs, there will be resentment over the city folk coming in droves into the area each Sunday. Yet the suburbanites flood into the core city each workday. Somehow, the suburbanite is not likely to feel that the one counterbalances the other. Clearly, the dispute over extraterritorial powers is a reflection of the inadequacy of uncoordinated independent municipalities in the metropolitan area.

Voluntary Cooperation.[24] The lack of an over-all government in the metropolitan area can be compensated for to a degree through the use of informal or contractual agreements between one or more cities in the area. Agreements may be made by one suburb with other suburbs, or by a suburb with the core city.

It is becoming increasingly common for such intergovernmental arrangements to be made for the disposal of sewage, garbage, and rubbish. It is also common to share police radio networks or to have the core-city police radio supply the suburban departments. Formal agreements or informal understandings concerning emergency stand-by assistance in the

[23] Data from a 1944 study cited in Jones, "Local Government Organization in Metropolitan Areas," in Woodbury (ed.), *op. cit.*

[24] G. W. Rutherford, *Administrative Problems in a Metropolitan Area: The National Capital Region* (1952) stresses that cooperative approaches, rather than the integration discussed above, offer the best solution to the problem. He presents views strongly dissenting against those of Jones and others, holding that their arguments for integration are based upon a priori reasoning, rather than empirical data.

case of unusual police or fire problems are also common. A large number of core cities sell water to the suburbs on a contractual basis. Baltimore and Cleveland, for the most part, sell the water directly to the suburbanite, but most cities sell it to the suburb itself at a master meter. Many cities have understandings of an informal type concerning traffic-flow patterns, including such necessities as the establishment of one-way streets through two or more communities. Dozens of other cooperative arrangements have been worked out in various parts of the nation.

Voluntary agreements are temporary solutions edged with a coloration of the haphazard. They represent an unsystematic and ultimately unsatisfactory approach, although in the short run they do ease some of the strains encountered in furnishing services to urbanites.

Concluding Statement. It seems fairly evident that each device so far tried for the government of metropolitan areas either is basically unacceptable politically to groups powerful enough to block adoption, or has proved to be inadequate as a solution. Cooperative arrangements and special districts have many times proved to be of temporary help, but do not offer permanent solutions. Any proposal that does not meet the requirement of responsibility and responsiveness to the general public must be dismissed as lacking accord with our basic concepts of democratic theory. Victor Jones, after long and careful study, believes that only some system based upon the federal principle has a chance of lasting success. And to date, that principle has proved politically inexpedient. Jones concludes:[25] "If the government of metropolitan areas is to be a local government, we still have before us the job of devising acceptable and effective ways of organizing it."[26]

[25] Jones, "Local Government Organization in Metropolitan Areas," in Woodbury (ed)., *op. cit.*, p. 605.

[26] This chapter has drawn heavily upon the works of Victor Jones. In addition to the bibliography already cited, the following are especially useful: Betty Tableman, *Governmental Organization in Metropolitan Areas* (1951) has a compilation of data on developments to that date. Don J. Bogue, *The Structure of the Metropolitan Community* (1949), shows that economic and social integration and population density vary directly with distance from the core city.

Earlier works include Paul Studenski and others, *The Government of Metropolitan Areas* (1930), the report of the committee on metropolitan government of the National Municipal League; and R. D. McKenzie, *The Metropolitan Community* (1933), by a sociologist.

H. A. Simon, *Fiscal Aspects of Metropolitan Consolidation* (1943), discusses the problem of finances that often lies at the base of metropolitan conflicts. The National Municipal League, *City Growing Pains* (1941), is a series of case studies. Annexation, intergovernmental cooperation, and other developments are reported in each volume of the *Municipal Year Book* and from time to time in the *National Municipal Review*. Jones offers a more complete bibliography and names studies of specific areas.

CHAPTER 12

INTERGOVERNMENTAL RELATIONS

The city in the metropolitan area must learn to get along with its incorporated and unincorporated neighbors. Up to the present time, it has not learned very well how to do this. It is meeting further problems, too, for it must also make a happy adjustment with both the state and national governments.

The state government, as a parent, occupies a special relationship to the city. It has sought to oversee many of the activities of cities through its administrative agencies. The national government, which has no control over cities per se, has nonetheless forged many connecting links between its own administrative structure and that of the cities. Especially in the last twenty-odd years have the number of national-city administrative contacts become numerous.

STATE ADMINISTRATIVE RELATIONS WITH CITIES

State Administrative Oversight of Cities.[1] The administrative branch of state government follows the typically Jacksonian pattern of decentralization. Because of the influence of this frontier philosophy, departments of local government, such as the Ministry of the Interior in France or the Ministry of Local Government in Great Britain, are not to be found in the United States. Administrative contacts between the city and the state are characteristically on a *functional* basis. That is, members of the state department of education oversee the activities of the local school district, the state department of health watches the activities of the local department of health, and so on. Canadian provinces, on the other hand, follow British and continental practices of consolidation for

[1] On this subject, the standard references are S. C. Wallace, *State Administrative Supervision over Cities in the United States* (1928) and *Report of the Council of State Governments, Committee on State-Local Relations* (1946). There are numerous articles in the professional journals and many studies of specific functions. See the series of monographs on *Research in Intergovernmental Relations* under the general editorship of William Anderson and Edward W. Weidner, 1950–1953; Dale Pontius, *State Supervision of Local Government: Its Development in Massachusetts* (1942). Charles M. Kneier and Guy Fox, *Readings in Municipal Government and Administration* (1953), chap. 6, give illustrative excerpts from state laws and administrative orders.

the most part, and perhaps five American states have made some move toward centralized supervision.[2]

Areas of Supervision. What local government functions are subject to state oversight today? Most of them, might be a brief answer. In particular, the state is especially watchful of municipal activities that involve (1) the expenditure of state grants-in-aid (e.g., in education, the building of expressways within cities); (2) those areas of national grants-in-aid which are administered through the states, but under conditions requiring state supervision of the expenditures (e.g., the building of airports in some states); and (3) those activities in which the state as a whole has a particular interest (e.g., the spread of communicable diseases, law enforcement, finances). The principal areas of control are those of education, finance, health, highways, and welfare, but to these must be added airports, fire prevention, libraries, housing, personnel, planning, police administration, and even control of municipally owned public utilities, among others.[3]

Techniques of Supervision. From all that has been said in this book and elsewhere about the tendency for the state to step in and take over much of the independence of local government, it might be assumed that the above-mentioned activities are controlled by heavy-handed bureaucrats from the state capital, armed with court decrees and administrative orders. While these devices do play a part, it has been the practice of most of the state agencies to try persuasion, education, and other noncoercive techniques wherever possible. The big stick is brought into play principally whenever the state overseers find evidence of incompetence, irresponsibility, or corruption.

State agencies exercising supervision usually start by requiring *reports* from local communities. This serves the purpose of warning the state agency when and where trouble spots begin to appear, and it tends to channel local activity, since the reporting official, knowing that he will be judged by his professional peers, will want to "look good." The state agency can furnish *advice and information.* This is especially important for the smaller communities, where amateurs may be floundering about seeking to do an adequate job with little experience, or where overworked professionals may not have time to keep up with the latest techniques in their fields. Unfortunately the relationship between the state and the large-city technical specialist may sometimes become strained when the city functionary thinks he is (or in fact is) professionally more competent than is his nominal supervisor on the state level. Is the manager of a large-city airport able to get along without advice from the state airports commissioner? He is likely to think so. It is by no means unheard-of for a running feud of many years' duration to color the re-

[2] See below, pp. 260–261.
[3] Control over some of these functions will be discussed further in chaps. 16–21.

lationships between a department of a large city and the corresponding agency of the state. Usually, however, relations are friendly and cooperative. The smaller cities and villages have technicians who are likely to recognize the genuine need for advice and to seek it. To simplify requests for such help, Tennessee has established a clearing house for information—the Municipal Technical Advisory Service—in connection with the state university, and some other states have municipal research bureaus which may or may not be connected with a state school.

One step beyond advice is *technical aid*. The state agencies, with (perhaps) a relatively larger budget and with more specialized equipment and personnel, are particularly in a position to help out the local amateur or semiprofessional. How effective can the chief of police in a village of 1,500 people be against the professional criminal? And how much experience or scientific equipment can be put to use if the rare event of a murder should take place in his town? What would his colleague, the water commissioner, know about the technical problems of drilling a new deep well for the town? And how much does the overworked local general practitioner really know about public health, even though he may bear the title of health officer? How much special equipment can the town afford when it is needed? The state agencies in these and in dozens of other circumstances and activities stand ready to offer technical information, advice, and equipment.

Other approaches failing, the state may also make use of its *coercive power*. Among other things, its agencies can *grant or withhold permits* for certain things (e.g., to dump raw sewage into a stream under prescribed conditions); or *issue orders* (e.g., to build a sewage-treatment plant); or *issue rules and regulations* which are technically called ordinances (e.g., to prescribe the technical standards for water-supply purification); or *withhold grants-in-aid* if standards prescribed by state, or sometimes federal, law are not complied with; or *review decisions* of local agencies (e.g., the power of the state tax-equalization board to review the determination of local boards and perhaps to order reassessment in extreme situations); or require *prior permission* from a state agency (e.g., the power of some state health departments to pass on the qualifications of local health-officer nominees); or *appoint certain local officials or remove them* (e.g., the local police chief). It is even possible in most states, as a last resort, to apply *substitute administration*. That is to say, in extreme cases the state may suspend local self-government altogether for some or all functions and allow state officials to govern instead. This is particularly true in the fields of finance, public health, and education.[4]

[4] This section borrows from Dale Pontius, *State Supervision of Local Government: Its Development in Massachusetts* (1942); *and Report of the Council of State Governments, Committee on State-Local Relations*, pt. 2.

Organization for Supervision. The increasing tendency in recent years to turn over state supervision to the administrative rather than to the legislative branch of government has probably changed the pattern of state-local relationships to a considerable degree. Local professional technicians feel more at ease and have less of a feeling that they will be exploited when they deal with state professionals rather than with the politicians of the state legislature. A smoother, more confident relationship is the result. The community is likely to gain, too, for the *motivation* of the professional administrator is different from that of the politician, and this is likely to have an important effect upon the eventual solution of local problems. The professional administrator has a pride and reputation at stake in everything he does, and his success is measured in terms of acceptance of his work by his professional peers, not only within the state, but also within the professional organizations to which he belongs. The politician has his job at stake in everything that he does, and his success is measured in terms of the number of votes he can get in comparison with those of his opponents. The administrator is hence interested in doing the best possible job in accord with the latest technical standards and techniques. The politician will meet the same problem with one thought in mind: what approach will produce the most votes? If he wishes to stay in office he has little choice but to appeal to the popular mind. That the administrator's approach will likely result in an enduring solution, while the politician's will only accidentally produce the same result, should be obvious. In a day of increasing numbers of governmental activities which are also increasingly technical and specialized, it is perhaps fortunate that supervision is more and more becoming the task of the state administrator rather than the legislator.

The problem still remains, however, of determining who is to do the actual supervising. Is the American or the Canadian-European approach the better one?

Functional Relationships or a Single State Agency? Because city-state relations have experienced a gradual unplanned growth on a piecemeal, function-by-function basis and because there have been few systematic overhauls of municipal government in this country of the type that have taken place in England, city-state relations are for the most part uncoordinated and subject to duplications and omissions. New Jersey, with a Division of Local Government in the state Department of Finance and Taxation, has gone the furthest toward an integrated bureau to direct state contacts with local governments.

The New Jersey division has the duty of investigating on a continuous basis the needs of local government and hence has information available for the legislature that does not exist in most states. The principal action of the division has been in the fiscal area. It has power to regulate local methods of budgeting and financial procedure. It makes certain that localities provide enough funds to service their debts and can even require local levies to reduce deficits. It supervises regular audits of the cities. Annual fiscal reports must be made by the cities on state-prepared forms. The Local Government Board, which sets policies for the division, may even take over control of a municipality if it falls into an "unsound financial condition," as defined by law.

While the board has been active primarily in the field of finance, it has become a general overseer of local government to a degree. It has made some investigations into conservation, public health, education, housing, planning, and metropolitan consolidation.[5]

Indiana has centralized fiscal control under the state Board of Tax Commissioners, but this agency does not act as a local government office otherwise. It has power to review local budgets and reduce appropriations, tax levies, and bond issues. It may prohibit the issuance of bonds. The commission has a wide range of discretion under the law.[6]

Without resorting to the use of an integrated agency for the supervision of local government, other states also control some aspects of local finance. A Local Government Commission in North Carolina has wide powers in controlling local bond issues, and Iowa and New Mexico exercise more direct fiscal supervision than does the typical state.

Some states prescribe uniform systems of accounts for municipalities. Thirty states have some degree of state jurisdiction over auditing of municipal accounts. Twenty-two states require municipalities to submit financial reports to the state periodically. Many states provide budget forms for municipalities, and the state form is compulsory in thirteen states. Nearly one-half of the states supervise municipal debt to one degree or another, often passing upon the legality of an issue before it is sold. Four states actually inquire into the necessity and wisdom of municipal bond issues. North Carolina and sometimes Virginia handle the sale of bonds to private investors on behalf of municipalities.[7] In most cases, however, these state activities are carried on in the time-honored decentralized manner.

Canadian Practices. Canada has followed the British, French, and general continental practice of centralizing control of municipalities in a single state (provincial) agency. Eight of the ten provinces have departments of municipal affairs or an equivalent.[8] The general practice is to

[5] *Report of the Council of State Governments, Committee on State-Local Relations,* pp. 37–38, 48–50.

[6] State-local fiscal relations are covered in Wylie Kilpatrick, *State Supervision of Local Budgeting* (1939); also his *State Supervision of Local Finance* (1941); and T. E. McMillan, Jr., *State Supervision of Municipal Finance* (1953).

[7] McMillan, *op. cit.,* provides details and has several charts showing the practice in various states.

[8] See Horace L. Brittain, *Local Government in Canada* (1951), pp. 34–39.

have a board or commission with quasi-judicial powers of debt and financial control, together with a department that performs the necessary administrative functions.

These provincial agencies have very broad control not only over finance, but also in supervising the service functions of municipalities. They are, in effect, responsible to the provincial governments for the honesty, sufficiency, and financial soundness of the municipalities.

A Comment on State Supervision. Two problems must be solved in determining the proper relationship of the state to local administration. One is that of the use of a single state agency over local affairs versus the use of functional relationships;[9] the other centers in the question of the desirable degree of state coercive supervision over cities, whatever the method of organization. It is not likely that an integrated department of municipal affairs is desirable in American states. Plans such as those in New Jersey, North Carolina, and Indiana appear to be reasonably successful, but they do not fit into the general trend. The over-all supervision of local government by a single central department, as in France, results in a high degree of central control, not only over techniques, but over programs and policies. One of the strengths of municipal government in this country lies in the initiative and autonomy exercised by local officials, in contrast with the French municipal officer, who must get approval of even small decisions from the prefect who represents the Minister of the Interior. Over-all supervision leads to uniformity, which in turn destroys the opportunity for experimentation. It is likely that in most states, improved administrative methods have more often originated in the city hall than in the state capitol. It is also important to note that state services to municipalities often tend to be mediocre in quality and that state departments sometimes have no real interest in rendering services to local government.

In general, technical assistance and advice rather than supervision and control are the ideal sought for in this country by both state and local officials. Although state supervision and control is sometimes used, the extent of state dictation to local officials has been relatively slight, and state officials have applied these sanctions only very reluctantly. The advancement of standards, education, and techniques is being achieved more through voluntary associations of city officials and professional technicians in the same field than through central tutelage of local officers.

---

[9] See *Report of the Council of State Governments, Committee on State-Local Relations;* and Joseph E. McLean, "Threat to Responsible Rule," *National Municipal Review,* vol. 40 (September, 1951), pp. 411–417.

NATIONAL ADMINISTRATIVE RELATIONS WITH CITIES

National Government Advice and Assistance to Cities.[10] There are more than 100 Federal government agencies that supply more than 500 services to cities in the United States. They range all the way from the well-known cooperation given to local police officers by the FBI to thousands of technical pamphlets on every subject from adequate specifications for firemen's gas masks to techniques for estimating land values.[11]

The United States Civil Service Commission furnishes local personnel agencies with information on examination techniques and will furnish testing materials. The Bureau of Standards makes a great deal of technical information available to cities concerning commodity specifications, a valuable service since not many cities can operate adequate testing bureaus. The Bureau will make performance tests on all kinds of material and equipment at cost. It also provides cities with model building, fire, plumbing, elevator, and other codes.

The Bureau of Mines gives technical advice on air-pollution problems. The Civil Aeronautics Adminstration tells city officials about the uses to which they might put airplanes, or furnishes them with a model airport-zoning ordinance, and may even give them a surplus Federal airport. The General Services Administration sells surplus Federal buildings to cities at "50 per cent off."

The U.S. Public Health Service furnishes a host of things: advice on sanitation problems; technical assistance, grants for planning and loans for constructing, sewage-treatment plants to overcome water pollution; advice on organizing and staffing a municipal health department; and cash grants through the state for research on heart disease.

FBI agents not only arrest local law violators who have left the state, but they testify without charge as experts in handwriting, tire treads, hairs and fibers, and shoe prints. The local police can find out from them without charge the marks made by a certain German typewriter, 1926 model, or the kind of headlight glass used in a 1930 Essex. The FBI

[10] See P. V. Betters, J. K. Williams, and S. L. Reeder, *Recent Federal-City Relations* (1936); Committee on Intergovernmental Fiscal Relations, *Federal, State and Local Government Fiscal Relations* (1943); National Institute of Municipal Law Officers, *Federal-City Relations* (1953); National Resources Committee, *Urban Government* (1939); D. W. Hanks, "Neglected Cities Turn to U.S.," *National Municipal Review*, vol. 35 (April, 1946), pp. 172–176; J. K. Williams, "Federal Aid Due to Continue," *ibid.*, vol. 37 (February, 1948), pp. 86–90; J. P. Harris, "The Future of Federal Grants-in-Aid," *The Annals of the American Academy of Political and Social Science*, vol. 207 (January, 1940), pp. 14–26. Detailed descriptions of federal-city relations are given in the Anderson and Weidner series previously cited. Convenient material is to be found in Kneier and Fox, *op. cit.*, chap. 8.

[11] See R. H. Blundred and D. W. Hanks, *Federal Services to Cities and Towns* (1950), from which the following illustrations are drawn. Some of them may have since been discontinued.

academy trains city police officers to serve as instructors in local police academies, while the Bureau of Narcotics instructs uniformed policemen in drug identification and enforcement methods at the bureau's training school.

Many other Federal agencies cooperate with local officials from time to time, giving advice or assistance upon request. Local administrators can go to the Housing and Home Finance Agency for advice on problems of race relations in unsegregated public housing; to the Bureau of Prisons for methods of designing, building, and operating a jail; to the Bureau of Public Roads for help in making a parking survey; to the Bureau of Ships for help in learning how to fight a harbor fire; to the Fish and Wildlife Service for surplus bison and elk for the local zoo; and to the Curator of the Navy for a list showing the shipping weights and handling charges on obsolete warships for the city park. But these are only a few of the total number of services available.

Federal Approval of Municipal Activities. The city, in its proprietary capacity, often acts as an ordinary corporation; and when it does so, it must get Federal approval wherever such approval would be necessary in the case of a private corporation. When Federal grants-in-aid are involved, the city must often get approval from the appropriate Federal agency for governmental functions, too. As examples, if a city operates a ferryboat, it must have its rates approved by the Interstate Commerce Commission; if it operates a radio station, it must get a Federal Communications Commission license; if it builds an expressway with the aid of Federal funds, it must have the proposed route approved by the Federal Bureau of Public Roads; if it builds a bridge, it must have the plans approved by the Corps of Engineers. Municipal administrators thus have frequent and varied contacts with Federal agencies.

Federal Grants-in-aid to Cities.[12] Beginning in the early 1930s, the national government began a policy of extending aid through loans and subsidies to municipalities, either directly or through redistribution of grants made to the states. The beginning of Federal-city direct relations came with the Emergency Relief and Construction Act of 1932 in the closing days of the Hoover Administration. The act permitted the newly created Reconstruction Finance Corporation (a Federal agency) to make loans to municipalities in order to finance self-liquidating projects. The act was notable in that it established not only the first Federal-city fiscal relationship, but also provided the beginnings of *conditional* grants to municipalities by establishing certain standards of labor that must prevail in any project receiving a grant. The act was not a success, for it in

---

[12] It might be well for the student, at this point, to review the introduction to grants-in-aid that may be found in any American government textbook. Or see Council of State Governments, *Federal Grants-in-Aid* (1949).

effect required interest rates higher than the cities would accept and the conditions of repayment were overly stringent. But it was a beginning.

The New Deal provided for a host of Federal-city financial arrangements. It began by tiding over the nearly bankrupt cities and states by making grants to the states to care for the unemployed under the Federal Emergency Relief Act of 1933. The Federal government later began to deal directly with the cities through projects financed by the Civil Works Administration and the Works Progress Administration, and sponsored and supervised by municipal and other local governments. It also made grants and loans to municipalities and school districts to construct athletic fields, water standpipes, hospitals, sewerage systems, and other permanent improvements through the Public Works Administration.

The Federal government began to offer grants-in-aid for highways in 1916, but streets within municipal boundaries were specifically excluded from the program. In the early days of the automobile, the problem was to build hard-surfaced highways between cities. Once these were built, the new problem of bringing the streams of traffic from the city limits into the downtown area arose. Funds became available for municipalities beginning in 1932, and the Federal Aid Highway Act of 1944 specifically provided that one-fourth of the aid funds were to be used for the extension of U.S. highways within cities.[13] All of this money, however, is channeled through the state highway departments.

Legislation during the Great Depression and also under the War Mobilization and Reconversion Act of 1944 permitted cities to receive Federal aid for planning public works, such as city halls, and water and sewerage systems. In the field of low-rent housing, the United States Housing Act of 1937 authorized the making of contracts with municipal, county, or state housing authorities to supply most of the money on long-term credit for building housing projects. The act also authorized Federal contributions to these authorities as a subsidy to keep rents low. Where these authorities are county or municipal organizations, the Federal Public Housing Authority deals directly with the local government unless state law prohibits it.

President Roosevelt's recommendation for a postwar Federal aid program to cities for several activities was lost in the conservative trend in politics after 1945. Most of the existing aids were continued, however, and in support of the popular belief that the airplane and helicopter would replace the automobile in the best of all possible postwar worlds, the Federal Airport Act of 1946 provided for Federal grants to cities (directly if state law allows) to buy sites and build airports.

The Small Business Administration, established in 1953 to replace the

[13] R. A. Gomez, *Intergovernmental Relations in Highways* (1950), chaps. 1, 4, and 9.

RFC, was authorized, among other things, to continue the RFC practice of making loans to municipalities in the event of emergencies and disaster. The Federal government also provided, in the postwar era, matching funds for hospital construction by states and municipalities. Some housing subsidies were continued. Aid for the control of communicable and venereal diseases was made available to cities via the states. Federal aid was offered for civil defense. Special aid was also provided for communities which may suddenly be overwhelmed by the influx of new people into a defense area. Another law provided that some Federal surplus properties could be made available to states for distribution to municipalities in the event of major disasters, such as floods or tornadoes.

Federal-city Relations and Postwar Problems. The trend, established in the thirties, toward closer and more direct Federal-city relations and increased financial aid to cities seems destined to continue and eventually to expand. This is so for several reasons: (1) Federal agencies have a great potential for assisting cities because they have both specialized personnel and equipment which the cities need but cannot afford and often cannot get from the state; (2) rural-dominated legislatures have often closed their eyes to the financial problems of the cities and wished them away, while the national government has met the call, at least to a degree—and if the national government has helped a few times when the states have failed, it is likely to be asked for help again; (3) the present level of taxes and the nature of the tax structure leave both the municipalities and the states in a position which will put them in financial distress in the event of even a moderate depression, and it is therefore becoming more and more clear that the only real solution to urban financial problems is for increased Federal government assistance.

The principal postwar issues are two: (1) Is it proper or desirable for the national government to deal directly with the cities, bypassing the parent state government? (2) What can or should the national government do to improve the financial condition of cities? Concerning the former, what damage is done by direct dealing? Does the state perform a function other than to provide another desk with an "in" and "out" box? Does direct relationship encourage greater Federal control of cities? Might Washington one day seize the state's children and adopt them forcibly? If the cities refuse Federal aid, or the states refuse to let them have Federal aid (as has happened in some cases involving housing and airports aid), how long must the cities wait before the states provide adequate substitute legislation?

Concerning the financial needs of cities and Federal government power, there are several questions. Since Federal instrumentalities are not taxable by the states, are present Federal payments in lieu of taxes to cities adequate? Is the Federal subsidy to cities in the form of tax exemption for income from municipal bonds a rational basis for aid? If not, what should be substituted? What tax areas should the national government stay out of and leave to the cities? What kind of grants-in-aid and of what size should the national government provide for cities beyond those already provided for? How much of the fiddler's bill is the national government willing to pay while still allowing the city governments to call the tune? Shortly after President Eisenhower took office he named a Commission on Intergovernmental Relations to make a study of national-state-local interrelationships. A complete reappraisal is no doubt needed.

A Closing Note. Increasingly it is true that the major functions of government can be performed only through the joint activity and cooperation of national, state, and local governments. It is not a question of which level is to carry on these functions, but rather how all three may effectively aid and participate. This is true in education, highways, health, welfare, housing, airports, law enforcement, and perhaps other functions. The pattern of the future will inevitably see more, rather than less, cooperation among the three levels of government in the United States.

CHAPTER 13

MUNICIPAL ADMINISTRATION

It is conventional, in the field of public administration, to say that there are two fundamental activities of government: (1) the determination of public policy, which is *political;* and (2) the putting into effect of that policy, which is *administration.* In a general sense this is true, but it must always be kept in mind that no sharp distinction can be made between the two. The determination of policy will also involve questions of the means of carrying it out. The execution of policy always involves modification of the policy and its selective application to actual circumstances as they arise. But basically, modern government requires that policy be determined by the political organs of government, representing the people, and that policy should be carried out by a professional staff of administrators.[1]

On the American frontier, government performed few functions, and their execution was relatively simple. Today, government performs a great many functions, and virtually all of them are complex and technical. Their execution requires specialized equipment in many cases. It is nearly always necessary to have trained personnel and an effective form of organization.

PRINCIPLES OF ORGANIZATION

Integration. Modern organization of government requires an *integrated* administrative structure—that is, one in which all authority and responsibilty are in the hands of a single individual or body. Where this is the case, the administrative structure is arranged so that each employee or officer is responsible to some one superior, who in turn must answer to his superior, until ultimately department heads are responsible to a single chief executive. This is the form of organization that long ago proved its effectiveness in large private corporations. Without such

---

[1] There are several good textbooks on modern administration. See especially John Millett, *Management in the Public Service* (1954); H. A. Simon, D. W. Smithburg, and V. A. Thompson, *Public Administration* (1950); and J. M. Pfiffner and R. V. Presthus, *Public Administration* (1953). There are also several books on municipal administration, as such. This chapter has drawn extensively from T. H. Reed, *Municipal Management* (1941).

a structure, government cannot be responsible to the public. Its various activities cannot be coordinated, and duplication and waste cannot be eliminated. A generally integrated structure of this desirable type is to be found in the manager and strong-mayor forms of city government, but not in the commission and weak-mayor forms.

Line and Staff. Under the chief executive, one finds two general types of agencies or departments. They may be classed as the line and the staff. *Line* agencies perform direct services for the public, or administer regulatory activities which directly affect the public. Police, fire, water, public transportation, and health departments are examples. *Staff* agencies have as their purpose the promotion of better public policy and better administration through assistance to the line agencies. They do not deal directly with the public. Finance, personnel, legal advice, and planning are examples.[2]

In early forms of municipal organization, it was common to divorce all staff agencies, except finance, from executive control, and even finance was often separated. Today it is widely believed by experts that these functions should not be under elective officials or independent boards, but should be direct aids to the mayor or manager and his subordinates and under the control of the chief executive.

The Administrative Code of the City. The administrative organization of cities in the past was established in state law. Changes could be made only by the legislature. Functions assigned to a particular department could not be changed to another department by order of the mayor or council, no matter how much of an improvement in municipal services might result from the proposed change. This is still the case in some states. Even in home rule cities, administrative structure can often be changed only by the local charter-amending procedures.

Modern charters, however, do not attempt to establish a rigid departmental structure, but rather authorize the council to adopt an *administrative code* for the city establishing a plan of organization. The council is then able to rearrange departments, bureaus, and lesser agencies as changing requirements dictate. This practice is not yet the rule, however. Too often city officials must go to the state legislature with a request for authority to transfer garbage collection, for example, from the public health department to the public works department. Even in home rule cities, the public is often expected to decide on referendum such things as whether there should be a separate department of traffic engineering or whether central purchasing should be consolidated with the controller's office. Some experts believe that many decisions on adminis-

---

[2] Pioneer students of public administration did not all classify the various agencies of government in the same manner. This author is here using the simplest classification. For an evaluation of traditional organization theory on this point, see Simon, Smithburg, and Thompson, *op. cit.*, chap. 13.

trative organization might well be left to the chief executive himself, without even councilmanic action being required.

A complete administrative code or manual is desirable in all except perhaps small cities not only to describe basic structure, but for another reason: it explains the responsibilities and authority of the various departments and their principal officers. The need for this is clearly illustrated in an example cited in the Stone, Price, and Stone study.[3] Some years ago in Austin, Texas:

> . . . there was a complete lack of agreement between the manager and several department heads about the responsibilities of each. The manager assumed, and it was clear in his own mind, that one department was composed of the water, the electric, and the sewage divisions, but the superintendent of one of these divisions had no such idea. He reported directly to the manager instead of to the supposed head of the department, whom he did not recognize as his superior. The manager and the division head never got together to reach a common understanding. Similarly, the health officer in Austin had the notion that he should report directly to the council, which appointed him, rather than to the manager. On the other hand, the manager believed that it was his job to supervise the health officer. No written record of the council's desire was available to the manager and the health officer for guidance.

Clearly such a situation does not aid in the development of effective organization. But confusion as to administrative responsibility is quite a common thing in cities, and Stone, Price, and Stone found that many managers did not seem to know what an administrative code was or how it operated. They found that in San Diego, officials paid no attention to the code and "most of them were unaware of its existence."[4] As municipal management becomes more professionalized, however, the flexible and complete administrative code becomes more important.

DEPARTMENTAL ORGANIZATION

Government must be divided up for purposes of specialization of effort. Departments may be organized in any of several ways.[5] Line departments are usually established roughly on the basis of *functions* of government so that all activities with a common *purpose* (e.g., public safety) may be grouped in a single department. Sometimes, however, they are grouped so that all activities using a common *process* or administrative method are in a single department (e.g., in general, public works). There are other means of classification, too, but the departments

[3] H. A. Stone, D. K. Price, and K. H. Stone, *City Manager Government in the United States* (1940), p. 84. By permission of the Public Administration Service.
[4] *Ibid.*, p. 85.
[5] If the instructor chooses to develop structural theory at length, the student will find it most helpful to read Simon, Smithburg, and Thompson, *op. cit.*, chap. 7.

of a typical city do not, as a rule, fall clearly into any one of them. Staff functions are usually organized roughly by process so that lawyers are in one department, budget officers in another, and personnel technicians in a third.

If departments do not contain reasonably related services that require similar administrative methods it is difficult to get a department head trained adequately in the various functions. Thus, for example, except in small cities, it is unwise to combine welfare and parks into a single department.

Number of Departments. It is not easy to determine how many departments a particular city should have, and there is a great deal of variation among cities. Large cities often have so many departments that the chief executive cannot keep track of what is going on in all of them. Public administrators say that when this is the case, the "span of control" is too great. There are so many department heads reporting directly that true accountability is lost and departments develop semiautonomous status. On the other hand, commission cities often have arbitrarily five departments into which all of the activities must somehow be stuffed. In a fair-sized city, five departments may be each of unmanageable size and may be made up of altogether unrelated activities.

If the number of departments that seem desirable or necessary results in too broad a span of control, the problem may be overcome to some degree by using additional levels of supervisory officials, thus enlarging the chain of command. This can be done by placing intermediaries between the chief executive and the department heads. This practice has not been followed to any extent in American cities. It is very practical, however, and is frequently done, in reducing the span of control of the large city department head over the various bureau chiefs within the department. Thus, if the police chief has more than six or eight bureaus reporting to him directly, the department might be reorganized with three assistant chiefs, one supervising operational agencies, another the service agencies (e.g., maintenance, the crime laboratory), and a third, administration (e.g., personnel, inspection). The chief would then have a span of control extending over but three assistant chiefs. This plan "relieves the head of much of the burden of command and gives him more free time to inspect the department and plan improvements. The extra level of authority interposed between him and the level of execution, however, lessens his personal participation in police operations, impedes somewhat the easy and rapid flow of information up and down the channels of control, lessens the ability of the leader personally to control operations, and may diminish the effectiveness of his personality and add to department red tape."[6]

[6] O. W. Wilson, *Police Administration* (1950), pp. 40–42.

The Department Head: Individual, Group, or Combination. In an earlier day, departments were often headed by boards or commissions, either elected or appointed for staggered terms. Departments with individual heads elected or appointed by the council were also common. The individual head, appointed by the chief executive and removable by him, is regarded as the modern form of governmental organization. In quite a few cities, however, boards are commonly used. Their membership may be either paid or unpaid, and the boards may be empowered to make policy for the departments or may serve only as advisory bodies. In the case of the former, it is common for an individual, perhaps called the executive secretary, to handle details of administration, although old-fashioned administrative boards still remain, especially in weak-mayor cities.

Except in small cities generally and small departments in any city, it is the department head's job to see to it that the work is done, not to do it himself. He need not usually be a technical specialist himself. The lay public often misunderstands the motives of the chief executive who appoints, say, an attorney who has never worn a uniform of any kind to be police commissioner. Actually, department heads are often chosen from among the career members of the particular department, but this need not usually be the case. The important qualifications for a department head are that he has administrative ability and that he has the confidence of the chief executive. In small departments, however, the head takes an active part in performing functions and hence must be qualified for this purpose.

Department heads should have an over-all view of the whole purpose of their departments. They are, of course, at an advantage if they have had experience in the functions performed by their departments. If they have not, it is vital that they be willing to listen to, and take the advice of, technicians who are their subordinates.

The department head establishes over-all departmental policy with the approval of the chief executive. He represents the department in conferences with the chief executive and before the council. Often he must be prepared to defend his subordinates (just as the chief executive must, in most instances, be prepared to defend him), and to smooth over frictions with other departments, with the chief executive, with the council, or with the public. If he fails to do this, morale in the department will be seriously damaged. He appoints subordinates and supervises and coordinates the work of the department.

Boards and Commissions. The use of boards and commissions (the terms are now virtually interchangeable) became very widespread after the War between the States. This marked a transition from control of departments by council committees to control by the chief executive. It also reflected a desire to take government "out of politics." Boards were either bipartisan or, later, nonpartisan in structure, members were usually appointed for long and overlapping terms, and their removal from office was normally very difficult.

T. H. Reed, reporting on the historical evidence, tells us that boards "seldom if ever worked anywhere in the case of police, fire protection, public works and personnel." They have been satisfactory in the case of libraries and planning, and have an in-and-out record in parks, recreation, health, and welfare.[7]

Librarians and educators strongly favor independent boards over their departments. Powerful and vociferous pressure groups often wish to take functions under their wings and protect them as infants that should not be exposed to the rigorous and competitive circumstances of the ordinary city agency. An attempt to make the agency autonomous almost always exists in the case of functions involving special-interest groups or special-clientele groups. Other instances of this sort of thing may be found in connection with public health, public transportation, airports, parks and recreation, art galleries, and museums.

The use of administrative boards is generally disapproved of because in most cases it has led to divided responsibility, conflict within the board or between it and agency leaders, delay in decision making, and lack of coordination of the department with other administrative departments. Advisory boards are still often used and have been successful where their activities are restricted to this function. They are used especially in connection with planning, personnel, welfare, and health, but may be found in various cities in connection with almost any function.

Mr. Inside, Mr. Outside. In small cities, administrative structure is likely to be simple and rather informal. Precise departmentalization is not necessary. In such cities, the success of governmental operations may depend upon having two key administrators, one an "outside" man, the other an "inside" man. The former may have such a title as "director of public works," but may handle many matters including streets, parks, building inspection, water supply, and planning. The latter may be called the "city clerk" or perhaps the "director of finance" and may handle finance, personnel, purchasing, and routine office duties. Of course, the larger the city the more specialization that is required. The type of administration just described may be found in connection with the manager plan, but it is also a requirement in many of those cities of a few thousand where the mayor is too busy with his own occupation to supervise the affairs of the city.

[7] Reed, *op. cit.*, pp. 86–89.

THE CHIEF EXECUTIVE[8]

The role of the executive in city government is as essential as it is in industry or in any sizable organization. The top administrator is the man who is in charge of the entire process of municipal administration, who serves as the liaison officer between administration and the legislative body, who is formally or informally a principal policy maker by the very fact that he does head administration, and who must find and develop latent administrative talent for use in the vital positions of department heads. The job of the chief executive is so important, in fact, that Chapter 9 of this book discusses in some detail the functions of this officer.[9]

MUNICIPAL STAFF SERVICES

Organization of Staff Services. The principal staff services, finance, personnel, legal advice, and planning, are today all considered to be aids to the chief executive. They help him to provide services to the public at the highest possible level of performance. At one time, all of these functions were considered to be checks upon the chief executive. That view has been abandoned by specialists in municipal administration today, but much of the public is still likely to be skeptical of entrusting the direction of these activities to the chief executive. These people are likely to argue that if personnel, for example, were under a director appointed by the mayor or manager, the chief executive would build up a machine through patronage appointments. If the public is at all alert, however, it does not work that way. The principal motivation of the modern chief executive is to achieve a successful administration that will impress his professional colleagues and the public favorably. He can achieve real success only by choosing the best possible advisers and appointing the best possible personnel.

Finance. The city treasurer and the controller were formerly often elective officials. Sometimes the control function scarcely existed at all in the modern sense of preauditing of expenditures. The budget in an earlier day was often made up by a council committee. Today modern municipal organization calls for an integrated finance department with a

---

[8] This text has usually used the term "chief executive" for the officer in charge of administration, partly because this conforms to popular usage, partly because the officer called a Chief Administrative Officer as discussed in chap. 8 is not actually the top responsible officer, and partly because the mayor is more than simply a chief administrative officer. The chief executive in this sense, then, is the mayor in mayor-council cities and the manager in council-manager cities. There is no true chief executive in commission cities.

[9] See especially p. 210 ff.

commissioner appointed by the chief executive and including divisions for assessing, control, budgeting, purchasing, and the custody of public funds. In this way the executive has a mechanism for watching the activities of all departments as they spend their appropriations. By having the budget officer as a staff assistant, he can apply his over-all view of municipal functions to the preparation of the annual budget.[10]

Personnel. In the nineteenth century, personnel administration was a matter of patronage appointments. As the need for specialists in government developed, the merit system came into use. It was generally believed by reformers that an independent civil-service commission would be necessary in order to keep corrupt politicians from destroying their efforts. Today, with responsible municipal administration, personnel is viewed as a proper function of management, just as it is in private industry.[11]

Legal Advice. In older forms of city government the city attorney (often called the corporation counsel) was frequently an elective official or an appointee of the council. Frequently there was no central pool of legal talent, but rather each large department would have its own independent legal staff. Modern management calls for a single legal department serving as a staff agency to the chief executive. This department can also provide advice to the council. The greatest advantage of a unified department is that it gives a single opinion to all concerned on each legal problem. Because of Dillon's rule, every department of the city is constantly seeking legal opinions as to its authority, and consistency among these opinions is highly desirable.

In small cities the attorney is commonly a part-time officer. In many states all but the largest cities depend for much of their legal advice upon the expert staff of attorneys of the state league of municipalities.

Planning. City planning is nothing more than long-range policy making: the development of broad outlines of policy into which detailed day-to-day policy should be fitted.[12] In addition to physical planning of the type discussed in Chapter 20, financial and administrative planning or research is carried on. This latter type is concerned with "the organization, efficiency and cost of local government."[13] Better means of organization and better methods of operation mean better municipal services at less cost, and the responsibility for achieving these goals rests with the chief executive, as does that of better physical planning.

The reasons why planning should be organized as an executive rather than an independent, function are clearly set forth by T. H. Reed:[14]

---

[10] See chap. 15, on financial administration.
[11] See chap. 14, on personnel administration.
[12] See chap. 20, on planning and zoning.
[13] See Reed, *op. cit.,* chap. 14.
[14] *Ibid.,* p. 305.

It is only by more closely associating the function of planning with municipal management that the hopes and aspirations of the planners can be translated into action. The weakness of planning in this country has been, and still is, that it is to a large degree carried on in a vacuum. It has produced a vast array of handsome volumes, maps, and sketches, which are mostly gathering dust on library shelves and have not accomplished much else, except the wide adoption in urban communities of so-called "zoning ordinances." These are frequently so badly enforced as to destroy most of their usefulness. It is more than probable that the average mayor, manager, and council member regard the local planning commission as an excrescence on municipal government, created to quiet a few cranks by allowing them to play with pretty pictures of the city's future so long as they do not interfere with the routine conduct of the government.

It is common to establish a planning commission as an advisory group, but in the past there has been a lack of understanding as to whom the commission is to advise. Generally, planners have talked to anyone who would listen. The result has been frustration for them and a city less attractive than it might be. T. H. Reed has concluded: "What is needed is not so much a reorganization of the planning authority . . . but a reorientation of planning in the scheme of local government. It should be regarded, not as an isolated service, but as part of the essential machinery of government. Its principal point of contact should be with the executive."[15]

The Chief Executive's Personal Staff. In addition to the assistants discussed above and such advisory commissions as may exist, the chief executive usually, except in small cities, chooses a staff of personal advisers and assistants. These may include an administrative assistant or two, or sometimes, especially in manager cities, an intern trainee just graduated from a university training program. In larger cities, the chief executive may have a personal, confidential secretary and a number of stenographers and office assistants.

The staff of the chief executive has the task of helping him keep abreast of the functions for which he is responsible. Needless to say, these persons must have his complete confidence, for they are often more closely associated with his success or failure in office than are his department heads.

Other Staff Functions. In addition to the staff functions already mentioned, there are numerous housekeeping functions which are sometimes operated by central agencies over which the chief executive has general supervision. These include:

1. The maintenance of building and grounds (except parks)
2. Janitorial service agency
3. Central heating for large buildings or groups of buildings

[15] *Ibid.*, p. 307.

4. Central lighting plant, either for furnishing electricity to the community (in which case it would be considered a line function) or, more commonly, to light streets and public buildings

5. Central telephone switchboard

6. Messenger and mailing service

7. Central stenographic pool, used in some cities but likely to encounter strong opposition from the operating departments, which want their own staffs

8. Central transportation pool and equipment-maintenance service[16]

ADMINISTRATION AND THE PUBLIC

Public Relations in City Government. Much of the activity of everyday administration goes along with little or no notice taken of it by the average citizen. His knowledge of the services that are available to him, or of the nature of bureaucrats or of the administrative process, is likely to be very skimpy indeed. But the average citizen does not automatically come by an understanding of these things. He must be told what his government is doing, and why.

It has already been noted that the political process involves not just one monolithic "public," but a series of *publics* each demanding satisfactions.[17] Citizens are rarely unanimous in their attitudes toward public matters. If they were, government officials would have few problems in public relations. Given the nature of the political process as involving the interaction of conflicting groups, public relations must normally be directed toward one or more of the interested groups in the community. Groups may be interested in municipal government because of their physical location within the community, their businesses, their tax bills, their income, their (high or low) status positions within the community, or for other reasons. Each individual belongs to several publics and can become displeased with city government in connection with any one of them. He can also be informed about the activities of his city by being reached as a member of any one of these publics.

Municipal departments often have peculiar publics of their own, and each of them must therefore be conscious of the importance of public relations. Departments dealing with particular professional or clientele groups are especially likely to have uniquely identifiable publics. The welfare department, for example, must please (1) welfare recipients; (2) the pillars of the community who take an interest in welfare as an avocation; (3) taxpayers who pay the bills; (4) editors, who may want to take the occasional welfare cheat and make a headline case out of him; (5)

[16] *Ibid.*, chap. 15.

[17] Whenever the term *public opinion* has been used in this text, it has been meant in the sense of "the attitudes of interested publics."

grocers and other businessmen who have welfare recipients as customers; (6) professional social workers, who may want the department to be established as an autonomous agency; (7) ordinary citizens, who are likely to believe that people on public relief are lazy, shiftless, and of a category akin to the criminal. The manager of the local airport must cope with publics that include passengers, pilots, airline officials, and people who live near airports or proposed airports; the health department must reach an understanding with the medical profession, with the Parent-Teachers' Association and other pressure groups interested in the schools, with social reformers who want expanded public health services; and so on.

The informed citizen should understand that, in the process of seeking to placate their various publics, the personnel in the various departments often come into conflict with one another. They compete over budgetary matters and in seeking status in the community. Some department heads feud publicly with other department heads—with resultant damage to all of local government, since the citizen is likely to believe the worst that each official says about other officials. In order for the individual citizen to get a proper view of his municipal government, therefore, it becomes important for public relations to be established as a vital staff function under the supervision of the chief executive.

Gauging Public Attitudes. The public official who would keep his publics informed through an active public relations program must first of all be acquainted with the attitudes existing in the community. This is no easy task to accomplish, as the student can learn from any councilman, mayor, or manager.

How can the public official go about gauging attitudes? He may employ one of the so-called public opinion polling organizations, or alternatively establish a polling unit within, say, the city complaint department. But public opinion polling is quite a technical task and therefore requires specially trained personnel. It is also too expensive for most cities to finance. It is time-consuming, and the information is therefore often not available when it is needed. Perhaps most difficult of all, poll results that are unfavorable serve as ammunition for opponents of the administration, and this discourages their use. Such results, if they fell into the hands of irresponsible persons, could produce a great deal of damage before the administration could correct the faults complained of.

The official is therefore likely to turn to older methods of measurement, most of which are of doubtful reliability. All persons in the political arena, for example, engage in *informal polling* by noting the views expressed by visitors and letter writers. But these views may be highly unrepresentative, and are of uncertain value at all times. *Advisory bodies* are often used as a means of measuring the attitudes and the intensity of attitudes of the important pressure group interested in a particular activity. *Letters, petitions,* and *resolutions* from groups are expressions of group attitudes and are useful as such. Usually they express protests rather than offer positive suggestions such as advisory bodies often make. *Elections,* of course, may serve as a final public opinion poll at which to measure important controversies. Ideally, municipal election campaigns should be conducted primarily over important policy issues, but this has often not been the case. Candidates usually prefer to deal in glittering generalities and indulge in name calling and other propaganda techniques rather than to take a stand on specific issues which may lose votes, and the citizen has unfortunately often permitted this practice.

Contacts with Citizens. Every public official has an obligation to help increase interest in government by informing the public of what government is doing, what it has done, and what it plans to do. Groundwork for future plans must be especially well laid if a city is to approach its problems on the basis of long-range planning. The public should know what services are available from each agency of government, what it is costing, and why it is costing what it is. On the other hand, no official has a moral right to use taxpayer money in a public relations program that is simply a defense of incumbent officeholders, although this is sometimes done.

Public employees who daily meet the ordinary citizen in the course of their work are probably the most important persons in helping to determine whether a public relations program is to be successful. Many public works employees are in a position to make city government either popular or unpopular. Refuse collectors, for example, meet the public daily. If they are efficient in their work and courteous in receiving complaints or informing citizens of ordinance violations, they can create much good will. So can public works foremen in replying to "sidewalk superintendents" who want to know what is being done, why, and what the cost will be.

Policemen are perhaps the most important public relations men the city government has. Their uniform makes them conspicuous. For that reason, the uniform itself must always be neat and properly worn. Policemen must be indoctrinated in the rules of courtesy and must be taught while in recruit training to be living city directories, for their responses to requests for information become in effect measurements of the efficiency of the force so far as the typical citizen is concerned. And, of course, one police officer seen in uniform in a bar or caught in some wrongdoing does untold harm. He may represent a tiny fraction of 1 per cent of the force, but he can do more damage than can be repaired by a dozen fancy annual reports.

Firemen have some special advantages in public relations. Fire fighting is dramatic and a public relations activity in itself. Firemen also gain good will by rescuing rat terriers from culverts and young boys from trees, and by making and repairing toys in their spare time for distribution to needy children at Christmas time. On the other hand, they must overcome the popular notion that firemen chop down doors, smash windows, and spill chemicals on the living-room rug with malicious glee. Fire fighting is a good example of the value in public relations of dramatic activities. Americans are quite generous in permitting the purchase of expensive fire equipment, although they are not very much interested in fire prevention, which would make the equipment less necessary. Lectures on fire prevention are normally not dramatic.

Departments vary a good deal in the nature of their public relations problems. Some of them must work hard to satisfy their clientele, but they do not often attract general public attention (e.g., recreation); some of them are vital but work largely in a manner that seldom attracts general public notice (e.g., public health); some perform functions that are generally approved of, but are potential public relations dynamite (e.g., public housing); some of them are constantly under public surveillance (especially police and public works). All of them have a good deal to do with the status position of public employees in the community and the general repute of local government.

Counter clerks and switchboard operators are key personnel in good public relations. They should not be allowed to develop the notion that their job is to get rid of persons lodging complaints or seeking information. Tact, courtesy, and pleasant personality are the traits required. "Every citizen complaint or request for information," E. D. Woolpert has said, "has the makings of a public relations asset for the city." Inquiries should be answered in clear, lay language. Gobbledegook does not impress the citizen; it annoys him. Complaints should be received courteously, and should be regarded as warning signals, not as an annoying characteristic of cranks. Explanations should be offered, if appropriate, but not arguments. Written records should be kept, and occasional statistical compilations of them can be of great value both in public relations and in improving the operations of line departments. Every complaint should be referred to the officer whose responsibilities are involved. If the complaint is justified, action should be taken at once. A follow-up system is required if the chief executive is to keep control over policy toward complaints. A file should be kept showing action taken, and the complainant should be informed of the disposition of the matter. In some cities this is done through a central complaint bureau.

City Officials and the Newspapers. Nothing is more important to the reputation that city government enjoys in the community than the relationship city officials have with the local newspapers. These publications, reflecting the varied views of their editors and publishers, take many different attitudes toward local governments. Many of them are responsible in their criticism and anxious to promote good government in the community. Others believe that criticism of any sort is good for circulation building. Some of them encourage the continued existence of popular superstitions, prejudices, and misconceptions concerning the nature of government. Some of them are ably edited; others are headed by men who run the newspaper as a profitable business, but who have no concept of social, economic, or administrative realities.

The department head may find the reporter or editor informed, responsible, and intelligent, in which case their relationship is likely to be happy and easy. On the other hand, he may consider the reporter or editor to be uninformed or simply stupid. But he should never for a minute forget that, whether responsible or not, the newspaperman controls the most important medium of communication in the city. Newspapers are normally of special influence in the formulation of *local* attitudes, as distinguished from attitudes on national or international matters.

Of course, the problem may be that the newspapers are represented by able men seeking to keep the public informed, while the councilman or department head has developed a confused notion of what the press is entitled to know. Arthur W. Bromage, a councilman–political scientist, has pointed out to public officials that:[18]

The only attitude appropriate to press and radio relations is one of open frankness. When a newspaper or radio representative calls, there is no use pretending that you don't know something which you actually know. If you do not wish to be quoted, you can always say so. One must keep constantly in mind that public office is not private business. The press and radio operate to convey news, and you are a source of local news.

City officials must learn not to be too easily annoyed by inaccurate reports in the newspapers. They should encourage friendly relations and should never turn down a request for information unless it is vital not to release it in advance of a certain time (some municipal officials find it desirable to "fill in" reporters on such material, but secure from them a promise not to release it prematurely.) One reporter has said, "If I were a city official, I would have a clearly defined and systematic policy in all press relations. I would either supervise execution of such policies myself or have a responsible person, preferably with a knowledge of news and reporting techniques, do so under my direction."[19] The picture that the average citizen has of city government is likely to·be the picture painted

[18] A. W. Bromage, *On the City Council* (1950), p. 73.
[19] Hal Hazelrigg, quoted in E. D. Woolpert, *Municipal Public Relations* (1940), p. 50.

by the local press. No municipal official can afford to forget that this is the case.[20]

Public Reports. Outside of direct contacts between public officials and employees and the citizen, and information distributed through the press, local governments can inform their publics in a variety of ways: through the use of annual reports, leaflets, radio and television programs, movies, "open house" days, and talks before clubs and groups. The infrequency of these reports (except for the personal appearances of officials) is one of the weaknesses in present-day city government and represents an area in which there is much need for improvement.

Cities have long been required to issue some sort of annual statement of finances for public consumption. Out of this background, some cities have come to issue general annual municipal reports aimed at the citizens of the community. Often these are in traditional form—dull, formal, and understandable only to persons having some knowledge of accounting. Other cities have produced clever abbreviated annual reports, with dramatic graphs, pictures, cartoons, and other eye-catching devises that still manage to convey a great deal of information. More of these are needed. In 1952, only 130 United States cities issued annual reports, and about one-third of these were of the dry, traditional type. (There are 1,346 cities of over 10,000 people in the United States, and 2,528 cities of over 5,000.) Smaller cities have been more successful in distributing their reports than have larger cities. Distribution of the reports together with utility or tax bills appears to have been successful in some cities. Reports in 1952 ranged in size from one folded page to 200 bound pages. Their cost was not great. The average city spent only $645, while the maximum, spent by New Orleans, amounted to just over $7,000.[21]

An increasing number of cities have adopted the practice of preparing leaflets in lieu of the more expensive report. They are usually enclosed with the annual property-tax bill. Some cities prepare a series of leaflets, each of which deals with a different city function. Others have used the leaflets to present the government's side of an issue: to tell of the need for new bond issues, to encourage homeowners to follow proper methods of garbage storage, to welcome new citizens in the community, or to explain the purpose of an annexation program.

Radio and television offer a fine communications medium for munici-

---

[20] This section has borrowed from E. D. Woolpert, *Municipal Public Relations* (1940). See also H. A. Simon, D. W. Smithburg, and V. A. Thompson, *Public Administration* (1950), pp. 415–421. Several of the books in the municipal-management series published by the International City Managers' Association and cited throughout this text devote a chapter to public relations. One of the most important areas demanding good public relations is that of police protection. See the chapter on the subject in O. W. Wilson, *Police Administration* (1950).

[21] Statistics for this section are taken from M. E. Keane, "Municipal Reporting in 1952," *Municipal Year Book, 1953*, pp. 259–264.

palities, particularly because a certain amount of time is usually available to city governments without charge. A few cities have brought radio and TV into the council chamber. The routine nature of most council meetings, however, makes it doubtful if they would appeal to many listeners and viewers. The practice in Austin of making tape recordings of council meetings and then editing them to fit a thirty-minute program helps to overcome many of the objections to live broadcasts. Important committee hearings and investigations might also be presented in this fashion. The radio and television medium, however, is certainly subject to abuse by unscrupulous persons seeking personal publicity.

Some cities have weekly television programs conducted by the mayor or by department heads taking turns. These may include panel discussions and round tables, but the use of filmed action programs on TV offers fine possibilities for the future. The professional organizations of municipal employees should not overlook the possibility of encouraging television producers to present semidocumentary programs in which the activities of local government functions are dramatized. In recent years, *Dragnet* has helped to make the Los Angeles police force famous and has given the public a generally realistic view of how a large-city detective division operates. Other programs have helped to glorify the unsung workers in public health, volunteer fire fighting, juvenile delinquency, social work, and other municipal activities. That such programs can do much to develop public good will was demonstrated years ago by several Federal agencies, notably the FBI and the Marines, using the movies as a medium.

A handful of cities have produced movies to be shown to various groups about town. It is likely that a great many public officials realize the value of this reporting device, but consider it too expensive. Only five such films were produced in 1952. Actually, San Diego produced a twenty-seven-minute, 16-millimeter film at a total cost of $7,500, or only slightly more than the cost of the New Orleans annual report of the same year. The city manager of Concordia, Kansas, doing nearly all of the work himself, produced a fifteen-minute film at a cost to the city of only $200.

A few cities have used the "open house" device for allowing citizens to get a first hand view of municipal operations. Only sixteen cities were reported as using this form of reporting in 1952, although it would appear to have fine possibilities, especially for middle-sized cities. These "open houses" have sometimes been held in connection with the dedication of a new building. They usually include exhibits from the various city departments and sometimes working models of municipal projects.

In a day of intensely competitive commercial advertising, city government must learn to sell itself. The public has been conditioned to expect representatives of all institutions to come to the individual and explain in a clear, firm voice and simple style the wares they have to sell. Most cities have a long way to go, however, before they succeed in doing their share toward making the public aware of its government.

Closing Statement. This chapter has discussed some of the principles and methods of municipal administration. The following chapters deal with the line and staff services furnished by the various departments of the city.[22]

[22] For material on municipal administration in addition to that cited in this chapter, see Charles M. Kneier and Guy Fox, *Readings in Municipal Government and Administration* (1953), chap. 12.

CHAPTER 14

THE MUNICIPAL CIVIL SERVICE

Issues of policy abound in the area of municipal employee-employer relations. Many of these issues are submitted from time to time directly to the voters of the city. Some of them become campaign issues. All of them relate to the effectiveness of city government.

Should public employees be allowed to join regular trade unions? Should they be allowed to join any kind of union at all? Should public employees have a right to strike? What sort of job security should they have? Are public employees' salaries adequate, or are they too high? These are some of the questions that the citizen may expect to be asked to know something about.

MODERN PERSONNEL PRACTICES

It seems likely that most urban citizens do not realize the degree of professionalization that has taken place in the municipal civil service in recent decades. Nearly two million people are employed in local government service in the United States (not counting school employees). Most of these are employed by municipalities, and most of them are performing specialized jobs that require special training of one degree or another. While the number of Federal employees has had a general downward trend since 1945, municipalities continue to expand their services, the total number of employees, and the total size of the payroll.

A great many people still believe, as they believed in the mid-1930s, according to a survey, and as Andrew Jackson believed well over a century ago, that government jobs are so "simple that men of intelligence may readily qualify themselves for their performance."[1] Of course, a moment's reflection by a thoughtful person leads to the conclusion that this is no longer the case. Government now performs a great many, rather than a few, functions. In the last century or so, the performance of most of man's activities has become specialized and mechanized. Governmental activities are no exception. Since the turn of the century, govern-

---

[1] See Commission of Inquiry on Public Service Personnel, *Better Government Personnel* (1935); and Andrew Jackson's first message to Congress (1829).

ment employment has become increasingly specialized and increasingly performed by professionally trained personnel with professional attitudes toward their work.

Civil Service and the Merit System. The term *civil service* refers to civilian employees of government. In practice it is often used interchangeably with *merit system*. The latter properly refers to a method of choosing government employees on the basis of examinations demonstrating the technical or professional competence of the applicant. The beginnings of a municipal civil service based upon the merit principle appeared in 1884, but, as in the case of the states, the principle did not become widely accepted until the 1930s. The national government, through its insistence upon professional competence of administrators for some programs receiving Federal grants-in-aid, prodded many cities and states along in this direction.

The Civil Service Commission. The acts establishing civil-service merit systems in 1883 (Federal) and 1884 (New York and Massachusetts) established a semi-independent civil service commission and began a pattern that is still typical in cities as well as higher units of government. It is common to have a three-member civil service commission appointed (usually by the mayor) for overlapping terms, not more than two of the members being of the same political party. An executive secretary is normally hired to handle the actual administration of its activities.

The commission makes rules respecting examinations, classifies positions, conducts examinations, and keeps a list of eligible appointees.[2] It establishes uniform wages, hours, and conditions of labor (so that two clerks doing about the same job, but in different departments, will receive the same pay). It makes rules on transfers and promotions. It may, especially in large cities, conduct training programs. It certifies the payrolls so as to discourage payroll padding. It may have other functions, too.

The Personnel Director. In recent years, students of public administration have often criticized the use of the civil service commission to head personnel recruitment. It is now argued that the commission competes with the mayor or manager for control over city employees. The resultant conflict is often harmful to administration and to morale. It is argued further that personnel control is inherently a function of management and hence should be handled as a part of the chief administrator's office.

It is probable that the commission system was necessary in the early days of civil-service reform because the administrative branch of government was corrupt and was opposed to the merit principle. Today, however, a chief administrator who wants to run a smooth, effective adminis-

[2] See T. H. Reed, *Municipal Management* (1941), chap. 12.

tration desires competent personnel. He dare not resort to spoilsmanship; if he tried to do so, he would in any case be detected immediately.

There is a trend, therefore, toward the establishment of a personnel department under a single head, the personnel director, who is responsible to the mayor or manager. Personnel then becomes an executive function and responsibility.[3] This form of organization has been used most often in manager cities, where it began. It is more easily accepted in such cities because the manager is himself a professional careerist.

Some people have accepted the idea of a single personnel director, but insist that he should be chosen on the basis of an open competitive examination. This approach is workable provided that the chief executive is free to remove the personnel director. If he does not have that power, the personnel agency becomes a self-perpetuating bureaucracy with no responsibility to the public.[4]

The old-fashioned independent civil service commission, usually consisting of three members selected on a bipartisan or nonpartisan basis, has had many weaknesses. Its most undesirable characteristic has usually been found in the hostility that it has encouraged, either deliberately or by the nature of its structure, between the personnel agency and the chief executive. Its very existence has implied that the chief executive was standing by, eager to return city employment to a patronage status at the first opportunity. Sometimes the commissions have been politics-ridden and actually less anxious than the chief executive to establish a true merit principle of employment. Some commissions have sought to administer their policies themselves, but have been lacking in the technical qualifications that a qualified personnel director would possess. Others, as independent agencies, have been unable to get funds in order to hire a technical staff capable of preparing and administering valid and reliable examinations—and neither the council nor the chief executive has had any incentive to go to bat for the commission at budget hearings.

Today it is generally realized that personnel administration needs to be a part of management, as it invariably is in private enterprise. Under the leadership of a director whose professional interest is in the improvement of personnel and the methods of selecting personnel, the chief executive is given one of his most effective tools for a successful administrative record.

Circumventing the Merit System. Regardless of the structural arrangement of the personnel department, the merit system will not operate un-

---

[3] Many would want this plan modified by the use of an *advisory* civil service commission, or by having the commission make policy provided that all administration of policy is left to the personnel director.

[4] See Reed, *op. cit.*, pp. 253–256; and the *Model City Charter* of the National Municipal League. The argument for a single personnel director has been restated in W. S. Carpenter, *The Unfinished Business of Civil Service Reform* (1952).

less the public demands that it be honored in practice. Some merit systems have been installed only to become the butt of city-hall jokes. A small amount, or a great deal, of evasion of the principle may be found in many cities nominally under a merit system. There are so many methods of evasion that even the most conscientious independent commission cannot make the system work if officeholders wish to violate its principles and if they believe the public will let them get away with it. And if in the commission itself the majority do not believe in the very system they are to administer, obviously the chances of prostituting the device become much greater.

These are some of the means of circumventing the merit principle: A large number of positions may be *exempted* from the classified service. Lawyers, physicians, department heads, and private secretaries to department heads are commonly so exempted. But the list may be greatly expanded so that in the end ample patronage appointments may be made available, while a façade of the merit system remains for window dressing.

Provisional appointments, for temporary service until a new examination can be given and a new eligible list can be prepared, offer the best of all opportunities for evasion. Provisional appointments are necessary for emergencies, and they usually have a three- or six-month time limit upon them. There are many ways in which these appointments can be continued for years if they are used as a method of placing political favorites in jobs. The department head may be allowed to certify that no other person is qualified for a "unique" job, or provisional appointees may be given some kind of preference when the examination is finally given, or there may be a series of reappointments. In any case, six months on the job as a "temporary" should be enough experience to allow the person to finish in the top three when the examination is given—and in most cities the department head may choose from among the three highest names certified by the commission or personnel director. There are other devices that may be used, too, such as giving bonus scores for certain reasons, or canceling eligible lists when a new administration takes office, so that new examinations must be given and many provisionals may be appointed in the meantime.

Artificial safeguards are inadequate protection for a merit system. Yet the professional, career approach *does* work in many cities because it has become a part of the local political cultural pattern. And in England, where there are no safeguards at all against making every appointment a political one, the system works very well indeed. The voters would not allow it to be otherwise.

It should thus be kept in mind that the *spirit,* rather than the letter, of the merit system is the important thing. Many small and middle-sized municipalities cannot afford to employ professional personnel directors and staffs. The mayor, manager, clerk, or some other official may act as personnel officer. Yet in many cities that have no organized merit system, there are no spoils, and existing policy is to get the best available man for the job. It should also be remembered that the personnel methods used in any city are not likely to be more modern in character than are those used in private enterprise in that community, and that the major personnel problem in municipal government today is likely to be, not spoils, but low pay, particularly in smaller communities.

Position Classification. In the establishment of a merit system of civil service, it is important that the various jobs of the municipality be categorized. Position classification consists of determining the duties and responsibilities of each individual job, whether occupied or vacant, and the assignment of that position to a class together with other positions of similar or related duties and responsibilities. Thus positions may be classified, for example, as junior clerk-typist, senior budget analyst, patrolman, chauffeur, or personnel director. Accurate and meaningful classification of positions is a technical and difficult job and can be done properly only by persons with training in personnel administration techniques. Once the duties of each position have been described, the number and type of classes needed for the particular city must be determined, classes must be given a descriptive title, and positions must be assigned to classes. This last activity may create a good deal of controversy. Since it is part of a supervisor's duty to look after the welfare of his subordinates, a bureau chief may well engage in a bitter controversy with the personnel agency over whether his best stenographer fits the job description of intermediate stenographer or senior stenographer.

Although a position-classification plan may be greeted as "red tape and bureaucracy" by the general public and municipal employees alike, it performs many useful functions if it is allowed to operate properly. Classification raises employee morale by standardizing job titles. Employees in the public works department who are referred to on the payroll as "bookkeepers" are not happy if persons doing the same job in the department of water supply are called "accountants." Morale drops if the mayor lists his favorite stenographer as an "office manager." Classification of positions prevents this sort of thing.

Classification permits the use of a uniform pay plan so that all persons doing approximately the same work receive the same pay. In an earlier day, the pay of employees depended largely upon the ability of the department head as a lobbyist before the mayor, the controller, or the council. Even today, of course, much pressure may be brought to bear against standardization of salaries, and city councils may refuse to base salaries upon the position classifications established by the personnel agency.

Modern policy, however, calls for the coordination of classifications and salary scales.

If salaries are standardized, classification permits the use of a system of periodic pay raises. These should be based on the employee's increased value and faithful service over a period of time, or on his receiving additional training. Often, however, they are based almost purely on the length of employment. Since the opportunities for promotion are necessarily limited, it is important to the morale of employees that they may be advanced in pay up to a maximum limit while continuing to perform the same type of duties. Such a policy can best be tied to a classification plan.

Classification allows for the transfer of employees among departments on the basis of their job descriptions. It simplifies recruitment, since a single standard examination may be given for a class, even though many positions in that class are to be filled.[5]

Training for the Municipal Service. Increasingly, public servants are receiving formal training for their jobs, both before and after entry into service. Some municipal positions require, as they always have, professional training. This is true of attorneys, accountants, and physicians, for example, although these persons are often untrained in the specialized aspects of their professions that deal with the public service.

For many routine positions only a general high-school education is necessary, or perhaps a business-school course. Training for these jobs involves no special difficulties. Many universities today offer general programs of training as preparation for public administrative positions such as those of city manager, finance officer, and personnel officer. Several schools now offer courses in police administration, health administration, and other special technical-professional areas.

Many positions in municipal government require, or are aided by, in-service training programs. A clerk-typist or an elevator operator does the same job in public as in private employment. On the other hand, police and fire departments, especially, have found it necessary to establish training academies. There are few opportunities to learn the technical aspects of these jobs in preservice training or in private employment.

Many state leagues of municipalities have sponsored training programs for various jobs, and they often provide technical manuals or booklets. The International City Managers' Association and other professional organizations offer correspondence courses for training in various fields. Quite a few universities offer professional in-service training courses for policemen, firemen, public health workers, and other municipal employees.

[5] Ismar Baruch, *Position-classification in the Public Service* (1942), is a standard reference.

Types of Examinations. Unlike the civil-service examinations in most other countries, those in the United States tend to be specific, technical, and designed to test a person only for one single position. The practice of the national government in this regard has been copied by most of the cities and states. In recent years, however, there has been somewhat of a change in the type of examination used. Newer ones follow some of the elements of the British system and some taken from American business practices. Education is given more importance. So is the record of previous employment. Intelligence tests and adaptability or aptitude tests are used to a greater extent, as are personal interviews to determine personality traits.[6]

The object of the new type of testing, of course, is to select persons who may be able to improve their job status over time—who will be able to move up into higher positions of responsibility. It is also desirable to have persons with enough flexibility so that they may switch from one job to another without too much inconvenience. The opportunity for promotion through the ranks is an important one for morale in the public service.

The Requirement of Local Residence. Except for teachers and city managers, it is a very common rule established by state law, the city charter, or the civil service commission that a city employee be a resident of the city—and often for a specified length of time, such as one year, before employment. This rule is an anomaly in a modern personnel system. It is based upon a *spoils*, rather than a *merit*, concept. It is a vestige of Jacksonian thinking, that government jobs should be reserved for home-town persons. A merit system assumes that employees are chosen for demonstrated competence. Clearly if that is the true criterion, then it matters not where the person may live or how long he has lived there. A residence requirement sometimes works a hardship upon the city administration by requiring the employment of a mediocre person when a superior one may live a few miles away outside the city limits. This problem may be especially acute in metropolitan areas with their numerous independent suburbs. Out of necessity, cities are increasingly waiving residence requirements in recruiting persons for positions demanding technical and administrative training and experience.

The Method of Dismissal. Much controversy may appear from time to time in local newspapers over the discharge of a particular municipal employee. The public's attitude concerning these widely publicized dismissals is often one of ambivalence. Nearly everyone today works for someone else—has a supervisory superior. Through the process of identification, therefore, the individual is likely to have an initial reaction of

[6] Reed, *op. cit.*, pp. 256–259.

sympathy for someone who is dismissed from his job. ("After all, the same thing might have happened to me!") But on the other hand, the lay citizen is likely to complain that—according to hearsay—no one is ever dismissed from a government job, that an incompetent may be transferred, or retired, or given nothing to do, but that he is never dismissed. Some will add that the law does not permit dismissal once the status of civil-service tenure is given.

This ambivalence has its counterpart among public administrators in the conflict over the "open back door" versus the "closed back door" methods of dismissal from the service. Should a supervisor have the authority to discharge an unwanted employee summarily? Or should he have to serve a notice and accord a hearing before removal, and then discharge the employee only for "cause" as described in the law? And should the decision be left to the department head, or should it be made by the civil service commission?

In the early days of merit practice, it was believed that department heads—political appointees—would dismiss employees of the "wrong" political faith if there were no safeguards, and so the back door was often closed. This was essentially a negative view of administration, of course. Today the emphasis is upon executive responsibility. This means that department heads must be given wide latitude of discretionary power in running their departments so that they may show they can produce worthwhile results. If they fail, or if they abuse the responsibility, they must be prepared to answer for it.

Yet many city charters provide that civil-service employees may be discharged only for cause, and give the employee the right to appeal the decision to the independent civil service commission, which may order his reinstatement. The results have not been fortunate, as a rule. Independent civil service commissions often order the employee reinstated if they think that dismissal is too severe a penalty for the charges made against him. Often the employee engages a skillful attorney to represent him at the hearings before the commission, and his attorney succeeds in turning the hearings into a trial of the head of the department, instead of an appraisal of the charges against the employee. After such an experience, the department head often decides that it is better to put up with employees who are incompetent, lazy, and even insubordinate rather than to go through the ordeal required to discharge them.

On the other hand, municipal civil-service employees should be accorded reasonable protection against arbitrary dismissal, or discharge for political reasons. This can be provided in one of several ways. The personnel director may be given, as one of his duties, the investigation of any cases involving suspension or discharge of employees, which will have a restraining influence on arbitrary actions by department heads.

Similarly, in cities where the personnel board is advisory rather than administrative, it may be authorized to investigate dismissals and to make recommendations to the manager or the mayor, who exercises final decision. This arrangement provides ample safeguard against abuse, without the faults of an independent review by a civil service commission with power to reinstate the employee.

THE PUBLIC ATTITUDE

Community Status and Municipal Employment. The Jacksonian frontiersman taught us to be skeptical of those who would "feed at the public trough." The lesson was taught so well that Americans are habitually infected with the notion that public employees are loafers, far less efficient than those in private employment. Some lay citizens believe that the *nature* of public employment itself makes people lazy and inefficient.

While students and practitioners of municipal government are in virtually universal agreement that this viewpoint is completely false, it is difficult to present conclusive evidence to that effect because there is no certain basis for comparing public and private employment. In the field of private endeavor, the test of profit exists. Cities, however, operate few services that are expected to be revenue-producing. Even where they do —such as in public transportation—the service is often one in which profit opportunities are too doubtful for most businessmen to be interested. The effectiveness of most city services—its recreation, welfare, highways, fire fighting, and other functions—can be given only a subjective evaluation. Where one person may think the city recreation program, for example, is inefficient and a waste of the taxpayers' money, two others may think it to be excellent. There is no clear standard of measurement, and the recreation program certainly cannot be compared in efficiency with the method by which some local manufacturer makes motorboats.

Analogies with Private Business. There is a tendency in the United States to deify "business efficiency." In the light of the rapid development of industrialization and the commensurate rise in the standard of living that have taken place in this country since the War between the States, it is understandable that the businessman and his methods should be greatly admired. But we should guard against exaggeration.

It is well to remember that a great deal of business is conducted today by large corporations, and that these corporations are operated for the most part by self-perpetuating bureaucracies. These bureaucracies enjoy the same advantages and suffer the same disadvantages, for the most part, as do public bureaucracies.

Like their sisters in the city hall, clerk-typists in private industry will start putting on their coats fifteen minutes before quitting time if the supervisor permits it. And he often does. The public employee has no monopoly on morning and afternoon coffee breaks. In many cities today, all of the stenographers would quit if a private company tried to stop this type of "loafing." Magazines are not read during working hours in the street commissioner's office alone. Minor forms of bribery—tickets to next Saturday's football game, a turkey at Christmas—are not limited to councilmanic recipients: they are standard operating procedure in business. Bureaucratic maneuvering for positional advantage and struggles for power exist in the city hall, in the corporation offices, and wherever else bureaucracies exist.

Obscure, ritualistic, and technical language—gobbledegook—exists in business and in government. Red tape—a necessary means of maintaining and identifying responsibility in a large, impersonal organization—exists in big business as well as big government. The mimeograph machine, the typewriter, and the ream of paper are everywhere today. Almost everyone, when he thinks about it, recalls incidents of excessive delays and excessive filling out of forms in connection with a business matter involving a private company, especially a large company.

Private endeavor may be more efficient than public endeavor. We do not know. We do know that they have much in common. We do know that each is dependent upon professional, technical specialists in a day of mechanization and specialization. It is time we re-evalued our attitude toward public employees.

MUNICIPAL EMPLOYMENT AND ORGANIZED LABOR

At least some employees in all of the largest cities in the United States are members of labor unions. The smaller the city, the less likely the employees are to be organized, but four out of five cities even in the 25,000 to 50,000 class have employees belonging to unions (see Table 22).

The AFL has two unions for municipal employees, the American Federation of State, County and Municipal Employees (AFSCME) and the International Association of Fire Fighters (IAFF). In addition, many city employees, such as truck drivers, belong to their own craft unions just as do persons in private industry plying the same trade. The CIO also has a public employee union, the Government and Civic Employees' Organizing Committee (GCEOC). The United Public Workers of America (UPWA) is an independent union. There are also many local, unaffiliated unions. Some of them are "company unions," which are illegal under the National Labor Relations Act, but the provisions of that act do not apply to municipal corporations.

Several large cities, chiefly in the South, do not permit, or at least do not encourage, organization of employees. Houston, in 1952, had only

Table 22. Organizations of Local Employees in Cities over 10,000

Population group	No. of cities in group	Cities with employees in one or more organizations	
		No.	Per cent
Cities over 500,000........	18	18	100.0
250,000 to 500,000........	23	20	87.1
100,000 to 250,000........	65	64	98.5
50,000 to 100,000........	129	121	93.8
25,000 to 50,000*........	276	222	80.4
10,000 to 25,000.........	836	367	43.9
All cities over 10,000.....	1,347	812	60.3

* Note the sharp decline in unionization in cities of under 50,000. This corresponds to the lesser importance of organized labor generally in these cities.

SOURCE: *Municipal Year Book, 1953,* p. 155.

the IAFF; New Orleans and St. Louis had only the IAFF and the AFSCME. Dallas, Memphis, San Antonio, and Montgomery were, however, the only cities of over 100,000 population prohibiting unionization of municipal employees. The nation's cities of over 500,000 have all of the unions listed above, plus local unaffiliated unions.[7]

Should Municipal Employees Be Unionized? In 1952, the city of New York had 126,250 employees, Chicago 26,694, Boston 17,187, and Richmond, Providence, and Miami over 3,000 each. Nearly all city employees have relatives and friends. Taken together, they constitute quite a pressure group and voting bloc. Fear of political power like this is certain to influence a city council when it determines wages and conditions of labor.

Many people argue that political power of this magnitude plus civil-service protection gives public servants adequate security. They hold that if unionization is added to the employees' weapons, they have a bargaining position that is disproportionate in comparison with employees in private business.

Certainly there is some merit to these arguments. In many cities, and especially in large cities, municipal employees with jobs comparable to those in private business sometimes receive a salary above the going market price. A New York study has indicated that in that city, salaries of public workers lag behind in times of inflation, but forge ahead in times of depression.[8] But in 1952, Chicago employees worked a thirty-five-hour week, and those in Philadelphia worked thirty-eight hours. A

[7] *Municipal Year Book, 1953,* pp. 156–187.
[8] Mayor's Committee on Management Survey, *Modern Management for the City of New York* (1953), vol. I, pp. 69–73.

work week of less than forty hours is not uncommon even in cities of less than 50,000. New Orleans employees received thirteen paid holidays in 1952; those in Boston received twelve. Even Lancaster, Pennsylvania (1950 population: 64,000), gave twelve, and dozens of medium- and small-sized cities allowed eleven days. Sick-leave days may accumulate to 300 in Buffalo and St. Paul, and 200 in Detroit. Pension plans are often generous.

While laborers, clerk-typists, draftsmen, and junior accountants may receive somewhat more than the market price for their services, this is often not the case with members of the semimilitary departments of the municipality, the policemen and firemen. Of course, there is no direct means of measuring the social value of a policeman or fireman, and he has few counterparts in private employment. Judging, however, by the quality of recruits and the success, or lack of it, that cities have in filling their quotas of need for these jobs, one finds that the salaries are not attracting men of sufficient ability in sufficient numbers. Quite a few cities have found it necessary in the postwar years to reduce physical and intelligence requirements in an attempt to get enough men on the force. Quality has been sacrificed.

The semimilitary services are barred from striking by one rule or another. This, plus the fact that the public will tolerate less "labor agitation" from them, has sometimes resulted in their salaries falling behind the trend of other employees. On the other hand, they often enjoy a pension plan that is more liberal than that of the other municipal employees. Firemen are commonly on duty for many hours consecutively, after which they have a long period off duty. In many cities, therefore, firemen take outside employment on their off days. Some policemen do too, although this is specifically prohibited in some cities because it might interfere with the policeman's duty to enforce the law impartially and for other reasons.

Labor unions have accomplished much good in cities, as they have in private industry. But public employee unions are subject to the same weaknesses as are all unions. They may be controlled by a small bureaucracy rather than by the general membership. Ambitious men struggle for their control. Unions may emphasize seniority and tenure rather than initiative and efficient management. They may resist mechanical improvements that they regard as speed-ups or that cause technological unemployment.

But the fact must be faced—unions are here to stay. Some writers have argued—from a theoretical standpoint—that there should be no organizations of municipal employees because "the civil service commission is their union." Such an argument is unavailing. To the rank-and-file worker, the civil service commission and its executive secretary or the personnel director are the *employer*—and hence the opposition when it comes to bargaining. Clearly the commission cannot serve simultaneously as employer and as employee representative. At least it cannot do so in the mind of the employee, and that is what matters.

A Suggested Policy. The question of whether municipal employees should be allowed to join a union is sometimes decided by the city council or the administration. Sometimes it is decided by a public referendum. It ought to be decided by the employees themselves.[9] If they desire unionization, they should have it. It is unrealistic to expect city employees to accept less than the equivalent status and security enjoyed by persons performing the same tasks in private endeavor. Cities cannot accept the remnants from the labor market. They must compete with private employers for qualified personnel, and the future health of city government demands that they come out of the competition not less than even.

Collective Bargaining. When it comes to differences of opinion between employees and supervisors, the employees are likely to demand collective protection. Many of their complaints lie outside the provisions of civil-service law. William S. Carpenter has made the point that "few genuine grievances arise as a result of violations of civil service laws and regulations."[10] Other machinery is needed—the same machinery that is used to settle these grievances in private employment. To a great many people today, the labor union is a basic part of that machinery.[11]

Negotiations between labor unions and private management normally reach their consummation in a formal written contract. To this extent, practice there varies from that in the field of public employment, for in the case of the latter, formal written contracts are very exceptional. The end result of negotiations is almost always either a gentleman's agreement or a unilateral statement of intended policy on the part of the civil service commission or the city council.

The Cincinnati Common Council, for example, passed a resolution in 1951, resolving "That it shall be the policy of the council of the city of Cincinnati through the City Manager and his designated assistants, to bargain collectively with city employees, their Unions, or other authorized representatives, on all matters pertaining to wages and working conditions before any final determination is made by City Council."

It is an established rule of law that a legislative body cannot contract

[9] Carpenter, *op. cit.*, p. 125 and chap. 3, makes this point. See also Sterling D. Spero, *Government as Employer* (1949).

[10] Carpenter, *op. cit.*, p. 125. On grievance machinery, see R. B. Posey, "Handling City Employee Grievances," *Public Management*, vol. 35 (March, 1953), pp. 54–58.

[11] British local government settles disputes with its civil servants through the use of the Whitley Councils. See L. D. White, *Whitley Councils in the British Civil Service* (1933); and C. J. Schneider, "The Revival of Whitleyism in British Local Government," *Public Administration Review*, vol. 13 (Spring, 1953), pp. 97–105.

away its powers and that it cannot bind future legislative bodies. Because of this, nearly all courts have held that, in the absence of express enabling law, a contract binding the city to certain wages, hours, and conditions of labor for a certain period of time is illegal and void.[12] Even given legislative permission, such agreements may be held to violate the state constitution. The gentleman's agreement or the statement of policy has usually served as a substitute. There is, however, some trend toward the increased use of contracts.[13]

An extensive study of the problem by Louis L. Friedland concludes that "the trend in personnel relations is away from unilateral dealings on the part of management with its employees.[14] He feels that "negotiated agreements whether formal or informal do not develop abstract rights destructive of management prerogatives"; and that "the end product is to provide employee associations a constructive place in the continuous improvement of the public service. The public and its government officials must establish democratic machinery for the adjustment of differences and provide for the synthesis of executive leadership and employee participation in public personnel administration."

The Right to Strike. The constitutions of some public employee unions contain a clause denying the strike as a weapon. State laws sometimes prohibit public employees from striking, as do city ordinances. A few judges have even found a similar prohibition in the common law. Policemen, firemen, employees of public hospitals, and others who perform services closely connected with the public health and safety are often prohibited from striking. Certainly the public itself is intolerant of strikes in these areas.

But strikes occur anyway. They are the one really powerful weapon of organized labor, and under certain conditions strikes will occur even in the face of a law to the contrary. Even policemen and firemen will on occasion become frustrated or desperate enough to strike. Laws will not prevent strikes where the employees consider themselves seriously wronged.[15]

Those who hold that no public employee should be allowed to strike make use of several arguments. The principal ones are two. First of all, it is said that public service is so closely connected with the health and welfare of society that it is dangerous to permit strikes. Secondly, it is said that the government is the people, that a strike against "the govern-

---

[12] See C. S. Rhyne, *Labor Unions and Municipal Employee Law* (1946), which cites leading cases.

[13] A list and illustrations of various types of policy statements and agreements will be found in Louis L. Friedland, "The Role of Collective Bargaining in the Public Service," *Papers of the Michigan Academy of Science, Arts and Letters* (1953).

[14] *Ibid.*

[15] See R. B. Posey, "Analysis of City Employee Strikes," *Public Management,* vol. 34 (June, 1952), pp. 122–127.

ment" is therefore a strike against oneself, that governmental employment is therefore substantially different in character from private employment and that a strike against the government is a disloyal act, a challenge to the sovereign.

The Need for Equality with Private Employees. Public service is certainly closely allied with the health and safety of society. So are coal mining, the operation of the railroads, and many other private activities. Yet strikes occur in these fields. A strike is never a pretty thing. It is nearly always a last resort. Where the weapon does not exist and where no substitute is provided for it, employee caliber is likely to deteriorate. A minority of scholars have argued, therefore, that even policemen and firemen should have the nominal right to strike. These people have a sense of responsibility and of loyalty to the city—otherwise they would not readily go into these services. The threat of a strike, if used responsibly, may be a necessary and permissible weapon. And a threat is meaningless unless it is an actual possibility.

Why do public employees strike? Because they are subversives? Because they are seditious? Of course not. They strike because they want an additional ten cents an hour in pay. It may be sound legally to say that striking public employees are striking against themselves or the state. It is unsound psychologically. The bus driver or city-hall janitor has no such thought in mind. He is striking against the boss—just as is his fellow worker in private employment. His last thought is to destroy the government, for that would destroy his job as well as his way of life.

If it is deemed to be wise public policy to forbid strikes, the laws must be carefully drawn to avoid gross inequities. Michigan law, for example, permits Dearborn bus drivers to strike, but prohibits Detroit bus drivers from doing so. Each performs the same service for society. But the one system is privately owned, the other publicly. There is no logical justification for such discrimination. If the law prohibits strikes in public utilities, it should certainly apply equally to all who are doing the same job.[16]

Compulsory Arbitration. Because strikes in the public service have grave consequences and are unpopular with the public, as may be seen in the trend toward state laws and city ordinances prohibiting them, many have suggested the use of compulsory arbitration as an alternative last resort. There has been an increasing amount of interest in *arbitration* in recent years. It must be distinguished from *mediation,* which is an older practice and refers to the calling in of a third person to hear arguments concerning a dispute and to make *recommendations.* Arbitration

---

[16] On strikes and the public service, see M. R. Godine, *The Labor Problem in the Public Service* (1951); Spero, *op. cit.;* and three articles debating the issue in the *National Municipal Review,* vol. 30 (September, 1941), pp. 515–528.

involves the turning over of the dispute to a third person or a team, with the disputants agreeing in advance to accept the findings as *binding* upon both parties.[17]

The use of arbitration involves legal complications, since the practice has the effect of establishing the arbitration team as a public body empowered to make decisions on wages, hours, and conditions of work that are normally within the province of the civil service commission or the council. Since the arbitration team is not directly responsible to the public—or to anyone except the consciences of the members of the team—democratic responsibility for government is interfered with. Yet if we say that our basic goals are (1) to avoid strikes and yet (2) to maintain the efficiency of public personnel at the same level as that in private employment, arbitration may well be worth a try as a means toward accomplishing both goals.

If arbitration is used, it would seem to be necessary for the following conditions to obtain: First of all, arbitration machinery must be put into action at the option of *either* party. If both sides must first agree before arbitration can be used, the whole plan may be unavailing, for the side with the support of public opinion may sabotage the machinery by refusing to arbitrate or to negotiate further. Secondly, a plan must be worked out that reasonably guarantees the selection of a balanced arbitration team that will also be aware of its grave obligations to the public interest. Lastly, the team must have sufficient powers to be able to obtain information and witnesses that may be necessary for it to arrive at a just and prompt decision.

PAY SCALES AND POLITICS

Salaries in Municipal Employment. It has already been noted that salaries of city employees tend to run somewhat above the average pay in comparable private employment. At least this is true of the lesser skills and the unskilled in large cities. It may also be more true of those positions—such as clerk-typists—that are directly comparable with private employment than it is of some that are not so easily comparable—such as policemen or firemen. It has been argued that equivalent pay should be enjoyed by public employees as compared with private employees. Superior pay is not justifiable. Yet it has also been held in this chapter that without the protection of the labor union many of these employees might

[17] Carpenter, *op. cit.*, pp. 70–72, favors the use of arbitration where honest differences of opinion cannot be settled by negotiation. For a debate on the subject, see C. R. Adrian, "Detroit Experiments in Arbitrating Labor Disputes," *Public Personnel Review*, vol. 13 (January, 1952), pp. 9–11; D. J. Sublette and C. A. Meyer, "Detroit *Does Not* Experiment in Arbitrating Labor Disputes," *ibid.* (July, 1952), pp. 134–136; and Adrian's surrebuttal, *ibid.* (October, 1952), pp. 161, 185.

fall below the pay in private fields and that this would be undesirable from the viewpoint of the public interest and needs.

If salaries at the lower levels tend to be above average, pay for top technicians and administrators is always well below the average paid to private employees. There is no labor union to look after the salary needs of the city attorney or the chief engineer at the city power station. Furthermore, persons in positions like these have, because of fewer numbers, far less political influence in getting pay increases.

If the rank-and-file workers in the street railways or public works department of the city ask for a raise, councilmen will consider the possible effect in the next election of their votes and those of their friends and relatives if they are refused. No such fears need sway the councilmen when it is suggested that $7,000 is an inadequate salary for the city attorney in a city of 150,000 people. Quite to the contrary, the Jacksonian tradition lends public support in opposition to an increase. Since the average citizen is making less than the present salary of the attorney, psychologically he is unsympathetic to arguments for an increase. A suggestion of $10,000 or $11,000 as being a necessary salary to get an able man will be greeted with jeers, for even today that is an income beyond the aspirations of the average citizen. Councilmen can thus make friends by refusing a raise to chief administrators and technicians.

Since late in 1948, rank-and-file city employees have been relatively well off in pay (see Table 23 and Figure 24). The need to improve the

Table 23. Salaries of Selected Municipal Officials, 1953†

Title of official	Cities over 500,000		Cities of 50,000 to 100,000	
	Mean average salary	Highest salary	Mean average salary	Highest salary
Mayor (mayor-council cities)....	$19,622	$40,000	$6,640	$12,000
Controller.....................	13,683	30,000	6,274	10,296
Engineer......................	11,420	15,672	6,776	12,600
Fire chief.....................	11,430	15,500	6,064	9,672
Chief personnel officer..........	10,384	14,500	5,861	9,367
City attorney..................	13,932	25,000	6,342	15,700
Health officer.................	13,020	20,805	7,039	12,000
Superintendent of schools.......	19,787	32,500	11,027	15,000

† Note that except for salaries of superintendents of schools and for mayors of the largest cities, the pay of top administrators and technicians is not outstanding. Note too the small pay gradation between medium-sized and very large cities for some of the offices.

SOURCE: *Municipal Year Book, 1953*, pp. 135–137.

pay of those in higher positions in city government is still very great, however, unless cities are willing to accept the leftovers—those who have failed in the competition of private endeavor—or to hope for the occasional individual who for personal reasons is willing to work for the city at a sacrifice in pay.

The Escalator Clause. In the sharp inflationary period following World War II, several labor unions effected contracts with management calling for a sliding pay scale to be related to the cost-of-living index of the Bureau of Labor Statistics. Under these plans, an increase of a certain amount in the index would mean an additional cent an hour in pay, and

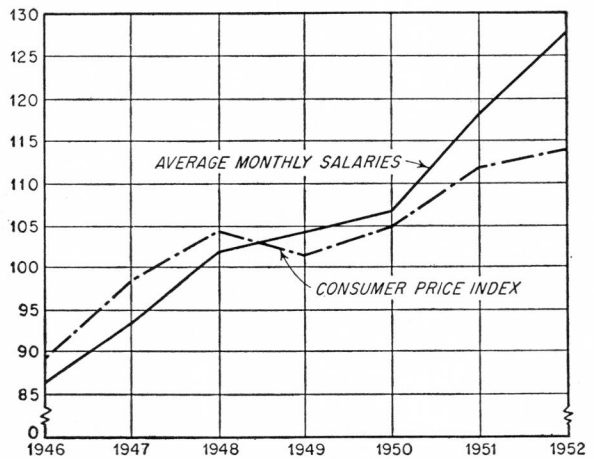

Fig. 24. Consumer price index and municipal salary index, 1946 to 1952. SOURCE: *Municipal Year Book* (1953), p. 147. Used by permission.

an equivalent decrease would mean a reduction in pay. The plan proved popular in a period of seemingly endless inflation.

More than thirty years ago St. Paul made use of the escalator clause for its own employees, and an increasing number of cities have adopted it recently. Needless to say, its popularity will decline in periods of declining prices.

Retirement System.[18] As a part of the total remuneration for public employment, municipal retirement systems are commonly provided. Nearly all cities of over 10,000 and many smaller municipalities provide old-age insurance for all of their employees. Many cities operate their own local systems, often with the police and fire services under a separate plan, but about one-half of them are members of state-administered systems. Smaller cities, in particular, are aided in maintaining solvency

---

[18] For a summary of developments to that time, see the *Municipal Year Book, 1951*, pp. 124–129.

by being banded together with other cities in a state system. Since 1951 there has been a sharp trend toward the covering of municipal employees in the Federal old age and survivor's insurance program ("social security"). Amendments to the Social Security Act in 1954 aided in bringing more local governments into the Federal program, which often provides more liberal benefits than do local systems.

Most retirement systems are "contributing" plans, that is, both the city and the employee contribute part of the cost. Many systems are not on an actuarial basis and are hence financially unsound, although this is not true of an increasing number of them. Retirement boards, often with employee representation on them, commonly administer the investment of the funds that accumulate as the system develops. Retirement plans must also provide for payments to persons who are permanently disabled before retirement, for payment to survivors if the employee dies before retirement, and for the return of funds invested in the system by the employee who is separated from the service before retirement. In the last case, he is always entitled to the total amount of salary that has been withheld from his pay checks, but he does not always receive the interest that has been accumulated by his money.

Municipal retirement plans of today are merely a parallel to the general pattern of old-age-security plans that have developed throughout private enterprise in recent decades. It is likely that they will become virtually universal phenomena for cities of all sizes in the near future. Smaller cities will have their employees covered in state or Federal systems.

Concluding Statement. In recent decades, Americans have expected more and more services from city government. As a result of this, the public employee has perforce become a technical specialist, skilled in his task. In order to obtain such persons for the public service, the elaborate art of modern personnel administration and management has been applied to our cities. The day has long since passed when city employment could serve as a reward for faithful political effort.

To those who work for the city, their positions are not far different from similar positions in private employment. As a result, the same problems of labor-management relations arise in the city hall and in the offices of the business corporation.

The labor union is a basic institution in American life today, and public employees usually desire to share in its benefits. Fortunately, therefore, the principle of unionism does not conflict with the merit system. This is true even of the union shop under which employees might be *required* to join a union after employment. The union sometimes is, in fact, the only collective method of settling employee-employer disputes.

There may be some areas of union interest that conflict with the merit system. A strict emphasis upon seniority, often a union goal, is not in harmony with the principle. The closed shop is certainly not possible in public employment, since it would require one to be a union member *before* employment, and this would enable the union to supplant the personnel director or commission. In general, however, city governments must—and can—learn to live with the labor union. While the two will have occasional conflicts, they can also work together toward the common goal of a better personnel system and a more satisfied group of employees. This in turn will mean better city government.[19]

[19] On the general subject of municipal personnel practices, see the many publications of the Civil Service Assembly of the United States and Canada dealing with specific practical problems of personnel administration. See also International City Managers' Association, *Municipal Personnel Administration* (5th ed., 1950); Robert L. Thorndike, *Personnel Selection Test and Measurement Techniques* (1949); Charles S. Rhyne, *Labor Unions and Municipal Employee Law* (1946); Leonard D. White and T. V. Smith, *Politics and Public Service* (1939). The *Municipal Year Book* annually reports new personnel developments, prevailing wages, hours, conditions of labor, and other information. It also lists a good bibliography. Convenient materials are found in Charles M. Kneier and Guy Fox, *Readings in Municipal Government and Administration* (1953), chap. 13.

CHAPTER 15

FINANCING MODERN CITY GOVERNMENT

A major cause of interest in municipal governments stems from the fact that these institutions possess the power of taxation—the power to exact from a person or a body of persons involuntary contributions to be used by the government for the benefit of society.

It is in the area of taxation that a possible technique for development of greater public interest in city government could be uncovered. Part of the interest constantly evoked in the affairs of the national government is a result of its taxation policies, which change on a virtual year-to-year basis. Local taxation is much more stable. This is partly because its basic type of tax is on general property. There are good reasons why the general property tax level should not be changed often, but if taxes were more variable—and perhaps more varied—on the local level, a greater interest in city government might be a result. Direct payments of an income type of tax, in particular, would tend to encourage interest in campaigns and council meetings. In recent years, a particularly seductive technique for tax payment has tended to remove the homeowner even further from the realities of taxation. Modern-day mortgages are usually paid on a monthly installment basis, with principal, interest, fire insurance, and taxes paid gradually in the "house payment." For the promotion of a sensitive political public, taxes should be out in the open where they can be seen.

EXPENDITURES IN PRESENT-DAY CITIES

Where Does the Money Go? The fiscal year 1952 marked the seventh consecutive one in which municipal expenditures exceeded revenues.[1] In a period of rising costs and increasing urban populations and birth rates, the demands for local government services have been regularly increasing. At the same time, however, revenue sources have remained relatively unchanged. The result is that local-government debt continues, year after year, to reach all-time highs. In 1952, it stood at 10.6 billion dollars (see Figures 25, 26, and 27).

[1] *Wall Street Journal*, Nov. 10, 1953 (Chicago ed.).

Cities of over 25,000 spent 7.2 billion dollars in 1952—a record. It was also an increase of 7 per cent over 1951 and of 12 per cent over 1950. The municipal function that usually involves the greatest expense is streets and highways. These cost municipalities 589 million dollars in 1952. Other functions are also expensive on a per capita basis (see Table 24).

REVENUE FOR PRESENT-DAY CITIES

All taxes are ultimately derived from either of two sources: property or income. Taxes are theoretically based upon some criterion of *ability to pay*, although the criteria used in various periods of history have not been the same, and a tax created in one period and logical and equitable at that time may live on into another time when its justification becomes less apparent. In some instances, payments to the government are based upon a *benefit theory* rather than on ability to pay, but such payments are more in the nature of service charges than taxes. The benefit theory is applied, for example, in cases of special assessments for street, sidewalk, street lighting, and similar improvements. It is also applied in determining water and light charges and, to a degree, in motor-vehicle license fees.[2]

State Limits on Taxing and Spending. Cities have only those powers of taxation which are granted to them by the state. The only exceptions to this rule are to be found in a few home rule states, notably California and Wisconsin, where court interpretations of the constitutional home rule clause have given cities a general grant of powers to levy taxes. (Even in Wisconsin a general act limiting municipal taxing powers in particular areas at the discretion of the legislature is valid.) States, either through the constitution or through statutes, will normally place limitations upon the taxing power of cities. The law usually states a maximum tax rate in terms of so many dollars per capita, or allows an increase of only a certain small percentage over the previous year's rate, or permits the city to levy a tax of only a certain percentage of the assessed value of the taxable property within the city. The last restriction is by far the most common. States also often impose conditions and regulations on the administration of municipal finances.[3]

Cities are limited in other ways, too. As a result of the famous case of *McCulloch v. Maryland,* Federal properties within the city are not taxable. The state may exempt many other categories, such as private educational and religious properties. Beginning in the days of the Great Depression, a large number of states have adopted "homestead exemp-

[2] On the general subject of taxes, see one of the textbooks on public finance. A standard text is Harold M. Groves, *Financing Government* (3d ed., 1950).

[3] Control over spending is described in T. E. McMillan, Jr., *State Supervision of Municipal Finance* (1953). See also chap. 12 above.

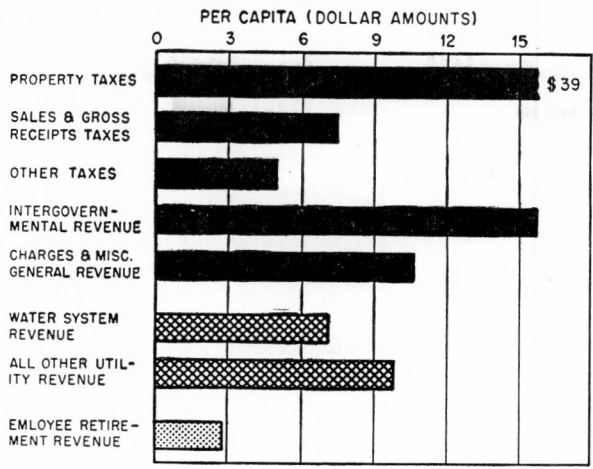

PER CAPITA (DOLLAR AMOUNTS)

PROPERTY TAXES	$39
SALES & GROSS RECEIPTS TAXES	
OTHER TAXES	
INTERGOVERNMENTAL REVENUE	
CHARGES & MISC. GENERAL REVENUE	
WATER SYSTEM REVENUE	
ALL OTHER UTILITY REVENUE	
EMLOYEE RETIREMENT REVENUE	

United States Bureau of the Census

Fig. 25. Per capita amounts of city revenue, by source, 1951. SOURCE: *Municipal Year Book* (1953), p. 230. Used by permission.

Table 24. Summary of City Finances: 1951

Item	All 481 cities over 25,000		
	Amount in millions	Per cent increase from 1950	Per capita
Total revenue and borrowing.................	$7,116	2.8	$114.85
Total expenditure and debt redemption........	6,767	4.9	109.23
Total revenue.............................	6,050	6.8	97.66
Total expenditure..........................	6,227	3.7	100.51
All general revenue (excludes utility and employee-retirement revenue)...............	4,813	6.5	77.68
Taxes, total..............................	3,187	6.4	51.43
Property..............................	2,416	5.7	39.00
Sales and gross receipts..................	466	12.2	7.52
Licenses and other......................	304	3.8	4.91
Intergovernmental revenue.................	971	2.7	15.67
From state governments only............	872	2.4	14.07
Charges and miscellaneous.................	656	13.3	10.58
All general expenditure (excludes utility and employee-retirement expenditures)........	4,797	3.5	77.43
Total debt outstanding......................	9,975	5.9	161.01
Long term, total...........................	9,628	6.7	155.41
Full faith and credit...................	8,123	4.9	131.12

SOURCE: *Municipal Year Book, 1953*, p. 232.

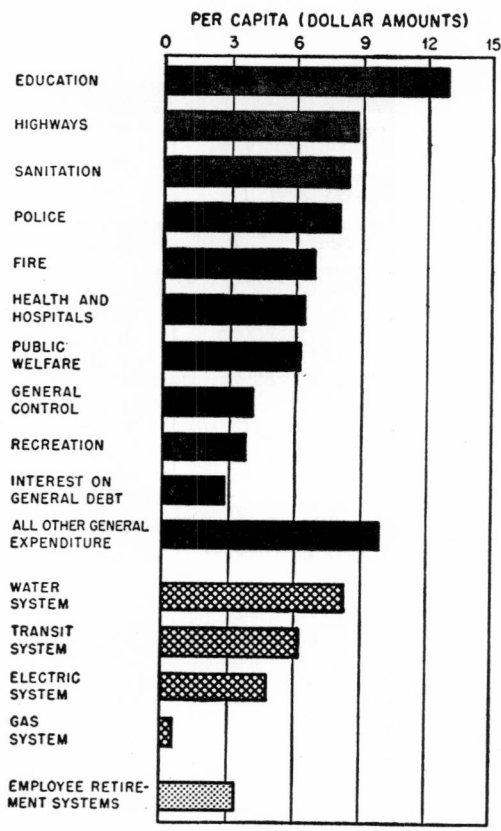

Fig. 26. Per capita amounts of city expenditure for various functions, 1951. Note: Education is shown here as a city expenditure, although in almost all urban areas this function is performed by an independent unit of government. SOURCE: *Municipal Year Book* (1953), p. 230. Used by permission.

YOUR GOVERNMENT DOLLAR

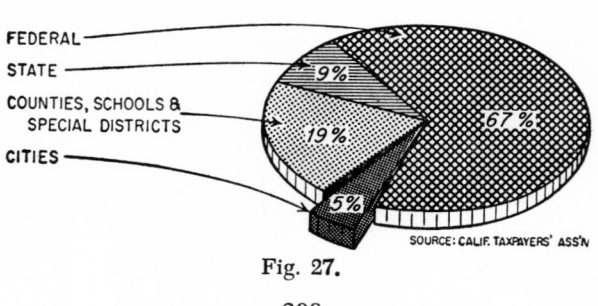

Fig. 27.

tion" laws, which exclude part or even all of the value of owner-occupied homes from the general property tax.

Limitations on Subjects of Taxation. The subjects that may be taxed by the municipality are normally strictly controlled by the state. Nearly all of the states tell their cities which taxes they may levy, for what period of time they may be levied, and under what conditions. A city that finds its property tax consistently inadequate may not, for example, decide to levy a payroll or a sales tax. The state must first authorize such a levy on a new subject.

Only a few states have been willing to trust their cities enough to allow them to choose from a wide variety of tax sources by adopting broad enabling acts. California and Wisconsin cities have wide taxing powers as a result of judicial interpretation of constitutional home rule clauses. Pennsylvania and New York have given their cities broad taxing powers through legislation.

Limitations on Borrowing Power. In addition to limitations upon taxation, the state normally also seeks to protect the public credit by limiting the *borrowing* powers of cities. Such a limitation may be written into the city charter or into state law or the constitution. The limit is usually expressed in terms of a percentage of the assessed value of the taxable property within the city, but it may also be a specific number of dollars, or the debt may be limited to a figure equal to the annual tax revenue of the city.[4]

Since these debt limits may be very unrealistic and since they bear no necessary relationship to the needs of the city, it is sometimes desirable or even imperative that the artificial limitations be circumvented. Many techniques have been devised for doing this. For example, bonds issued for certain purposes, especially public utilities, may not be included under the limitation if they may theoretically be retired through revenue from the proposed project. Bonds to build a stadium, an auditorium, or a toll bridge might be paid out of revenues, and hence the courts or the legislature will sometimes exempt them from the limitation. In some states, the voters (in a few states, the property-tax payers) of a city may vote to raise the debt limit.

If either the debt or the tax limit is expressed in terms of a percentage of the assessed evaluation, the city can nearly always—and frequently does—resort to raising the assessed value of property in order to raise both the debt and tax limits. In the days before the Great Depression, when many states depended heavily upon the general property tax, a serious inequity resulted when large cities, encountering increasing costs per capita, had to assess property at or above full value in order to get around debt and tax limits. Suburbs, country towns, and rural areas

[4] McMillan, *op. cit.*, appendix E.

might at the same time be at one-third or one-fourth of market value. Obviously, this meant that the city, with a higher evaluation criterion, would pay a much larger proportionate share of the state tax. Few state governments today utilize the general property tax as a source of revenue, most states leaving the field for local taxation. Large cities, however, still pay a disproportionate share of the *county* property tax wherever proper equalization of local assessing unit evaluations is not made. This is also sometimes a problem when rural and urban areas are combined in a school district.

Limitations on Use of Dedicated Funds. The income of cities, instead of being channeled into the general fund to be used as the council sees fit, is sometimes diverted into a series of special funds each dedicated to a particular use. This may be required by either the city charter or state law. It is common, for example, to provide that the city's portion of a state-shared gasoline tax is to be placed in a special fund for highway use only. Or one mill of the property-tax levy may go to the library fund, for library use only.

Dedicated funds promote inflexibility in budget planning, since their use is dictated not by need but by the amounts received. They are a carry-over from Jacksonian distrust of public officials.

Some sinking funds represent money that has been set aside to pay off bonds that will become due in the future. Others are not really funds at all, but merely appropriations from the general fund, but titled "funds" in the auditor's reports.

According to modern budgeting practices, the use of special, earmarked funds should be kept at a minimum. They are needed for reserves to pay off term bonds and to meet the costs of pensions for retired municipal employees. For most other purposes, the council should be given a free hand to appropriate moneys on the basis of the needs of the various services of government which fluctuate greatly from one year to the next.

Some cities have few funds. Hanover, Pennsylvania (1950 population: 14,048), has only three. But Bloomington, Illinois (1950 population: 34,163), has twenty, as required by state law. These include various pension and retirement funds, four different sewer funds, a motor-fuel tax fund, and even a municipal-band fund.[5]

The General Property Tax.[6] It was stated earlier that all taxes must ultimately come from either income or property. A tax must produce adequate revenue, but a long-range tax policy must be concerned with equity, too. *Equity* is usually thought of as meaning *ability to pay*. In

[5] City of Bloomington, *Auditor's Report* (1953).

[6] On the sources of local government revenue, see A. M. Hillhouse and Muriel Magelsson, *Where Cities Get Their Money* (1946). There is a 1947 supplement by Hillhouse, and others in 1949 and 1951 by M. B. Phillipps. The *Municipal Year Book* also furnishes data on trends.

colonial America, ability to pay could best be measured in terms of property, or total wealth. Today, when most people receive a regular pay check (unlike the situation in the predominantly agricultural colonies), income is generally considered to be a better criterion.

The income tax takes into consideration the fact that not all property is equally able to pay taxes. A home, most Americans would agree, is less suitable for taxation than is a factory. A factory that is losing money is less a subject for taxation than one that is making a profit (although it should still pay some taxes). The property tax makes them pay equally, the income tax does not. Saxophones, to an amateur musician, are as much a consumer good as are rutabagas, yet the former are (theoretically) taxable in many states as property. The income tax, in a complicated modern world, can be much more equitably administered and is less subject to evasion than is the property tax.

Yet in colonial America, the property tax was a fairly good measure of ability to pay. There was then a much closer relationship between property owned and income received than is the case today. Despite the fact, however, that the property tax has been bitterly attacked in more recent years as being unsuitable for a modern world, and especially for urban society, it remains as by far the most important source of revenue for local government. It furnished 74 per cent of all city *tax* revenues in 1952.

The great authority on the property tax, E. R. A. Seligman, once suggested that there is nothing the matter with the general property tax except that it is wrong in theory and does not work in practice. What are the objections to the tax?

It has already been suggested that the property tax is no longer a very good measurement of ability to pay and is hence inequitable. It taxes consumer goods. It sometimes results in double taxation, as when a tax is levied both upon a mortgaged home and upon the mortgage. Today, when very large incomes are sometimes possible from relatively small investments, it seems especially unfair for the city to derive a major portion of its income from a tax upon homes, many of which are owned by relatively low-income persons.

The general property tax has often been poorly administered. A large proportion of property today is intangible: stocks, bonds, mortgages, and the like. These are easily hidden from the assessor. So are much jewelry and other small tangible valuables. Depreciation allowances on automobiles, furniture, and other properties far in excess of what is reasonable are claimed by taxpayers—and are frequently allowed by assessors.

The arbitrariness of property assessment and the failure to relate it to market value is indicated in a recent study conducted by the Oregon state tax commission. It found that local assessments in one county ranged from 6.5 per cent to 187.5 per cent of the commission's figures on residential properties. Such extremes are no longer typical, however (see also Figure 28).

Assessors are often elected, even though theirs is a job requiring technical competence. Others are appointed on the basis of political considerations. Most assessors are honest, but too few of them are trained for

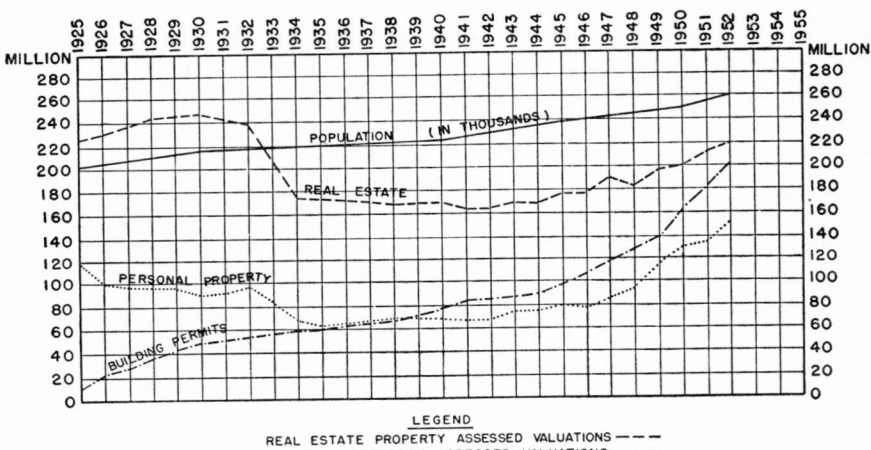

Fig. 28. Note that assessed valuations bear little relationship to market prices but are rather fictional values. Despite a transition from a depression to a wartime boom, real estate and personal property assessment totals remained almost constant between 1934 and 1946. It will easily be noted that Omaha's population increased by 25 per cent and that over 200 million dollars in building permits were issued from 1925 to 1952. However, at the close of 1952 assessed real estate valuations were still about the same as in 1925. SOURCE: City of Omaha, *A Financial Report for the Year 1952*.

their jobs. In the largest cities, necessity has required the development of a trained staff. Assessment in large cities is usually technically superior to the job done in small places.

Some attempts, none of them adequate, have been made to improve the general property tax in recent years. The withdrawal of the state from the scene has reduced or eliminated the old evils of competitive underassessment to reduce the burden of the state tax. Some states have classified property, taxing some of it at lower rates. Others have exempted intangibles or provided for the taxation of some of them at a low rate. An increasing number of them have virtually or completely exempted personal, as distinguished from real, property. The general property tax is not so inequitable nor so poorly administered as it once was, but it is still not a good tax.[7]

Why Is the Property Tax Retained? If there are so many objections to the general property tax, why does it remain as the core of financial support of the local government? For one thing, inertia itself helps to preserve the tax. It would seem that taxpayers generally do not support improved property-tax assessments. In Wisconsin, for example, they have repeatedly turned down referendum proposals to place assessors on a professional basis and have rejected the efforts of governing bodies to provide a fair reassessment of all property within some municipalities. Hence inertia works against either elimination or improvement of the tax and its administration.

A second reason is to be found in the venerable argument holding that any old tax is a good tax and any new tax is a bad tax. The argument, to the extent that it is true, is based upon the fact that society has accommodated itself to the old tax. Property values are adjusted to the property tax. When a person buys a home, he considers the annual tax levy as a maintenance cost, and its relative size is a factor in determining the price he is willing to pay.

A third reason for the continued use of the property tax is to be found in the fact that the subjects of local-government taxation must necessarily be things that will "stay put"—and most real property (if not personal property) is not easily moved out of the city the day the assessor comes around. Sales taxes on the local level tend to drive shoppers and buyers out of the city. Taxes upon income tend to cause political complications if levied upon nonresidents and if not, tend to drive people into the suburbs. On the other hand, the real property tax does not stay perfectly put, either. High property taxes tend to drive homeowners, businesses, and industry outside the municipal limits and thus undermine the tax base.

A fourth reason for retaining the tax is that it produces a very high yield, except in severe depressions. It probably meets the test of *adequacy* better than does any other tax with the exception of the retail sales tax, which is collected a bit at a time and often upon the necessities of life.

Lastly, the general property tax is retained because cities need money and no one has suggested a substitute satisfactory enough to replace the tax. The best that cities have been able to do up to now is to ease the burden upon the property owner by diversifying the tax base through the addition of other taxes.

[7] A restatement of its weaknesses is to be found in the New Jersey Commission on State Tax Policy, *The General Property Tax in New Jersey* (1953).

The Search for Property-tax Relief. In looking for likely subjects of local taxation, it is necessary to consider whether or not a subject will stay in one place long enough to be taxed there and whether or not the field has already been completely pre-empted by the national or state government. These considerations are in addition, of course, to the famous requirements for a tax system stated by Adam Smith: certainty, equity, economy, and convenience.

The *sales tax* became popular during the depression because it yielded well even in such times. It became the backbone of many state tax systems and has had limited use as a secondary tax for city governments. The city of New York adopted it in 1934 as a "temporary" expedient. As is the fate of most "temporary" taxes, it has become a permanent fixture in that city, varying over time from 1 to 3 per cent. New Orleans, Denver, and other cities in New York and elsewhere have adopted sales taxes. It has become especially popular in postwar California, where more than 160 cities (over one-half of the state's total) have adopted such a tax ranging up to 1 per cent, but with most of them at 0.5 per cent. In California cities and in most others, the regressive tendency[8] of the tax has been ameliorated to a degree by exempting foods and other necessities.

The *income tax* supplanted the tariff as the principal source of revenue for the Federal government during World War I and has become increasingly important since that time. In recent years, many states have turned to this tax. Cities have, therefore, found the field largely pre-empted. Philadelphia, however, adopted an income tax in 1939 which has come to produce about one-fourth of the city's revenue. More than forty other municipalities in Pennsylvania, several in Ohio, St. Louis, Louisville, and in other parts of the nation levy an income tax. Toledo, since 1946, has made it an especially important part of its tax structure. Eight cities adopted the tax in 1952. Most city income taxes might more accurately be called "payroll taxes," for they normally do not permit any deductions, but are simply a certain percentage of the total amount of money earned by individuals, and sometimes corporations, within a city. The payroll tax has the great advantage of forcing suburbanites to help bear the cost of maintaining the city in which they earn their living and whose facilities they use daily. It is in effect regressive, however, if it allows no deductions or exemptions.[9] The Philadelphia tax, moreover, taxes only earned income and not income from stocks, bonds, and rents.

Organized labor has tended to oppose the payroll tax because of its regressivity. In 1954, for example, a Cincinnati councilman who was also

[8] A regressive tax is one the burden of which is lessened as ability to pay increases. A sales tax on necessities is considered regressive, since low-income people spend a larger percentage of their income on necessities than do high-income people.

[9] See, L. J. Quinto, *Municipal Income Taxation in the United States* (1952); and R. A. Sigafoos, *The Municipal Income Tax: Its History and Problems* (1954).

a CIO official resigned from the Charter party after that organization helped adopt a payroll tax in that city.[10]

Cities secure some revenue from *business taxes*. These may be primarily levies to pay the cost of supervising a business directly affecting the public health, but some of them are higher levies and are designed to produce revenue beyond the cost of inspections. A city may, for example, levy a modest tax in the form of restaurant licenses, most of which must be spent upon health inspections of eating places. But other taxes may be levied upon businesses in which there are no regulatory activities under the police power.

Public utilities often, and other businesses sometimes, are taxed upon gross earnings. One version of this tax, called an "occupational tax" (usually upon gross earned income, but excluding unearned income) is becoming widely used, especially in the South and West. Because it is difficult to determine the value of inventory and other personal property for tax purposes, experts in public finance sometimes advocate the use of such a tax on business in lieu of the personal property tax. It is often used in addition to other taxes, however.

Baltimore, Chicago, and Joplin, Missouri, are among the cities with a local cigarette tax. Some resort and vacation cities, such as New York and Atlantic City, tax hotel-room occupancy. Mount Clemens, Michigan, another resort center, levies a tax upon every mineral bath taken within the city limits. Tourists and transients are favorite objects of taxation: they cannot vote in local elections.

It has often been argued in recent years that admissions taxes upon theatrical, motion-picture, and sports events would be a desirable subject for taxation—if the national government would but vacate the field.[11] This tax has the advantage of "staying put," since theaters and stadiums are relatively immovable. It also would spread the tax over a large number of persons, including many from outside the city limits. The councilmen of Ann Arbor looked hungrily a few years ago at the mammoth University of Michigan stadium which seats more than 90,000 potential taxpayers. They stood ready to place a price upon the head of every fan attending football games, and the plan was popular—most of the stadium being filled each Saturday by Detroiters—until the state Attorney General held that such a tax would actually be levied upon an instrumentality of the state, that is to say, the University.

Unfortunately, in a search for taxes other than that on general property, cities have often followed the practice of using any subject that will yield well and will not be moved away. Equity is a secondary consideration, and taxes are added piecemeal rather than combined into a system.

[10] *The New York Times,* Feb. 28, 1954.
[11] See Charles S. Rhyne, *Admissions Taxes* (1949).

Paul E. Malone has said that "local financial practices are becoming more a process of scrounging than of revenue administration."[12]

Nontax Revenues. Cities receive some money annually from fines and fees. The fines are paid for violating city ordinances and state laws. The fees are charges for certain services such as issuing marriage licenses and transferring the title of real estate.

Rather than pay for many services from general taxes, an increasing number of municipalities are levying service charges. These have traditionally been used for water supply. In recent years, they have also been levied in the form of charges on sewerage, garbage collection, street lighting and cleaning, snow removal, weed cutting, and others. Various formulas are used in determining these charges, but in general they are based upon the concept of payment according to benefits received.

Often service charges are levied as a means of avoiding a raise in the general tax rate. It is a means of making the tax level appear to be lower than it actually is. This can be done effectively, for example, if the sewerage charge is a flat rate or a percentage of the water bill and is added to the periodic water bill. On the other hand, service charges may serve as a means of promoting equity in local taxation. Sewerage charges, for example, may be used as a method of charging tax-exempt property, of which there is a good deal in some cities, so that the cost of this service does not fall upon the rest of the public. Such charges are also useful where some industries contribute disproportionate amounts of sewage to the system while others contribute nothing, and where cities are close to their tax limit (service charges are not usually counted as taxes for limitation purposes).

Some cities make a small profit from the operation of utilities. This is seldom an important source of revenue. Few transportation systems meet operating expenses today. Water departments and other utilities generally charge only enough to meet costs and to permit a reasonable allowance for depreciation and potential expansion. Sometimes, however, a surplus will be turned in to the city treasury.

Some villages and cities own and operate municipal liquor stores. These may be package stores or ordinary liquor-by-the-drink bars. Where these have been permitted by state law they have often proved immensely profitable. Needless to say, powerful pressure groups oppose enabling legislation for such stores.

Grants-in-aid. Grants-in-aid are distributed from the state or national government by appropriation for particular local functions in which there is a state or national interest.[13] The amount of a grant is generally independent of the yield from any particular tax. Grants are now sec-

[12] *Wall Street Journal,* Nov. 10, 1953 (Chicago ed.).
[13] John R. McKinley, *Local Revenue Problems and Trends* (1949), pp. 22–27.

ond in importance only to the general property tax as a source of local revenue.

The grant-in-aid has been described as a device for bridging the gap between the appropriate spending unit and the most efficient tax-raising unit.[14] It is also an emergency solution to serious financial problems, and grants are sometimes made simply in response to sufficiently powerful pressures.

Federal grants have been made to cities for housing, public works, and expressways, among other things. Grants are also made by most of the states and for a great variety of functions. Most states follow the practice of giving specific annual grants for certain projects or functions, in contrast to the British and Canadian practices of lump-sum, or block, grants on a per capita basis. New York, however, furnishes a local government general assistance grant (see Figure 29).

Specific grants are normally made with conditions attached—"he who pays the fiddler calls the tune." These conditions may require, for example, the putting up of matching funds; the use of technically trained personnel in administering them; the maintenance of technical standards of equipment or material; or the use of the money only for certain very specific purposes.

Three principal objections are usually levied against the use of grants-in-aid.[15] First, it is said that they may stimulate extravagant expenditures because the locality is spending funds which are not an immediate and obvious burden upon local taxpayers. It is said that if local officials spend money that they need not solicit from the voters of the city, they may feel no need to spend it wisely or on necessities. Secondly, grants are considered a threat to local self-government and local responsibility. Since the state or national government provides the funds only if certain conditions are met, they may come to supplant local government in the making of policies in these areas. Lastly, grants are held, potentially at least, to lead toward disproportionate expenditures in favor of those functions receiving grants. In other words, regardless of the merits or need of the various functions performed by the city, some will always have a plentiful budgetary appropriation because of the grants, while others, perhaps more needy and deserving, may be skimped. Grants for venereal-disease and tuberculosis control may promote these services nicely while other functions of the health department shrivel for lack of funds. While these objections arise virtually every time grant-in-aid problems are discussed, there appears to be little empirical study to support their validity. They may well be proper objections, but further research is needed on the matter of the harmful effects of grants-in-aid.

---

[14] Robert S. Ford, "State and Local Finance," *The Annals of the American Academy of Political and Social Science,* vol. 266 (November, 1949), pp. 15–23.
[15] *Ibid.*

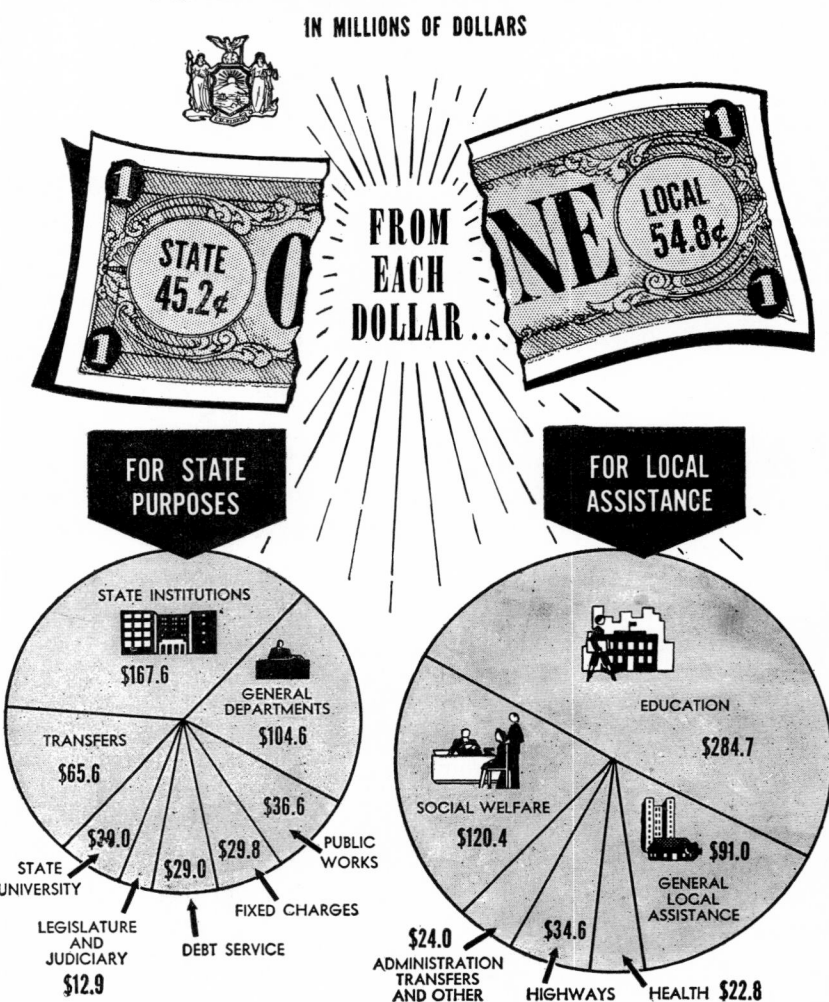

GENERAL FUND EXPENDITURES

IN MILLIONS OF DOLLARS

FROM EACH DOLLAR..

STATE 45.2¢

LOCAL 54.8¢

FOR STATE PURPOSES

FOR LOCAL ASSISTANCE

STATE INSTITUTIONS $167.6

GENERAL DEPARTMENTS $104.6

TRANSFERS $65.6

$36.6

$39.0

$29.8

$29.0

PUBLIC WORKS

STATE UNIVERSITY

LEGISLATURE AND JUDICIARY $12.9

DEBT SERVICE

FIXED CHARGES

EDUCATION $284.7

SOCIAL WELFARE $120.4

$91.0

GENERAL LOCAL ASSISTANCE

$24.0

$34.6

ADMINISTRATION TRANSFERS AND OTHER

HIGHWAYS

HEALTH $22.8

Fig. 29. New York State local-assistance grants. Note: More than one-half of the state general fund goes to local assistance. About one-half of this, in turn, is paid to local school districts. Much of the remainder, such as social welfare and highways payments, goes to the counties. "General local assistance" payments are block grants made to cities, villages, and towns (townships). The state gives aid to veterans' service agencies, housing subsidies, and youth programs. In addition, since 1945, the state mortgage tax has been returned in full to cities, villages, and towns. SOURCE: Comptroller, State of New York, *Annual Report* (1953), p. 7.

In connection with Federal grants to cities, two further issues arise. Should Federal grants be made directly to cities and not through their parents, the states? And should the Federal government make grants to the cities at all?[16]

There are no ready answers or solutions to the questions and problems that have been raised concerning grants-in-aid. Enough is not yet known about their economic and psychological effects. We do know that they have come to be an important timber in shoring up the increasing inadequacies of the local tax base.[17]

Shared Taxes. A shared tax is one imposed by the state but shared with local governments according to a fixed percentage. This percentage is often intended to be representative of the portion of the tax produced within the area of the local unit, but shared taxes may be distributed on any basis the legislature chooses. Unlike the grant-in-aid, a shared tax delivers no fixed amount; rather, local receipts are entirely dependent upon the yield of the tax.[18]

Shared taxes have become increasingly popular in recent decades, and they seem to be preferred by local officials to either grants-in-aid or an enlargement of the taxing powers of the local government. Part of the reason for this is to be found in the fact that fewer strings are normally attached to shared taxes than to grants. Shared taxes also bring less criticism from local citizens than does the enactment of additional local taxes.

Taxes that are most often shared by the state with local units of government include those on motor fuel, motor vehicles, liquor sales, and income. Shared taxes are sometimes defended as being less in the nature of charity than the grant-in-aid, for although they are state-imposed and state-collected, they are levied upon *local wealth* and hence are not a largess. Since they are viewed as a local tax with the state acting as a collecting agent, cities are usually more free in using the revenue as they see fit than they are in the case of grants.

There are, however, grave weaknesses in the shared tax. New York state commissions, both in 1936 and again in 1946, discouraged their use.[19] These study groups pointed out that shared taxes cannot be adjusted to local needs. Some areas with little need receive more from such taxes than they can spend, while others receive much less than their

[16] See above, pp. 264–267.

[17] On the topic of grants-in-aid and shared taxes, see Committee on Intergovernmental Fiscal Relations, *Federal, State, and Local Government Fiscal Relations* (1943); U.S. Bureau of the Census, *State Aid to Local Governments* (1948); R. S. Stout, *Recent Trends in State Grants-in-Aid and Shared Taxes* (1948).

[18] McKinley, *op. cit.*, pp. 22–27.

[19] See *Report of the New York State Commission on State Aid to Municipal Subdivisions* (1936); *Report of the New York State Commission on Municipal Revenues* (1946).

greater needs require. Grants-in-aid are better adjustable to need. Shared taxes, further, do not help to stabilize local revenues. They yield well in prosperous times, but tend to be withdrawn by the state during depressions, when local need for funds is most critical. Lastly, the manner in which shared taxes are used is less subject to control than are grants. From a philosophical viewpoint this may be argued as either an advantage or a disadvantage. But from the viewpoint of improving local government or administration, it is clear that the state cannot very well approach this problem through shared taxes as it can through grants. However, a long look into the future will no doubt reveal the shared tax still with us.

The Need for a Better Tax Base. In a day when relatively low-income people are attempting to buy homes, property is a poor measure of ability to pay taxes. A broader base is needed, incorporating taxes that can more equitably be administered. Many students of taxation have said that the property tax can never be well administered, but there is no point in discussing the abandonment of the tax; it is still the core of local-government taxation and is too badly needed for its repeal even to be considered. Furthermore, the tax is so deeply incorporated into the calculation of property values that its repeal or substantial reduction would be an unwarranted gift to the person who happens to be the owner at the moment.

It can be argued, however, that the property tax should not be increased and that further sources of local-government revenue should be found elsewhere. The problem then, is: Where is elsewhere? There are psychological, and perhaps economic, objections to a much greater dependence upon grants-in-aid. Shared taxes present even greater objections. Both of these devices have become important parts of the local financial web, but they cannot serve as complete solutions.

What sort of taxes are needed? Certainly taxes that are coordinated with those of the state and national government so as to keep inequities to a minimum. Taxes ought to be such that they will encourage local self-government and local autonomy. They should affect all or most of the citizens of the community directly. They should not be regressive.

If these are desirable prerequisites, a new tax is not going to be easy to find. The income tax does not produce a very stable yield. Sales taxes and payroll taxes appear to offer the greatest hope so far as adequacy of yield is concerned. But do they meet the requirement of equity? Although the city retail sales tax has yielded well in New York, California, and elsewhere, and although it broadens the tax base considerably, it tends toward regressivity even if many necessities are exempted. There is also the danger that a sales tax that exempts food and clothing in prosperous times will become seriously regressive in depressions through repeal of the exemptions. Payroll taxes tend to be even more regressive than sales taxes if they allow no exemptions or deductions. On the other hand, the general property tax may be more regressive than the sales or payroll tax, so that a shift of emphasis toward the newer tax may reduce the total regressivity of the tax load, especially as it affects the lower-income homeowner.

Several suggestions have been made for locally levied, state-collected taxes. Thus a local sales tax might be collected through existing administrative machinery for the state sales tax, as is done in Mississippi. A local income tax could be made more equitable than is the payroll tax by assessing each individual at a certain percentage of his state or national income-tax bill. These taxes would have the merit, from a local viewpoint, of passing some administrative costs on to other units of government.

The Moore Plan Act of 1947 in New York grants extensive taxing powers to cities. It allows them to levy taxes on retail sales, restaurants, admissions, vending machines, the retail licenses of the State Liquor Authority, and the use of motor vehicles. This helps to diversify the tax base, but it should be noted that the last two tend to pile local taxes upon state taxes, which is likely to be politically inexpedient even though not necessarily inequitable. The Federal government has failed to abandon the admissions field, and this has made local adoption politically more difficult. Admissions levies have, however, been widely used in the postwar era in Ohio, Pennsylvania, and Washington. In all, more than 300 cities have such taxes.[20]

A conclusion on municipal taxation might hold that the general property tax will remain the backbone of the system. There are several possible supplementary taxes, the use of which should be considered, but all of them have shortcomings, and none of them can replace the outmoded, inequitable, and poorly administered tax that has held the center of the stage for so long. The problem must be solved, however, for it is impossible to have self-reliant municipal government without adequate revenue (see Figures 30 and 31).

Special Assessments.[21] Special assessments have become less important since the Great Depression than they were before that time, but they are still used to a considerable extent. They are especially used in rapidly expanding suburbs with their gross lack of services and conveniences. Special assessments are extra levies upon specific pieces of property de-

---

[20] Clyde F. Snider, "What Can Cities Tax Next?" *National Municipal Review*, vol. 38 (May, 1949), pp. 212–216, reprinted in Charles M. Kneier and Guy Fox, *Readings in Municipal Government and Administration* (1953), chap. 15. See also Mayor's Committee on Management Survey, *Modern Management for the City of New York* (1953), vol. I, chap. 7.

[21] A recent study is W. O. Winter, *The Special Assessment Today* (1952).

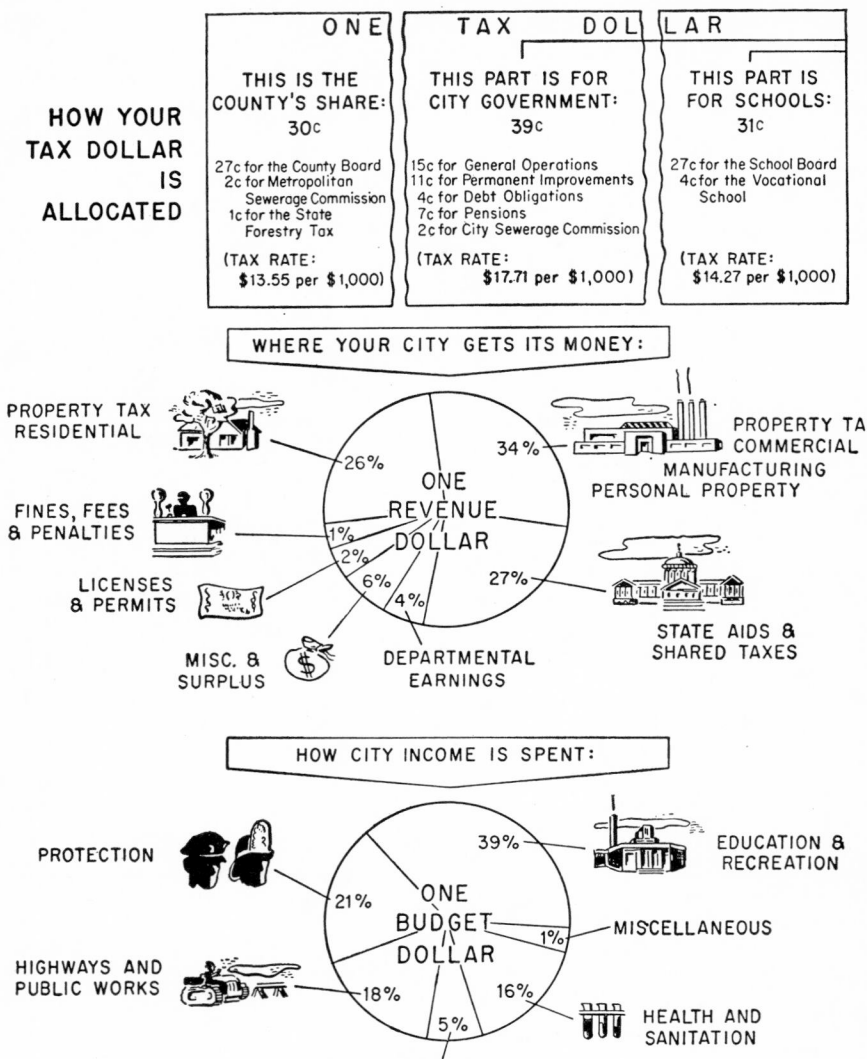

Fig. 30. SOURCE: City of Milwaukee, *The Milwaukee Way* (1952).

signed to defray the costs of services or conveniences of particular value to that property.

By far the most common use of special assessments is to pay all or part of the cost of new street paving, installation of water lines, construction of off-street parking areas, and street lighting. In the last case, special assessments are most commonly levied only for ornamental lighting and not for the ordinary type. In smaller suburbs, however, and especially in unincorporated places, special-assessment "districts" are often created for all street lighting. Some cities defray part of the cost of developing new parks and playgrounds by special assessment.

The theory behind the special assessment is that certain neighborhood improvements installed by the city are of greater value to the nearby

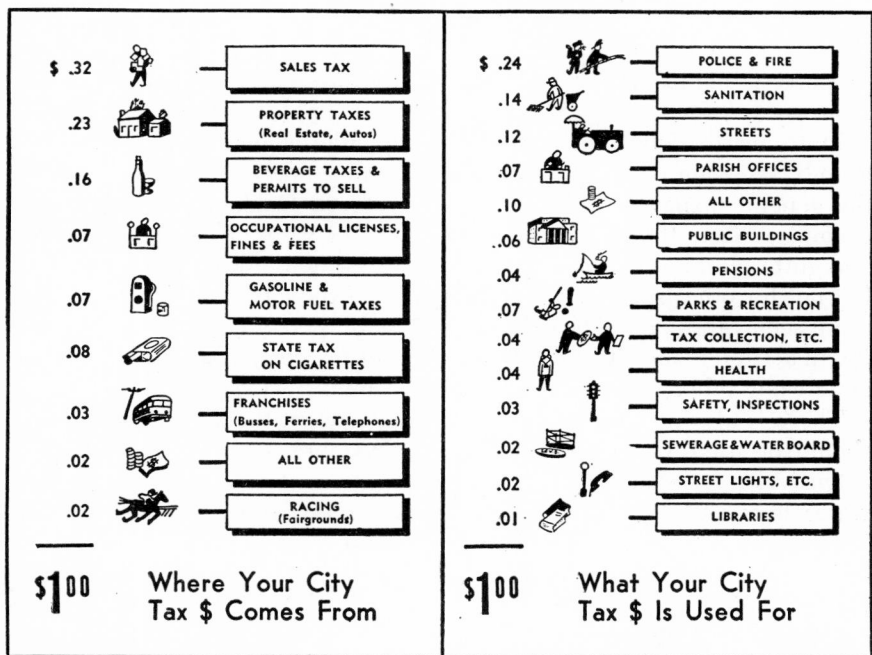

$ .32		SALES TAX
.23		PROPERTY TAXES (Real Estate, Autos)
.16		BEVERAGE TAXES & PERMITS TO SELL
.07		OCCUPATIONAL LICENSES, FINES & FEES
.07		GASOLINE & MOTOR FUEL TAXES
.08		STATE TAX ON CIGARETTES
.03		FRANCHISES (Busses, Ferries, Telephones)
.02		ALL OTHER
.02		RACING (Fairgrounds)

$1.00 Where Your City Tax $ Comes From

$ .24		POLICE & FIRE
.14		SANITATION
.12		STREETS
.07		PARISH OFFICES
.10		ALL OTHER
.06		PUBLIC BUILDINGS
.04		PENSIONS
.07		PARKS & RECREATION
.04		TAX COLLECTION, ETC.
.04		HEALTH
.03		SAFETY, INSPECTIONS
.02		SEWERAGE & WATER BOARD
.02		STREET LIGHTS, ETC.
.01		LIBRARIES

$1.00 What Your City Tax $ Is Used For

Fig. 31. Note: The Milwaukee chart includes expenditures for schools, while that of New Orleans does not. The two are hence not directly comparable. Note, however, that Milwaukee revenue sources are traditional, with 60 per cent coming from property taxes. The New Orleans tax base is more diversified, particularly by the addition of a municipal sales tax. SOURCE: City of New Orleans, *Annual Report of the Mayor* (1952–1953).

property owners than they are to the citizenry at large. On the other hand, they are not of *exclusive* interest to the nearby property owners, and the citizenry at large profit, as does perhaps the city government itself. Because of special benefit, special charges should be levied. Yet it is difficult to determine a formula.

Obviously, you benefit greatly if the street in front of your home is paved. You should pay for this benefit and not enjoy this advantage at the expense of the general taxpayers of the city. Should you pay *all* of the cost, however? The neighbor on the next street now finds your street a handy short cut when he wants to get to the arterial highway.[22] Should he pay, too? How about the Torkelsons, who are your best friends? They live miles away, but they use the street almost every day. And how about Cousin Alfreda, who comes to visit once a year? Or the department store that delivers parcels on the street? Obviously the cost cannot be apportioned directly and precisely in relation to benefit. The problem is even greater in connection with the construction of boulevards, parks, and playgrounds. Cities do not often try to determine the economic benefits from such improvements. They may assess owners other than those whose property is immediately abutting, but the formula is likely to be rather arbitrary.

In trying to determine actual benefit, cities generally use a rule of thumb, assessing part of the cost to the local property owner, and having the general taxpayers of the city pay the rest. Oakland, California, for example, shares the cost of assessments for new street paving and curbs and gutter, but not for sewers or sidewalks. Syracuse helps pay for sewers, but not for other special assessments. Where the city does share the cost, there seems to be no reasonable basis for the percentage of the cost that it will accept. Some cities pay 25 per cent of the cost; others pay 50, 80, or almost any other percentage one might name.

There is also no general agreement as to when the special assessment should be used. Cleveland, Ohio, and Alhambra, California, use it very extensively, for example. But Cranston, Rhode Island, uses it only for water lines; Albuquerque only for new street paving; and Fall River, Massachusetts, only for sidewalks.[23]

In newly developed urban areas, the older residents are likely to feel that special assessments should be used for nearly all capital improvements and that approximately 100 per cent of the cost of improvements should be paid by the benefited property owner. Older residents often contend that they have already met all the costs of their own improvements and they do not think they should be required to help pay for those of the newcomers. This type of controversy is likely to be a part of the fringe-area problem.

There is always the problem on the part of the property owner of paying for the special assessment. Four principal methods of financing are used. One is to demand advance payments from property owners. This requires them to be prosperous or to borrow the money from a private source. The use of this method is not uncommon. Secondly, the city may make temporary loans from a revolving fund. The property owners must repay these within a relatively short length of time. Thirdly, a few cities

[22] Special assessments are sometimes used for arterial streets and highways. Since traffic on these streets may actually depreciate the value of homes along them, special assessments should not logically be used to pay for their surfacing.

[23] The *Municipal Year Book* annually reports extensive data on special assessments.

still issue property liens to the contractor who did the work, with the contractor then selling the liens to a local bank at a discount. These liens must usually be paid off in a time period of less than a year. They are lucrative for the bank, but are not otherwise very satisfactory. Lastly, and most commonly, cities issue special-assessment bonds in order to get cash to pay the contractor. The bonds, with interest charged on the unpaid portion, must then be paid off over a period of time, usually several years. This is simply another application of that popular institution, the installment plan. In Chicago, bonds must be paid in five years, in New York in fifteen. At one time these bonds were commonly nothing but liens against property and hence could be sold to investors only if they bore a rather high rate of interest. Today, about two-thirds of the cities over 10,000 pledge the full faith and credit of the city as a guarantee that the bonds will be paid. This serves to safeguard the money of the investor and the good standing of the public credit and to make special improvements available to more property owners by reducing their interest costs.

Pay Cash or Issue Bonds? A debate that arises in every city from time to time centers in the alternatives of paying for capital improvements by issuing bonds or by increasing taxes and paying cash. The principles of borrowing on the municipal level are far different from those on the national level. The national government itself is the principal institution for the establishment of credit-creating institutions, chiefly the banks. If the national government borrows from banks, it is borrowing credit made possible largely by its own rules. Furthermore, the internally held national debt is not passed on to other generations. The credit of the United States is psychologically intertwined with nearly all that is held worthwhile by most Americans. Its borrowing power is limited only by the faith the American people have in their government, and that faith is enormous.

Municipalities enjoy none of these advantages of the national government when it comes to borrowing. Cities cannot create credit. Municipal debt can be, and is, passed on to future generations. When it is paid off, it is not a matter of taxing Americans to pay other Americans, as is the case with the national government. The debt of Nashville is held in many parts of the nation. If it is paid off in later years, Nashvillians must pay increased taxes, the proceeds of which are then distributed throughout the nation to bondholders. The result is a lower standard of living for the people of Nashville. The public faith in any given city is also immensely less than the public faith in the United States. Municipal borrowing power is accordingly greatly limited. Except for the nontax feature, municipal bonds are treated with no more respect on the open market than are the bonds of private corporations.

When should a city borrow money? Almost everyone is agreed that it should never be in a position of having to borrow to meet current operating expenses. In the past this has happened, either because a depression has dried up the revenue sources and the city was desperate, or because local officials desired to keep taxes low as a vote-gathering technique for the next election. Borrowing to pay for permanent improvements is another matter, especially if the bonds are to be paid off well before the improvement becomes obsolescent or dilapidated. In fact, borrowing to cover a period greater than the life of the improvement is under no circumstances *economically* sound, although city councilmen find that it is often *politically* sound to postpone payment as long as possible—if not longer. Cities sometimes borrow in anticipation of receipts that are scheduled to come in later in the fiscal year. They also borrow sometimes in the face of unanticipated emergencies.

Some people have argued that municipal-bond rates are so low that cities cannot afford *not* to borrow; other argue that cities should not borrow at all and should use a pay-as-you-go approach. It is sometimes said that cities should always pay cash because in this way they avoid the decades of interest payments that are often involved in borrowing, payments that may total several times the original cost of the improvement. There is also no chance of default or of bankruptcy if the city pays cash. And the city is less likely to be extravagant and buy more than it can afford.

Unfortunately, while a cash-payment system may mean that the city will buy fewer improvements, it is likely to mean that it will buy *too* few. There is no intrinsic value in a low budget. The question that is more important is: Are the services that are needed, and that can be afforded, being performed?

Furthermore, operating a city on a strict cash basis is impossible so long as the general property tax is the basic form of revenue. A cash basis means that the expenditures of the city will vary greatly from year to year, for one does not build a municipal auditorium, a new sewer system, or an expressway every year. If expenditures vary, the tax levy will also vary, and this is undesirable in the property tax. This tax tends to become capitalized, affecting the value of the property directly. A varying tax would add a great element of uncertainty to the real estate market. People also prefer to know in advance what to expect in the way of taxes.

Some municipalities attempt to reduce the need for borrowing by the use of reserve funds which may be built up in anticipation of expenditures on capital improvements. Through the use of this device, tax rates can be kept stable and yet interest need not be paid on money used for many improvements. If the municipal government can determine the normal amount of annual capital outlay, the tax rate can be set high enough to provide funds for this purpose. Often, however, cities do not plan this well, or the money on hand is used for other than capital-development purposes.

Bonds, then, appear to be desirable and necessary provided that good judgment is used, a low rate of interest is obtainable, and certain rules, such as the one limiting the length of bond issues to less than the life of the improvement, are followed.[24]

Characteristics of Municipal Bonds. Traditionally, municipal bonds were paid off by the establishment of a *sinking fund* which would, in theory, provide sufficient funds to retire the bonds when they came due. Most of the bonds of this type would be issued so that all of them would fall due at the same time. The sinking-fund method has proved to be seriously defective in several respects, particularly because (1) the council often failed to make adequate appropriations to the fund, which must be built up regularly and systematically, or the fund was otherwise tampered with for "political" reasons; and (2) the sinking fund could come to disaster in depression times if its investments failed.[25]

More recently, most cities have tended to favor the use of *serial bonds*. Under this plan the bonds mature gradually, a certain percentage of them each year. The council then, instead of appropriating money into a sinking fund, appropriates the amount for the direct retirement of part of the debt. This is the same plan that is so popular in bank loans to private individuals today: part of the principal is paid back each month, simplifying the planning for retiring the debt.

Another recent development is the inclusion of a call provision in municipal bonds.[26] This is a feature, long included in many private bond issues, whereby the bonds can be paid off at any time prior to the date of maturity at the option of the debtor. Naturally, exercising such a privilege must be offset by paying a premium—a higher price—for the bonds than would otherwise be necessary.

The call provision is nevertheless likely to be worthwhile, for a sharp drop in interest rates or a suddenly increased income of the city might make it very desirable to pay off debts ahead of maturity dates. The U.S. Treasury and the Federal Reserve Board of Governors reached an "accord" on March 4, 1951, which served to begin a trend toward an increase in all interest rates by lowering the support price on government bonds. The financial policies of the Eisenhower administration directly after it entered office in January, 1953, also raised interest rates throughout the

[24] See C. H. Chatters and A. M. Hillhouse, *Local Government Debt Administration* (1939); A. M. Hillhouse, *Municipal Bonds: A Century of Experience* (1936).

[25] Sinking-fund managers, if they act responsibly, may be successful in their efforts. See F. E. Wood, *The Louisville Story: A Century of Fiscal Integrity* (1951).

[26] Commission on Municipal Debt Administration, *The Call Feature in Municipal Bonds* (1938).

nation. These policies made it more expensive for cities to borrow money. If the national government should return again to the lower-interest policies of an earlier day, it would certainly be advantageous for cities to have a call provision in bonds issued in 1951 and thereafter.

Types of Municipal Bonds. In addition to the special-assessment bonds already mentioned above, cities commonly issue three types of bonds: general obligation, mortgage, and revenue. General-obligation bonds are secured through a pledge that the full faith and credit of the local unit of government is available to pay them off. The community thus agrees to levy whatever tax is necessary in order to pay the interest and eventually to retire the bonds. Unless constitutional tax limits threaten to make this pledge meaningless, general-obligation bonds normally bear a relatively low rate of interest.

Mortgage bonds are normally used in connection with the purchase or construction of utilities, and they offer a mortgage on the utility as security. This type of bond has usually required a higher rate of interest than bonds of general obligation and as a result has been less popular. Sometimes mortgage bonds also involve a pledge of full faith and credit.

Revenue bonds have become increasingly popular in the years since the Great Depression. These bonds are secured by a pledge of the revenue from some self-liquidating project. Toll bridges, tunnels, and electric-light and water-supply systems may be financed in this way. Municipalities must agree to set rates high enough to pay the debt charges. Sometimes the bondholders are also given a mortgage on the utilities. Revenue bonds have several advantages. This type of debt is often not counted as part of the debt where a statutory or constitutional limitation exists. The ease with which their provisions can be enforced has made them very attractive to bond buyers.

Bond Prices and National-government Policies. It has been noted that the monetary policies of the national government are a major factor in determining the interest rates that must be paid by cities on their bonds. This is not the only factor: the credit standing of the city, the amount of existing debt, state restrictions upon taxing powers of the city, and other items are included in credit ratings. But United States Treasury and Federal Reserve System rules restricting credit can offset the best efforts of a city to reduce its interest payments. Conversely, in times of depression, the national government can help to lower interest rates or to keep them from rising. It can also make loans available to cities directly from its own vastly superior borrowing facilities.

Out of a series of nineteenth-century Supreme Court decisions was evolved the principle of intergovernmental tax immunity. According to this concept, cities cannot tax the instrumentalities of the national government and the national government cannot tax the income of persons when it is received from interest payments on municipal bonds. While the Court has shown a tendency to narrow the scope of tax immunity,[27] this principle still stands. There has been much debate as to whether municipal bonds should continue to enjoy their immunity. The advantage of tax exemption to the city is clear. With no taxes to be paid on interest income, the city can sell the bonds at a lower rate of interest and thus, in effect, receive a subsidy from the national government. This might be a desirable thing if it were not for the fact that municipal bonds are purchased in large part by persons of high income who are seeking to avoid being placed in a still higher income-tax bracket. The exemption feature thus, in effect, subsidizes individuals who least need subsidization. It is also possible that this results in a greater loss in Federal revenue than the amount that it saves the cities.

Some students of taxation have urged that municipal bonds should be made taxable by the Federal government and that the cities should receive a federal grant-in-aid to replace their lost interest-rate advantage. There are many complications involved in such a proposal, however, and municipal finance officers undoubtedly prefer to keep the present system rather than to experiment with something new and unknown.[28]

Municipal Tax Exemption for Industries.[29] For a long time some of the states have authorized or sometimes even required cities to exempt from property taxation for a certain number of years the manufacturing establishments of new industries in the city. The aim, obviously, is to attract industry to a city and thus provide greater wealth for the community. In some cases, tax exemption of a negative sort has been granted, too: an industry will threaten to leave the city and the state unless it is granted special tax consideration.

Beginning in 1936, the state of Mississippi went one step further with its "Balance Agriculture with Industry" program. It authorized cities to borrow money and to spend that money to buy or build industrial plants which would, in turn, be rented at a low rate to newly arrived industries. The bonds were to be retired from the rentals. Since 1951, Alabama, Florida, Illinois, Kentucky, and Tennessee have adopted similar laws. These programs, like ordinary tax exemption, have been used particularly in the South in attempts to attract industry. The textile industry has been most often enticed by them.

How effective has tax exemption been in attracting wealth-producing industries to a community? No complete studies have been made, but there is some evidence to show that industries consider other factors as

[27] Note the mood of the Supreme Court in *Graves v. New York ex rel. O'Keefe,* 306 U.S. 466 (1939); and *Helvering v. Gerhardt,* 304 U.S. 405 (1937).

[28] See Lyle C. Fitch, *Taxing Municipal Bond Income* (1950).

[29] J. S. Floud, Jr., *Effects of Taxation on Industrial Location* (1952), provides a recent study.

more important in determining situs, especially the availability of ample nonunion labor, and that cities offering special inducements gain little by such activity. In contrast, the risk is considerable, for the local tax base is undermined, and this produces serious problems in the event of a depression. When bonds have to be issued in order to build factories, a depression will find the community saddled with both the bonds and a "white elephant" factory. The Investment Bankers Association of the United States has condemned the practice for these reasons.

Tax exemptions are inequitable, too, for they are unfair to businesses and private homeowners that do not receive exemptions. They are demoralizing to those who pay taxes faithfully. Tax exemptions assume that all in the community gain enough to warrant charging the cost to all the other taxpayers. Such is not necessarily the case, however. The system is also likely to attract unstable, fly-by-night industries that are the least desirable to have.

Most students of taxation and of general economics condemn tax exemption or the use of public credit to attract industry. If economic conditions are favorable, if the city is well and honestly run, and if local groups such as the chamber of commerce are active, there is no need to resort to inequitable and unsafe subsidies.[30]

War-plant Tax Exemption. An extension of the theory of intergovernmental tax immunity is costing cities hundreds of thousands of dollars annually. Present Federal statutes exempt from local property taxes all federally owned real estate, regardless of use.[31] As a result government-owned plants leased to private manufacturers are exempt, as are manufactured goods, raw materials, tools, and machinery when the title is technically vested in the United States. The Federal government has worked with manufacturers to allow them to place title in the United States from the time the manufacturing process starts, thus enabling the company to avoid its just share of the taxes needed to maintain the community in which these concerns are located. Such federal policy has the improbable effect of requiring local units of government to subsidize the federal government. This policy resulted in a 1953 tax loss of $376,420 in St. Paul and of over 18 million dollars in Los Angeles County.

There is perhaps no reason why cities should not make a direct contribution to the national defense effort, except that their financial condition does not permit it. There is enough Federal tax-exempt property located within our cities now without adding to the list those things that will some day in the future be a part of the Federal government's property.

---

[30] The contrary argument is given in W. E. Barksdale, "Mississippi's BAWI Program," *State Government*, vol. 25 (July, 1952), pp. 151–152.
[31] *National Municipal Review*, vol. 42 (April, 1953), pp. 191–192.

FINANCIAL ADMINISTRATION IN THE CITY[32]

The Financial Officers. To most of the public, the city treasurer sounds like a very important person indeed, while the controller is an obscure bureaucrat who might do almost anything—or nothing. The auditor performs functions but hazily conceived of, but there is no doubt as to the duties of the tax collector. It is well, at this point, to examine the functions of the top fiscal administrators (see Figure 32).

The Council. The city council makes basic financial policy for the city. It determines the tax rate, adopts the budget, and demands an accounting of the funds subsequently spent by the city. The budget is so much thought of as an administration document today that these facts of the case are often overlooked.

The Chief Administrator. The mayor or manager (in commission cities, the finance commissioner) acts as the chief fiscal officer of the city. Not only is he responsible for proper administration, but he often takes the lead in determining policies both of raising and of spending money.

The Treasurer. The office held by this person is one of the oldest in local government. As a traditional office, it was one that Jacksonians insisted upon making elective. As a result, most Americans think of the treasurer as being a very important person entrusted with major policy-making responsibilities. Actually, such is almost never the case. The treasurer is really a glorified bookkeeper. He receives moneys according to law, the amounts of which have been determined by others. He is custodian of the city funds, although these are normally actually deposited in local banks. He must be able to account for each cent received. He pays out moneys only on orders from the controller. In none of these acts does he exercise any discretion, and he is not often called upon to advise the mayor or council on fiscal policies. His is a ministerial office. There is no logical basis, therefore, for electing the treasurer. Yet more than one-third of the cities still do elect him. He might better be appointed, and there is no overriding reason why he should not be a civil servant.

The Tax Collector. At one time, especially in New England, an officer of this title commonly existed. Today tax collection is merely one of the jobs of the treasurer in nearly all cities. In a few places, the job is retained as a separate one from that of the treasurer, who keeps and disburses the funds.

The Controller. The controller, or comptroller (pronounced "controller" in either case), is an obscure officer so far as the general public is con-

[32] The Municipal Finance Officers' Association has published a large number of pamphlets and monographs on financial and debt administration. The series is designed to aid the practical administrator.

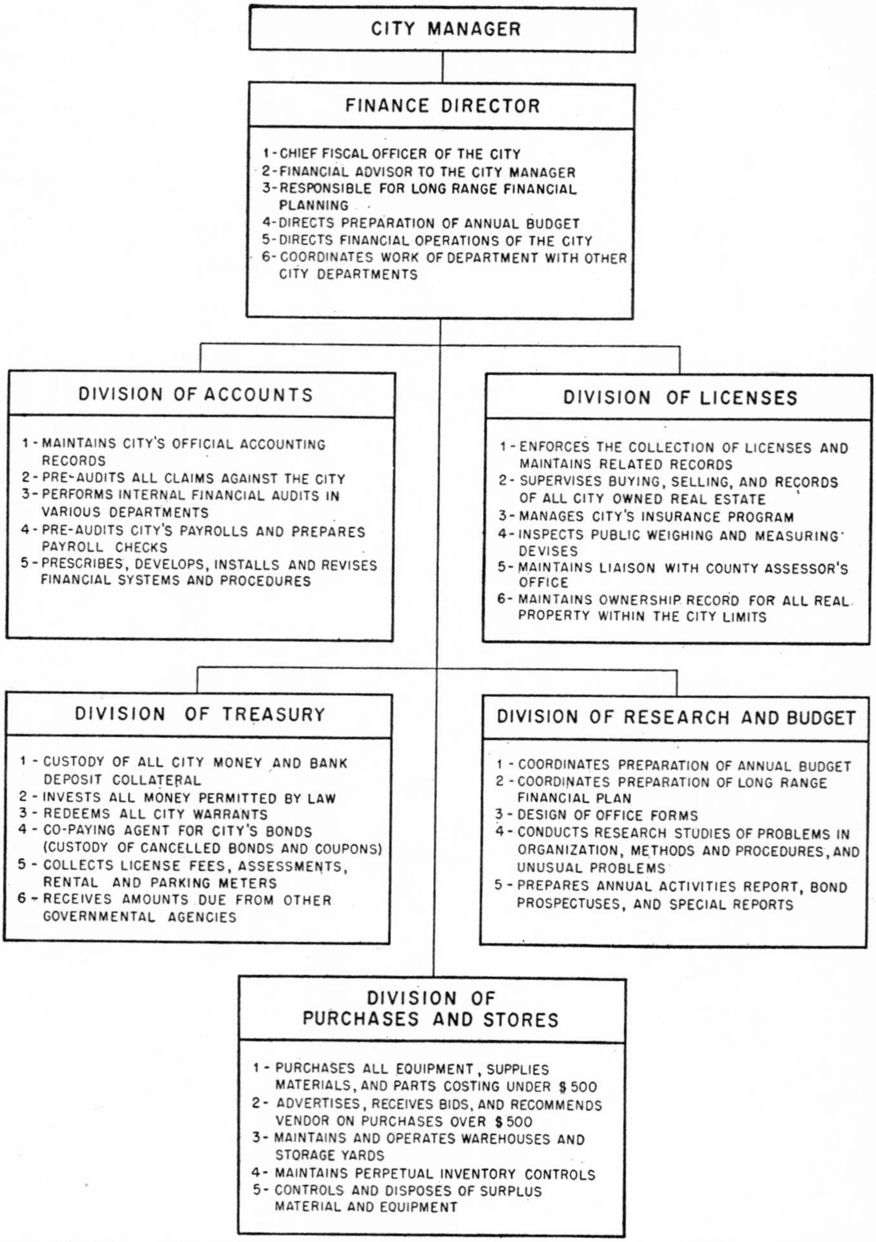

CITY MANAGER

FINANCE DIRECTOR

1 - CHIEF FISCAL OFFICER OF THE CITY
2 - FINANCIAL ADVISOR TO THE CITY MANAGER
3 - RESPONSIBLE FOR LONG RANGE FINANCIAL PLANNING
4 - DIRECTS PREPARATION OF ANNUAL BUDGET
5 - DIRECTS FINANCIAL OPERATIONS OF THE CITY
6 - COORDINATES WORK OF DEPARTMENT WITH OTHER CITY DEPARTMENTS

DIVISION OF ACCOUNTS

1 - MAINTAINS CITY'S OFFICIAL ACCOUNTING RECORDS
2 - PRE-AUDITS ALL CLAIMS AGAINST THE CITY
3 - PERFORMS INTERNAL FINANCIAL AUDITS IN VARIOUS DEPARTMENTS
4 - PRE-AUDITS CITY'S PAYROLLS AND PREPARES PAYROLL CHECKS
5 - PRESCRIBES, DEVELOPS, INSTALLS AND REVISES FINANCIAL SYSTEMS AND PROCEDURES

DIVISION OF LICENSES

1 - ENFORCES THE COLLECTION OF LICENSES AND MAINTAINS RELATED RECORDS
2 - SUPERVISES BUYING, SELLING, AND RECORDS OF ALL CITY OWNED REAL ESTATE
3 - MANAGES CITY'S INSURANCE PROGRAM
4 - INSPECTS PUBLIC WEIGHING AND MEASURING DEVISES
5 - MAINTAINS LIAISON WITH COUNTY ASSESSOR'S OFFICE
6 - MAINTAINS OWNERSHIP RECORD FOR ALL REAL PROPERTY WITHIN THE CITY LIMITS

DIVISION OF TREASURY

1 - CUSTODY OF ALL CITY MONEY AND BANK DEPOSIT COLLATERAL
2 - INVESTS ALL MONEY PERMITTED BY LAW
3 - REDEEMS ALL CITY WARRANTS
4 - CO-PAYING AGENT FOR CITY'S BONDS (CUSTODY OF CANCELLED BONDS AND COUPONS)
5 - COLLECTS LICENSE FEES, ASSESSMENTS, RENTAL AND PARKING METERS
6 - RECEIVES AMOUNTS DUE FROM OTHER GOVERNMENTAL AGENCIES

DIVISION OF RESEARCH AND BUDGET

1 - COORDINATES PREPARATION OF ANNUAL BUDGET
2 - COORDINATES PREPARATION OF LONG RANGE FINANCIAL PLAN
3 - DESIGN OF OFFICE FORMS
4 - CONDUCTS RESEARCH STUDIES OF PROBLEMS IN ORGANIZATION, METHODS AND PROCEDURES, AND UNUSUAL PROBLEMS
5 - PREPARES ANNUAL ACTIVITIES REPORT, BOND PROSPECTUSES, AND SPECIAL REPORTS

DIVISION OF PURCHASES AND STORES

1 - PURCHASES ALL EQUIPMENT, SUPPLIES MATERIALS, AND PARTS COSTING UNDER $500
2 - ADVERTISES, RECEIVES BIDS, AND RECOMMENDS VENDOR ON PURCHASES OVER $500
3 - MAINTAINS AND OPERATES WAREHOUSES AND STORAGE YARDS
4 - MAINTAINS PERPETUAL INVENTORY CONTROLS
5 - CONTROLS AND DISPOSES OF SURPLUS MATERIAL AND EQUIPMENT

Fig. 32. City of Phoenix, Ariz., Finance Department functional chart. SOURCE: City of Phoenix, *Annual Financial Report* (1953).

cerned, but he is actually the chief fiscal assistant to the mayor or manager.[33] He is thus the person who performs the functions that the public often attributes to the treasurer. In more than 100 cities, the controller is elected, but in over 95 per cent of the cities in which the office exists he is appointed.

The budget is often assembled, in the name of the mayor or manager and under his direction, by the controller or the budget officer in the controller's office. After the budget is assembled, it is reviewed and revised by the mayor or manager, and is then submitted to the council, which usually may alter it in any way it sees fit. After the council has adopted the budget for the ensuing year, the controller assumes the task of administering it. He must see to it that no department spends more than is authorized, that no department spends all of its appropriation in the first quarter and is then without funds for the rest of the year, that all expenditures are legally authorized in every way, and that the departments have permission to spend *before* they proceed to make purchases. He must sign every payment voucher, and normally the treasurer can pay no claim against the city without the approval of the controller. He also serves constantly as the chief adviser to the mayor or manager on financial and frequently on other matters. In some cities he serves as deputy mayor.

In small cities, and often in larger ones, the functions of the controller are performed wholly or in part by the council itself. Many a council session is devoted in large part to the approval of routine bills. Even in small places where no officer resembling a controller exists, this work could be done more efficiently by an administrative officer. In some cases, of course, state law requires the council to perform this ministerial function.

The Assessor.[34] The assessor (or board of assessors) is responsible for the valuation of property to serve as a basis for determining the general property tax. The assessor is sometimes located within the department of finance, but often he has a separate office. And not all municipalities serve as assessing units. It was once common to elect the assessor, and more than 15 per cent of the municipalities in the country still do so. There is no logical justification for this, however, since the job is not a policy-making one, but is rather one for a technician.

The assessor's office, once it has prepared the tax rolls after assessment, may send out tax bills, although this is more commonly the job of the treasurer and many tax jurisdictions do not send a bill to the taxpayer

[33] There is no standard terminology for the office. He may be called the director of finance, the finance commissioner, the budget director (only one of his jobs, really), or by some other term. In many cities, no single officer enjoys all of the powers of a controller.

[34] Many technical pamphlets and monographs on desirable assessing practices are published by the National Association of Assessing Officers.

at all because of the cost involved. The assessor may also handle condemnation proceedings.

The Purchasing Agent. Modern finance departments contain a division of purchasing. Through it most of the city's needs for supplies, materials, and equipment are procured so that savings of large-scale purchasing may be achieved. In large cities the purchasing division contains experts who understand differences in quality and who are acquainted with the technical advice available from the U.S. Bureau of Standards and other Federal and state agencies.

The division reduces the possibility of agencies purchasing beyond their needs. It is also often given responsibility for handling the details of contract procedure for commodities, services, land purchase, and construction projects.

The purchasing officer is most logically a civil servant with special training. Often, however, he is an appointee of the mayor or controller. There is no strong objection to this, provided the appointing officer acts responsibly and remembers that the job is technical and not political.[35]

The Department of Finance. In some cities all of the above officers are grouped together into a Department of Finance headed by a director. Authorities on financial administration agree that this is a desirable organization, since it provides for direction and coordination of these several financial activities. Council-manager cities, especially smaller ones, are likely to have an integrated department of this type. But in many cities each of the finance officers is independent and may be popularly elected.

The Auditor. The auditor is the agent for the *legislative* branch of government whose job it is to check upon the executive branch to make certain that the expenditures it has made were according to appropriation and were otherwise legal. In a few cities the auditor also makes recommendations to the council concerning the effectiveness of operation of the administrative agencies.

Because the job is an old one, one auditor in eight is still elected. But since the position requires a knowledge of accounting, there is no logic in choosing the incumbent in this fashion. The job is technical, not policy-making. (The auditor sometimes performs some of the functions described in this chapter as belonging to the controller, but these are not tasks that belong to an elective official either.)

Where the auditor is not elected, he may be chosen by the council, or he may be sent to the city periodically from the state auditor's office or the council may hire a private accounting firm to do a periodic audit.

[35] Russell Forbes, *Government Purchasing* (1929), is the classic work in the field. A more recent book is S. F. Heinritz, *Purchasing: Principles and Applications* (1951).

Large cities are likely to have their own auditing officers, smaller cities to use private firms or be subjected to a check by the state office, or both.

The important thing is that the auditor be sufficiently expert in accounting methods and procedures and that he be responsible to the legislative branch in making his reports. This requires, of course, that he be in no sense a part of the executive branch, and he should never be appointed by or removable by the mayor or manager.

The Executive Budget.[36] The trend toward centralized administration, the increasing number of functions of government, and the increasing complexity of those functions have contributed to the rapid rise in the use of the executive budget in the United States since the turn of the century. In an earlier day there was no systematic approach to budget making or administration. Expenditures and revenues were not brought together in a benefit-versus-cost sense. The council voted the funds of the various departments without a view to over-all needs. Each department succeeded according to its relative political influence with the councilmen. When government was simple and performed few functions, as on the frontier, this system could be made to work.

Today the budget process is divided up so that the executive branch makes a recommendation for revenues and expenditures in the form of a systematic, comprehensive statement of income and outgo. The council then adopts this budget, nearly always with some, and perhaps with many, modifications. The executive branch then oversees the expenditure of the appropriations by the various departments. Finally, the legislative branch, through its auditors, checks to ascertain whether or not its instructions have been carried out and whether or not appropriate provisions of the state law have been followed by the executive.

Until recent years the municipal budget dealt with all of the minutiae that are needed to operate an office or a city function. The emphasis was upon the things to be acquired—paper clips, snow shovels, wheelbarrows —rather than upon the services to be rendered. This was necessary when public funds had to be guarded at all times against ingenious attempts at fraud. It encouraged, however, the citizen's habit of disassociating taxes from services provided.

Today, the trend is toward what is called the *performance* budget, such as was recommended for the Federal government by the Hoover Commission. "In its simplest terms the goal of performance budgeting is to prepare, analyze and interpret the financial plan in terms of services and activity programs, rather than limiting the budget to a detailing of objects

---

[36] See the citations at the end of this chapter. The National Municipal League has prepared a *Model Accrual Budget Law* (1946) and a *Model Cash Basis Budget Law* (1948). For a distinction between the two budgeting methods, see T. H. Reed, *Municipal Management* (1941), pp. 154–156.

of disbursement. . . . "[37] This type of budget emphasizes that taxes are collected, not to pay salaries or to buy typewriters, but to operate swimming pools, provide pure water, and construct expressways.

The Parts of the Budget. The municipal budget is a broad outline of (1) proposed expenditures for all purposes (expenditures to be financed by borrowing should be included in a general or special budget but in many municipalities are not budgeted at all); (2) anticipated revenues for the coming year from all sources except from the annual property-tax levy; and (3) the property-tax levy necessary.[38] State law usually requires that step 3, in form at least, bring the budget into balance.

Preparing the Budget. In some cities, such as Chicago, the budget is still prepared by a committee of the council. In other cities it is prepared by an independently elected controller. Practically all students of public administration agree, however, that the job should be done under the supervision of the mayor or manager. The budget is, after all, the clearest possible statement of policy by the executive. It is a plan of work for the coming year.

The preparation of the budget begins with the collection of estimates for the following year's needs from the various departments. These must be gone over carefully by budget analysts, who look for padding, inaccuracies, and inconsistencies. There may be conferences between the departments and members of the budget division when differences arise.

When detailed estimates of the needs of each department for the coming year are available, they are set out in parallel columns with statements of the estimated expenditures for the same items in the current year and the actual expenditures for those items in the fiscal year just completed.

The budget officer next must go over the document in detail with the mayor or manager so that proposed changes in policy may be incorporated in the estimates. If the chief executive proposes to suggest that the city's parks program is now up to date and that in the coming year the paving of side streets should be emphasized, the budget must be changed accordingly.

The completely assembled budget, often with a summary intended for public consumption, is then ready to be sent to the council. A budget message is often included. It may say simply, in effect, "Here is the budget for the next fiscal year," or it may explain new policies in expenditures, tell why tax changes are requested, and otherwise explain and summarize the budget. One municipal authority has added, perhaps

[37] S. M. Roberts, "Trend toward Performance Budgeting," *Public Management,* vol. 34 (October, 1952), pp. 223–226. The quotation is from p. 224. See also Orin K. Cope, "The Performance Budget," *Tax Digest,* vol. 30 (December, 1952), pp. 419–422.

[38] Reed, *op. cit.,* p. 137.

a bit cynically, "The budget message should contain one item which will be read by everyone, for every newspaper will quote it—a statement of the tax rate for the ensuing year. This is something any citizen can grasp."[39]

Enacting the Budget. The council will usually next hold budget hearings, either before the full body or before the tax and appropriations committees, depending upon its form of organization. These hearings do not often give the councilmen information they do not already have, but they serve to allow pressure groups and individuals to vent their annoyances, bitterness, or frustrations. They are an important part of the democratic process. A large-city budget hearing, however, is nearly always attended by representatives of pressure groups, rather than by a representative cross section of the general public. In large cities, some of the city departments may lobby at this time to get a bigger share of the pie than was given to them in the budget division. In small cities, this will probably be done *sotto voce* and informally, as may also be the case in large cities. In weak-mayor cities or those in which the budget-making officer is elected, these demands may be more open and vigorous than in a strong-mayor or manager city, where a dissident department chief risks his job by "going over the head" of the executive. Pressure groups at this time seek to protect their pet projects and agencies, city employees try to improve their working conditions and pay, and the newspapers may take the opportunity to view with alarm the ever increasing cost of local government.

Some charters in mayor-council cities limit the powers of the council in modifying the budget submitted by the executive. The council may be allowed, for example, to reduce but not to increase the amount of a budget item. It may be prohibited from entering new items. These restrictions seem undesirable. The council is the policy-making body of the city, and it should have the responsibility for the final constitution of the budget.

The council finally adopts a budget through an appropriation ordinance and through other ordinances providing for the tax rate and for the issuing of necessary bonds. Often the mayor has the final word through use of the item veto.

Administering the Budget. In cities with a modern budget system, the head of each department must submit a work program to the chief executive before the beginning of a new fiscal year. This program will show how much of the total appropriation for that department is desired in each month or quarter of the coming fiscal year. This is known as the *allotment system.* After the chief executive has approved, the allotments are turned over to the controller, who will then refuse to allow any money to be spent by that department unless it is both authorized by the council-

[39] *Ibid.*, p. 157.

manic appropriation ordinance (or by state law) and falls within the time provided in the allotment schedule. This practice prevents overspending and assures a systematic approach to the performance of the city's functions. In small cities where control and auditing functions are inadequate, the council may exercise control only through monthly reports from officers.

The control division of the finance department performs two tasks in ensuring a systematic administration of the budget. First of all, the division maintains an appropriation ledger, in which each appropriation is encumbered as the department spends the money. In the second place, before any department can spend any of its appropriation, it must have the approval of the controller. Since the treasurer will not pay a warrant without the signature of the controller, the department has no choice but to submit its proposed expenditures to him. The control division then checks the request against the appropriation and allotment, approving or disapproving as may be appropriate. Doubtful cases may be referred to the mayor or manager. The chief executive may refuse to approve a proposed expenditure even though it is clearly authorized by appropriation and is within the allotment for the month or quarter. Whether or not the chief executive can legally thwart the implied wishes of the council in this fashion is a matter for the courts to decide. They tend to uphold the chief executive. (A manager could not do the same thing and keep his job, of course, without the consent of the council.)

Not all of the accounts of the city are always kept in the finance department's division of accounting and control. Where some of them are kept, for some reason, in the operating departments, the division is, or should be, authorized to prescribe the form of all accounts.

After the moneys have been spent, the auditor checks to ascertain the legality of all expenditures and reports his findings to the council and sometimes also to the state auditor. Even as the money is being spent throughout the year, however, the budget officer is surveying the scene for possible alterations in the next budget, for the governmental process is an unending one.[40]

[40] Details of financial management may be found in T. H. Reed, *Municipal Management* (1941), pt. III, from which the author has drawn extensively. See also the bibliography in the current *Municipal Year Book* as well as the following: International City Managers' Association, *Municipal Finance Administration* (1949); Municipal Finance Officers' Association, *Municipal Accounting and Auditing* (1951); C. H. Chatters and Irving Tenner, *Municipal and Governmental Accounting* (1947); and a short work, John McMahon, *Municipal Budget Making and Administration* (1952). Convenient further reading may be found in Charles M. Kneier and Guy Fox, *Readings in Municipal Government* (1953), chaps. 14 and 15.

CHAPTER 16

THE CITY AND ORGANIZED CRIME

The alliance between crime and local government has become so legendary that one wonders if the whole picture has not been exaggerated. Do police captains actually send policy memos such as the following to their vice-squad sergeants? Or is this the sort of thing that takes place only in television dramas? "Make your raids specifically at 10 o'clock. At that time, the gambling tables will be covered. Observe the girl show and then leave. During that time, there will be no gambling conducted so your officers will not be embarrassed." Such a note was actually sent by a captain of the Los Angeles County sheriff's office who admitted to the Kefauver committee that he had written it.

A PUBLIC ATTITUDE OF *LAISSEZ FAIRE*

An Old Story. In 1951, American televiewers were fascinated by the unsystematic but overwhelming collection of evidence concerning organized crime activities in the United States gathered by the staff of a Senate committee and presented, largely through the interrogation of witnesses, to the public. The Special Committee to Investigate Organized Crime in Interstate Commerce, headed first by Senator Estes Kefauver of Tennessee and later by Senator Herbert O'Conor of Maryland, amazed even the more cynical Americans. It frightened some local officials, if no professional gamblers. It made Senator Kefauver a hero to many Americans and made him a formidable presidential candidate at the 1952 Democratic National Convention. The investigation did considerable damage to the already shaky reputation of local-government officials and, unfortunately, reinforced many misconceptions of long standing concerning public officials.[1] But whether any permanent diminution in the

[1] The Kefauver hearings and reports include some twenty-five volumes. See *Hearings before the Special Committee to Investigate Organized Crime in Interstate Commerce* (1951). There were also three *Interim Reports* and a *Final Report* of the Special Committee (1951), cited hereafter as Kefauver committee, *Third Interim Report*, etc. Other useful investigations and studies include those of the California Crime Commission, *Combined Reports of the California Crime Commission* (1950); and the *Reports of the New York State Crime Commission* (1953). There are earlier studies, too, such as the report of the Lexow Committee: *Report and Proceedings* of the Senate Committee Appointed to Investigate the Police Department of the City

activities of organized criminals will result is doubtful. With the exception of a few communities, the ordinary citizen did not rise up in wrath at the reports. The problem of a policy toward the social functions performed traditionally by organized crime is yet to be met, or even faced frankly. Certainly it was not much considered in the Kefauver reports.

The situations uncovered by the Kefauver committee are not new or different: they are a restatement of long-existing practices. In fact, they may be viewed as one aspect of old-time machine politics that has not been eradicated.

The professional criminal is sometimes strictly predatory—the bank robber and the pickpocket, for example—but those who are organized into crime "syndicates" are normally providers of services to the general public. These services differ from those of the butcher, physician, or insurance salesman chiefly in that they are illegal and are usually considered immoral or detrimental to health. It was concerning these services that the Kefauver committee made the flat statement that "these operations could not continue without the protection of police and without the connivance of local authorities."[2]

What Makes Organized Crime Possible? Judging from the editorial efforts of newspapermen or the occasional sermon from the pulpit, one might conclude that organized crime exists in defiance of society, that it is wanted only by those who profit from it. A moment's reflection should convince anyone that such is not the case. Why, then, do we have organized crime?

Sociological Factors. Part of our difficulty in suppressing crime stems from an ambivalent attitude. We have inherited certain puritanical values which condemn gambling and purely pleasurable activity. On the other hand, we live in a culture that is dynamic, complex, impersonal, and materialistic.[3] Our whole economic and cultural pattern is based upon competition and "getting ahead." Gambling, therefore, is partly a result of a *hope for gain,* a desperate need to succeed. Establishments for performing abortions—another illegal occupation—exist because women have a great fear of loss of status through the bearing of an illegitimate child. Loss of status comes easily in our culture and symbolizes failure.

In our competitive society, it is often difficult to distinguish the criminal from the noncriminal. Many business activities verge on the classification of racketeering; certainly they often violate the moral values of many individuals. "Anything's fair in business that you can get away with." If so, how does one distinguish legitimate and illegitimate businesses? Many

---

of New York (5 vols., 1895); and the Illinois Association for Criminal Justice, *Illinois Crime Survey* (1929).

[2] Kefauver committee, *Second Interim Report,* p. 3.

[3] D. R. Taft, *Criminology* (1950), pp. 198–201 and chap. 15.

Americans believe that you cannot do so. Americans have never strongly believed that *all* laws should be obeyed.[4] A multimillionaire once told a Senate committee that it was morally right for an individual to avoid paying all taxes that he could possibly shirk. "Anything is legal that you can get away with" and "everyone has his racket." So why should we condemn the gamblers, prostitutes, abortionists, or bootleggers?

An additional complication arises as a result of the fact that we are a heterogeneous population consisting of many subcultures, each with a variant set of values. There is no general agreement as to what is right and what is wrong. So the individual follows his own value pattern. He does not agree with the views of his neighbor, but he tolerates them. ("I wouldn't do that myself, but every man to his own way!")

The *Uniform Crime Reports* of the Federal Bureau of Investigation year after year indicate that of all crimes, murder is the one most likely to be solved. This is partly because solution is aided by a strong and obvious motive which is usually present whenever this crime is committed. But it is also partly because the public *wants* murderers to be apprehended. The punishment for the crime is likely to be severe. This is largely a result of the fact that what the public *says* is its attitude toward murder agrees with what the public actually *does* hold as its attitude toward murder. Unfortunately, social mores and criminal law do not always agree so nicely.

Prostitution and the sale or use of narcotics are everywhere illegal. Gambling, with certain exceptions, is illegal in all states except Nevada. Yet it is safe to say that in every large city and in a great many medium- and small-sized cities, one may find gamblers, prostitutes, and narcotics peddlers engaging in their occupations. The fact of the matter is that there is a very sizable demand for these services, and hence there are those who will supply them in spite of almost all hazards. Unlike murder, gambling is not accorded identical viewpoints by the citizen in his public and his private opinions. For the sake of social appearances, the individual is likely to condemn it publicly regardless of his real views. The same thing is true, in lessening degrees, of prostitution and narcotics peddling.

Laws in serious conflict with the mores of society become unenforceable. The public, or at least a large segment of it, does not want the laws on gambling rigidly enforced. An even larger segment is indifferent to the question of how they are enforced. Many people do not gamble, but they do not object if their neighbors do.[5] Likewise, there are some cultural

---

[4] *Ibid.,* p. 236.

[5] Virgil W. Peterson, "Obstacles to Enforcement of Gambling Laws," *The Annals of the American Academy of Political and Social Science,* vol. 269 (May, 1950), pp. 9–20, holds that "self-interest, personal conveniences, and expediency" are the principal motivating factors in law evasion and in the public attitude toward law enforcement. But this does not fully explain the tolerance of nonparticipants of some types of law evasion and intolerance of others.

groups in our society that accept the existence of the prostitute as an ordinary part of life. And a large number of persons who would themselves never enter what was once called a "house of ill fame" are not incensed at the thought that such places exist in their city. A few persons are the slaves of narcotics. The use of narcotics produces so many undesirable physical, psychological, and social effects that it is indeed fortunate that in this case society actually does not approve of its sale or use. Yet the cravings of the addict are so powerful—the demand for the product is so inelastic—that this risky business remains alive if for no other reason than that it is greatly profitable.

Psychological Factors. In our society, gambling often serves to fill important psychological needs. To some it is an escape from a troublesome, or unsuccessful, or dull world. To others, it is, like liquor, a crutch, and hence something highly necessary. To others it is simply enjoyment, but one strangely exhilarating. To others, it is excitement and the vicarious conquering of worlds that will not lend themselves readily to conquering outside the gaming casino. Millions of Americans—psychopaths and normal people—spend greater or lesser amounts of time gambling.[6]

The psychological factors behind such other illegal occupations as prostitution and narcotic-drug sales are complex and beyond the scope of this text. It must be borne in mind that psychological factors are stimulated and conditioned by their sociological environment. There is, for example, almost certainly no inherent desire or need to gamble. But there is a need for security, and this psychological desire may be directed toward gambling as a possible means of fulfillment.

Legal Factors. Americans, especially of the middle classes, have a rather naïve faith in law and punishment as solutions for social problems.[7] As a result, the superficial action of making an occupation illegal is mistaken for a move toward the abolition of the occupation. Psychological and sociological phenomena cannot be legislated away, for their causes are complex and deep-seated. Since demand is not eliminated by making the occupation illegal, such action merely has the effect of creating racketeering, gangsterism, and an increased disrespect for the law.

The Pattern of Corruption. It should not be assumed, because a certain number of houses of prostitution are known to exist in the city, or because rumors have it that there are some narcotics peddlers about, or because the numbers racket is still in business, that the officer on the beat is being bribed, or that the city administration is necessarily corrupt. It is

[6] On the pathological aspects of gambling, see Robert M. Lindner, "The Psychodynamics of Gambling," *The Annals of the American Academy of Political and Social Science*, vol. 269 (May, 1950), pp. 93–107. On people of normal personality who gamble, see David D. Allen, *The Nature of Gambling* (1952), pp. 30–32.

[7] Taft, *op. cit.*, p. 235.

true that none of these things could take place without the knowledge of the city administration and police officials. That does not always mean that they *want* or *like* it that way.

In a large city, it is almost inevitable that at least a small amount of prostitution exists. An honest administration may want to eliminate all of it, but it will find this to be an impossibility, practically speaking. The administration may decide upon a compromise with the strict letter of the law, permitting prostitution within narrowly defined areas of the city and with the stipulation that it not attract unfavorable publicity. A policy such as this does not necessarily indicate corruption, and the administrators who establish it would defend it as "practical."

While quite a few city administrations may cooperate with gambling and some with prostitution, few will make an alliance with purveyors of narcotics. Even if they should want to, state and Federal law-enforcement officers are particularly alert and active in seeking out these persons. Yet large cities are quite certain to have dope peddlers. There is no simple formula for destroying the elaborate and extensive narcotics rings that are organized to carry on this profitable business.

Gambling. Gambling, which is an ancient type of human activity, is very widespread, and it takes many forms: the policy racket or numbers game; the bookmakers who take bets on horse races, athletic events, and even the outcome of presidential elections; the casinos with a great variety of card and dice games; the slot machines, which add mechanical ingenuity to the pattern. There are others, too.

The police can never escape knowing of the existence of gambling, but they may not be able to eliminate it even when they wish to do so. Often, of course, they have no such wish. The attitude of a city administration toward gambling can be determined to some degree simply by observing the type of gambling that is tolerated. The policy racket, for example, probably could not be completely eliminated in large cities. Convictions are difficult, the evidence is easily hidden, and the operators are highly mobile. On the other hand, gaudy casinos in the Monte Carlo tradition, or heavy, bulky slot machines, cannot be operated except with the passive cooperation of the police (see Figure 33).

Gambling is big business in many American cities. Around 1950, Miami bookmaking was grossing 26 million dollars annually. Rough estimates by Kefauver staff workers found that nationwide illegal off-track betting on horse racing totaled from 3 to 5 *billion* dollars annually. This was in addition to some 2 billion dollars legally bet each year at the race tracks. It was estimated that the net profit on 3 billion dollars to illegal bookmakers would be not less than 600 million dollars each year.

Similarly, "In Chicago some $10,000,000 is spent annually on policy

MEETING OF THE BOARD OF DIRECTORS
APRIL 14, 1950

Fig. 33. SOURCE: By permission of Daniel R. Fitzpatrick and the *St. Louis Post-Dispatch*.

playing alone; no other business in the Negro community is so large or so influential. As elsewhere in Negro communities, the policy racket in Harlem is the most widespread form of law breaking."[8]

The Kefauver committee concluded that at least 20 billion dollars changed hands each year in organized, illegal gambling of all kinds. No estimate was attempted as to the amount of this that was paid in protec-

[8] Maurice R. Davis, *Negroes in American Society* (1949), p. 254.

tion money, except to state that it must amount to millions of dollars annually.[9]

Police Graft. Where illegal occupations take place with the permission of the police, graft may be collected at either the top or the bottom of the hierarchy. The cop on the beat may receive petty bribes. If payments are at the top, however, the money is not likely to be passed along downward. But in that event, the effect upon the morale of the ordinary patrolman cannot be anything but unhappy. An honest policeman under these circumstances will meet with nothing but futility and frustration. He will find that, even if he is not personally bribed, there is no point in his attempting to enforce laws which it is not the policy of the department to have enforced. He will not secure convictions—or promotions for himself —if he does. He may become cynical and resort to picking up graft on his own. The knowledge of rookie officers that the top administration does not respect the law will lead to a low morale that will reflect itself in poor law enforcement in all fields, not in just the "protected" areas.

The Kefauver investigations demonstrated some of the methods of graft payments to top police administrators and to members of the city administration.[10] The hearings and the summaries of conditions in various cities in the reports show that traditional techniques are still being used:[11]

In some cases the protection is obtained by the payment of bribes to public officials, often on a regular basis pursuant to a carefully conceived system. In other cases, the racketeering elements make substantial contributions to political campaigns of officials who can be relied upon to tolerate their activities. Sometimes these contributors will support a whole slate of officers in more than one political party, giving racketeers virtual control of the governing body.

The Vice-squad Pattern. Where a city government, or merely the top police leadership of a city, has been corrupted by organized crime, it is necessary to find a method of making certain that promised protection is actually afforded. A police commissioner and his chief lieutenants will not wish to share their payments with ordinary policemen, yet the rank and file of the departments are sworn to enforce the law. To circumvent the ordinary policeman—who may, after all, be a completely honest individual who took his job thinking that it was the task of policemen to enforce laws —police heads commonly resort to what the Kefauver investigators called the "vice-squad pattern":[12]

[9] Kefauver committee, *Second Interim Report,* pp. 13–14.
[10] A history of the relationship of crime and politics in Chicago is given in Virgil W. Peterson, *Barbarians in Our Midst* (1952).
[11] Kefauver committee, *Final Report,* p. 5.
[12] Kefauver committee, *Third Interim Report,* pp. 95–96. Most police departments have vice squads. It should not be inferred that the existence of such a group implies corruption.

This device is used in many cities where the rackets thrive. The political department bosses set up a vice squad composed of a chosen few directly accountable to them. They instruct the remaining law enforcement officers to stay away from gambling and vice and to channel any complaints to the vice squad for action or, in most cases, inaction. By this device a small clique frequently controls the collection of the protection pay-off.

The person who observes the existence of corruption in some particular city should not assume that the cop on the beat is lining his pockets with illegal payments or that he is callously unconcerned with the law. His hands are tied.

THE PROBLEM OF A SOLUTION

The Results of the Kefauver Investigation. In the years following the Kefauver investigation of 1951, there were clean-up efforts in several American cities. Miami, a winter playground, had been an obvious congregating place for gamblers and other illegal operators. The publicity (it would be inaccurate to say revelations) of the investigation produced a reaction that closed up the gambling places and drove the gamblers from the city. In 1953 they still had not been allowed to return.

Other cities changed their public policies, too. And some had from time to time enjoyed reform administrations without benefit of Senate committees—for example, Minneapolis in the period directly after World War II.

It would be wrong, however, to think that a majority of urbanites were incensed by the findings of the investigations. Fascinated by the unraveling tale? Yes. But aroused to angry action? No, at least not in many places. In some cities, racketeers found that they could prevent embarrassment and punitive action by disappearing briefly. In other places reform efforts were either unsuccessful or of temporary effect.

In many cases, conscientious administrations were handicapped by the political atomization of the metropolitan area. The racketeers simply moved across an artificial line called the city limits into a hospitable suburb.[13] Some enforcement officers were frustrated by lack of jurisdiction and lack of cooperation in nearby areas. The Kefauver investigators discovered, for example, that in the late 1940s Los Angeles County was more "tolerant" than the city government. One of the peculiar county "islands," conveniently located and known as the Sunset Strip, "became a natural haven for those engaged in activities offensive to the Los Angeles police."[14] But there was nothing that they could do about it with-

---

[13] See the editorial "Escape to the Suburbs," *National Municipal Review,* vol. 40 (April, 1951), p. 184.
[14] Kefauver committee, *Third Interim Report,* p. 95.

out the cooperation of the Los Angeles County sheriff's office—which at that time was not forthcoming.

The Recommendations of the Kefauver Committee for State and Local Governments.[15] A reading of the suggestions made by the Kefauver committee for eliminating the unsatisfactory conditions that it uncovered is likely to leave one with a feeling of disappointment. This may be because the committee discovered no magic formula—as indeed could scarcely be expected—or because the committee placed such heavy emphasis upon the *legalistic* rather than the sociological and psychological aspects of the problem. In any case, its recommendations are not in any way startling or even particularly imaginative.

Some of the suggestions are of a routine character: that more and better facilities for the treatment of drug addicts be provided; that there be better coordination among local prosecutors so as to have a collective effort against racketeers; and that there be more state-local and national-local coordination of effort. Another set of recommendations urged the calling of investigating grand juries in every community where extensive gambling and racketeering exist; the use of state legislative and executive investigations in individual states to carry on the work begun by the Senate committee (such as the California Crime Commission); state sponsorship of crime conferences made up of citizen groups in order to sustain a public interest in the problem; and the organization of racket and special-purpose squads on the state and local level with enough manpower and authority to make investigations and arrests wherever crime is uncovered.

The committee also suggested the utilization of state income-tax data and of federal occupation-tax data (which is required of liquor retailers, gamblers, and operators of slot machines) in developing leads on persons engaged in illegal occupations. There are some legal and moral questions involved in the possible use of these data, however. It was also suggested that "racketeers" (presumably persons engaged in illegal occupations) should be prohibited from making political contributions. In light of the fact that all previous attempts at limiting or prohibiting certain types of contributions have been failures, the author knows of no way of enforcing this last rule, if adopted.

Two recommendations of the committee seem to be particularly important. One urged that all state laws on gambling and other illegal occupations be modernized, since most of them are outmoded to one degree or another and cannot therefore be used effectively in fighting crime. It also pointed out the advantages of uniform state crime laws. The second recommendation was that state legislatures consider laws to deprive any establishment of all of its state and local business and pro-

[15] Kefauver committee, *Final Report*, pp. 11–13.

fessional licenses if the owner or operator is convicted of permitting gambling games on the premises. Such a statute, rigorously enforced, succeeded in eliminating pinball and slot machines from the state of Minnesota in the late 1940s. It is doubtful, however, that such a law would win popular support in many states.

The Question of Legalizing Gambling.[16] Nevada legalized gambling in 1931. Great Britain permits certain types of bookmaking, and Sweden has a state-controlled monopoly with limited possible winnings and the profits going to the state. Gambling in Great Britain is organized, and there is considerable illegal betting in addition to the legalized types, but neither there nor in Sweden have criminals infiltrated the business. Numerous efforts have been made to legalize gambling of one kind or another in many states, but in most of these cases either the effort has failed or the enabling act has been shortly repealed. In November, 1950, Arizona, California, Massachusetts, and Montana voters rejected legalized gambling. So did Oregon voters two years later.

The question of the success of the Nevada experiment is a subject of much debate. One writer, opposed to legalized gambling, has said that "legalized gambling in Nevada has been a success in terms of the fact that it does not corrupt the government. However, it is a failure in terms of the fact that it has led to an increase in bankruptcies and an increase in crime.[17] The state has taken over much supervision of the occupation, and its license is required first before those of the county and city may be requested. Each jurisdiction may refuse.

A Nevada editor has said, "The infiltration of mobsters has been more or less blocked. There has been no trouble in Reno aside from an attempt by 'Bugsy' Siegel, shortly before he was killed, to move in with a race-track wire. . . ."[18] But the Kefauver investigators reported, "Before he was shot to death in 1947, Benjamin 'Bugsy' Siegel was undoubtedly the gambling boss of Las Vegas, Nevada."[19] The Senate investigators also said, "The committee's inquiries revealed that the caliber of the men who dominate the business of gambling in the State of Nevada is on a par with that of professional gamblers operating illegal gambling establishments throughout the country."[20] Some observers do not agree with this, however.

[16] See Allen, *op. cit.*; Peterson, "Obstacles to Enforcement of Gambling Laws"; this same author's *Gambling: Should It Be Legalized?* (1951); and Kefauver committee, *Final Report*. The entire issue of *The Annals of the American Academy of Political and Social Science*, vol. 269 (May, 1950), is devoted to a study of gambling.

[17] Allen, *op. cit.*, p. 96.

[18] Joseph F. McDonald, "Gambling in Nevada," *The Annals of the American Academy of Political and Social Science*, vol. 269 (May, 1950), pp. 30–34.

[19] Kefauver committee, *Third Interim Report*, p. 91.

[20] *Ibid.*

The general arguments in favor of legalizing gambling run somewhat as follows: that unenforceable laws should not remain on the books, for they merely spread contempt for the law and make the enforcement of all laws more difficult; that, since gambling apparently cannot be stopped, the state may as well share the profits of human weakness, rather than give it all to the gamblers; that the state could control gambling as it has controlled the sale of intoxicants and thereby could keep out dishonest persons; that the liquor business was made legitimate and most criminals were eliminated from the field after the repeal of prohibition; that gambling against honest odds is a relatively harmless escape mechanism and that the number of persons who would bankrupt themselves would not be great, not greater, in any case, than under present illegalization.

These arguments are countered by those who hold that legalizing gambling is wrong because it would encourage corruption of public officials rather than abate it, since there would be great competition for licenses; it would lead to greater problems of law enforcement, since legal gambling spawns increased illegal gambling; it is economically undesirable, since it is an occupation that particularly exploits those least able to pay, and a tax on gambling would be a regressive tax hitting hardest those least able to pay; it would increase the total amount of gambling, since it would be easier to gamble and the moral problem of violating the law would be absent; gambling is, in any event, suppressible and not an uncontrollable activity, as has often been argued. It is held that gambling can be suppressed by normal public opinion, supported by effective and honest police departments and adequate laws.[21] Minnesota eliminated slot machines in this fashion under Luther Youngdahl in the late forties. Bookmaking in California was greatly reduced at this same time as a result of action following the reports of the California Crime Commission.

The debate over the legalization of gambling rages on among both the informed and the uninformed. *Life* magazine, a veritable symbol of middle-class respectability and a close reflector of middle-class values, has suggested that New Jersey might well conduct a useful experiment by licensing bookmakers. The arguments and evidence are inconclusive, the magazine editorial held, but such an experiment might tell all states more about the effect of legalization upon the amount of gambling, better enforcement, and more effective laws.[22]

Senator Estes Kefauver, on the other hand, was convinced after the investigation that legalization would only make gambling worse and that

[21] Allen, *op. cit.*, pp. 104–106, cites examples.
[22] Editorial, *Life*, Jan. 21, 1952, p. 28.

racketeers would control it anyway. He also felt that the nation would be less worthy morally if it began to depend upon gambling receipts for revenue.[23]

The investigating committee opposed legalization:[24] "In states where gambling is illegal, this alliance of gamblers, gangsters and government will yield to the spotlight of publicity and the pressure of public opinion, but where gambling receives a cloak of respectability through legalization, there is no weapon which can be used to keep gamblers and their money out of politics."

One is tempted to ask why publicity and public opinion are not weapons against dishonest politicians receiving bribes from *legal* gamblers as well as from *illegal* gamblers, but this would merely reopen the argument for another round.

Conclusions. The evidence that gambling is a social evil is overwhelming. The arguments for and against legalization are inconclusive and evidence is lacking. Perhaps it would be best not to try to develop a national policy, but to make allowances for variations in local value patterns.

It may be that one of the faults of the American approach to gambling has been in the centralization of policy in the hands of the state legislatures and state administrators. These people, however well meaning, may not understand the desires and values of urban communities. It is necessary to have *all* of the following before honest government can be achieved:[25]

1. A policy that is locally acceptable and that conforms to local standards must first of all be developed.

2. The policy must be an honest one, clearly expressed so that it is understood by all.

3. The policy, once established, must be rigidly enforced. There must be no exceptions to, or deviations from, the established and understood policy, and *all* violators must be punished.

It is no argument to say that because local officials are more likely to be corrupt, gambling must be controlled by state or national officials only. The proposition itself need not be granted. In a long-range solution, public cynicism concerning the ethics of local-government politicians will not help to destroy the cynicism these local officials have concerning the public's attitude toward gambling.

With adequate and effective laws supporting policies that accurately reflect local opinion, the only additional need is for honest, courageous,

[23] *U.S. News and World Report,* Apr. 20, 1951, pp. 28–29.

[24] Kefauver committee, *Third Interim Report,* p. 93.

[25] The viewpoint here expressed is that of the present author, but see the conclusions of H. A. Bloch, "The Sociology of Gambling," *American Journal of Sociology,* vol. 57 (November, 1951), pp. 215–221.

and confident law-enforcement officers and city administrations to carry out the law. Americans are becoming more and more aware of the need for a higher level of ethical conduct on the part of government officials. Criminal alliances by politicians do not exist in Scandinavia or Great Britain because the general public would permit no such thing. Americans must find that the only solution for obtaining better and more honest politicians on the local or any other level is for them, the ordinary citizens, to insist upon better and more honest politicians and to accept no substitutes. As Adlai Stevenson said during the 1952 presidential campaign: "Your public servants serve you right. Indeed, often they serve you better than your apathy and your indifference deserve." The cultural value patterns in other nations have changed in the direction of such expectations. Those in the United States can, too.[26]

[26] Ethics in government and the problems connected with their improvement are discussed in George A. Graham, *Morality in American Politics* (1952); Paul H. Douglas, *Ethics in Government* (1952); Paul H. Appleby, *Morality and Administration in Democratic Government* (1952); Wayne A. R. Leys, *Ethics for Policy Decisions* (1952); Fritz Morstein Marx, "Ethics in Local Government," *National Municipal Review*, vol. 41 (October, 1952), pp. 438–442.

CHAPTER 17

PUBLIC SAFETY

A great many of the functions of municipal government are related to the safety of the public. In this chapter, fire protection, smoke abatement, traffic engineering, civil defense, and, in particular, police functions will be discussed. Except in a relatively few cities, these functions are not grouped together into a single department. Their methods of operation and their technical requirements are so different that most cities assign police and fire to separate departments.

POLICE PROTECTION[1]

Some aspects of the problem of adequate policing of cities have already been discussed in Chapter 16. While vice and organized crime are not the major police problems of today, they are among the most difficult to combat. In the typical city, these occupations exist in spite of the efforts of the police department, if they exist at all. Most departments, it should be understood, enforce the law to the extent that they are permitted by public opinion as reflected in the political process. Two of the major problems in connection with police work in recent years have been the continuing increase in the crime rate in postwar America and the increasing cost of police protection (see Figure 34).

The insecurities of continued international tensions have added a new psychological factor to the many other reasons for a high American crime rate.[2] The number of serious crimes committed in the United States, according to the *Uniform Crime Reports* of the FBI, increased by more than 5 per cent in 1951 and by more than 6 per cent in 1952. In the first half of 1953, the rate was one-third greater than the 1937 to 1939 aver-

---

[1] This section draws extensively from O. W. Wilson, *Police Administration* (1950). See also the detailed manual on administration which is published by the International City Managers' Association, *Municipal Police Administration* (3d ed., 1950); W. C. Reckless, *The Crime Problem* (1950); "New Goals in Police Management," *The Annals of the American Academy of Political and Social Science*, vol. 291 (January, 1954), entire issue; and Bruce Smith, *Police Systems in the United States* (rev. ed., 1949).

[2] See D. R. Taft, *Criminology* (1950), or one of the other textbooks in that field.

age.[3] The most alarming increases have been taking place in the various types of robberies. One reason for this, perhaps, is that the odds are in favor of the robber, auto thief, or burglar each time he commits a crime (unless he resorts to violence). The police catch relatively few thieves—only in about three cases in ten is anyone even charged with the offense. Under these circumstances, an increasing number of men seem to be making a career of crime. The public does not tolerate a similar lack of success where crimes of violence against the person are involved.[4] But these crimes are increasing, too, especially among juveniles.

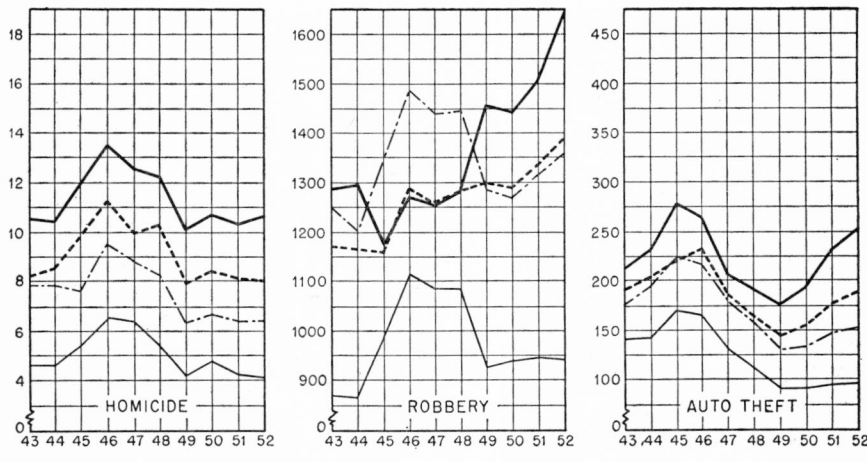

Fig. 34. Urban crime rates per 100,000 population in the United States by population groups, 1943 to 1952. SOURCE: *Municipal Year Book* (1953), p. 410. Used by permission.

The American crime rate is several times as high as that of any European nation, yet as in the case of the fire department, the police are the best equipped in the world. An outstanding police chief has said: "Despite the technology that has been acquired through no small effort and expense, the police service today fulfills its task with no greater success than it did a quarter- or half-century ago."[5]

Americans tend to be careless of property losses resulting from robbery just as they tend to be careless of fire losses. The poor record of American police is, therefore, in large part a result of public apathy. Furthermore,

[3] Figures quoted in *Newsweek*, Feb. 8, 1954.
[4] See *Municipal Year Book, 1950* for comparisons of offenses known and offenses cleared. An offense is "cleared" when a person is charged with a crime.
[5] William H. Parker, "The Police Challenge in Our Great Cities," *The Annals of the American Academy of Political and Social Science*, vol. 291 (January, 1954), pp. 5–13. The author is the chief of police in Los Angeles.

"the individual police officer operates with a remarkable lack of public support, cooperation, or trust."[6] The police are sometimes hampered partly by unwise efforts on the part of public officials and the citizenry at large to "save" tax money. American police forces are small by comparison with European forces. To be sure, manpower is less expensive there than in the United States, but our great wealth should be protected from the predatory—and the existence of the wealth is itself proof that we can afford to pay for adequate protection.

Police Organization. Police and fire departments, by long tradition, are organized along quasi-military lines. The head of the police department is commonly a professional policeman called the chief.[7] In some cities, especially in the largest cities, the highest-ranking uniformed officer may be subordinate to a lay department head, called the commissioner, director, or in a few cities, the chief. The lay department head does not perform, or should not be allowed to perform, details of departmental administration. His job is to serve as liaison officer between the force and the chief executive. At one time a council committee administered the police department, and in the last half of the nineteenth century it was common for the department to be operated by a semi-autonomous board. This is still the case in about seventy cities,[8] but is increasingly giving way to control of the department by the chief executive.

When the head of the department is a professional policeman, he should serve the chief executive at his pleasure. Under this arrangement, if the appointing chief executive or his successor wishes to appoint a new chief, the incumbent is not dismissed from the service, but is dropped back to a lower position in the departmental hierarchy.

Under the chief, and depending largely upon the size of the city, are numerous supervisory officers arranged in a hierarchy. They are traditionally given military titles. Under the chief, there may be assistant chiefs, then majors or inspectors (especially if the city is large enough to have precinct or district stations), captains, lieutenants, and sergeants. The patrolmen make up the broad base of the pyramid. Detectives may outrank patrolmen, or they may merely be patrolmen with a special position classification.

The force is organized according to the nature of the tasks performed (e.g., patrol and traffic divisions). Larger cities are divided into geographical districts, or precincts, especially for administering the patrol force. In some cities, some of the specialized divisions may also be de-

[6] *Ibid., p. 5.*
[7] Terminology for various ranks is not standardized. The most common titles will be used in this section.
[8] See the current edition of the *Municipal Year Book* for statistics. The department head is still appointed by the council in about eighty cities.

centralized so that they operate out of the district stations. Since police work, especially that of the patrol division, is continuous, the force is also divided into platoons, or shifts.

Specialized Units. Even fairly small departments have some degree of specialization, and most departments of more than about 100 men have all of the following operational divisions:[9]

Patrol—to repress criminal activity, regulate conduct, and perform a number of services to the public

Detective—to apprehend criminals, recover stolen property, and gather and prepare evidence for the prosecution of criminals

Traffic control—to prevent accidents and congestion

Vice control—to eliminate commercialized vice and safeguard the morals of the community

Juvenile—to prevent the development of delinquent tendencies in children and to aid in the correction of such tendencies when they do develop

Women's—to perform police duties that can be done best by police-women

Only a few cities have separate women's divisions. In other places, policewomen are often assigned to the juvenile division and are made available to other divisions as needed.

Police departments, except small ones, must also be organized with several staff, or service, divisions to aid the operational divisions. The common ones are:

Records—to record, classify, index, file, and tabulate facts relating to crime, criminals, and other police matters

Communications—to receive and transmit police information and orders, using the telephone, teletype, radio, and other communications devices

Crime laboratory—to identify or establish other facts relating to physical evidence by examining it scientifically

Jail duties—to provide suitable custodial care of prisoners

Property management—to care for department-owned property and property temporarily in police custody

Maintenance—to service, repair, and maintain police buildings, vehicles, and other property

The Patrol Division. The largest division, and the core of police-department operations, is the patrol division. Patrol attempts to eliminate opportunities or desire for misconduct, it investigates offenses, apprehends offenders, recovers lost or stolen property, aids lost or distressed persons, and performs dozens of other tasks.

In an earlier day, the patrolman followed his established beat alone.

[9] Wilson, *op. cit.*, pp. 22–24.

He could call for assistance by using a whistle, but he was largely on his own. Later, telephone call boxes with red or amber signal lights were established so that the patrolman could call in to his supervisor or be called. But today the foot patrol is being used less and less, and the motor patrol has become the standard operation. Only about fifty municipalities still use the foot patrol throughout the city; about 140 cities, including some as large as Memphis, Wichita, and Berkeley, have abandoned the foot patrol completely. Most cities still use it for the business district, however.

In an effort to explain the rising rate of crime to their own satisfaction, some laymen have in recent years come to the conclusion that one fault is to be found in this trend in patrol usage. They argue that the cop on the beat is more effective in *preventing* crime than is the patrol car, since the latter can arrive on the scene only *after* the report of a crime or a suspicious person. The foot patrolman, it is argued, may surprise a burglar at work, and his very presence on the sidewalk is a deterrent to potential lawbreakers. Experts in police administration point out that actual experience does not support this viewpoint. In fact, the motor patrol with its constant communication, speed, range, and other advantages is not only the least expensive form of patrol, but it is for most purposes far more effective than is the old-fashioned foot patrol.[10]

Partly as a result of attempts to reduce the wage bill and partly because some authorities on police administration believe them to be more efficient, a trend has developed toward the use of one- rather than two-man patrol cars. Over 200 cities, including some as large as Berkeley, Hartford, and Wichita, use one-man patrol cars exclusively, and a majority of municipalities over 10,000 now use the one-man patrol for some shifts. O. W. Wilson, an authority on police administration, has urged the use of one-man cars because "a patrolman who is able to perform his duty satisfactorily while alone on foot should not find it necessary to have a brother officer accompany him when he is equipped with the most modern means of transportation and communication. Actually he works more efficiently, effectively, and safely when alone." Wilson believes that this system provides more patrol units, with each officer giving his job undivided attention with no visiting, swapping of stories, or neglect of safety precautions.[11]

Bicycles were once used for patrol by many police forces, and they have not completely passed from use today. Horses were once common, especially for controlling crowds and traffic, and for mobility and range before

[10] O. W. Wilson, "Put the Cop Back on the Beat," *Public Management,* vol. 35 (June, 1953), pp. 122–125; S. R. Schrotel, "Changing Patrol Methods," *The Annals of the American Academy of Political and Social Science,* vol. 291 (January, 1954), pp. 46–53.
[11] Wilson, *Police Administration,* pp. 101–102.

the auto. Today, departments that retain a mounted division do so as a luxury. The beautiful animals are impressive at parades, but they have been supplanted for useful purposes. The three-wheeled motorcycle is used a good deal for chalk marking and ticketing parked autos and is apparently the best piece of equipment for this purpose. The two-wheeled motorcycle is still used a good deal, especially in large cities, because of its high maneuverability and acceleration rate, but it has little to recommend it over patrol cars and its operation is extremely hazardous.[12] Cities as large as Boston and Cincinnati have virtually abandoned its use.

The Detective Division. Laymen may be surprised to learn that until recent years detectives had no greater training or education than uniformed patrolmen. In fact, the two classifications were commonly interchangeable. This situation still exists in many cities, but it is now generally recognized that detectives should be specialists. O. W. Wilson says:[13]

Routine patrol service with its manifold problems and experience in preliminary investigations provides invaluable training for future detectives. The qualities of a good detective are an abundance of physical and nervous energy, considerably more-than-ordinary persistence, imagination, and ingenuity with the initiative and force to apply them, and a broad background of experience with special reference to information sources. Psychological and physical tests may one day be developed to measure these qualities, but at present the best method of discovering latent investigative talents is to observe preliminary investigations by patrolmen for the purpose of selecting those who give evidence of investigative ability for trial service in the detective division.

The detective, although he is experienced in investigation and interrogation, today leaves much of the work that he himself once attempted to specialists in the records and crime laboratory divisions of the department. Examinations for physical evidence and measurements, diagrams, and photographs at crime scenes, for example, have been turned over in larger cities to specialists from the laboratory who are assistants to the expert criminalist.

It is quite common, especially in larger cities, for detectives to work in pairs. Some police authorities believe, however, that cities can economize while at the same time improving service by using them singly. It is argued that detectives operate better alone for the same reasons that patrolmen do, and therefore should do so except when making a dangerous investigation or arrest.[14]

---

[12] *Ibid.*, pp. 95–96.
[13] *Ibid.*, pp. 124–125. See also P. L. Kirk, "Progress in Criminal Investigation," *The Annals of the American Academy of Political and Social Science*, vol. 291 (January, 1954), pp. 54–62.
[14] Wilson, *Police Administration*, p. 127.

The Traffic Division. In handling traffic, the department is concerned with many problems that are not police problems within a narrow sense. It also deals with law violators who are not usually criminals in the popular sense. Because this type of police work is specialized, traffic divisions were organized in a great many cities beginning in the late twenties and early thirties, when the increasing number of automobiles created congestions, hazards, and accidents against which the public rebelled.[15]

More than any other police division perhaps, traffic control is forced to tread a narrow path between public indignation over law violations that lead to hazards and accidents on the one hand, and public objection to vigorous enforcement programs on the other. Almost every citizen is directly and constantly affected by the activities of the traffic division. As is the American habit, driver-citizens are quick to criticize no matter how lacking in technical knowledge of traffic enforcement they may be, and they often expect miracles from those entrusted with solving the traffic problem.

The traffic division is made up of policemen using specially equipped vehicles who are specially trained to investigate accidents and record data and evidence. Traffic policemen sometimes help handle the enforcement of parking regulations, the regulation of moving traffic, and intersection and crosswalk duty in addition to their principal functions. The division also records and analyzes accident and traffic-flow data so as to be able to judge enforcement effectiveness and to plan changes in the traffic pattern. For this function, the division requires the help of traffic engineers, who may be inside or outside the police department. In policing traffic and accidents, the division is partly dependent upon support and cooperation from other divisions, especially patrol, and in investigations, the detective division as well. Furthermore, traffic officers have a responsibility to aid other divisions in ordinary law enforcement in the course of their regular duties.

Since the police cannot issue warning or citation tickets for every violation, a policy of *selective enforcement* must be followed. Under these circumstances, the traffic division has an important responsibility in safety education. It must educate not only school children but the adult public to be better drivers. Seeking to do this, the division tries to develop desirable driver attitudes and habits. (There is a well-known tendency for the motorist to use his auto as a weapon for working off aggressive and rebellious feelings and thus to act selfishly and differently

[15] See F. M. Kreml, "The Specialized Traffic Division," *The Annals of the American Academy of Political and Social Science,* vol. 291 (January, 1954), pp. 63–72; and W. S. Smith, "Widening the Traffic Enforcement Front," *The Annals of the American Academy of Political and Social Science,* vol. 291 (January, 1954), pp. 73–77.

Table 25. Reductions in Death Rate in Cities Having Specialized
Traffic Divisions†

City	Year of adoption	Death rate per 10,000 registered motor vehicles in	
		Year of adoption	1952
Atlanta................	1938	7.3	4.5
Chattanooga...........	1938	10.5	2.4
Chicago...............	1948	7.0	5.2
Cincinnati.............	1936	13.3	3.8
Cleveland.............	1937	10.2	3.8
Detroit...............	1937	6.9	3.1
Los Angeles...........	1941	8.9	4.1
Oakland..............	1939	7.5	2.4
Portland, Oreg.........	1940	6.1	2.8

† Specialization of personnel and effort is the great advantage of large-city administration. Its effectiveness in meeting one major police problem is shown in this table.

SOURCE: National Safety Council, cited in F. M. Kreml, "The Specialized Traffic
Division," *The Annals of the American Academy of Political and Social Science,* vol. 291
(January, 1954), p. 65. By permission.

from the way he does when not behind the wheel.) It cooperates with
schools, safety patrols, safety councils, radio and television stations, and
other agencies in seeking to inform the public and to get a better public
understanding of police problems.

There are three principal methods of enforcing traffic regulations, other
than through a general-education campaign: through use of the warning,
the traffic-violator school, and the citation. The warning is relatively inexpensive both as to administrative costs and as to costs in public good
will. It is very successful in controlling a very large part of the driver
population. The traffic-violator school is a product of depression days,
when few people could afford to pay traffic fines. It is the most effective
treatment, according to studies, although violators resent the time they
must spend at traffic school.[16] The citation, ordinarily followed by fine
or jail, is the traditional treatment for traffic violators, but its effectiveness
is more limited than the lay public realizes. Criminologists know that the
threat of punishment, including that of incarceration, is of limited value
as a deterrent to law violation. In the case of traffic violation, punishment
is even less effective because the public is often unsympathetic to police
efforts toward rigid enforcement. While the police can, through education, build up traffic "enforcement tolerance," it is not high in any American community.

[16] See Wilson, *Police Administration,* pp. 158–166 and 171–177.

The Vice Division.[17] Enforcement of laws dealing with the moral code is the duty of the vice division. The term *vice* includes gambling, prostitution, and the illegal use of narcotics and intoxicants. Because this task involves problems and techniques differing from those of ordinary criminal investigation, a separate division handles vice in larger cities, and even in middle-sized cities a squad or a detective or two will normally be assigned exclusively to vice control.

Contrary to what much of the public believes, the professional policeman is ready, willing, and able to suppress organized vice whenever the public demands that he do so. In the typical middle-sized or small community little or no organized vice exists. Despite this, however, and as a result of public tolerance, vice operations are active in many cities, and the need for their suppression is everywhere continuous for reasons discussed in the preceding chapter.

Although police officers, especially those in command positions, are not infrequently corrupted by organized crime, this cannot happen if the city administration is opposed to it; and it will never happen if the public desires to have the law enforced. While an element of selective enforcement of vice laws must always exist (it would be immensely expensive, for example, for the police to attempt to eliminate all private, small-stakes gambling), professional law-enforcement officers are prepared to enforce the laws, and they do not consider vice control a hopeless, uncontrollable problem as the layman often holds it to be.

The Juvenile Division. Police administrators consider the juvenile division to be in the same class as preventive medicine and fire prevention —it deals with the prevention of crime "by correcting conditions that induce criminality and by rehabilitating the delinquent."[18] In seeking to do this, the police must cooperate with schools, probation officers, social agencies, recreation departments, and public welfare agencies, but they should not attempt to duplicate or usurp the functions of those agencies.

According to O. W. Wilson, a well-rounded program should include the following activities:[19]

1. The eradication, by patrol, inspection, supervision, and investigation, of elements that induce criminal tendencies and of conditions that promote criminal activities, especially among children;

2. The discovery of delinquents, near delinquents, and those exposed to high-risk situations, and the treatment of the poorly adjusted;

[17] In the previous chapter, the term *vice squad* was used because it was found in the Kefauver reports. In this chapter, "division" is used as the principal subdivision of a department. Vice control may be invested in a division, bureau, squad, unit, or a subdivision with some other designation.

[18] See Wilson, *Police Administration*, chap. 11; and Jane E. Rinck, "Supervising the Juvenile Delinquent," *The Annals of the American Academy of Political and Social Science*, vol. 291 (January, 1954), pp. 78–86.

[19] Wilson, *Police Administration*, pp. 210–211.

3. The planning, promotion, and direction of recreation, character building, and other group activities that provide wholesome influences.

The Staff Services. Serving all of the operating divisions are the specialists in the staff divisions. A small city or village cannot afford specialists, has only a rudimentary police laboratory, and must depend on state detective bureaus and the FBI for technical assistance. Larger cities have elaborate crime laboratories under the direction of a *criminalist* trained in chemistry, biology, and related fields. The advantages of scientific crime detection have caught the public's imagination and interest. The polygraph, or lie detector, is also operated by special personnel at headquarters. The police department needs a records division providing classified, indexed, and filed records of complaints and arrests, together with property-control and identification records, the latter including fingerprint, photograph, and *modus operandi* ("M.O.") files. In large departments these cards may be sorted by electrical International Business Machines (IBM) equipment to narrow down the search for a criminal.

Recruitment. American policemen, although improving in ability, are generally considered by authorities to be of inferior quality when compared with European policemen. A part of the cause of this may be traced to our salary schedules. New York, in 1952, expected to attract adequate personnel while paying an entrance salary of $3,400. Chicago and Detroit were paying just over $4,000. Los Angeles was paying the best beginning salary, $4,260. These offers, in inflationary times, were not very attractive, especially when one considers the qualifications required of competent police officers. Furthermore, the prospects for better pay are not at all good. In 1952, New York, Chicago, or Philadelphia patrolmen could not earn more than about $4,500 even at maximum salaries unless they were promoted to higher jobs.

Large cities pay good salaries, however, in comparison with smaller places. Only one city in the 250,000 to 500,000 class paid a 1952 entrance salary of over $4,000 (Oakland), and many of them offered less than $3,250. Cities of under 100,000 typically pay less than $3,250, and many pay well under that figure.

The earliest salaried policemen in America were political appointees. Gradually appointments came to be subjected to physical, mental, and moral examinations or scrutiny. In many cities of all sizes, the recruitment and disciplining of police are under the control of the municipal personnel agency. Police administrators in general disapprove of this practice and desire independent control over personnel.[20] The method of recruitment is, of course, less important than the results.

---

[20] Police administrators, like members of other professions, desire autonomy for their function of government. Because of the unique nature of their task, they often succeed in securing independence from central municipal staff services in budgeting,

Local residence requirements are contrary to sound practice, and should be abandoned for police applicants, as they have been for teachers. A desirable candidate is one in his early twenties, who has a high-school education or better, is above average in size, is in very good health, is psychologically stable, and has an above-average intelligence quotient. Police recruits must be of unimpeachable character and should have a suitable personality as determined by psychological tests and interviews. One of the grave faults of recruiting in an earlier day was that sadists, overly aggressive persons, and other undesirables often chose to become policemen, and there was no process for weeding them out.

Promotions within the department should be made primarily on the basis of leadership ability, probably without formal examinations. No reliable written examination has yet been developed to test leadership potential. In the actual practices of many departments, promotions are often made because the officer has been an excellent patrolman, has given faithful service for many years, has a large family and needs the money, or has committed acts of heroism. Efficient leadership, however, does not result from sentimentality in the promotion process.

Training.[21] Police departments usually encourage some preservice training in the form of useful high-school and college courses, but the superintendent of the Cincinnati Police Academy believes that correspondence courses, "cram" courses to pass the entrance examinations, and college courses in police administration are of little or no value. Concerning the last of these, he believes that a person should not be prepared for a high police administrative post before he has become even a policeman.[22]

In recent years, efforts to raise the caliber of personnel has led to the establishment of police academies in most larger cities and the operation of hundreds of police institutes for smaller cities under the sponsorship of the FBI. In Los Angeles, for example, the recruit is put through a thirteen-week training course in police law and procedures, first aid, self-defense, physical conditioning, and discipline. Emotionally unstable men and others who should not have passed the entrance examinations are eliminated at this time. Patrolmen must undergo periodic retraining during their years on the force. Other training takes place constantly on the job, of course, as supervisors correct the mistakes of subordinates.

---

personnel, purchasing, and maintenance, and from traffic engineering. On police personnel, see R. A. Lothian, "The Operation of a Police Merit System," *The Annals of the American Academy of Political and Social Science*, vol. 291 (January, 1954), pp. 97–106; and Wilson, *Police Administration*, chaps. 19–20.

[21] See R. E. Clift, "Police Training," *The Annals of the American Academy of Political and Social Science*, vol. 291 (January, 1954), pp. 113–118; and Wilson, *Police Administration*, chap. 21.

[22] Clift, *op. cit.*, p. 114.

MUNICIPAL COURTS

Courts are essentially state institutions, and their operation is discussed in all courses in American or state and local government. Outside of cities, the justice of the peace has traditionally handled minor civil and criminal cases, with county, district, superior, or other trial courts of record handling the major cases. Within cities, where a large number of misdemeanors, especially by traffic violators, take place, it is common to provide so-called "municipal" courts, although major civil and criminal cases are usually handled by the regular court system. In the largest cities, however, special courts often exist for each type of case.

Magistrates' and Municipal Courts. W. V. Holloway says:[23]

In many cities there are no justice of the peace courts, but in their place are local tribunals known as "magistrates' courts," "police courts," or "recorders' courts." While frequently referred to as "city courts," they are actually a part of the state judicial system. They exercise jurisdiction similar to that of the justice of the peace courts but are limited to cases arising within the boundaries of the city. They may also hear cases involving violations of city ordinances. The judges of these courts are more frequently trained in law than their rural counterparts and are paid salaries instead of fees, but on the whole their records are little better; in many cities they are worse. The judges are elected by popular vote or are appointed by the city council or commission, and their salaries are so low that qualified men are seldom attracted, though, of course, there are exceptions. Political contact—or the lack of it—may be of more significance in the disposition of a misdemeanor case than the real innocence or guilt of the accused. The court is held in a police station or city hall, frequently in a dirty and noisy room, and the proceedings are usually informal and undignified. The decisions of the magistrates are not final, and appeals may be taken to higher courts. However, the penalties are usually small, appeals are slow, expensive, and uncertain, and in many instances no appeals are taken at all.

When there is a considerable amount of litigation and of law violation, as in some of the larger cities, including New York, Chicago, Detroit, Philadelphia, and Cleveland, unified municipal courts are maintained to hear and decide minor criminal and civil cases. These courts may also hear appeals from the magistrates' courts. They are organized on either a functional or geographical basis, and if the functional basis is used, as in Chicago, there are specialized divisions to deal with certain types of cases, such as civil cases, misdemeanors, domestic relations, traffic, and other matters. The actual organization of municipal courts varies from city to city, but usually there is a chief judge to supervise the whole system, and presiding judges, elected or appointed, are in charge of the other courts or divisions. If needed to prevent congested dockets, the judges may be transferred from one court or

[23] W. V. Holloway, *State and Local Government in the United States* (1951), pp. 264–265.

division to another. The unified courts are much superior to the justice of the peace and the magistrates' or police courts, and they have wider jurisdiction in both civil and criminal matters. Better salaries are paid, and as a rule better trained judges are secured.[24]

FIRE PROTECTION

Color, Drama—and Carelessness.[25] American cities have the finest fire equipment in the world, but they also have the greatest annual fire losses. Such losses in the United States exceed 800 million dollars annually —most of it in cities (see Figure 35). Americans are not very economy-

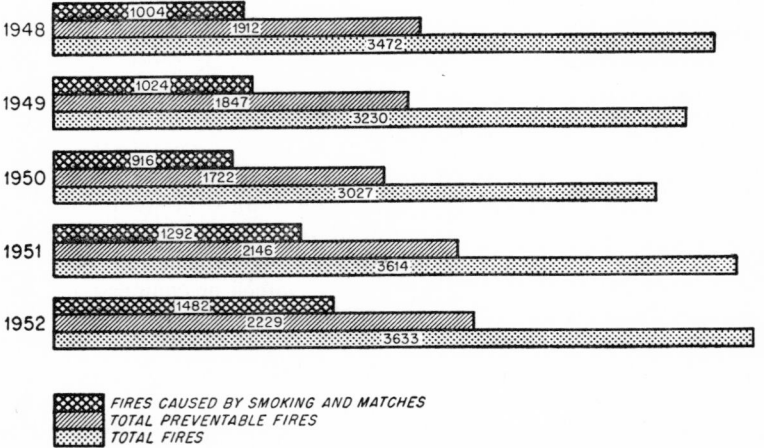

Fig. 35. American carelessness produces an annual fire loss far greater than is necessary. Results in one city. Note that in each year more than one-half of the fires were rated by the Division of Fire as preventable. Many of the others were potentially preventable. Note, too, that more than one-half of the preventable fires were caused by careless smoking and use of matches. SOURCE: *Cincinnati Yearbook* (1952).

conscious. Europeans, endowed with fewer of nature's gifts, must be conservationists. Americans, for example, are seldom prosecuted for contributory negligence in cases of fires. Losses, it is felt, are somehow "paid

[24] See also H. M. Curran, *Magistrates Courts* (1942); Raymond Moley, *Our Criminal Courts* (1930); George Warren, *Traffic Courts* (1942); Roscoe Pound, *Criminal Justice in America* (1945).

[25] A detailed manual of administration is published by the International City Managers' Association, *Municipal Fire Administration* (5th ed., 1950), from which the author has borrowed for this section. See also President's Conference on Fire Prevention, *Reports of Committees* (1947); and an urban case study by J. K. Trump, Morton Kroll, and J. R. Donoghue, *Metropolitan Los Angeles: A Study in Integration. VI. Fire Protection* (1952).

by the insurance company." Insurance rates are not associated with fire rates. (It might be noted that in nearly all American states, fire-insurance rates are determined by the quality of *fire defense equipment* in each community, with no consideration given to actual *fire-loss* experience.)

The core cities of urban areas typically have modern, professional fire departments. The larger the city, the more specialized the equipment is likely to be. Suburbs and small cities, on the other hand, often depend upon amateur departments. Some small residential communities make it a practice to hire a few full-time members who man the station and equipment, with volunteer amateurs on call to follow along at each fire alarm. Other municipalities are following the practice, quite common in the province of Quebec, of training men as both police and firemen.[26]

It is a peculiar phenomenon of American life, best left to the explanation of psychologists, perhaps, that citizens will be apathetic in responding to calls for volunteers for blood donations, civil defense, or even the manning of a charity booth at a church bazaar, but will establish waiting lists to join a volunteer fire department. In fact, volunteer companies were such powerful pressure groups in New York and Philadelphia that they were able to prevent the installation of professional systems in those cities until 1865 and 1870, respectively, even though the first paid department had been inaugurated in Boston as early as 1837. This urge to assist, or to offer "helpful" information, is useful to the city government, but is is also a nuisance at times.

Fire Prevention. Fire departments have a responsibility for preventing fires that is equal to that for fire fighting. Europeans have long placed heavy emphasis upon fire-prevention procedures, but the idea has received serious and general attention in the United States only since about the mid-1920s. In their prevention activities, fire departments depend heavily upon routine inspections performed by the men of neighborhood fire stations. They seek to correct common hazards (e.g., accumulated rubbish, dirty chimneys, defective heating equipment). Periodically, technical surveys by trained engineers are made in some cities to suggest major improvements in the use and construction of buildings.

Fire prevention also involves the granting of permits, licenses, and certificates of approval (e.g., for the design of fire escapes, the use of dry-cleaning materials, the licensing of motion-picture operators, and the installation of oil burners). It is the responsibility of the city council (and in some cases of the state legislature) to provide adequate fire-prevention codes. The department also investigates the causes of fires and seeks to give publicity to fire statistics so that the public may learn from the experiences of others. Firemen cooperate with municipal, school, and

[26] See C. S. James, "The Integration of Fire and Police Services," *Public Management,* vol. 36 (February, 1954), pp. 26–29.

private agencies in teaching school children and the adult public the principles of fire prevention.

Fire-fighting Equipment. Cities are heavy concentrations of what the professional fire fighter calls "burnable values." Fighting fires in cities crowded with people, with buildings close together and with some of them reaching many stories into the air, is a technical and complex profession. The basic equipment for all urban departments includes internal-combustion pumpers, ladder trucks, hose, and nozzles. High-pressure pumpers capable of delivering 1,000 gallons of water a minute are now available and within the budget possibilities of middle-sized cities. Mechanical aerial ladders are today used to reach the higher stories of buildings. They are expensive for the city to buy, but they are safer than old-style ladders, can be put into use more quickly, and have a low operating cost. Cities of all sizes also need chemical equipment for fighting various types of fires against which water is ineffective or dangerous to use.

Larger departments must be equipped with gas masks, asbestos suits, pulmotors, and other rescue-squad equipment. Often they use fire boats. Recent developments in equipment include the increasing use of water-fog and water-spray nozzles that were developed by the United States Navy and Coast Guard during World War II. (The fog or spray turns to steam. Expansion then pushes smoke and heat out of the building, thus greatly reducing the temperature, clearing smoke and gas from the building, and putting out the fire. The method is fast acting and results in reduced smoke and water damage.)

Fires were once commonly reported by following the instructions to "break glass, pull lever" at the nearest alarm box, but the increasingly commonplace telephone has now largely supplanted the boxes in use. About 400 cities of over 10,000 population no longer use alarm boxes. Cities as large as Little Rock and Des Moines have none.

Larger fire departments, with their decentralization of equipment, must have elaborate methods of relaying alarms to the station in the vicinity of the fire, of indicating the intensity of a fire, of sending additional equipment by a prearranged plan when the original equipment answering a call cannot cope with the problem it encounters, of keeping track of equipment that is out of the stations, and of transferring equipment to unguarded sections of the city if some area's regular equipment is out on call.

Departmental Organization. Fire-department organization in general parallels that of the police department. At least fifty cities still have a lay fire commissioner in charge, although in others the departments are headed by a professional chief chosen from the department or, in a few instances, from fire departments in other cities. Fire or safety boards still appoint the chief in quite a few cities, and in nearly 100 weak-mayor cities the council makes the appointment. Normally, however, the appointment is made by the chief executive. In all but small cities, district stations are established with a company under the command of a lieutenant or captain. In very large cities, several companies in a section of the city may be organized into a battalion or district. Because of the expense involved in their construction, it is especially important that fire stations be carefully planned in accordance with advice from the planning commission on the future uses of land and the probable movement of population.

Professional firemen work a platoon (shift) system, since stations must be manned at all hours. It was once common for them to be on duty for an eighty-four hour week. Much duty time is, of course, spent in eating, sleeping, and card playing, and many firemen take outside employment on their days off, thus there is no doubt that firemen must spend a great deal of time away from their homes and families. The average duty hours have been decreasing, especially in large cities, and since 1947 the average duty week has been seventy-two hours, with continuing pressure for further reduction.

Training. Stemming from the traditions of volunteer days, fire departments did not have trained personnel until recent decades. The result of lack of training was, of course, unnecessary property damage and unnecessary fire losses. Today large cities have facilities for training their own recruits in the use of the highly complicated equipment that is now common. About two-thirds of the states provide for state-wide training courses which are available to all cities and villages in the training of their personnel. Training programs involve not only physical conditioning, but also instruction in the use of equipment, chemicals, and explosives, in fire-fighting techniques, in ventilation, and in making fire-prevention inspections. It seems a bit surprising that, in the light of the importance of physical stamina and dexterity in fire fighting, over 85 per cent of cities of over 10,000 population have no plan for regular physical examinations of firemen.[27] Without doubt adequate training and physical conditioning are important prerequisites to any program designed to reduce America's great annual fire toll.

OTHER PUBLIC SAFETY FUNCTIONS

Weights and Measures. One of the oldest functions entrusted to local government, first in England and then in the United States, was the task of overseeing the use of devices for determining weights and meas-

[27] Percy Bugbee, "Fire Administration Developments in 1952," *Municipal Year Book, 1953*, p. 368.

ures. The job of checking for honesty and accuracy is handled in larger cities by specially trained persons and in smaller places by the police department.

Smoke Abatement. In years past, American industrial plants concentrated exclusively upon maximizing profits and increasing size. There was little interest in the side effects of factory life or in the community results of releasing smoke to irritate lungs and blacken buildings. Today factory management is much more aware of its responsibility to the rest of society. City ordinances are coming to assert more and more the fact that smoke, dirt, and noise from a factory are damaging to society and that their abatement is part of the cost of doing business.

Smoke-abatement ordinances with real enforcement provisions are coming into being. The problem has been one, not of complexity of administration, but of a willingness to enforce such ordinances. "The most important element in handling the problem," T. H. Reed has said, "is an ordinance clearly defining prohibited practices and then a courageous and personable inspector to enforce it. Even in a large city, no considerable force is necessary for this purpose."[28] Cincinnati, for example, employs about twenty persons in its bureau (see Figures 36 and 37).

Traffic Engineering. T. H. Reed has said:[29]

So far as the traffic problem is concerned with laying out new thoroughfares, widening old ones, locating traffic circles and medial strips, and placing buildings toward which traffic naturally converges, [traffic engineering] belongs to the local planning agency. Actual construction of new traffic facilities is a matter for the department of public works. The enforcement of traffic regulations and reporting of accidents are clearly part of the duty of the police department. There is much, however, which can be done by studying the movement of traffic to determine what regulations should be made for the use of existing streets and where traffic signals should be located. This is the field of traffic engineering in its narrower sense.

In the past, traffic engineering was often decentralized. There might be a traffic-safety bureau in the department of public works, another in the police department, and a traffic-study group in the planning agency. Today there is an increasing trend toward centralizing these functions in a separate agency whose main problem is to keep the principal business districts and the main traffic arteries from becoming choked with automobiles. As the number of automobiles increases, this function increases in importance.

Civil Defense. Despite the threatened use of thermonuclear weapons in the event of war, the American public, even in metropolitan areas that would appear to be prime H-bomb targets, has been almost completely

[28] T. H. Reed, *Municipal Management* (1941), p. 401.
[29] *Ibid.*, p. 405.

HOW DID YOU MANAGE TO QUIT SMOKING?

SATURDAY, DECEMBER 21, 1940.

Fig. 36. Note: St. Louis has an excellent smoke-control ordinance, but it was achieved only over powerful political opposition. Fortunately for the core city, uncooperating industrial suburbs in Illinois are downwind. SOURCE: Used by permission of Daniel R. Fitzpatrick and the *St. Louis Post-Dispatch*.

apathetic toward the development of a system of defense. The public regards the problem either as futile or as a technical one not involving popular participation at this time. Even industry has resisted Federal-government policies of deconcentration.

The Federal government has developed a civil-defense program in cooperation with state and local agencies, but many cities have done little to further planning and preparation. While others have worked at the problem, they have had great difficulty in getting volunteers to fill vital roles. An extensive study has been made of the problems and methods to be used in preparing a defense of prime metropolitan targets.[30] But state-

COMPARISON OF OBSERVED SMOKE VIOLATIONS

Fig. 37. Note: Adequate ordinances and vigorous enforcement can rid a city of smoke damage. SOURCE: *Cincinnati Yearbook* (1952).

ments made in 1954 by authorities on nuclear physics, after extensive H-bomb tests in the Pacific Ocean, added to resigned apathy by indicating that there was no real defense of these areas except by evacuation. The warning system established at that time, furthermore, was inadequate to

[30] See the ten-volume *Report of Project East River* (1953).

allow for evacuation. It would appear, then, that the best defense for American cities is the prevention of World War III. It is likely, however, that a municipal civil-defense program is of *psychological* value as a means of reminding the public of the danger and horrible destructiveness of war. Some city officials have effectively combined the program with a disaster plan, so that the city is prepared for such emergencies as floods and tornadoes.

CHAPTER 18

PUBLIC UTILITIES AND TRANSPORTATION

Public utilities provide services that are essential to urban living. Of them all, public transportation has probably offered the biggest problem to municipal administrators in all except the smallest cities in the period after World War II. In addition to public utilities, this chapter will also examine the general topic of urban transportation.

PUBLIC UTILITIES[1]

Public utilities are not necessarily *publicly* owned. Many of them are, but the majority are actually owned and operated by private corporations, and some by individual proprietors. A list of utilities within a municipality would include street railways and buses, and telephone, telegraph, electricity, water, and gas services. Other functions that are of the nature of utilities, although not always fully accepted as such, are auditoriums, port facilities, slaughterhouses, airports, and possibly toll bridges, toll roads, sewers, and public markets.

Public utilities, then, are businesses affected with a more than usual amount of public interest, which therefore require a greater than normal amount of governmental control. They are usually granted a monopoly within their areas of operation. This is because experience has shown that competition in these areas is impractical and uneconomical. Competitive utilities have existed in the past—a few still do—but generally they have proved to be wasteful of resources and have offered inferior and costly services to the public. A public utility normally has a right to use public property (over which to string electric wires, or to operate buses) and to exercise the state's power of eminent domain. It usually charges for services rendered on a benefits-received basis, and it is subject to the control of some type of public service commission whose responsibility it is to protect both the provider and the purchaser of services.

[1] Many manuals and pamphlets on applied administration of public utilities are published by the American Public Works Association, the Public Administration Service, and other professional organizations.

372

Regulation. In the nineteenth century, utilities were normally operated on the basis of a *franchise* which was granted to local utilities, most commonly, by the city government. A franchise is a license stipulating the conditions under which a utility may operate and the privileges it is to enjoy. The franchise usually stated the quality of service that was expected of the utility and the rates that could be charged. In practice, the utilities were often little inhibited by their franchises. Sometimes they resorted to bribery of public officials, sometimes they won judicial interpretations of ambiguous provisions of the franchise by the use of superior legal talent, and in almost no cases was there a public body that had the legal authority to hold the utility to the terms of its agreement.

One of the major areas of activity of reform forces at the turn of the present century was that of public utility regulation. The modern method of control that gradually evolved calls for a public service commission (bearing various titles in various states) whose duty it is to determine rates after investigations and hearings, and to supervise both the service and the management of the utilities. Most commissions prescribe uniform accounting methods, they often must approve the issuance of new securities and of expansion plans, and they may sometimes even be authorized to order such expansions. Commissions are constantly at work overseeing the activities of the utilities, but there is considerable variation in the degree to which they are effective.

Franchises are still granted, but they are no longer so detailed as they were in the days before public service commissions. They are usually limited to a term of years (perhaps twenty-five) rather than made to exist in perpetuity, as was once common. The franchise usually provides for the privileges to be enjoyed by the utility, it may provide for a special tax structure for it, and it prescribes some conditions which must be met by the utility. It leaves most other controls to the public service commissions.

In the worst of nineteenth-century corruption, control over franchises was assumed by the state, in most cases in a desperate attempt to achieve better franchises more honestly administered. Control of franchises has remained in the state for the most part.

The major questions in connection with public utilities today seem to be three. First, how are utility rates to be determined? Second, should the state or the city control utilities operating in the city? Third, should utilities be privately or publicly owned?

The Determination of Rates. The question of rate determination is one that can easily take up most of a semester in a college course in public utility regulation without a satisfactory answer being arrived at. The problem in practice has evolved around a question that is almost impossible to answer: What is the true value of a large and complex corporation? If rates are so low that the utility does not receive a fair rate of return on its investment, confiscation of private property results, and this is prohibited by the due-process clause of the Fifth Amendment. But what is the "investment" or "worth" of a utility? Is it more equitable to calculate the revenue that a rate should produce on the basis of a percentage of the present cost of replacing the capital equipment of the utility, or of the actual total investment made over the years? Should changes in the price index be considered? Should any value be placed on the franchise, "good will," or "going concern"?

In an attempt to answer these questions, public service commissions have made valuation studies; but these often take years and are inconclusive, and by the time they are completed their results are no longer applicable to existing conditions. Since due process of law is involved, utilities controversies are commonly adjudicated in the courts on appeal from the commissions. In seeking equity, the United States Supreme Court has for years struggled between the "cost of reproduction" and the "actual amount of prudent investment" theories.[2] While the most recent decision leans toward actual investment in capital without considering the problem of subsequent influences of inflation or deflation, the Court still has not settled on a definitive formula. Even with a formula, there are many questions and problems. Rate determination, despite able research staffs, is still in large part based upon folklore and subjective evaluations, and it is very costly.[3]

Should the State Control Local Utilities? Advocates of a maximum of local self-government sometimes hold that utilities should be controlled by municipal public service commissions, since they operate locally, local people are their customers, and they make use of city property. Some cities do indeed control local utilities in this fashion. The general pattern, however, is for the state to control. An exception is often made in the case of *city-owned* utilities, where quality of service and charges made are left to local authorities.

A state commission is normally in a better position to control utilities, since it has more adequate jurisdiction. A utility is seldom limited to the boundaries of one city. The "local" telephone company of the Bell system will usually cover one or more states; bus systems include some of the suburbs in their operation. Even the state does not always have enough breadth of jurisdiction, so that the Federal Power Commission must con-

---

[2] See *Smyth v. Ames,* 169 U.S. 466 (1898), the first landmark case; *Southwestern Bell Telephone Co. v. Missouri,* 262 U.S. 276 (1923); *F.P.C. v. Hope Natural Gas Co.,* 320 U.S. 591 (1944), the ruling case at present.

[3] See John Bauer, *The Public Utility Franchise; Its Functions and Terms Under State Regulation* (1946); I. E. Barnes, *The Economics of Public Utility Regulation* (1942); J. M. Bryant and R. R. Hermann, *Elements of Utility Rate Determination* (1940).

trol interstate shipment of electricity, while the Interstate Commerce Commission controls interstate telephone rates.

It is especially important that the state can afford a more adequate technical staff. Its agency can use the experience gained in a utility proceeding in one community in other proceedings throughout the state. The regulation of utilities is an enormously complicated problem of economics, law, accounting, and engineering. In general, most municipalities are helpless in seeking to compete with the skilled experts of the large utility corporations. Even the largest cities and the states can rarely match them.

Should Utilities Be Privately or Publicly Owned? In nineteenth-century America, when the businessman was paid great homage and when business subsequently attracted the lion's share of talent, utilities were commonly privately owned. This was in contrast to the practice in Europe, where, apart from any arguments concerning the merits of socialism, state and municipal ownership of utilities has always been the rule.

Americans in the past did not trust government, and, with business proving on all sides that it could "get things done," it was quite natural for Americans to expect private business to operate utilities. Nevertheless, starting in the nineteenth century it became customary for some functions to be publicly owned. Water supply, which is closely related to public health and to fire protection, was the earliest to become commonly a public function.

Most utilities are still privately owned, however, and probably most citizens regard this as preferable. This despite the fact that the reform movement around the turn of the century had included in it persons who strongly advocated the need for municipal ownership of utilities. They argued that private ownership had failed because the utilities acted irresponsibly, with little effective state control and with a policy of maximizing profits and minimizing service. They therefore argued for municipal ownership of various utilities, but especially of urban transportation.

Even up to the present day, charges made by private utilities have often been excessive, and regulation has been ineffective as a means of securing reasonable rates. Municipalities have sometimes threatened to bring private utilities into line by establishing competing services. Sometimes they have carried out this threat, expensive as it is, with ultimate improvement in public service.

Those who today advocate municipal ownership hold that such a system has many advantages. It creates a system of operation for *use* rather than for *profit*. It is pointed out that private companies often have watered stock, they fail to pass on to the consumers the economies of technological developments, and they frequently fail to pay off their indebtedness, continuing it in order to boost the rate base. But public services are not a proper area for profit-making activities. Municipalities expand their services less expensively than do private companies because they can normally borrow money at lower interest rates than can private companies. The great cost of determining net investment, which must be done each time a private company asks for a rate increase, is eliminated. Control of the utility is held entirely within the city, for state public service commissions often do not extend their control over functions that are municipally owned. The utilities magnate, with bribe—or at least campaign contribution—in hand is eliminated from local politics.

There are, however, arguments, presented with equal vigor, against municipal ownership. It is held that private utilities have cleaned their own houses since the worst days of blatant corruption and rate gouging in the 1870s and 1880s. American business has proved its ability to produce needed goods and services. A change to relatively untried public ownership and especially public *management* involves an unnecessary risk. The absence of the profit motive produces lethargy, inefficiency, and a lack of interest in technical experimentation. Policy is based on political, rather than economic, considerations. Patronage in small or large degree creeps into the system. Workers who also act as voters—especially if organized into a trade union—are able to exert undue control. They force the wage bill to disproportionate levels. Management is transitory, depending upon elections that may turn on trivial or irrelevant issues, instead of being stable.

Emotion, rather than reason or empirical study, is often the basis of argumentation on both sides. In particular, there is an insufficient amount of data available to prove or disprove many of the arguments. Most of them involve the propaganda technique of "card stacking"—the use of half-truths, or the emphasizing of favorable statistics and considerations and the de-emphasizing of the unfavorable.

No categorical argument can be made for or against municipal ownership. It has worked well in some places, poorly in others. The local environment is an important consideration. So is the relative effectiveness of the local privately owned utilities. If these are very unsatisfactory, municipal ownership may be less unsatisfactory. A city with a reputation for good government may be more confidently entrusted with the operation of a utility than a city with a reputation for corruption and ineffectiveness. There is neither intrinsic good nor evil in public ownership, nor is it part of a philosophy of socialism. In typical American fashion, the question of its desirability must be decided on the merits of the individual situation.[4]

[4] C. W. H. Bangs, *The Case for Public Ownership of Electric Utilities* (1937), and John Bauer and Peter Costello, *Public Organization of Electric Power* (1949),

The Extent of Municipal Ownership Today. Certain functions have become very commonly municipally owned today. Nearly three-fourths of the cities of over 5,000 own their own water-distribution systems. Nearly all of them own their own sewerage systems, and one-half of them own sewage-treatment plants. Municipal airports and auditoriums are quite common, and large cities often own incinerators. (See Table 26.)

Electricity is in the large majority of cases in private hands, although many cities own plants and lines for distributing power to street lights and traffic signals. In some parts of the nation, especially in relatively isolated cities, municipal systems exist—over 500 of them. Of America's eighteen largest cities (those over half a million), only Cleveland and Los Angeles have city-owned electrical generating and distributing systems for general use. Municipal gas plants are very rare. Of these largest cities, only Philadelphia and Houston produce and distribute gas.

The street railway is fast disappearing in America, and only nine municipal systems remain, most of them in the largest cities. Fort Collins, Colorado (1950 population: 14,937), is the smallest city with a publicly owned system. Twenty-three cities of under 25,000 own bus systems, however, and there are thirty-eight municipal systems in the nation, in addition to the Boston transit, which is controlled by a separate unit of government.

All of the largest cities own some utilities, except for Boston, which has them operated on a regional basis by the Massachusetts Metropolitan District Commission. One city in eight, however, owns no utilities of any kind, and private ownership is the overwhelming rule even today for most functions.

The question of whether municipal ownership becomes more or less popular in the future will turn primarily upon the relative improvements made by private companies on the one hand and municipal administration on the other. Thus there is the question of the future success or failure of public regulation of privately owned utilities, and of whether privately owned utilities will be able to provide the level of service required at acceptable rates. And there is also the question of the future success or failure of cities to achieve effective *administration* of utilities, removing them from spoilsmanship, giving them long-range policy planning, and securing able administrators. Many have argued that, in order to achieve these things, utilities should be operated by independent or semi-independent authorities so that they are not a regular part of the city government. This plan suffers from the defects, discussed previously,

seem to show that in this field public ownership offers slightly lower rates. For elaborate statistical data, see Burns and McDonnell Engineering Co., *Results of Publicly Owned Electric Systems* (9th ed., 1948).

Table 26. Ownership and Operation of Utilities in Cities over 5,000 Population

Type of utility	Number of cities	Per cent of cities	Over 500,000	250,000– 500,000	100,000– 250,000	50,000– 100,000	25,000– 50,000	10,000– 25,000	5,000– 10,000
Auditorium..........................	406	16.6%	8	17	21	34	43	136	147
Bus or trolley bus system...............	38	1.6	4	1	1	4	5	16	7
Elec. generation & distribution...........	290	11.9	2	3	6	12	30	84	153
Elec. distribution only..................	212	8.7	0	1	3	3	15	70	120
Gas. mfg. & distrib....................	42	1.7	2	3	3	2	5	19	8
Gas distribution only...................	66	2.7	0	1	1	2	6	20	36
Incinerator...........................	421	17.2	14	10	38	49	77	129	104
Port facilities........................	78	3.2	10	8	11	4	16	18	11
Street railway........................	9	0.4	5	1	1	0	1	1	0
Sewage-treatment plant................	1,203	49.3	12	16	35	51	135	416	538
Slaughterhouse........................	26	1.1	0	0	4	2	1	10	9
Water supply and distribution...........	1,648	67.5	16	20	54	90	177	521	770
Water distribution only.................	151	6.2	0	0	3	10	20	56	62
Airport...............................	510	20.9	12	17	46	48	74	157	156
Cities having none of above.............	300	12.3	1	0	1	7	23	104	164
Total number of cities reporting*.........	2,441	96.6	17	23	65	129	276	815	1,116

* Of the 2,528 cities of over 5,000, eighty-seven (3.4 per cent) did not report and are not included in the table.
SOURCE: *Municipal Year Book, 1953*, p. 67.

of the special-purpose district.[5] No pat answer has been devised for the question of the proper organization of municipally owned utilities.

MUNICIPAL SERVICES AND UTILITIES

Books have been written about each of the services performed by the modern city. They are available to the student who desires to make a detailed study of the various municipal services. This and following chapters treat municipal functions not from the point of view of the technician, but rather from that of the citizen or the layman who needs a basic understanding but not a technical account of them.

Highways. All cities must cope with the problem of street paving, cleaning, and lighting, and sidewalk installation. While basic engineering and financing practices have come to be applied to these functions, more perplexing problems have arisen in recent years in connection with the building of high-speed, limited-access expressways and with the finding of off-street parking.

It has become generally accepted, for example, that street width should be measured in terms of automobile lanes, 10 feet to a lane. The actual width of a particular street and its sidewalk is determined on the basis of traffic studies and surveys. The type of surfacing material is today determined largely upon the basis of technical studies known to qualified engineers. The abutting property owners were once permitted to choose the material, but this method is so obviously unsatisfactory and unscientific that it has been abandoned nearly everywhere. Engineers know the relative merits of concrete, asphaltic concrete, asphalt, macadam, stone blocks, wood blocks, and bricks. They know, for example, that concrete is fine for suburban residential streets and that asphalt is better for most thoroughfares, but that the warehouse district needs something like stone blocks.[6] They, not the property owners, are in a position to choose the best material.

Sidewalks are usually installed shortly after an area is subdivided for development. The principal question of public policy in connection with their construction and maintenance is that of financing. In former days, the property owner constructed the sidewalk, which was then inspected by the municipality to ensure its meeting specifications. A crumbling sidewalk could be condemned by inspectors who would order the owner to replace it, if necessary. This practice is still quite common, although it would seem that a better quality of concrete and a more uniform and

---

[5] See above, pp. 247–248.
[6] The national government furnishes specifications for many technical functions of the municipality. The Public Roads Administration of the Department of Commerce does this for streets. See *Highway Practice in the U.S.A.* (1949).

satisfactory job could be had if the city did the job itself, either from general taxes or by special assessment.[7]

Mighty Rome had no street lighting and neither did any city of Western civilization until the eighteenth century. Occasional delegations of housewives waiting upon the mayor in his office today sometimes suggest that things have not changed much even after twenty centuries. Although technical specifications as to the proper height, spacing, intensity, and maintenance of street lighting exist, most city streets are inadequately lighted.[8]

Expressways. In large cities, the principal postwar problem and political issue has been in connection with the construction of modern highways within the city. What route should they follow? How often should there be an entrance-and-exit interchange? Expressways are enormously expensive. The Hollywood Freeway in Los Angeles cost about 5 million dollars per mile. The John Lodge and Edsel Ford Expressways in Detroit cost almost 8.5 million dollars per mile. How should they be paid for? Would a toll road be feasible? Should they be paid for out of a rebate to the city from the state gasoline tax? Out of the general revenue fund? Out of a local tax on each automobile? Expressways damage property values along their routes but enhance the values of property at either end of them. One of their main purposes is to shore up sagging property values in the downtown area and to keep up the dollar volume of business in downtown stores. If these establishments benefit particularly from the highways, should they be asked to pay an extra tax to compensate for this advantage?

Congress anticipated a postwar need for road building after a backlog of several years had built up during the war. It also recognized that additional autos would soon be on the road and therefore provided in the Federal Aid Highway Act of 1944 that one-fourth of such Federal funds should be used for the extension of U.S. highways within cities. As a result, many cities are now building such roads with one-half of the cost being paid out of Federal grants-in-aid. Because this is the case, many questions of routing and technical specifications are settled, not by local political considerations, but by the Public Roads Administration. This agency must approve the route and all technical details before the Federal funds are made available. In most cases the cost of building is so great that without these funds there could be no expressway.

Many states are granting aid money to cities for building these high-speed, limited-access highways, and they have helped in other ways, too.

[7] Street construction and maintenance, sidewalks, lighting, and cleaning are covered in the International City Managers' Association, *Municipal Public Works Administration* (4th ed., 1950).

[8] See American Public Works Association, *Public Lighting Practice* (1945).

Michigan, for example, has allowed its cities to issue bonds in anticipation of their future receipts of state-collected, locally shared gasoline taxes.[9]

The use of Federal and state grants and the use of revenue from gasoline taxes have been the most popular methods of financing highways. Asking the downtown property owner to contribute a larger share has been suggested by some labor-backed candidates for municipal office, but this has not proved popular with the owners or the public. In several cities the county has paid part of the cost.

All large cities developed postwar plans for expressways. Los Angeles has an elaborate plan (see Figure 38) that will eventually provide 150 miles of such roads. Expressways under construction in 1953 in Chicago will total 67 miles, in Pittsburgh 28, and in Detroit 23. Toll roads within cities have generally been rejected as impractical, although the Denver-Boulder Turnpike is used by many commuters, as is the prewar Merritt Parkway in Connecticut.

Where Shall I Park? Some 20,700 miles of new highways were built in 1950, which seemed impressive—until someone calculated that that could just about provide for the parking spaces needed to accommodate the 6 million autos built in that year.[10] The postwar development of the expressway has made it easier to get downtown, but it has not solved the problem of what to do with the auto once one leaves the expressway. In fact, this problem is becoming greater rather than less each year. Nothing like enough parking space exists in downtown areas. Land is too valuable and wrecking operations are too expensive to clear away existing buildings for parking. Multistory parking garages are very expensive, too. It has been estimated that one-third of the buildings in downtown Boston would have to be torn down to provide adequate parking space for the patrons of the remaining structures. The larger the city, the smaller the proportion of residents using their cars to get downtown. But despite this, the larger the city, the more difficult it is to find adequate parking.[11]

Beginning with its use in Oklahoma City in 1935, the parking meter has become an almost universal phenomenon along commercial streets in American cities. The meters are, in effect, yet another tax upon the motorist. They serve as a good source of revenue for cities. This income is used for street maintenance and traffic control in some cities and to construct off-street parking facilities in others. The meters themselves do not solve the parking problem, except perhaps to speed up the shopper

[9] Norman Hebden and W. S. Smith, *State-City Relationships in Highway Affairs* (1950).

[10] *National Municipal Review*, vol. 42 (March, 1953), p. 151.

[11] J. D. Carroll, Jr., "The Future of the Central Business District," *Public Management,* vol. 35 (July, 1953), pp. 150–153.

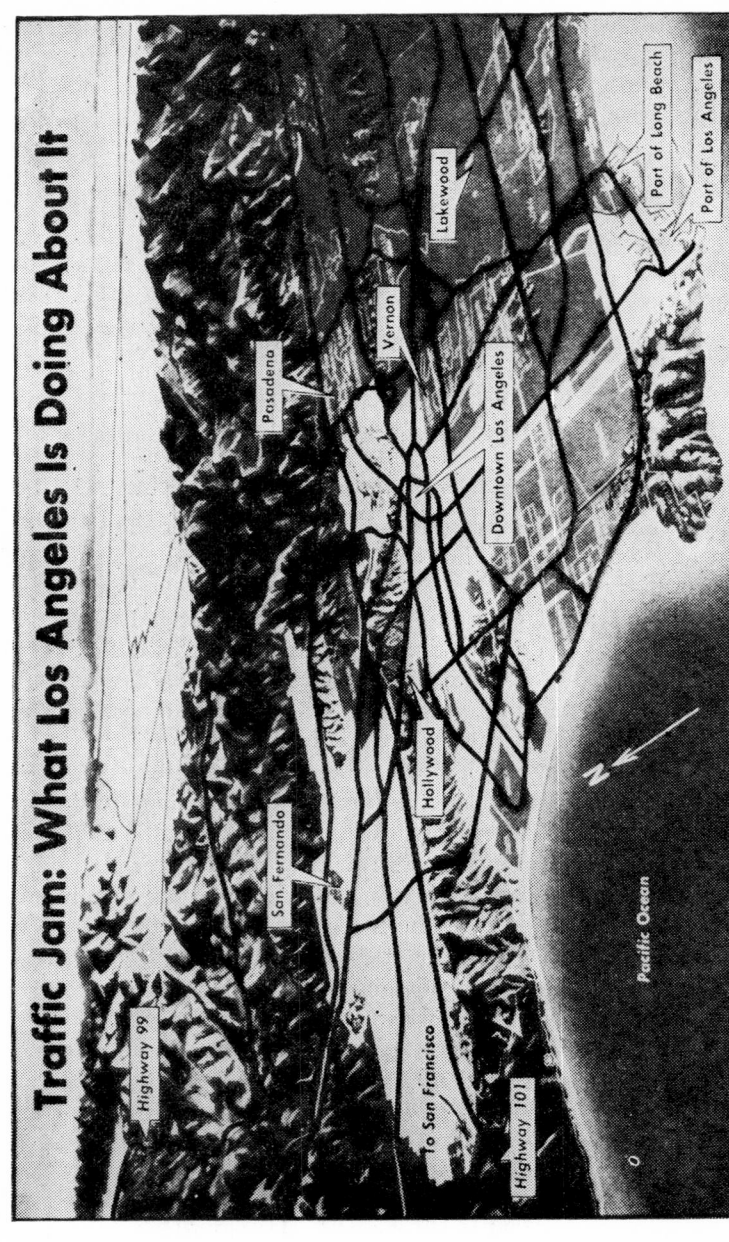

Fig. 38. Network of expressways (projected and completed) to keep millions of Angelinos moving long distances fast. SOURCE: *Newsweek* (Aug. 3, 1953), p. 66. Used by permission.

and other parker and to discourage all-day parking along downtown streets (see Figure 39).

Adequate parking space is, economically speaking, a responsibility of the firm for whom the driver works or the store to which the driver-shopper is headed. Because the business districts were built before the automobile was developed, such provisions have not been made. Most cities now attempt to require all new commercial places to furnish adequate parking spaces off the street. There is no justification for any other policy, either in the core city or in the suburbs, yet the practice is not universal.

PARKING METER RECEIPTS—MORE PARKING METERS MEAN MORE PEOPLE USING AVAILABLE PARKING SPACE

= $10,000.00

Fig. 39. SOURCE: *Cincinnati Yearbook* (1952).

A problem in many cities in procuring sufficient parking lots from private sources is found in the fact that the business is monopolized in the hands of one or a few large lot owners possessing considerable political power. There are several parking-lot corporations organized on a nationwide basis, each operating lots in numerous cities.

Cities are trying to keep up with the great increase in the population both of people and of autos. Buffalo offers a tax exemption on buildings used for off-street parking if they house at least 150 autos and are basically parking facilities. To hurry conversion of buildings, a time limit in order to qualify has been set. Milwaukee charges persons who park all night on the streets and uses the money to pay for off-street parking lots. Baltimore makes long-term loans from a 5-million-dollar fund for use in constructing parking garages by private operators. There is no tax exemption.

The Municipal Parking Authority in Detroit acquires land by condemnation, issues revenue bonds, and constructs garages. The finished structures are then leased to private operators who run them at cost plus a fee. Other profits go to the Authority. Low interest rates on bonds are secured by pledging garage revenues plus parking-meter profits.

Municipal Parking Lots. In 1952 almost one-half (46 per cent) of the cities over 10,000 had one or more publicly owned municipal parking lots. Los Angeles had the largest number of such parking spaces at that time, but many cities are following the trend in this direction. In the same year Chicago announced plans for a 50-million-dollar development, and other large cities also entered the field.

Financing has been principally through general taxes or often through general-obligation bonds. Revenue bonds are also issued, and parking-meter receipts are often used as a partial method of financing. Four cities have used special assessments against the benefiting property owners. This is sound practice, but it often encounters legal and political obstacles. Lots are usually administered by either the police or the public works departments. Over one-half of them in 1952 provided free parking, and in those where a charge was made, it was through the use of meters in the overwhelming majority of cases.[12] It seems likely that the municipal parking lot, together with such elaborate devices as underground parking garages, will become increasingly common as municipal authorities fight to keep the streets clear and free for traffic.[13]

Airports: Public Subsidy for Transportation. American governments have traditionally subsidized methods of transportation, especially when they are new. We have subsidized facilities for canalboats, railways, automobiles and trucks, ocean transportation, and, after World War I, air travel. Beginning in the 1920s, cities were authorized to construct, and usually to operate, municipal airports. Today almost all of the nation's largest cities have city-owned airports. In some cases this is a county function and there are several *ad hoc* airport authorities to cover the metropolitan areas, while in other cities the airports are leased to private operators. But in most places the city owns and operates the facilities.

So optimistic have people been about the future of air travel that municipal airports are common even in cities of under 10,000 population. The Federal Aid Airport Act of 1946 undoubtedly encouraged many cities that did not need, and for a long time will not need, airports to construct them with the help of matching Federal funds. The act made no allowance for aid in operation and maintenance, however, and these costs have proved to be a great burden for many municipalities.

---

[12] See the current issue of the *Municipal Year Book* for data.

[13] See Ben Solomon, *Parking—A 1951 Guidepost to Municipal Action;* and D. Grant Mickle, "What to Do about Parking," *Public Management,* vol. 34 (September, 1952), pp. 198–200.

In the first years after World War II, there were many rosy dreams in the thoughts of air-transport promoters, private flyers, returning armed forces pilots anxious to retain their newly learned skill, and the general public concerning the future of aviation. Some authorities believed that the number of airplanes would increase by 30 per cent a year in the ten years following the war—or by more than thirteen times the 1945 figure of 30,000 planes.[14] Airports were built and expanded. Helicopters were to carry people from far-outlying airports into the heart of the city. Airplanes that "anyone can fly" were soon to be on the market. Many cities over-expanded their facilities.

Air transportation is important, but it has not as yet supplanted the auto or train. There are many problems to be solved in airport facilities. Almost everyone in an urban area wants an airport, but no one wants it near his own home because of the noise, dirt, traffic, and threat of an accident. So airports are constructed many miles from the heart of the city, yet the time-saving helicopter has not come into use because it is too expensive a device to serve as a shuttle bus. Many cities find themselves maintaining airports which are used to far less than capacity, some of them being hardly used at all. Almost no cities have broken even, much less shown a profit, on their airports, yet in some cases they are subsidizing airlines that are making comfortable profits on over-all business.

It is doubtful if airport ownership and management should have been made a municipal function to the extent that it has been. At any rate, state subsidies to cities performing this function seem to be in order. Certainly the Federal government, which regards airports as a part of the national defense pattern, should bear a considerable share of the loss that airports show annually. Such aid is now forthcoming for construction and improvements; it should probably also be available for maintenance. The Federal government, if it chooses to promote the construction of new airport facilities, should do so under a more selective formula than the one used in the 1946 act. The decision as to whether a new airport is needed can be made much more realistically by the Civil Aeronautics Authority and the Department of Defense after comprehensive surveys of nationwide traffic patterns than by local city councils or local air interests. Congress certainly should remember this in devising future aid programs.

Airport Management. Municipal airports are administered in a variety of ways. They may be under the control of departments of public works, parks (because early airport management consisted largely of grass cutting), utilities, public service, or finance. Others are directly under city airport commissions enjoying semiautonomous status.

[14] See, for example, T. P. Wright, "The National Airport Program," in *City Problems of 1945–1946*, pp. 83–94.

The airport manager, in cities with modern forms of government, is appointed by the chief executive, or by the department head if the airport is a division of a larger department. The principal qualification for an airport manager is not that he be a pilot (although that is not undesirable), but that he have administrative and business ability. He must have high courage, too, for his airport is not unlikely to show a deficit despite his best administrative efforts.[15]

Water and Sanitation. The major issues in water and sanitation facing urbanites today deal with the procurement of water in sufficient quantities and the financing of adequate sewage-disposal systems.

Water Supply. Many small municipalities receive their water supply from wells. This is a relatively inexpensive method for small cities and villages, although the water is often very hard and, until one becomes accustomed to it, unpalatable. As core-city suburbs increase in size, their wells tend to become dry, for the table level of the ground water drops. It has been predicted, for example, that all of the thirty-odd suburbs of Chicago using wells in 1953 will eventually be forced to abandon them and obtain water from the core city.[16]

Few of the larger cities use wells. Memphis uses them. Brooklyn once did, but for many years citizens objected that the water was salty and brackish. This led to an abandonment of the privately owned wells in 1947 and the use throughout New York City of water from the Catskill reservoirs. In large cities, however, many wells have been sunk by business firms for air-conditioning purposes. In many cities the table level is sinking rapidly as a result, and it is now clear that strict regulation of these practices has become necessary. It is probable, for example, that the city should require all water withdrawn from the ground for air-conditioning purposes to be returned to the ground. New York has had such a law since 1933. Business firms are not likely to do this voluntarily, since it adds to the expense of the system.

Most large cities depend for their water supply upon rivers or the damming of small streams, or they make use of lakes. The problem of securing a supply of relatively unpolluted water becomes increasingly difficult as urban populations grow and the amount of industrial and human waste dumped into streams increases. Cities along the Great Lakes have been able to get palatable, germ-free water with a minimum of treatment. Some cities, such as Philadelphia, which uses the Delaware River, must use a great amount of filtration and chemical treatment, for their sources are badly polluted.

Cities along the ocean, such as New York and Los Angeles, have not

[15] For airport developments immediately after World War II, see the *Municipal Year Book, 1948*, pp. 309–323; and for airport administration, International City Managers' Association, *op. cit.*

[16] Illinois Legislative Council, *Chicago Sanitary District* (1953), p. 28.

been able to convert sea water inexpensively and have had to bring their supplies hundreds of miles from the mountains. The 82d Congress authorized the Secretary of the Interior to cooperate with state and local governments in an effort to devise a process for making use of salt and brackish water for home and factory consumption.[17] Some growing inland cities, such as Denver, are faced with acute water problems in the near future.

A political issue in the area of water supply in the postwar period has centered in the fluoridation of water in an effort to reduce dental caries. For reasons that are not evident, fluoridation has been opposed by very conservative, and particularly isolationist, groups as being "un-American."[18] Others have questioned whether its beneficial results have been adequately demonstrated and the dangers of harmful side effects disproved. The American Dental Association favors the adding of fluorides, and in 1954 over 800 water systems were adding small amounts of it.[19]

Sanitation. Boston, in 1823, was the first American city to install a system of sanitary sewers. Other cities followed as their populations increased. In those early days, the sewage was commonly dumped into a nearby stream or other body of water. This was in itself a scientific method of disposal. Contrary to a popular impression that the downriver town drank the raw sewage of the one above it, the chemical reaction of the oxygen in the water with the sewage would convert the organic matter into nitrates and other non-disease-bearing by-products. If a sufficient supply of water was available and cities were not too close together, this approach was reasonably safe.

Today, as a public health precaution, sewage must be treated before disposal. There are several methods of treatment, and they are all normally expensive. Because cities, and often their suburbs, may try to avoid this expense, several states have established water-pollution commissions. These commissions may, if they find that a municipality is endangering the public health or the fish and wildlife of the state, order a municipality to construct a sewage-treatment plant. Unfortunately, some municipalities have been so irresponsible that the state has sometimes had to resort to its coercive power and force them into safety precautions.

Sewage-treatment plants, like those for water treatment, are least expensive if used to full capacity and if one rather than a series of them

[17] R. D. Bugher, "Public Works Developments in 1952," *Municipal Year Book, 1953*, p. 345. See C. B. Ellis, *Fresh Water from the Ocean* (1953).

[18] See James M. Burns, "The Crazy Politics of Fluorine," *New Republic*, vol. 128 (July 13, 1953), pp. 14–15.

[19] A worthwhile case study on water is Vincent Ostrom, *Water and Politics: A Study of Water Policies and Administration in the Development of Los Angeles* (1953).

exists in a metropolitan area. A major postwar issue has been in connection with meeting the treatment problem adequately.

Municipal sanitation also involves the disposal of ashes, rubbish, and garbage. These may be collected separately or in various combinations, depending upon the method of disposal. Ashes are becoming less of a municipal task. Industries normally dispose of their own, while each year fewer homes are heated by coal (see Figure 40). Ashes, together with street dirt, make good fill for low places and are commonly disposed of in this fashion. Sometimes they are simply dumped.

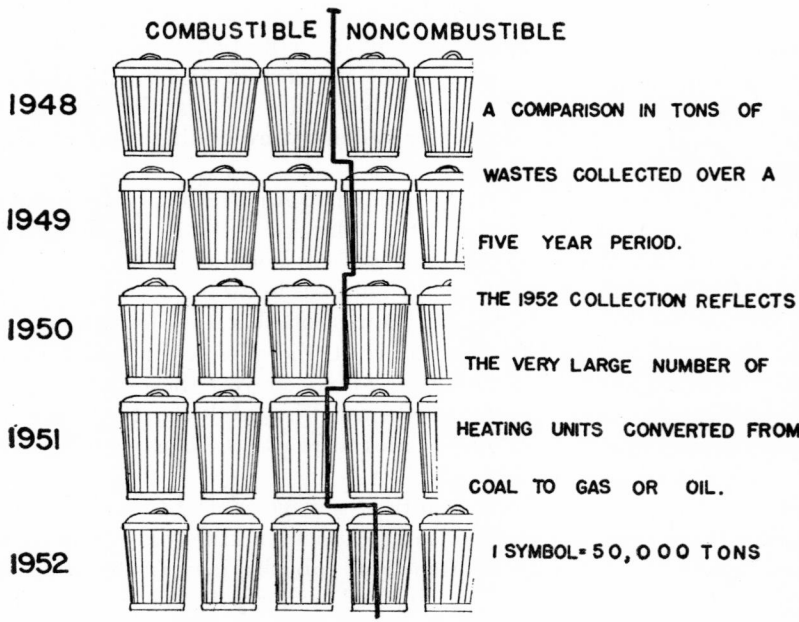

Fig. 40. SOURCE: *Cincinnati Yearbook* (1952).

Rubbish (nonorganic trash and discards) is also used for fill, or it may be dumped. Sometimes it is incinerated. Garbage (organic waste) may be disposed of by incineration, use of the reduction process, the sanitary fill, feeding to hogs, dumping, grinding at central locations, or grinding in the home. Incineration is expensive, but very effective. It is used particularly in larger cities and is becoming increasingly popular. The expensive reduction process, which is used to recover waste fats, has been tried in large cities but is passing from favor. The sanitary-fill method is used quite extensively, especially in small or medium-sized cities.

Feeding to hogs has been popular, since a part of the cost of collection and disposal can thereby be recouped. It is believed, however, that the feeding of raw garbage may be a method of transmitting vesicular exanthema among hogs and cholera and trichinosis to human beings. As a result, at least one-fourth of the states now require precooking of the garbage. This additional cost is causing municipalities to switch to other disposal methods, especially to incineration.

Garbage is sometimes dumped, either into a pit to be buried, or into a body of water. This is usually a temporary measure, although some small places use it as a regular disposal method.

Grinding of garbage has the effect of converting it into sewage. This is a method of robbing Peter to pay Paul, for in solving the garbage problem, it adds to the sewage problem. Grinding at central locations is quite common and works satisfactorily if an adequate sewage-disposal plant exists. The home garbage grinder has become extremely popular in the postwar period. In 1953 these units were being installed at a rate of 10,000 a month in the Los Angeles area, and new homes throughout the nation are frequently built to include them. In some places they are causing problems by overtaxing the sewerage system or the disposal plant. The increased amount of organic matter that is thereby dumped into bodies of water may constitute a threat to fish and wildlife by removing oxygen from the water to a dangerous extent.[20] But the grinders symbolize, to the housewife, another step in America's material progress.

Municipalities do not necessarily collect and dispose of ashes, rubbish, or garbage themselves. In some places the job is done by a collector holding a contract from the city. In others the city licenses several collectors. A great many cities do the job themselves, however, through a department of public works. The sewerage system is almost always operated by the city itself, but an important question to be settled in connection with this activity is whether storm drains should be connected to the regular sewers or constructed separately. The present trend is toward the latter method.

Public Transportation. Public transportation systems within cities are becoming white elephants at an alarming rate. The development contains some elements of serious maladjustment, for while *most* people have automobiles and could get along entirely without public transportation if necessary, it still remains an absolutely vital utility to an important minority.

Virtually all transit systems in the United States were losing money in the 1950s. This was true of those privately owned as well as those publicly owned. No large-city system was earning the current rate on its investment. There were several reasons for the failure of these utilities to be able to pay their costs. First of all, of course, is the switch to auto transportation. There were 28 million autos in 1946 and over 44 million

---

[20] See the comments of William Vogt, *Road to Survival* (1948), pp. 34–35.

in 1953. Largely because of this, the number of passengers carried by transit systems fell from 23 billion to 15 billion in the same space of time[21] (see Table 27).

Table 27. Trends in Public Transit, Selected Cities†

City	Revenue passengers % decrease 1946–1951	% decrease vehicle miles operated 1946–1951	Cash Fares			% increase auto use of streets
			1946	1951	% increase	
Baltimore....	31	12	10¢	15¢	50	
Chicago......	28	4	8	17	112	72
Cleveland....	27	4 (increase)	10	15	50	40
Dallas.......	31	5 (increase)	8	15	87	77
Denver......	22	..	10	12	20	114
Des Moines..	43	12	10	15	50	67
Detroit......	43	38‡	10	15	50	61
Knoxville....	38	16	10	10	...	48
Los Angeles..	27	12	10	10	...	52
New York....	24	7	5	10	100	68
Oakland.....	39	24	10	11	10	
Rochester....	45	15	10	12	20	40
Toledo.......	18	12	10	13	30	51
Wilmington..	36	6	8	10	25	88

† Most fares have been increased since these data were gathered. For example, New York subway fares in 1954 were 15 cents, a 200 per cent increase over 1946. In 1954, Detroit fares were 20 cents, a 100 per cent increase in the same period.

‡ Detroit decrease was due in part to a two months' strike in 1951.

SOURCE: Adapted from *Municipal Year Book, 1953*, p. 353.

Further factors in reducing the load of transit systems include the suburban movement and television. Suburbanites, too far out to go to work or to shop downtown by public transportation, use commuter trains, or more likely, the auto. The lessening density of population of the core city spells trouble for transit lines. Television has a tendency to reduce entertainment travel, which does further damage. Entertainment travel is important to transit systems which are constantly confronted with the problem of the waste involved when equipment needed for peak-load hours lies idle in the evening.

As long ago as 1940, the number of persons entering the Chicago central business district daily by elevated train, streetcar, or bus amounted to only 47.8 per cent of the total number.[22] In 1916, 82.8 per cent of persons entering the St. Louis central business district each day came by

[21] *Wall Street Journal*, July 20, 1953 (Chicago ed.).
[22] G. W. Breese, *The Daytime Population of the Central Business District of Chicago* (1949), pp. 106–109.

streetcar. By 1946, only 46.9 per cent came by streetcar and bus. Almost an equal number came by private automobile (see Table 28). And there

Table 28. Persons Entering St. Louis Central Business District, 7 A.M. to 7 P.M. Daily, 1916 to 1946, in Thousands

Year	Total	Means of Transportation Used			
		Private automobile	Streetcar	Bus	Miscellaneous*
1916	180	31	149		
1926	275	71	158	18	28
1937	310	140	84	37	49
1941	335	150	90	45	50
1946	375	160	110	65	40

* Includes trains and service cars, but not pedestrians.

SOURCE: St. Louis City Plan Commission, *Comprehensive City Plan* (1947), p. 59.

has been a very sharp decline in public transportation patronage since that time (see Figure 41).

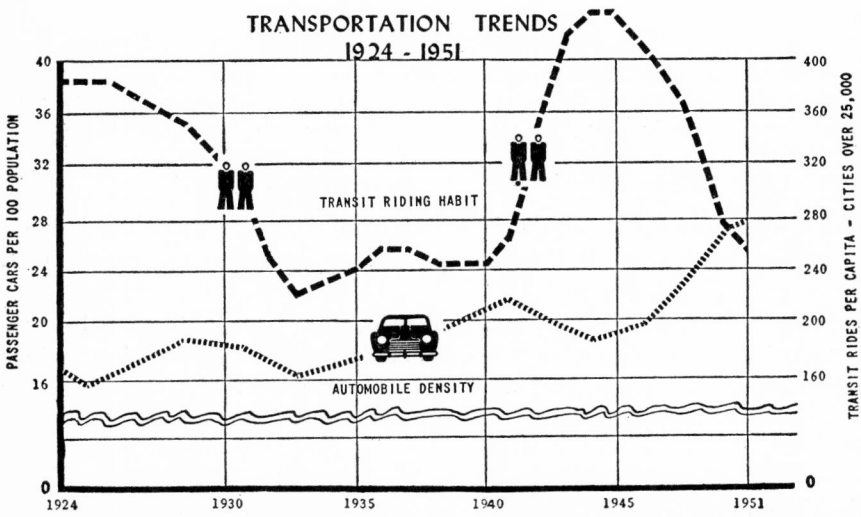

Fig. 41. SOURCE: H. S. Simpson, "Mass Transit Can Be Saved," *Public Management,* vol. 35 (April, 1953), p. 79. Used by permission.

The abnormal circumstances of World War II helped stave off the inevitable for a few years for many systems, but the shift from the six-day to the five-day work week since 1945 has reduced the number of riders considerably. In addition to the decreasing number of riders, postwar inflation brought increasing costs of operation and maintenance. This forced fare increases, which in turn encouraged switching to auto transportation. The transit managers were then forced to reduce service or ask for another fare increase or both. Furthermore, the greater number of autos on the streets made it increasingly difficult to maintain schedules that were fast enough to satisfy the public. All of this added to the snow-balling effect toward fewer passengers and greater deficits.[23] The problem was not helped by the rise of the bus as a replacement for the streetcar. The bus takes up less room on the street, interferes less with traffic, and costs less to buy and maintain, but it is uncomfortable, vexatiously slow, and, if diesel fuel is used, a source of unpleasant odors.

The Solution. In an attempt to solve the increasing financial difficulties of transit systems, various desperate measures have been recommended. There are some who urge that subways, monorails, or elevated-train systems be built, but it is unlikely that any but a few cities could, at this time, meet operating expenses out of fares from these, much less pay off any of the original capital investment.

Some laymen have urged that all would be well if cities would sell their systems to private companies, as if that were a panacea. Clearly, it is not, for Chicago had to take over its transportation system in 1947 after the private company had gone bankrupt and the system had been administered for years under the eye of a federal judge. The Boston system lost money first under private and then under public management.

Other laymen, as well as some professional students of public administration, have said that the transit systems should be "taken out of politics," an old American antidote. Governor Thomas E. Dewey caused the New York transit system to be separated from the city government in 1953, and it was set up under an authority partly appointed by the governor. The plan produced numerous cries of interference with local self-government.

Some have urged that people stop using their own autos and be persuaded to ride the public transit. This could be done by applying various pressures, such as a special tax on downtown parkers.[24] Few municipal or private managements, however, have made genuine appeals with meaningful promises behind them. As a result, urgings have fallen on deaf ears. For all except those who have no choice in the matter, public transportation is too slow and the fare is too high. Besides, the problem is social as

[23] John Bauer, "Municipal Utilities Developments in 1952," *Municipal Year Book, 1953*, pp. 352–357. The experience of the city where the population is most dependent upon public transportation is related in Mayor's Committee on Management Survey, *Modern Management for the City of New York* (1953), vol. 1, chap. 6.

[24] H. S. Simpson, "Mass Transit Can Be Saved," *Public Management*, vol. 35 (April, 1953), pp. 77–81; John Bauer, "The Crisis in Urban Transit," *ibid.*, vol. 34 (August, 1952), pp. 176–178; and John Bauer and Peter Costello, *Transit Modernization and Street Traffic Control* (1950).

well as economic, and for that reason the solution is not easy. One authority on the subject has explained the shift as follows:[25]

. . . devolution of transit traffic and earning power has doubtless been due in part to gradual shifts in community life. But it has been due chiefly to everyone's desire to own an automobile and to have the satisfaction of driving to and from work in his own or jointly in his neighbor's car. This is not only a matter of assumed riding convenience and advantage, but perhaps principally one of inferred prestige.

The expressway, the off-street parking lot and garage, and the prestige factor seem to assure us that transit systems cannot hope to recapture much of their lost ridership. Should cities abandon public transportation as a thing of the past? This would work a great hardship upon enough people to be an unthinkable solution at this time. Furthermore, there are almost no cities that could handle either the street traffic or the parking problem if everyone were to ride by auto.

It seems likely that privately owned companies will have to be taken over by the cities in the future—perhaps as bankrupts. Municipally owned systems are faced with the need for subsidies in order to make up the difference between earnings and costs. Most such systems already enjoy some subsidies. Very often, for example, they need not pay property taxes. Sometimes the department of public works maintains the space between the tracks in the few remaining street railway systems, although private companies normally pay this cost themselves.

But is a subsidy equitable? If the loss is made up from the general-revenue fund, it means that the taxpayer is subsidizing the bus rider. If municipally owned transit systems are exempted from the property tax, the same result is obtained. Is this logical? Property-tax payers, for the most part, are not wealthy people.

Is a transit system a convenience to business? If it is, should some of the deficit be paid by a special tax on business? This plan is being tried in New York. The New York system receives a total subsidy equal to about 40 per cent of its expenses. This comes from business and real estate taxes.

It would seem desirable that if a subsidy is necessary—and this seems to be the case—a broader tax base, and perhaps one more diversified than the present one, should be used. In any case, it seems unlikely that many transit systems will be able to break even in the future, given any type of ownership, management, or equipment.

[25] Bauer, "Municipal Utilities Developments in 1952," p. 355.

THE ADMINISTRATION OF PUBLIC WORKS

Whenever a city is large enough to be organized on a departmental basis, it will have a department of public works operating under one title or another. The department usually includes many utility and other service functions—for example, divisions in charge of street maintenance, cleaning, and lighting, of bridges, of sewers and sewage disposal, of refuse collection and disposal, and of public property. Traffic engineering is frequently in the department of public works, as are municipally owned utilities, such as electricity, gas supply, public markets, and slaughterhouses, although any of these may be established as independent departments. Public transportation, airports, and water supply are in the great majority of cases, but not always, organized as separate departments.

The Department Head. The general view of authorities on municipal management holds that the public works department should be organized with a single department head responsible to the chief executive. The once-common autonomous board was unsuccessful and has generally been abandoned. This is not true, however, in the case of public transportation and water supply, where the board is still often found, even in strong-mayor and manager cities.

The director of public works (often called the city engineer, especially in smaller cities) is normally an engineer of one kind or another. In small cities, it is most important that the director possess technical qualities. In large cities, administrative ability is imperative, while engineering ability is less important and may not be necessary at all. In smaller cities, the director must supervise many technical functions himself. In large cities, say of over 100,000, the director often turns over technical matters to one or more assistant directors while he concerns himself with general administration. There may be two assistant directors, for example, one in charge of operations, the other in charge of departmental staff services.

In large cities, some of the functions performed by the public works department may be decentralized on an area basis. The object of such geographic decentralization is to save time and expense in moving men and materials about the city as they are needed. In most cities, however, the department is organized on a functional basis, each division operating under centralized control.

The Staff Services. In cities of less than about 10,000, the head of the public works department is likely to take care of the staff services himself —he does the planning, surveys, and inspections. In larger cities there are usually several divisions within the department which provide these services. The common ones deal with research and planning, design, and inspection. There may be a purchasing division, or the department may use the purchasing services existing for the city as a whole. Large departments need a personnel officer even though most personnel services are handled by the general agency established for that purpose. Cost accounting, a vital service that determines unit costs, may be performed by a staff division, or the service may be provided outside of the department by the central finance agency. Cost accounting is used by the department head to locate areas for possible economies, to compare costs with those of other cities, to compare costs from one year to the next, and for many other purposes.

The division of research and planning uses the city's master plan as a point of departure. It must establish priorities for the various projects proposed in the plan and then a timetable and capital budget for them. It takes careful planning to finance in the proper order such things as a new city hall, an additional water-pumping station, and a system of expressways. Planning provides further for the allocation of parts of the long-range plan in the annual budget and in the quarterly or monthly allotments within the department. Thus the division completes its job when work programs for construction and maintenance for each of the operating divisions have been readied for the next allotment period. Research and planning are part of a continuous, never ending process. The division works closely with the division of design, which deals with the technical matters of the design of bridges, buildings, and other structures.

Because much of the work of construction and some of the maintenance is done by private contractors, it is important that the department of public works have a division of inspection manned by able and honest inspectors. They must make certain that contracts are fulfilled and that the quality of materials and workmanship meets the required standards. It was in the area of public works contracts that much corruption in city government once took place. There have been many forms of collusion among contractors and between city officials and contractors, not to mention the practices of skimping on materials and workmanship and the technical and financial incompetence of many contractors. Proper inspection, supported by capable and honest administration at the highest levels, eliminates these problems. The modern chief executive considers the public works department one of the best mediums through which to demonstrate his administrative ability in bringing better services to the public.[26]

[26] For an elaboration on the subjects of this section, see International City Managers' Association, *op. cit.* T. H. Reed, *Municipal Management* (1941), chap. 23, explains the common methods of cheating used by private contractors.

CHAPTER 19

URBAN HOUSING

Issues that urban citizens must now settle or must cope with in the future include these, among others: Should slum clearance be integrated with the development of public low-rent housing? Should slum clearance be effected by public or by private effort? If private effort is used, should the municipality grant a subsidy, or purchase land by condemnation for private companies, or otherwise grant assistance? Should low-rent housing be built only on the site of cleared slums, or should some or all of it be built upon vacant land? What policy should be followed in choosing vacant sites, if they are used? If cleared sites are used, where should the displaced families live while new projects are being constructed? Is it desirable or undesirable to clear slums and then build housing upon the site that the persons displaced cannot afford to rent?[1]

THE DIRECT APPROACH THROUGH GOVERNMENT

The Present Situation. American urban housing conditions improved in the decade preceding 1950 despite the fact that several years of war delayed home building and slum clearance. In 1950, almost all urban dwelling units had electricity, 97.2 per cent had radios (television had not yet become commonplace at that time), 89.0 per cent had reasonably adequate indoor plumbing, and 86.1 per cent had mechanical refrigerators. Nonfarm owner occupancy was at an all-time high of 53.4 per cent of the dwelling units, up from 41.1 per cent in 1940. Most of these figures exceed by far the comparable statistics in almost any other nation in the world.

But American cities still had their slums. In 1950, one-third of urban dwellings were over thirty years old. Over 1,850,000 occupied urban units were rated as dilapidated by American standards. More than 100,000

[1] For a description of existing slum areas, see any textbook on urban sociology; or Edith E. Wood, *Slums and Blighted Areas in the United States* (1938). Several books on city planning, cited in chap. 20, also deal with the subject, as do M. L. Walker, *Urban Blight and Slums* (1938); Newark Housing Authority, *The Costs of Slums in Newark* (1946); and Edith Abbott, *The Tenements of Chicago* (1936).

units were in such bad shape that they stood unoccupied. The amount of dilapidation was especially high in units occupied by urban nonwhites:[2]

	Total, %	Nonwhite, %
Dilapidated..	6.4	27.5
Not dilapidated, but with no running water............	1.9	9.1

Improvements had been made. But it seemed clear that some outside help would be needed before American homeowners could or would eliminate slums.

Some Background. City governments have long had building codes providing for minimum standards for building and for human occupancy. The code (or series of codes, for they are not always unified or administered by a single agency) makes provisions for standards of lighting and ventilation, sanitation, and fire prevention and protection. Historically, these codes have often been subject to pressure demands of manufacturers, builders, real estate people, tenement owners, and building-trades unions. As a result they have often established minimum standards well below those that the contemporary society would accept as a rock-bottom minimum. Codes often become seriously outdated, so that their already meager standards in one era become grotesquely inadequate a few decades later as society's concept of a minimum standard of living changes. Trade unions have frequently used the code as a device to establish make-work rules or to prevent the use of cheaper and faster techniques of home building. Manufacturers have sometimes been able to get codes to require the use of their patented materials, thus creating a monopoly situation. Out-of-date codes have sometimes prevented the introduction of new devices, such as prefabricated homes or dry-wall construction, simply because they are not provided for in a code drawn up decades before these things appeared on the market.

It is important that the building code keep pace with changes in the accepted concept of a minimum standard of living. Many cities have recently been bringing their codes up to date, yet scores of others permit jerry-built housing, or do not allow modern building techniques, or permit the construction of low-rent housing (most likely by the *conversion* of old homes and apartments into tenements) that does not meet present standards for human living.

The ecological pattern in American cities has been one of allowing the central parts of the city to decay and become low-rent housing while higher-priced housing moves outward along the periphery. Traditional American housing policy has been to let low-income people live in what-

---

[2] Statistics from the U.S. *Census of Housing* (1950). For technical criteria of dilapidation, see *ibid.*, introduction.

ever is left over. In the days before the automobile some exceptions to this were made, since factories were located near the downtown area and workers were dependent upon public transportation or their own legs. In cities such as New York and Chicago, therefore, tenement buildings (multistoried apartments with minimal conveniences) were constructed specifically to provide housing for these people and to provide lucrative investments for absentee owners. In cities that have done most of their growing since World War I, however, few such buildings exist, and the poor live in converted and subdivided homes and apartments abandoned by the fleeing middle class.

A conservative writer has said, "In some respects, a 'slum' is like a used car lot. A 'slum area' offers a supply of second-hand housing of the kind which satisfies a need until such time as a person can afford and wants a better home." He argues further that "if people really want houses, let new ones be built or bought by those most able and anxious to build or buy."[3]

Public Housing. This approach to housing lasted until the Great Depression. At that time, the New Deal sought to encourage a revival of the home-building industry, which had ground to a complete stop, and at the same time to clear away some of the nation's worst slums. (Note that this was a characteristically New Deal effort in that it attempted to do two things simultaneously: to help business recover from the depression and to effect social reforms.) In 1933, Federal offers of conditional loans for private housing projects were unsuccessful because, with only a few exceptions, private companies did not meet the established standards. Some states also attempted to encourage low-rent private housing, but almost all of these efforts were essentially unsuccessful. It was, and still is, more profitable, or at least a safer investment, to build homes for higher-income families.

Public housing had long been practiced abroad, but prior to 1933 it was generally regarded as unconstitutional in this country. The need for low-cost housing was especially great during the depression, however, and the national government next turned its attention to public housing. Some fifty projects in thirty-six cities were federally constructed and administered by the Public Works Administration (PWA). It was not, however, until the United States Housing Authority (now the Federal Public Housing Authority of the Housing and Home Finance Agency) was created under the Federal Housing Act of 1937 that public housing could become a new national policy.[4]

[3] The laissez-faire argument against subsidized housing is presented in a pamphlet by Paul L. Poirot, *Public Housing* (1954).

[4] For historical background, see Jack Levin, *Your Congress and American Housing* (1952), a history of Congressional housing policy from 1892; Housing and Home Finance Agency, *Evolution of Housing Activities in the United States* (1950); Com-

The act was bitterly opposed, however, as have been all subsequent acts and propositions calling for public housing. Opposition has come partly from realtors, bankers, and others who profit from the private housing industry. Others have said that public housing is wrong in theory, that housing, within the concepts of our prevailing economic system, belongs properly in the realm of private and not public endeavor. A third type of opposition has come from those persons who fear that public housing projects would in one way or another damage existing property values.

The Federal Housing Act of 1937. The act of 1937 provided for quasi-public corporations known as "housing authorities" to be established wherever state laws permitted. The authorities were made up of appointed officials serving without pay, in most cities. The authorities drew up the plans for Federal approval, received the loan, and constructed and operated the projects.[5] The authorities had to sign three contracts with the Federal agency. One provided for the loan and established conditions for qualifying. A second provided for conditions under which the United States would pay a *subsidy* to help bridge the gap between rent receipts and actual costs. A third provided for Federal accounting control and debt control. The city had to agree to eliminate unsafe and unsanitary dwelling units equal in number to the new units to be constructed. State and local governments had to contract to furnish municipal services either free or for a small payment in lieu of taxes by the national government. This generally meant that public housing would be subsidized, not only in the process of building, but afterward, too, and by both the national and local governments.

The status of the housing authority as a separate corporation had the advantage of relieving the municipality of responsibility for its debts and could be used to avoid state constitutional debt limits. The local housing units, once constructed, remained to a large degree under Federal control, since questions of rent levels and eligibility to reside in the project were decided by its agency. Persons whose incomes came to exceed the established maximum were required to leave the projects.

Shortly before the start of World War II, by June, 1940, 210 local housing authorities had been established. During the war years, all public policy was directed toward a winning effort. Housing programs were aimed at giving millions of migrating people a place to live. A large number of units were constructed, mostly by private builders under a guaranteed profit contract with the national government. These units

---

mittee on Banking and Currency, *Federal Housing Programs: Chronology and Description* (1948).

[5] This section borrows from T. H. Reed, *Municipal Management* (1941), pp. 506–512.

were constructed in those cities with populations swollen by the construction of new war plants. Unfortunately, many of them were unsuitable for permanent postwar occupancy.

Postwar Policy. Since 1945, running warfare has been conducted between pressure groups representing or acting in the interest of low-income urbanites on the one hand, and the pressure groups of real estate interests on the other. The battle has been fought in Washington, in the state capitals, and in the city halls. By 1954 it appeared that the opponents of public housing were winning a clear-cut victory.

It was not even possible to get a new housing act through Congress until 1949, despite the powerful support given public housing by three leaders of the liberal Democrats, the southern Democrats, and the Republicans, in the Wagner-Ellender-Taft Bill (see Figure 42). The Federal Housing Act of 1949 reaffirmed the principle that providing for housing was basically a private business matter, and it did not change the fundamentals of the 1937 act. It made adjustments, however, in order to recognize inflation and the changing concepts of a minimum standard of human living.

The provisions of the act for an extensive Federal-municipal public housing program were immediately placed under attack by opponents. The opponents, again, were largely successful. In subsequent amendments, the number of unit starts authorized for each fiscal year was steadily whittled away:[6]

Year	No. of unit starts authorized
1949	135,000
1952	50,000
1953	35,000
1954	None
1955	35,000

Public housing accounted for only 5 per cent of the housing starts in 1952, but 446 projects were begun or added to, and for 57,000 units actual construction was begun. Of these, 54,930 were under the Housing Act of 1949 (as amended),[7] while 2,070 were state- or city-aided projects only. By the end of 1952, 68,472 units in 612 public housing projects had been completed under the 1949 act in addition to prewar construction under the 1937 act. Furthermore, 156,060 units were in various phases of construction in 1,040 projects.

Opposition to public housing was strong, however. On the state level,

[6] These statistics and those that follow are chiefly from John D. Lange, "Housing and Development," *Municipal Year Book, 1953,* pp. 331–336. By a vote of almost 2 to 1, the House of Representatives voted against authorizing any public housing starts in fiscal 1954, other than those already contracted for.

[7] Note that these statistics do not conflict with the 50,000 authorized starts cited above. Many starts had earlier been authorized.

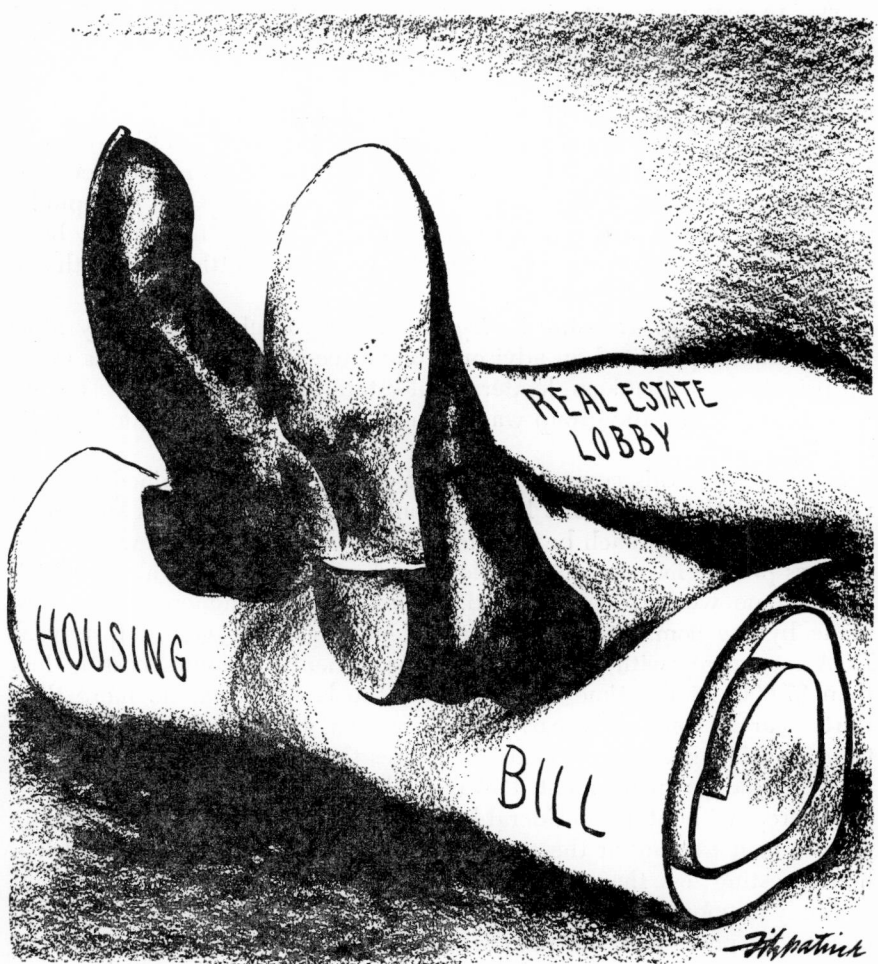

WHO'S WHO ON CAPITOL HILL
FEBRUARY 16, 1948
Fig. 42. The passage of a post—World War II housing bill was delayed for several years. The dean of American cartoonists depicted the real estate lobby "playing footie" with Congressmen while low-income families went without adequate shelter. SOURCE: By permission of Daniel R. Fitzpatrick and the *St. Louis Post-Dispatch.*

attempts were made to require a local referendum before a public housing project could be begun. Five legislatures defeated such proposals in 1952, while Virginia passed one. On the local level, proposals were also placed before the voters to require referendums before launching into public housing. Toledo and Cincinnati defeated such proposed charter amendments by votes of about 3 to 2, in November, 1952.

The 1949 Detroit and 1953 Los Angeles municipal campaigns turned largely on the question of public housing policy. Los Angeles, Toledo, Indianapolis, Helena, and other municipalities attempted in 1952 to cancel their cooperation agreements on public housing with the Federal government. They were generally blocked in the courts until Congress, by a 1953 law, prohibited new public housing units, even if under contract or construction, if the governing body of a municipality or a public referendum rejects the proposal. If some Federal money has already been spent in such cases, the municipality must make a "settlement" with the Public Housing Administration.

The Eisenhower Housing Policy. President Eisenhower, shortly after taking office, appointed an advisory committee on housing. It was made up principally of bankers, lenders, real estate men, and builders. Democrats charged that the group was prejudiced against low-rent and public housing.

Late in 1953, this committee made a report which contained no new recommendations on public housing, but committee members suggested that the whole approach be discontinued "when and if the new program induces private industry to provide enough good housing at a cost which low income workers could afford."[8] Some fifty recommendations were made by the committee. For low-cost housing, it suggested forty-year FHA mortgages with almost no down payment on homes costing less than $7,600. At the time of the report, the law allowed no more than thirty-year mortgages. In early 1954, however, bankers were not willing to make FHA-guaranteed loans for longer than *twenty* years, even with a substantial down payment. It was doubtful if longer mortgages would be offered without a considerable increase in interest rates above the 4.5 per cent existing at the time of the report. It was also doubtful if a house costing less than $7,600 would be habitable for forty years; and certainly a mortgage should not exceed the expected lifetime of the house. Prospects that the plan would provide a substantial number of low-cost housing units and thus eliminate the need for public housing appeared to be small. Perhaps in recognition of this, President Eisenhower, in his 1954 housing message, urged that the public housing provisions of the 1949 act be continued.

It seems unlikely that new low-cost housing can be built except as subsidized public housing or by having the Federal government take the mortgage on low-cost homes directly through one of its own agencies. Because this is so, and despite strong opposition from persons arguing from both theoretical and economic viewpoints, municipally administered public housing projects appear to be a permanent fixture as a local function of government.

[8] Associated Press dispatch, Dec. 16, 1953, citing the Housing Administrator.

THE INDIRECT APPROACH THROUGH GOVERNMENT AID

Private Redevelopment with Public Assistance. A few efforts were made by state and city governments during the thirties to encourage private endeavor to clear slums and build new homes. For the most part, this consisted of tax-exemption provisions and in most instances was an inadequate inducement. The New York Urban Redevelopment Act of 1941 would have established limited-dividend urban-development corporations subject to close supervision by municipal authorities and with certain tax exemptions. However, the coming of World War II prevented experimentation with this device.

The Federal Housing Act of 1949 provided for continued extension of credit by the government to home builders, home buyers, mortgage lenders, and sometimes directly to veterans. A great number of homes have been built with FHA- and VA-guaranteed loans, most of them in the suburbs and fringe areas. Undoubtedly these policies have aided greatly in the decentralization of urban America.

The act, however, also made some provisions to aid the core city (and, of course, many suburbs), by including a new policy for slum clearance and urban redevelopment. Provision was made for grants to local units of government to acquire, clear, and prepare blighted areas for the construction of new dwellings. The cleared land could then either be used for public housing projects, or be resold to private builders for redevelopment.

The redevelopment provisions of the act have been used to aid public housing construction, but to a greater extent they appear to have encouraged a trend toward stimulation of private building on slum sites. The first such project—Penn Towne—was completed in Philadephia in 1952. It included rehabilitated old structures combined with new buildings.[9] Numerous cities, including most of the largest, were acquiring or already clearing land for sale to private builders in 1953. In addition, Indianapolis completed a redevelopment project without Federal funds and Pittsburgh finished a 2-billion-dollar job, but its redeveloped area was not reserved exclusively for home-occupancy uses.

The old problem of the constitutionality of a new municipal function has arisen in connection with this type of redevelopment. In several state courts it has been argued that public condemnation and clearance of land is not for a public purpose if it is then immediately resold to a private firm, even though extensive conditions as to the use of the land and the type and quality of construction are provided. In many states, however, the high court has validated the action of the cities. Redevelop-

[9] Lange, *op. cit.,* p. 335.

ment laws in such urban states as Michigan and Illinois have been upheld, and the United States Supreme Court added a further stamp of legality by refusing to review the Illinois case. By the end of 1953, only the Florida courts had held that condemnation for sale to private redevelopers was not for a public purpose and was therefore unconstitutional. A 1951 state constitutional convention in Rhode Island refused to grant municipalities the power to condemn land for redevelopment, but in 1952 the state high court nevertheless ruled such legislation valid.

Complaints frequently heard against the private-redevelopment plan include the objection that adequate provisions are not made in advance for housing the families displaced when the slums are torn down, and that the evacuated persons cannot afford to rent the dwelling units built on the cleared sites by private builders. The latter charge appears to be well founded. Slum clearance that merely forces people in the lowest income brackets to move into other areas only creates new slums.

During the 1949–1951 period quite a few public housing projects were built on vacant lands, but after that time public and private developments alike were usually built upon cleared slum sites. There have been several reasons for this. By 1952, the postwar construction boom of one- and two-family dwellings had taken up most of the suitable sites in most cities. Perhaps there was by then slightly less pressure to provide rapidly for more dwelling units without decreasing the number already in existence.

There has been much opposition to the building of multiunit projects in areas of single-family homes. And there has been strong objection in many cities to government-assisted invasion by racially or socially "inferior" (in the minds of the objectors) groups into middle-class neighborhoods. Racial conflicts may produce opposition to government-assisted housing from another source, too: a 1948 slum-clearance bond issue in St. Louis was overwhelmingly voted against by low-income Negroes in the area to be cleared because they believed that they would be displaced while the eventual new structures would probably be occupied by whites.

In 1954, President Eisenhower asked for nearly 1 billion dollars in Federal aid funds for the "renovation" of run-down neighborhoods and the elimination of slums. He urged liberal loans with Federal guarantees to conserve older homes, pointing out that there are over 19 million frame homes in the United States over thirty years old. He also asked for continued Federal aid for slum clearance.

Municipal Action against Blighting. It is likely that many deteriorated neighborhoods could be rehabilitated and others that are declining could be saved without rebuilding. This could be done by requiring landlords (largely absentees) to repair their properties and raise conditions to a minimum standard. An ordinance providing that the city would do the job if the owner failed to do so after adequate notice, with the cost being assessed against the property, would be greatly helpful in retarding deterioration. Unfortunately, political pressure by owners to prevent the adoption or enforcement of such ordinances has been so great that little of this kind of experimentation has taken place. But in the fifties an increasing amount of interest was being taken in this approach. Milwaukee and Baltimore have led the way to this type of activity.

Rent Control as Municipal Policy. The same pressure groups that were lined up on public housing also took an interest in Federal laws on postwar rent control. In June, 1952, Congress extended rent control in critical defense areas. In other areas (and not many were deemed critical), rent control was to die the following September unless city councils or other local bodies, by resolution, decided to retain it. Such action by Congress had the effect of passing another responsibility along to the local community which ought to be in a good position to judge local needs.

Actually, the change to local option was a political compromise when outright abolition could not be achieved. Probably most real estate groups felt that they could be more effective before the city council than before Congress. This may well have been the case, for a large number of cities failed to extend control, even though many of those cities had severe housing shortages and a large number of workers and others who favored rent control. More than 1,400 communities voted to retain control, however, either at referendums or by council action.[10] The large number of councils that acted to kill rent control, even though the cities contained many people whose best interests would call for a continuation of it, raises some interesting implications concerning the representativeness of city councils.

Closing Note. More than 1 million housing starts were made in the United States in each year beginning in 1949. In 1950 an all-time record of 1,396,000 starts was made. Yet several authorities have estimated that 2 million dwelling units must be built yearly in order to keep pace with the deterioration of old dwellings and the increase in population. It has also been estimated that 135,000 annual units must be constructed in a slum-clearance program that is to make any progress against continuing deterioration. In 1952 the number of one- and two-family units being constructed was increasing, contrary to the pattern for multifamily units.

Despite a considerable amount of postwar building, a housing shortage still exists in most parts of the United States. The problem of housing low-income people in an adequate fashion has still not been solved.[11]

[10] *Ibid.*, pp. 333–334.
[11] See the remarks and statistics presented to Congress by President Eisenhower in his housing message, Jan. 25, 1954.

Private endeavor has persistently failed to do the job in the past. There is little reason to hope that it will do so in the future.

Public housing, for the moment at least, appears to be politically unpopular. Private redevelopment techniques, on the other hand, are not making dwelling places available for people of the rent level that their projects are displacing. In contrast to the great success that the British, Dutch, and Scandinavians have had in slum clearance and provision for low-rent housing, America has not yet solved its problem.[12] The opportunity for municipalities to aid in finding a solution exists, and the challenge is a great one.[13]

[12] See John Graham, Jr., *Housing in Scandinavia* (1940); Leonard Silk, *Sweden Plans for Better Housing* (1948); and the considerable literature on the British Town and Country Planning Act.

[13] For further material on housing, see Coleman Woodbury, *The Future of Cities and Urban Redevelopment* (1953), especially Catherine Bauer, "Redevelopment: A Misfit in the Fifties," pt. I, chap. 1, and Victor Jones, "Local Government Organization in Metropolitan Areas," pt. IV, chap. 3; Miles L. Colean, *American Housing; Problems and Prospects* (1944); Charles Abrams, *The Future of Housing* (1946); Nathan Straus, *Two-Thirds of a Nation* (1952); Clarence S. Stein, *Toward New Towns for America* (1951); Edward B. Olds, *How Does Your City Rate?* a comparison of fifty-seven metropolitan areas on population and housing characteristics; P. D. Angell, *The Case for Slum Clearance by Private Enterprise* (1939). There are several case studies of individual cities. See, for example, Arthur Hillman and R. J. Casey, *Tomorrow's Chicago* (1953). A most readable brief summary of progress and problems is Miles L. Colean, *Renewing Our Cities* (1953).

CHAPTER 20

PLANNING AND ZONING

Planning "involves the appraisal of all manner of resources in men and materials and the marshaling of them in the community interest."[1] Zoning, which is an aspect of applied planning, is "the practice of restricting the height, area and use of buildings or premises by districts."[2] While planning in the United States might be said to date from William Penn's 1682 layout of the city of Philadelphia, most American cities had a chaotic growth until recent decades.

In the nineteenth century, informal committees composed of people interested in realty development or simply in civic improvement would sometimes present city plans to the council for consideration. Later, committees of the same sort were sometimes appointed by the mayor or council to study and make recommendations on city plans. Once they made a report, like most study groups, their task was finished.

It was not until 1907 that a permanent planning commission as a municipal agency was established. In that year, Hartford, Connecticut, took this important function out of the hands of private citizens and set a pattern that has commonly been followed ever since. Once begun, the movement spread rapidly, and today over one-half (56.1 per cent) of the cities of 10,000 population or larger have an official planning commission. Some others have unofficial planning agencies or committees. Of the cities over 50,000, three-fourths have permanent commissions.

The beginnings of zoning go far back into American urban practices. In the nineteenth century it was common for the council to control the location of industries capable of creating a public nuisance, such as animal-rendering plants or stockyards. The traditional common-law police power over the health, safety, and morals of society was invoked to give a piecemeal sort of zoning. In the 1880s New York began to control the height of dwellings, and in the 1890s Boston the height of nonresidential buildings. But it was not until New York took action in 1916 that a comprehensive zoning ordinance was adopted by an American city. As in so many matters of protecting a community-wide interest, the United States was slower in acting than many of the European nations.

[1] T. H. Reed, *Municipal Management* (1941), p. 304.
[2] *Ibid.*, p. 311.

By 1952 well over one-half (58.7 per cent) of the cities of 10,000 population or larger had comprehensive zoning ordinances, and 72 per cent of those over 25,000 had such ordinances. These figures for planning and zoning fail to account for areas having these functions in the hands of county or city-county bodies. All large cities have planning agencies, and almost all of them also have zoning ordinances. The modernization of these zoning rules has been taking place at a rapid rate since the end of World War II. Some large cities, however, including Detroit, Houston, and San Francisco, lack a *comprehensive* zoning ordinance covering use, height, bulk, and area control.[3]

Many aspects of planning and zoning involve issues of public policy. Practices of good planning and zoning are violated annually in dozens of cities without the persons who are thereby injured being clearly aware of it. But many other phases of the functions become important in elections and in lobbying before city councils.

A LONG-RANGE APPROACH TO LAND USE

Planning. The central planning agency is almost always a commission, but all city officials and departments engage in planning. The council plays a decisive role, while the city manager, the mayor, and department heads prepare plans, both long range and short range. The central planning agency coordinates the plans of the several departments and carries on certain planning activities of a city-wide nature. The city planning commission usually has five or seven members, but may have as many as fifty. It may be entirely ex officio, consisting of designated city officials, or it may be made up of citizens serving without pay, or some combination of these two. Ex officio boards are generally unsatisfactory because members are likely to be too busy and have too many other interests to spend much time or thought on planning.

Planning deals not only with streets, utilities, and the regulation of private property, but also with parks, recreation, housing, slum clearance, airports, traffic, parking, public health, and a host of other things (see Figure 43). Unfortunately, the reports of planning commissions often gather dust or are even greeted with scorn. Sometimes the commission reports directly to the council and as a consequence loses the cooperation of the administrative branch of government. It is probably desirable to have the commission report to the mayor and to serve as one of his advisory staff agencies.[4]

Adequate planning requires expert attention, yet as a result of historical

[3] *Municipal Year Book*, 1953, pp. 284–297. The most recent *Year Book* contains data on planning and zoning practices in individual cities.

[4] See Reed, *op. cit.*, chap. 14. The problem is less acute in manager cities, but here too the commission should probably report to the administrative head.

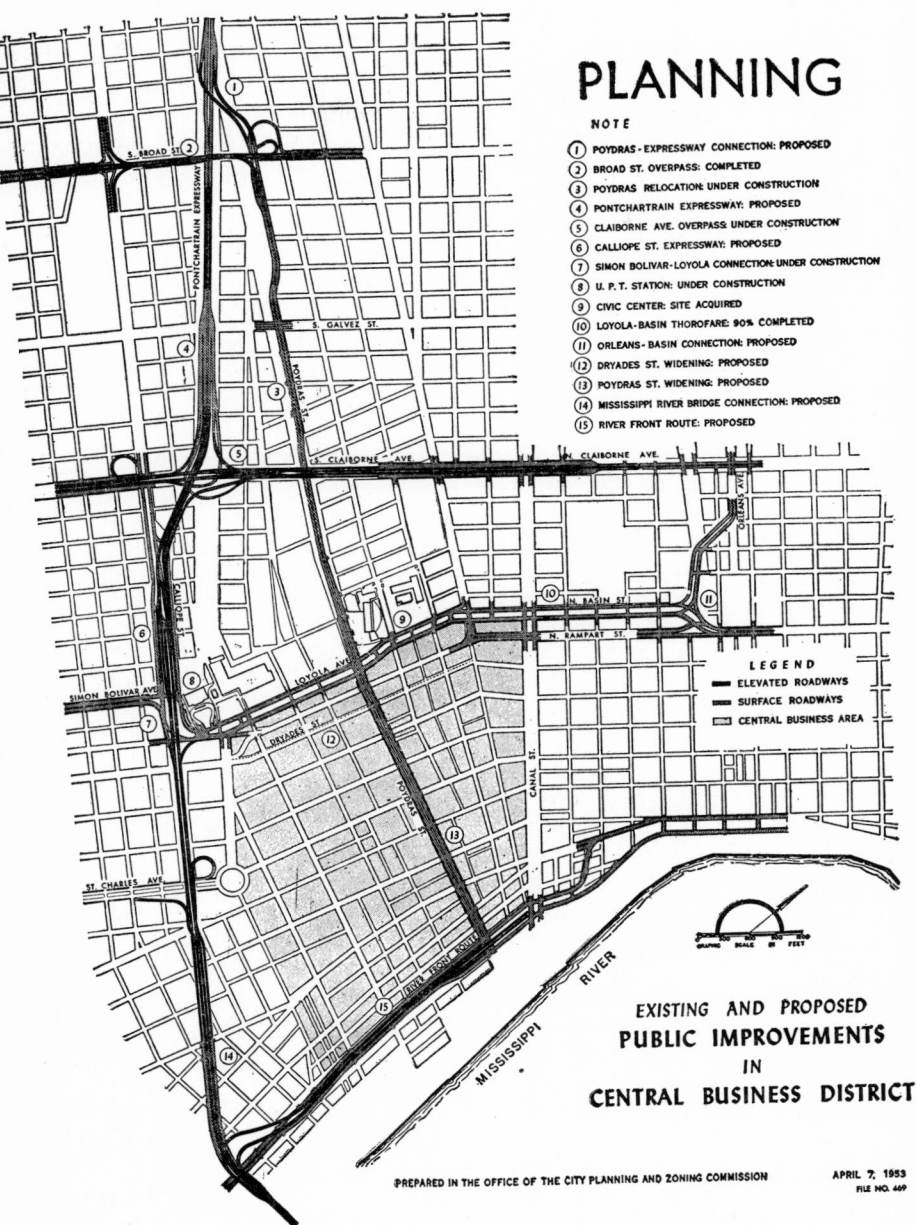

PLANNING

NOTE

① POYDRAS - EXPRESSWAY CONNECTION: PROPOSED
② BROAD ST. OVERPASS: COMPLETED
③ POYDRAS RELOCATION: UNDER CONSTRUCTION
④ PONTCHARTRAIN EXPRESSWAY: PROPOSED
⑤ CLAIBORNE AVE. OVERPASS: UNDER CONSTRUCTION
⑥ CALLIOPE ST. EXPRESSWAY: PROPOSED
⑦ SIMON BOLIVAR-LOYOLA CONNECTION: UNDER CONSTRUCTION
⑧ U. P. T. STATION: UNDER CONSTRUCTION
⑨ CIVIC CENTER: SITE ACQUIRED
⑩ LOYOLA-BASIN THOROFARE: 90% COMPLETED
⑪ ORLEANS - BASIN CONNECTION: PROPOSED
⑫ DRYADES ST. WIDENING: PROPOSED
⑬ POYDRAS ST. WIDENING: PROPOSED
⑭ MISSISSIPPI RIVER BRIDGE CONNECTION: PROPOSED
⑮ RIVER FRONT ROUTE: PROPOSED

LEGEND

▬ ELEVATED ROADWAYS
▬ SURFACE ROADWAYS
▦ CENTRAL BUSINESS AREA

EXISTING AND PROPOSED
PUBLIC IMPROVEMENTS
IN
CENTRAL BUSINESS DISTRICT

PREPARED IN THE OFFICE OF THE CITY PLANNING AND ZONING COMMISSION   APRIL 7, 1953
FILE NO. 469

Fig. 43. Existing and proposed improvements for the city of New Orleans. SOURCE: City of New Orleans, *Annual Report of the Mayor* (1952–1953).

development, planning commissions are commonly made up of laymen. Most of these groups have consisted of sincere, conscientious workers, but they have often been oriented toward the interests of the building and real estate groups or the general business community rather than toward the interests of the population as a whole. And very few planning-commission members are qualified to do the actual planning work. For this reason, it is very important for the planning commission to employ a widely trained professional planning director and a staff. But relatively few cities under 100,000 have full-time directors, and many cities use the city engineer in this position, especially cities under 50,000. Of course, planning is much more than engineering. It also involves economics, geography, architecture, human ecology, demography, aesthetics, and other matters in which the typical engineer may have little training or interest. About two-thirds of the cities of over 50,000 with official planning agencies have at least one full-time employee, but few smaller cities feel that they can or need afford such assistance.[5]

Few cities, even today, appropriate very much money for the planning function, although variation among them is great. Not many cities under 50,000 consider planning a very important part of the budget, and fewer than one-fourth of America's cities of over 10,000 spent $1,000 or more on planning in 1952.

The Plan. After the council authorizes a planning commission to go to work, a staff of experts is usually hired (in other than large cities, a consulting firm may be retained instead). Surveys are made and basic data are gathered. It is then the job of the commission to interpret the data and to develop plans to fit it. Planning must be continuous, however, and new data and new interpretations of the data must be constantly made by the commission.

It is important that planners allow for flexibility. Master plans suffer from fairly rapid obsolescence. It is true that in 1791 Pierre L'Enfant was asked to draw up a master plan for the new city of Washington and that his imagination was so wonderful and his foresight so great that the plan has never needed serious alteration. In fact, subsequent alterations have marred, rather than improved, it. Washington is the one truly comprehensively planned city in America—but then few people have ever had the opportunity to lay out a full city *in advance* of its construction as did L'Enfant.

Most planners are confronted with a *fait accompli* and must make changes slowly and against the resistance of inertia and vested interests. The planners are rarely men of the vision of a L'Enfant. Even if they should be, they would encounter difficulties in long-range planning. A plan in the early nineteenth century founded upon a system of water transportation would have to be seriously altered with the coming of the rail-

[5] See *Municipal Year Book, 1953,* pp. 278–297, for data.

road. Later, the automobile would require even greater changes. And the best plans laid out in 1850 or 1900 could not have made proper arrangements for an airport at a logical and convenient location.

The master plan drawn up by the commission in many cities is not enacted into law, but serves as a basic guide for the council and administrative officials. The council may instead formally adopt a *map* that becomes the official statement of policy. This map, logically, should not be modified without consultation with the commission.

The commission may also control subdividing. In the past, ambitious real estate operators have subdivided far beyond the foreseeable needs of the community and have often talked or pressured the council into furnishing utilities to an otherwise vacant subdivision. This, in effect, forces the taxpayers to subsidize speculation in real estate and is scarcely to be justified.

The model city charter of the National Municipal League and the standard city-planning enabling act recommended by the U.S. Department of Commerce call for subdivision platters to provide for the financing of adequate streets, parking, water, sewers, and other utilities, or to post a bond guaranteeing their installation. "No one should be permitted to put lots on sale which are not provided with the facilities for decent living any more than he should be allowed to sell adulterated foodstuffs or fake securities. Nor, on the other hand, should a municipality be allowed to provide such facilities indiscriminately at public expense before taxable values have been created which can be relied on to pay for them"[6] (see Table 29).

In New York and a few other cities, the planning commission prepares a capital budget with long-range plans for urban development. The com-

Table 29. Number of Cities over 10,000 Requiring Improvements in New Subdivisions: 1953

Population group	No. of cities in group	Grad-ing streets	Grad-ing and surfac-ing streets	Curbs and gutter	Side-walks	Water mains	Sani-tary sewers	Storm sewers	Street trees	No im-prove-ments required
Over 500,000....	18	0	5	5	5	5	5	5	1	10
250,000–500,000.	23	2	11	13	11	11	12	11	1	5
100,000–250,000.	65	8	25	18	21	23	26	20	1	11
50,000–100,000..	129	17	52	42	42	44	52	38	12	19
25,000–50,000...	276	38	103	85	72	89	110	83	23	48
10,000–25,000...	836	81	236	192	147	239	266	185	43	82
All cities over 10,000......	1,347	146	432	355	298	411	471	342	81	175

SOURCE: *Municipal Year Book, 1953*, p. 286.

[6] Reed, *op. cit.*, p. 319. Philip H. Cornick, *Premature Subdivision and Its Consequences* (1938), is a basic source.

mission often, and probably desirably, also functions as the zoning board. In some cities, however, there is a separate zoning board. Since this body is certain to make some mistakes and to create inequities, an appeal board must be established in order to hear property owners who feel that they have been wronged. The planning commission may act as the board of zoning appeals, if it is not the zoning board itself, but this function is more commonly assigned to a separate board.

APPLIED PLANNING

Zoning.[7] The control of the height, area, and use of buildings or lots may be achieved either by zoning or by subdivision deed restrictions. The former is public policy enforceable at law, while the latter are *private* contractual relationships enforceable in civil action. Land values are often protected in areas of expensive homes by writing restrictions into the sale contracts providing, among other things, that homes of not less than a specified minimum floor space may be built. Subdivision deed restrictions are often used to protect property values where no zoning or inadequate zoning exists. They are not a substitute for good zoning practice, however, for in order to enforce their provisions, a resident of the restricted area must bring a civil action against the violator. This is expensive, time-consuming, clumsy, perhaps embarrassing, and often "not worth the bother."

Zoning has now become the standard method of ensuring the efficient use of land and of promulgating many of the provisions of the city plan. A city is virtually always divided up into at least three zoning classifications: for manufacturing, for commercial operations, and for residences. There may be a division of each of these categories into two or more subcategories. For example, the city may be divided into zones for heavy industry, light industry, general commercial, local business, multifamily dwellings, and single-family dwellings.

In addition to restrictions concerning *use* of land, the zoning ordinance will usually restrict the *height* of buildings in relation to the width of the street, the size of side yards, and the use to which the area is put. Residential and commercial zones normally have such restrictions. Further limitations are placed on *area* that is usable for building. In single-family home sections, the building line may be twenty or thirty feet back of the sidewalk, for example. And apartment buildings are no longer allowed to take up the whole of the lot with little provision for sunlight and air. A building in a residential area is today generally required to come no nearer than a specified distance to the lot line—the distance being determined by the height of the buildings in the neighborhood.

[7] On the legal basis of zoning, see above, pp. 137–138.

In the years since 1945 there has been a strong trend toward the adoption of zoning ordinances, and many existing ones have been modernized. Of about 800 cities over 10,000 that have such ordinances, 278 revised theirs between 1946 and 1950. On the other hand, however, nineteen cities have not made a basic change in their zoning ordinances since at least 1925.

Competent planning and zoning will not in itself guarantee a "city beautiful." This is clearly demonstrated by recent developments in New York skyscraper construction. Since the war a large number of moderate-sized skyscrapers—twenty to thirty stories in height—have been built. The financiers of these projects are anxious to make a maximum utilization of Manhattan's expensive land. The architects have therefore been forced to plan them, not with aesthetic considerations paramount, but rather so as to fit the minimum setback requirements of the zoning ordinance.[8] Lewis Mumford has given a fitting title to the resulting "style": wedding-cake modern.

Spot Zoning. Zones of a city should not be taken too literally as being belts or areas of the city. A zone may be very small: it may be a narrow strip along a street or railroad track, or—unfortunately—it may be only one lot. The single-family "zone" may be interlarded with zones of commerce, industry, and multifamily dwellings in a pattern that is confusing and sometimes difficult to rationalize.

The location of a single lot or of a few lots of one classification in the midst of a more preferred type—"spot zoning" so called—is not a part of zoning at all, but rather a deterioration of it, or a refusal to recognize it. It may be very profitable to an owner to be able to sell a lot in an area zoned for single-family homes to a filling-station or grocery-store operator. But it means a loss in the total value of the community. Because this loss is socialized among many persons who individually have less incentive to pressure the council than does the single profiteer, such practices take place with considerable regularity in some cities, sometimes reducing to an absurdity the principle of zoning. It is something that should not be allowed to become a part of public policy, and in quite a few states it is held to be illegal.

The Zoning Ordinance. Zoning is intended, of course, to do more than merely protect property values. It is also used to ensure that adequate light, air, and accessibility are made available to all property. It protects the public health and minimizes the number of fire hazards. The zoning ordinance—which is sometimes the only formal and legal promulgation of

[8] The zoning rules regarding the height of buildings usually require a certain amount of *setback* as the number of stories increases. Thus, a building may use the full ground space for perhaps ten stories, after which there must be one foot of setback from the building line for, perhaps, 4 feet of height. This allows air and sunlight to reach the lower floors.

the efforts of the planning commission—must, it goes almost without saying, conform to the city's master plan and must be adjusted to conform with the almost constant changes in that plan.

The zoning ordinance, likewise, should not be primarily the product of councilmanic efforts, nor should it represent a mosaic of the pressures applied upon the individual councilmen. Rather, it should be drawn up by the planning commission as part of its plan, with a long-range, community-wide view. Amendments to the ordinance should be made by the council, not on a spot-zoning basis, but only after consultation with the planning commission and with the burden of proof being on those who would not follow the recommendations of the commission. Any other policy will likely result in an unplanned, unsystematic approach to land use which is inevitably wasteful of both resources and property values.

Planning in the Suburbs. Urban areas have achieved procedures and practices of planning and zoning—long after they were first needed, to be sure. Today, the principal growth in urban areas is on the periphery, chiefly in the suburbs. And it is here, where planning and zoning are most needed today, that they are most often inadequate or entirely absent.

Suburbs, especially in their earliest years of development, suffer from several things that lead to blight. Premature subdividers are normally little enough controlled within the core city. In suburbs, and especially in unincorporated areas, they may encounter virtually no restrictions at all. They may be responsible for erratic and inefficient use of land. The outer fringe, which in a few years is to become an inner fringe, is characteristically the area where individuals try to build their own homes, or purchase jerry-built shacks. With no building code, or a very inadequate one, it may be possible for the person who cannot afford to build or buy a home in the city to construct one in the fringe area. He may be able to afford one that has too little floor space or is of too flimsy construction to meet the core-city building regulations.

In a few years, the outer fringe becomes truly suburban, with a great amount of subdividing and building. But the new homes are now interspersed with dilapidated shacks and nonconforming buildings according to the belatedly adopted zoning regulations. In quite a number of metropolitan areas, there is a greater percentage of substandard and dilapidated homes in the suburbs than in the core city.[9]

A few suburbs stand out in sharp contrast from the usual, for in a small number of industrial and wealthy residential suburbs, an excellent master plan has been drawn up in advance of occupancy and has been adhered to, sometimes by writing the major part of the plan into the contracts for purchase of the land. Most fringe subdividers have maintained the unimaginative, severe, but more profitable gridiron pattern for residential

[9] Compare the approach in Australia: A. J. Brown and H. M. Sherrard, *Town and Country Planning* (1951).

streets, and many times they have been allowed to make use of inexcusable 40- and 45-foot-wide lots.

The tragedy of planning and zoning on the fringes of most American cities has been that it has come on a too-little-and-too-late basis. The core city has not often had zoning powers, much less planning powers, beyond its own boundaries, except perhaps for nuisance industries. The fringe frequently has no local government at all, or only a township government, often run by political hangers-on from the rural days of the area. There is little incentive from these sources for the development of a systematic approach to land use. In a few urban areas, the county does now zone the unincorporated sections, but this is not the general rule. Some states, years too late, have authorized townships to perform planning and zoning functions, at least in urban areas.

The major problem remains, however: chaotic land usage until the area becomes quite heavily populated and then a belated attempt to prevent the building of any more individual shacks and shanty towns. But by this time the opportunity for maximum efficiency of land use is probably gone forever.

Efforts at Metropolitan Planning. Because our metropolitan areas are atomized politically while planning is not of that nature, a hiatus exists between the need for planning and its political practicality. In order to fill this gap, there has been somewhat of a trend recently toward the development of metropolitan planning commissions or joint city-county commissions. Often these groups are private and unofficial, sometimes they are extralegal, sometimes they are provided for by state enabling acts, but almost always they are *advisory* only in nature and have no coercive powers. Some of them have their own staffs, large or small, but quite a few of them share the staff of the core-city planning commission. Some of them have no staffs at all, but are merely operated through occasional meetings.

These organizations do a considerable amount of research, and some of them draw up elaborate master plans for the metropolitan area. They seek to publicize the importance of long-range, area-wide planning, something in which the general public is not easily interested. They attempt to influence the planning efforts of local communities in the area and to keep them informed of what other communities are doing.

In some states the official planning map of the core city can be extended into the satellite communities, and this offers some control over the future development of the entire community. An increasing number of states are authorizing counties to perform planning and zoning functions, but ordinarily these powers are restricted to unincorporated areas. Even where this is the case, the developing urban fringe may be controlled by this unit of government. County planning and zoning on a comprehensive scale has the great advantage of channeling the direction of urban development before it takes place, of preserving the beauty of scenic highways and historic cities, of preventing the development of shanty towns and such things as indiscriminately located roadside stands or trailer camps, of establishing building-setback lines so that highway lanes may be added less expensively as they become transformed into urban arterial routes, and of controlling the use of that abominable nuisance, the billboard. Several states, especially Wisconsin and California, have made use of county zoning, but its value in controlling the development of fringe areas has been limited up to the present time.

Planning for utilities, parks and recreation, highways, the location of industry, and many other urban matters should logically be approached on an area or regional rather than a city basis. Yet it has been most difficult to work out any sort of metropolitan planning group with more than advisory powers, for the problem of an equitable and yet politically expedient method of representing the many communities in the area is a formidable one. Some of the suburbs are so suspicious of the core city that they will not even cooperate with an advisory planning group.

To say that regional planning should have been begun—and upon a coercive basis—in the days when America's cities were beginning their great spurt in development is to speak the truth, but the statement is unavailing. The plain fact of the matter is that it was not done then and is little done today. The slipshod manner in which we have allowed our urban areas to grow from infancy to adulthood is one of the tragedies of the American scene.[10]

[10] There is considerable material dealing with planning and zoning. A reconsideration of much of the problem is to be found in the two volumes edited by Coleman Woodbury, *Urban Redevelopment: Problems and Practices* (1953); and *The Future of Cities and Urban Redevelopment* (1953). Lewis Mumford has written much on planning, especially of its aesthetic aspects. See his *City Development* (1945), and his occasional articles in *The New Yorker*. The great French architect and planner Le Corbusier (Charles E. Jeanneret-Gris) has a book, *Concerning Town Planning* (1948).

Other works, emphasizing various aspects of planning, include Harold M. Lewis, *Planning the Modern City* (2 vols., 1949); Gerald Breese and Dorothy E. Whitman, *An Approach to Urban Planning* (1953); A. B. Gallion, *The Urban Pattern* (1950); S. E. Sanders and A. J. Rabuck, *New City Patterns* (1946); American Municipal Association and others, *Action for Cities: A Guide for Community Planning* (1943); R. B. Mitchell (ed.), *Building the Future City, The Annals of the American Academy of Political and Social Science*, vol. 242 (November, 1945); International City Manager's Association, *Local Planning Administration* (2d ed., 1948); John D. Millett, *The Process and Organization of Government Planning* (1947); M. C. Branch, *Urban Planning and Public Opinion* (1942). There are many studies of various cities and areas. See, for example, Judith N. Jamison, *Metropolitan Los Angeles: A Study in Integration, III. Regional Planning* (1952); and R. L. Duffus, *Mastering a Metropolis* (1930), a fine summary of the great study toward a plan for the New York region which was originally published in ten volumes. See also Charles M. Kneier and Guy Fox, *Readings in Municipal Government and Administration* (1953), chap. 16.

CHAPTER 21

PUBLIC HEALTH AND WELFARE

Few functions of municipal government affect more urbanites in a greater variety of ways than do those involving health and welfare (which, for purposes of this chapter, includes recreation). Yet these are also largely technical and professional functions, and much of their activity takes place below the level of the attention of the general public. Some political controversy arises in connection with them at times, however, and they are always an important part of a municipal budget.

PUBLIC HEALTH

The Nation's Health Is a Municipal Trust. Great cities, with their high concentration of people in confined areas, are natural targets for communicable diseases. For this reason, local governments have long had responsibilities toward the protection of health. The idea that some diseases were in some manner contagious was discovered long ago. Resulting from this knowledge came the practice of having cities require the isolation of afflicted persons. The pesthouse was an early form of isolation. Quarantining of such persons in their houses also became a municipal responsibility. A flag or sign beside the doorway of the homes of those with contagious diseases was the responsibility of the public health officer.

During the Great Plague (bubonic plague) that struck London in 1665–1666, for example, the houses of the afflicted were marked with red crosses on the door, "searchers" were sent out to certify as to the cause of deaths, and municipal authorities sent a man out to kill the dogs of the city, for these well-loved creatures were mistakenly blamed for spreading the disease. Cities, aided by a considerable amount of progress in medical knowledge, still perform these functions. In recent decades, their tasks have become ever greater and their successes in lowering the death rate ever more impressive.

Another development in municipal health activities, and a logical development out of the older practice of isolation, came with the discovery of the techniques of vaccination and inoculation against communicable diseases. A conflict has developed over the question of whether these practices are "treatments" that should be cared for by private physicians, or preventive medicine, and as such a public health function. In the United States, the former view has generally prevailed, except for the vaccination of school children in some cases and the emergency treatment of populations in the event of epidemics.[1]

A third factor in the development of public health departments was the popularity of the filth theory of disease in the middle years of the nineteenth century. This notion led to heavy emphasis upon sanitation, especially on the construction of sewers, the collection of garbage, and the abatement of nuisances. It was during this period that public health departments became common and were expanded in size beyond that of a local physician acting on a part-time basis. Although the collection and disposal of sewage and garbage is still a function of the health department in some cities, it has generally been transferred to the more logical public works department. But the health department is still responsible for the health supervision of such activities, and it has been entrusted with an ever increasing number of other functions.

Public Health Administration. The American Public Health Association believes that specialization is so important in a proper health program that its Committee on Local Health Units has recommended the establishment of health units so organized as to contain not less than 50,000 people in each of them.[2] Smaller units not only cannot develop specialization, but are likely to be unable to finance a successful program. This means, of course, that the county or a special-purpose district would have to be used as the health unit, except for fair-sized cities. The professional organization also suggests that there should be one public health nurse for each 5,000 people and one sanitarian for each 25,000 people. Few communities in the nation meet these and other standards of the Association, however. Cities and villages are still the standard units established by state law, although county and city-county departments are increasingly taking over health functions in urban areas and standards are rising. For example, Michigan law provides that any city failing to maintain a full-time health officer comes automatically under the county health department, and that the city and county may, by mutual agreement, share the services of a single health officer to supervise both departments. It is likely, however, that health units will be rapidy consolidated in the future only through the incentive of conditional Federal or state grants-in-aid.

There is a trend today toward municipal health departments under a single head responsible to the chief executive. Most municipalities, how-

---

[1] Parts of this chapter borrow from T. H. Reed, *Municipal Management* (1941), chap. 18.

[2] American Public Health Association, *Local Health Units for the Nation* (1946).

ever, still make use of the traditional board of health. (General municipal health departments first became popular in the heyday of the independent board and commission.) Quite a few cities still have boards, but have stripped them of administrative powers, leaving them with but an advisory function. This is, in fact, the structure recommended by the American Public Health Association.

The board of health is often made up partly of physicians and partly of interested laymen. In some cities, at least one seat must be given to an engineer. The American Public Health Association and other medical groups favor a heavy representation of physicians on the board. This can perhaps be justified on the basis of the superior interest of these men, but undoubtedly they are also wanted there to "protect" the private medical profession against those who would greatly expand the scope of public health functions. Board members ought logically to be appointed by the chief executive, and certainly less than a majority of them should be professional medical people.

The old-style administrative boards were inadequate because they gave amateur, lay control to a highly technical function of government. The modern department, headed by a public health officer, with or without an advisory board, has the professional leadership that is needed. The health officer in small cities is a local physician, often working on a part-time basis. In larger cities, a person with professional training in public health and the degree of Doctor of Public Health, as well as that of M.D., is often employed. The specialized professional degree affords training in sanitation, public administration, and other fields in addition to medical training. In the largest cities, the health officer's time is fully occupied with administration, and technical functions are left to his subordinates.

Public Health Functions. A great many health activities are performed or aided by state health departments and by Federal agencies, especially by the United States Public Health Service of the Department of Health, Education and Welfare. But the principal direct health services are performed by local governments. Except in small communities, the health department is normally divided into several specialized line and staff divisions.

Communicable-disease Control. The traditional function of the health department deals with communicable-disease control. Despite limited funds, health departments have been so effective in reducing, with the help of private medicine, the incidence of these diseases that they have almost eliminated the need for this function. Almost—but never entirely. The communicable-disease division receives the required reports from physicians and enforces isolation in those cases where it is still required. It must sometimes prod lax physicians into the prompt reporting of diseases.

By keeping watch over water and milk supplies this division has almost eliminated typhoid fever. At the turn of the present century, there were more than thirty times as many deaths from this disease in the United States as there are today. Yellow fever and malaria, once common in swampy areas frequented by certain types of mosquitoes, have been virtually eliminated in this country by the draining of swamps and the treatment of other standing water. Typhus has been controlled through ratproofing programs and through health education, which has taught the dangers to be found in the body lice that transmit the disease. Smallpox is almost unknown today as a result of educating the public and the occasional use of compulsory vaccination laws.

In recent years, trends in communicable-disease control have included (1) reduced emphasis upon strict and protracted isolation of patients for many diseases, (2) the development of immunization techniques for an increased number of diseases, and (3) a tendency to abandon fumigation of the premises after a patient has recovered. It has been discovered that disease germs do not linger in a corner of the living-room sofa for weeks or months, as was once believed.

Tuberculosis, less contagious than most communicable diseases, but requiring special equipment and methods, is handled by a separate division of the health department in larger cities. Clinics and special hospitals or hospital sections are needed for its treatment. The prevention of tuberculosis is possible largely through conditions beyond the control of the health department—through better housing and conditions of labor for many urban citizens.

Venereal diseases are also usually treated by a special division of the department. These diseases, like tuberculosis, must be controlled through treatment. Protection against them can be achieved only through health education. The venereal-disease-control section has the major task of persuading people to apply for its help voluntarily and of overcoming the sufferer's wish to keep secret his socially disapproved ailment. Health departments have sought to encourage people to come forward for treatment by making their services available to all, regardless of ability to pay, and by locating treatment clinics as inconspicuously as possible.

Federal grants for venereal-disease control have been of help to local units, as has the fact that some of the postwar "wonder drugs" have been very effective in treatments. However, an unknown, but no doubt very large, number of cases requiring treatment are never brought to the attention of either private practitioners or public health clinics.

Maternal and Child Care. The principal functions of this division are of an educational nature. It offers lectures, pamphlets, publicity releases, and other information services designed to reduce the great areas of ignorance concerning childbearing that are so common among prospective mothers and fathers. The division also gives advice on child care and child rearing. Many cities operate prenatal and postnatal clinics and provide for home visits by public health nurses. The division works closely with hospitals offering free maternity service to the indigent, and it licenses and regulates midwifery in those states where its practice is still permitted.

Sanitation. Many municipal functions related to sanitation are administered outside of the health department. Swamps are drained, water is supplied, and sewage is disposed of by the public works department, or by independent departments, but health aspects are supervised by the health department.

The municipal department shares many inspection duties with state and federal agencies. Milk must be inspected to guard against watering and against the presence of tuberculosis and typhoid as well as several other types of germs that may be found in raw milk. Local slaughterhouses, if not inspected by representatives of the U.S. Department of Agriculture, are often inspected by the local health department. Retail food establishments are inspected and food handlers examined for communicable diseases by the health department, or under its supervision.

In checking the premises of retail food establishments, sanitation-division personnel usually follow the practice of unexpected and irregular inspections. If illegal and unsanitary conditions are found, the usual practice is to issue a warning. In the case of extreme or repeated violations, licenses may be suspended or revoked.

Municipal Hospitals. Municipal hospitals have become common throughout the nation as part of a public health program. There are over 250 city hospitals and over 60 city-county hospitals in the United States. Hospitals in cities under 100,000 are usually managed by semiautonomous boards, while in larger cities they tend to be controlled by the city health departments. In smaller cities, the budget is also usually autonomous, with the council having no power of review, but in larger cities, municipal hospitals as a rule are treated as simply another city agency.

Generally speaking, the smaller the city, the more likely its hospital is to be completely self-supporting, or nearly so. In very few cities of over 50,000 is the municipal hospital even 50 per cent self-supporting. The difference is made up from funds appropriated by the city, or sometimes the county or state. Municipal hospitals in larger cities, it should be explained, exist to a large extent to care for police and indigent cases. The smaller the city, generally speaking, the more likely is the hospital to be a general-service institution. Larger cities are also likely to operate special hospitals for contagious diseases, tuberculosis, poliomyelitis, and mental disorders.[3]

[3] Statistics are taken from the *Municipal Year Book, 1953,* pp. 310–326.

The oldest municipal hospital in the United States, the Philadelphia General, dates from 1732. The largest municipal institution, New York's famed Bellevue, is only four years younger. The city of New York also operates thirteen other hospitals and sanatoria. There are, however, municipal hospitals in cities of all sizes, including almost 100 cities of under 5,000 population.

Public Health Education. This division seeks to increase longevity by teaching members of the public the principles of personal hygiene and the need for proper medical care and consultation, and warning them about certain dangers to health. The division may conduct public lectures, issue news releases and public service announcements to press, radio, and television, and furnish lecturers to clubs, school assemblies, and other get-togethers. For example, the division may help the National Cancer Society warn the public of the "seven danger signals of cancer"; in the summer it may issue public service announcements to local radio stations reminding parents of the symptoms of poliomyelitis in children (or themselves); or it may issue news releases to the press warning of the dangers of food poisoning in an unrefrigerated cream puff.

The Staff Services. A staff function of general public interest is the collection of *vital statistics* for the community: records of births, of deaths and their causes, and of communicable diseases. The *public health laboratory* furnishes analyses of blood, sputum, and other samples in helping physicians diagnose diseases. It also may analyze food suspected of being tainted. As a staff service, *public health nurses* are furnished to aid the divisions in charge of communicable diseases, tuberculosis, venereal diseases, maternal and child care, public health education, and outpatient care.

Public Health and a Healthy Public. T. H. Reed, city manager, municipal consultant, and professor, writing in his usual style of realism tinged with satire, has said:[4]

There is no field of local public administration in which the professional staff comes into so many and so varied contacts with the public as does that of a department of health. Furthermore, it comes into contact not with any special section of the public but with representatives of every social and economic group. The marvelous development of the technical side of health work in the past generation has scarcely, if at all, reduced the importance of its human side. Health administration cannot, in spite of its scientific flavor, be reduced to a series of rigid formulas. It is still a matter of making rich landlords provide suitable sanitary conveniences for people who have to be taught not to use bathtubs for storing coal. It is as much as ever a question of inducing ignorant and wayward men and women to submit to restraints and treatments the nature of which they cannot understand. It furnishes the clearest

[4] Reed, *op. cit.*, p. 448.

possible illustration of the distinction between the pursuit of professional techniques and the application of such techniques to the service of real human beings. It is the human relationships involved which separate the science of epidemiology from the art of municipal management.[5]

PARKS AND RECREATION

Recreational Administration.[6] In few areas of municipal activity have so many disputes arisen over the proper forms of organization as in the field of parks and recreation. Although the general public probably thinks of parks and recreation as two aspects of a single function, professionals in the field are not so sure. In the past, it was common for the city government to have separate departments for parks and for recreation, but the postwar trend has been away from this.[7] In many cities, the school board also provides an organized summer recreation program.

In the past, parks and recreation departments were commonly set up under autonomous administrative boards, and it was not uncommon for them to have independent sources of income so that they existed practically as separate *ad hoc* units of local government, similar in status to the school boards. Parks and recreation boards were (and still are) very often made up of well-known and prosperous members of the community —the type known to the irreverent as "do-gooders." Professional recreation workers have generally tended to favor the independent board because of the support which it gives to the recreation program, particularly when the budget is under consideration. They also argue that such a board offers a continuity of policy not to be found when the head of the department changes at the pleasure of the chief executive.

General administrators in the field of municipal management are in agreement, however, that the parks and recreation function is not unique in its problems of management and that it should be administered as a regular department of the city under the control of the chief executive. They contend that this activity should be financed out of the general fund rather than a separate tax levy, that its budget should be treated like those of other city departments, and that the department should make use of the municipal staff services for purchasing, personnel, maintenance,

[5] For further reading on public health functions, see Ira V. Hiscock, *Community Health Organization* (4th ed., 1950); W. G. Smillie, *Public Health Administration in the United States* (1947); H. S. Mustard, *Government in Public Health* (1945); B. J. Stern, *Medical Service by Government* (1946); and an administrative study, L. W. Wyatt, *Intergovernmental Relations in Public Health* (1951).

[6] See International City Managers' Association, *Municipal Recreation Administration* (2d ed., 1948); H. D. Meyer and C. K. Brightbill, *Community Recreation* (1948); G. D. Butler, *Introduction to Community Recreation* (1949); J. L. Hutchinson, *Principles of Recreation* (1951).

[7] G. D. Butler, "Parks and Recreation Developments in 1952," *Municipal Year Book, 1953*, p. 470.

and the like. Only in this way can a modern, coordinated city government be achieved. In order to maintain organized community interest in parks and recreation, some people urge that a board be retained as an *advisory* body and hence a watchdog, while at the same time leaving administrative control under the chief executive.

Concerning the question of combining parks and recreation, T. H. Reed has said:[8]

Many recreational facilities can be located most conveniently in parks. Recreationists used to deplore the preoccupation of park authorities with shrubs and flower beds. The idea, however, that parks are for the use of the public, not merely for the delectation of their eyes, has gained ground rapidly in recent years. A considerable portion of the area of all large parks within or adjacent to cities is nowadays devoted to active recreation. In other words, our traditional parks—laid out on the pattern of an English country gentleman's estate—have gone recreational in a large way. Today if there is any tendency which threatens the dominance of the recreational motive it is a weakness for turning park drives into motor speedways in an effort to relieve traffic congestion elsewhere.

Perhaps the number one problem of administration in the postwar era —at least in many cities—has been that of recruiting recreational leaders, and especially persons for top executive positions. In some cities salaries have increased at a greater rate than the cost of living, but leadership salaries have generally failed to keep pace with those offered in related professions. Qualified persons have thus been difficult to obtain, and turnover has been high.[9]

The Recreation Program. Recreationists believe that every municipality should have a program designed to provide equal opportunity for all. It should provide a wide range of individual choices in different types of activities, not just sports, but games, music, arts and crafts, nature, drama, and social recreation. A good recreation program may include "rifle clubs, junior symphonies, dog obedience classes, toy workshops, baton twirling classes, charm schools, Hallowe'en window painting classes, show wagons and drama clubs."[10] Passive forms of recreation should not be neglected—watching, listening, and contemplation. The program should continue throughout the year and should serve people of all ages and of both sexes. As the normal work week decreases in length, the problem of providing for constructive and acceptable ways of using leisure time becomes ever greater. Attention should be given to the needs of special groups, such as the family, the handicapped, and service personnel. The long-range goals of a recreation program include the development of creative expression as well as good citizenship through safe,

[8] Reed, *op. cit.*, p. 461.
[9] Butler, *op. cit.*, p. 470.
[10] *Ibid.*, p. 471.

healthful, and socially approved activities, and the teaching of activities that will persist after children reach adulthood.[11]

Federal-government restrictions on recreation construction during World War II and for most of the period since that time have retarded the development of an adequate program, but many cities have long-range plans for expansion of facilities. In anticipation of a lifting of restrictions, several municipalities have in recent years conducted community-recreation surveys to determine long-range needs and their proper distribution. Such studies have been made by recreation departments themselves, by state agencies, by private consultants, and by the National Recreation Administration.

Parks. The inhabitants and public officials of cities have often been slow in recognizing the need for spacious, beautiful, and useful parks. They are of great psychological value, especially to the apartment or slum dweller, to whom a park may be the only available substitute for a front lawn or a back yard.

Cities such as New York and Philadelphia were allowed to grow up with almost a criminal disregard for the need for large open spaces for grass, trees, and shrubs. Even cities that expanded at a much later date, such as Detroit, failed to consider adequate park needs. Today, a belated attempt is being made in all large cities to provide small recreational playgrounds and indoor gymnasiums and swimming pools. In most cities it is now too late to provide areas for large parks that should have been set aside twenty-five, fifty, or more years ago. In an attempt to correct these errors, quite a few cities (or *ad hoc* park districts) have constructed parks and beaches outside of the urban areas. This practice began as long ago as 1893 in the Boston region. Unfortunately, outlying parks and "reservations" must sometimes be located twenty, thirty, or even more miles from the heart of the city. Where this is so, it at the least causes inconvenience and traffic hazards on week-ends. To those in the lowest-income group, who have no automobiles, but who most need the facilities, these areas are often quite inaccessible.

Some municipalities have sought to require provisions for a reasonable amount of park and playground area at the time of, or in advance of, subdividing. The courts have not been particularly cooperative, however, and several types of such laws and ordinances have been declared unconstitutional. Of course, some cities have planned their parks well, fitting them into the long-range scheme of things and not waiting for someone to donate the land in a hit-or-miss fashion. Quite a few American cities have beautiful park systems. Minneapolis has a particularly beautiful system, but Chicago, Boston, and other cities rate near the top, too.

Neighborhood parks offer a spot for relaxation, and their greenery

[11] For an elaboration on the criteria for a successful recreation program, see International City Managers' Association, *op. cit.*

breaks the monotony of a drab or uninteresting neighborhood. Large parks add to the beauty of a community and give opportunity for forms of recreation impossible in the small playground, such as golf, walking, bicycling, skiing and, very importantly, picnicking. With a lake, they may provide facilities for boating and swimming, and their trees and shrubs offer hours of pleasure to the nature lover and to that butt of television jokes, the bird watcher.

A large city often makes a zoo out of one of its parks. Zoos are sometimes operated by a board and department separate from the parks department, although this does not seem to be necessary. They are expensive to maintain but are immensely popular with children and adults alike. Today, zoos such as those in Chicago, Philadelphia, St. Louis, and Washington are among the finest in the world. All municipal institutions seem to have their opponents. Some people, for example, consider zoos to be either a waste of the taxpayers' money or a cruelty to the confined wild animals. But most people love animals and like to observe them, provided that they are given adequate and expert care and attention.

Places to Read and Learn. Libraries have been a municipal function for over a century. The first one that was tax-supported was established in Peterborough, New Hampshire, in 1833. Libraries are sometimes privately endowed and privately operated, but indirectly agencies of the city because they receive an annual appropriation either from the council or from a special property-tax levy. This type of library, especially common in New England and the South, is controlled by a self-perpetuating board of trustees. Other libraries are entirely public, controlled either by the school district or by the city government. They usually have autonomous control through a library board, but a few cities have a single librarian reporting directly to the chief executive.

Three problems, in particular, have vexed librarians in recent years. In the first place, the decentralizing tendency of cities means, in many places, that the main public library is often isolated in the center of the city from which the population is receding. This poses the threat that fewer people will use the libraries. The answer seems to be in a greater use of branch libraries in outlying residential areas. Such a movement has been under way for years but is now being accelerated. Connected with the problem is also the question of allowing suburbanites to use the core-city library, for which they do not pay taxes. Some cities allow free use of the library to anyone who is *employed* in the city regardless of where he may live. This is another form of subsidizing the suburbs and is inequitable. County libraries and *ad hoc* library districts are arising to supply the suburbs in many places.

A second problem lies in the threat posed by the coming of television. Will the people stop reading after they buy a TV set and thus make the library obsolete, or a luxury maintained only for scholars? Studies conducted to date indicate that people do, in fact, read less shortly after purchasing a television set, but that after the novelty wears off, they return to approximately their old habits.[12] There has been a decrease in library use in recent years, but television is probably only one of several causes.

A third problem confronting librarians is the threatened censorship of reading materials that has been made by well-meaning but misguided persons in the postwar period. In times of tension, unrest, confusion, and doubt, people seek security through unity and conformity. Alien ideas become enemies to be fought along with the human enemies. Overzealous individuals have somehow confused a study of communism with allegiance to it. Such a viewpoint contains an implicit doubt as to the sturdiness of democracy and the overwhelming loyalty of Americans to its ideals. Communism surely does not offer so much hope to the casual reader that he will leap to it instantly, forgetting of a sudden a lifetime of accumulated devotion to an entirely different philosophy!

Yet in 1952 the *Boston Post* conducted a campaign to have all materials concerned with communism removed from the public library. The effort was not successful, but similar movements have been made elsewhere. The American Library Association has taken a strong stand against such attacks upon intellectual freedom.[13]

Museums and Art Galleries. There are far fewer museums and art galleries in the United States than there are libraries. Most large cities operate them, however. They are usually autonomously controlled in the same fashion as are libraries, and they enjoy the protection of the "patrons of the arts" in the political process. These patrons are often well-to-do and influential persons.

PUBLIC WELFARE

The ancient power of the state to protect the "welfare" of the people is not limited to public assistance programs. The problems of caring for the unemployed and those injured in industrial accidents, and of providing old age and survivors' insurance, are largely beyond the scope of municipal administration. They are discussed in textbooks dealing with American and with state and local government. But many other welfare functions are handled by municipalities, or jointly with the state. This

[12] S. Janice Kee, "Public Libraries Developments in 1952," *Municipal Year Book, 1953,* p. 484.
[13] On libraries, see E. W. McDiarmid and John McDiarmid, *The Administration of the American Public Library* (1943); Arnold Miles and Lowell Martin, *Public Administration and the Library* (1942); Oliver Garceau, *The Public Library in the Political Process* (1949).

includes the care of the poor, including children whose parents cannot or will not support them, and old people who can neither work nor support themselves from their savings. Delinquents, disabled persons, and the mentally handicapped are also taken care of by welfare agencies in some cities and states, as is the entire recreation program sometimes.

Persons Dependent upon Public Aid. The responsibility for public assistance aid rests with the state, but it has been delegated to local units of government ever since the Elizabethan Poor Law of 1601, the principles of which were adopted in colonial America. The basic approach to the care of the poor taken in the days of the first Elizabeth in England remained unchanged in the American states until its archaism became obvious in the Great Depression. In the years since the Federal government set up its so-called categorical grants-in-aid program in the Social Security Act of 1935, however, there has been a shift of emphasis from the city or township as the administrative unit to the county or to the state itself.

The Federal government furnishes grants-in-aid to the states to help in caring for certain categories of persons: old-age assistance, aid to the blind, aid to dependent children, and (since 1950) aid to the permanently and totally disabled. Some of the states administer these programs themselves; others are handled locally, but far more often by the county than by the municipality.

In some states, although the above categorical aids are administered by the county, general direct relief is left to the cities. The administration of these "welfare cases" is a major task taken alone. City public welfare agencies are often entrusted, in addition, with responsibility for the licensing of private child-caring agencies, the provision of foster care for children unable to live in their own homes, adoption services, work with children's courts, provision for medical and dental care for the needy, and the supervising of private charities.[14]

Welfare Administration. The department of welfare is ordinarily a separate agency of city government, although not all welfare functions are placed in such a department by any means. This is another function of government that has often been supervised by an administrative board, and weak-mayor cities, especially small cities, still treat it as an autonomous function. Modern municipal organization regards public assistance as but another of the responsibilities of government, and it is therefore normally organized under a single head, although quite a few cities retain an advisory welfare board. Professional social case workers and

---

[14] Elizabeth Wickenden, "Public Welfare Developments in 1952," *Municipal Year Book, 1953*, pp. 302–306. On welfare administration in general, see R. Clyde White, *Administration of Public Welfare* (2d ed., 1950); Wayne McMillan, *Community Organization for Social Welfare* (1945); and an administrative study, Ruth Raup, *Intergovernmental Relations in Public Welfare* (1952).

the influential persons of the community who frequently interest themselves in social work as an avocation tend to favor an independent board to whom the department head is responsible. This is the case for the same reasons that recreationists favor such a plan. General administrators oppose it because they believe that local government must be an integrated whole with the needs of the various departments balanced against one another. Social workers point out, however, that in times of depression, the direct-relief agency has one of the biggest budgets in local government and that, considering the directness of the relationship between the provision of relief funds and the use of the vote as a means of saying "thank you," the temptation for improper meddling in the department by nonprofessionals is very great.[15]

Of course, the social worker is mistaken in believing that the autonomous board eliminates political pressures. Experience during the Great Depression indicated that boards could be politically oriented and could override the professional opinions of their staffs with their own lay views, down to even the smallest details. It is likely that as municipal government matures administratively, this controversy, and similar ones in recreation, health, and elsewhere, will tend to disappear and governmental structure will tend to become integrated.

Public Assistance Policies. Since colonial days, American public relief has taken two forms.[16] One is so-called "outdoor relief," or the granting of money, food, clothing, fuel, and other necessaries to people in their own homes. The other, "indoor relief," involves care in institutions, the almshouses and poor farms of an earlier day, which have not yet entirely disappeared. The pattern of relief did not change fundamentally from colonial times until the Great Depression. In well-governed communities, the system once worked adequately, since the poor were few and were usually restricted to widows, dependent children, invalids, the disabled, the aged, and the mentally ill.

In the nineteenth century, however, outdoor relief in many communities came to be granted purely on the basis of political considerations. Indoor relief was commonly inadequate, with the institutions operated by callous and sometimes sadistic incompetents and with no segregation of the senile, the tubercular, the mentally ill, or the blind. Late in the nineteenth century, persons interested in social welfare began to organize private charities on an increasing scale, and these institutions came to dominate the relief scene from that time until after World War I. It was through these organizations that the "case work" system was developed, resulting in the use of administrative techniques still employed

---

[15] See Reed, *op. cit.*, chap. 20.
[16] *Ibid.*, pp. 490–491. The history of public welfare in America is discussed in Abraham Epstein, *Insecurity: A Challenge to America* (1938).

today. These charities became so accepted that they were frequently subsidized by local governments, and they began to attract university-trained social workers.

With the coming of the Great Depression, mounting unemployment proved to be too great a financial strain for private charities, which could not meet the demands of the millions who were forced to "go on relief" after October, 1929. Local public agencies were also unable to meet the depression load, so that the states and the Federal Emergency Relief Administration had to provide funds.

Today, private charities carry only a small part of the welfare load. But their techniques and their trained social workers were incorporated into government programs in the thirties and today form the basis of this governmental function.

Under the contemporary case-work system, a social worker is assigned to interview each person asking for assistance. He or she determines whether the individual is eligible for help on the basis of his residence, ability and willingness of the family to work, and reason for lack of self-support. Pending investigation of the facts gathered, temporary relief may be ordered. If investigation substantiates the facts gathered at the initial interview (called the "intake"), the budget to be granted is determined on the basis of established standard allowances. Since the purpose of the case-work method is to provide individual attention, social workers follow up each relief case to ascertain whether there has been any change in eligibility status, to give advice, to try to bolster morale, and to help the family regain its self-support.

Despite many changes in the administration of governmental services in recent years, public relief, by its very nature, must be administered by some unit of local government. Any substantial unemployment in the future will find local relief agencies that have, for the most part, become professionalized, modernized, and prepared to fulfill their very necessary role. Perhaps the major obstacle remaining in their way is the low grants provided in the standard allowances of many state laws or city ordinances. The old misconception that the poor and the unemployed must be lazy and shiftless has not yet left our philosophy of welfare, and the result is often gross inadequacy of assistance grants.

FAIR EMPLOYMENT PRACTICE COMMISSIONS

" . . . Because of Race, Color or Creed." In an attempt to bring social democracy abreast of political democracy, there was a movement after World War II to secure the adoption of municipal, state, and national fair employment practices commissions (FEPC laws). No nationwide FEPC has been adopted, but several states have established them.

Where this is the case, the state enforces fair practices both among private employers in the cities and within the personnel structure of municipalities themselves.

By early 1954, more than thirty cities had adopted charter amendments or ordinances providing for an FEPC, among them Chicago, Minneapolis, Cleveland, Philadelphia, and Pittsburgh. These regulations seek to prevent discrimination in employment because of race, religion, color, or national origin of the employee. They apply to cases of private employment in business and industry, to labor-union membership, and to discriminatory practices toward employees in governmental agencies.

Discrimination in employment is certainly not uncommon. Even city personnel agencies have permitted discrimination in the hiring of municipal employees, though their rules may formally forbid it. In some instances, personnel agencies have actually abetted such discrimination.

Most FEPC agencies have avoided coercion or punishment in attempts to eliminate discrimination. In fact, most municipal commissions have only advisory and noncoercive powers, although some of them, such as that of Clairton, Pennsylvania, have power to bring court actions against offenders which may result in both restraining orders and criminal punishments. Most FEPCs, however, depend upon education, conferences, persuasion, social pressure, and threat of unfavorable publicity to produce compliance.

There is some question as to whether the municipality is the proper agency to operate fair employment practices commissions. The problem is really at least state-wide in nature.

Conservatives in general oppose FEPC legislation, not because they are bigoted, but because they feel that such legislation represents another area of governmental interference in private enterprise. They believe that it does more harm to freedom than it does good and are likely to argue that progress comes through education, not laws.

Some cities which lack FEPCs have established interracial or intergroup committees to help improve relations between persons of different ethnic, racial, or religious group membership. These committees have no coercive powers, but they are sometimes objected to by improvement associations whose members fear that equal treatment of all groups would threaten property values.

CHAPTER 22

THE FUTURE OF AMERICAN CITY GOVERNMENT

No American political institution has made greater progress in the last half century than has municipal government. But no institution has had further to go in order to accommodate itself to modern society's needs. Today, it is clear that most cities have succeeded in bringing their governments at least partly up to date. Their record is far more impressive than is that of the states and counties. Many problems remain to be solved—problems of securing adequate legal authority from the state, of making municipal government more fully representative of the interests and desires of the community, of developing high standards of municipal service and administration, and of providing the municipal government with financial means to meet the increasing demands for services. The municipal reformer still has much work to do.

THE PAST

Reforms and Progress. The Jacksonian democracy of the 1820s and 1830s was a genuine reform movement. It helped to restore the common man's faith in government, it destroyed control of government by the aristocratic class, and it narrowed the gap between the people and those who operated the government. Even the much-criticized spoils system helped to do these things by putting the common man in control not merely of the elective positions, but of all the lesser positions of routine administration as well.[1] This movement accomplished much in bringing government into accord with the needs of the America of over a century ago. It produced universal manhood suffrage, which meant that all men could help choose their leaders. It devised a form of government to fit the personal politics of the informal, sparsely settled frontier. It applied this same type of democracy to our budding cities. But the movement also helped to make possible the city boss and machine. Its concepts proved to be inadequate when government became too complicated for

[1] See A. M. Schlesinger, Jr., *The Age of Jackson* (1945), chap. 5.

"anyone" to hold official positions—positions which came to require professional and technical skills. Its weak-mayor system could not provide satisfactory services to impersonal, complex cities of a size unknown in Jackson's day.

A reaction to the demoralization of urban government that resulted when a theory of government developed in one epoch of history was applied to a different set of environmental circumstances came about in the shape of a reform movement headed largely by middle-class businessmen. The forty-year span from the 1880s until after World War I brought a great many improvements in the apparatus for operating the present-day city. Modern forms of government—the strong-mayor and council-manager—evolved and have proved to be applicable to contemporary needs. The ballot was shortened somewhat so as to make it more comprehensible. The merit system for choosing employees was slowly but progressively applied to cities. New administrative techniques were developed. The idea that salaries of municipal employees should be equivalent to those in private endeavor was advanced. Graft and corruption in local government—and in private business, from whence the practices had come—was attacked until it has today declined to a tiny fraction of what it once was. The boss and the machine suffered a similar fate. Home rule and broad optional charter plans were devised so as to help fit government to the unique needs of particular cities and to free it from inappropriate state control. The number and scope of municipal functions was—and has since continued to be—increased as demand for them arose.

But the reform movement, like Jacksonianism before it, had its limitations and defects. By the time of the onset of the Great Depression, it had become in part outmoded. Many of the reformers, in their distaste for the boss and machine, mistakenly named "politics," rather than "unethical politics," as the villain of the day. They condemned "political parties," rather than "political parties that are corrupt," as well. They were so concerned with the need for "efficiency and economy" in government that they overlooked the need for representativeness (except for the advocates of the ill-fated proportional representation). They were so vitally interested in what they were doing that many of them did not recognize that the great majority of urbanites were apathetic toward the problems of reform and would quickly forget reform campaigns. Many of them did not seem to realize that the common man might not respond to the same value appeals that inspired reformers, that he might want something in addition to "efficiency and economy" from government. The movement, which had developed in a day prior to the social-service state and the rise of organized labor as a powerful urban force, often found itself in opposition to interest groups that represented great numbers of working-class urbanites who had, by and large, been excluded from the movement.

Many of the reformers confused themselves through an exaggerated use of the business analogy. It is unrealistic to suppose that by the simple method of selecting businessmen to apply business principles, satisfactory urban government can be achieved. Some reformers recognized this. One of them said, "Any plan of government based on the belief that municipal government is solely a business institution is wrong in principle and will not in the long run produce the desired results. City government is more than a business. . . ."[2] Business institutions have profit making as their objective. Municipal governments have public service as their objective. The two can use the same techniques of *administration* to reach their goals; they cannot use the same techniques in *policy formulation.*

THE FUTURE

The Need for Increased Responsibility and Representativeness. Many problems remain to be solved in the field of municipal government. State legislatures which are more representative and responsible are needed before city governments can be expected to be granted adequate powers and financial resources for self-government. Better judges with a better understanding of social and economic realities could help reduce the excessive legalism that often confounds the efforts of city officials. Experimentation in metropolitan-area government has had only the barest beginnings. The practice of dispersing powers of local government among independent units of government such as *ad hoc* districts or among autonomous boards and commissions has not yet been stopped—with the result that municipal governments still often lack powers adequate to coordinate the various public functions on the local level. But the greatest need of city government today is for a development of interest in it by the general public. This cannot take place unless the city is conceived of as an institution which administers public policies that have been established through the operation of the *political* process.

Unless government is responsive to changing demands of the public and unless it represents a cross section of that public, it is not democratic government. In fact, despite all the clichés of the past concerning local government as a laboratory for training in democracy, its frequent failure to be responsive and representative—especially in large cities— has made it less truly democratic than the national government, although it has certainly in most cases been more successful in this respect than has state government.

[2] W. P. Capes, *The Modern City and Its Government* (1922). Capes was director of the New York State Bureau of Municipal Information.

Nonpartisanship has proved to be a useful device in small, and perhaps most middle-sized, cities; and these places usually have few problems of representativeness. However, the nineteenth-century machines and the reformers' nonpartisan elections both failed to bring more responsive and representative government to our large cities. In some such cities, the premises upon which nonpartisanship is based require re-examination. Actually, some urbanites have argued in recent years, there *is* a Democratic way to lay a sewer and a Republican way to pave a street. At least both of these functions involve issues of policy that should be so treated in the municipal political process. The questions of *which* sewer is to be laid and how much money is to be spent in paving *which* streets are questions of public policy—that is to say, of politics. Nonpartisan ballots, in large cities, also strongly tend to produce unrepresentative and conservative governments for reasons that have been discussed in this text. But few cities have a *two*-party system, and so national parties seldom compete on the level of large-city politics. One party is normally far more powerful than the other. For this reason, the reintroduction of national parties into city elections would be of very doubtful value. The problem of a satisfactory ballot and political structure still awaits solution in most large cities.

The Public Must Be Made Aware of Its Government. Making city government more responsive and more representative is not enough. People cannot claim their rights in a democracy unless they are aware of them. We have greatly improved the quality of city government, but we have not raised the level of interest in its activities and its elections. People feel the need for the functions of city government and for their improvement—but they do not seem to have learned how to go about achieving their needs.

Many everyday complaints of the citizenry center in functions which lie wholly or partly within the sphere of city government. Elmo Roper, the pollster, found that residents of New York felt a need for (in order of their importance):[3]

1. Good housing;
2. Better transportation;
3. Better recreation facilities;
4. Cleaner streets;
5. Better schools;
6. Better city government;
7. A solution to the problem of taxes;
8. Better police protection;
9. A solution to the problem of juvenile delinquency;
10. A solution to the problem of the unassimilated foreign groups in the slums.

[3] A Roper study cited in the *National Municipal Review*, vol. 42 (June, 1953), pp. 268–269.

It is interesting to note that, allowing for differences in local conditions, Arthur Kornhauser found in Detroit a remarkably similar set of problems as "matters people think it is important to do something about":[4]

1. Housing needs;
2. Negro-white relations;
3. The bus and streetcar system;
4. Garbage collection and street cleaning;
5. City government;
6. Traffic and parking;
7. Spare-time activities (recreation);
8. Labor-management relations;
9. The public schools;
10. The activities of labor unions;
11. The police department.

Many of these problems are basically the responsibility of municipal government; most of the others can be met by cities acting in conjunction with national and state governments and private groups. *Yet vast numbers of persons who see a need for better housing, cleaner streets, and more parking spaces do not vote in municipal elections.* They do not seem to conceive of voting as an avenue toward reaching these ends.

Citizen Participation. Much has been said over the years concerning the apathy of the urbanite toward his local government. He has long been exhorted to become active in "the government closest to himself." He has been urged to take part in "citizen action" groups. For the most part, he has preferred national politics—or baseball.

Perhaps a major cause of failure to interest the typical citizen in local political activities has been a lack of understanding of the urban political process. Floyd Hunter has stated the problem clearly:[5]

The notion that city dwellers can or will act like persons inhabiting small New England towns and accustomed to town meetings has . . . been a pitfall for many efforts in community organization. Urban life is organized along the lines of organized interest groupings whether the particular interest be higher wages, higher profits, lower tax rates or lower disease rates. Basic organizations have sprung up around a multiplicity of interests in urban communities and the possibility of the so-called "face-to-face relationship" of city dwellers is an illusion. . . .

Citizen action must therefore be *group* action. It must also be *pluralistic* in organization. No single "citizens' action league" can permanently

[4] Arthur Kornhauser, *Attitudes of Detroit People Toward Detroit* (1952), pp. 22–23. By permission of the Wayne University Press.
[5] Floyd Hunter, *Community Power Structure* (1953), p. 256. By permission of the University of North Carolina Press.

reform a city or bring it democratic government. Many groups—business, labor, social, religious, reform, and others—must exist, and all of them must be free to participate in the political process. The more groups that are active, the more chances the individual has of having some group represent his interests. Public policy is a result of compromise among these groups in the legislative process.

Political parties—national or local—exist for the citizen and welcome his help. They need better and more extensive organization. The citizen can and should work through them. In all cities, and especially in cities with weak party organization or nonpartisan ballots, the pressure group is more likely to be the important unit of political action. There are groups for persons of all interests. The individual should be made to understand that his interests can be furthered through *group* action and that such action is a legitimate part of the democratic process.

Expanded citizen participation also involves the induction of more able men into the political process. Yet some business firms and banks even today informally prohibit their employees from entering local politics. Some school systems apply the same rule to teachers. A recent poll indicated that 70 per cent of America's parents do not want their children to enter politics. Archaic attitudes toward politics and the politician can greatly damage the prospects for better city government. Nineteenth-century viewpoints toward political institutions are not appropriate to twentieth-century conditions. They must go.

City participation requires more than interest and activity. It requires a better understanding of the democratic process on the part of public servants as well as private citizens. Certainly there is needed a clearer concept of the process than that which was demonstrated by Dallas election judges a few years ago, when they confiscated all of the lists of candidate slates that had been brought to the polls by voters who were seeking to overcome the problem of remembering the identities of all of the names on the ballot. Surely the voter is entitled to cast his vote for a team—for a group of men who have agreed that they are willing to try to work together if elected.

The Responsibility of Officials to Inform the Public. The failure of the citizen to take interest in or to understand municipal government is by no means his fault alone. In an America characterized by energetic advertising, public officials have very frequently made the mistake of assuming that municipal activities will "sell themselves." The failure of the public official to inform his "customers" of his activities is a fault that must be overcome in developing a better city in the future and in creating a more responsive and responsible public.

The Future City Will Be Costly to Operate. At the turn of the century, the city of New York was dominated by the Tammany machine under the control of Richard Croker. In 1901, various reform groups joined together in a strong effort to defeat the machine. They presented a slate to the voters, headed by Seth Low as the candidate for mayor. At a fusion ticket conference, a "declaration of principles" was drawn up which included a promise for "a progressive, businesslike and nonpartisan administration of municipal affairs, with a special view to cutting down public expenses and reducing the present excessive burden of taxation."[6]

Seth Low was elected mayor. But his first budget, to the dismay and disillusionment of a great many reformers, was $600,000 *higher* than the estimates made by his Tammany predecessor. A wise editorial writer separated reality from wishful thinking:[7] "Some reformers expected a large reduction from Tammany expenditures, but the leaders of the reform movement have long since learned that good government means better public service rather than cheaper public service. The more alert the citizenship of a place and the greater their confidence in their city officials, the larger is the work which the municipality is required to perform for its members."

This might be the text for today's lesson in city government. While the desirability for honest and competent government should not be in the least minimized, there is little prospect of the future city government's spending less money than it does today. It will be called upon to perform an increasing number of functions and to perform its present ones better. For this reason, the long-standing need for a more equitable municipal tax base will become even greater in the future.

We expect city governments to perform many functions for us today that were at one time within the scope of family activities. The time has therefore come to stop viewing government negatively, to stop finding ways of handcuffing officials and circumventing the normal channels of policy making. A mature society must have a mature government and a mature attitude toward that government. Government must now be recognized in theory, *as it is in practice,* as a useful thing, not as an evil monster to be caged.

American cities and their governments have come a long way in the direction of the satisfaction of modern needs. Most of the tools and techniques that are needed have been found. The future of American cities looks bright. All great civilizations have centered in great cities.

[6] Quoted in *The Outlook*, vol. 69 (Sept. 28, 1901), p. 199.
[7] *Ibid.*, vol. 71 (May 10, 1902), pp. 100–101.

SUGGESTED READINGS

PERIODICALS

In order for the student to keep abreast of current development in the fields of local government and administration, it is necessary for him to be acquainted with the periodical literature. The following are important periodicals, but they do not necessarily exhaust the field. In many states, the student can learn much about local municipalities through the periodical of his state municipal league. For a list of these publications, see the *Municipal Year Book*.

American City. Monthly. Much detail on administrative developments and less attention to politics and reform action than is found in the *National Municipal Review*. Many pictures and a great deal of advertising of the most recent municipal equipment.

American Journal of Public Health. Monthly. American Public Health Association.

American Municipal News. Monthly. Current municipal developments and practices.

City Managers' Newsletter. Biweekly. International City Managers' Association.

Journal of Housing. Monthly. National Association of Housing Officials. Housing and redevelopment news.

Municipal Finance. Quarterly. Municipal Finance Officers' Association. Also publishes a biweekly *News Letter*.

National Municipal Review. Monthly. Perhaps the best source of news of a general nature. Emphasizes political action, especially of the reform type.

National Tax Journal. Quarterly. National Tax Association. Features information on municipal taxation.

Newsletter. Monthly. American Society of Planning Officials.

New York Times. Daily. Reports important political and administrative developments throughout the country if of general interest.

Police Chiefs. Quarterly. International Association of Chiefs of Police.

Police Journal. Quarterly. Published in Great Britain.

Public Employee. Monthly. The American Federation of State, County, and Municipal Employees of the American Federation of Labor. The labor viewpoint, especially on personnel practices.

Public Management. Monthly. International City Managers' Association. A major source of news on administration.

Public Personnel Review. Quarterly. Civil Service Assembly. Includes developments in municipal personnel administration.

Public Utilities Fortnightly. Management and technical problems of utilities operation.

Public Welfare. Quarterly. American Public Welfare Association.

Recreation. Monthly. National Recreation Association.

State Government. Monthly. Occasional articles on state-local relations.

The Tax Digest. Monthly. By California Taxpayers' Association, but with items of nationwide interest.
Taxes—the Tax Magazine. Monthly. Commerce Clearing House. Reports on local developments.
United States Municipal News. Monthly. U.S. Conference of Mayors.
Wall Street Journal. Daily, Chicago and New York. Frequent articles on municipal finance and other developments.

FOR SPECIFIC LOCALITIES

The following are some of the books and phamphlets dealing with particular communities. Other works have been cited in the text, and it is likely that there are publications that are not known to the author. The student should consult his instructor concerning local materials.

Alabama: Weldon Cooper, *Metropolitan County: A Study of Government in the Birmingham Area* (1949).

California: The lengthy series of studies on the Los Angeles metropolitan area published by the Haynes Foundation have been cited several times in the text. There are also J. C. Bollens, *The Problem of Government in the San Francisco Bay Region* (1949); and J. C. Bollens and Stanley Scott, *Local Government in California* (1951).

Illinois: On Chicago, C. E. Merriam, S. D. Parratt, Albert Lepawsky, *The Government of the Metropolitan Region of Chicago* (1933).

New Jersey: S. H. Friedelbaum, *Municipal Government in New Jersey* (1954).

New York: Mary Field Parton, *Metropolis: A Study of New York* (1939). See also the report of the Mayor's Committee on Management Survey, *Modern Management for the City of New York* (1953).

Ohio: Clara L. Chambrun, *Cincinnati: Story of the Queen City* (1939); and Charles P. Taft, *City Management, the Cincinnati Experiment* (1933).

South Carolina: G. R. Sherrill and R. H. Stoudemire, *Municipal Government in South Carolina* (1950).

Tennessee: L. E. Abbott and L. S. Greene, *Municipal Government and Administration in Tennessee* (1939).

Some of the textbooks dealing with state and local government in particular states also contain valuable chapters on municipal government in those states.

BOSSES AND MACHINES

The old-time bosses, because they were glamorous, dramatic and, to many people, immensely frustrating, produced perhaps more source material than any other aspect of city government. Since this material is now principally of historical value rather than a reflection of the contemporary scene, it is listed here rather than in the main part of the text. The following list is not complete; further material is cited in textbooks on political parties.

General materials that should be cited include H. Zink, *City Bosses in the United States* (1930), a standard reference that draws conclusions from a study of twenty of them; F. R. Kent, *The Great Game of Politics* (1923); and C. W. Van Devander, *The Big Bosses* (1944), journalistic surveys; J. T. Salter, *Boss Rule: Portraits in City Politics* (1935), a study of political-leadership qualities in ward committeemen, based principally upon the Philadelphia machine; S. Forthal, *Cogwheels of Democracy: A Study of the Precinct Captain* (1946). There are also famous early studies by Lincoln Steffens. *The Shame of the Cities* (1904), which examines former machines in St. Louis, Minneapolis, Pittsburgh, and Philadelphia; and his noted *Autobiography of Lincoln Steffens* (1931).

New York: There is a long list of books on politics in New York, dealing especially with Tammany Hall. A classic study is that of Gustavus Myers, *History of Tammany Hall* (1917); an always popular and entertaining work is W. L. Riordon, *Plunkitt of Tammany Hall* (1905), which was reissued in 1948 with an interesting introduction by R. V. Peel; M. R. Weiner, *Tammany Hall* (1928); L. Stoddard, *Master of Manhattan* (1931); N. Thomas and P. Blanshard, *What's the Matter with New York?* (1932). The colorful, infamous Tweed Ring is reported in James Bryce, *American Commonwealth* (rev. ed., 1911), vol. 2, pp. 379–396; and in T. Lynch, *Boss Tweed: The Story of a Grim Generation* (1927). The fascinating story of a contemporary district leader is told in Richard Rovere, "The Big Hello," *New Yorker,* Jan. 12 and 19, 1946; reprinted in H. M. MacDonald, et al., *Outside Readings in American Government* (2d ed., 1952), pp. 240–268. A frank, revealing, and interesting autobiography is told by the man who was boss of the Bronx Democratic machine from the mid-1920s until 1953, in E. J. Flynn, *You're the Boss* (1947).

Philadelphia: Bryce, *op. cit.,* pp. 354–371, deals with the "Gas Ring"; W. S. Vare, *My Forty Years in Politics* (1933), is an autobiography of one of the bosses; a more recent work is D. H. Kurtzman, *Methods of Controlling Votes in Philadelphia* (1939).

Chicago: See footnote, p. 122, above.

Kansas City: R. Coghlan, "Boss Pendergast," *Forum,* vol. 97 (February, 1937), pp. 67–72; M. M. Milligan, *Missouri Waltz: The Inside Story of the Pendergast Machine by the Man Who Smashed It* (1948), that being the United States District Attorney; W. M. Reddig, *Tom's Town: Kansas City and the Pendergast Legend* (1947).

Jersey City: The best work is D. D. McKean, *The Boss: The Hague Machine in Action* (1940).

A West Coast machine of the early twentieth century is covered in Walton Bean, *Boss Ruef's San Francisco* (1952). Politicians who fought machines give their stories in the article by F. H. LaGuardia, "Bosses Are Bunk," reprinted in C. M. Kneier and Guy Fox, *Readings in Municipal Government and Administration* (1953), pp. 243–248; and in Brand Whitlock, *Forty Years of It* (1916), the autobiography of a famous Toledo mayor.

INDEX

Administrative code, 269–270
Administrative organization, municipal, 268–277
Administrative oversight of cities, state, 53–54, 162
(*See also* City–state relations)
Admissions tax, 315, 321
Airports, 384–386
management, 385–386
Aldermen, 174
(*See also* Council, city)
Amateurism in suburban government, 43–44
American Heritage Foundation, 69
American Labor party (New York), 80, 82
American Legion, 12, 115
American Political Science Association, 68
Annexation, 244–246
Annual reports, 282
Apathy toward municipal government, 4–5, 7, 57, 435–436
(*See also* Nonvoting)
Art galleries, 427
Arvey, Jacob, 122
Assessor, municipal, 312, 333–334
Attorney, city, 275
Auditor, municipal, 334–335, 338
Austin, Texas, 270

Baker, Newton D., 209
Ballot, long or "bedsheet," 51, 60, 83
nonpartisan, 83–84
partisan, 84
Banks and bankers, political influence of, 106
Baton Rouge, city-parish consolidation, 250
Beard, Charles A., 74, 77
Beverly Hills, California, nonvoting in, 70
Billboard regulation, 137–138
Boards and commissions, rise of, 52
use of, 272–273

Bonds, municipal, affected by national-government policies, 327–329
characteristics of, 327–328
types of, 328
use of, debate on, 325–327
(*See also* Debt, municipal)
Borough, meaning of term, 14
Bosses and political machines, 74, 118–131
bibliography of, 440–441
challenged by reformers, 57–59
in Chicago, 122–126
contemporary pattern, 126–131
decline of, 119–122
relation of, to business community, 105–106
to form of government, 178–179
social function of, 118–119
(*See also* Tammany Hall)
Boston, 9, 25
Curley machine, 122
nominations by petition, 84
nonpartisan ballot, 76
strong-mayor plan, 57
use of chief administrative officer, 187
Bowron, Fletcher, 133
Brennan, George, 124
Bridgeport, Socialist party in, 78–79
Bromage, Arthur W., 281
Brooklyn, 9
strong-mayor plan, 57
water supply, 386
Budget, municipal, administration, 337–338
enactment, 337
executive function, 274–275, 335
parts of, 336
performance type, 335–336
preparation, 336–337
Bureau of Municipal Research (New York), 60
Burgess, E. W., 22
Burke, Thomas A., 209
Burton, Harold H., 209
Buses, 392
(*See also* Transportation)

Business taxes, 315
Businessmen, influence on municipal politics, 105–109, 131–134
  bankers, 106
  contractors, 106
  professional men, 107–108
  realtors, 108
  taxicab owners, 107

Canada, centralized control over municipalities, 261
  municipal government in, 67, 68
Carpenter, William S., 297
Case studies, boss, contemporary example, 126–131
  bosses in Chicago, 122–126
  metropolitan federation in Toronto, 251–253
  metropolitan panorama, 6–11
  nonvoting, 69–71
  portrait of small city, 11–13
  problem of adequate legal authority for municipalities, 137–138
  recall in San Francisco (1946), 90–92
Caste system, urban, 24–25
Central purchasing, 332, 334
Cermak, Anton J., 124
Chambers of commerce, interest in reform, 60
  local, as pressure group, 12, 106
  support of manager plan, 205–206
Charter, city (*see* City charters)
Charter party (City Charter Committee of Cincinnati), 80–81
Chicago, Commission on Human Relations, 26
  growth of, 18, 20, 33, 122
  machines in, 110, 122–126
  political influence of business groups, 105–106
Chicago Tribune, 110, 125
Chief administrative officer, as aid in strong-mayor city, 184–187
  current use of, 187–189
  value of, 189
Chief executive, 274
  (*See also* City manager; Mayor)
Childs, Richard S., 189, 196
Cicero, Illinois, riot in 1952, 26
Cincinnati, Charter party, 80–81
  collective bargaining by municipal employees, 297
Cities, administrative oversight of, 53–54, 62
  corrupt government in (*see* Corrupt government in cities)

Cities, development patterns, theories of, 21–23
  grants-in-aid to, 264–266, 316–319
  growth of, 2, 15–18, 48
    theory of, 18–21
  legal status of, 2–3
  state fiscal control over, 260–261
  taxing power, 3, 143, 306
  (*See also* City-nation relations; City-state relations)
Citizens' Union (New York), 79, 102
City, meaning of term, 13–14, 16*n.*
City charters, nature of, 139
  types of, classified, 149
    general act, 145, 147–149
    home rule, 152–161
    multiple systems, 161–162
    optional, 150
    special act, 145–147
City employees (*see* Municipal employment)
City government, attitudes toward, 2–6
  in early America, 48–49
City manager, criticisms of, 201–202
  duties of, 222–223
  and elections, 224
  as professional, 225
  and public relations, 224–225
  qualifications of, 219–220
  relations with council, 202–203, 223–224
  salary, 222
  selection and tenure, 220–222
  (*See also* Council-manager plan)
City-national relations, advice and assistance to cities, 263–264
  approval of municipal activities, 264
  grants-in-aid to cities, 264–266
  postwar problems, 266–267
City planning (*see* Planning)
City-state relations, 162–165
  state administrative oversight of cities, 53–54, 162
  state judicial oversight of cities, 163
    taxpayer's actions, 163–165
  state legislative control over cities, 53–54, 162
  state limits on taxing and spending, 306–310
Civic associations (*see* Improvement associations)
Civic pride as community identification, 5–6, 28–29, 42
Civil defense, 368–371
Civil service (*see* Municipal employment)
Class system, urban, 24–27

Cleveland, mayors of, 209
use of proportional representation, 93, 96
Close corporations, 49, 67
Cobb, Irvin S., 5
Cobo, Albert E., 133
Columbus, Ohio, 9
Commision plan, appraisal, 191–194
characteristics, 190–191
development, 61, 189–190
present use of, 194–195
Communicable-disease control, 419–420
Communication media in municipal public relations, 282–283
radio use by municipal officials, 6
television use by municipal officials, 6
Complaints, 280
Consolidation, city-county, 249–250
Contract liability, municipal, 165–170
Controller, municipal, 331–333, 337–338
Cooley, Thomas M., 55–56
Cooperation, voluntary intergovernmental, 255–256
Corporation, public, city as, 138–145
contrast of, with private corporation, 139–140
creation and dissolution of, 144–145
distinguished from quasi, 141–142
elements of, 140–141
nature of, 138–140
powers of, 142–144
Corporation counsel, 275
Corrupt government in cities, 4, 53–54, 79, 123–124, 342–346
prevention of, 346–351
in relation to public utilities matters, 373, 376
Cost-of-living pay plans, 302
Council, city, 8, 11–12
members, personal qualities of, 226–227
practical problems of, 239–241
salaries of, 229–230
women as, 229
minority group representation, 227–229
organization and procedure, 236–238
powers, 238–239, 331
presiding officer, 236
structure, 229–235
bicameral, 57, 232–233
election by wards versus at-large, 233–235
size, 231–232
term of office, 230–231
type of ballot, 235

Council, city, structure, unicameral, 232–233
Council Bluffs, Iowa, 18
Council-manager plan, 11–12, 61, 78
appraisal, 200–205
characteristics, 197–199
development, 195–197
politics of adaption, 205–206
(*See also* City manager)
County, consolidation with core city, 249–250
as metropolitan unit, 253–254
separation from core city, 250–251
Courts, municipal, 363–364
Crime, organized, clean-up efforts against, 346–348
as means of corrupting officials, 342–346
as municipal problem, 4, 10
as pressure group, 108–109
problem of legalized gambling, 348–350
reasons for, 339–342
Crime laboratory, police, 355, 357
Crime rates, urban, 352–354
Croker, Richard, 438
Crump, Edward H., 122, 128
Curley, James M., 84, 122

Dallas, 76, 77
annexation of territory by, 245
Dayton, early use of manager plan, 196, 206
Dearborn, strong-mayor plan, 181
study of politics in, 126–131
Debt, municipal, debate concerning, 325–329
limitations on, 309–310
(*See also* Bonds, municipal)
Democracy, assumptions of, 86
Departmental organization, 270–273
boards and commissions at head of, 272–273
number of departments, 271
single head of, 272
in small cities, 273
"Des Moines plan," 61, 190
abandoned in Des Moines, 61, 194
Detective division, police, 357
Detroit, attitudes toward city government, 71
community identification in, 29
growth of, 21
political pattern of, 76, 77, 131, 133
public awareness of power structure, 116–117

Detroit, social tensions, 25
Detroit News, 110–111
Dewey, Thomas E., 131, 188, 392
  recommends manager plan for New
    York, 203
Dillon's rule, 142, 154
Dodge City, Kansas, 18
Duluth, Minnesota, 18, 195

Ecological patterns, urban, 21–23
Education, board of (*see* Schools)
Efficiency and economy movement, 56–
  63, 65, 433–434
  (*See also* Reform movement)
Eisenhower, Dwight D., 402, 404
Elections, municipal, 74–84
    nonpartisan, 57, 62, 76–78, 80, 83–
      84, 132, 435
    partisan, 74–76, 78–82, 132
Electrical power, 20
Expenditures, municipal, 305–306
Expressways, 13, 380–382
Extraterritorial jurisdiction, 254–255

Fair Employment Practice Commission,
  101, 113, 430–431
Federal-city relations (*see* City-national
  relations)
Federation, metropolitan, 251–253
Finance, municipal, expenditures, 305–
  306
    financial administration, 331–338
    budget, 335–338
    financial officers, 331–335
    future trends in, 437–438
    nontax revenues, 316–320
      grants-in-aid, 264–266, 316–319
      special assessments, 321–325
      state-shared taxes, 319–320
    state limits on taxing and spending,
      306–310
  (*See also* Bonds, municipal; Taxes)
Fire-fighting equipment, 366
Fire prevention, 365–366
Fire protection, organization for, 366–367
  problems, 12, 364–365
  training for, 368
Fordham, J. B., 160
Forms of city government (*see* specific
  names of plans)
Fort Worth, 77
Franchises, public utility, 373
Friedland, Louis L., 298
Fringe area, urban, 9–10, 13
  (*See also* Suburban movement; Sub-
    urbs)

Fromm, Erich, 23
Fusion party in New York, 80

Galveston, adoption of commission plan,
  61, 189–190
Gambling as municipal problem (*see*
  Crime)
Garbage disposal, 388–389
Gobbledegook, in public relations, 280
  meaning of, 294
Good-government groups, 102–103
Gosnell, H. F., 123, 125
Governmental functions of city defined,
  166
Grants-in-aid to cities, 264–266, 316–319
Great Depression, effect of, on municipal
  government, 3–4, 124–126
Gross earnings tax, 315
Growth, city, 2, 15–21, 48
Gulick, Luther H., 189

Hague, Frank, 122
Hare, Thomas, 94
  (*See also* Proportional representation)
Harrison, Carter H., 123
Health, public, as municipal function,
  417–418
Health administration, 418–419
  functions, 419–422
    communicable-disease control, 419–
      420
    education, 422
    hospitals, 421–422
    maternal and child care, 420–421
    sanitation, 421
  staff services, 422
Hibbing, Minnesota, 20
Hoan, Daniel W., 208
Hoboken, abandonment of commission
  plan, 194
Holloway, W. V., 363
Home rule, municipal, 54, 57, 139, 149
  appraisal of, 161
  definition of, 152–153
  legislative type, 160
  origin and spread of, 155–158
  practical value of, 158–160
  procedure for adopting charter, 153–
    155
  states providing for, 154–155
Hospitals, municipal, 421–422
Housing, public (*see* Public housing)
  urban, continued shortage, 405–406
    municipal control of, 397–398
    municipal rent control, 405

Housing, urban, present status of, 396–397
(*See also* Urban redevelopment)
Houston, Texas, 19
Hoyt, Homer, 23
Hubbard, Orville L., contemporary boss, 126–131
Hunter, Floyd, 436

Identification, community, 5–6, 28–29, 42
Improvement associations, 26, 135
as pressure groups, 104–105
Income tax, municipal, 314, 320–321
Indiana, centralized municipal fiscal control, 261
classified charters, use of, 149
Industry, decentralization of, 35–36
Inherent right of local self-government, 55–56
Initiative and referendum, 60, 78
appraisal of, 86–88
arguments concerning, 86
definition of, 61, 85
procedure, 85–86
Insull, Samuel, political influence of, 123–124
Intergovernmental relations (*see* City-national relations; City-state relations; Cooperation; Extraterritorial jurisdiction)
International City Managers' Association, 225, 290
Invasion, meaning of term, 25–26
as political issue, 25, 135

Jacksonian democracy as theory of local government, 50–52, 174, 178, 201, 285, 432–433
Jefferson, Thomas, on cities, 50
Jersey City, 122
nonpartisan ballot, 76
Johnson, Thomas L., 209
Jones, Samuel M., 208
Jones, Victor, 242, 246, 249, 256
Juvenile division, police, 360–361

Kansas City, Missouri, fine for nonvoters, 73
Pendergast machine, 121
Kefauver committee, 4, 339–340, 346, 349
recommendations of, 347–348
(*See also* Crime)
Kelly, Edward J., 125

Kelly-Nash machine, 122
history of, 125–126
Knox, Harley, 133
Kornhauser, Arthur, 436

Labor, organized, attitude toward manager plan, 205–206
interest of, in getting out vote, 69, 73
in municipal employment, 294–300
arbitration, 299–300
collective bargaining, 297–298
right to strike, 298–299
in municipal politics, goals of, 112–113
history of, 132
as pressure group, 103, 111–112
La Guardia, Fiorello H., 80, 121, 208
Lapham, Roger D., 90–92, 133
Lausche, Frank J., 209
Law enforcement (*see* Police)
Leadership, political, 12, 115–116
League of Women Voters, 12, 60, 135
as pressure group, 103
Leagues of municipalities, state, 65
Legal status of cities, 2–3
(*See also* City-state relations)
Legislative control over cities (*see* City-state relations)
L'Enfant, Pierre, 410
Liability, municipal, 165–170
for tort, 166–171
Liberal party (New York), 80, 82
Libraries as municipal function, 426–427
Line agencies, 269
Liquor control, municipal, 4
London, England, 4
metropolitan federation in, 251
Los Angeles, 33, 77, 79
decision makers in, study of, 115–116
expressway system, 380, 382
interest in chief administrative officer, 188
political pattern, 133
recall, use of, 61
voting behavior, 70
Los Angeles County, chief administrative officer, 254
as metropolitan area government, 254
voting behavior, 70–71
Los Angeles Times, 111
Low, Seth, 208, 438

McCormick, Robert R., 125
McGeary, M. Nelson, 239–240

Machines, city, and bosses (*see* Bosses and political machines)
McKean, Dayton D., 122
Manager (*see* City manager)
Mason, Haven A., 195
Massachusetts Metropolitan District Commission, 249
Maternal and child care, 420–421
Mayor, ceremonial head of city, 214
  as lobbyist, 214
  personal qualities, 208–209
  powers, 210–215
  removal, 217–218
  salary and term of office, 216–217
  selection method, 215–216
  (*See also* Strong-mayor–council plan; Weak-mayor–council plan)
Mayor-council plan (*see* Strong-mayor–council plan; Weak-mayor–council plan)
Mayor's Commission on Management Survey (New York), 188
Memphis, Tennessee, 53
  machine in, 122
Metropolitan area government, atomization of, 242–244
  need for, 242
  proposals, 244–256
    annexation, 244–246
    city-county consolidation, 249–250
    city-county separation, 250–251
    county as metropolitan unit, 253–254
    extraterritorial jurisdiction, 254–255
    metropolitan federation, 251–253
    special districts, 246–248
      multipurpose, 248–249
    voluntary cooperation, 255–256
Metropolitan areas, importance of, 17
  meaning of term, 14, 16n.
  need for planning in, 415–416
Metropolitan-wide planning, 415–416
Middle class, urban, 24
    importance of, in municipal elections, 73, 126–127
Milwaukee, annexation in, 244
  receipts and expenditures, 322
  Socialist party, 78–79
Minneapolis, 20, 76, 77n., 144
  as weak-mayor city, 176
Minority groups, in municipal politics, 113–114
  representation on council, 227–229
Mississippi, municipal suffrage, 68
  tax subsidy for industry, 329–330
Moberly, Missouri, 19
Mobile, Alabama, 53

Model City Charter provisions, council-manager plan, 222
  sponsor system of nomination, 84
  subdivision requirements, 411
Modesto, California, use of council-manager plan, 199
Moore Plan Act (New York), 321
Muckrakers, 62
Mumford, Lewis, 413
Municipal employees as pressure group, 114–115
  (*See also* Municipal employment)
Municipal employment, circumvention of merit system in, 287–289
  civil service defined, 286
  civil-service commission, 286
  dismissals from, 291–293
  examinations for, types of, 291
  history of, 285–286
  local residence requirement, 291, 362
  merit system defined, 286
  and organized labor, 294–300
  personnel director, 286–287
  position classification for, 289–290
  public attitude toward, 293–294
  retirement systems, 302–303
  salaries, 300–302, 361
  training for, 290, 362, 367
  (*See also* Municipal employees)
Municipal home rule (*see* Home rule)
Municipal liability, contract, 165–170
  for tort, 166–171
Municipal research bureaus, 60, 103
Municipal Voters' League (Chicago), 60, 79
Municipality, meaning of term, 14n.
Murphy, Frank, 208
Museums, 427

Narcotics trade (*see* Crime)
Nash, Patrick A., 125
National Association for the Advancement of Colored People, 69, 114
National Civil Service Reform League, 57
National Municipal League, 60, 84, 90, 196
National Municipal Review, 75, 439
National Popular Government League, 60
National-city relations (*see* City-national relations)
Negroes, 22
  influence of machines on, 120
  involvement in political process, 24–27, 128–129
  as pressure group, 113–114

Negroes, representation on city councils, 228–229, 234

New Deal, effect of, on municipal government, 4, 63–64, 78, 265, 398

New Jersey Division of Local Government, 260–261

New Orleans, 19, 33
  city planning, 409
  receipts and expenditures, 323
  use of chief administrative officer, 185, 187

New York City, metropolitan integration, 251
  public transportation, 392, 393
  recent growth pattern, 33
  use in, of chief administrative officer, 188–189
  of proportional representation, 93, 96
  water supply, 386

New York Herald-Tribune, 111

New York State, local assistance grants, 317–318
  municipal taxing powers, 321

New York Times, 111

Newspapers, as community influence, 109
  importance of, reasons for, 109–110
  relationships of city officials with, 280–282
  role of, in local politics, 110–111
  suburban and neighborhood, 111

Nomination of candidates, methods of, 82–84

Nonpartisan elections, 74–76, 78–82, 132

Nonvoting, consequences of, 71–72
  extent of, 68–69
  in Los Angeles County, 70–71
  in St. Louis, 69–70

North Carolina Local Government Commission, 261

Omaha, assessment pattern, 312
  commission plan, 192

Ordinance defined, 143n.

O'Rourke, Lawrence W., 70

Parent-Teachers Association as pressure group, 103, 278

Paris, France, 15

Parking, 7, 13
  municipal lots for, 384

Parking meters, 381

Parking problem, 381–384

Parks, administration, 423–424
  need for, 425–426
  zoos in, 426

Patrol division, police, 355–357

Patterson, John M., 196

Payroll tax, 314–315, 321

Pendergast, Thomas J., 121

Personnel administration (*see* Municipal employment)

Philadelphia, 54
  corruption in, 4, 120
  coterminous city and county, 251n.
  machine in, 121
  use of chief administrative officer, 187
  water supply, 386

Philadelphia Inquirer, 111

Pittsburgh, 53, 251

Planning, definition of, 407
  as executive function, 275–276
  history of, 407–408
  metropolitan, 415–416
  official map, 411
  organization, 408–409
  preparation of plan, 410–412
  subdivision control, 411
  suburban, 45, 414–415
  (*See also* Zoning)

Plunkitt, George W., 119

Police, chief, 354
  commissioner, 354
  crime laboratory, 355, 357
  detective division, 357
  graft, 342–346
  juvenile division, 360–361
  organization, 354–361
  patrol division, 355–357
  problems confronting, 352–354
  recruitment, 361–362
  staff services, 361
  traffic division, 358–359
  training, 362
  vice division, 345–346, 360

Political parties, local, 78–82
  reform, 78–82
  small-town, 79
  Socialist, 78–79
  national, in municipal elections, 74–76

Political process, decision makers in, role of, 115–116
  importance of, 99
  nature of, 99–100, 436–437

Population, urban, mobility of, 5, 28–29

Port of New York Authority, 249

Poulson, Norris, 133

Preferential voting, 61, 97–98

Pressure groups, characteristics of, 101–102
  definition of, 100–101
  function of, 100–101, 131
  lobbying activities, 100

Pressure groups, in municipal politics, list, 102–115
(*See also* specific pressure groups)
Primary elections, 83–84
Proportional representation, 60, 234
present use of, 93, 96–97
process of, description, 92–96
Proportional Representation League, 60
Proprietary functions of city defined, 166
Prostitution as municipal problem (*see* Crime)
Public health (*see* Health)
Public housing, 398–402
history of, 398–400
postwar policy, 400–402
(*See also* Housing, urban)
Public libraries, 426–427
Public relations, municipal, contacts with newspapers, 280–282
as departmental problem, 277–278
as duty of manager, 224–225
gauging of public attitudes, 278–279
good, methods of, 279–280
public reports, 282–284
Public utilities, 60, 78
definition of, 372
franchises, 373
issues in, private versus public control, 375–376
state versus local control, 374–375
municipally owned, 377–379
as pressure group, 106
rate determination, 373–374
regulation, 373
(*See also* Transportation)
Public works department, head, 394
staff services, 394–395
Purchasing agent, municipal, 334

Quasi corporation, 141–142

Racial and ethnic groups, importance of, in politics, 106
as lobbies, 113–114
Radio, 6
Recall, 60, 78
arguments concerning, 88–90
of city managers, 221
definition of, 88
in San Francisco (1946), 90–92
Recall procedure, 88
Reconstruction Finance Corporation, 264, 266
Recreation administration, 423–424
Recreation programs, 424–425

Reed, T. H., 273, 276, 368, 422, 424
Referendum (*see* Initiative and referendum)
Reform movement, municipal, 5, 433–434
appraisal of, 62–63
contemporary, 65–66
goals and aims, 57–62
history of, 56–57
in support of public utility regulation, 375
Religious groups as lobbies, 114
Reporting, public, 282–284
Representative town-meeting plan, New England, 206–207
Respondeat superior, rule of, 169
Restrictive covenants, 26
Revenue, municipal (*see* Finance; Taxes)
Rhode Island, municipal suffrage in, 68
Riesman, David, 23–24
Rochester, New York, 20
Roosevelt, Franklin D., 64, 124, 265
Roper, Elmo, 70, 435
Roselle, New Jersey, 67
Rubbish disposal, 388–389

St. Joseph, Missouri, 18
St. Louis, 33, 36
home rule, 156
partisan elections, 76
public transportation, 390–391
voting behavior, 69–70
St. Louis Post-Dispatch, 120
Salaries, municipal, 300–302
Sales tax, municipal, 314, 320–321
San Antonio, adoption of manager plan, 203
annexation, 245, 246
San Diego, liability insurance carried, 171
political pattern, 77, 133
public relations, 283
San Francisco, 37, 76, 77
recall election (1946), 90–92
use in, of chief administrative officer, 186–187
of initiative, 61, 85
Sanitation, 387–389
Schools, 46
relationship of, to municipality, 11, 44
Seasongood, Murray, 208
Seattle, 19
municipal league, 103
Seidel, Emil, 208
Self-government, local (*see* Theory of local self-government)
Seligman, E. R. A., 311

Separation, city-county, 250–251
Sewage disposal, 387–388
Shaw, Frank, 133
Sidewalks, 379–380
Slums, 396–397
Small Business Administration, 265
Smoke abatement, 368
Socialist party in municipal government, 78–79, 208
Special assessments, 321–325
Special districts, *ad hoc*, 246–248
  multipurpose, 248–249
Special legislation, 53–54
  special act charters, 145–147
Sprague, J. Russel, 126, 131
Staff services, 269, 274–276
  in police work, 361
  in public health, 422
  in public works, 394–395
Stare decisis, principle of, 142
Stassen, Harold E., 76
State-city relations (*see* City-state relations)
State fiscal control over cities, 260–261
Staunton, Virginia, early use of manager plan, 196
Steffens, Lincoln, 120, 172
Street railways, 378, 391
  (*See also* Transportation)
Streets, 13, 379
  expressways, 380–382
  lighting of, 380
Strikes, municipal employees, 298–299
Strong-mayor–council plan, appraisal, 183–184
  characteristics, 180–183
  with chief administrative officer, 184–189
  development, 61, 180
  (*See also* Mayor)
Suburban movement, effect of, on core city, 37–41
  problems of suburbs created by, 41–47, 324
  reasons for, 30–34
Suburbs, growth of, 32–34
  planning in, 45, 414–415
  politics of, 134–136
  types of, 34–37
Suffrage, municipal, extension of, 51
  present qualifications for, 67–68
Sullivan, Roger, 124
Sumter, South Carolina, early use of manager plan, 196
Superhighways (*see* Expressways)

Tammany Hall, 58, 79, 80, 96, 119, 437
  current status, 59, 121
  (*See also* Bosses and political machines)
Tax collector, 331
Tax exemption, for homesteads, 306
  for new industries, 329–330
  on war and defense plants and materials, 330
Taxes, admissions, 315, 321
  business, 315
  cigarette, 315
  equalization of, 44–45
  general property, 3, 12, 46, 310–313
  gross earnings, 315
  income, municipal, 314, 320–321
  need for diversification, 319–320
  occupational, 315
  payroll, 314–315, 321
  sales, municipal, 314, 320–321
  state-shared, 319–320
  (*See also* Finance)
Taxing power of cities, 3, 143, 306
Taxpayers, action of, 163–165
  leagues, 60, 105
Television, 6
Theory of local self-government, colonial, 48–50
  contemporary, 64–66
  inherent right, 55–56
  Jacksonian, 50–54
  New Deal, 63–64
  reform movement, 56–63
Thompson, William H., 118, 123–125, 129
Toledo, Ohio, 9
  mayors, 208
  proportional representation, use of, 93, 96
Toronto, metropolitan federation in, 251–253
Tort, definition of, 165*n.*
  municipal liability for, 166–171
Town, meaning of term, 14
Town-meeting plan, New England, 206–207
Township, meaning of term, 14
Traffic division, police, 358–359
Traffic engineering, 358, 368, 394
Transportation, public, problems, 8, 389–392
  proposed solutions for, 392–393
Treasurer, municipal, 331, 332
Truman, Harry S., 68
Tucker, Raymond R., 76

Urban areas, definition of, 14–15
Urban League, 114
Urban life, characteristics of, 10–11, 23–29
Urban redevelopment, history of, 403–404
 prevention of blight through, 404–405
Urbanization (*see* Cities)

Van Antwerp, Eugene, 133
Veterans as pressure group, 115
Vice division, police, 345–346, 360
Village, meaning of term, 14
Virginia, annexation, 244, 246
 municipal suffrage, 68
Voting, compulsory, 73
 limited, 93
 preferential, 61, 97–98
 qualitative make-up of participants, 72–73
 (*See also* Elections; Nonvoting; Suffrage)

Wagner, Robert F., Jr., 189
Walker, "Jimmie," 121

Washington, D.C., 19, 25, 186
Water supply, 12, 19, 386–387
Weak-mayor–council plan, appraisal, 178–180
 characteristics, 174–178
 development, 178–180
 (*See also* Mayor)
Weights and measures, control of, 367–368
Welfare, public, administration, 428–430
 case-work system, 430
 history, 427–428
Whitley Councils in England, 297n.
Whitlock, Brand, 208
Wichita, Kansas, 19, 20
Wilson, O. W., 356, 357, 360
Women in politics, 135, 229
Woolpert, E. D., 280

Zoning, 9–10, 45
 definition of, 407–408
 development of, 412–413
 spot, 413
 suburban, 414–415
Zoning ordinance, 413–414